About Island Press

Island Press is the only nonprofit organization in the United States whose principal purpose is the publication of books on environmental issues and natural resource management. We provide solutions-oriented information to professionals, public officials, business and community leaders, and concerned citizens who are shaping responses to environmental problems.

In 2000, Island Press celebrates its sixteenth anniversary as the leading provider of timely and practical books that take a multidisciplinary approach to critical environmental concerns. Our growing list of titles reflects our commitment to bringing the best of an expanding body of literature to the environmental community throughout North America and the world.

Support for Island Press is provided by The Jenifer Altman Foundation, The Bullitt Foundation, The Mary Flagler Cary Charitable Trust, The Nathan Cummings Foundation, The Geraldine R. Dodge Foundation, The Charles Engelhard Foundation, The Ford Foundation, The Vira I. Heinz Endowment, The W. Alton Jones Foundation, The John D. and Catherine T. MacArthur Foundation, The Andrew W. Mellon Foundation, The Charles Stewart Mott Foundation, The Curtis and Edith Munson Foundation, The National Fish and Wildlife Foundation, The National Science Foundation, The New-Land Foundation, The David and Lucile Packard Foundation, The Pew Charitable Trusts, The Surdna Foundation, The Winslow Foundation, and individual donors.

About 4Ever Land Conservation Associates

4Ever Land Conservation Associates, Inc., a woman-owned firm with principal offices in St. Paul, Minnesota, and York, Pennsylvania, provides various land and natural resource conservation and planning design services to a variety of clients throughout the Midwest and Mid-Atlantic regions. Our staff of scientists, land planners, and landscape architects combine their knowledge of design, site planning, and environmental analysis with the broad talents of our nearly eighty associates who work throughout the region in areas such as land conservation, restoration, land management, planning, and sensitive areas development. This unique structure enables 4Ever Land to offer clients a comprehensive source of nearby expertise for innovative and workable solutions to complex land problems. This facilitates a greater level of efficiency and cost savings and increases the capacity and standards of land conservation organizations and agencies. Our endeavors to be pioneers have facilitated the development of many collaborative partnerships with numerous nonprofit organizations. Unique in our approach, 4Ever Land endeavors to understand both the human and environmental constraints of each individual project through an integrated approach that facilitates a sound relationship between people, their communites, and the natural environment.

Protecting the Land

*To those who have not relegated to abstraction
the connections between our actions and the
impacts they make on the land.*

Protecting the Land

Conservation Easements Past, Present, and Future

Edited by
Julie Ann Gustanski
and Roderick H. Squires

ISLAND PRESS
Washington, D.C. • Covelo, California

ISLAND PRESS is a trademark of The Center for Resource Economics.

Cover photo: Orchard along the Hudson River in the historic "Olana Viewshed," Columbia County, New York. Protected by The Scenic Hudson Land Trust, Inc., with a conservation easement restricting the land's development in perpetuity. Courtesy of Scenic Hudson, Inc.

Library of Congress Cataloging-in-Publication Data

Protecting the land : conservation easements past, present, and future
/ edited by Julie Ann Gustanski, Roderick H. Squires
    p.   cm.
    Includes bibliographical references and index.
    ISBN 1-55963-654-8 (paper : acid-free paper)
    1. Conservation easements—United States. I. Gustanski, Julie.
II. Squires, Roderick H.
KF658.C65P76   2000
346.7304'35—dc21   99-37173
                                                                    CIP

Printed on recycled, acid-free paper

Printed in Canada
10 9 8 7 6 5 4 3 2 1

Contents

List of Figures, Photographs, and Tables

Figures

Photographs

Tables

Foreword

೪ ೮

In 1959, William H. Whyte wrote a technical bulletin for the Urban Land Institute called *Open Space for Urban America: Conservation Easements.* "It was probably the first time an entire publication had been devoted to explaining and promoting this then-obscure conservation tool," he said. It certainly was a major step forward in educating planners, conservationists, and policy makers about a new way to protect open land without acquiring it.

Not that conservation easements were brand new, even then. In fact, the first conservation easements in the United States were written in the late 1880s to protect parkways designed by Frederick Law Olmstead in the Boston area. In the 1930s, the National Park Service made extensive use of easements to protect land along the Blue Ridge and Natchez Trace Parkways. And in the early 1950s, the state of Wisconsin established a highly successful easement acquisition program to protect land bordering the Great River Road along the Mississippi River.

When Whyte wrote his small bulletin, however, easements were neither well known nor much used, even among those whose business was land conservation. One of the stumbling blocks was that lawyers found a number of legal uncertainties with conservation easements.

Conservation easements are not like easements lawyers were used to. First of all, they do not grant the holder the right to do something on another person's land, the way a utility or road easement does. Rather, they give the holder the right to *prevent* certain uses. A negative easement was not a common idea. Moreover, conservation easements usually run in perpetuity, something the common law does not like very much.

Finally, conservation easements are usually "in gross," that is, they benefit the public at large, rather than benefiting an adjacent or nearby property, as does an "appurtenant easement." There were questions about whether an easement in gross would be enforceable over time. As Russell Brenneman, a Connecticut attorney who was an early proponent of conservation easements, once observed, "An easement in gross is a very bad thing to be if you are an easement."

Thus, in the 1960s, thanks largely to the work of William Whyte and the dedication of lawyers like Brenneman, states began to enact legislation specifically dealing with conservation easements. California, Connecticut, Massachusetts, New York, and eventually many other states designed state laws to clarify the uncertainties. If a state statute was well drafted, it defined what a conservation easement was, stated how they could be created, said that they are valid even though they are in gross, and declared how they could be enforced and by whom.

Not all the statutes were well designed, however, and by the late 1970s, there were enough states still without easement laws, or with inadequate laws, that the National Conference of commissioners on Uniform State Laws began work on a Uniform Conservation Easement Act (UCEA). This model conservation easement law was approved by the Commissioners in August 1981 and recommended for enactment by all states. A few months later, the American Bar Association gave its approval of the UCEA. It was a significant advancement for conservation easement law, prompting a number of states to adopt or revise easement statutes.

As this book points out, few states have adopted the UCEA exactly as written. Some have modified it quite a bit, perhaps to appease political interests or to address issues the enactors believed unique to their jurisdictions. The results vary and can be confusing for landowners and easement holders alike. Moreover, as conservation easements have become a commonly accepted conservation tool, some practitioners may even have forgotten that, in most places, conservation easements are creatures of state law.

Not surprisingly, land conservationists have paid a lot of attention to the requirements of federal tax law that govern deductibility of charitable gifts of easements, but enforcement of easements over time will depend heavily on state laws. This book not only reminds us of that, but also provides a wealth of information and analysis about those laws.

Anyone who has watched the use of conservation easements burgeon understands what a compelling tool easements are for protecting endangered natural areas, scenic properties, and working farms and forests. For many properties, it is hard to imagine a more appropriate tool. The case studies in this book recount some outstanding successes, painting a vivid picture of the complexity that can be involved in crafting sound easement transactions and building the partnerships necessary to ensure their success. These stories also demonstrate the extraordinary tenacity and skill of dedicated land conservationists who work through land trusts and the enormous difference their work is making in the lives of their communities.

Yet anyone who understands conservation easements is also acutely aware of how much of the work of protecting land begins *after* the easement is signed. Some of the case studies remind us that consistent attention is required if easements are to work as planned. Monitoring and enforcement are tasks for perpetuity.

Finally, as the land trust movement and the use of easements matures, we are faced with questions born of our success: When do easements work and when is a different tool more appropriate? What land should be protected, and how do we choose? How does land conservation intertwine with the economic and social goals of our communities? How do we convey an understanding of the benefits of land conservation? The book suggests some ways of thinking about those questions.

The years since William Whyte wrote his technical bulletin have brought enormous changes to land conservation. Although then land conservation was largely a job for government, today the job is shared by public and private efforts, with nonprofit groups often providing the innovation. Although then the number of nonprofit land trusts was fewer than 200, today the number exceeds 1,200. Although then the emphasis was on public land acquisition, today the focus is increasingly on private lands and a panoply of conservation methods to protect them.

Perhaps nothing better illustrates these changes than the evolution in the use of conservation easements. Used wisely and well, easements will continue to be a major conservation tool for the twenty-first century, protecting precious natural areas and green space for generations to come.

Jean Hocker

Preface

ᘗ ᘘ

The conservation easement has proved to be an effective tool for protecting the historical and ecological characteristics of particular buildings and land-scapes, contributing in a unique way to the stock of protected landscapes in the United States. Using such easements, private landowners first decide to protect the land and second to do so by conveying some of their rights to use the land to a nonprofit organization or a government agency that is then charged with the responsibility of ensuring that the requirements of the ease-ments are fulfilled.[1] They decide to do so because the benefit to them exceeds the cost involved the limited ability, to use the land surface in the future. For some, the prime benefits are intangible, the satisfaction at preserving a his-toric building or a spectacular scenic view, for example, and purely personal. To such individuals, the cost is inconsequential, even irrelevant. For most landowners, however, the prime benefits, although not the prime motivation, are the economic rewards they receive when they protect the land surface. They receive such rewards because land protection is considered a public, not merely a private, benefit, one that is widely shared. Consequently, protection receives the support of multiple jurisdictions that determine that its eco-nomic costs should be borne by all who will benefit. Landowners receive income and/or estate and/or property tax relief in return for conveying their real property rights; the community pays for those rights in the form of lost governmental income.

Contributors to this book describe examples of conservation easements with which they have been associated. The land protection purposes to which easements have been put are diverse. From protecting blufflands along the Upper Mississippi River, preserving a historic landscape in the Hudson River valley and farmland in Wisconsin and Pennsylvania, and providing buffers from sprawling urban development along national park system units in Ten-nessee and North Carolina, conservation easements have played a key role.

The conservation easement is a recent method of protecting the land sur-face. In many ways, it is a hybrid of the tools that have been used to protect lands throughout the twentieth century. Some of these earlier methods focus, as does the conservation easement, on the decisions that private landowners make about land use, with federal, state, and local governments providing financial incentives to persuade owners of lands with specific ecological characteristics into protecting their land. In such an approach, private landowners convey no real property rights but are merely compensated for exercising them in a particular way. In a somewhat different approach, federal, state, and local governments prevent owners of lands with specific ecological characteristics from using land in ways that will destroy these characteristics. Regulating how landowners can exercise their real property rights without compensation involves considerable political will on the part of governments and has elicited charges of "taking" real property rights. These approaches share two characteristics: The land remains in private ownership, and the public has no right of access.

Other methods of protecting land do not focus on private landowners. Federal and state governments actually acquire land with specific ecological characteristics from private landowners and protect the surface. Sometimes such lands become part of a management unit that emphasizes protecting the surface and may, or may not, provide public access. Governments have acquired a range of private landowners real property rights. Until recently, they acquired all the rights and became fee owners; the lands became public and, usually, exempt from ad valorem real property tax. Because of the actual cost of acquiring fee title and the resultant lost of tax revenue to local governments, however, the federal and state governments are increasingly opting to acquire only some of the real property rights from private landowners. In some cases, they acquire a possessory interest and thus become partial owners of a particular tract of land. In some cases, they acquire a nonpossessory interest and thus have no ownership claims, and the lands remain private.

The conservation easement possesses the compensation characteristic of the first-described methods of land protection and the conveyance characteristic of the last-described method. Completely avoiding the imposition of regulatory controls on private landowners, land protected through a conservation easement typically remains in private ownership and thus remains on the real property tax rolls. The easement, a nonpossessory interest in the land, is conveyed to a government agency or a nonprofit organization that has land protection as a prime goal.

> Conservation easements occupy an appealing niche in the array of land protection techniques—halfway between outright public or nonprofit ownership, at one extreme and government land-use regulation at the other. Easements are more permanent and often restrictive than land use regulation, which can shift with the political winds. At the same time, easements are tailored to the protection requirements of the par-

ticular property and to the desires of the individual landowner. Easements keep property in private hands and on the tax roles, and also carry a lower initial price tag than outright acquisition.[2]

The main difficulty associated with conservation easements is how the real property interests created by them, and qualifying as a charitable deduction for federal income tax purposes, have been treated by individual states and incorporated into the existing framework of real property law. Contributors to this book describe in some detail how different states have overcome this difficulty.

An Evaluative Context for Land Use Decisions

We need to use a broad perspective in evaluating conservation easements, a particular tool designed to achieve a particular goal in a particular way.[3] The decision of a current landowner to protect the land and the governments to promote land protection through this particular tool is merely the latest decision in a long line of decisions that both have made and have resulted in the very land surfaces that we now wish to protect.

Explaining how owners make such decisions demands that we look at decisions from a temporal perspective because the current ecological characteristics that are being protected owe their existence to decisions of successive landowners. Many landowners, however, have decided not to protect the land surface but to use the land to produce marketable goods and services. So, throughout the United States, protected lands exist alongside lands used for other purposes. Explaining why and how some owners decide to protect land and why and how some owners decide not to protect land demands that we also look at decisions from a spatial perspective.

Viewing conservation easements in this way places them in an appropriate social framework. After all, landowners who have decided to encumber their titles to land as a way of protecting it are merely part of a society consisting both of landowners, some of whom have decided to protect the land surface in other ways and some of whom have decided not to protect the land surface at all, and nonlandowners, who demand a variety of goods and an array of services that can only be produced or provided by landowners using the land surface in "nonprotective" ways. The various protected lands compose part of the kaleidoscope that is the American landscape.[4]

There is a problem in viewing conservation easements in this way. Conservation easements are tools that are specific to particular landowners. To examine how landowners make decisions, we need to create some general models of land use behavior. These models omit some of the specific details that characterize an easement but rather illustrate how all land use decisions, that both protect and do not protect the land surface and contribute to the American landscape, get made. Such models possess the additional advantage that they can also illustrate the fundamental characteristics of the democracy in which we live, a significant personal freedom with significant social controls on those freedoms. The resultant visible landscapes provide evidence, "of the kinds of people we are and were, and are in the process of becoming," a public document that reflects the complexities, ambiguities, contradictions, and paradoxes that characterizes our democracy.[5] We just need to know how to read it.

Landowners construct artifacts, produce goods, and provide services for a marketplace. They seek to satisfy a goal or goals based on their knowledge about the temporal and spatial ecological characteristics of the land they own, not unusually distilled into an index of productivity, their access to mechanical skills, including capital, and their a priori evaluation of the likelihood of a particular action achieving a desired result: to take advantage of place (Figure P.1). These goals, along with the available empirical information, the access to mechanical skills, and the evaluation procedures, compose interacting elements in all land use decisions. They create an evaluative context in which particular landowners make decisions to use land. The varying importance of each element to different landowners and the varying nature of these elements across space and in time explain the tremendous variety in the uses to which the land is put.

Despite this variety, however, there are geographies of land use. Different landowners, making decisions within a different context, make similar land

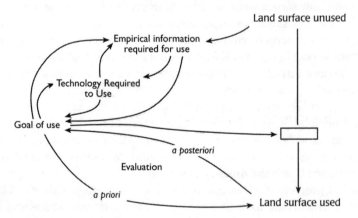

Figure P.1. A general land use model
Source: R. H. Squires

use decisions. Thus, individuals owning land on the margins of urban areas tend to make similar choices, as do individuals owning land in the corn belt of the Midwest. Moreover, a landowner tends to make the same sorts of decisions over short periods of time at least. There is some spatial and temporal consistency, some inertia, in land use decisions. How can we explain this phenomenon? Landowners are faced with a great deal of freedom in making land use decisions. Their freedom is not unlimited, however. In part, they are restricted by decisions they previously made. Any land use decision is really part of a temporal sequence of such decisions as each landowner evaluates the future, the likelihood of achieving a particular objective, in the light of the past and the present. Each land use decision is incremental, reflecting a past, a present, and a perceived future.[6]

Most of the restrictions on the freedom of a landowner derive largely from the relationship between landowners and nonlandowners. Some nonlandowners create the elements that form the evaluative context of the landowner, by promoting new goals, creating new technologies and new empirical information, and establishing new ways of assessing the outcomes of land use decisions. Other nonlandowners consume the goods and services landowners produce. Landowners, making decisions about how to use land, are faced with a constant stream of new technology, new information, and new ways of predicting and evaluating the outcomes of land use decisions. At the same time, they are also faced with a constantly increasing demand for goods and services.

How do conservation easements fit into this general land use decision model? Landowners establish easements on their property as one way of protecting land surfaces with particular ecological characteristics. The goal is to protect the land, the empirical knowledge concerns the characteristics that are to be protected, and the mechanical skill is the easement itself. Landowners who choose to use their land in this manner anticipate that their efforts at protecting the land surface will be successful although the easements need constant monitoring by those nonprofits or government agencies to which they are conveyed.

A Structural Context for Land Use Decisions

Landowners are part of an organized society in which relationships between all individuals, organizations, and governments are defined, a society in which some behaviors are encouraged and rewarded and other behaviors discouraged and penalized.[7] They are steered into making decisions about how to use their land by the rewards and penalties that stem from statutes, rules, and judicial opinions of multiple jurisdictions.[8] Appreciating social organization and the rewards and penalties faced by landowners is key to understanding landscapes. It would be a mistake, however, to focus solely on the behavior of landowners as a way of explaining landscapes. Landowners are enmeshed in complex relationships with nonlandowners, and their land use decisions reflect the decisions of all who live in a jurisdiction. Every land use decision, in fact, must be set against the rewards and the penalties that steers the behavior of all members of a jurisdiction. Described in this manner, all land use decisions should be examined against the backdrop of the continuous and acrimonious debates about the role and responsibilities of governments for producing goods and providing services.

The outcome of these debates, the statutes, rules, and judicial opinions that make up the law, defines sets of expectation and obligations for everyone. The law provides a structural context for all land use decisions creating a set of alternatives for landowners faced with choosing how to use land. Multiple jurisdictions have elegantly and inelegantly defined, differentially promoted, partially enforced, and variably protected the rights of use that give landowners expectations and obligations in making land use decisions. Expectations create opportunities for particular landowners and may require compensation if not met. Obligations, or duties, imposed on landowners effectively limit those expectations, and, if not fulfilled may result in penalties. In a similar manner, multiple jurisdictions have also elegantly and inelegantly defined, differentially promoted, partially enforced, and variably protected the rights that give nonlandowners expectations and obligations in making decisions about what goods and services to demand and actually acquire. Like landowners, if nonlandowners expectations are not realized, some compensation may be owed, and if nonlandowners do not fulfill obligations, they may be assessed penalties.

Viewed this way, landscapes document how individuals, organizations, and governments exercise rights that are channeled in certain directions by jurisdictions with powers to control those rights. Governments "steer" the exercise of all freedoms in particular directions, responding to public debate about the role and responsibility of governments to produce goods and services.

The Production Spectrum

Landscapes, created by landowners who evaluate alternatives created by the law and decide to use land in particular ways, can be summarized as a production spectrum (Figure P.2). Private land use and their artifacts reflect public policy as much as national parks. Both arise out of the debate regarding the role of governments and their responsibilities.

At one end of the spectrum are the public lands, owned by jurisdictions that use lands to produce goods and provide services that both supplement

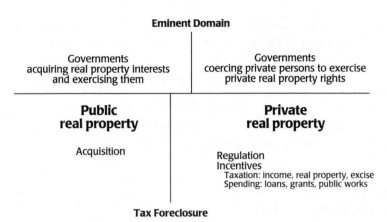

Figure P.2. A Production Spectrum
Source: R. H. Squires

and complement those produced by private landowners. Such goods and services include those not produced at all by private landowners—defense, justice, education, and wilderness, for example—and those produced in part by private landowners, outdoor recreation, lumber, and, most important for our viewpoint, land protection. The amount of public land and how it is used changes as constituents in a jurisdiction change their minds about what goods and services government should produce and whether such goods and services should be produced from publicly owned, rather than privately owned, land.

At the other end of the spectrum are the private lands owned by individuals and organizations. Governments play a vital role in the production of goods and services from such lands by coercing private landowners into making specific land use decisions. There are two principal forms of coercion. The first is a general coercion, unfocused on any specific decision. Governments have constructed transportation systems permitting private landowners to produce good and services and move them to market via road, rail, waterway, and airways. The second form of coercion is more direct and focused. Governments discourage certain land use activities, prohibiting some activities or assessing financial penalties. They also reward certain land use activities, by providing financial incentives, for example. In addition, governments prohibit or reward landowners for producing specific goods and services by placing limits on the quantity and quality of goods and services produced. In such instances, governments focus their attention more on the rights of the consumers than on the landowners and producers, ensuring safe products, healthy food, effective services, clean air and water, and goods and services that no landowners provide without coercion. The nature of the coercion changes from time to time as constituents in a jurisdiction collectively change their minds about what goods and services they require and how government should ensure private landowners produce those goods and services.

Conclusion

Conservation easements necessitate, first, laws defining the role and responsibility of governments in encouraging the protection of land, creating a context in which private landowners will choose to protect their land. Second, they require action by individuals and organizations in response to the law. The federal government encourages conservation easements through the federal income tax code. Individual states define, protect, and enforce the real property interests created by conservation easements. They also encourage their use by offering income and property tax incentives. Landowners exercise their real property rights to protect a particular land surface and to take advantage of monetary compensation offered by the governments, conveying part of their bundle of sticks to a third party. Organizations, especially land trusts, provide the third party oversight required by federal and state law. How state and local units of government have carried out this task and how landowners and nonprofit land trusts have responded is the focus of this book.

Such an analysis may help explain why particular individuals, particular organizations, and even particular governments do not favor the use of conservation easements. Some may argue that land protection is best produced from public lands or from private lands by governments regulating the behavior of private landowners rather than governments creating a new class of property rights. Some may not regard land protection as a responsibility of governments at all. In a democracy, such as ours, there will always be opponents of any goal that is established. Such opposition is both the blessing and the curse of a democracy. As Ackermann wrote,

> No longer a night-watchman the state surveys the outcome of market processes and finds them wanting. Armed with a prodigious array of legal tools, it sets about improving upon the invisible hand—taxing here, subsidizing there, regulating everywhere. The result of all this motion may well be something that redounds to the public good—a cleaner environment, a safer workplace, and a decent home. Nonetheless, these welfare gains can rarely be achieved without social cost—though many may gain, some will lose as a result of the new government initiative.[9]

This book concerns the implementation of a particular types of legal tool aimed at producing a particular type of land use, or rather avoiding a particular type of land use, with a specific goal in mind, protecting the ecological characteristics of the land surface.

Roderick Squires
University of Minnesota

Notes

1. Conservation easements, like other easements, run with the land and are encumbrances to the title. They are also nonpossessory. Easements and licenses are widely employed land use devices that have proved to be a source of frequent litigation and a topic of much legislation. Moreover, the variety of easements and licenses has steadily expanded over time. See Jon W. Bruce and James W. Ely Jr., *The Law of Easements and Licenses in Land,* rev. ed. (Boston: Warren, Gorham, and Lamont, 1995), p. vii.

2. Janet Diehl and Thomas S. Barrett, *The Conservation Handbook, Managing Land Conservation and Historic Preservation Easement Programs* (San Francisco: Trust for Public Land, 1988), p. 2.

3. My research and teaching focus on describing and explaining, first, the location and appearance of specific landscapes and second, the connections and disconnections between different landscapes in various contexts and at different spatial and temporal scales. I emphasize that our democracy requires public debates, and the outcomes of those debates, given legitimacy through statutes, rules, and judicial opinions, frame the decisions that individuals, organizations, and governments, landowners and nonlandowners alike, make, many of which influence land use activities and the landscapes. The framework was developed and is used to teach students about land use and about governments, not merely about conservation easements or land protection. This preface, then, is a statement of an approach, which seems to coherently explain the visible landscape, in terms of the society that created it, on the one hand its diversity from place to place and its apparent dynamism, and on the other, its apparent inertia. In my classes, I use a large number of disparate examples and case studies, many of them beyond the scope of the present work. My research into public land history has benefited considerably from such an approach. Clearly, the framework must be refined when applied to specific cases that deal with particular locations, time periods, and individuals, organizations, and governments.

4. Landscapes comprise visible objects although they clearly embody and reflect a range of human emotions. Although landscapes reflect how we use land, water, wildlife, minerals, and air, I specifically restrict my comments to activities influ-

encing the land surface because this is the principal focus of conservation easements. Land use activities have profoundly altered the nation's surface and underground waters, the biota, with which humans share Earth, and the envelope of air
above.

5. Peirce F. Lewis, "Axioms for Reading the Landscape, Some Guides to the American Scene," in *The Interpretation of Ordinary Landscapes,* edited by Donald W.
   Meinig, 11–32 (New York: Oxford University Press, 1979).

6. The term *muddling through* was introduced by Charles Lindblom to characterize
   the disjointed incrementalism process of making public policy. "The Science of
   Muddling Through" *Public Administration Review* (Spring 1959): 79–88. The
   same sort of analytical approach can be used to examine how decisions of all sorts
   get made, not just the decisions that involve several hundred individuals and
   questions of national and statewide significance that comprise public policy. Warren Johnson, *Muddling Toward Frugality* (San Francisco: Sierra Club Books,
   1978), noted: "The process of muddling through is a gutsy, down-to-earth
   process full of inefficiencies and inconsistencies. It takes an inordinate amount of
   time to take modest incremental steps forward and significant bold steps are
   clearly not in the cards. . . . It keeps this country pretty close to the middle of the
   road, while permitting slow faltering adjustments to change" (p. 151). Johnson
   argues that such a characterization conforms to Plato's definition of democracy,
   "a charming form of government, full of variety and disorder and dispensing a
   sort of equality and inequality to equals and unequals alike" (p. 151).

7. As William Blackstone noted, "Every man, when he enters into a society, gives up
   part of his natural liberty, as the price of so valuable purchase . . . obliges himself
   to conform to those laws which the community has though proper to establish."
   *Commentaries on the Laws of England. A Facsimile of the First Edition of
   1765–1769* (Chicago: University of Chicago Press, 1979), vol. 1, p. 121.

8. Such steering has long been accepted: "Every holder of property, however
   absolute and unqualified may be his title, holds it under the implied liability that
   his use of it may be so regulated that it shall not be injurious to the equal enjoyment of others having an equal right to the enjoyment of their property, nor injurious to the rights of the community. All property in the commonwealth is
   derived directly or indirectly from the government, and held subject to those regulations, which are necessary to the common good and general welfare. Rights of
   property, like other social and conventional rights are subject to such reasonable
   limitations in their enjoyment, as shall prevent them from being injurious, and to
   such reasonable restraints and regulations established by law, as the legislature
   may think necessary and expedient." (*Commonwealth v. Alger,* 7 Cushing's (Massachusetts) Reports 51 at 84, 1851.

9. Bruce A. Ackermann, *Private Property and the Constitution* (New Haven: Yale University Press, 1977) p. 1.

Acknowledgments

❦ ❦

The underlying premise for *Protecting the Land* began in 1995 when 4Ever Land Conservation Associates initiated a project to take a collective and reflective look at the current nature of the legal and practical framework of land conservation across the United States.

Initially, the project's aims were limited to a critique of land conservation legislation across the nation. From this maiden concept, it was concluded that a broader context for examination was important in understanding where we as a nation have been, where we are, where we are going in our ever evolving relationship with the land, and what role conservation easements have played in facilitating this evolution. Consequently, the project began to take on a broader aspect, which is reflected in the structure of the book. The views expressed throughout the book do not necessarily represent the views of the sponsoring organizations or those working or represented on their various governing boards, nor are the views expressed to be taken as those of 4Ever Land itself. Rather, they are the views from a broad spectrum of professionals working to protect cherished landscapes across the country.

We are indebted to a great many people for their help and guidance with this book. In particular, we are enormously grateful to our editor at Island Press, Heather Boyer, and all individual contributors and their research associates for their knowledge, insights, advice, and support. We have gained immeasurably from our numerous enjoyable and wide-ranging discussions and advice and could not have written such a volume without their help. We are also grateful to the many people who gave of their valuable time to speak with us and share their ideas, insights, and hospitality. We would also like to specially thank Barbara Warren; general manager of 4Ever Land for her countless hours dedicated to orchestrating the organization of conference calls, correspondence, and various aspects of proposal preparation and the emerging manuscript.

It is as appropriate here as anywhere else to say that none of the people mentioned herein bears any responsibility for what we have written. We have greatly appreciated assistance of those at both the University of Edinburgh and University of Minnesota, and those contributors whose knowledge of transferring electronic images greatly outweighed our own.

In addition, we would also like to thank our friends and colleagues at the University of Edinburgh Institute of Ecology and Resource Management and at the University of Minnesota Department of Geography for the opportunity to share their insights and to reflect on the importance of land protection in light of recent questions and on conservation and sustainability. Particular thanks must be given to friends Nantana Gajaseni, Lise Tole, and Isaac Odeyemi for their support and tolerance.

We would also like to thank our families for their forbearance at too many months of weekends spent writing and editing, and particularly to Ariel who, at the age of six, gave as much love, patience, support, and assistance as those many times her age.

J.A.G.
R.H.S.

Introduction

༯ ༞

Julie Ann Gustanski and Roderick H. Squires

The Contextual Setting

In laying the groundwork for the book in part I, chapters 1, 2, and 3 give the reader a broad context in which to consider conservation casements, their creation, and their use. Here the profound nature of the relationship between individuals and their environment is examined. Realizing that these relationships are not philosophical, abstract, and generalizable, each chapter focuses on a more narrowly defined context for understanding conservation easements.

Unlike the direction of many such texts that have touched on the use of conservation easements, this book looks to the legislation put into play in the Tax Reform Act of 1976.[1] This single piece of legislation has played an instrumental role in providing guidance to states, enabling legislation, and launching easements into widespread use by explicitly recognizing them as tax-deductible donations.

Chapter 1 reviews the role of the nation's land trusts as the principal employers of conservation easements and the capacity of easements to give individuals and their communities control to achieve their land conservation goals in the long term. Here Julie Ann Gustanski imparts information from current research, tying together the various strands that link conservation easements and land trusts, laying a foundation for following chapters.

Chapter 2 stages an overview of the state of the nation's conservation easement legislation. Todd Mayo makes some interesting comments and visionary insights. He reflects on the past, discusses the present, and makes some predictions for the future of conservation easements and the laws that give them firm ground.

Chapter 3 presents Stephen Small's views on how a once obscure tax code provision forged a role as a major land use planning tool and is taking private land protection into the twenty-first century.

In part II, the authors take an in-depth look at each states' unique interpretations of the UCEA. In addition, the authors explore the handful of "holdout" states that have not adopted some form of conservation easement enabling legislation. Here are offered interpretations on the various attempts to get conservation easement laws on the books.

1

In the introduction to part II, Rod Squires offers guidance to assist the reader through subsequent chapters that examine the nature of the nations' conservation easement enabling laws.

To group states into manageable chapters, the regional system of the federal judicial circuit structure has been used, which works well on several levels. First, states with geographic proximity frequently share similar legislative histories. Second, to the extent case law exists, it is more likely that neighboring states will look to precedent within the same circuit. Chapters 5, 15, and 19 have combined more than one federal circuit, largely to even the distribution of the number of states covered by each chapter.

Following each regional analysis of conservation easement enabling legislation are case studies in which the authors highlight some interesting and often unique applications of conservation easements.

The First and Second Federal Circuits

In chapter 5, Karin Marchetti and Jerry Cosgrove look at conservation easement legislation in those states within the First (Maine, Massachusetts, New Hampshire, and Rhode Island) and Second (Connecticut, New York, and Vermont) Federal Circuits.

Chapters 6 and 7 are case studies from two different states within the Second Circuit. Seth McKee recounts the unique process used to protect a historic viewshed in New York's Hudson River Valley, and Leslie Reed-Evans shares the journey of one rural Massachusetts land trust to combine the use of conservation easements with a limited development to protect farmland.

The Third Federal Circuit

Chapter 8 covers the Third Federal Circuit, which encompasses Delaware, New Jersey, Pennsylvania, and the Virgin Islands. Here Melanie Pallone examines the enabling legislation across the region. Pennsylvania, one of the nation's five states without conservation easement enabling statutes is within this circuit. Although Pennsylvania lacks easement enabling legislation that speaks to easements being held by nonprofit organizations, it maintains one of the nation's most active and thriving land trust communities. Currently, more than seventy land trusts serve nearly every corner of this vast state. Pennsylvania also has its share of case law challenging various aspects of easement validity.

In chapter 9, Dennis Collins reviews the trials and tribulations of a situation in which one landowner, after granting an easement, desired several substantive changes to the easement. The lessons learned about easement language and content are shared and discussed. The author, a longtime leader in the struggle to get enabling legislation on the books in Pennsylvania, reflects on its implications for conservation easements in the state.

In chapter 10, Tom Daniels presents an inclusive discussion on one of the country's most successful farmland preservation efforts. He suggests how communities can pursue dual goals of farmland protection and growth management through a comprehensive strategy that includes the use of conservation easements.

The Fourth Federal Circuit

Chapter 11 explores the enabling laws in the Fourth Federal Circuit states of Maryland, North Carolina, South Carolina, Virginia, and West Virginia. T. Heyward Carter Jr., W. Leighton Lord III, and Chalmers W. Poston Jr., present an illustrative examination of the legislation in this circuit.

In chapter 12, Sharon Richardson presents an interesting discussion on the impressive land conservation efforts in South Carolina's ACE Basin. The author reflects on South Carolina's Uniform Conservation Easement Act as the "foundation that has enabled some 80,460 acres of biologically diverse land to be protected in coastal South Carolina."

Chapters 13 and 14 again illustrate the land protection feats that that have been accomplished due to the enactment of conservation easement enabling legislation. In chapter 13, Charles Roe goes to the spectacular landscape of North Carolina's Blue Ridge Parkway, revealing how conservation easements have long been used to protect the nation's premiere scenic "motor road." He explores an impressive long-term project launched in 1996 when the city of Asheville conveyed a conservation easement over more than 17,000 acres of land.

In chapter 14, Randolph Brown looks at protecting the foothills of the Great Smoky Mountains of Tennessee. He recounts a project that has enabled the strategic protection of land to create a buffer zone between the Great Smoky Mountains National Park and the suburban sprawl of the greater Knoxville metropolitan area.

The Fifth and Eleventh Federal Circuits

In chapter 15, easement-enabling legislation in the southern states of Louisiana, Mississippi, and Texas comprising the Fifth Federal Circuit and Alabama, Florida, and Georgia in the Eleventh Federal Circuit is covered by Beth Davis, Laurie Fowler, Scott Fitch, and Hans Neuhauser.

In chapter 16, David Bezanson aptly introduces land conservation efforts in the Texas hill country. He recounts the efforts of a statewide land trust given solid footing with the enactment of the Texas UCEA. Here he discusses the dedication and valuable contributions of three landowners to preserve the natural ecosystems, wildlife, and rural character of Texas.

The Sixth Federal Circuit

Chapter 17 examines the differences, shared aims, and unique features of conservation easement enabling legislation in the Sixth Federal Circuit states of Kentucky, Michigan, Ohio, and Tennessee. John Rohe, drafter of the State Model Conservation Easement in Michigan, deftly presents the status of enabling statutes across this circuit.

In chapter 18, Linda Mead provides insights on one particularly interesting effort of the Little Travis Conservancy, located in Michigan's Upper Peninsula. Through the assistance of a firsthand account provided by the conservancy's director, Tom Bailey, Mead recounts how the unique partnership between a foundation, a land trust, and state and local governments worked cooperatively toward the protection of 600 acres of land in the Mackinaw Headlands.

The Seventh and Eighth Federal Circuits

Chapter 19 examines the diversity of legislation and conservation activity across this vast expanse of land that covers much of the U.S. agricultural heartland. The Seventh Federal Circuit encompasses Illinois, Indiana, and Wisconsin, while the Eighth Federal Circuit consists of Arkansas, Missouri, Iowa, Minnesota, North Dakota, South Dakota, and Nebraska. The level of conservation easement activity within this region varies as dramatically as the landscapes. Brian Ohm, Matthew Cobb, Julie Ann Gustanski, and Larry Meuwissen assess the varied patterns of conservation easement enabling legislation touching on other conservation efforts in the region. North Dakota, one of the "holdout states," is in the Eighth Federal Circuit. Mark Ackelson of the Iowa Natural Heritage Foundation provides a case study for chapter 19 that bespeaks the creativity and cooperative alliances characteristic of the conservation community. He travels to the blufflands of the upper Mississippi River, where land trusts from four states have come together to protect this scenic and diverse region.

Chapters 20 and 21 arise from Wisconsin, part of the Seventh Federal Circuit. In chapter 20, Tom Quinn presents an intricate scenario in which one Wisconsin land trust has joined forces with a conservation-oriented landowner to link the protection of a farm and river greenway along the St. Croix River with a community supported agriculture farm. In chapter 21, Christine Thisted shares insights on a cooperative venture with the Wisconsin Department of Natural Resources and the National Park Service to protect lands along the more than 1,000-mile-long Ice Age Trail.

The Ninth Federal Circuit

In chapter 22, William Hutton, one of the nation's leading tax law experts in this field, heads a team of coauthors in assessing the state of conservation easement enabling laws in the Ninth Federal Circuit. The Western and island states that comprise this circuit are Alaska, Arizona, California, Hawaii, Idaho, Montana, Nevada, Oregon, and Washington.

Chapter 23 details the protection efforts of New Mexico's Santa Fe Conservation Trust. Here John Wright explores land protection amidst a complex pattern of land tenure in northern New Mexico.

Chapter 24 describes how one land trust in California has addressed prioritizing proposed greenbelt lands for conservation using a geographic information systems approach. Brian Stark describes how the Conservancy of San Luis Obispo developed a GIS tool to assist this California land trust in identifying specific lands for protection.

In chapter 25, Robert Myhr reveals how conservation easement enabling laws in Washington State made a unique neighborhood conservation easement project on Orcas Island possible.

The Tenth Federal Circuit

In chapter 26, Heidi Anderson and William Silberstein of Colorado together with Matthew Cobb and Kelly Kindscher of Kansas analyze the unique and varied laws from Colorado, Utah, Wyoming, New Mexico, Kansas, and Oklahoma, which form the Tenth Federal Circuit. Oklahoma (in this circuit) and Montana (in the Ninth Federal Circuit) are two of the nation's five states without any form of enabling legislation. Here the multifaceted and largely political foundations that ground the status of enabling laws in these two states are examined.

In chapter 27, John Wright reflects on the use of conservation easements in Montana to protect agricultural land. Like Pennsylvania in the Third Federal Circuit, Montana has been repeatedly unable to get conservation easement enabling legislation passed. Similarly, Montana also has a thriving land trust community, yet it has not experienced the legal challenges found in Pennsylvania. Wright shares his experiences and insights on protecting agricultural lands in this Rocky Mountain state.

Case study chapters, drawing on examples from land trusts around the country, are intended to show the impact enabling legislation has had in the actual protection of land. The case studies reflect a broad range of interdisciplinary perspectives on the balance and connections between landscape and society. They explore some of the most innovative uses of conservation easements, including examples of easements on agricultural and natural lands, private development initiatives, and multiparty partnerships.

In part III, Julie Ann Gustanski stretches the boundaries of current decision making in the land trust–land conservation context in chapter 28. Land conservation practices *must* reflect the reality and "values" of the places we are seeking to protect. Integration of current land conservation practices, policies, and decision making are examined in the closing section of chapter 28 through the use of an integrated land conservation decision support model as a tool for evaluating lands for protection.

Finally, chapter 29 pulls together thoughts and reflections on the nature of land-saving actions given vigor through the UCEA and various state enabling laws. John Wright encourages our interpretations on the use of conservation easements to be as flexible as the tool itself.

Note
1. Public Law 94-455, The Tax Reform Act of 1976, § 2124.

Part I

❧❧

A Context for
Conservation Easements

Chapter 1

✺ ✺

Protecting the Land: Conservation Easements, Voluntary Actions, and Private Lands

Julie Ann Gustanski

Various legal instruments aim to protect, preserve, and defend the unique natural resources that provide meaning to the very fabric of the nation. Today, there is little doubt that an orchestrated tapestry of protected lands will only be achieved through the artistic use of a battery of legal mechanisms and administrative procedures. Among these measures is one tool that has now earned the position of being the most widely used private sector land conservation tool across the nation: the conservation easement (Figure 1.1).[1] Simply put, a conservation easement is a legally binding agreement that permanently restricts the development and future use of the land to ensure protection of its conservation values. The first American conservation easement, which permanently limited the development of land, was written in the late 1880s to protect the parkways in and around Boston designed by renowned landscape architect Frederick Law Olmsted.

Scores of articles, newsletters, and books have now been dedicated to covering the implementation, benefits, and requirements of qualified conservation easements. This book is an investigation into both the legal framework that fences our grasp of land and nature and our interpretations that guide us in its conservation. It is a search into the past, present, and future of what has become the single most important tool to protect privately owned land across the nation, the conservation easement.

Although much has been written about conservation easements, much remains to be shared, explained, and explored. Refining our knowledge about easements is the central purpose here. In fact, the title of this book presents an interesting and perhaps an unusual thought: that conservation of land should be about taking account of the *past* and *present* as well as looking to the *future*.

9

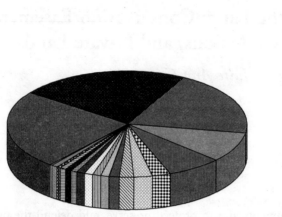

Legend:
- Land Donation
- Land Purchase
- CE Donation
- CE Part Purchase
- Preacquisition
- Limited Development
- Options
- Land Exchanges
- 3rd Party Negotiation
- CE Purchase
- Deed Restrictions
- Manage
- Nature Preserve
- ROFR
- Lease
- Lease & Management
- Restricted Sales
- Testamentary
- Agreements

Figure 1.1. Conservation methods used by U.S. land trusts.
Source: J. A. Gustanski (1997)

Naturally, most actions involving the protection of land are investments in the present made for the future often with respect to the past. For example, setting up national parks or nature preserves, passing protective enabling legislation, and educating people about the importance of the land are all investments in the *future,* made in the *present* based on experience. Until recently, however, the driving force behind most conservation work has been about hanging onto what we have inherited from the past. In this sense, the conservation of land resources has often had much in common with the protection of our heritage. Indeed, preservation of the natural and cultural heritage often occurs in a policy context. Globally, for example, the World Heritage Convention sought to protect natural and historic sites of "outstanding universal significance." In the United States, U.S.C. Title 16, Conservation, provides for the conservation "of the scenery and the natural and historic objects and wildlife therein."

Protecting the best lands we have inherited, be they agricultural, cultural, scenic or otherwise, is a vital part of all conservation work, but the world is not a historic relic, rather, it is a living, evolving, and dynamic entity.

At the heart of all land use and conservation issues are the laws designed to bring about collective decisions about this important resource. The Uniform Conservation Easement Act (UCEA) and related state enabling laws have laid the legal foundations enabling land trusts, working with local, state,

The Uniform Conservation Easement Act: An Overview

The UCEA was approved in 1981 by the National Conference of Commissioners on Uniform State Laws.[3] Its purpose is to enable durable restrictions and affirmative obligations to be attached to real property to protect natural and historic resources and to remove obsolete common law defenses that might obstruct such efforts (see Appendix A). Although the UCEA does not itself impose restrictions or affirmative duties, it does allow consenting parties to do so within an arrangement free from common law impediments, as long as the conditions of the act are met.

The conditions of the UCEA are designed to ensure that transactions serve defined protection purposes and that such interests are placed with a "holder" that is either a governmental body or a charitable organization with an interest in the subject matter. Conservation easements may be created in the same manner as other easements in land. The UCEA also enables the parties to establish a right of a third party to enforce the terms of the transaction if the possessor of the right is also a governmental unit or charity.

In designating these interests so protected by the UCEA as "easements," the terminology reflects the rejection of other options that exist in some state laws that contend with nonpossessory conservation interests. First, common law disabilities associated with real covenants, equitable servitudes, and those of easements are removed. As altered by statute, these three common law interests retain their existence as tools used to meet conservation and preservation goals. Second, the UCEA seeks to create a unique additional interest. Although unfamiliar to common law, it is, in some fuzzy sense, a revised mixture of the three traditional common law interests.

In adapting conservation easements to conventional easements, the UCEA permits great freedom by allowing the parties to such easements to arrange their relationship as they see fit. The UCEA differs in this respect from some of the state enabling laws, in particular those that require planning or other governmental agency review. In addition, with the exception of the requirement of section 2(b) that the acceptance by the holder be recorded, the formalities of recording such easements are left to individual states.

The UCEA enables the creation of conservation easements of unlimited duration subject to the power of a court to modify or terminate them in states whose case or statutory law allows their courts such power. There are, however, supplementary safeguards; as mentioned earlier, easements may only be created for specified purposes and may only be held by certain government or nonprofit organizations. Enabling the creation of such easements also makes it possible for the donor to fit within federal tax law requirements that the interest be "in perpetuity" if certain tax benefits are sought.

Restrictions burdening real property in perpetuity or for long periods can fail due to changed conditions affecting the property or the surrounding area, because the holder of the conservation easement may cease to exist, or for other reasons not anticipated at the time of its creation. An array of doctrines, including the *doctrines of changed conditions* and *cy pres*, has evolved through the judicial system and, in many states are legislatively sanctioned as a basis for responding to these unpredictable occurrences. Under the doctrine of changed conditions, privately created restrictions on land use may be terminated or altered if they no longer achieve their intended purpose due to the changed conditions. As seen in later chapters, some state laws provide that the court's order limiting or terminating restrictions may include certain terms and conditions, including monetary adjustments, as it finds necessary to protect the public interest and to ensure a fair resolution of the problem. The doctrine is applicable to real covenants and equitable servitudes in all states, although its function concerning easements is, in many states problematic.

The doctrine of *cy pres* provides that if a charitable trust cannot carry out its purposes due to a change in circumstances, courts may impose terms and conditions that may facilitate achievement of the general charitable objectives while altering specific provisions of the trust. The same is true in cases where a charitable trustee ceases to exist or can no longer carry out its responsibilities; the court will appoint a substitute trustee upon proper application and will not allow the trust to fail.

It can be difficult to determine through casual observation whether a state has adopted the major provisions of the UCEA. Some states have departed from the title and have even omitted the term uniform. Some states have altered the language of the uniform act to suit their specific conditions, their political history and legal traditions, and in particular their approaches to real property rights and land uses targeted in the UCEA.

and federal government agencies, to protect nearly 1.4 million acres of private lands across the United States through conservation easements.[2]

Conservation Easements, Voluntary Actions, and Private Lands

The cultural value of our landscape and the economic impact of land conservation and general environmental improvement are matters of concern to a widening audience in the United States. In recent years, at every level, legislation and programs have been enacted to protect a diversity of land resources. At the heart of many of these efforts are land trusts that either facilitate the protection of lands through these devices or in supplement to public agency efforts.

Land trusts are predominantly nonprofit local, regional, or statewide organizations that work with private landowners to protect their land for conservation, recreation, and other public benefit. They work to conserve land that is important to the communities and regions in which they operate by undertaking or assisting direct land transactions. Typically, these organizations act to acquire land, conservation easements, management agreements, or other interests in real property for the purpose of enabling public benefit from the land.

Lands acquired or otherwise protected by land trusts may include but are not exclusively limited to scenic vistas, urban parks, gardens, greenways and wildlife corridors, open space, wetlands and groundwater recharge zones,

Table 1.1. Attitudes Toward Open Space and Land Conservation in the United States

Statement	Level of Agreement (%)		Total (%)
	Agree	Strongly Agree	
Preserving open space			
Too much is already done to protect open space.	1.2	3.5	4.7
Policies protecting open space could be stronger.	22.0	55.7	77.7
Responsibility			
Farmers and other owners of land should look after rural lands.	13.1	53.6	66.7
Everyone should look after open space.	31.9	54.6	86.5
Access			
Everyone should have access to outdoor recreational areas.	22.7	59.0	81.7
Farmland and farming			
Policies protecting farmland from development should be stronger.	25.1	46.1	71.2
Protecting other lands			
Lands providing habitat for rare or endangered species are the most important lands to protect.	21.8	32.6	54.4
More areas should be set aside as national parks so that they are protected from development.	30.4	40.3	70.7
More emphasis should be place on protecting historical landscapes.	13.8	43.3	57.1

Source: J. A. Gustanski, Survey, "Public Attitudes Towards Land Use and Conservation" (1996).

farmland, cultural and historic lands, habitat, and river corridors. Each land trust has its own mission statement, specific to its setting and region, although there is a common intent among land trusts, the protection of land resources.

Recent research in the United States shows that most people believe that the conservation of land and its appurtenant resources, be they historic, natural, agricultural, or scenic, makes a major contribution to the economic and social well-being of the places where we live (Table 1.1).[4] Derived from the August 1996, phase II mail survey entitled "Public Attitudes Towards Land Use and Conservation," Table 1.1 reflects dominant attitudes expressed by the survey population. Shifts in attitudes toward the environment since the 1960s have acted to strengthen both legislative protection and policy guidance on conservation of the environment, of which land is a critical component. Changes to tax law and passage of the American Farm and Ranch Protection Act (see chapter 4) are the most recent examples of the far-reaching effects such laws may have at the local level.[5]

Conservation Easements

The fastest-growing method for protecting land is the conservation easement (Table 1.2). Across the nation, landowners have shown a growing commitment to limiting future development on their land by working through land trusts. Nearly 1.4 million acres of land have been protected by conservation easements (Figure 1.2).[6]

A conservation easement is a less than fee, nonpossessory interest in a parcel of land created by deeds executed with the same formalities associated with the other forms of real estate conveyances. Although conservation easements can be conveyed by a landowner to either a qualified tax exempt 501(c)(3) land trust or a government agency, it is the growing band of land trusts that have capitalized on the strength and flexibility of this land protection tool.[7] With the advent of the reforms to the tax code in 1976, the popularity ascent of conservation easement use by land trusts began.[8]

The bundle of rights analogy used by property law professors across the

Table 1.2. Growth in Acres Protected with Conservation Easements, 1988-98

Method of Protection	1988 (acres)	1990 (acres)	1994 (acres)	1998 (acres)	Ten-Year Growth (%)
Fee title ownership by land trusts	300,000	440,000	535,000	828,000	176
Conservation easements held by land trusts	290,000	450,000	740,000	1,385,000	377

Source: Compiled using data obtained from Land Trust Surveys (1990 and 1995) and Land Trust Census, 1998.

Note: Due to inconsistencies in data collection over the period, data do not reflect the acreage of land acquired by land trusts and transferred to government or other third parties.

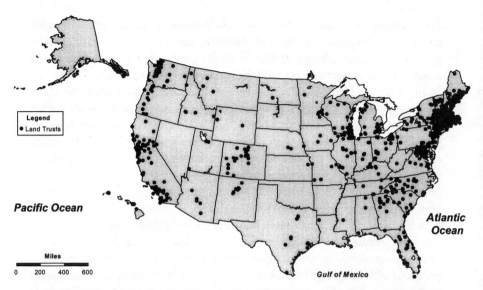

Figure 1.2. Distribution of land trusts in the United States.
Source: J. A. Gustanski (1998)

nation works well to explain the nature of this nonregulatory, voluntary conservation tool. Essentially, the rights of landownership, or the proverbial "ownership bundle," is much like owning a bundle of sticks. Each stick represents a different right that is attributable to landownership, such as, development, forestry, mining, farming, or recreation. Rights typically removed from the land by a conservation easement include development and mining. Those rights that remain with the land are generally those seen as nondestructive and otherwise conducive to the protection of the resource itself.

Some people have come to refer to such easements as development rights, which in turn has sprung the term *purchase of development rights,* or PDR. Although a conservation easement is not actually equivalent to a "development right," both may be thought of as one stick from the infamous bundle that contains those rights of development associated with landownership. In practice, PDRs are generally programs enacted at the state, regional, or local level that allow governments to acquire development rights to private property.[9]

As revealed throughout this volume, conservation easements—although given life and power through the UCEA and myriad state enabling laws—are neither mandatory nor a governmental regulatory tool.[10] Rather, easements are entirely voluntarily and are donated or sold by landowners at their discretion. Resulting restrictions on the land are arrived at jointly, a concerted effort between the landowner and the organization or agency accepting the easement.

This synergetic relationship fosters the development of a long-term vision for perpetual management of the land. Although easements may occasionally be granted for a specified period, this course is unusual, due to provisions of the Internal Revenue Service Code and most state enabling legislation.[11]

In essence, granting a conservation easement creates a legal partition of the ownership bundle of rights. The recipient organization retains the rights associated with development. In turn, the landowner continues to hold fee simple title to the property, with an understanding that uses must be in keeping with the terms of the easement. The organization, in accepting the easement, assumes perpetual responsibility for ensuring that neither the grantor nor successors violate the terms set forth in the easement, hence the need for annual monitoring of easement protected lands. If the terms of the agreement have been breached, the easement holder is under obligation to take necessary action to ensure that the landowners make required corrections. Although such transgressions occur infrequently with the grantors, there is increased potential with successive landowners for easement infringement. Assumption and enforcement of a conservation easement is a lofty responsibility, as is pointed out in chapter 18. Fortunately, it is rare that those organizations that have included easements in their conservation tool chests have had to resort to court action to uphold the integrity of an easement. Conservation easements have now been used since the late 1920s, yet only since the 1980s have their application become popular,[12] thus increasing the likelihood of growth in the number of easement challenges in the future.

Most private land trusts believe that every conservation easement should be unique and specifically adapted to the needs of the individual landowner and the features of the land. Their public counterparts, however, more oft than not, use a more standardized or "cookie cutter" approach to easement design. Regardless, all conservation easements meeting UCEA requirements run with the land, binding all future landowners to the restrictions of the easement. Conservation easements derive their strength in part from their binding connection to title and genuine custodial commitments of landowners to the land. Unlike government-issued policies and regulations on land use, easements have the distinction of redefining traditional models of land ownership. Some may argue that the history of conservation easement use is not sufficiently long enough to determine what the long-term effects may be, but if the increase in their use is any measure, it seems that only a positive judgment can be made.

The passage of the UCEA was a monumental advance for conservation easements, the organizations that employ them, and landowners wanting to protect their cherished lands. Although most probably not his original intent, Stephen Small, in chapter 3, deems the tax code as it applies to conservation easements as a "major land use planning tool." One thing is clear: with the enactment of the UCEA, the granting of a conservation easement to a qualified organization is ensured the same treatment under federal law as other charitable contributions, such as a cash donation to the United Way.

In general, the tax benefits to the landowner generated by a conservation easement are determined by subtracting the value of the land after the easement from its value before granting the easement. The difference between these two values is essentially the amount assigned to the charitable donation. Just as before, the landowner continues to own the fee title to the land, to govern public access, and in most cases to pay taxes on the land. Although legislation in some jurisdictions has been adopted to ensure that easement conservation are taxed in accordance with their restricted nature, this treatment is by no means universal. Land protected by a conservation easement may continue to be bought, sold, or otherwise conveyed by inheritance as usual.

The origins of conservation easements are in use by government agencies to protect scenic routes and wildlife habitat.[13] Today, lands protected through the donation of conservation easements to land trusts across the nation outweigh those so protected by government agencies. Despite the efforts of countless planning commissions and local and regional government agencies, many people across the country have become frustrated and disillusioned by the failings of various government programs to adequately protect cherished lands from sprawling development. This disappointment factor has played a significant role in the phenomenal growth of land trusts.

Land Trusts, Past and Present

Since the mid-1980s, more than 650 land trusts have been formed across the United States and Canada. Their present vogue and influence conceals a remarkably long chronicle. The grandfather of all land trusts, the Trustees of Reservations in Massachusetts, was formed in 1891.[14] Whether in 1891 or 1991, land trusts have largely formed in response to two predominant factors: rapid growth in population and the development of land.

Halfway through the twentieth century, just over 50 land trusts existed, predominantly in New England. By 1965, the number of land trusts had grown to 132, with a geographic spread that now included some two dozen states. At that time, nearly all organizations were located in the Northeast and Mid-Atlantic states.[15] By 1980, the number of such organizations had expanded fourfold. The explosive development trends of the 1980s across the United States spurred conservation efforts throughout the country. Today, more than 1,200 land trusts exist, supported by more than 900,000 members across the country.[16]

At the 1995 National Land Trust Rally, Jean Hocker, president of the Land Trust Alliance (LTA), remarked in her opening address that the growth of the land trust movement was unsurpassed by any other sector of the larger "envi-

Table 1.3. Growth in Land Trusts by Region, 1988–98

Region	Base Year 1988[a]	1990	Increase (%)	1994	Increase (%)	1998	Change +/- (%)	Ten-Year Growth (%)
Rocky Mountains	20	28	40.0	42	50.0	52	23.8	160.0
Southwest	15	19	26.6	27	42.1	37	37.0	146.0
South	65	74	13.8	114	54.0	142	24.5	118.0
West Coast	83	119	43.4	173	45.4	173	0.0	108.0
Mid-Atlantic	117	154	31.6	202	31.2	222	10.0	89.7
Great Lakes	84	97	15.5	116	19.6	145	25.0	72.6
New England	336	374	11.3	395	5.6	417	5.7	24.1
Plains	21	23	9.5	26	13.0	23	−11.5	9.5

Source: Compiled using information obtained from Land Trust Surveys (1990 and 1995); and, Land Trust Census, 1998 J. A. Gustanski, Phase III Expert Interviews (1996–98). States comprising the named regions are as follows: South (AL, AR, FL, GA, KY, LA, MS, NC, SC, TN, VA, WV); Rocky Mountains (CO, ID, MT, UT, WY); West Coast (AK, CA, HI, NV, OR, WA); Southwest (AZ, NM, OK, TX); Mid-Atlantic (DE, MD, NJ, NY, PA); Great Lakes (IL, IN, MI, OH, WI); Plains (IA, KS, MN, MO, ND, NE, SD); New England (CT, MA, ME, NH, RI, VT). The District of Columbia is included in the Mid-Atlantic region.

[a] The base year of 1988 was established because it was the first year that the Land Trust Alliance actually disseminated surveys to known land trusts across the United States.

ronmental movement" umbrella. Between 1990 and 1994 alone, local and regional land trusts in the United States increased by 23.3 percent, or approximately one new land trust per week over this four-year period.[17]

Since their early beginnings, land trusts in the United States have protected over 4.7 million acres of land, some 300,000 acres more than the total land and water area of the District of Columbia, Connecticut, and Rhode Island combined.[18] Although the concentration of land trusts remains strongest in New England, which boasts more than a third of the nation's land trusts, recent years have seen rapid growth in both sheer numbers and activity in other areas of the country (Table 1.3). Between 1994 and 1998, the Southwest, for example, saw the most rapid growth, with the number of land trusts increasing by more than 37 percent and an increase of protected lands of nearly 61 percent. The South, Southwest, West Coast, and Rocky Mountain states have all shown impressive growth and strengthened land trust activity since 1988. The 1998 National Land Trust Census reported that were 1,213 land trusts in the United States, an increase of 470 organizations since 1988. The growth trend that began at the end of the 1980s set the pace for the next ten years, when more than 63 percent of the nation's land trusts formed.[19]

Growth in Acreage Protected

Through 1998, land trusts in America have helped to protect an area larger than the District of Columbia, Connecticut, and Rhode Island combined: a total of 4.7 million acres of land (see Table 1.4). This is an increase of 2 million acres, or approximately 135 percent, since 1988.[20] Protected acreage includes:

Land owned by land trusts	828,000 acres
Conservation easements held by land trusts	1,385,000 acres
Land acquired and transferred to third parties	2,487,000 acres

Although the conservation easement has taken lead as the most widely used conservation tool among the nation's land trusts, the LTA reports that an additional 1,764,000 acres have been protected through other methods.[21] Among these are deed restrictions, acquisition of mineral rights, preacquisition by other organizations or government agencies, and limited developments. Between 1990 and 1994, the South had both the greatest proportional growth in the number of land trusts and the greatest percentage increase in acreage protected: approximately 190,000 acres, or more than a doubling of land trust-protected acreage in the region. Other regions with impressive growth were the West Coast with 170,000 acres (a 42 percent increase) and the Mid-Atlantic with an additional 160,000 acres (a 37 percent increase).[22]

Table 1.4. Land Protected by State and Method by U.S. Land Trusts

State	Number of Land Trusts	Total Acres	Acreage Breakdown			
			Owned	Easement	Transferred to Third Party	1995 Protected Other Methods
AL	3	31,472	5,472	0	26,000	2,385
AK	4	1,312	395	917	0	0
AZ	10	3,339	280	857	2,202	0
AR	2	1,666	1,581	85	0	0
CA	119	536,922	235,571	78,099	223,252	59,813
CO	29	95,593	6,124	79,783	9,686	10,105
CT	113	54,094	38,694	12,946	2,454	2,973
DE	4	33,883	20,537	1,527	11,819	10,571
FL	29	56,839	9,899	17,071	29,869	9,110
GA	23	7,646	1,457	6,189	0	10
HI	4	7	2	5	0	0
ID	8	23,042	778	8,315	13,949	100
IL	31	43,834	8,309	3,498	31,577	7,645
IN	6	3,461	3,247	209	5	16
IA	5	39,825	5,392	3,445	30,988	21,379

(continues)

Table 1.4. Continued

State	Number of Land Trusts	Total Acres	Acreage Breakdown		Transferred to 3rd Party	1995 Protected Other Methods
			Owned	Easement		
KS	2	219	0	219	0	0
KY	9	2,997	1,296	12	1,689	8,298
LA	1	15,555	651	14,604	300	0
ME	80	82,038	19,218	59,141	3,679	52,202
MD	41	93,114	6,938	79,342	6,834	2,177
MA	137	150,515	91,259	35,811	23,445	15,635
MI	38	46,929	30,338	10,648	5,943	334
MN	2	8,450	1,250	4,855	2,345	0
MS	1	2,973	1,098	1,875	0	0
MO	9	6,438	6,426	12	0	0
MT	9	296,840	261	258,416	38,163	0
NE	3	16,846	15,146	1,700	0	0
NV	4	4,843	0	118	4,725	94,111
NH	32	127,662	48,215	65,659	13,868	820,032
NJ	34	90,403	24,765	4,800	60,838	1,453
NM	7	28,986	873	28,113	0	12,317
NY	68	345,034	49,855	190,924	104,255	34,933
NC	22	37,741	6,259	26,564	4,918	23,302
ND	1	4,834	4,154	0	680	0
OH	27	10,732	7,374	2,885	473	677
OK	1	0	0	0	0	0
OR	17	11,711	386	2,654	8,671	204
PA	75	348,239	54,014	59,774	234,451	80,614
PR	1	2,131	1,176	0	415	
RI	29	12,544	8,795	3,519	230	483
SC	14	29,747	4,978	22,071	2,700	256
SD	1	9,062	0	7,760	1,302	0
TN	13	23,637	6,932	1,797	14,908	9,896
TX	20	11,531	3,244	3,823	4,464	1,275
UT	4	22,805	19,787	3,000	18	467,972
VT	26	193,061	41,647	138,769	12,645	8,668
VI	1	50	50	0	0	0
VA	16	132,953	11,368	118,402	3,183	0
WA	29	27,230	10,219	11,949	5,062	4,298
WV	9	364	289	75	0	0
WI	43	15,117	9,560	5,141	416	400
WY	2	37,752	1,467	7,585	28,700	0
TOTAL	1,218	3,184,018	827,026	1,384,963	961,445	1,763,644

Source: Land Trust Alliance; Land Trust Survey, 1995; and, Land Trust Census, 1998.

Note: The 1998 land trust census conducted by the Land Trust Alliance, unlike previous surveys, does not include land protected through other methods (deed restrictions, acquisition of mineral rights, or negotiating acquisition for other organizations or agencies). According to the Land Trust Alliance, some 1.5 million additional acres are protected using such tools.

Type of Land Protected

Land trusts protect a diversity of land resources. Phase II research interviews conducted between 1996 and 1998 on a minimum 10 percent representative sampling of 120 land trusts revealed that wildlife habitat ranked as the number one resource to which land trusts devote attention (76.6 percent).[23] By comparison, the 1994 Land Trust Survey reflects some 80 percent of land trusts respondents protected wildlife habitat as a primary goal, whereas the 1998 National Land Trust Census indicates only 38 percent of survey respondents "primarily or very involved" in the protection of wildlife habitat.[24] Table 1.5 identifies those land resources protected by land trusts included within the phase III representative research sample.[25] Other leading efforts of the nation's land trusts include the protection of forests (70.5 percent), open space (69.5 percent), and watersheds (64.3 percent). Closely behind in the fifth, sixth, and seventh positions are wetlands (60.4 percent), scenic views and roads (55.7 percent), and ecosystems (55.2 percent). Protecting recreational resources is also a high priority for land trusts: 50.3 percent focus on greenways and another 49 percent on trails; and an equal number focus on the protection of floodplains and their affiliated amenity values. Land trusts also help in the plight to conserve productive lands: more than half (51 percent) participate in farmland protection and some 34 percent work with the protection of ranch lands.

Table 1.5. Land Resources Protected by U.S. Land Trusts

Land Features Protected	Land Trusts Interviewed (%)	Land Features Protected	Land Trusts Interviewed (%)
Wildlife habitat	76.6	River corridors	35.3
Forests	70.5	Coastlines	35.2
Open space	69.5	Ranch land	34.3
Watersheds	64.3	Mountains	34.3
Wetlands	60.4	Hillsides	33.8
Scenic views and roads	55.7	Lakes	32.9
Ecosystems	55.2	Urban land	28.9
Farms	51.0	Islands	28.9
Greenways	50.3	Prairies	27.6
Recreation and trails	49.0	Archaeological sites	25.7
Floodplains	49.0	Community gardens	22.9
Historic and cultural areas	46.2	Deserts	15.8

Source: J. A. Gustanski, Phase III: Land Trust Interviews (1996–98).

Although land trusts are principally concerned with direct land protection initiatives, they also undertake many other related efforts. Some 78 percent of all land trusts report maintaining land for public access or recreational purposes, 75 percent conduct public education and outreach activities, and 60 percent now undertake land use planning.[26] From detailed analysis provided through on-site visits and the interview process, it is clear that no two land trusts are alike. Each organization experiences its own evolution, adapting both the protection of particular land resources and the services provided, unique to the location. Although some land trusts may participate in the development of land policies, others may play an active role in providing urban populations with gardening opportunities and still others may take part in affordable housing initiatives.

Conclusion

Historically, land has represented power and influence. Landowners across the nation have increasingly used conservation easements to help them achieve land protection goals, thereby permanently altering traditional notions of land tenure by partitioning the "bundle" of rights.

The provisions in the Tax Reform Act of 1976 and Tax Treatment Extension Act of 1980 have led the way for the use and success of conservation easements. The estate tax savings from such charitable donations encourage transfers of real estate to philanthropic and public uses. In addition, they have worked to save many hundreds of thousands of acres from inheritance tax breakups, accelerated conversion, subdivision, and development.

Conservation easements have the capacity to give individuals and their communities control to achieve their land conservation objectives in the long term. In the legal analysis chapters, legal authorities from across the nation illuminate that individual states, embracing their uniqueness and given set of land resources have produced enabling legislation to meet their own needs.

The case studies presented throughout this book show how the dynamic and entrepreneurial character of land trusts across the nation have pushed, pulled, and stretched the dimensions of easement application. The range of applications to which conservation easements can and have been put are countless.

Notes

1. J. A. Gustanski (1996–98). Data derived from Phase III Expert Interviews conducted in conjunction with doctoral research. The operative framework of this research is a comparative analysis of private land conservation in the United States and Britain. Focus groups, mail surveys, and expert interviews were used to verify, test, and ground the development of an integrated land conservation decision support (ILCDS) tool. The conceptual model applies an integrated

approach that extends beyond traditional bioecological constraints through incorporation of both and qualitative social and quantitative economic information. Between July and October 1996 and November 1997 and June 1998, 120 land trust professionals across the United States were interviewed to explore a range of issues linked to the three dimensions of the research paradigm. Interview questions focused on (1) considering how land trusts measure their success, (2) the decision processes employed, (3) land conservation tools used, (4) perceptions about public attitudes toward land conservation, and (5) applicability of the proposed ILCDS model and uses envisioned. The interview process gathered a wealth of detailed information and presented several advantages for obtaining information pertinent to the land trust setting. Principal among these are that the nature of the information sought is not easily quantified, complexities of real world experiences are not oversimplified, relationships among variables do not favor statistical interpretation, and an understanding of the "big picture" is facilitated. The interview technique adopted is best characterized as a standardized open-ended approach. See also Land Trust Survey (1990 and 1995), Land Trust Alliance: Washington, D.C.; and National Land Trust Census 1998, Land Trust Alliance: Washington, D.C., hereinafter Land Trust Census, 1998.

2. Uniform Conservation Easement Act (UCEA) § 1 et seq.; Title 26 U.S.C. § 170(h); I.R.C. § 170(h). The Land Trust Alliance, the umbrella organization for the more than 1,200 land trusts across the nation, reports in its 1998 survey that some 1,385,000 acres have been protected using conservation easements. Land Trust Census, 1998.

3. *Uniform Laws Annotated,* master edition (St. Paul: West Publishing, 1968), 1998 pocket part 10.

4. J. A. Gustanski, Phase II mail survey, "Public Attitudes Towards Land Use and Conservation" (August 1996). The survey was distributed to a cross section of 2,000 individuals across the United States to identify particular attitudes, key issues, values, and preferences toward land conservation objectives of the general public. In keeping with the aims of the related research, the survey was administered in both Britain and the United States. Developed using information derived from Phase I focus groups together with information distilled from interviews with appropriate officials and organizations, the mail survey was sent to a stratified random sampling of people aged eighteen or over, with an equal distribution by gender, geographic location, and socioeconomic profiles in each country.

5. American Farm and Ranch Protection Act, sec. 508 of the Taxpayer Relief Act, enacted August 5, 1997.

6. Land Trust Census, 1998.

7. U.S. Code, Title 26, §170(h).

8. U.S.C. § 170(f)(3)(b)(iii).

9. See T. Daniels, *Holding Our Ground: Protecting America's Farms and Farmlands* (Washington, D.C.: Island Press, 1997) for detailed coverage on PDR programs in the United States.

10. Uniform Conservation Easement Act of 1981.

11. Several state statutes do not have perpetuity requirements or language specifically enabling term easements.

12. B. Ohm (1998) and J. A. Gustanski (1997) research findings.

13. In 1951, the Wisconsin state Highway Department purchased easements along Great River Road. The National Park Service purchased scenic easements as early as the 1930s for lands adjacent to the Blue Ridge and Natchez Trace Parkways. Among other early users of conservation easements were the U.S. Forest Service and the U.S. Fish and Wildlife Service, who have used easements to protect scenic areas and habitat.

14. This Boston-based organization began in response to land development spurred by a growth in the country's population from 38 million to 76 million between 1870 and 1900. Newsletters and information pack supplied by the Trustees of Reservations, September 1997.

15. J. A. Gustanski. The figures represented have been determined through the compilation and aggregation of data and information collected in connection with doctoral research.

16. Land Trust Census, 1998; J. A. Gustanski (1999). Zip code data files of U.S.-based organization (1996–98) compiled from information obtained from organizations themselves and other miscellaneous sources were entered into Excel-formatted files. Geocoding and plotting of points were accomplished by integrating files with BusinessMAP Pro 1.1 (1995–97), Environmental Systems Research Institute, Inc., Redlands, Calif.

17. Land Trust Survey (1995).

18. Total area was calculated using information from the U.S. Bureau of the Census, *Statistical Abstract of the United States,* 11th ed. (Washington, D.C.: U.S. Government Printing Office, 1991). Total area includes dry land and land temporarily covered by water as well as water areas within a state's boundaries (i.e., inland, coastal, and Great Lakes waters). Total area cited includes (1) District of Columbia, 68 square miles (43,520 acres); (2) Connecticut, 5,544 square miles (3,548,160 acres), and (3) Rhode Island, 1,231 square miles (787,840 acres).

19. Land Trust Surveys (1991 and 1995); Land Trust Census, 1998; J. A. Gustanski, Land Trust Interviews (1996–98).

20. Land Trust Census, 1998.

21. J. A. Gustanski (1996–98). Research interviews conducted with the sample population revealed that conservation easements (donated, purchased in whole or in part, or given through bequest) have become the most widely used conservation tool among U.S. land trusts.

22. J. A. Gustanski, Phase III Expert Interviews (1996–98); Land Trust Surveys (1990 and 1995); Land Trust Census, 1998.

23. J. A. Gustanski, Phase III Expert Interviews (1996–98). In both the United States and Britain the subject land trust population was divided into distinct geographical units or clusters. The interviewed subpopulation was then selected from within each cluster. This technique worked well given the size and dispersion of organizations, and the expense and effort of travel involved. The minimum sample population of 10 percent for each country percent was drawn from those

organizations known to exist, resulting in 120 interviews in the United States and 19 in Britain. A standardized question set was used to ensure reliability and validity of data. Expert interviews centered on eliciting information to further explore five general areas: (1) organizational success, (2) land conservation tools used, (3) attitudes expressed by general public (specific to given regions), (4) use of decision-support process or ranking procedures, and (5) usefulness of proposed ILCDS model.

24. Land Trust Survey (1995); Land Trust Census, 1998.
25. J. A. Gustanski (1996–98) Phase III Expert Interviews. Data prepared from responses generated at the land trust level in response to the interview question, "What are the principal land protection tools, techniques, or mechanisms used by your land trust?"
26. Land Trust Census, 1998.

Chapter 2

A Holistic Examination of the
Law of Conservation Easements

Todd D. Mayo

There is considerable diversity among state statutes establishing conservation easements. There are, of course, discernable patterns, too. Massachusetts's statute, for example, inspired a small cadre of other states, including Connecticut, Delaware, New Hampshire, and Rhode Island, to enact such legislation; consequently, there is a great deal of consistency between the statutes of these states. Not surprisingly, the greatest degree of uniformity and consistency is found among the states that have adopted the Uniform Conservation Easement Act (UCEA).

Differences between state statutes are illustrated even in their choice of terminology. For example, the term *conservation easement,* which enjoys widespread usage in common parlance, is not always used. A conservation easement may be called a conservation easement in gross, a conservation restriction, a preservation restriction, an agricultural preservation restriction, a conservation right, a conservation agreement, a preservation agreement, or a land use easement, depending on the state and, in some cases, the purpose of the easement.[1] For convenience, the term *conservation easement* is used in this chapter, although a particular state may have adopted a different term.

This diversity makes a comparative examination of state law regarding conservation easements fascinating. Similarities between statutory language suggest similarities in the way state law developed and, at the same time, reveal surprising omissions. The ensuing romp through the state laws explores the nature of a conservation easement, the conservation values that it is able to protect, the nature of the restrictions and obligations through which it achieves this protection, and the types of organizations that are entrusted with the responsibility of holding and enforcing the easement. This exploration also looks at the ways a conservation easement may be modified or even terminated.

Easement as Rights

A conservation easement generally is described as a right, an interest in real property, or an interest in land. Massachusetts, for example, defines a conservation easement as "a right . . . whether or not stated in the form of a restriction, easement, covenant or condition,"[2] a definition that is used in a handful of other states. California defines a conservation easement as "any limitation in a deed, will, or other instrument in the form of an easement, restriction, covenant, or condition."[3] The UCEA describes a conservation easement as a "nonpossessory interest . . . in real property," noting that its designation as "a conservation easement or a covenant, an equitable servitude, a restriction, an easement, or otherwise" is irrelevant. As Attorney John F. Rohe observes in chapter 17, "One develops a sense that the chosen terminology is often a matter of preference, rather than substance."

When coupled with the statutory abolition of the common law impediments to easements in gross, such as lack of privity of estate or assignability, Rohe's observation is correct. The name or terminology is irrelevant. The conservation easement statute purposefully creates and defines a specific right or interest in property having, at least to some extent, its own set of rules.

Purposes

The most fundamental question of a conservation easement is, What can it protect? (Table 2.1, also see Table 2.3). The statutes vary as to the nature of the permissible restrictions and obligations. The UCEA allows states to create a conservation easement (1) to retain or protect natural, scenic, or open-space values of real property; (2) to ensure the availability of real property for agricultural, forest, recreational, or open-space use; (3) to protect natural resources; (4) to maintain or enhance air or water quality; and (5) to preserve the historical, architectural, archeological, or cultural aspects of real property.[4] Alabama permits conservation easements to protect silvicultural resources and paleontological characteristics of property.[5] Maine, on the other hand, does not allow conservation easements to preserve historically, architecturally, archeologically, and culturally significant property.

Although not expressly recognized, habitat protection may be inferred from the UCEA. Several nonuniform states specifically describe such a purpose, however, allowing conservation easements to protect wildlife habitat, including fish habitat. Four states allow easements for the protection of plants. The UCEA clearly allows conservation easements to protect property

Table 2.1. What Conservation Easements Protect

STATE	UCEA	HOLDER'S PURPOSES	NATURAL	SCENIC	OPEN SPACE	AGRICULTURAL	SILVICULTURAL	FOREST	RECREATIONAL	AIR QUALITY	WATER QUALITY/WATER	HISTORICAL	ARCHITECTURAL	ARCHEOLOGICAL	PALEONTOLOGICAL	CULTURAL	CONSERVATION OF LAND	PROTECTING NATURAL RESOURCES	SPECIAL NOTES
Alabama	U	X	X	X	X	X	X	X	X	X	X	X	X	X	X	X		X	
Alaska	U	X[a]	X	X	X	X			X	X	X	X	X	X		X		X	[a] "Empowered to"
Arizona	U	X	X	X	X	X			X	X	X	X	X	X		X		X	
Arkansas	N	X	X	X	X	X			X	X	X	X	X	X		X		X	
California	N		X	X	X	X			X			X							
Colorado	N																		
Connecticut	N	X			X						X[b]	X								[b] Conservation of land or water area
Delaware	N	X			X						X[c]	X								[c] Conservation of land or water area
Florida	U	X	X	X	X	X			X	X	X	X	X	X		X		X	
Georgia	U	X	X	X	X	X			X	X	X	X	X	X		X		X	
Hawaii	N	[d]																	[d] whose original purpose is designed to facilitate the purpose of this chapter
Idaho	U	X	X	X	X	X			X	X	X	X	X	X	X			X	
Illinois	N		X		X						X[e]	X	X	X		X	X		[e] Primary purpose
Indiana	U	X	X	X	X	X			X	X	X	X	X	X		X		X	
Iowa	N																		
Kansas	U	X	X	X	X	X			X	X	X	X	X	X		X		X	
Kentucky	U	X	X	X	X	X			X	X	X	X	X	X		X		X	
Louisiana	U	X	X	X	X	X			X	X	X	X	X	X		X		X	Also immovable property and unimproved immovable property
Maine	U	X	X	X	X	X			X	X	X	X	X	X		X		X	
Maryland	N																		
Massachusetts	N	X			X						X	X						X	
Michigan	N																		
Minnesota	U	X	X	X	X	X			X	X	X	X	X	X		X		X	

STATE	UCEA	HOLDER'S PURPOSES	NATURAL	SCENIC	OPEN SPACE	AGRICULTURAL	SILVICULTURAL	FOREST	RECREATIONAL	AIR QUALITY	WATER QUALITY/WATER	HISTORICAL	ARCHITECTURAL	ARCHEOLOGICAL	PALEONTOLOGICAL	CULTURAL	CONSERVATION OF LAND	PROTECTING NATURAL RESOURCES	SPECIAL NOTES
Mississippi	U	X	X	X	X	X		X	X	X	X	X	X	X		X		X	Also property available for educational use
Missouri	N																		Silent; wildlife habitat
Montana	N	f																	f Original purpose designate to further purpose of this" wildlife habitat
Nebraska	N	X	X	X	X	X		X	X	X	X	X	X	X		X		X	Also wildlife habitat
Nevada	U	X	X	X	X	X		X	X	X	X	X	X	X		X		X	
New Hampshire	N	X				X					X	X						X	
New Jersey	N	X	X	X	X						X							X	
New Mexico	N	X	X		X	X		X	X									X	Also mountain production uses of real property
New York	N																	X	For conservation or preservation of real property
North Carolina	N	X	X	X	X	X		X				X	X	X					Also horticulture and farming
North Dakota	N																		
Ohio	N																		
Oklahoma																			
Oregon	U	X	X	X	X	X		X	X	X	X	X	X	X		X		X	
Pennsylvania	N																		
Rhode Island	N	X									X	X					X		
South Carolina	U	X	X	X	X	X		X	X	X	X	X	X	X		X		X	Also educational use
South Dakota	U	X		X		X	X		X	X	X	X	X	X	X	X			
Tennessee	N																		Silent
Texas	U	g	X	X	X	X		X	X	X	X	X	X	X		X		X	g Created or empowered to

(*continues*)

Table 2.1. Continued

STATE	UCEA	HOLDER'S PURPOSES	NATURAL	SCENIC	OPEN SPACE	AGRICULTURAL	SILVICULTURAL	FOREST	RECREATIONAL	AIR QUALITY	WATER QUALITY/WATER	HISTORICAL	ARCHITECTURAL	ARCHEOLOGICAL	PALEONTOLOGICAL	CULTURAL	CONSERVATION OF LAND	PROTECTING NATURAL RESOURCES	SPECIAL NOTES
Utah	N																		Silent
Vermont	N	X		X	X		X					X[h]							[h] One of its stated purposes
Virginia	U																		
Washington	N	X	X									X						X[i]	[i] One of the holder's principal purpose; also, scientific research.
West Virginia	U	X	X	X	X	X	X		X	X	X	X	X	X	X	X	X	X	Wildlife
Wisconsin	U	X	X	X	X	X	X		X	X	X	X	X	X	X	X	X	X	
Wyoming	N																		

U = Conservation easement legislation directly influenced by UCEA.
N = Conservation easement legislation absent or not influenced by UCEA.

for recreational use, whereas a number of nonuniform states are silent on the issue. Most states expressly allow conservation easements to preserve agricultural lands, although Hawaii, Illinois, Mississippi, Missouri, New Jersey, New York, and Washington are notable exceptions. In Colorado, Nebraska, North Carolina, and Ohio, a conservation easement may protect horticultural resources. In Arizona, Mississippi, and South Carolina, a conservation easement may protect the educational value of the property.

Delaware's statute is ambiguous regarding purpose. Although a conservation easement may be established to maintain land predominantly in its natural condition and, to that end, the easement may restrict "activities adversely affecting the fish and wildlife habitat," the easement may not "restrict or abridge . . . the rights of any present or future fee simple owner from permitting or denying the use of the land for hunting, fishing or other recreational purposes."[6] Undoubtedly, such language will lead to situations in which the landowner's ability to hunt, fish, or use the property for other recreational activities will significantly impair, if not destroy, the very conservation purposes for which the easement was created. This particular statute, unfortunately, seems unforgiving, and it subordinates conservation purposes to recreational activities.

Delaware's statute has the effect of denying landowners any benefit under recently enacted federal legislation concerning estate taxes. Under section 2031(c) of the Internal Revenue Code, a landowner's estate may exclude up to 40 percent of the value of land subject to a conservation easement. Among the numerous criteria required for such a qualification, however, is a requirement that the conservation easement contain "a prohibition on more than a de minimis use for a commercial recreational activity."[7] The legislative history of the section indicates that "de minimis commercial recreational activity that is consistent with the conservation purpose, such as the granting of hunting and fishing licenses, will not cause the property to fail to qualify" under section 2031(c). Delaware's statute, however, makes no distinction between commercial and noncommercial activities, providing a blanket prohibition against an easement provision that infringes upon the landowner's right to use the property for hunting, fishing, or other recreational activities. Landowners in Delaware would therefore be unable to establish or modify conservation easements to receive section 2031(c)'s benefits.

Restrictions and Obligations

Second to the question of what a conservation may protect is, How does a conservation easement achieve its purpose? Table 2.2 reflects on how states across the United States have dealt with this question. A conservation easement is a collection of restrictions and obligations, at a minimum, restricting the activities that may occur on the property and thus limiting a landowner's use of the property. A conservation easement also may impose affirmative obligations on both the landowner or the holder. State statute, of course, defines the nature of such restrictions and obligations. In all cases, the restrictions and obligations are intended to serve the conservation purposes of the easement.

A preliminary observation is in order. The effectiveness of a conservation easement is largely dependent on the commitment of the easement holder. The holder's diligence in monitoring the easement and its willingness and ability to enforce the easement are two of the cornerstones of an effective easement. A third cornerstone is a well-drafted easement document, but without the commitment of the easement holder, the restrictions and obligations expressed in that document are all but meaningless. Although third-party enforcement rights and vigilant attorneys general can help to ensure an easement achieves its purpose, the holder must be prepared to undertake long-term monitoring of the easement and stewardship of the property.

Conservation easement statutes universally recognize the ability of the

Table 2.2. How Conservation Easements Protect

State	UCEA	Negative Rights	Affirmative Rights	Holder's Right of Access	Nonpossessory Interest	Restriction	Easement	Covenant	Condition	Equitable Servitude	Interest in Land	Incorporeal Right	Interest in Property	Contractual Right	Special Notes
Alabama	U	X	X		X	X	X	X		X					
Alaska	U	X	X		X	X	X	X		X					
Arizona	U	X	X		X	X	X	X		X					
Arkansas	N	X	X		X	X	X	X		X					
California	N	X				X	X	X	X				X		Massachusetts model
Colorado	N	X	X										X		
Connecticut	N	X				X	X	X	X						Massachusetts model
Delaware	N	X				X	X	X	X				X		Massachusetts model
Florida	U	X	X			X	X	X	X						Massachusetts model
Georgia	U	X	X		X	X	X	X		X					
Hawaii	N					X		X	X						
Idaho	U	X	X		X	X	X	X		X					
Illinois	N	X	X			X	X	X	X						
Indiana	U	X	X		X	X	X	X		X					
Iowa	N					X	X		X		X				
Kansas	U	X	X		X	X	X	X		X					
Kentucky	U	X	X		X	X	X	X		X					
Louisiana	U	X	X		X[a]	X		X		X					[a] Nonpossessory interest in immovable property
Maine	U	X	X		X	X	X	X		X					
Maryland	N	X				X	X	X	X			X[b]			[b] Incorporeal property interest
Massachusetts	N	X	X			X	X	X	X						Massachusetts model
Michigan	N	X	X			X	X	X	X		X				
Minnesota	U	X	X		X	X	X	X		X					
Mississippi	U	X	X		X	X	X	X		X					

STATE	UCEA	NEGATIVE RIGHTS	AFFIRMATIVE RIGHTS	HOLDER'S RIGHT OF ACCESS	NONPOSSESSORY INTEREST	RESTRICTION	EASEMENT	COVENANT	CONDITION	EQUITABLE SERVITUDE	INTEREST IN LAND	INCORPOREAL RIGHT	INTEREST IN PROPERTY	CONTRACTUAL RIGHT	SPECIAL NOTES
Missouri	N					X	X							X	
Montana	N	X											X		
Nebraska	N	X	X			X	X	X	X				X		
Nevada	U	X	X		X	X	X	X		X			X		
New Hampshire	N	X	X			X	X	X	X						**Massachusetts model**
New Jersey	N	X				X	X	X	X		X				
New Mexico	N	X	X		X	X	X	X		X					
New York	N	X	X			X	X	X					X		
North Carolina	N	X				X	X	X	X		X				Also, reservation
North Dakota	N														**No state enabling Act as of 10/1/99**
Ohio	N	X				X	X	X	X		X	X			Also, articles of dedication
Oklahoma	N														**No state enabling Act as of 10/1/99**
Oregon	U	X	X		X	X	X	X		X					
Pennsylvania	N														**No state enabling Act as of 10/1/99**
Rhode Island	N	X	X			X	X	X	X						**Massachusetts model**
South Carolina	U	X	X		X	X	X	X		X					
South Dakota	U	X	X		X	X	X	X		X			X		
Tennessee	N	X	X				X								
Texas	U	X	X		X	X	X	X		X					
Utah	N					X	X	X	X						
Vermont	N	X	X			X	X	X	X				X		
Virginia	U	X	X		X		X								
Washington	N					X	X	X					X		
West Virginia	U	X	X		X	X	X	X		X					
Wisconsin	U	X	X		X										
Wyoming															

U = Conservation easement legislation directly influenced by UCEA.

N = Conservation easement legislation absent or not influenced by UCEA.

easement to impose restrictions and limitations on the activities of the landowners. In addition, the UCEA and some states with nonuniform statutes expressly sanction the imposition of affirmative obligations on the landowner.[8] In the UCEA, a conservation easement is defined as "a nonpossessory interest of a holder in real property imposing limitations or *affirmative obligations*" (emphasis added). The UCEA also expressly affirms the validity of a conservation easement that "imposes affirmative obligations upon the owner of an interest in the burdened property or upon the holder." The nonuniform statutes tend to speak in terms of requiring certain acts or requiring an obligation to perform certain acts. Colorado, for example, allows a conservation easement to "prohibit or require a limitation upon or an *obligation to perform acts* on or with respect to a land or water area"[9] (emphasis added). Vermont's statute goes one step farther, stating that a conservation easement may give the holder "rights to perform, or require the performance of, specified activities."[10] Thus, in Vermont, the holder could have the right either to require the landowner to remove and destroy any nonnative vegetation or to enter the property and remove the vegetation.

The Massachusetts statute arguably allows such affirmative obligations. The statute declares that a conservation easement is a right "*appropriate to* retaining land or water areas predominantly in their natural, scenic or open condition or in agricultural, farming or forest use, to permit public recreational use"[11] (emphasis added). Note that the term *appropriate* is used to describe the nature of a right that a conservation easement may contain. Negative and affirmative rights are not mentioned. A right appropriate to accomplishing the conservation purposes of the easement could clearly include an affirmative obligation.

One of the most serious shortcomings of some of the nonuniform acts is the failure to specifically authorize conservation easements to impose affirmative obligations on landowners. In California, Connecticut, Delaware, and Montana, the statutes speak in terms of prohibiting or limiting certain activities, but they are silent with respect to whether a conservation easement may impose any affirmative obligations on the landowner.[12] Despite the lack of specificity in the statutes, however, conservation easements in those states routinely impose affirmative obligations. In most instances, of course, the ability to restrict certain acts by landowners may be the practical equivalent to imposing an affirmative obligations on them. For example, a prohibition against the use of motorized vehicles, by implication, seemingly would impose an obligation to undertake reasonable efforts to prevent the use of motorized vehicles on the land by third parties. This exercise of extracting an affirmative from a negative is not wholly satisfying; like walking atop ice-encrusted snow, you are never quite sure when you might step through. The statutes would be improved irrefutably by expressly sanctioning affirmative obligations and thus eliminating any uncertainty.

In some situations, affirmative obligations are unquestionably necessary to fulfill the conservation purposes of the easement. Nonetheless, land trusts must recognize the practical limitations on their use because they are more likely to encounter easement violations when easement documents incorporate affirmative obligations. Suppose that a landowner, a generation or more removed from the grantor of the easement, is unwilling or unable to perform the required acts. The land trust must enforce the affirmative obligations, either by assuming the responsibility of performing the acts, and then only if the landowner is willing to accommodate incursion onto the property, or by initiating litigation to force the landowner to perform the required acts. There is, of course, a third possibility: The land trust may opt not to enforce the affirmative obligations. This option raises a thicket of issues. As Andrew Dana, an attorney in Bozeman, Montana, has observed, "As a practical matter, the more intrusive a land trust's rights to govern land use decisions (i.e., through affirmative obligations), the less sympathy the land trusts will receive from the courts."[13] It is the very susceptibility of affirmative obligations to being disregarded by landowners and by courts that necessitates that land trusts treat such obligations with care and attention.

Eligible Holders

The statutes achieve a high degree of uniformity with respect to the type of entities that may hold conservation easements. In Table 2.3, the variations that exist are compared. Under the UCEA, the holder may be a governmental body, a charitable corporation, a charitable association, or a charitable trust.[14] Among the states adopting the UCEA, there are some minor differences. For example, Alaska and Maine use the term *nonprofit corporation* in their statutes.[15] On a more substantive level, Mississippi adds private corporations and educational corporations to the list.[16] New Mexico, on the other hand, omits governmental entities from its list of eligible holders, and Arizona excludes charitable associations.[17] Among nonuniform states, the statutory language may differ, but the general effect is to allow governmental bodies, charitable corporations, charitable associations, and charitable trusts to be holders.

In New Hampshire and Rhode Island (both nonuniform states), the statutes define eligible holders somewhat obliquely. In both states, "any governmental body or by a charitable, educational or other corporation, association, trust or other entity whose purposes include conservation of land or water areas or of a particular such area" may hold conservation easements without fear that their easements could be defeated by common law rules.[18]

Table 2.3. Who May Hold Conservation Easements

STATE	UCEA	GOVERNMENT	CHARITABLE TRUST	CHARITABLE ASSOCIATION	CHARITABLE CORPORATION	SECTION 501 (C)(3) TAX-EXEMPT ORGANIZATION	SPECIAL NOTES
Alabama	U	X	X	X	X		
Alaska	U	X	X	X	X	X	Nonprofit corporation
Arizona	U	X	X		X		Trustee of charitable trust
Arkansas	N	X	X	X	X		
California	N	X	X		X	X	Tax exempt nonprofit organization
Colorado	N	X	X		X	X	Charitable organization in existence at least two years
Connecticut	N	X	X		X		
Delaware	N	X	X		X		
Florida	U	X	X		X		
Georgia	U	X	X	X	X		
Hawaii	N	X[a]	X		X	X[b]	[a] "public body" [b] 501(c) organization
Idaho	U	X	X	X	X		
Illinois	N	X	?		X		Not-for-profit corporation
Indiana	U	X	X	X	X		
Iowa	N	X	?	?	?		Private, nonprofit organization"
Kansas	U	X	X	X	X		
Kentucky	U	X	X	X	X		
Louisiana	U	X	X	X	X		
Maine	U	X	X		X		Nonprofit corporation
Maryland	N						
Massachusetts	N	X	X		X		
Michigan	N	X	X	X	X		Charitable or educational . . . or other legal entity
Minnesota	U	X	X	X	X		
Mississippi	U	X	X	X	X		Private, nonprofit, charitable, or educational organization
Missouri	N	X	?	?	?		Nonprofit organization
Montana	N	X	X		X	X[c]	Qualified private organization [c] 501(c) organization
Nebraska	N	X	X		X		
Nevada	U	X	X	X	X		
New Hampshire	N	X	X	X	X		
New Jersey	N	X	X		X	X[d]	Charitable conservancy [d] 501(c) organization

STATE	UCEA	GOVERNMENT	CHARITABLE TRUST	CHARITABLE ASSOCIATION	CHARITABLE CORPORATION	SECTION 501 (c)(3) TAX-EXEMPT ORGANIZATION	SPECIAL NOTES
New Mexico	N		X	X	X		Nonprofit organization (not charitable)
New York	N	X			X	X	Not-for-profit conservation organization
North Carolina	N	X	X		X		Private corporation or business
North Dakota							
Ohio	N	X					
Oklahoma							
Oregon	U	X°	X	X	X		° Modified UCEA
Pennsylvania							
Rhode Island	N	X	X	X	X		
South Carolina	U	X	X	X	X		Charitable not-for-profit or educational organization
South Dakota	U	X	X	X	X		
Tennessee	N	X	?	?	?	?	Confused terminology
Texas	U	X	X	X	X		
Utah	N	X	X		X	X	Charitable organization
Vermont	N	X	X		X	X	Also, a 501(c)(2) organization controlled exclusively by a 501(c)(3) organization
Virginia	U	ƒ	X	X	X	X	ƒ Implied but not stated
Washington	N	X			X	X	Nonprofit nature conservancy corporation
West Virginia	U	X	X	X	X	X	
Wisconsin	U	X	X	X	X		
Wyoming	N						

U = Conservation easement legislation directly influenced by UCEA.

N = Conservation easement legislation absent or not influenced by UCEA.

Although the statutes define conservation easements as rights designed to achieve certain conservation purposes, they do not expressly require a conservation easement to be held by one of those types of organizations. Thus, a business corporation seemingly could hold a conservation easement, but that easement would be susceptible to the common law impediments. Another nonuniform state, North Carolina, includes private corporations and business entities among the list of eligible holders, although the purposes of the corporation or business must include one or more of the enumerated conservation purposes.[19]

Ten states, including some that adopted the UCEA, require a land trust to be a tax-exempt organization. Alaska, New York, Utah, Virginia, Washington, and West Virginia require the holder to be exempt under section 501(c)(3) of the Internal Revenue Service Code.[20] In Vermont, the holder must be exempt under section 501(c)(3) or under section 501(c)(2), as long as it is "controlled exclusively" by an organization exempt under section 501(c)(3).[21] Hawaii, Montana, and New Jersey, three nonuniform states, broaden the scope of tax-exempt organizations that are eligible holders, requiring them to be exempt under section 501(c) of the Internal Revenue Service Code. As a practical matter, the state law requirement for federal tax exemption will usually have little significance. Land trusts generally will avail themselves of tax-exempt status under section 501(c)(3) so that their donors can enjoy the benefits of tax-deductible contributions, including contributions of conservation easements.

Almost all states describe, with some specificity, the purposes for which holders of conservation easements can be organized. Many of these echo the purposes for which a conservation easement may be established, but there are some differences. Nebraska, borrowing the UCEA's list of purposes, adds ensuring the availability of property for horticultural use.[22] In Massachusetts, whose statute served as the model for a handful of states, the holder's purposes must include the "conservation of land or water areas" or the "preservation of buildings or sites of historical significance or of a particular such building or site."[23] Although the states adopting the UCEA clearly allow the protection of water quality, only a few of the nonuniform states expressly reference the protection of water quality or water areas. Those states are California, Connecticut, Delaware, Illinois, Massachusetts, New Hampshire, New Jersey, Rhode Island, Vermont, and Washington.

Preserving agricultural land appears almost a universal purpose in the enabling statutes, although Illinois and Montana notably fail to include the preservation of agricultural land among the holder's purposes.[24] In Illinois, the holder's primary purpose must include "the conservation of land, natural areas, open space or water areas, or the preservation of native plants or animals, or biotic communities, or geographic formations of scientific, aesthetic, or educational interest, or the preservation of buildings, structures or sites of historical, architectural, archeological or cultural significance."[25] In Montana, the holder's "organizational purposes are designed to further" the voluntary "preservation of native plants or animals, biotic communities, or geological or geographical formations of scientific, aesthetic, or educational interest" or "the preservation of other significant open-space land."[26]

Among states adopting the UCEA, the holder's purposes may include the preservation of the historical, architectural, archeological, or cultural characteristics of real property. Similarly, some nonuniform states include the preservation of historical, and architectural, archeological property among the holder's required purposes.[27] Commonly, however, the statutes of nonuniform states omit the preservation of cultural aspects of real property.[28] In Vermont, the holder's purposes must include the acquisition of property rights "to preserve historic, agricultural, forestry or open space resources."[29] The statute unfortunately omits any reference to the preservation of architectural, cultural, or archaeological property, although those are purposes for which a conservation easement may be established.[30]

Most states, including those adopting the UCEA and those that do not, simply require the holder's purposes to include certain conservation purposes.[31] Some states, however, impose higher standards. In California, the holder's *primary* purpose must be to preserve, protect, or enhance land in its natural, scenic, historical, agricultural, forested, or open-space condition or use.[32] Similarly, Illinois requires that the holder's *primary* purposes include the conservation of land, natural areas, open space, or water areas; the preservation of native plants, animals, biotic communities, or geographic formations of scientific, aesthetic, or educational interest; or the preservation of buildings, structures, or sites of historical, architectural, archeological, or cultural significance.[33] In Washington, one of the holder's *principal* purposes must be conducting or facilitating scientific research, conserving natural resources, including biological resources, conserving natural areas, including wildlife habitats, or conducting or facilitating the preservation of historic sites, districts, buildings, and artifacts.[34]

The standards in Hawaii and Montana fall below the primary purpose requirement of California and Illinois and the principal purpose requirement of Washington. Under Hawaii's statute, the holder must be a tax-exempt organization "whose organizational purposes are designed to facilitate the purposes" of preserving and protecting land predominantly in its natural, scenic, forested, or open-space condition.[35] Montana employs similar language requiring the holder be an organization "whose organizational purposes are designed to further the purposes" of preserving open space.[36] Although the preservation of open space arguably is a purpose that facilitates or furthers the conservation purposes of the statute, both Hawaii and Montana seem to call for something more than simply the inclusion of a conservation purpose.

Land trusts assume a significant responsibility when they accept conservation easements. Somewhat surprisingly, only two states impose requirements on how long the organization must have been in existence before they can accept a conservation easement. Colorado requires a organization to have been formed at least two years prior to accepting an easement.[37] Virginia, on the other hand, requires an organization to have had a principal office in the commonwealth for at least five years prior to accepting a perpetual easement,[38] thus prohibiting new organizations and out-of-state organizations from holding conservation easements. Interestingly, no state requires a land trust to have a minimum net worth or otherwise demonstrate the financial wherewithal to serve as the steward of the land and easements.

Duration of Conservation Easements

To some extent, there is a philosophical proclivity toward perpetual easements, evident in Table 2.4. They are regarded, rightly so, as worthwhile endeavors to protect land permanently so that succeeding generations can share the values of such land. Nonetheless, the history of conservation easements is quite short, and the expectation that a conservation easement will serve its purpose *forever* requires some degree of hubris.

The majority of states allow easements to last perpetually or for a limited duration. In most states, the statutes establishes a default rule favoring perpetual easements, the approach found in the UCEA. Thus, if the easement is silent as to duration, then the statute provides that the easement will be perpetual. In Alabama, Kansas, and West Virginia, the opposite is true; duration of an easement is limited unless the easement states that its duration is perpetual. In Alabama, the term of the easement is the lesser of (1) thirty years, (2) the grantor's lifetime, or (3) the sale of the protected property. In Kansas,

Table 2.4. Duration of Conservation Easements

STATE	PERPETUAL MANDATORY	PERPETUAL BY DEFAULT	TERM BY DEFAULT	SILENT
Alabama			X	
Alaska		X		
Arizona		X		
Arkansas		X		
California	X			
Colorado	X			
Connecticut				X
Delaware				X
Florida	X			
Georgia		X		
Hawaii	X			
Idaho		X		
Illinois				X
Indiana		X		
Iowa		X		

STATE	PERPETUAL MANDATORY	PERPETUAL BY DEFAULT	TERM BY DEFAULT	SILENT
Kansas			X	
Kentucky		X		
Louisiana		X		
Maine		X		
Maryland				X
Massachusetts				X
Michigan				X
Minnesota		X		
Mississippi		X		
Missouri				X
Montana		N/A	N/A	
Nebraska				
Nevada		X		
New Hampshire				X
New Jersey				X
New Mexico		N/A	N/A	
New York				X
North Carolina		N/A	N/A	
North Dakota N/S				
Ohio				X
Oklahoma N/S				
Oregon		X		
Pennsylvania N/S				
Rhode Island				X
South Carolina		X		
South Dakota				X
Tennessee				X
Texas		X		
Utah				X
Vermont				X
Virginia		X		
Washington				X
West Virginia			25 years	
Wisconsin		X		
Wyoming N/S				

Notes: N/A = not applicable. N/S = no enabling statute.

the easement ends upon the death of the grantor or upon revocation by the grantor. In West Virginia, the easement must last for at least twenty-five years.

Four states—California, Colorado, Florida, and Hawaii—require easements be perpetual, denying landowners and land trusts the flexibility to create an easement that lasts for a period of time. In Massachusetts, conservation restrictions and historic preservation restrictions may be perpetual or for a limited duration, but agricultural preservation restrictions and watershed restrictions are perpetual.[39]

A significant number of state statutes are silent on the issue of duration.[40] By their silence, we may presume that these states tacitly sanction perpetual easements, because the legislatures could have easily limited the maximum duration of conservation easements. In these states as well as in Montana, New Mexico, and North Carolina, whose statutes address duration but do not establish default rules, however, an easement document must state its duration. Easements that are silent as to duration contain an inherent and serious ambiguity.

There is a federal tax overlay to the issue of an easement's duration. A conservation easement must be perpetual to bestow upon the donor the benefits of the charitable deductions and possible estate tax exclusion. Yet, as a practical matter, the Internal Revenue Service's interest in a conservation easement is short-lived. With some exceptions, their interest ends three years after the donor contributes the easement. Nonetheless, the requirement of perpetuity remains, and only those easements that are granted in perpetuity enjoy the tax breaks.

The federal tax law encourages the contribution of perpetual easements and simultaneously discourages the contribution of term easements. A contribution of a perpetual easement entitles the donor to an income tax charitable deduction and possibly to a partial estate tax exclusion for the land subject to the easement. In contrast, not only does the contribution of a term easement fail to yield an income tax charitable deduction, but it is a taxable gift because it violates the gift tax partial interest rule. The unfavorable tax consequence arises even though the easement provides a public benefit during its (albeit less than permanent) life span, and it may provide a land trust with the time to fashion a strategy for permanently protecting the target property.

Modification

Recent tax law changes have sparked interest in amending easements that already exist. Some landowners, seeking to benefit from the estate tax exclusion for land subject to a conservation easement, want to add a prohibition against commercial recreational activity to their easements. The motivation for such amendments is the estate tax requirement that the easement contain "a prohibition on more than a de minimis use for a commercial recreational activity, " and few existing easements contain such a prohibition.[41] Table 2.5

Table 2.5. Permissible Modifications, Terminations, and Assignability of Conservation Easements

State	UCEA	Released	Terminated	Termination by Court (under the principles of law and equity)	Termination by Taking	Abandoned	Terminated by Merger	Modified	Modified by Court	Assignable	Special Notes
Alabama	U	X	X	X				X	X	X	
Alaska	U	X	X	X				X	X	X	
Arizona	U	X	X	X^a				X	X^a	X	^a Requires consideration of public interest
Arkansas	N	X	X	X				X	X	X	
California	N									X	
Colorado	N	X	X			X	X			X	
Connecticut	N									X	
Delaware	N				X					X	
Florida	U									X	
Georgia	U	X	X	X				X	X	X	
Hawaii	N										
Idaho	U	X	X	X				X	X	X	
Illinois	N	X			X					X	
Indiana	U	X	X	X				X	X	X	
Iowa	N									X	
Kansas	U	X	X	X				X	X	X	
Kentucky	U	X	X	X				X	X	X	
Louisiana	U	X	X					X		X	
Maine	U	X	X	X^b				X	X^b	X	^b If in public interest
Maryland	N	X	X							X	
Massachusetts	N	X^c								X	^c Requires public hearing or legislative action
Michigan	N									X	
Minnesota	U	X	X	X				X	X	X	
Mississippi	U			X^d		N			X^d	X	^d Land trust is compensated for the value of the conservation easement
Missouri	N										
Montana	N										
Nebraska	N	X^e	X^e	X				X^e	X	X	^e Must be but only if approved the conservation easement's purpose is not substantial

(continues)

Table 2.5. Continued

STATE	UCEA	RELEASED	TERMINATED	TERMINATION BY COURT (UNDER THE PRINCIPLES OF LAW AND EQUITY)	TERMINATION BY TAKING	ABANDONED	TERMINATED BY MERGER	MODIFIED	MODIFIED BY COURT	ASSIGNABLE	SPECIAL NOTES
Nevada	U	X	X	X				X	X	X	
New Hampshire	N				X		X			X	
New Jersey	N	X[f]								X	[f] Public hearing required
New Mexico	N	X	X	X				X	X	X	
New York	N		X	X	X						
North Carolina	N	X	X		X					X	
North Dakota	N										
Ohio	N										
Oklahoma	N										
Oregon	U	X	X	X				X	X	X	
Pennsylvania	N										
Rhode Island	N	X[g]								X	[g] In accord with the terms of the conservation easement
South Carolina	U	X	X	X				X	X	X	
South Dakota	U			X							
Tennessee	N										
Texas	U	X	X	X				X	X	X	
Utah	N	X	X			X	X				
Vermont	N										
Virginia	U	X	X	X	X[h]			X	X	X	[h] Compensation required
Washington	N										
West Virginia	U	X	X	X[i]				X	X[i]	X	[i] If consistent with public policy.
Wisconsin	U	X	X	X				X	X	X	
Wyoming											

U = Conservation easement legislation directly influenced by UCEA.

N = Conservation easement legislation absent or not influenced by UCEA.

compares permissible modifications, termination, and assignability of conservation easements as handled by individual state statutes.

The UCEA allows a conservation easement to be modified in the same manner as any other easement, and it allows a court to modify an easement in accordance with the principles of law and equity.[42] The nonuniform states are almost universally silent regarding the ability of a landowner to modify a conservation easement.

One interesting issue is whether a conservation easement may be modified by the exercise of eminent domain. This issue explores the interplay between the means by which a conservation easement may be modified and the statutory rules on acquiring or terminating easements by the exercise of eminent domain. The answer to this question has two parts. First, does the modification expand or contract the protective scope of the conservation easement? Second, does state law allow the holder to acquire or destroy a conservation easement by taking?

State law would have to allow the acquisition or expansion of a conservation easement by the exercise of eminent domain. Similarly, to the extent that the proposed modification contracts the scope of the easement, state law must allow the (at least, partial) destruction of a conservation easement by the exercise of eminent domain. Alabama expressly addresses that issue. Under Alabama's statute, a conservation easement may not be expanded by the exercise of the power of eminent domain.[43] The proposed modification, of course, may simultaneously expand and contract the scope of the easement. For example, the proposed modification may increase a building envelope while enhancing the protection of the remaining property. In such a case, state law may allow the contraction of the easement, but prevent the expansion of the easement. That seemingly would be the result in Alabama, California, Florida, Iowa, Oregon, and Tennessee, where the acquisition of a conservation easement by taking is prohibited.

Termination

The idea that a conservation easement may be terminated is anathema to some landowners and land conservation professionals, yet it is a real possibility. A term easement, of course, terminates at the end of its term. A perpetual easement, however, is intended to last forever. In truth, circumstances—and doctrines of law—may shorten the life of a conservation easement. For example, a conservation easement may be terminated if the conservation purposes for which it was created cannot be achieved.[44] Recognizing this reality, the UCEA provides that "a conservation easement may be . . . terminated . . . in the same manner as other easements." For example, an easement may be terminated by abandonment, merger, or taking.[45]

Abandonment

All easements may be extinguished by abandonment. A conservation easement may be extinguished by the holder's failure to enforce the restrictions and obligations expressed in the easement, for example. Of course, the prospect that a conservation easement could terminate by abandonment flaunts the perpetual nature of most easements. Colorado and Utah expressly recognize termination by abandonment.[46] In contrast, New York's statute effectively prevents the termination by abandonment.[47] In practice, the issue of abandonment is only likely to arise when a land trust becomes defunct and fails to transfer its conservation easements to another holder or when a land trust loses track of a particular easement and fails to monitor it as it does with the rest of its easements. Both situations are, unfortunately, likely to occur as the land trust community continues to mature.

Merger

Under the common law doctrine of merger, an easement is extinguished when the easement holder acquires fee title to the property subject to the easement.[48] Conservation easements are susceptible to termination by merger. The statutes in Colorado and Utah specifically refer to termination by merger.[49] Because the UCEA provides that "a conservation easement may be ... terminated ... in the same manner as other easements," in states adopting the UCEA, merger may extinguish a conservation easement. Similarly, in New Hampshire, the conservation easement statute does not defeat any doctrines of law with respect to which the statute is silent. By implication, therefore, the statute allows the application of the doctrine of merger to extinguish a conservation easement.[50]

Mississippi and New York specifically repudiate the termination of a conservation easement by merger. In Mississippi, a "conservation easement shall continue to be effective and shall not be extinguished if the easement holder is or becomes the owner in fee of the subject property."[51] New York achieves the same result via a less obvious route, allowing a conservation easement held by a land trust to be extinguished only by the terms of the easement or through judicial action or the exercise of eminent domain.[52] The statute does not mention merger, and, by inference, conservation easements are not terminated by merger in New York. In Rhode Island, a conservation easement is shielded against "any other doctrine of property law that might cause the termination of the restriction."[53] Rhode Island arguably, then, joins Mississippi and New York as states carving out conservation easements as an exception to the doctrine of merger.

Of course, there may be no one to enforce a violation of the easement held by the land trust on its own land. The statutory exceptions to the doctrine of merger may have no practical effect as long as the land trust owns the land. The conservation easement statutes may include a third-party enforcement right. Mississippi and New York specifically sanction third-party enforcement rights, granting the party standing to enforce the easement.[54] Mississippi also grants standing to the attorney general and the Mississippi Department of Wildlife Conservation, although they may never become aware of a violation.[55] In contrast, the Rhode Island statute is silent as to both standing and third-party enforcement rights.

A conservation easement that has been extinguished needs to be re-created. A land trust can do so by creating an easement and either conveying it to an eligible holder or conveying fee title to some other party and reserving the easement. Even in Mississippi, New York, and Rhode Island, a land trust would be wise to reference or restate the conservation easement in the deed by which it transfers the property to the new owner, thus ensuring that the new owner has notice of the easement.

Termination by Taking

A conservation easement may be terminated by taking.[56] Five states— Delaware, Illinois, New York, North Carolina, and Virginia—specifically provide that a conservation easement does not impair the exercise of a power of eminent domain.[57] Virginia requires the easement holder to be compensated for the value of the easement, although this requirement is inherent in state and federal constitutions.[58] Under the UCEA, "a conservation easement may be . . . terminated . . . in the same manner as other easements."

Arbitration

With increasing frequency, land trusts and landowners are inserting arbitration provisions in conservation easements. The use of arbitration provisions raises two issues. First, what is the impact of arbitration provisions on the development of a strong body of law favorable to the conservation purposes of the easements? Second, to what extent is arbitration appropriate for conservation easements?

As the subsequent chapters illustrate, the field of conservation easement law is strikingly devoid of judicial precedents. The increasing use of arbitration provisions will undoubtedly perpetuate that condition and, in fact, may encourage unfavorable precedents. Over the past several years, the land conservation community has become more savvy and experienced, and the quality and specificity of language in conservation easements has consequently improved. With more experience, more improvement is expected. The increasing usage of arbitration provisions means that the older and presumably less effective easements will be the primary sources of litigation—and will serve as precedent.

To what extent is arbitration appropriate for conservation easements? Arbitration is attractive. It may be less costly than a lawsuit, sometimes a dubious proposition, and through the use of this process, which is less public than a lawsuit, a land trust can avoid creating an image of being litigious. There are compelling public policy reasons for having the judicial system address easement violations. The easement usually involves dedicating property to a charitable purpose and usually is intended to provide a public benefit. Where is the attorney general left if the easement violations are subject to private arbitration? Although the attorney general would be bound by the arbitrator's decision, there is a real risk that the parties would fail to notify the attorney general of the controversy. Also, and perhaps most important, the courts are much better suited to providing injunctive relief than arbitration. Both the arbitrators and the courts can provide monetary damages, but if landowners can only be assessed monetary damages, then they can effectively force the termination of easements by violating the terms of arbitration. The land trust, however, is apt to want to maintain the easement and see the continued enforcement of the restrictions and obligations that serve the easement's conservation purposes.

Third-Party Enforcement Rights

A third-party enforcement right is an important tool in ensuring the long-term vitality of a conservation easement.[59] Table 2.6 charts the different ways states have addressed third-party enforcement rights. Should the holder of an easement fail to enforce the terms of the easement, the burden of enforcement falls on a third-party organization. Whether or not a conservation easement grants a third-party enforcement right, the attorney general is apt to have the power to enforce the terms of the easement.[60] The UCEA defines a third-party enforcement right as "a right granted in a conservation easement to enforce any of its terms granted to a governmental body, charitable corporation or charitable trust, which, although eligible to be a holder, is not a holder." In Virginia, it means, in the case of a perpetual easement, that a third-party enforcer must have had a principal office within the commonwealth for at least five years.[61] In some states, the third-party enforcer must assent to the responsibility by signing the easement.[62]

Third-party enforcement rights remain solidly in the province of states that have adopted the UCEA. Of the states that have not adopted the UCEA, only three states—Arkansas, New Mexico, and New York—expressly authorize third-party enforcement rights. Each of these states enacted or revised

Table 2.6. Rights of Third-Party Enforcement

STATE	UCEA	THIRD-PARTY ENFORCEMENT	NO STATUTORY REFERENCE	SPECIAL NOTES
Alabama	U	X		
Alaska	U	X		
Arizona	U	X		
Arkansas	N	X		
California	N		X	
Colorado	N		X	
Connecticut	N		X	
Delaware	N		X	
Florida	U	X		
Georgia	U	X		
Hawaii	N		X	
Idaho	U	X		
Illinois	N		X	
Indiana	U	X		
Iowa	N		X	
Kansas	U	X		
Kentucky	U	X		
Louisiana	U	X		
Maine	U	X		
Maryland	N		X	
Massachusetts	N		X	
Michigan	N		X	
Minnesota	U	X		
Mississippi	U	X		
Missouri	N		X	
Montana	N		X	
Nebraska	N			
Nevada	U	X		
New Hampshire	N		X	
New Jersey	N		X	
New Mexico	N	X[a]		[a] "specifically identified"
New York	N	X		
North Carolina	N		X	
North Dakota	N			
Ohio	N		X	
Oklahoma	N			
Oregon	U	X		
Pennsylvania				

(*continues*)

Table 2.5. Continued

STATE	UCEA	THIRD-PARTY ENFORCEMENT	NO STATUTORY REFERENCE	SPECIAL NOTES
Rhode Island	N		X	
South Carolina	U	X		
South Dakota	U	X		
Tennessee	N		X	
Texas	U	X		
Utah	N		X	
Vermont	N		X	
Virginia	U	X		
Washington	N		X	
West Virginia	U	X		
Wisconsin	U	X		
Wyoming	N			

U = Conservation easement legislation directly influenced by UCEA.

N = Conservation easement legislation absent or not influenced by UCEA.

their conservation easement statutes after the publication of the UCEA. The New Mexican legislature seems to have had some wariness of third-party enforcement rights, and there the third-party enforcer must be "specifically identified" in the easement.[63] With some redundancy, the statute adds that "[n]o party shall have any third-party enforcement right unless that right is expressly provided for in a land use easement."[64] In the other states, a third-party right of enforcement may be crafted as an executory interest. Despite the lack of statutory authority for third-party enforcement rights in many states, the use of third-party enforcement rights appears widespread throughout the nation.

Notes

1. Connecticut, Massachusetts, New Hampshire, and Rhode Island use the terms *conservation restriction* and *preservation easement.* Conn. Gen. Stat. § 47-42a; Mass. Gen. Law ch. 184, § 31; N.H. Rev. Stat. Ann. § 477:45; and R.I. Gen. Laws § 34-39-2. Massachusetts and New Hampshire use the term *agricultural preservation restriction.* Id. Massachusetts also uses the term *watershed preservation restriction.* Id. Illinois uses the term *conservation right.* Ill. Comp. Stat. 120/0.01(a). North Carolina uses the term *conservation agreement* as well as the term *preservation agreement.* N.C. Gen. Stat. § 121-35(1) and (3). New Mexico uses the term *land use easement.* N.M. Stat. Ann. § 47-12-2(B).
2. Mass. Gen. Laws ch. 184, § 31.
3. Cal. Civ. Code § 815.1.

4. See, e.g., Tex. Nat. Res. Code Ann. § 183.001(1).
5. Ala. Code § 35-18-1(1).
6. Del. Code Ann. tit. 7, § 6901(c).
7. I.R.C. § 2031(c)(8)(B).
8. The states that expressly allow conservation easements to impose affirmative obligations are Alabama (Ala. Code § 35-18-1(1)); Alaska (Alaska Stat. § 34.17.060(1)); Arizona (Ariz. Rev. Stat. Ann. § 33-271(1)); Arkansas (Ark. Code Ann. § 15-20-402(1)); Colorado (Colo. Rev. Stat. § 38-30.5-102); Georgia (Ga. Code Ann. § 44-10-2(1)); Idaho (Idaho Code § 55-2101(1)); Illinois (Ill. Comp.) Stat. 120/0.06(a)); Indiana (Ind. Code § 32-5-2.6-1); Kansas (Kan. Stat. Ann. § 58-3810(a)); Kentucky (Ky. Rev. Stat. Ann. § 382.800(1)); Louisiana (La. Rev. Stat. Ann. § 9:1271(1)); Maine (Me. Rev. Stat. Ann. tit. 33, § 476(1)); Michigan (Mich. Comp. Laws § 399.252(a)); Minnesota (Minn. Stat. § 84C.01(1)); Mississippi (Miss. Code Ann. § 89-19-3(1)); Nebraska (Neb. Rev. Stat. § 76-2,111(1)); Nevada (Nev. Rev. Stat. § 111.410(1)); New Hampshire (N.H. Rev. Stat. Ann. § 477:45); New Mexico (N.M. Stat. Ann. § 47-12-2(B)); New York (N.Y. Agric. & Mkts. Law § 305(5)(e)); Oregon (Or. Rev. Stat. secs. 271.715(1)); Rhode Island (R.I. Gen. Laws § 34-39-2); South Carolina (S.C. Code Ann. § 27-8-20(1)); Tennessee (Tenn. Code Ann. § 66-9-303(1)(A)(iii)); Texas (Tex. Nat. Res. Code Ann. § 183.001(1)); Vermont (Vt. Stat. Ann. tit. 34, § 821(a) and (b)); Virginia (Va. Code Ann. § 10.1-1009); West Virginia (W. Va. Code § 20-12-3(a)); and Wisconsin (Wis. Stat. § 700.40(a)).
9. Colo. Rev. Stat. § 38-30.5-102. For similar language, see N.H. Rev. Stat. Ann. § 477:45, I, and R.I. Gen. Laws § 34-39-2(a). See also Mich. Comp. Laws § 399.252(a) (defining a conservation easement as an interest in land that provides limitation on the use of land or a body of water, or *requires* or prohibits *certain acts* on or with respect to the land or body of water" [emphasis added]).
10. Vt. Stat. Ann. tit. 10, § 821(a).
11. Mass. Gen. Laws ch. 184, § 31. Florida's statute uses similar language. See Fla. Stat. § 704.06(1).
12. Cal. Civ. Code § 815.1; Mont. Code Ann. § 76-6-203.
13. E-mail from Andrew Dana, Esq., November 17, 1998.
14. See, e.g., Ky. Rev. Stat. Ann. § 382.800(2).
15. Alaska Stat. § 34.17.060(2)(B); Me. Rev. Stat. Ann. tit. 33, § 476(2)(B).
16. Miss. Code Ann. § 89-19-3(2)(b).
17. N.M. Stat. Ann. § 47-12-1(A); Arizona.
18. N.H. Rev. Stat. Ann. § 477:46. For similar language, see R.I. Gen. Laws § 34-39-3(a).
19. N.C. Gen. Stat. § 121-35(2).
20. Alaska Stat. § 34.17.060(2); N.Y. Agric. & Mkts. Law § 303(2); Utah Code Ann. § 57-18-3; Va. Code Ann. § 10.1-1009; Wash. Rev. Code § 64.04.130; W. Va. Code § 20-12-3(2). The Virginia statute unadvisedly requires the holder to be "declared exempt" under section 501(c)(3). As a matter of federal tax law, an organization is (or is not) exempt under section 501(c)(3). An organization generally must apply for *recognition* of its tax-exempt status. If the organization meets the

requirements of section 501(c)(3), then the Internal Revenue Service will issue a determination letter indicating that it recognizes the organization's tax-exempt status. The Internal Revenue Service, however, does not *declare* that an organization is exempt under section 501(c)(3).

21. A section 501(c)(2) organization is a type of title-holding company that is organized as a corporation and whose activities are limited to holding title to property, collecting income from the property, and distributing any net income to the parent organization. The two latter activities would be unlikely in a title-holding company that only held conservation easements.

22. Neb. Rev. Stat. § 76-2,111(3)(b).

23. Mass. Gen. Laws ch. 184, § 32. Massachusetts distinguishes conservation easements by their purpose. The statute recognizes four types of easements: (1) conservation restrictions, (2) agricultural preservation restrictions, (3) watershed preservation restrictions, and (4) preservation restrictions. Mass. Gen. Laws ch. 184, § 31. With respect to conservation restrictions, agricultural preservation restrictions, and watershed preservation restrictions, the holder's purposes must include the "conservation of land or water areas." In contrast, with respect to a preservation restriction, the holder's purposes must include the "preservation of buildings or sites of historical significance or of a particular such building or site." Mass. Gen. Laws ch. 184, § 32.

24. Although states such as Connecticut, Delaware, Massachusetts, and Rhode Island do not include the preservation of agricultural land among the holder's purposes, that purpose is implicit. In those states, an easement may be established for the purpose of preserving agricultural land, and the holder's purpose must include the "conservation of land." See, e.g., Conn. Gen. Stat. §§ 47-42a(a) and 47-42b.

25. Ill. Comp. Stat. § 120/0.02.

26. Mont. Code Ann. §§ 76-6-103 and 76-6-104(5)(c).

27. See, e.g., Massachusetts, North Carolina, and Rhode Island.

28. Those states are California, Connecticut, Delaware, Massachusetts, Missouri, Montana, New Hampshire, New Jersey, New Mexico, New York, Ohio, Rhode Island, Tennessee, Vermont, and Washington.

29. Vt. Stat. Ann. tit. 34, § 821(c)(2).

30. Vt. Stat. Ann. tit. 34, § 821(b). See Vt. Stat. Ann. tit. 34, § 821(c)(2).

31. See, e.g., Ariz. Rev. Stat. Ann. § 33-27(3)(b); Me. Rev. Stat. Ann. tit. 33, § 476(2)(B); Mass. Gen. Laws ch. 184, § 32; and R.I. Gen. Laws § 34-39-3(a). Vermont also seems to fall into the group of states requiring only that the holder's purposes include certain conservation purposes. In Vermont, one of the holder's *stated* purposes must be "to acquire property or rights and interests in property in order to preserve historic, agricultural, forestry or open space resources." Vt. Stat. Ann. tit. 34, § 821(c)(2).

32. Cal. Civ. Code § 815.3(a).

33. Ill. Comp. Stat. 120/0.02.

34. Wash. Rev. Code § 64.04.130.

35. Haw. Rev. Stat. § 198-3.

36. Mont. Code Ann. § 76-6-104(5)(c).

37. Colo. Rev. Stat. § 38-30.5-104(2).
38. Va. Code Ann. § 10.1-1009.
39. Mass. Gen. Laws ch. 184, § 31.
40. The states whose statutes are silent on the issue of duration are Connecticut, Delaware, Illinois, Maryland, Massachusetts, Michigan, Missouri, New Hampshire, New Jersey, New York, Ohio, Rhode Island, South Dakota, Tennessee, Utah, Vermont, and Washington.
41. I.R.C. § 2031(c)(8)(B).
42. See, e.g., Ala. Code § 35-18-2(a) and 35-18-3(b).
43. Ala. Code § 35-18-2(a).
44. See William T. Hutton and Walter T. Moore, "Easements in the Wake of Catastrophe: The Legal Fallout," *The Back Forty*, April 1991, pp. 1–7 (reprinted in *The Back Forty Anthology*, pp. 3.23–3.29). See also Jeffrey A. Blackie, "Do Conservation Easements Last Forever? Conservation Easements and the Doctrine of Changed Conditions," *The Back Forty*, July/August 1990, pp. 1–5.
45. Marketable title acts also can function to defeat conservation easements. See William R. Ginsberg, "Marketable Title Acts: Traps for the Unwary," *The Back Forty*, May/June 1992, pp. 8–10 (reprinted in *The Back Forty Anthology*, pp. 4.11–4.13).
46. Colo. Rev. Stat. § 38-30.5-107; Utah Code Ann. § 57-18-5.
47. N.Y. Agric. & Mkts. Law §§ 305(2) and 307(1).
48. For an excellent discussion of the doctrine of merger, see William R. Ginsberg, "The Destructibility of Conservation Easements through Merger," *The Back Forty*, August 1991, pp. 5–8. See also Paul Doscher and Sylvia Bates, "Merging Ownership of Conservation Easements with Fee Interests: The Experience of the Society for the Protection of New Hampshire Forests," *The Back Forty*, August 1991, pp. 1–4.
49. Colo. Rev. Stat. § 38-30.5-107; Utah Code Ann. § 57-18-5.
50. N.H. Rev. Stat. Ann. § 477:46.
51. Miss. Code Ann. § 89-19-5(5).
52. N.Y. Agric. & Mkts. Law §§ 305(2) and 307(1).
53. R.I. Gen. Laws § 34-39-3(a).
54. Miss. Code Ann. §§ 89-19-3(3) and 89-19-7(1)(c); N.Y. Agric. & Mkts. Law §§ 303(4) and 305(5).
55. Miss. Code Ann. § 89-19-7(1)(d) and (e). Under Mississippi law, the attorney general and the Department of Wildlife Conservation receive copies of any instrument conveying a conservation easement, but they do not necessarily receive notice of a conveyance of the encumbered land. See Miss. Code Ann. § 89-19-15.
56. For a general discussion of eminent domain and conservation easements, see Gregory Bialecki, "What Must the Taking Authority Pay for Land Subject to a Conservation Easement," *The Back Forty*, July/August 1990, p. 6, and Gregory Bialecki, "Eminent Domain Takings of Land Subject to Conservation Easements," *The Back Forty*, September 1990, pp. 8–9 (compiled as "Eminent Domain Takings of Land Subject to Conservation Easements," *The Back Forty Anthology*, pp.

6.3–6.5). See also Terri Finkbine Arnold, "Condemnation and Conservation Easements," *The Back Forty Anthology,* pp. 6.7–6.9.

57. Del. Code Ann. tit. 7, § 6905; Ill. Comp. Stat. 120/0.06; N.Y. Agric. & Mkts. Law § 309; N.C. Gen. Stats § 121-36(c); and Va. Code Ann. § 10.1-1010(F).

58. Va. Code Ann. § 10.1-1010(F).

59. See Ann Grimaldi, Kelly Moffat, and Eric Singleton, "Back-Up Enforcement of Conservation Easements," *The Back Forty,* September 1991, pp. 1–6 (reprinted in *The Back Forty Anthology,* pp. 3.71–3.76).

60. In the states adopting the Uniform Act, the attorney general is named inferentially as a party who can enforce the terms of a conservation easement. See, e.g., Tex. Nat. Res. Code Ann. § 183.003(a)(4). Under principles of charitable trusts, the attorney general is apt to have standing to sue to enforce the easement.

61. Va. Code Ann. § 10.1-1010(C).

62. See, e.g., Va. Code Ann. § 10.1-1010(B).

63. N.M. Stat. Ann. § 47-12-1(B).

64. N.M. Stat. Ann. § 47-12-1(B).

Chapter 3

🦋 🦋

An Obscure Tax Code Provision Takes Private Land Protection into the Twenty-First Century

Stephen J. Small

The growth of the land trust movement in the United States accelerated through the 1980s as land trusts became increasingly familiar with section 170(h) of the tax code and its possible uses. Passage of section 170(h) in 1980 was not the only reason for the land trust boom, but the conditions were certainly ripe for capitalizing on tax incentives. Across the country, land values were on the rise and there was an increasing demand for land. These factors, coupled with continued and growing estate tax problems, made the perfect setting for section 170(h).

The Land Trust Exchange, now called the Land Trust Alliance (LTA), formed in 1981. The first two years of its existence was not particularly noteworthy. In November 1983, a small group of land trust representatives, attorneys, and other interested parties met at the Feathered Pipe Ranch in Helena, Montana. There were two items on the agenda of what is referred to as the Feathered Pipe Conference: an attempt to elicit comments from the land trust community in response to the income tax regulations on conservation easement donations published in the Notice of Proposed Rulemaking under section 170(h) in May of 1983; and the continued viability of the young and struggling LTE. At that conference, the most vocal critics of the Land Trust Exchange, who had threatened to withdraw their support from LTE and possibly start a new organization to take its place, agreed to turn over the reins of the organization to Ben Emory from Maine. He was given a year or so to see if he could make the organization work. In November of 1985, two years later almost to the day, LTE held its first annual conference in Washington, D.C., with 200 people in attendance. The tax code had created a tool for protecting private lands and gave land trusts a focus for their efforts, and the land trust movement was growing by leaps and bounds.

The easement provisions added to the Internal Revenue Code in 1976 occurred virtually without debate and without any notice whatsoever.[1] A search of the legal literature before 1976 shows almost nothing being written about conservation and preservation easements.[2] When the statute was amended in 1980, only a few interest groups were involved. Once section 170(h) became law in 1980, however, the fledgling land trust movement around the country began to pay attention to the new statutory language and to the subsequent regulation writing process. Thirty-seven individuals were on the scheduled speakers' list for the hearing on the Notice of Proposed Rulemaking at the IRS national office in Washington, D.C., on September 15, 1983. According to an LTA 1998 survey, in 1988 there were 743 land trusts in the United States responsible for securing protection of approximately 2 million acres of land, of which 290,000 acres were under easement.[3] There are now more than 1,200 land trusts around the country that have helped to protect more than 4.7 million acres of land, and nearly 1.4 million of these used easements.[4] This number is rising rapidly as land trusts take on and complete more and more conservation easement projects each year.

In 1980, the legal provisions for conservation easements were obscure and poorly understood. Congress certainly believed that such provisions would provide useful incentives for protecting important conservation values. Between the relative obscurity of the provision and the relatively low land values at that time, both the House and Senate committee reports on the 1980 legislation estimated that the federal government would lose $5 million annually in income tax revenue through conservation easement donations. At least one easement donated in 1998 had a value of more than $10 million.

With very little debate, as part of the Tax Reform Act of 1976, Congress adopted the Historic Structures Tax Act. This legislation codified for the first time the deductibility of conservation and historic preservation easement donations.[5] This new tax code provision, section 170(f)(3)(b)(iii), allowed a taxpayer to claim an income tax deduction for the charitable donation of a thirty-year easement to a qualified charitable donee. A year later, in 1977, the law was amended to make such a deduction available only if the taxpayer donated a *perpetual* (emphasis added) easement.[6]

The 1976 statute had a five-year so-called "sunset" provision, which meant that absent any further congressional action the provision would expire and disappear from the tax code in 1981. By early 1980, the Treasury Department had decided that Congress would extend and, very possibly, would amend the 1976 legislation. Consequently, the Treasury Department instructed work on draft regulations for the 1976 statute to cease.

Again, few interest groups were involved in the congressional hearings and debate over the 1980 statute. Some of these, including The Nature Conservancy (TNC), the Trust for Public Land (TPL), and the American Farmland Trust (AFT), had contacted the IRS during the process of drafting regulations for the 1976 statute. If someone had suggested in 1980 that within twenty years the land trust movement around the country would be in a period of explosive growth, the speaker would have been dismissed as a dreamer, but this trend of explosive growth may well continue over the next twenty years.

In December 1980, President Jimmy Carter signed new tax legislation that, among other things, amended the 1976 provision and slightly modified the rules for deductibility of conservation easement donations. Modest as it was at the time, the general conservation community was pleased with the changes, particularly since this provision had been made permanent by eliminating the "sunset" date. Yet, organizations were still concerned about exactly what the new statutory provisions meant. The new U.S.C. section 170(h) contained terms such as "clearly delineated governmental policy," "for the scenic enjoyment of the general public," and "significant public benefit," terms that were both essential to the workings of section 170(h) but without precedent in the tax code.

"What does this mean?" some land trust people asked. "How can we ever advise a landowner that there is sufficient 'significant public benefit' associated with a donation to meet the requirements of the tax code when we do not know what that is?" These were valid questions. The regulations project then underway at the Internal Revenue Service would provide a sound framework for the answers and ensure that conservation easement donations would become an accepted land protection tool.

In 1983, when the Notice of Proposed Rulemaking on section 170(h) was published, again some land trust people expressed dismay. "What does this mean? How will the IRS deal with these donations? How can we advise landowners? This will never work," were among the most popular questions of the day. Throughout 1983 and 1984, many people did not believe that they would eventually become comfortable with this new tax language and the provisions for conservation easements.[7]

Over time, it was hoped that land trusts would see that the IRS would treat conservation easements in a sensible and sensitive manner and that the regulations would provide a sensitive and meaningful framework for them to carry on their work and for easement donations to proceed. As the IRS issued letter rulings under the new section 170(h), it was hoped that the comfort level of the land trust community would grow.[8]

Over the following years, these assertions proved to be true. Beginning early in the 1980s the IRS started issuing private letter rulings under section 170(h).[9] In 1982, five such rulings, all favoring individual taxpayers, were issued. In 1983, three more rulings were issued, and 1984 brought issuance of another nine favorable rulings. The language in these early letter rulings, some of which are abstracted here, and in dozens more since that time, was familiar to land trusts and helped reassure them that their efforts were on track. Excerpts of these rulings are as follows:

> Aspen, willows, and meadow have been identified as the three major vegetation types located on the property. The aspen provides a habitat for a wide variety of birds and escape and resting cover for large mammals. The willow vegetation is used as browse by moose that also breed on the property. Elk migrate across the property, crossing from P to islands in S in order to breed. The property has been observed as being in an elk migration corridor. It has also been recognized as a substantially unaltered natural setting of the nearby rugged mountains of southern P and the adjacent S flood plain and its riparian community.[10]

> [T]he viability of the agriculture industry is very important for a number of reasons. It is a low service-requiring industry, which constitutes a sizeable portion of the tax base. It is largely responsible for the scenic and open space amenities in the County. It is primarily important to the planning process. Without its continued existence, the . . . concept of orderly development will be doomed. . . . Without substantial effort to protect the agricultural industry, [other goals of the plan] will be next to impossible to attain.[11]

> Taxpayer, a resident of W, is a general partner in a limited partnership in the process of being formed for purposes of acquiring, preserving and selling property located in C. The property consists of 5,367 acres of F. It is represented that the property is unique in that it is the largest private land holding in C, containing valuable ground and surface water, mature woodlands, habitat for uncommon flora and fauna, acres of agricultural land, significant historic structures and sweeping scenic vistas. It includes 4,300 acres of active farmland, 1,000 acres of woodland, more than seven miles of streams and is dotted with historic farmhouses and buildings.[12]

> Revenue derived from agricultural production is a substantial component of the County's economy. In an effort to direct nonagricultural land development in the County and prevent the conversion of prime agricultural land to other uses, County has established a land preservation program for farmland and

placed it under the responsibility of X. Taxpayers' property is included within a proposed agricultural preserve under the County's comprehensive plan for land use and is the type of land over which conservation easements are sought pursuant to X's deed restriction program. Farmland also provides scenic open areas between developed areas and a variety of wildlife habitats. Consequently, we conclude that the contribution of the proposed deed of easement will be made for a conservation purpose within the meaning of section 170(h)(4)(A)(iii)(II) of the Code.[13]

In 1994, the Township Board of Supervisors designated the Property as part of the Township ASA, which qualifies the property for special protections designed to discourage development. The Property is within the Y Corridor, which has been designated as a National Historic Landmark and also is adjacent to the X Historic District, which was listed on the National Register of Historic places in 1984. The X Historic District was established by Township, which has indicated that it strongly supports the donation of the conservation easement and that protection of the property will have important public benefits. In addition, other properties nearby are the subject of conservation easements.[14]

A letter from Donee to taxpayers' representative indicates that Donee is familiar with Ranch, that it is one of the most scenic, ecologically important, and developable properties in the region and that considers Ranch to be 'exceptionally important from a conservation viewpoint.' An Easement Documentation Report prepared by Donee in connection with the easement indicates that Ranch contains two globally rare plant species. In addition, Ranch provides significant open space and natural habitat in the form of sagebrush, grassland, and native grass meadows, which provide prey for raptors, including golden eagles, northern harriers, red-tailed hawks, kestrels, and great-horned owls. Ranch contains more than five miles of riparian habitat along the two creek drainages, both of which consist of pristine riverine plant communities with a large variety of trees and many species of shrubby plants, all of which provide excellent habitat, as well as shelter for waterfowl. The riparian areas and adjacent meadows and fields provide habitat for small mammals, bobcat, cougar, bear, elk, white-tail and mule deer, and moose.[15]

Just as tax code provisions can create income tax deductions, income tax deductions can spawn tax court cases. There are now more than twenty reported conservation easement donation cases. However, as noted in the 1995 Second Supplement to *The Federal Tax Law of Conservation Easements,* "it would not be inaccurate to say that the most significant development in the law concerning easements is simply the continuing development of favorable law for easement donors and charitable donee organizations, including land trusts." (emphasis in the original; p.1).[16] A series of favorable letter rulings from the IRS under section 170(h) has increased landowner and advisor confidence in the workability of the tax code rules, and a series of generally positive court cases has assured practitioners that section 170(h) works and that a sound and professional appraisal will result in the anticipated income tax benefits.

A discussion of section 170(h) and its happy history would not be complete without a look at the first new tax code incentive for private land conservation to pass Congress in more than a decade—section 2031(c) of the tax code.

In mid-1997, President Bill Clinton signed into law the Taxpayer Relief Act of 1997. That legislation included a modified version of the American Farm and Ranch Protection Act, the original version of which was first introduced in Congress in 1990 by Senator John Chafee and Congressman Richard Schulze. The proposal originated with the Piedmont Environmental Council (PEC), based in northern Virginia. Some PEC supporters and representatives became convinced of the need for additional tax code incentives for land protection and proposed, rather simply and directly, that land subject to a conservation easement under section 170(h) of the tax code should be totally exempt from estate tax. This was essentially the provision introduced by Senator Chafee and Congressman Schulze in 1990, although over the next several years, as the federal legislative process moved forward, the proposal became less simple and less comprehensive. It nonetheless became an important new incentive for private, voluntary land conservation that landowners, their advisors, and land trusts must become familiar with.

How the New Law Works

The American Farm and Ranch Protection Act added section 2031(c), "Estate Tax With Respect to Land Subject to a Qualified Conservation Easement" to the tax code. All of the existing conservation easement rules of section 170(h), the current conservation easement section, are still intact and section 170(h) works exactly the same way it did before the 1997 tax code changes. If you donate an easement on land you own, and if the easement meets the requirements of section 170(h), you are entitled to an income tax deduction for the value of the conservation easement. In addition, the value of your land may be reduced for estate tax purposes.

Consequently, after meeting the requirements of section 170(h), you may benefit additionally under section 2031(c). It is entirely possible, however, that you may not be eligible for the additional benefits of section 2031(c). In addition, although you may be eligible for the benefits of section 2031(c), the executor of your estate may decide not to take advantage of section 2031(c). Put another way, an easement *must qualify* under section 170(h) for you to be eligible for the benefits of section 2031(c), but if the easement *does not* qualify under section 2031(c) or if you decides not take advantage of section 2031(c) there are no consequences to you under section 170(h).

In a nutshell, this is what section 2031(c) says: if you have land subject to a conservation easement that meets the requirements of section 170(h), if you own that land when you die, and if you meet the requirements of section 2031(c), then you can exclude *an additional percentage of the value of that land* from your estate in addition to the reduction in value already attributable to the easement.

The new law allows an executor to elect to exclude up to 40 percent of the value of land (not structures) that is subject to a conservation easement from a decedent's estate for federal estate tax purposes if:

- the land is within a 25-mile radius of a metropolitan statistical area, as defined by the Office of Management and Budget as typically an area with a population over of 50,000, or a national park or wilderness area, or within 10 miles of an urban national forest;
- the easement was donated, is perpetual, and otherwise meets the requirements of section 170(h). Easements qualifying solely because they protect historic assets are not eligible for section 2031(c) benefits;
- the land was owned by the decedent or a member of the decedent's family for at least three years immediately prior to the decedent's death;
- the easement was donated by the decedent or a member of the decedent's family; and
- the easement prohibits all but minimal commercial recreational use of the land (see more on this in the text that follows).

The maximum amount that may be excluded from an estate was $100,000 in 1998, increasing by $100,000 each year up to the maximum exclusion of $500,000 in 2002 and after. The exclusion applies regardless of when the easement was donated.

Here is the simplest possible example of how the new exclusion will work:

John owns land worth $2 million. In 1998, he donated a qualifying conservation easement that reduces the value of his land to $1 million. He dies in

2003. The land is valued in his estate at $1,000,000. His executor elects to take the section 2031(c) exclusion: 40 percent of the $1,000,000 land value is excluded from John's estate and the remaining $600,000 of land value is subject to estate tax.

Finally, note that if an easement *does not prohibit* all but what the law calls de minimis commercial recreational activities, the estate will not be eligible for the section 2031(c) exclusion.

Some Important Issues

Prior to the new law, if a landowner died without having either donated an easement during lifetime or included an easement donation in a will, the estate tax was based on the full and fair market value of the land. The new law includes a very important provision that allows an executor, a trustee, or an heir to elect to donate a qualified conservation easement *after the death of the landowner.*

"Post-Mortem" Easement Donation

The opportunity to donate a post-mortem easement is incredibly important yet very poorly understood. The legal rules concerning the circumstances in which such a donation can be made varies widely from state to state and may require changes in some state laws. In some states, for example, title to real estate vests in the *heirs* at the date of death, while in other states the executor of the estate may hold title. In the latter case, state law may prevent an executor or a trustee from making charitable contributions from the assets of the estate or the trust without either explicit authorization in the governing instruments (the will or trust) or without court approval. Addressing this particular problem, Colorado and Virginia passed legislation that allows executors and trustees to make conservation easement donations.

If these state law issues can be satisfactorily addressed, here is the simplest possible example of how the post-mortem donation will work.

Mary owns land worth $2,000,000. She did not donate an easement during her lifetime and she did not include an easement in her will. She dies in 2003 and leaves the land to her children. The land is valued in her estate at $2,000,000. Her executor and her children agree to donate a conservation easement. Assume the easement reduces the value of her land to $1,000,000 and that $1,000,000 of value is subject to estate tax. *In addition,* her executor elects to take the section 2031(c) exclusion whereby an additional 40 percent of the $1,000,000 land value is excluded from Mary's estate, and the remaining $600,000 of land value is subject to estate tax. (Under these circumstances, even though the easement met the requirements of section 170(h), apparently neither the estate nor the children will be able to take an *income tax deduction* for donating the easement.)

Commercial Recreational Activities

Here is another important post-mortem planning opportunity. Assume Mary dies owning land restricted by an easement that met the requirements of section 170(h) but that the easement does not prohibit commercial recreational activity and therefore the estate is ineligible for the section 2031(c) exclusion. Since the executor can in fact make a post-mortem *easement donation* in order to qualify for section 2031(c), it also appears that the executor can make a post-mortem *easement amendment* in order to eliminate any prohibited commercial recreational activity so as to be eligible for section 2031(c).

Note of Caution

The post-mortem easement donation and the post-mortem easement amendment are important. However, while these planning opportunities are useful additions to the planner's toolbox, a landowner, family, or an advisor should not take the position that comprehensive planning during a lifetime should be put off because of the availability of post-mortem planning opportunities. For one thing, the law is *absolutely clear* on the income tax and estate tax savings that are available when an easement is donated during lifetime. All of the issues are *not clear* in the case of a post-mortem donation. In addition, using these post-mortem tools successfully means addressing a complex array of state law and other related questions and reaching agreement among all necessary parties within a relatively short period after the death of the decedent. It is certainly better to see to it that the proper planning is done during the lifetime of the landowner.

Planning Observations

Every single conservation easement must now take into account the provisions of section 2031(c) as part of the planning process. Land that falls outside the geographic limitations of section 2031(c) simply will not be eligible for the benefits of that section. However, continued urban sprawl will inevitably result in the addition of new metropolitan statistical areas to the map, which will mean greater coverage under section 2031(c).

Every single-family lands planning situation must now take into account the provisions of section 2031(c) as part of the planning process. Do the current owners want to gift the property to children over a period of years as part of the estate planning and succession planning process? Does the family want to remain eligible for the section 2031(c) benefits? There is no "right" answer to these questions, but now we have an important additional planning tool in the landowner's toolbox.

Every recorded easement should be reviewed with section 2031(c) eligibility in mind (to look for a prohibition on commercial recreational activities, for example) if the land is still owned by the same family that donated the easement.

Section 2031(c) is a very important incentive for land conservation. It will take some time to sort out all of the planning issues and to answer some of the questions that have already come up, but landowners and their advisors and land trusts must begin to work with the law. The fact that this incentive is a part of the tax code is also testimony to the growing strength of the land trust movement.

Given the success story of section 170(h) and section 2031(c), we are seeing a historically unique combination of circumstances that will fuel the continued growth of conservation easements and the land trust movement. First, high real estate values continue to collide with the heavy burden of the estate tax system. For the first time in the history of the United States, the family that just wants to leave important family land to the children may not be able to do that without tax and legal planning, and that planning often will involve the family donating a conservation easement to lower the estate tax value of the land.[17] Second, the nation as a whole, including private landowners, is aging. Combining the demographics of the United States and the estate tax burden, between 2005 and 2020 *many millions of acres* of farmland, forestland, ranchland, wildlife habitat, *of important family land* will change hands and potentially change use.[18]

At the same time, there is another fundamental matter that needs attention. In every single community in this country, if you have a piece of land that you want to *develop,* an entire infrastructure exists to support you. There are attorneys, engineers, land use planners, surveyors, appraisers, and planning board or zoning commission members who know all about how to develop a piece of land. There is a whole support network of professionals and technicians who make a living doing real estate development. If you have a piece of land to develop, the question is not "How can I find help?" If you have a piece of land to develop, the question is, "Let's see, of all of the available choices, who shall I choose to help me and to work with me?"

But consider this. In every single community in this country there are landowners who love their land and do not want to see that land developed. And most of them have *absolutely nowhere to turn.* In many communities around the United States there are absolutely no professionals who understand how to protect a piece of land. There are no attorneys, no accountants, no "planners," no zoning commission members, no appraisers, no real estate brokers, no advisors at all who understand the concept of private land protection and how to go about it.

On one hand, we have a real estate development infrastructure permanently in place and highly visible after 200 years of real estate development in the United States. On the other hand, a landowner with a farm, a ranch, working forestland, country property, or open space has absolutely no idea where to turn for help.

This must change.

The single best tool available to preserve family lands and open space is the conservation easement. The income and estate tax incentives and land protection benefits of section 170(h) and of section 2031(c) will continue to play a pivotal and critical role in private land protection efforts around the country as we move into the twenty-first century.

Finally, a few personal observations about state conservation easement statutes. First, as far as the organized bar is concerned, almost no one knows anything about state easement enabling legislation. Second, and perhaps in spite of this, the *existence* of state easement enabling laws has made a difference in some states. Many landowners or, perhaps more accurately, many professional advisors to landowners, have been reluctant to encourage (or agree to) conservation easement donations in the absence of a state statute. I do not share their reluctance. Currently there is no state statute in Wyoming, where there are active conservation easement programs, or in Pennsylvania, which has one of the most active government and land trust easement programs in the nation. Certainly, however, *passage* of enabling legislation in states where none currently exists will have a favorable effect. Third, statutes exist and where they do they must be reviewed and attended to, but the terms have had little or no effect in the marketplace of conservation easement donations.

Notes

1. Federal Tax Law, at 1–5 and Appendix D.
2. The sole significant exception is Browne and Van Dorn, "Charitable Gifts of Partial Interests in Real Property for Conservation Purposes," *Tax Law* 29 (69) (1975).
3. 1998 National Land Trust Survey, Washington, D.C.: Land Trust Alliance, September 1998.
4. Land Trust Survey, 1998.
5. See Small, S. J. "The Tax Benefits of Donating Easements in Scenic and Historic Property," *Real Est. L. J.* 7 (304) (1979).
6. Small, S. J. "The Tax Benefits of Donating Easements in Scenic and Historic Property."

7. See Small, S. J. "Working with the 1980 Amendments to the Internal Revenue Code," in *Land-Saving Action,* Sarah M. Bates and Russell L. Brenneman, eds. (Washington, D.C.: Island Press, 1984).

8. See Small, S. J. "Working with the 1980 Amendments to the Internal Revenue Code," in *Land-Saving Action.* (Washington, D.C.: Island Press, 1984), pp. 156–164.

9. See Small, S. J. "The Federal Tax Law of Conservation Easements," *Land Trust Alliance,* 1986.

10. P.L.R. 8243125.

11. P.L.R. 8422064.

12. P.L.R. 8450065.

13. P.L.R. 8544036.

14. P.L.R. 9603018.

15. P.L.R. 9632003.

16. Small, S. J., *The Federal Tax Law of Conservation Easements, Second Supplement* (Washington, D.C.: Island Press, 1995), p. 1.

17. See Small, *Preserving Family Lands: Book I,* 3rd ed. (Boston: Landowner Planning Center, 1998).

18. See Small, S. J., *Preserving Family Lands: Book II* (Boston: Landowner Planning Center, 1997).

Part II

❦ ❦

Conservation Easements: Regions, Regulatory Framework, and Protected Lands

Chapter 4

❦ ❧

Introduction to Legal Analysis

Roderick H. Squires

Legislation allowing nonprofit conservation organizations to hold conservation easements has been enacted by forty-five states and the District of
Columbia.[1] In this book, we have used the familiar federal circuits to divide
the country into manageable chapters. This also works on a practical level in
that neighboring states frequently share some legal similarity and courts from
neighboring states are more likely to look to laws from states from within the
applicable circuit (Figure 4.1).[2]

Conservation easements are the product of both federal and state legislation. The initial impetus, and, perhaps, key to their widespread popularity
and utility as a land protection tool, is the potential federal income tax benefits to landowners. These benefits, described in federal statutes and Internal
Revenue Service regulations, reflect national consensus following public
debate about the desirability of protecting parcels of land having specific ecological characteristics and using the tax code to do so, in essence to compensate landowners who own specific types of real property for not exercising the
most valuable stick of their real property bundle.

In 1976, following a number of years of favorable tax rulings by the Internal Revenue Service, Congress enacted seminal tax legislation allowing
landowners of certain types of land, and who donated a portion of their real
property interests to a government agency or nonprofit organization, to claim
a deduction on federal income tax forms for such a "qualified conservation
contribution"[3] (Figure 4.2). This legislation introduced a new tool to organizations and agencies interested in protecting the ecological characteristics of
land surfaces, the conservation easement.[4] It provided an important tool to
nonprofit organizations, like land trusts, established solely to protect land and
specific artifacts, because it allowed them to solicit donations of real property

Figure 4.1. U.S. federal circuits.
Credit: Cartography Lab, University of Minnesota

rights from private landowners. It provided government agencies with a low-cost alternative to purchasing private ownership rights. Provisions in the Tax Reduction and Simplification Act of 1977 and the Tax Treatment Extension Act of 1980, along with more favorable rulings by the Internal Revenue Service in actual instances of taxpayers claiming a deduction for such donations, encouraged more widespread interest in conservation easements.[5]

There was a potential barrier to the widespread use of such a tool because the federal tax legislation necessitated that the landowner create a new type of real property interest. To achieve the necessary tax reduction, landowners had to encumber their fee title with a conservation easement and convey that easement, and their real property rights, to another party. Such easements could only be created and conveyed if made legal through state legislation defining them as valid real property interests. Surprisingly, some states had created conservation easements even before the 1976 legislation. California, Connecticut, Maryland, New York, Oregon, and Pennsylvania had all enacted legislation specifically or generally allowing landowners to create and convey conservation easements and realize the promised tax benefits.[6]

In an effort to help all states develop statutory language that would permit landowners to create and convey conservation easements and government agencies and nonprofits to hold such easements, the National Conference of Commissioners on Uniform State Laws adopted the Uniform Conservation

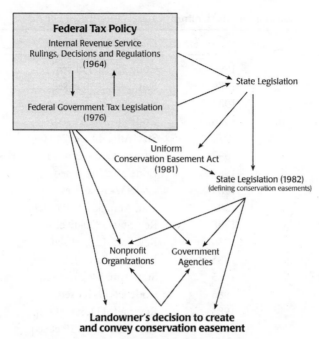

Figure 4.2. Elements involved in creating conservation easements (dates refer to start of legal elements).
Credit: R. H. Squires (1998)

Easement Act (UCEA) in 1981.[7] Aimed at restricting land use activities that would alter the nature of the land surface while keeping the land in private ownership, the act took advantage of federal tax provisions. The UCEA was not designed to be comprehensive but to provide a blueprint for the legislatures of the various states. The act was intended to create a conservation easement that could be designed for the specific circumstances of a particular place and take into account both the land's ecological characteristics and the landowners' present and future economic circumstances. The UCEA reflected the collective wisdom of lawyers from all the states about how state legislatures could, first, take advantage of the federal tax code to protect land via conservation easements on private land and, second, overcome some of the common-law problems associated with such easements.

Since 1981, twenty-one states have adopted the UCEA with or without modifications (Table 4.1). Twenty-five other states—including California, which was the earliest to adopt statutory language permitting conservation easements—have enacted legislation that reflects the intent, if not the word-

Table 4.1. States Adopting the Uniform Conservation Easement Act

State	Legislation Enacted	Current Code Citation
Alabama	1997	Code 35-18-1 et seq.
Alaska	1989	Stat. 34.17.010 et seq.
Arizona	1985	Rev. Stat. 33-271 et seq.
District of Columbia	1986	Code 45-2602 et seq.
Florida	1976	Stat. Ann. 40 sec. 740.06
Georgia	1992	Official Code Ann. 44-10-1 et seq.
Idaho	1988	Code 55-2101 et seq.
Indiana	1984	Code 32-5-2.6-1 et seq.
Kansas	1992	Stat. Ann. 58-3810 et seq.
Kentucky	1988	Rev. Stat. 382.800 et seq.
Louisiana	1986	Rev. Stat. 1271 et seq.
Maine	1985	Rev. Stat. Ann. 476 et seq.
Minnesota	1985	Stat. Ann. 84C.01et seq.
Mississippi	1986	Code 89-19-1et seq.
Nevada	1983	Rev. Stat. 111.390 et seq.
Oregon	1983	Rev. Stat. 271-719 et seq.
South Carolina	1991	Code 27-8-10 et seq.
South Dakota	1984	Codified Laws 1-19B-56 et seq.
Texas	1983	Natural Resources Code 183.001 et seq.
Virginia	1988	Code 10.1-1009 et seq.
West Virginia	1995	Rev. Code 20.12.1 et seq.
Wisconsin	1981	Stat. Ann. 700.40

ing, of the UCEA, designed to enable "private parties to enter into consensual arrangements with charitable organizations or government bodies to protect land and buildings without the encumbrances of certain potential common law problems"[8] (Table 4.2).

Across a large part of the nation, state statutes define how conservation easements may be created and conveyed and who may hold them. They describe any real property tax benefits to the landowner, and the future obligations such easements place on the landowner, future landowners, and the holder. For the landowner, the obligations concern future land use activities. For the holder, the obligations concern monitoring future land use activities and enforcing the terms of the easement. Broadly speaking, such statutes reflect the consensus reached by the citizens of those states about the importance of protecting particular lands and the desirability of using conservation

Table 4.2. States Adopting Conservation Easement Enabling Laws Other Than the UCEA

State	Legislation Enacted	Current Code Citation
Arkansas	1983	Code Ann. 15-20-401 et seq.
California	1979	Civil Code 815 et seq.
Colorado	1976	Rev. Stat. 30.5
Connecticut	1971	Gen. Stat. Ann. 47.42a et seq.
Delaware	1978	Code 7 6901 et seq.
Hawaii	1985	Rev. Stat. 98-1 et seq.
Illinois	1977	Comp. Stat.c. 30 sec. 401 et seq.
Iowa	1970	Code 475A.1et seq.
Maryland	1977	Ann. Code Real Property 2-118
Massachusetts	1969	Ann. Laws c. 184, sec. 31 et seq.
Michigan	1980	Comp. Laws 399.251 et seq.
Missouri	1971	Rev. Stat. Ann. 67.870
Montana	1969	Code 76-6-101 et seq.
Nebraska	1981	Rev. Stat. 76-2,211 et seq.
New Hampshire	1973	Rev. Stat. Ann. 477.45 et seq.
New Jersey	1979	Stat.13:8B-1 et seq.
New Mexico	1991	Stat. Ann. 47-12-1 et seq.
New York	1983	Environ. Cons. Laws 49-0301 et seq.
North Carolina	1979	Con. Stat. 106-735 et seq.
Ohio	1980	Rev. Code 5301.67 et seq.
Rhode Island	1976	Gen. Laws 34-39-1 et seq.
Tennessee	1981	Code 11-15-101 et seq.
Utah	1985	Code 57-18-1 et seq.
Vermont	1977	Stat. 34 sec. 821 et seq.
Washington	1979	Rev. Code Ann. 64.04.130 et seq.

Source: Squires, R.H. (compiled 1998).

easements to do so. This consensus reflects both a willingness to accept and advance land protection as a goal and a willingness and ability to weave conservation easements into the existing real property law of the state.

Throughout such debates the states are influenced by their history, by the choices previously made about private land ownership, land use, and protection. This history explains, in part, why state legislatures did not immediately adopt the UCEA and why, when they did, they made changes in its language.

The provisions in the UCEA did not, and could not, address the variety of conditions in states. Therefore, considerable differences exist from state to state in the language of statutes permitting conservation easements, including those that follow the UCEA.[9]

The differences in statutory language reflect the way in which different states have historically defined land ownership and land use and particularly how they have protected valuable land. In some instances, conservation easement legislation created an entirely new category of real property interests, whereas in others it merely made explicit what was already being practiced.[10] Some states were slow to adopt the UCEA because they already had statutorily defined conservation easements in 1981; some have not adopted the UCEA or have adopted it only recently because they already possess a variety of ways to protect land.[11]

Forty-five states and the District of Columbia have adopted either the UCEA or similar legislation that protects lands with characteristics described in the UCEA and in the federal tax code.[12] A majority of states have thus accepted that a conservation easement is a useful land protection tool incorporating it into existing real property law. They have accepted that protecting land efforts through tax breaks to individual landowners, who voluntarily donate sticks in their bundle of real property rights to a nonprofit group or a government agency, possesses advantages over other ways of protecting land. Such a method avoids the costly fiscal efforts of government acquiring fee title to the land or the costly political efforts necessary to regulate the land use activities of private landowners.

Each state is unique. The choices that each state's citizens have made over a period of time to organize themselves according to federal constitutional principles and to use their natural resources, in essence to take advantage of the opportunities afforded by their location and to overcome the limitations imposed by it, have made states dissimilar. Not surprisingly, the history of land ownership and land use and the history of land protection and of accepting conservation easements are also dissimilar.

New Estate Tax Incentives for Landowners

In mid-1997, President William Clinton signed the Taxpayer Relief Act of 1997 into law.[13] For landowners and land trusts, the act included several positive additions. The new legislation also included a modified version of the American Farm and Ranch Protection Act and important new tax incentives for landowners.

Senator John Chafee and Congressman Richard Schulze first introduced a version of the Farm and Ranch Protection Act in 1990. Convinced of the need for additional tax incentives for land conservation, the Piedmont Environmental Council initiated the proposal. The proposal for tax relief was simple and direct: Land subject to a conservation easement under section 170(h) of the tax code should be totally exempt from estate tax. In essence, this proposal was the provision introduced by Chafee and Schulze in 1990. As the legislative process moved forward over the next several years, this once simple proposal became convoluted and less comprehensive. It remains, however, an important new tax incentive for private conservation and one with which landowners, their advisers, and land trusts should become familiar.

The new law adds to the tax code a new section 2031(c), "Estate Tax with Respect to Land Subject to a Qualified Conservation Easement." The new law does not replace section 170(h). To the contrary, all the existing rules of section 170(h) are intact, and it works precisely the same way it did before the 1997 tax code changes. If a person owns land and donates a conservation easement that meets the criteria of section 170(h), he or she is entitled to an income tax deduction for the value of the easement. The value of the land is also reduced for estate tax purposes.

Once meeting the requirements of section 170(h), the landowner can look to the potential additional benefits available under section 2031(c). Two things can happen at this point, however. First, it is possible that although the easement met section 170(h) requirements, the landowner may not be eligible for additional benefits provided by section 2031(c). Two, the landowner may be eligible for new benefits of section 2031(c), but the executor of that person's estate may decided not to elect section 2031 (c).

Essentially, section 2031(c) states, that if land one owns is subject to a conservation easement that meets section 17(h) requirements that land is owned when the landowner dies, and that section 2031 (c) requirements are met, a landowner is entitled to exclude *an additional percentage of the value of that land* from his or her estate. This exclusion is in addition to the reduction already attributed to the easement.

There are several important observations and impacts of section 2031(c):

- Every conservation easement must now consider section 2031(c) as part planning process.
- Easements already in place and recorded should be reviewed in light of the new legislation.
- When deliberating the future of family held land, provisions of both section 170(h) and section 2031(c) should be considered in the planning process.
- With good comprehensive planning, landowners can protect and pass land to heirs as well as reap additional savings on estate taxes than is possible under section 170(h) exclusively.

Although it may take some time to sort through the various planning issues and implications tied to the new section 2031(c), it provides some new and potentially important incentive for land conservation. Although it was once sufficient to have a sound understanding of the tax and planning implications of section 170(h), land trusts, landowners, and their advisers must now also become familiar with the provisions of section 2031(c) to ensure that it is used to its full advantage in the protection of private lands and saving tax dollars.

Notes

1. An introduction to this section, in which legislation is described and, to some extent, compared, should perhaps offer a datum from which we might measure the success or failure of legislation in particular states. I do not think such a datum is appropriate, because states should be considered unique, so here I describe the way I think about the origins of conservation easement legislation in various states and the differences in such legislation from one state to another, a framework that addresses the following questions. Why is the language enabling individuals to create and convey conservation easements different from state to state? Why did states enact conservation easements at different times? Why do several states still not allow such easements?

2. Most authors of the legal analysis chapters are practicing lawyers and are therefore familiar with such an arrangement.

3. The federal income tax benefits are defined, first, by federal statutes enacted by Congress and currently described in Title 26 section 170(h) of the *United States Code* and, second, by federal regulations promulgated by the Internal Revenue Service and currently described in Title 26 part of the *Code of Federal Regulations*. Stephen J. Small has traced the history of federal legislation and regulation from 1976 to 1986 and provides copies of key congressional documents that explain the purpose of the legislation in his book *The Federal Tax Law of Conservation Easements* (Bar Harbor, Maine. Land Trust Exchange, 1986), which he describes as annotated commentary on the final regulations concerning "qualified conservation contributions" under section 170(h) of the Internal Revenue Code (26 *United States Code* 170(h)).

4. Although Congress made statements that partial interests in real property were to be regarded as charitable contributions, specific language was not included in the Tax Reform Act of 1969. See Kingsbury Browne Jr. and Walter G. Van Dorne, "Charitable Gifts of Partial Interests in Real Property for Conservation Purposes," *Tax Lawyer* 29 (1975): 69–93; see also Stephanie J. Wilbanks, "Qualified Conservation Contributions: Analysis of Proposed Regulations," *Virginia Tax Review* 3 (winter 1984): 323–345.

5. Public Law 95-30, the Tax Reduction and Simplification Act of 1977, 94 Stat. 3204; Public Law 96-541, the Tax Treatment Extension Act of 1980, 94 Stat. 3204. For a list of IRS rulings, see Small, note 3, and Wilbanks, note 4.

6. Section 2124 of Public Law 94-455, the Tax Reform Act of 1976 (90 Stat. 1916)

created tax incentives to encourage the preservation of historic structures and removed tax incentives to demolish such structures. The legislation was a mammoth 413-page overhaul of the Internal Revenue Code of 1954. Among the states with such legislation in place were California, New York, Maryland, Connecticut, Pennsylvania, and Oregon.

7. The National Conference of Commissioners of Uniform State Laws was organized in 1892 to promote uniformity in state laws; it includes a representative from every state, the District of Columbia, and Puerto Rico. Each proposed act is "subjected to the criticism, correction and recommendation of the Commissioners who represent the experience and judgment of a select body of lawyers from every part of the United States." *Uniform Laws Annotated* vol. 12 (St. Paul, Minn.: West Publishing) p. iv. The UCEA is reproduced in Russell L. Brenneman and Sarah M. Bates, eds., *Land-Saving Action: A Written Symposium by 29 Experts on Private Land Conservation in the 1980s* (Washington, D.C.: Island Press, 1984).

8. Brenneman and Bates, 1984, p. 112.

9. An interesting question concerns the actual language of legislation. How far must the language be altered from the UCEA before it can no longer be defined as falling under the guidelines of the UCEA?

10. The history of particular states may answer a number of questions posed by both the timing and wording of state conservation easement legislation. The timing of the legislation reflects that particular states accept that conservation easements are valid tools to help protect land at that point in time. The next question is, Why then? The language of the legislation clearly reflects the state's attempt to create the legal device and so allow landowners to take advantage of federal income and estate tax deductions. In doing so, the state has to ensure that this easement can be incorporated into the real property law of the state, existing without conflict with other easements and real property interests.

11. Such an explanation raises questions, of course. Why was Wisconsin so receptive to the UCEA and why did neighboring Minnesota take four more years to accept its provisions? Why didn't Georgia adopt the UCEA until 1992, even though the Georgia legislature had enacted a Conservation Easement Act, fifteen years earlier, in 1976? Why has Pennsylvania never enacted conservation easement legislation?

12. K. H. Garrett, "Conservation Easements: the Greening of America," *Kentucky Law Journal* 73 (1984–85): 255–273

13. Taxpayers Relief Act of 1997 (Pub. L. 65-34, 111 Stat. 788).

Chapter 5

🙚 🙚

Conservation Easements in the First and Second Federal Circuits

Karin Marchetti and Jerry Cosgrove

In the United States, laws concerning land are based on state statutes and court precedent, making the interpretations and applications of laws pertaining to conservation easements unique across the states. All easement enabling statutes are aimed at overcoming long-standing and antiquated legal obstacles that deter landowners from placing restrictions on land use. Without such statutory authority that modifies the common law, conservation easements as we know them may enjoy only a presumption of validity and enforceability as easements in gross. Enabling laws vary considerably from state to state within the First and Second Federal Circuits (Figure 5.1). Maine and Massachusetts were the first to adopt easement enabling legislation in 1969. While Maine's statute has been amended to mimic the UCEA, Massachusetts's statute has remained unchanged and continues to impose the most complex requirements. New Hampshire, Vermont, Connecticut, and Rhode Island's legislation predate the UCEA, and New York's conservation easement statute was passed after the uniform act but bears little resemblance to it. Puerto Rico's Natural Patrimony Act essentially creates a state-run centralized land conservation program for Puerto Rico and simply makes a definitional reference to conservation easements. Despite their differences and the complexity of some, all states enjoy an active and healthy conservation easement program. Tables 5.1 and 5.2 give a schematic comparison of conservation easement enabling legislation across the First and Second Federal Circuits.

Connecticut

In 1971, at the same time that the Internal Revenue Service recognized charitable gifts of land use restrictions, Connecticut passed one of the nation's first conservation easement enabling laws.[1] The law established two new

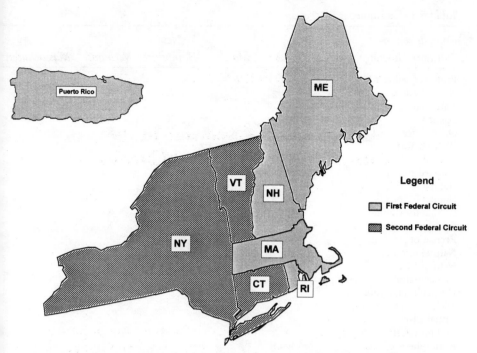

Figure 5.1. States and territory of Puerto Rico comprising First and Second Federal Circuits.
Credit: J. A. Gustanski (1999)

Table 5.1. Comparison of Statutory Language and Terminology in the First Federal Circuit

Comparison of Statutory Language	UCEA	Maine	New Hampshire	Vermont	Massachusetts
Description of Interest					
Nonpossessory interest	X	X			
Easement	X	X	X	X	X
Restriction	X	X	X	X	X
Equitable servitude	X	X			
Covenant	X	X	X	X	X
Articles of dedication					
Condition			X	X	X
Interest in land			X	X	
Incorporeal right					
Easement of view					
Obligation					
Affirmative duty	X	X	X	X	
Negative duty (limitations/ restrictions)	X	X	X	X	X
Holder's access to ensure compliance	X	X		X	
Encourage limited public use					

(*continues*)

Table 5.1. Continued

Comparison of Statutory Language	UCEA	Maine	New Hampshire	Vermont	Massachusetts
Protected Subject Matter					
Natural values	X	X	X	X	X
Natural beauty					
Scenic values	X	X	X	X	X
Open-space values	X	X	X	X	X
Wetland area					
Agricultural resources	X	X	X	X	X
Wooded condition					
Habitat for fish					
Habitat for plants					
Habitat for wildlife				X	
Forest resources	X	X	X	X	X
Recreational resources	X	X			
Natural resources	X	X			
Natural area					
Archeological resources			X	X	X
Horticultural resources					
Silvicultural resources					
Visual effect					
Audible effect					
Atmospheric effect					
Air quality	X	X			
Water quality	X	X			X
Historical aspects	X	X	X	X	X
Architectural aspects	X	X	X	X	X
Facade/external appearance					X
Cultural aspects	X	X		X	X
Historical value on designated registers					
Permissible Conservation Easement Holder					
Authorized governmental body	X	X	X	X	X
Charitable corporation	X	X	X		X
Charitable association	X		X		
Charitable trust	X	X	X		X
Authorized tax-exempt section 501(c) charitable organization				X	
Permissible Third-Party Enforcer					
Governmental body	X	X			
Charitable corporation	X	X			
Charitable association	X	X			
Charitable trust	X	X			
Beneficiary					
Real property owner	X	X			
Conservation easement holder	X	X			
Authorized third party	X	X			
Person authorized by law	X				
Legal and equitable principles unaffected	X	X			

Comparison of Statutory Language	UCEA	Maine	New Hampshire	Vermont	Massachusetts
Creation, Conveyance, Acceptance, and Duration					
Same as other easements	X	X		X	
Same as other interests in land			X	X	X
Holder's acceptance prerequisite to enforcement	X	X			
Recordation of acceptance prerequisite to enforcement	X			X	
Notify assessor					
Duration unlimited	X	X			
Duration for life of another					
Duration for owner's life					
Duration as stated	X	X			X
Written consent of state and town required for both acceptance and release					X
Fee simple					
Acquisition by donation					
Acquisition by purchase					X
Cancel after thirty years if not rerecorded					
Enforcement					
Action at law			X		
Injunction			X		X
Equitable action			X		
Civil action					
Specifically enforceable				X	
Superior Interests					
Existing interests absent written consent	X	X			
Surrounding coal mining operations					
Surrounding coal transportation					
Innocent bona fide purchaser protected					
Eminent domain not impaired					X
Defenses Specifically Eliminated					
Not appurtenant	X	X		X	
Assignability	X	X	X	X	X
Not recognized by common law	X	X			
Imposes a negative burden	X	X			
Imposes affirmative obligations	X	X			
Benefit does not touch/concern real property	X	X	X	X	X
No privity of estate	X	X	X		X
No privity of contract	X	X	X	X	X

(*continues*)

Table 5.1. Continued

Comparison of Statutory Language	UCEA	Maine	New Hampshire	Vermont	Massachusetts
Applicability of Statute					
Interests created after effective date of statute	X	X	X		
Permissible interests created before effective date	X	X	X		
Does not invalidate other lawful interest	X	X			X
Only in counties over 200,000 people					
Only in approving county/ municipality					
Uniformity of Application and Construction					
Applied to effectuate uniform law	X	X			
Construed to effectuate uniform law		X	X		
Tax Valuation					
Taxable at eased value					
Public body tax exemption					

Table 5.2. Comparison of Statutory Language and Terminology in the Second Federal Circuit

Comparison of Statutory Language	UCEA	New York	Connecticut	Rhode Island
Description of Interest				
Nonpossessory interest	X			
Easement	X	X	X	X
Restriction	X	X	X	X
Equitable servitude	X			
Covenant	X	X	X	X
Articles of dedication				
Condition			X	X
Interest in land		X	X	X
Incorporeal right				
Easement of view				
Obligation				
Affirmative duty	X			X
Negative duty (limitations/restrictions)	X	X	X	X
Holder's access to ensure compliance	X	X		
Encourage limited public use				
Protected Subject Matter				
Natural values	X	X	X	X
Natural beauty		X		
Scenic values	X	X	X	X
Open-space values	X	X	X	X
Wetland area		X		
Agricultural resources	X	X	X	X
Wooded condition				
Habitat for fish				

Comparison of Statutory Language	UCEA	New York	Connecticut	Rhode Island
Habitat for plants				
Habitat for wildlife				X
Forest resources	X	X	X	X
Recreational resources	X	X		
Natural resources	X	X		
Natural area				
Archeological resources		X		X
Horticultural resources				
Silvicultural resources				
Visual effect				
Audible effect				
Atmospheric effect				
Air quality	X			
Water quality	X			
Historical aspects	X	X	X	X
Architectural aspects	X	X		X
Facade/external appearance				
Cultural aspects	X	X		
Historical value on designated registers				
Permissible Conservation Easement Holder				
Authorized governmental body	X	X	X	X
Charitable corporation	X	X	X	X
Charitable association	X			X
Charitable trust	X		X	X
Authorized tax-exempt section 501(c) charitable organization				
Permissible Third-Party Enforcer				
Governmental body		X	X	
Charitable corporation	X	X		
Charitable association	X			
Charitable trust	X			
Beneficiary				
Real property owner	X			
Conservation easement holder	X	X		
Authorized third party	X			
Person authorized by law	X			
Legal and equitable principles unaffected	X			
Creation, Conveyance, Acceptance, and Duration				
Same as other easements	X			
Same as other interests in land		X	X	X
Holder's acceptance prerequisite to enforcement	X			
Recordation of acceptance prerequisite to enforcement	X	X		
Notify assessor				
Duration unlimited	X			
Duration for life of another				
Duration for owner's life				

(continues)

Table 5.2. Continued

Comparison of Statutory Language	*UCEA*	*New York*	*Connecticut*	*Rhode Island*
Duration as stated	X			
Written consent of state and town required for both acceptance and release				
Fee simple				
Acquisition by donation				
Acquisition by purchase				
Cancel after thirty years if not re-recorded				
Enforcement				
Action at law	X		X	
Injunction			X	X
Equitable action		X	X	X
Civil action				
Specifically enforceable				X
Superior Interests				
Existing interests absent written consent	X			
Surrounding coal mining operations				
Surrounding coal transportation				
Innocent bona fide purchaser protected				
Eminent domain not impaired		X		
Defenses Specifically Eliminated				
Not appurtenant	X	X		
Assignability	X	X	X	X
Not recognized by common law	X	X		
Imposes a negative burden	X	X		
Imposes affirmative obligations	X	X		
Benefit does not touch/concern real property	X	X	X	X
No privity of estate	X	X	X	X
No privity of contract	X	X	X	X
Applicability of Statute				
Interests created after effective date of statute	X			
Permissible interests created before effective date		X		
Does not invalidate other lawful interest	X			
Only in counties over 200,000 people				
Only in approving county/municipality				
Uniformity of Application and Construction				
Applied to effectuate uniform law	X			
Construed to effectuate uniform law	X			
Tax Valuation				
Taxable at eased value				
Public body tax exemption				

statutory estates in real property, conservation restrictions, and preservation restrictions. The former includes limitations "to retain land or water areas predominately in their natural, scenic or open condition or in agricultural, farming, forest or open space use."[2] The latter covers limitations "whose purpose is to preserve historically significant structures or sites."[3] To achieve these goals, both estates were made assignable. Under the statute, landowners could now convey restrictions to another party and both governmental bodies and charitable corporations had the ability to acquire such restrictions and enforce their provisions in a variety of ways, such as through injunctions. The statute explicitly overrides the traditional common law defenses to enforcement of privity of estate or contract and lack of benefit to particular land.[4]

The statute is silent on how such restrictions may be extinguished, but it does make reference to a provision in Connecticut's parks' statutes that covers "alienation."[5] Connecticut's parks law provides that once the state acquires a conservation restriction, the restriction may only be alienated or put to uses other than as a natural area preserve if either of two findings are made by the commissioner of the Department of Environmental Protection: (1) "such alienation or other use serves a public necessity and that no prudent alternative exists" or (2) "the features of the land found worthy of preservation have been destroyed or irretrievably damaged so that the public purpose in preserving such land has been frustrated." Any alienation is subject to just compensation by the state and requires a public hearing.

In 1978, Connecticut established a state program to preserve agricultural land.[6] It defines "development rights" as "the rights of the fee simple owner of agricultural land to develop, construct on, sell, lease or otherwise improve the agricultural land for uses that result in rendering such land no longer agricultural land."[7] The statute also defines a "restriction" as "the encumbrance on development uses placed on restricted lands as a result of the acquisition of development rights by the state of Connecticut." The commissioner of agriculture can only remove the restriction from the land if the owner of the land or the town legislature petitions the commissioner. All petitions must be submitted to the voters of the town in a referendum called for that particular purpose. The commissioner must also determine that the public interest is such that there is an overriding necessity to relinquish control of the development rights.

One of the beauties of Connecticut's easement enabling legislation is its brevity. Addressing only the basic issues of purpose, enforcement, and holdership, it leaves the details of the contractual relationship between landowner and easement holder to the agreement between the parties and to interpretation by the courts.

Maine

Since the mid-1960s, Maine has been considered a national leader in the use of conservation easements. Maine's legislative history reflects a commitment to preserving the state's unique natural features, in particular its 3,500 miles of coastline. The state legislature first adopted a statute that eliminated many of the common-law impediments to conservation easements in 1969. Amendments made in 1983 enabled nonprofit entities, in addition to government, to hold conservation easements.[8] In 1985, the state adopted a modified "Maine" version of the Uniform Conservation Easement Act, a law that remains.[9] Maine also boasts one of the most broadly applicable, and effective, landowner liability protection acts in the nation, an act that encourages landowners to allow others access to their land for outdoor recreation and traditional harvesting activities along the shore and in forests.[10] It is also one of the few states with a current-use property tax program that offers a specific equation for taxing land under conservation easement.[11] All these statutes serve to allay the fears of landowners who are eager to permanently protect their land and allow the public to enjoy it, fears about property taxes on land whose use is restricted and about their liability for anyone injured while enjoying their property.

Analysis of the existing Maine statute requires some familiarity with the uniform act after which it was modeled. The UCEA was adopted by the Uniform Law Commissioners in 1981 and endorsed by the American Bar Association House of Delegates in 1982, which encouraged all states to adopt it (see appendix A). The UCEA allows parties to create and convey "conservation easements," nonpossessory interests in real property, to conserve or preserve land. Such easements can impose restrictions on the use of the land and impose affirmative duties on the donor of the easement and successive landowners. Only governmental entities or charitable organizations with an interest in conservation or preservation can hold easements. Both of these entities must record their "acceptance" of the easement.[12]

The UCEA endows conservation easements with several other important legal characteristics not possible under common law. For example, they may be created and conveyed in the same manner as other easements in land, and they are unlimited in duration unless otherwise specified. An easement cannot impair any preexisting legal interest in the affected property unless the owner of that interest consents, thus protecting both recorded interests, such as mortgages and liens, and unrecorded interests, such as leases and adverse possession. The statute does not invalidate any legal interest in the land arising under other laws, even if the document that gives rise to the interest is designated as a conservation easement. Hence, a conservation easement can also be an express charitable trust, subject to special oversight by the court and the state's attorney general. It might also include executory interests to other qualified entities, rights of first refusal, and affirmative management rights. Judicial actions concerning a conservation easement may be brought by the owner of an interest in the land, the holder, or a third party with rights of enforcement or by any person authorized by another law. A court may modify or terminate an easement under the doctrine of *cy pres,* or changed conditions.[13] Finally, a transaction is entitled to the protections of the statute regardless of date and regardless of what it is called as long as complies with the requirements of the statute. Thus, documents created before the UCEA was enacted in Maine but having the requirements specified in the UCEA— a conservation purpose and a qualified holder having the right to enter and enforce any land use restrictions, for example—will be protected from the existing common law prohibitions against enforcing such restrictions.

Maine's Conservation Easement Act enjoys all the remedies to common law impediments to restricting land use found in the UCEA, with differences that reflect the state's unique resources and its legendary "Downeast" independence. For example, nongovernmental holders of conservation easements must be nonprofit corporations or charitable trusts. Associations are not permitted to hold easements. Maine's legislature indicates that such language was designed to ensure that legal entities without a perpetual life could not hold easement, although it probably does not succeed, because nonprofit corporations can certainly be dissolved. For several reasons, the elimination of associations from the pool of possible easement holders is certainly appropriate. Associations are not subject to the laws that define the fiduciary relationship between donor and donee, in the case of nonprofit corporations, and between trustor and trustee, in the case of charitable trusts. Neither are they subject to the laws requiring nonprofit corporations and charitable trusts to use or dispose of their holdings in accordance with their charitable or trust purposes. The legal protections afforded these nonprofits and charitable trusts are critical if the easements they hold are to have integrity or to be perpetual. A charitable nonprofit, such as a land trust, cannot simply ignore its easement obligations to the inurement of the landowner without risking the loss of its tax-exempt status and hence its ability to raise funds. In addition, when a nonprofit charity dissolves, its holdings must be distributed to other entities with similar purposes.[14]

The Maine statute requires that the proposed holder and third party accept the easement, but it does not require that the acceptance be recorded. Although current practice encourages all acceptances to be recorded, there are many older unrecorded easements signed only by the grantor. The UCEA would not protect such easements, but in Maine, acceptance is inferred by action. The requirement of acceptance is still quite important, however, because it preserves a holder's right to decline an easement made unilaterally by a landowner.

Maine's easements can restrict not only private land use but also the use of privately owned surface waters, giving owners the power to restrict aquaculture and even limit motorized watercraft.[15]

Maine demonstrates its tradition of individualism and protecting private rights in the unique way it modified the UCEA provision on who may initiate judicial actions affecting easements. The statute limits standing to initiate litigation to the owner, the holder, or a "third party with rights of enforcement." The Maine legislature expressly rejected the UCEA provision that recognized the legal standing of "a person authorized by another law" and expanded the group of potential litigants. The legislature feared that "potential donors would be deterred from making a gift by the appearance that unknown persons, other than those named in the easement . . . might have a right to bring an action to enforce or modify the easement."[16] This rejection apparently disenfranchises individuals claiming rights in the easement property under other laws, such as the attorney general in the capacity as supervisor of a charitable trust, the original grantor who is no longer an owner, or a public representative who argues rights under the public trust doctrine. This departure from usual protections afforded the assets of nonprofits is mitigated by an explicit provision that state and local government may intervene in lawsuits initiated by one of the parties with statutory standing to sue.[17] Moreover, the effort to disenfranchise under the conservation easement statute may prove illusory. The Maine statutes include a seemingly contradictory provision validating rights created under "other laws of this State."[18]

Most easements are drafted in a way that makes them either hybrid statutory easements/express charitable trusts or hybrid statutory easements/contracts.[19] Consequently, in Maine, conservation easements may be subject to actions initiated under contract law either by the original grantor or under charitable trust law initiated by the state's attorney general. This provision can be of critical importance if the easement holder inadvertently or intentionally breaches the trust obligations by failing to enforce the easement. One example illustrates the interplay of the statutes. A town wanted to sell the easement it held back to the developer owner, terminating the land use restrictions on the property, to permit development. This effort was forestalled by a well-placed inquiry to the town by the attorney general, who noted that the easement was granted "in trust," and despite the enabling statute's limits on standing to sue, the law of charitable trusts might entitle the attorney general to sue. Such a comment is especially useful in the case of easements held by municipalities, which are notoriously subject to political change and influence. The ability to enforce the initial conservation intent of the parties and its intrinsic, public benefit is critical to maintaining public confidence in easements.

Maine's independence emerges again in section 478(3) of the statute in its attempt to limit a court's power to modify or terminate an easement under the doctrine of *cy pres* or changed circumstances. The UCEA simply acknowledges the court's right to "modify or terminate in accordance with the principles of law and equity." Maine specifically declares that a court may deny equitable enforcement, and effectively terminate an easement, if it finds that changed circumstances have rendered the easement no longer "in the public interest." The Maine statute, seeking to limit the power of a court to modify or terminate an easement, goes on to clarify that economic circumstances cannot be considered to determine whether an easement is in the public interest.[20] This section is a new expanded alternative to the usual standard for *cy pres* modification, which requires the court to find that the original intent of the parties cannot be carried out. Under the Maine language, an easement designed to preserve an endangered species that becomes extinct or delisted could not be terminated if there is some other important public conservation goal satisfied by the easement, such as wildlife habitat or scenic protection.

Another important deterrent to terminating easements is a provision for awarding damages to the holder if a court allows termination. Of course, easements are not immune to eminent domain takings by government for public purposes.

Very similar standards to those enacted in section 478(3) have been adopted by the American Law Institute in their recent draft of the Restatement of the Law of Property (Servitudes), a treatise much relied upon by courts.[21] Although there may be constitutional questions as to whether the legislature has the authority to affect the power of a court to exercise its equitable jurisdiction, courts are highly likely to follow these standards.

Massachusetts

Massachusetts's Restriction Statute, originally enacted in 1969, combined with its Marketable Title Act makes Massachusetts one of the most challenging venues for voluntary land conservation,[22] yet it still enjoys a long-standing and highly effective easement program. The Massachusetts Restriction Statute defines "qualified restrictions" as real property rights appropriate for conservation, preservation, agricultural preservation, watershed preservation, and affordable housing. Conservation restrictions themselves are rights appropriate to retaining land or water areas "predominantly in their natural, scenic or open condition, or in agricultural, farming or forest use, to permit public use, and to forbid or limit any or all" specified construction, changes to the landscape or terrain, or other acts detrimental to conservation.[23] Using such a definition, individuals claimed that an easement, which allowed limited development, was void because such development was not a contemplated purpose under the statute.[24] After an initial ruling for the plaintiff, the

Massachusetts Supreme Judicial Court upheld the easement in *Parkinson vs. Board of Assessors of Medfield.*[25]

The Restriction Statute effectively eliminates several common-law impediments to placing restrictions on the use of real property, such as the requirements of appurtenancy, privity of estate or contract, touch and concern, the prohibitions against affirmative obligations, and assignability of easements in gross.[26] The statute confers the right of access to monitor and enforce a restriction on the holder of the restriction. The statute is silent on who, other than the holder, may enforce a restriction, but Massachusetts case law provides some authority for individual citizens having such standing in cases where the restriction grants public access or in cases where the restriction is held by a governmental unit.[27]

The statutory requirements faced by those wanting to create conservation restrictions, particularly the necessary certification of approval, are quite daunting. The agencies and land trusts are accustomed to the process, which facilitates a quick turnaround for approvals, often not more than two weeks. Each restriction must be accepted and approved by a recorded certification by a bureau of state government.[28] The secretary of the Executive Office of Environmental Affairs must also approve all conservation restrictions. If the proposed holder is a nonprofit entity, municipal approval is also required. The approval process is initiated on a standard form and includes an inspection of the land. A similar process is required to terminate restrictions. All holders must secure a recorded certificate of approval for release from the same division of state government that originally accepted and approved the restriction. Government holders must hold a public hearing and get legislative approval for the release. If a restriction is purchased with state funds, its release will also require the fee owner to repurchase the restriction at its then-current fair market value.

The Restriction Statute imposes some limitations on the right of public bodies to take easements for public utilities under eminent domain.[29] Any such action involving, for example, the addition of a utility easement on farm property already encumbered with a conservation restriction must be limited so as to impose "the minimum practical interference with farming operations with respect to width of easement, pole location and other pertinent matters."[30] In addition, the compensation paid to the owner must be based on an appraisal of the fair market value of the taking as though the land was not already encumbered. Compensating the owner of the fee in such cases does not help the holder of the conservation restriction, which in most states is entitled to a share of the proceeds of the compensation in proportion to its interest in the land, but it certainly encourages landowners to grant restrictions.

Easements face the impediments imposed by the common law on real covenants and equitable servitudes and those imposed by the Marketable Title Act.[31] This law, like most marketable title laws, limits all restrictions to a thirty-year duration unless the owner and holder record a notice that it is extended before it expires. It goes further, however, and effectively eliminates any possibility of a perpetual restriction unless such restriction is either held by a government entity or qualifies as a "publicly approved restriction" under the Restriction Statute. This requirement, while making easement practice cumbersome at the outset, helps to ensure that easements are responsive to public interests in conservation and that they will meet standards imposed by the bureau.

New Hampshire

As with the rest of New England, New Hampshire has been a leader in the use of the conservation easement to preserve land, primarily forest and farmland. The Town of New London acquired the first New Hampshire easement in 1967, protecting 703 acres of forest and farmland from development. By 1985, forty-three land trusts and government agencies held easements in New Hampshire. As of 1995, more than 100,000 acres of land had been protected by over a hundred public and private organizations across the state.[32]

The New Hampshire Conservation and Preservation Restrictions legislation, enabling the creation of conservation easements, was passed in 1973. It was truly a pioneering effort because, at the time, there were none of the income tax advantages associated with today's easements. The IRS did not pass statutory authority for the income tax deductibility of donated conservation easements until 1976.[33] The New Hampshire legislation, accomplishing the same goals articulated in the UCEA nearly a decade later, marked a significant advance over reliance on common law to establish conservation restrictions. It replaced common-law language by statutory language and so permitted conservation easements and restrictions that were void under the common law. As an example, owners of easements were no longer required to own land appurtenant or adjacent to the encumbered land for the easement to be a valid real property interest. Conservation and preservation restrictions could no longer only exist "in gross"; they could be assignable as such, which was not possible under the common law. In addition, New Hampshire's law specifically allows limitations on the use of land, which under the common law were prohibited as being negative easements. In 1992, New Hampshire modified the statute to require the grantees of such restrictions to accept the deed creating the restriction in the form of a notarized document.[34]

New Hampshire's statute specifically authorizes easement restrictions for conservation, historic preservation, and farmland preservation. It describes legal parties eligible to hold such restrictions as "a governmental body or by a charitable, educational or other corporation, association, trust or other entity whose purposes include" conservation of land or water, preservation of structures or sites of historic significance, or preservation of agricultural land or water. This language is significantly broader than either the "qualified donee" status defined in IRS regulations or the UCEA requirement that the grantee be a nonprofit corporation or charitable trust.[35] Hence, the broad scope of New Hampshire's law enables organizations such as nonincorporated neighborhood associations to hold enforceable restrictions to preserve their communities. These types of organizations, and certainly business corporations, however, do not have the kind of accountability nonprofit entities have under other laws that make them reliable permanent stewards of conservation.

The New Hampshire statute seems to impose conditions on qualification for statutory protection that are inconsistent with the purposes of the law. For instance, the definitions of conservation restriction and preservation restriction could be construed to require a standard of "appropriateness" for the specific restrictions in a deed.[36] The statute simply defines the restriction as a right, limitation, or obligation that is "appropriate to the retaining or maintaining such land or water area, including improvements thereon, predominantly in its natural, scenic or open condition, or in agricultural, farming, open space or forest use, or other use consistent with the protection of environmental quality" or "appropriate to the preservation or restoration of such [historic] structure or site."[37] It is unlikely that the drafters intended the word *appropriate* to imply a limitation on qualification for statutory protection and rather used the term as a way of describing the purpose and subject matter of the restriction. Contrary to the purposes of the law, this language might be used by a party to ask a court to determine whether a particular restriction is inappropriate under the statute, thus causing the easement, along with the deed that created it, to be wholly or partly voided.

Another problematic oversight concerns the definition of agricultural preservation restriction.[38] The statute specifically calls for such restrictions to prohibit or limit the "construction or placement of buildings, *except those used for agricultural purposes or for dwellings used for family living by the landowner, his immediate family or employees*" (emphasis added). This wording implies that an agricultural preservation easement cannot impose limitations on the number, size, or location of buildings used for agriculture or the owner's family. This interpretation is inconsistent with the general statutory purpose of a conservation restriction to maintain the scenic characteristics of the land and the specific statutory purpose of an agricultural preservation easement to prohibit "any other acts or uses detrimental to such retention of the land for agricultural use." If, as is common nationally, a New Hampshire restriction encompasses both conservation and agricultural preservation purposes, one hopes that courts will view limits on the size, number, and location of structures, regardless of their intended use or occupancy, as promoting preservation of agriculture and scenic character. Certainly, donors and donees of restrictions intend to limit development rights that conflict with those qualities, regardless of who lives in the buildings.

New York

New York's conservation easement statute was enacted in 1983 and received a substantial facelift the following year.[39] It incorporates two provisions of the UCEA but also varies considerably from the UCEA in several respects. One of the more unique variations is a provision that requires the Department of Environmental Conservation (DEC) to draft regulations to establish standards for conservation easements.[40] As might be expected, this provision prompted some vigorous discussion between the conservation community and DEC several years ago.

The declaration of purposes in New York's enabling legislation covers the full range of imaginable resource protection rationales: from open space to agricultural and forestland, to areas of scenic, natural beauty, or ecological character, to cultural and historical areas.[41] Language in the statute is consistent with these broad public purposes.

The statute authorizes public bodies and nonprofit conservation corporations to hold conservation easements.[42] To qualify, the nonprofits must be tax exempt under section 501(c)(3) of the Internal Revenue Code.[43] New York's law also authorizes the UCEA third-party enforcement right, which empowers a public body or a nonprofit conservation organization that is not a holder of the easement to enforce any of the terms of the easement. New York's law explicitly states that it "may be enforced in law or equity by its grantor, holder or by a public body or any not-for-profit conservation organization designated in the easement as having a third party enforcement right, and is enforceable against the owner of the burdened property." It also spells out the UCEA provisions relating to traditional common law defenses that cannot be used to challenge statutory conservation easements, stating:

> It is not a defense in any action to enforce a conservation easement that:
>
> • Is not appurtenant to an interest in real property;
> • Can be or has been assigned to another holder;
> • Is not of a character that has been recognized traditionally at common law;

- Imposes a negative burden;
- Imposes affirmative obligations upon the owner of any interest in the burdened property, or upon the holder;
- The benefit does not touch and concern the real property; or
- There is no privity of estate or of contract.[44]

The New York statute permits easements to be modified or extinguished in three ways—according to the terms of the easement itself, in a court proceeding showing "changed conditions," or by eminent domain.[45] Particular easements, held by the state, may also be modified or extinguished if the land is required for a major utility transmission facility or a major steam electric-generating facility. Of course, an easement held by a nonprofit conservation organization could be extinguished by eminent domain for the same purpose.

In New York, there is another statutory authority for land protection, enacted in 1960, more than twenty years before the UCEA.[46] General Municipal Law section 247 states: "The acquisition of interests or rights in real property for the preservation of open spaces and areas shall constitute a public purpose for which public funds may be expended or advanced. . . . " For the purposes of the statute, open spaces meant scenic and natural resources, including agricultural lands.[47] The law applies only to counties, cities, towns, or villages that, after notice and a public hearing, "may acquire, by purchase, gift, grant bequest, devise, lease or otherwise, the fee or any lesser interest, development right, easement, covenant, or other contractual right necessary to achieve the purposes of this chapter, to land within such municipality." Unlike New York's conservation easement statute, section 247 does address the thorny property tax issue. It states: "After acquisition of any such interest pursuant to this act the valuation placed on such an open space or area for purposes of real property taxation shall take into account and be limited by the limitation on future use of the land."[48] In New York, the provision has been used to support the argument that property restricted by a conservation easement, regardless whether the holder is a public body or a nonprofit, should be taxed on the value of the property subject to the restriction.

Two important local land protection initiatives relied on the authority contained in section 247. In Suffolk County, it was used to establish a purchase of development rights program in 1975.[49] Similarly, the towns of Perinton, Penfield, and Webster outside of Rochester and the town of Clifton Park, north of Albany, have enacted term conservation easement programs based on this law.[50]

A recent case involving the issue of standing may offer some comforting precedent both to the holders of conservation easements and to the owners of land encumbered by such easements. In *Bleier v. Board of Trustees of Village of East Hampton,* the court ruled that an abutting owner, who was not an original party to the easement and did not claim to be a successor in interest, heir, or assignee of original parties, lacked "standing" to sue to enforce a scenic easement.[51] Limiting standing to sue to the parties to the easement should help avoid the difficult situations when neighbors attempt to use the easement to redress some perceived wrong to their interests.

Puerto Rico

The Puerto Rico Natural Patrimony Act was enacted in 1988.[52] The legislation defines "conservation easement" as a "lien imposed on real property for the purpose of guaranteeing the protection and management of a natural resource of recognized value which makes the area worthy to be included in the Natural Patrimony Program."[53] The program gives broad powers to the secretary of natural and environmental resources to work with other government agencies, as well as nonprofit corporations, to designate, acquire, and manage these natural areas. The secretary is empowered to accept donations of money and property from individuals and organizations. Presumably, these donations could include conservation easements. The statute explicitly encourages donations to the program and states that such donations will be deductible for tax purposes.

One interesting aspect of the program is that title to any lands purchased by a nonprofit with funds matched by the program must be conveyed to the Commonwealth of Puerto Rico. The lands conveyed might also be encumbered by a conservation easement held by an organization to guarantee the protection of the resources that made the area worthy of being included in the program. Such lands become exempt from property taxes.

The Natural Patrimony Program is an ambitious natural lands protection program. The program, however, only mentions conservation easements briefly and seems to center its efforts squarely on fee acquisition as its principal protection strategy. Undoubtedly, Puerto Rico could benefit from adopting the UCEA, enabling landowners to create conservation easements. A more broadly based easement statute could complement this program by facilitating less-than-fee protection strategies for agricultural, recreational and natural lands.

Rhode Island

Enacted in 1976, Rhode Island's statute preceded the UCEA by five years.[54] Like its neighbor Connecticut, it establishes "conservation restrictions" and "preservation restrictions." The language of these provisions is strikingly similar to Connecticut's, lending credence to the theory that lawyers often start with existing statutory language and adapt or add to it. Rhode Island's act includes "public benefit" as a consideration and adds "wildlife" as an explicit conservation use. In addition, it requires that the conservation uses be "consistent with the protection of environmental quality." The "preservation restriction" language also resembles that found in Connecticut's statute. Rhode Island, however, moves toward explaining what is historically significant ("architecture, archeology or associations") and includes restoration of the structure or site as appropriate.[55]

Rhode Island's statute includes the same basic enforcement (override of common-law defenses) and holdership provisions (public bodies and nonprofit) as Connecticut's law, but it adds a bit more detail in several respects. Specifically, the statute states that these restrictions shall not be subject to the state's thirty-year limitation on restrictive covenants. It also includes a statutory section on "release." Strictly speaking, it allows release of the restriction in accordance with the terms of the restriction and in the same manner as land held by the state or cities and towns. Thus, it enables nonprofits or other charitable entities holding restrictions to release them. Such release is subject to the terms of the restriction and applicable bylaws, charter provisions, and statutes and regulations. Because the power to dispose of property by the state and local governments appears to be quite broad, any conservation easement must explicitly address such issues that may result in an easement's termination.

As in Connecticut, Rhode Island's statute presents a concise version of enabling legislation. The absence of extensive statutory guidance again requires those who draft easements and the courts to set the standard for both interpretation and enforcement of any conservation and preservation restrictions.

Vermont

Vermont has an extraordinarily effective farmland preservation program. Much of its success is due to conservation-friendly state policy, which includes a unique program to combine farmland preservation with affordable housing under the aegis of the Vermont Housing and Conservation Board. The Vermont Land Trust (VLT), the state's most prominent land trust, accepted its first easement in 1978. Since then, the VLT has worked effectively with partner agencies, communities, and more than twenty-five local land trusts to make the conservation easement a well-known and successful tool for conservation.

The language of Vermont's conservation easement statute, enacted in 1977, is as beautiful as the landscape it seeks to protect.[56] The law enables both conservation and preservation "rights and interests," its term for easements or restrictions. It cites in appropriately broad terms, the conservation intent for which "rights and interests" must be established to meet the requirements of the statute. Through this broad definition, Vermont avoids some of the pitfalls of other states, such as New Hampshire, which seem to mandate or proscribe certain goals, albeit inadvertently. The statute designates the type of entities that can hold preservation rights and interests more narrowly than the UCEA and many other states' enabling acts. It requires that any nongovernmental holder be "an organization qualifying under §501(c)(3) of the Internal Revenue Code of 1986, as amended [or its wholly owned and controlled subsidiary], provided one of the stated purposes of the organization is to acquire property or rights and interests in property in order to preserve historic, agricultural, forestry or open space resources."[57] Although this standard is not as strict as the public-support requirement imposed by the IRS on nongovernmental holders, it does serve to eliminate the possibility of casual easement trading between, for instance, developers and their homeowner's associations. The statute effectively abolishes the common-law impediments to preservation rights and interests, such as the requirement of appurtenance to another property, and privity of contract between the owner of the land and the enforcer of the restriction. The latter impediment, by implication, eliminates the common-law prohibition against assignability of preservation rights and interests by the holder. The statute also requires that the instrument creating the preservation right be recorded. The law does not address perpetuity directly, but expressly makes the "right and interest" deed subject to Vermont's Marketable Title Act's requirement of filing a notice of the instrument at least every forty years. Under the 1977 amendments to Internal Revenue Service Code section 170(h), requiring easements to be held in perpetuity, this requisite might have posed a problem for deductibility. Treasury regulations for qualified conservation contributions, however, expressly remark that the likelihood of extinguishment due to a state's rerecording requirement is so remote as to be negligible and does not render a conservation easement nonperpetual.[58]

Vermont promotes conservation through a current use property tax program.[59] Recent amendments to the current use statutes have created a new "conservation land" category in addition to farmland and forestland. Landowners who do not register their land under the current use program can register under a certification program guaranteeing that the municipal tax assessor will take into account the severance of any development rights due to "conservation rights and restrictions" on the land.[60] For a landowner to receive tax benefits under the program, the state commissioner of taxation must certify that the conservation rights and restrictions on the land are valid under the statute and are held by a qualified organization.[61] As a matter of practice, however, local assessors have been known to evade the purpose of this program either by finding little reduction in property value or by shifting any loss of value estimated on the restricted portion of a landowner's property to the owner's unrestricted land.

Yet another unique piece of artillery in Vermont's conservation store is an aggressive land gains tax.[62] The land gains tax program attempts to discourage individuals from speculating in land or for purchasing land for development. An owner who sells land within six years of acquiring it is subject to a gains tax, which varies from 80 percent of the profit on sales made within six months of acquisition to 20 percent on sales made between years five and six. There is an exemption from the tax for sales of land and conservation rights and restrictions to entities qualified under the Vermont law for farmland or open-space conservation, regardless of date.[63] Finally, such sales, called conservation sales, are also exempt from the state's real estate transfer.[64]

Conclusion

Although statutes within the First and Second Federal Circuits vary considerably and commentators have identified certain potential problems, there is no case law to justify significant revamping. The coming years will undoubtedly provide this guidance. Meanwhile, each state has its long-standing traditions, and conservation seems to be progressing briskly everywhere. It would seem worthwhile, however, for Massachusetts to adopt a UCEA model and eliminate the extraordinary government approval process. In addition, every state would benefit from some of Vermont's more innovative ancillary programs, such as the certification program for municipal tax recognition of restrictions and, most especially, the speculation gains tax.

New York Spotlight: Proposed Regulations for Conservation Easements: "If It Ain't Broke, Don't Fix It"[65]

In August 1991, New York's DEC sent a seemingly innocuous letter to the state's land conservation community. The letter set forth proposed conservation easement regulations in accordance with the statutory provisions of the Environmental Conservation Law. This very law not only created statutory conservation easements, but it required DEC to promulgate regulations. The response was loud and clear: The proposed regulations presented major obstacles to negotiating and drafting easements and would drastically reduce the ability of nonprofit groups to preserve open space and natural resources. The response, conveyed directly at a meeting in November 1991 and in written comments submitted by conservation organizations, was vehement enough to prompt the DEC representative at the meeting to pronounce the draft regulations dead on the spot.

The regulations as proposed would have created mandatory standards for easements. Included in the draft regulations were six "official" subcategories, each with corresponding required restrictions and affirmative rights. They also directed DEC to review each conservation easement before it could be recorded "for review with the standards stated in Section 506.3 of this part; and will, within thirty (30) days after receipt, return any easement that does not comply with such standards."

Some specific objections and concerns were outlined in a letter to then deputy commissioner, Robert Bendick, by Glenn Hoagland, formerly of the Open Space Institute.[66] These included objections to mandatory drafting standards for easements; concerns over the need or utility of "classifying" easements and the apparent inconsistency with the Internal Revenue Code section 170(h); concerns over requiring affirmative land management plans for forest, farmland, and natural habitat easements; and infeasible and vague filing procedures.

Not surprisingly, the proposed regulations were declared dead and the corpse disappeared with hardly a trace. The statutory requirement that DEC promulgate regulations, however, has not been repealed, leaving the door open for a well-intentioned bureaucrat without a painful institutional memory to revisit the issue in the future.

The question remains then, What is the appropriate role for the state in the administration of private, albeit publicly sanctioned and subsidized, land protection transactions? As the New York experience shows, the land conservation community was very clear about what it did not want. Reaching consensus will certainly be more difficult.

Notes

1. Title 47, Land and Land Titles (C.G.S.A. § 47-42a et seq.).
2. Title 47, Land and Land Titles.
3. Title 47, Land and Land Titles.
4. Title 47, Land and Land Titles (C.G.S.A. § 47-42a et seq.).
5. Title 47, Land and Land Titles.
6. Title 22, Agriculture (C.G.S.A. § 22-26aa et seq.). Created in 1978, it was amended in 1988.
7. Title 22, Agriculture (C.G.S.A. § 22-26aa et seq.). Created in 1978, it was amended in 1988.
8. Title 22, Agriculture (C.G.S.A. § 22-26aa et seq.).
9. Title 22, Agriculture (C.G.S.A. § 22-26aa et seq.).
10. Title 22, Agriculture (C.G.S.A. § 22-26aa et seq.).
11. Title 22, Agriculture (C.G.S.A. § 22-26aa et seq.).
12. The principal legal characteristic of these easements is that they are generally free from the impediments to restrictions on land use developed in feudal England and later exported to the United States under the guise of common law. The

UCEA abolished requirements of appurtenancy, privity of estate or contract, touch and concern, and the prohibitions against affirmative obligations and assignability of easements in gross.

13. Such actions may be brought by the owner of an interest in the land, the holder, a third party, or a person authorized by another law.

14. These obligations are based on the common law of charitable uses and trusts, IRS requirements, and state requirements for nonprofit corporations.

15. Great ponds in Maine, for instance, are subject to state ownership and control, but ponds fewer than 10 acres are owned and controlled by the owner of the surrounding upland.

16. Title 33 M.R.S.A. § 478(1), Maine Comment.

17. Title 33 M.R.S.A. § 478(2).

18. Title 33 M.R.S.A. § 479-A(3).

19. Under § 479-A (3) of the Maine statute (and UCEA), these legal instruments are not invalidated even if the instrument creating the interest is designated as a conservation easement.

20. This can be critical, because easements do tend to render land less economically valuable, and a court might well find a public interest in converting an open field to a motel or stadium.

21. Restatement of the Law Property (Servitudes), Restatement of the Law Third, American Law Institute, Tentative Draft No. 7 (April 15, 1998), § 8.5.

22. Massachusetts's Restriction Statute at G.L. c. 184, §§ 31–33; Marketable Title Act at G.L. c. 184, §§ 23–30.

23. Massachusetts's Restriction Statute at G.L. c. 184, §§ 31 (Paragraph 1)

24. *Parkinson v. Board of Assessors of Medfield*, 395 Mass. 643 (1985).

25. *Parkinson v. Board of Assessors of Medfield*, 398 Mass. 112 (1986).

26. See appendix A.

27. *Springfield Preservation Trust, Inc. v. Springfield Historical Commission*, 380 Mass. 159 (1980) (dismissal for lack of jurisdiction, but good discussion).

28. Different types of restrictions require acceptance and approval from different bureaus, hence the catch-all term *publicly approved restrictions.*

29. Massachusetts's Restriction Statute at G.L. c. 184, § 32, seventh paragraph (effective date November 15, 1977).

30. Massachusetts's Restriction Statute at G.L. c. 184, § 32.

31. Marketable Title Act at G.L. c. 184 §§ 23–30.

32. *Forests Forever,* New Hampshire Conservation Institute and Society for the Protection of New Hampshire Forests (1995).

33. Internal Revenue Code § 170(h).

34. Following what had become the practice of many states adopting the uniform act. This prevents the unilateral transfer of the easement without the grantees consent and presumably collaboration on the plan.

35. For tax-deductible conservation contributions, organizations must possess publicly supported section 501(c)(3) status.

36. New Hampshire RSA 477:45(I) and (II).

37. NH RSA 477:45.
38. NH RSA 477:45(III).
39. N.Y. Environmental Conservation Law Article 49, Title 3, §§ 49-0301 et seq.
40. N.Y. Environmental Conservation Law § 49-0305 (7). Regulations have never been promulgated, although some were prepared in 1991.
41. N.Y. Environmental Conservation Law § 49-0301.
42. N.Y. Environmental Conservation Law § 49-0303.
43. N.Y. Environmental Conservation Law.
44. N.Y. Environmental Conservation Law.
45. N.Y. Environmental Conservation Law § 49-0307.
46. N.Y. General Municipal Law 247.
47. N.Y. General Municipal Law 247(1).
48. N.Y. General Municipal Law 247(3).
49. Suffolk County Code (1976).
50. Town of Perinton (1972), town of Penfield (1992), town of Webster (1992), and town of Clifton Park (1996).
51. 191 A.D.2d 552, 595 N.Y.S.2d 102 (2d Dept. 1993).
52. Title 12, Chapter 124, §§ 1225 et seq.
53. Title 12, Chapter 124, §§ 1225 et seq.
54. Title 34, Property, Chapter 39, Conservation and Preservation Restrictions on Real Property, Sections 34-39-1 et seq.
55. Title 34, Property, Chapter 39, Conservation and Preservation Restrictions on Real Property, Section 34-39-2(b). "A 'preservation restriction' shall mean a right to prohibit or requires a limitation upon an obligation to perform acts on or with respect to or uses of a structure or site historically significant for its architecture archeology or associations, whether stated in the form of a restriction, easement, covenant, or condition in any deed, will, or other instrument, executed by or on behalf of the owner of the structure or site or in any order of taking, which right, limitation, or obligation is appropriate to the preservation or restoration of the structure or site."
56. Vermont Conservation and Preservation Rights and Interests Law, Title 10 [10 V.S.A. § 821 et seq.].
57. Title 10 V.S.A. § 821(c)(2) and (3).
58. Treas. Reg. § 1.170-14A(g)(2).
59. Title 32 V.S.A. chapter 124.
60. Title 10 V.S.A. chapter 6306(b).
61. Note that this does not require perpetuity.
62. Title 32 V.S.A. chapter 236.
63. Title 32 V.S.A. chapter 236.
64. Title 32 V.S.A. chapter 236.
65. Author's note: This seemed like an interesting sidebar, especially since the LTA-NY Advisory Committee, of which I am a member, is now looking at the issue of easement quality.
66. Hoagland is currently serving as executive director of the Mohonk Preserve in New York.

Chapter 6

✄ ✄

Conservation Easements to Protect Historic Viewsheds: A Case Study of the Olana Viewshed in New York's Hudson River Valley

Seth McKee

Olana, a picturesque Persian-style villa constructed between 1860 and 1900 by Frederic Church, is located in the Hudson River valley of New York State (Figure 6.1). Here Church, a student of renowned landscape artist Thomas Cole, painted many of his dreamy nineteenth-century landscapes, typical of the Hudson River School of painting that sought to celebrate the romantic and mysterious character of the American wilderness, especially in the Catskill Mountains and the Hudson River valley.[1] Church in particular was inspired by the sweeping views of the Hudson River, the Catskills, and the pastoral "working landscapes" of Columbia County (Photograph 6.1).[2]

Remarkably, the view that Church painted from Olana remains: a foreground of farmland, woodlands, and scattered rural residences; a middle view of the mighty Hudson; and a background made up of the majestic Catskills with the river winding its way south toward New York City and the Atlantic Ocean 120 miles away. Olana is an important site celebrating the birth of American landscape painting, which itself served as an inspiration for the growth of the modern American conservation movement.[3] A visit here gives a mere glimpse of what inspired Church and the Hudson River School.

Olana, now owned and operated by the New York State Office of Parks, Recreation and Historic Preservation, is one of the most popular historic sites in New York and attracts some 200,000 people annually.[4] Visitors experience the Persian/Moorish architecture of the mansion, the carriage roads and designed landscape of Church, and the spectacular view. The 250-acre site draws art and architecture lovers, history buffs, bird-watchers, cross-country skiers, and families looking for unique picnic places. The site is a vital part of

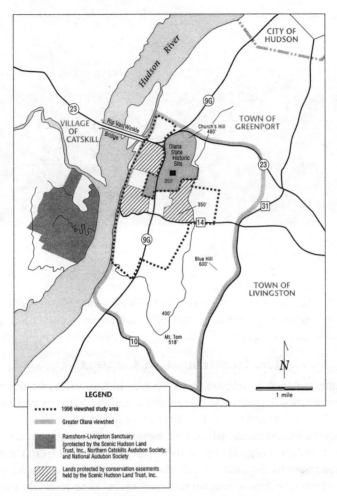

Figure 6.1. Hudson River Basin and Olana viewshed.
Source: USGS 1:2000 topographic map
Credit: Cartography Lab, University of Minnesota

the Hudson River valley's heritage and as such is also being discovered by a new generation of "heritage tourists," those seeking a connection with the land and its history.

Despite Olana's history and growing public support, the view is threatened by the same suburban sprawl that affects the visual character and historic setting of many unique sites nationwide. The municipality in which Olana is situated has no zoning regulations in place to guide land uses, thus

Photograph 6.1. View from Olana.
Photo credit: Joyce Rowley, Scenic Hudson, Inc.

inviting industrial, commercial, or residential land uses that could gradually overwhelm the historic landscape and blot out scenic vistas visible from Olana.

The Importance of Context

Increasingly, managers of unique places such as historic sites are concerned not only with a site's upkeep and maintenance but also with the quality and character of the surrounding landscape: the visual context in which the historic site exists. This context includes the views from the historic sites, called *viewsheds* or integral vistas, as well as the quality of the views from the entry routes or gateways to the site. After all, these gateways make a visitor's experience of arriving either a special moment to be long remembered and savored or just another trip in the car. At Olana, the gateways are currently intact. A working orchard graces the shoreline of the Hudson River directly below Olana, and a vineyard and woodlands greet visitors along the major route to Olana from the south (Photograph 6.2).

Protecting the Olana Viewshed

The groundwork for protecting the viewshed of Olana began in 1983, when the state of New York passed enabling legislation allowing conservation easements to be conveyed to land trusts or government entities.[5] This landmark legislation set the stage for the protection of land throughout New York and the growth of the land trust movement in New York.[6] Today, approximately sixty operating land trusts protect open space throughout the state, from the suburbs of New York City to the wilderness of the Adirondacks.

Photograph 6.2. View of Cherry Ridge Farms from Olana.
Photo credit: Steve Rosenberg, Scenic Hudson, Inc.

Efforts to make a case for protecting the Olana viewshed began in 1986 with claims that it was being compromised by inappropriate land uses. The National Park Service declared Olana a Priority II site, determining that the pressure to develop the surrounding land posed considerable threat to the future of Olana.[7] The New York State Olana State Historic Site also cited similar pressures in a master plan written the same year.[8]

In September 1986, Scenic Hudson, Inc., a nonprofit conservation organization and land trust dedicated to preserving, enhancing, and restoring the scenic, historic, natural, and recreational resources of the Hudson River valley, issued a report documenting the characteristics of the privately owned properties that could be seen from Olana and its gateways, those with structures and those without.[9] This analysis, noting such features as the size and location of buildings and the scenic and historic elements of the properties, was essential in determining the significance of the various properties to the viewshed and thus in identifying those properties that, if developed, would undermine the viewshed's character. The report recommended specific action, including land protection tools that could be used to protect the view.

The 1986 report was a springboard for actions designed to protect a significant portion of the Olana viewshed. First, the state of New York acquired fee title to a parcel of land along the Hudson River adjacent to an existing

Photograph 6.3. Ramshorn Marsh–Livingston Sanctuary.
Photo credit: Seth McKee, Scenic Hudson, Inc.

state-owned river island and marsh, a key gateway to Olana. Since then, Scenic Hudson has worked with willing landowners to purchase conservation easements that today protect over 400 acres of the Olana viewshed, including a working orchard, a vineyard, and several largely wooded residential proper-ties, restricting in perpetuity the amount of development that can occur on the land. Scenic Hudson has also protected 280 acres of Ramshorn Marsh by acquiring the fee on 236 acres and by placing easements on 45 acres. The marsh is the largest tidal swamp forest along the Hudson River and forms part of the longer view from Olana (Photograph 6.3).

Scenic Hudson purchased the conservation easements with the assistance of the Lila Acheson and DeWitt Wallace Fund for the Hudson Highlands, established by the founders of the Reader's Digest Association, Inc., to sup-port the acquisition and preservation of land in the Hudson River valley for the benefit of the public. The purchase price for the easements were sup-ported by qualified independent appraisals and ran to several thousand dol-lars per acre.

The Orchard at the Foot of Olana:
The First Conservation Easement

Scenic Hudson first approached the family owning the 130-acre Cherry Ridge Farms about the possibility of conveying a conservation easement in 1990.

This orchard is located on the Hudson River at the foot of Olana. It lies next to the Rip Van Winkle Bridge, the principal means of entry into Columbia County from the New York State Thruway. This feature is a key component in the Olana viewshed, with its apple, cherry, peach, and pear trees covering the landscape. At first, the family was skeptical: How could they consider encumbering their land, which had been a family-owned working orchard since 1923 and which represented their only substantial asset? The parents had their retirement to think of, and their riverfront property, with its sweeping views of the Hudson River and the Catskills, was certainly attractive to developers who had approached them several times over the years. All felt strongly about the property remaining an orchard and, fortuitously, their son was actively involved in the orchard's operation. Each time, they had turned the developers away, but were they prepared to foreclose that option forever?

Scenic Hudson formulated a conservation plan to protect the farm's scenic character while still allowing orchard operations to continue and even expand. The conservation easement eventually agreed upon allowed only agricultural and passive recreational use of most of the 130 acres. A 5-acre "building envelope," around the existing cluster of buildings was identified to allow additional farm structures, thus permitting the family to expand the business and the son to build a house of his own. The easement included strict limitations on the height, bulk, colors, and character of any new structures, however, so that the view of the orchard from Olana was not adversely affected.[10] In addition, Scenic Hudson was able to pay cash for the easement, which enabled the family to convert some of their capital asset, their prized orchard, into a form that the parents could use for their retirement without having to sell off all or a portion of the farm. In the end, the family was satisfied that their future farming and financial needs had been met and that their son's future on the farm was secure. Scenic Hudson was satisfied that its goal of preserving the visual and agricultural character of the property was protected, and the easement was executed in 1992.

A Budding Vineyard is Protected

Frederic Church was a painter for all seasons at Olana; he found grace in the state of nature and in the human-altered rural landscape at all times of the year. Nowhere is this more evident than in his painting "Winter at Olana," which prominently featured a rolling, snow-covered meadow and farm buildings below the icy Hudson River and snow-capped Catskills. Since Church's day, that rolling meadow has supported orchards and other crops, and by the early 1990s, it was being converted into a vineyard.

As the Cherry Ridge Farm conservation easement was nearing completion, Scenic Hudson contacted the owner of the vineyard, a corporate executive whose dream was to eventually work full-time on the land to ensure that it was not developed. The easement eventually negotiated included the usual prohibitions on residential, commercial, or industrial land use. The landowner was permitted to construct two additional buildings, a single-family house and a structure for use as a winery, with limitations on their height, bulk, color, and character.[11] Both of these structures were to be sited out of the view from Olana.

Protecting the view from Olana was straightforward in this instance. All new structures could easily be sited behind topographic or vegetative features. Part of Scenic Hudson's raison d'être, however, is the visual quality of the Hudson River corridor, and thus the easement needed to safeguard the quality of the river's shoreline. The siting of the proposed new structures was debated at length.

The road into the property and the existing residence were perched overlooking the Hudson (Figure 6.2). The landowner thought the new house and the winery building should be sited next to the existing structure overlooking the river, and thus would not interfere with either the view from Olana or the vineyard operation. Scenic Hudson's concern that any new

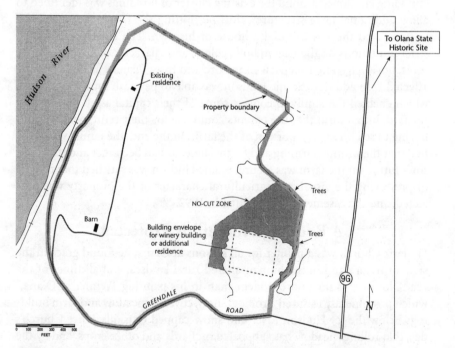

Figure 6.2. Lot Plan showing location of existing residence and building envelope.
Original: Rockefeller & Nucci Professional Land Surveyors, Claverack, NY.
Redrawn: Cartography Lab, University of Minnesota

Photograph 6.4. Vineyard in Olana Viewshed protected by conservation easement. Ramshorn Marsh and sanctuary in background.
Photo credit: Steve Rosenberg, Scenic Hudson, Inc.

building not detract from the river corridor's visual quality needed to be addressed, however. As negotiations continued, alternative sites for the winery and the home were identified, away from both the riverfront *and* the vineyard, much closer to New York State Route 9G, a major thoroughfare that serves as the southern gateway to Olana. This site was not easily visible from the road, and trees would block the view of any structures from both Olana and the Hudson River. The easement was executed in 1993. In this instance, the landowner was able to preserve his ability to expand his operation into the vineyard of his dreams, and Scenic Hudson was able to preserve 90 acres of the Olana viewshed and the view form the Hudson (Photograph 6.4).

One year later, the trust acquired a conservation easement on a 25-acre rural residential property immediately adjacent to the vineyard, a significant element in the view from Olana and from the southern gateway. This easement allowed one additional single-family residence, mostly shielded from Olana's view by trees.

Olana's Southern Boundary Protected

In 1994, Scenic Hudson secured a conservation easement protecting 175 acres directly south of Olana, property that forms southern views from the mansion. The easement capitalized on existing topography in identifying a suitable location for an additional single-family residence, which may be built on the low side of a hill facing away from Olana.

The challenge in negotiating this easement centered on the landowner's desire to construct an addition to the existing residence. The addition was permitted by the easement but, now that it has been constructed, is more visible from Olana than anticipated or acceptable. Fortunately, the easement required the landowner to plant vegetative screening and use earth tone–colored paints; as a result, Scenic Hudson is currently working with the landowner to plant white pine or other fast-growing conifers and to repaint the structure in the shortest possible time.

What became apparent in this case was that a higher standard needed to be maintained regarding the placement, scale, and color choice of structures that are planned for visually prominent, largely wooded ridgelines. The same addition to a residence, if located in an already visible cluster of buildings, would not have nearly the negative visual impact on the viewshed that the structure actually has on this more pristine setting.

Recent Developments

In addition to monitoring these four conservation easements annually to ensure compliance, Scenic Hudson has worked with a number of additional landowners to protect other properties identified in the 1986 report. For various reasons, many of these landowners have elected not to proceed with easements. Scenic Hudson continues to work to bring other viewshed landowners into the fold of conserved properties.

An Expanded Viewshed Study

The 1986 report focused primarily on the short views from Olana, the highly visible lands within one to two miles of Olana to the south and west. A conscious choice was made at the time of the report to rank these lands to give Scenic Hudson's efforts some structure and focus. Approximately 4,000 additional acres of land, however, form part of the long-distance views from Olana, lands to the south, southeast, and east, including several prominent hillsides two to three-and-a-half miles away, that provide integral vistas.

In 1996, the Columbia Land Conservancy, a local land trust serving Columbia County, carried out a viewshed analysis looking at the potential visibility of structures up to four miles away from Olana. In this analysis, topographic, vegetative, and property ownership data were fed into a geographic information systems program, which generated maps showing the visual sensitivity of various land parcels within the viewshed.[12]

The new study updated Scenic Hudson's original report and used current technology to expand the geographic and programmatic scope of the earlier protection efforts. The analysis identified portions of properties where additional development could be accommodated without jeopardizing the visual quality of the viewshed. In addition, the analysis identified portions of properties where a forty-foot structure, a typical residential dwelling, would be visible from Olana.[13] This analysis will significantly assist in the efforts to protect additional portions of the Olana viewshed.

Lessons Learned

The protection of a historic viewshed is a long-term undertaking that occurs over many years and constantly evolves due to the real estate market, landowner needs and life stages, and land trust priorities. Several issues worth considering emerge from such a sustained effort.

Long-Term Perspective

Taking the long view on landscape protection is essential. In the life of a landscape and of any property owner who contributes to that landscape, there are windows of opportunity that may compel the landowner to make decisions regarding the future of the property in ways that might have previously been undesirable or impractical but that secure the property's integrity for the future.

Forming a Land Protection Strategy

Scenic Hudson faced many questions: What is the most appropriate way to protect an entire viewshed, an assemblage of individual properties owned by assorted individuals possessing different plans for their lands? Is it best to proceed strategically, to secure options to acquire easements, and wait for a sufficient number of commitments to be made to provide a coherent geographical and visual "whole" before exercising the options? On the other hand, is it better to proceed opportunistically, to secure easements whenever landowners become receptive and accept some geographical and visual gaps in the protected landscape?

The first approach is preferable because it ensures that a conservation easement designed to protect a particular parcel would not be undermined by the inappropriate development of an unencumbered nearby property. The latter approach, however, offers some advantages. The first conservation easement executed in a project can open doors to new opportunities. The easement over Cherry Ridge Farms became the basis for negotiating easements on the subsequent three properties. In addition, the first easement became a reference point in those negotiations, offering guidance to the landowners grappling with the major decision to protect their land and with assurance of the Trust's competence.

Another consideration is that landowners arrive at the decision to sign conservation easements independently. They are not all ready to agree to restrict the development of their land in perpetuity at the same time. Each is faced with financial considerations, family dynamics, and other factors at play in every negotiation, factors that may or may not lead to a decision to grant an easement. Clearly, it is not a journey that will be taken simultaneously by multiple landowners.

For several reasons, Scenic Hudson elected to proceed both strategically and opportunistically in acquiring conservation easements to protect the Olana viewshed. Although lands were ranked through both the 1986 report and the 1996 Columbia Land Conservancy study, Scenic Hudson was opportunistic, working with willing landowners and pursuing land protection opportunities as they arose. In this way, the trust has protected 400 acres of the Olana viewshed gradually over a span of four years rather than by securing options and executing the easements all at once.

Scenic Hudson's strategy may well change over time. The trust may choose to secure options on assemblages of properties in specific parts of the viewshed before negotiating and acquiring easements. For example, Scenic Hudson may choose to work with landowners whose holdings make up a significant hillside or open plain visible from Olana, securing options on the cluster of lands before executing the easements. In any case, the track record established through protecting the first 400 acres will help.

Balancing Historic View Protection with Economic Viability of the Land

Conservation easements need to accomplish the dual goals of protecting the significant resources of the property while anticipating and accommodating the landowner's needs for the future. In the case of the Olana viewshed, the preservation of a historic landscape and the continuation of an orchard and a vineyard needed to be ensured.[14] This was accomplished by allowing landowners to develop their property in a limited way in preidentified locations. On Cherry Ridge Farms, for example, the building envelope surrounding the farm complex resulted in a blueprint for clustered future development. On the vineyard and on the two other residential properties, the locations where additional structures necessary for the economic viability of the farm would not harm the visual character of the property, especially the historic view from Olana, were identified.

The easements accommodate the future needs of the landowner by providing for the review and approval of additional structures not directly contemplated in the easement.[15] At the same time, Scenic Hudson retains control over such development, possessing the right to review any building proposals. Such provisions in the easement mean that a healthy relationship needs to be created between the landowner and the easement holder to facilitate good communication and trust between the parties.

Measuring Historic Significance?

Is it possible or even desirable to freeze the landscape at a particular moment in time? At what point does additional development on a property undermine its historic significance? Any historic viewshed protection effort must answer these questions. Purists might decry any development that does not either conform to the period or add to the context that gives the landscape significance. Others might say that any landscape must be allowed to evolve if it is to remain a place where humans can live and work, lest it become an open air museum, useful only as a history tool.

This debate is particularly pronounced with regard to working landscapes: the farms and forests that make up significant portions of New York's Hudson River Valley and much of rural America. If a farmer cannot adapt to changing markets, technologies, and consumer tastes and demands, the farm will not remain viable and the working landscape will inevitably change. In such a case, the farm landscape, treasured as part of the historic view, might end up as fallow fields, which will ultimately be reforested as nature reclaims what humans have abandoned.

At Olana, Scenic Hudson took the position that the easements should protect the historic landscape and views while accommodating landowners economic needs. The trust did not attempt to preserve the nineteenth-century farms and homesteads that Frederic Church painted. It did, however, attempt to keep intact those elements of the landscape that were important in Church's day while accommodating today's needs. Thus, a metal-roofed cold storage facility at Cherry Ridge Farms, despite its modern appearance, is allowed because it is most practical for today's orchards. Clearly, this building is not something that Church would have seen as he gazed out from Olana in the late nineteenth century. Nevertheless, it will be located within a cluster of farm buildings in the building envelope and not spread out across the prized landscape.

Preserving the historic landscape visible from Olana depends on crafting conservation easements that ensure sound land use practices and rural design, through clustering structures, restricting their height, scale, and color, and limiting timber cutting. The easements prohibit the uniquely American tendency to spread houses evenly across a landscape, a destructive, unsustainable practice that maximizes infrastructure costs, visual impacts, and short-term profits. In large part, only by prohibiting such land uses is historic landscape preservation accomplished.

Maintaining Historic Structures

Another element of historic view protection is the tricky question of maintaining historic features of structures in the landscape. Some of the lands within the Olana viewshed contain homes and barns that date to Church's era or earlier; some date to the late eighteenth century. How to deal with the maintenance of such structures is a challenge faced by all land trusts seeking to protect historic landscapes, and Scenic Hudson's efforts to protect the Olana viewshed are no exception.

Conservation easements normally seek to prevent certain actions, such as development, timber cutting, and road building. Preserving historic structures implies more than simply prevention, however. The prohibitions inherent in most conservation easements will not be enough to prevent a historic structure from simply crumbling away to ruin if not maintained properly. The logical solution is to provide affirmative obligations on the landowner to maintain the historic structures. The U.S. Department of the Interior has promulgated useful guidelines for the effective preservation of historic structures, guidelines that must be followed by anyone using federal funds to preserve buildings.[16]

Some of the Interior Department guidelines stress actions that landowners should avoid because they would tend to compromise historic integrity. Other guidelines stress the positive actions that landowners must take to maintain a structure's integrity, such as using period materials rather than modern, less expensive options. These latter guidelines impose affirmative obligations on landowners, and such obligations are anathema to many landowners. Any landowner that agrees never to develop a property has made a major decision, one that affects the landowner and his or her family and provides substantial benefits to the general public. This decision does not involve a commitment to maintain the property and the improvements on it to a certain standard in perpetuity, however. In addition, knowing the implications of such a commitment, financial and otherwise, has been an issue on which conservation deals have foundered.

Rather than requiring a landowner take positive steps to maintain historic structures in the Olana viewshed, Scenic Hudson seeks to provide guidelines for repairing and replacing historic structures and the various components or elements in its conservation easements. These guidelines include suggestions for repairing rather than replacing historic elements, using materials that match the historic ones in appearance if not substance, and requiring the landowner to take "practicable" steps to maintain the historic integrity of the structure. Scenic Hudson also prohibits any changes to any such structure if they would undermine its historic integrity.[17] Through these provisions, landowners are encouraged to be proactive in taking steps to preserve their historic structures while preventing actions that would directly undermine their historic significance. In reality, perhaps conservation easements cannot effectively prevent the benign neglect of historic structures, and they may not be the most appropriate tools for such a task. Instruments that offer a direct financial incentive to the individual landowner—such as a historic preservation grant, a tax deduction for a historically sensitive renovation or an accelerated depreciation schedule on a federal income tax return—may be more appropriate tools for encouraging active preservation of historic structures.

Conclusion

Scenic Hudson's efforts to protect the Olana viewshed are very much a work in progress. This multiyear effort has yielded significant benefits to the Olana State Historic Site and the surrounding region, but more remains to be done. Ideally, the surrounding communities will become more involved in viewshed protection, and the trust has been discussing how best to achieve this with other local organizations. Building on the experience to date, the cause of protecting this historic and breathtaking landscape in the heart of New York's Hudson River valley should advance.

Notes

1. Frances F. Dunwell, *The Hudson River Highlands* (New York: Columbia University Press, 1991), p. 51.
2. Dunwell, p. 52.
3. Dunwell, p. 140.
4. New York State Environmental Conservation Law, Article 49, Title 3.
5. N.Y. Environmental Conservation Law Article 49, Title 3, §§ 49-0301 et seq.
6. James Ryan, *The Master Plan for Olana State Historic Site.* M.A., State University of New York-Oneonta, 1984. The master plan set the direction of the historic site for several years.
7. A Priority II designation by the National Park Service signifies that the surrounding development pressure exhibits a greater potential threat to the resource than ever before.
8. James Ryan, *The Master Plan for Olana State Historic Site.*
9. Scenic Hudson, Inc., "Opportunities for Protection of the Viewshed of the Olana State/National Historic Site," Sept. 1986 (self-published).
10. The easement states that "no additional residential dwellings or structures shall be permitted, except (i) within the Building Envelope, and (ii) if such residential dwelling or structure is proposed to be taller . . . than any existing residential dwelling on the Property or proposed to contain more gross, above-ground volume than the largest existing (on the date hereof) residential dwelling on the Property, with Grantee's prior written approval. . . . " The easement also states that exterior surfaces shall "be of a design and color that is visually unobtrusive and consistent with other similar structures already on the Property."

11. The easement permits one additional residential dwelling with a ground-floor footprint no larger than 2,000 square feet and no taller than 27.5 feet in height and "of the same general rural farmhouse style and design as the existing residence." The winery structure can be no taller than 26 feet in height and can have a ground-floor footprint of no more than 4,200 gross square feet, with a possible variance to 5,600 square feet. The winery's designated location is screened from view from Olana by trees.

12. The GIS analysis was carried out by Saratoga Associates of Saratoga Springs, New York, using ARC-INFO software on a Unix Sun Workstation (personal conversation, Marcie Clark of Saratoga Associates). The GIS incorporated digital elevation models for topography, aerial photos for vegetation cover, and tax parcel maps for land ownership.

13. The views were then field-verified so as not to be overly reliant on computer modeling.

14. Indeed, part of the Olana viewshed's stunning quality is the presence of working landscapes, agricultural lands that, if abandoned, would eventually become reforested, which would be a significant loss to both the viewshed's character and to the agricultural economy and way of life in the Hudson River valley. Thus, it was important for the conservation easements to accommodate the business needs of the orchard and vineyard.

15. Most of the easements have a "design review" clause that allows additional structures to be reviewed and approved by Scenic Hudson at its discretion provided they "will not have a material, negative impact on views of the Property from Olana, the Hudson River, or State Highway 9G, and that such approval is otherwise consistent with the purposes of the Conservation Easement." The clause usually allows Scenic Hudson to attach conditions such as restrictions on height, bulk, materials, color, or tree removal or to require new plantings.

16. "The Secretary of the Interior's Standards for Rehabilitation and Guidelines for Rehabilitating Historic Buildings (36 CFR 67)," a detailed set of principles and guidelines that promote sound historic preservation principles.

17. Scenic Hudson has used the following language in easements regarding historic structures, which are based in part on the secretary of the interior's standards. The trust also prohibits any changes to such structures if they would undermine their historic integrity.

Chapter 7

✂️ 🐚

A Limited Development and Conservation Success Story

Leslie Reed-Evans

The Williamstown Rural Lands Foundation (WRLF) is a community-based land trust operating in a small college town in the rural northwest corner of Massachusetts. The foundation's membership is its primary financial support, and the small staff consisting of an executive director and a part-time administrative secretary, carries out the goals of the organization. Since its inception in 1986, the WRLF has helped to preserve almost 4,000 acres of productive farmland and forest. The foundation's role in many projects has been one of coordinator and facilitator, often providing funds for appraising and surveying private lands targeted for public acquisition. In some cases, because it can act more quickly than the state, the foundation has acquired title, owning them only until the state was able to become the owner. In the WRLF's experience, these projects have generally not proved to be financially high risk.

Should land trusts become involved in subdividing or developing land? This very question was faced by the WRLF in 1994 when a local dairy farmer voiced his concern over the future of a 44-acre parcel of land between Oblong and Hancock Roads in historic South Williamstown that provided him with twenty-five acres of good-quality hay land (Figure 7.1). The property, with an asking price of $350,000, provides spectacular views of Massachusetts's highest peak, Mount Greylock, and the Taconic Ridge between Massachusetts and New York, was part of the estate of a long-time Williamstown resident, and had been on the market for a considerable time (Photograph 7.1).[1]

The heirs hoped to keep the land undivided but were financially unable to sell the property at a bargain sale or through long-term financing, nor were they willing to consider donating a conservation easement. The rolling open land with considerable highway frontage appeared appropriate for both sub-

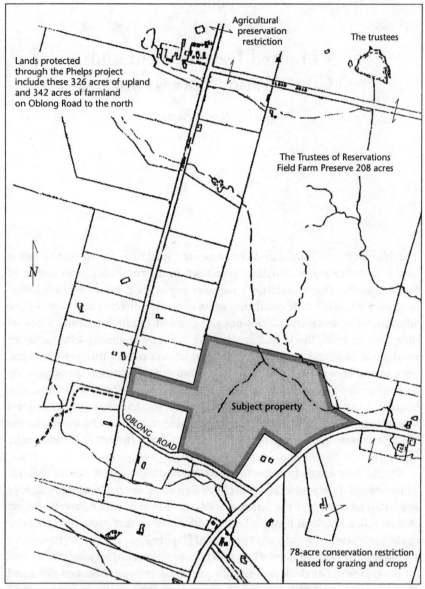

Figure 7.1. Williamstown Rural Lands Foundation's limited development, protected land and neighboring parcels.
Source: Leslie Reed, Williamstown Rural Lands Foundation
Credit: Cartography Lab, University of Minnesota

Photograph 7.1. Massachusetts's highest peak, Mt. Greylock, as seen from WRLF parcel.
Photo credit: Leslie Reed-Evans

division and conservation. Fortunately, two years prior, following an inquiry by the heirs regarding conservation possibilities, the WRLF had drawn up a limited development plan for the property, limiting the number and location of buildable lots (Figure 7.2).[2] The family had embraced the concept, but the foundation did not have the funds to purchase the parcel at that time. The dairy farmer notified WRLF that a seven-lot subdivision was proposed for the parcel, which would have not only drastically impacted his livelihood but would change the character of the rural neighborhood forever.

The foundation contacted the estate representatives, a daughter and son-in-law living in the Boston area, and the real estate firm with whom the property was listed. The son-in-law not only accepted an offer of $300,000 but was also willing to carry a short-term mortgage at an interest rate well below current mortgage interest rates. A 20 percent down payment and a two-year balloon mortgage at 6 percent interest were agreed upon. WRLF had to decide how to fulfill these terms with the least amount of risk. The decision was made to create several desirable house lots that would sell quickly while preserving the bulk of the land as open space, thus maintaining some land use consistency with other nearby protected parcels and allowing agriculture to continue on those lands best suited.

The immediate challenge for the foundation was raising the necessary down payment. One 5-acre lot on the east side of Oblong Road (lot A, Figure 7.2) already existed. This parcel, currently used by a neighboring farmer for corn, abutted a historic house and helped to provide the structure with its bucolic setting. WRLF first contacted the owners of the house to determine

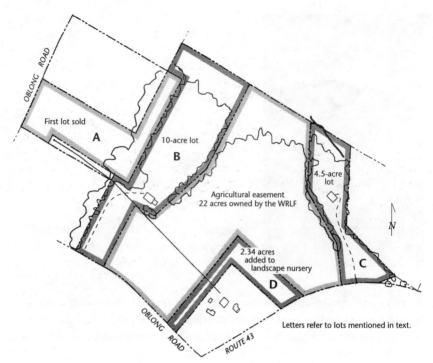

Figure 7.2. Williamstown Rural Lands Foundation's limited development and conservation project plan.
Source: Leslie Reed, Williamstown Rural Land Foundation
Credit: Cartography Lab, University of Minnesota

their interest in purchasing the 5-acre parcel to protect their surroundings. They were very receptive to the idea, and, in fact, their son purchased the property in July 1994 for $90,000, $85,000 cash with $5,000 to be paid in six months.[3] When this sale closed, the WRLF used the funds it received as the down payment for the entire 44 acres, leveraging the sale of part of what it did not own to acquire the larger parcel. The foundation did not have an option; rather, it made an offer to the heirs through the real estate agency that was accepted according to the terms described. The foundation made a down payment of $75,000 and acquired a mortgage of $225,000 with quarterly interest-only payments until June 1996, when the balance of the money would be due. The WRLF thus launched an ambitious project. The board had great confidence in this project despite the large interest payments and the short time given to raise the money needed to pay off the mortgage. Without complete support from the board, the project would not have moved forward.

The foundation hired a surveyor to establish building lots on those lands

Photograph 7.2. View across protected land toward barn-house. Taconic Ridge in background.
Photo credit: Leslie Reed-Evans

composed of both open and wooded areas that were divided by hedgerows and intermittent streams (Photograph 7.2). Natural boundaries were used to mark the lines of two additional building lots, one approximately 10 acres abutting the lot that had already been sold (Lot B) and the other approximately 5 acres at the east end of property (lot C). These boundaries resulted in lot shapes that may have looked strange on paper but were well-defined on the ground. Each lot passed a percolation test once the subdivision plan was drawn up.[4] Importantly, both of these building lots were of marginal agricultural value, and so the loss to the dairy farmer, whose concern prompted the foundation's initial interest in the project, was minimal.

A third, smaller lot was created to allow an abutting landscape nursery operator, who did not possess the 5 acres in cultivation required to qualify for the Massachusetts agricultural tax abatement program, to expand his operations (Lot D).[5] Since maintaining the agricultural viability of the parcel was a strong factor of the WRLF's involvement in the project, this action seemed appropriate, although it decreased the acreage of the hayfield.

The foundation's goal was to maintain as many of the open-space and agricultural values of the original 44-acre property as possible. Before lots B and C were put on the market, the real estate agent, the dairy farmer, and members of the WRLF board of directors walked each lot to determine how best to integrate all aspects of the residential properties, right down to landscape plantings, with continuing agricultural activities. Based on such site visits, the foundation attached a number of restrictions to each lot. The restrictions limited potential owners as to where they could build houses, driveways, and underground utilities and prohibited them from cutting certain parts of the hedgerows.[6] In addition, driveway screening would be limited to small shrubs, because trees would grow and eventually shade the good hay fields.

The lots were first advertised in late summer 1994, and lot B immediately sold for $129,000. The buyers were Williamstown residents who had long wanted to live in a more rural part of town and were in complete agreement with the restrictions. At closing in October 1994, they had already contracted with an architect to build a barnlike complex behind the existing hedgerow, clearing only where allowed for a view over the fields to Mount Greylock. The owner of the landscape nursery bought the small 2.34-acre parcel in February 1995 for $4,500. A no-subdivision clause and plant material height restrictions were used to ensure that the new larger nursery would not be subdivided and that the shade from mature trees would not interfere with hay quality.

The two sales quickly reduced the amount of the interest payment. The sales also allowed the WRLF to initiate negotiations with the Massachusetts Department of Food and Agriculture to sell the development rights on the remaining 22 agricultural acres to the commonwealth under its Agricultural Preservation Restriction (APR) Program.[7] The foundation maintained that an APR on this parcel would both support efforts to keep the area's agricultural community viable and would help to safeguard the commonwealth's investment in an earlier project protecting more than 300 acres on an adjacent Oblong Road dairy farm (see Figure 7.2). Ensuing to an appraisal, the commonwealth agreed to pay $124,500 for the development rights on the remaining 22 acres. An additional $500 would come from the town of Williamstown as the required municipal contribution under the APR program. In July 1995, one year after the project began, the WRLF retired the mortgage.

In November 1995, the final lot, lot C, was sold to out-of-town buyers looking for land in Williamstown on which to build a second home. They were thrilled with the opportunity to acquire property next to conserved land *and* endorsed the restrictions on their use.

At the end of the day, with all project expenses computed, WRLF had netted close to $90,000 (see the accompanying box for a financial summary). With other conservation projects waiting in the wings, the proceeds from this project will make possible the purchase of a conservation restriction on a historic, archetypal New England dairy farm.

Financial Summary of WRLF Limited Development and Conservation Plan

Cost of 44.52 acres, 7/94	$300,000
Project costs	
Interest payments	$7,210
Real estate and abatement taxes[a]	$12,001
Survey, engineering	$9,218
Registry, closing fees, legal	$3,052
Real estate commissions	$13,660
Miscellaneous (photos, etc.)	$39
Staff time (approx. 150 hours @ $10/hr)	$1,500
TOTAL EXPENSE	$346,680
Sales Income	
Sale of initial lot (5.7 acres), 7/94	$90,000
Sale of 10-acre lot, 10/94	$129,000
Sale of 2.34 acres to landscape nursery, 2/95	$4,500
Sale of development rights to DFA for agricultural restriction, 7/95	$124,500
Municipal contribution to restriction purchase	$500
Sale of 4.5-acre lot, 11/95	$89,000
TOTAL INCOME	$437,500
TOTAL PROJECT NET	$90,820

[a] The entire property was originally enrolled in the Massachusetts agricultural tax abatement program, Chapter 61A. When the property was subdivided, the lots were removed from Chapter 61A and a corresponding portion of the abated tax repaid to the town of Williamstown. Lot prices were set to reflect these payments.

The first parcel to be sold by the foundation, lot A, carried very few land use restrictions. Unfortunately, this lot was resold within two years when the couple, whose view it protected, decided to move. Their son, who had acquired the property to protect their view, had no reason to continue to do so and constructed a house where there was once a cornfield. Because the WRLF did not own the property, when it was sold it was not possible to place restrictions similar to those in force on the other lots. This lot has been the least successful element of the project. The house on lot B is a red barnlike structure complete with cupola that graces the edge of the field as if having been there for years (Photograph 7.3). The owners of lot C have built an unobtrusive cape-style house in the shelter of the hedgerow and named their retirement home Hidden Meadow, which was the name given to the lot by the real estate agent (Photograph 7.4). Both structures enhance rather than detract from the landscape.

Photograph 7.3. The barn-house on Lot B showing thinning cuts for view.
Photo credit: Leslie Reed-Evans

Photograph 7.4. Lot C—"Hidden Meadow."
Photo credit: Leslie Reed-Evans

Conclusion

Without a doubt, the WRLF experienced some incredibly good luck, good timing, and very cooperative people in making this project work. The following factors, led to the project's overall success.

- The executors of the estate gave the WRLF the time and flexibility essential to the project's success. In addition, their willingness to accept a lower sale price to jump start the project helped immensely. The low interest rate charged on the mortgage further demonstrated their endorsement of the project.
- The WRLF's relationship with the real estate agent was an example of how a partnership like this can work and work well. Not only did he do a tremendous marketing job; he liked the project so much that he charged the WRLF lower-than-average commission of 4 percent.
- The real estate market in this part of Massachusetts was hot, as evidenced by the quick sale of lots B and C.
- The buyers were excited to be supporting a project that combined preservation with providing the town with some revenue. In this case, the site restrictions did not seem to affect lot salability.
- Since a preliminary plan existed, the WRLF was able to act quickly when the need arose, with strong neighborhood support.[8]

Finally, return to the question posed at the start. Should land trusts be in the business of developing land? There is certainly a risk involved in undertaking such projects. If the lots had not sold as quickly as they did, the WRLF would have had to scramble to find the funds needed to retire the mortgage at the end of the two-year period. The interest payments alone would have strained its budget. In this case, the property, with its views and connection to other preserved areas, was highly attractive.

For a land trust the size of the WRLF, this project was a daring undertaking and one that has been well worth doing. Three years later, the foundation is still receiving high marks from a broad range of residents. The dairy farmer has since traded in his milkers for beef cows, strawberries, and greenhouses filled with organic tomatoes; he still relies on the many tons of good hay he harvests from the land. The WRLF has money to preserve an additional 55 acres. In addition, for many town residents, the project has shown that WRLF does care about the fiscal health of the town. Limited development in this case provided the WRLF a chance to site houses in a way that made the best use of the land's assets. Instead of seven houses sprawled over productive farmland, this corner of Williamstown retains its scenic rural character for all to enjoy.

Notes

1. Adding to the interest in this property was that it is abutted by a 78-acre conservation restriction to the east and a 200-acre conserved property to the north.
2. The sale of building lots in Williamstown had slowed in the early 1990s, but demand for property in this part of town continued.
3. Allowing six months for the final remaining payment was a condition of the cash sale.
4. Percolation testing is required under Massachusetts Title V regulations. In areas where municipal water and sewer are not available, percolation tests are the first engineering step taken in developing a site. There was an element of risk in waiting until after the property purchase to perform percolation tests on the proposed house sites.
5. A constitutional amendment passed in response to rising property values in Massachusetts in the 1970s allowed for preferential assessment of farm and forestland. In 1973, Massachusetts voters approved legislation with three laws: Chapter 61, the Forestland Act; Chapter 61A, the Farmland Assessment Act; and Chapter 61B, the Open Space Act.
6. Because the hedgerows provided natural screening and wildlife habitat, WRLF sought to preserve their integrity as much as possible. To justify the lot sale prices, however, view cuts were allowed in certain areas of the hedgerows.
7. 330 C.M.R. § 22.
8. Neighbors other than the dairy farmer were relieved to hear of the WRLF's interest in preserving the open space. Their support would have been a critical part of any fundraising effort had one been necessary.

Chapter 8

❦ ❦

Conservation Easements in
the Third Federal Circuit

Melanie Pallone

The Third Federal Circuit is composed of Pennsylvania, New Jersey, Delaware, and the Virgin Islands (Figure 8.1). Delaware is currently the only state or territory within this federal circuit to have passed a model form of the Unified Conservation Easement Act (UCEA). Of the other two states, New Jersey has both its own version of conservation easement enabling legislation and a body of court cases regarding long-term validity of easements. Pennsylvania relies on case law. Neither New Jersey nor Pennsylvania case law, though, is consistent or protective enough to give potential easement grantors confidence that their wishes will be remain intact in the next generation, let alone the distant future. Both states could benefit from the passage of a form of the UCEA, which in concert with tax legislation would make for financial incentives coupled with guarantees of permanency for land preservation. The Virgin Islands is basically regulated only by federal coastal zone growth barrier legislation. This chapter focuses on the fundamental variations and similarities of the state's common law and statutory laws as they apply both to the UCEA if in effect or to the need for its passage if not.

Delaware

Delaware has enacted a statute encompassing all the important provisions of the UCEA.[1] Delaware's model statute completely replaces 7 Del. C. §6901 et seq., Conservation and Preservation Easements, which included the same progressive language as New Jersey's Conservation Restriction and Historic Preservation Restriction Act prohibiting road signs, landfills, logging, mining, dredging, and damming. The new act is broad in scope and aims to protect natural, scenic, or open-space values; ensure availability of property for agricultural, forest, recreational or open-space use; protect natural resources, fish

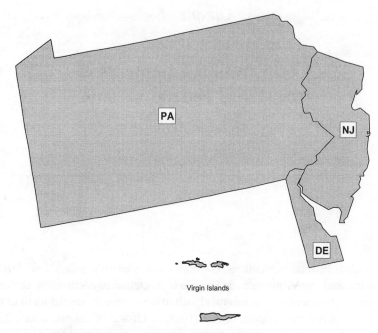

Virgin Islands

Figure 8.1. States comprising the Third Federal Circuit.
Credit: J. A. Gustanski

and wildlife habitat, rare species, and natural communities; maintain or enhance air or water quality; and preserve the historical, architectural, archaeological, or cultural aspects of real property.

Delaware's act authorizes government bodies and qualified charitable corporations to hold easements, and it allows third parties to enforce the easement provisions. A conservation easement created after the effective date of July 18, 1996 (or even one created prior to, if containing the necessary provisions) is valid despite lack of two adjacent estates where one property is principal, or benefited, and the other property is subservient, or detrimented (called "appurtenance"), despite lack of direct succession of the estates or the contract involved (called "privity"), or despite lack of a discrete benefit involving the physical use or enjoyment of the land by the holder of the restriction (called the "touch and concern" factor). Such an interest would also be valid despite assignability, distinction from common-law traditions, the imposition of negative burdens on the easement donor, or the imposition of affirmative obligations on the easement holder interest or the owner of the fee (meaning full property rights of a parcel).

Just like the model UCEA, Delaware's Conservation Easement statute includes the caveat: "This chapter does not affect the power of a court to modify or terminate a conservation easement in accordance with the principles of law and equity." Unfortunately, the act purposefully allows the existing case and statute law of adopting states to remain intact relating to modification, termination, and enforcement of easements and charitable trusts. Also, the doctrine of changed conditions is specifically recognized by that subsection.[2] Fortunately, though, the common law of easements in Delaware appears to be better equipped to preserve easements than in other states in the Third Federal Circuit. A quick survey is instructive. In 1952, the state supreme court stated that the facts and circumstances surrounding an easement's creation must be used to determine its true construction.[3] Furthermore, when the extent of the interest is doubtful, the manner in which the holder has exercised the rights must be examined, along with the grantor's assent to that exercise. Finally, any ambiguous words in the grant are to be construed in favor of the grantee. The Court of Chancery of Delaware followed this holding, finding that easement rights still existed in *Woods v. Maciey*, even though the rights were never used before they were challenged.[4] The court there looked at the nature of the grant and that its existence was referenced in relevant deeds. In Delaware, as in the other states of the Third Federal Circuit, nonuse does not mean that an easement has been abandoned.[5] In one case, a court has argued that nothing short of an express written statement may release an easement.[6] In a modern case, though, the Delaware Court of Chancery ruled squarely on behalf of grantor's rights.[7] Unlike the New Jersey courts, the tribunal ruled that the burden of an easement on the burdened estate cannot be materially increased, even when that estate has changed in nature, nor may an easement be relocated without the consent of both the burdened and benefited estates.

Beyond case law, Delaware goes further in its commitment to land conservation with the Delaware Land Protection Act.[8] The act creates an Open Space Council to advise the secretary of the Department of Natural Resources and Environmental Control on implementing a protection program.[9] Like New Jersey's Green Acres Act, the Delaware Land Protection Act acknowledges that providing recreational and conservation lands is "a proper responsibility of government." It also says that (1) the existing amounts of such lands are insufficient for an expanding population that continues to deplete the supply and increase the costs, and (2) rapid urban sprawl is eliminating much open space. Although the act's stated purposes are not all-encompassing, Delaware's General Assembly displayed great awareness of informed conservation policy in seeking to "protect and conserve biological diversity of plants and animals" and "to connect existing open spaces into a cohesive system of greenways and resources areas."

To ensure "the unique ecological functions" of recreation and conservation areas, county governments are authorized to develop and incorporate "overlay zoning ordinances" and "technically based environmental performance standards" and to structure "design criteria" into their land use ordinances. Like New Jersey, Delaware has included development rights as a potential property interest to be acquired through the Delaware Land and Water Conservation Trust Fund. The legislation requires county governments to fashion legislation granting landowners tax credit or other incentives for imposing land use restrictions on their land by transferring their rights to develop undeveloped property to other, already developed land that is already limited by zoning ordinances and the like. Unlike New Jersey, Delaware has not authorized state agencies to acquire open-space land interests through condemnation proceedings.

The Delaware Open Space Council has extensive powers and duties, progressive enough to sound as if The Nature Conservancy helped to write them. The council is to review and recommend "state resource area maps" for the state and "a ranking system to establish . . . permanent protection priorities" in accordance with them every five years. It must establish financial incentive programs seeking private sector contributions for funds to operate and maintain the resource areas. In addition, the council must analyze state and local tax codes for "incentives to encourage landowners and developers to donate or retain ownership of their lands in an undeveloped state." The legislature has even asked the council to evaluate giving the state a right of first refusal to purchase property within the state resource areas. One difficulty with the council's operations, however, is that many of their basic actions are subject to public hearings.

To fund the acquisition efforts, the legislature appropriated $6 million to the Land and Water Conservation Trust Fund for local and greenway projects, and provided additional funds to the secretary to purchase approved land and conservation easements when funds are matched by land trusts.[10] This act also created a Fund for Farmland Preservation, allowing the secretary of agriculture to help with purchases of development rights as approved by the Aglands Preservation Foundation.

Delaware does not possess the same agricultural prominence as Pennsylvania or New Jersey, but it has enacted a farmland preservation bill similar to that of Pennsylvania. Although Delaware's farmland preservation act does not include some of the restrictions regarding designated agricultural areas as Pennsylvania's does, it includes some added incentives. In hopes of encouraging landowners to voluntarily place protective restrictions on viable agricultural lands, the legislature provides for the sale of development rights and the purchase of easements.[11] Once a landowner so restricts his or her property, any violation of the restrictions give way to the imposition of civil penalties as well as recovery of rollback taxes with interest, compounded from the date of the agreement's inception. Delaware authorizes the exercise of eminent domain by state agencies within an agricultural preservation district as long as compensation is "based on the highest and best development use of the property with no consideration given to the restrictions and limitations imposed."

The Aglands Preservation Foundation created to administer the act's provisions is composed of state agency heads, representatives of the state Farm Bureau and State Grange, and active farmers from all counties. The foundation's duties and authority are many. It is charged with responsibilities such as forming a statewide preservation strategy, designing purchase criteria, developing cooperative working agreements with county governments, adopting procedural rules and regulations for designating districts and acquiring easements, approving and reviewing applications for districts and easements, and monitoring and enforcing restrictions imposed. Other functions include conducting public hearings and investigations, obtaining federal and private funding, receiving and investing funds from bonds and other monies to support the Preservation Fund, acquiring easements, and preparing an annual report. Each county has a Farmland Preservation Advisory Board, inclusive of several resident active farmers or agribusiness persons.

To establish an agricultural preservation district, an owner in fee of at least 200 productive farm or forest acres in an agricultural zone may submit an application for the designation of district directly to the foundation.[12] Eligibility criteria to be reviewed are thorough viability of the land based on a scoring system, the potential that agricultural easements will also be acquired by the foundation, the extent that long-term preservation is consistent with state and county land use plans, the likelihood that the district will be expanded, and so forth. If criteria are met, the foundation forwards the form to the county's board for a recommendation as well as to the county's planning and zoning commission, which reviews the form at one of its regular meetings. Thereafter, the foundation renders a decision at its next regular meeting. With the approval of two of the three bodies, the agricultural preservation district is established. Expansions occur in much the same way. The secretary of the Department of Agriculture, however, may reject the acquisition of an easement or the establishment or expansion of an agricultural preservation district, although applicants may reapply in a year.

Agreements of ten years may then be formed in which eligible property is limited to agricultural and related uses, and dwelling houses on the property are limited for owners (10 acres total) and those who work the land, on lots of 1 acre within 20-acre segments. No "major subdivision" is allowed, but is not defined beyond that above. All unimproved land enjoys *full* property tax exemption, not merely a reduction in assessment. Inheritance tax may be waived if all co-owners sign a document extending the agreement for another ten years. Within districts, normal agricultural activities are protected from nuisance claims. Local ordinances that would ordinarily permit such claims must include notification to buyers of existence of the district in agreements of sale; developers of nearby subdivision plans must also notify buyers of the existence of the district. After ten years, the owners may request withdrawal from the foundation; otherwise, the covenant is extended in five-year intervals. Notably, all tax relief, even from realty transfer tax, is subject to recovery if the property is released from the district within the first five years, if the land is subdivided, or if the land is rezoned. The back tax requirement will help to avoid later efforts to subdivide. Nevertheless, the act of rezoning is one taken by the municipality or government body, out of the landowner's control, and so seems unfairly punitive to the landowner.

Regarding agricultural easements, the foundation has discretion to acquire them in perpetuity within established agricultural preservation districts or to form new districts upon their acquisition. Easements are reviewed under the same criterion given above, with the potential for conversion to nonagricultural use. Agreements for agricultural easements must be at least twenty-five years in duration. They are valued for state purchase by the foundation's appraiser according to the difference between fair market value and agricultural value as of the date of application. As well as exemption from property tax, owners who contract for agricultural preservation easements are entitled to relief from gift, inheritance, estate, and realty transfer taxes.

After twenty-five years, the owner may request review for possible termination, at which time the foundation conducts an inquiry of the continued feasibility of profitable farming on the subject land. Included in the inquiry is an inspection, review under the scoring system, public hearing after notice, and approval of termination by the board of trustees of the foundation. If termination is denied, the landowner may make a new request in five years. Upon complete approval of the request, the fee owner may repurchase based on the difference between market and agricultural value (or, at very least, the state's original purchase price), provided he or she also pays the cost of reappraisal and the sum of any tax benefits enjoyed during the easement's duration.

Delaware's statutory scheme appears to be a logical one, without unnecessary bureaucratic complication or the trappings of antiquated property laws. It is encouraging to land conservation as well as giving due to key environmental values, yet is not completely inflexible as to the possibility of future changes. That Delaware is the one state having passed a conservation easement act in the Third Federal Circuit is somewhat ironic, because its body of court rulings was probably the most likely to protect common-law easements anyhow. The combination of statutory and common-law easement protections strengthen guarantees that parties placing an easement on their land can enter into such agreements with confidence their wishes will not be easily overturned.

New Jersey

Although New Jersey has adopted its own variation of easement enabling legislation, it has not adopted the UCEA. The state legislature has enacted several progressive land use statutes in the last few decades, however, and the state courts have accorded deference to the goals expressed in the legislation. In particular, the courts have made note of the rapidly diminishing fertile farmland of the state, for decades used as bedroom communities for New York City and Philadelphia, and a shoreline developed for tourism in one of the nation's most densely populated states.

In the New Jersey Conservation Restriction and Historic Preservation Restriction Act enacted in 1979, effective February 5, 1980, as in the UCEA, most easements and other land use covenants held by government units and charitable trusts are enforceable.[13] Any easements, covenants, and restrictions in existence when the act was passed are unaffected. Similar to the provisions of the UCEA, local assessment authorities must consider the restrictions when establishing the value of land subject to them and acquired under the provisions of the statute. Unlike the UCEA, though, New Jersey's act does not mention what happens to other problematic common-law characteristics of easements.[14]

All easement holders are entitled to reasonable access to ensure compliance with restrictions. Other crucial provisions attempt to ensure that easements remain permanent. The commissioner of environmental protection must review every easement whenever the holder of the easement proposes to convey it to another entity or to terminate it. When reviewing proposals to terminate easements, the commissioner "shall take into consideration the public interest in preserving these lands in their natural state." Terminations are to be legally recorded in the same formal manner as the restriction was recorded.[15] In addition, the municipality in which the land is located must hold a public hearing prior to termination. Despite such forethought, there are no guidelines for terminating easements, nor is there a minimum required time for maintaining easements and restrictive covenants.

New Jersey's Conservation Restriction and Historic Preservation Restriction Act, although similar to Pennsylvania's conservation and land development statute, is less specific about its purposes. The goal is to retain "land or water areas predominantly in their natural, scenic, or open or wooded condition, or for conservation of soil or wildlife, or for outdoor recreation or park use, or as suitable habitat for fish or wildlife." Importantly, however, the New Jersey statute defines more precisely what a conservation restriction may prohibit. "Construction of buildings, roads, signs, billboards, or other advertising"; "dumping . . . material as landfill"; "removal or destruction of trees . . . or other vegetation"; "excavation, dredging or removal of peat, gravel, soil, rock, or other mineral substance"; "surface use except for purposes permitting the land or water area to remain predominantly in its natural condition"; and "activities detrimental to drainage, flood control, water conservation, erosion control or soil conservation, or fish and wildlife habitat preservation" are all prohibited activities.

The New Jersey Green Acres Land Acquisition Act of 1961 authorizes the state's commissioner of conservation and economic development to conserve natural resources and to purchase lands for public outdoor recreation purposes.[16] Initially $60 million was raised through a voter-approved bond issue. A decade later, the Green Acres Bond Act of 1971 appropriated an additional $80 million for such purposes. These monies were to be expended by state agencies to acquire land and to help local units of government acquire land. Local units of government seeking assistance must formally adopt a comprehensive development plan stating what lands, easements, and water rights are to be acquired and why and must draft regulations ensuring that the lands will be managed in an appropriate manner. The commissioner must approve all such plans.

The legislature's findings for the act conclude that (1) the "expansion of population" increases "the need for" and "the cost of public acquisition of" such lands, yet "will continually diminish the supply" of "available and appropriate" lands; (2) provision of such lands "promotes the public health, prosperity, and general welfare and is a proper responsibility of government"; and (3) "special attention should be focused" on providing land "in the urban sectors of the State . . . since the most critical need for open lands now exists" there.

Under the related Green Acres Bond Act, the commissioner of conservation and economic development is directed to minimize purchase costs by seeking predominantly open and natural lands for acquisition. Furthermore, he or she is to achieve a balance among all areas of the state regarding the adequacy of recreation and conservation facilities, to anticipate future needs, and to coordinate plans for land use or acquisition with other state agencies such as the Water Policy and Supply Council, the Fish and Game Council, the Planning and Development Council, and the Shell Fisheries Council.[17]

In addition, in 1974, New Jersey passed a statute making all real property owned by nonprofit corporations or organizations "actually and exclusively used for conservation or recreation purposes," "owned and maintained or operated for the benefit of the public," exempt from taxation. The commissioner of the Department of Environmental Protection certifies both the group and the property as qualified.[18] Determining that "natural open space areas for public recreation and conservation purposes are rapidly diminishing," the legislature also provided additional funds for acquiring and maintaining privately owned open space.

Perhaps due to the desire to keep agricultural lands in the hands of farmers, the Green Acres Act advocates that such lands should be protected through government agencies and nonprofits acquiring easements and development rights. Far less complicated than Pennsylvania's Agricultural Security law, the Farmland Assessment Act allows owners of 5 acres or more of agricultural or horticultural land and earning $500 per year or more in gross sales for at least two years to apply for a reduced tax assessment.[19] The law penalizes those farmers who pay reduced taxes and subsequently alter land use, assessing back taxes for two years before the change in use.

Steve Small notes the potential for federal tax complications in the case of one New Jersey farmland easement in the second supplement to the *Federal Tax Law of Conservation Easements*.[20] A landowner's estate took advantage of an Internal Revenue Code provision to lower estate taxes by making the requisite ten-year agreement with the IRS that the farm remain in the family and in agriculture. Within the ten-year period, however, the state of New Jersey acquired a perpetual conservation easement on the farm. The IRS argued that the conveyance to the state violated the estate's agreement with them and assessed an additional estate tax. The estate maintained that the easement only made permanent the ten-year servitude promised to IRS, and the IRS refunded the additional estate tax without a ruling on the issue. Small thought that the IRS's decision to refund might have been based on New Jersey court's treatment of easements, as contract rights rather than real property interests. Although the status of New Jersey law concerning the nature an easement may be open to debate, Small's point is clear and reasonable. State law treatment of easements may have ramifications on federal tax assessment, which should be considered when planning for farmland preservation, especially in light of the many incentives offered in the new federal tax laws regarding exclusions from the gross estate for permanent conservation easements.[21]

The courts have interpreted various state statutes involving easements favorably to conservation aims. For example, the New Jersey Supreme Court overturned the Tax Court of New Jersey in holding that a taxpayer may reduce the value of property upon which a conservation easement was granted in perpetuity to a qualified conservation foundation for real estate tax assessment purpose.[22] The high court cited the statutes discussed above, stating: "the public benefits flowing from such a conservation easement are beyond debate. . . . By giving up the right in perpetuity to do anything with the property other than keep it in its natural state, defendant has . . . seriously compromised its value as a marketable commodity." To its credit, the New Jersey Supreme Court, unlike the Tax Court, recognized that the modern distinction between an easement in gross (where the easement only benefits the holder of the easement, without necessarily burdening any other property's rights) and an easement appurtenant (where the easement requires some kind of detriment to an adjacent parcel of land) is minimal. The court there wrote: "Conservation easements of the kind here are considered easements in gross. While there is no identifiable dominant estate that directly enjoys the benefit thereof, obviously such an easement can enhance the value of other property in the area."

The only difficulty with these two rulings, as noted by the Tax Court in its earlier ruling, was its form, essentially a scenic easement with added protections for soil and water.[23] The taxpayer had exclusive use of the land, the public had no right of access, and the holder of the easement could only enter the property to ensure compliance. According to the Tax Court, that some form of public use was stipulated was the reason that two earlier cases regarding deed restriction had different outcomes. So, the property in *Borough of Englewood Cliffs v. Estate of Allison* was kept for use as a free public park, and thus the easement's value was deducted from the market value of the land for assessment purposes.[24] In contrast, *In re Appeal of Neptune Township*, deed restrictions benefited only members of a private club and could be nullified by the grantor at any time; thus they could not be considered in assessing the market value of the land.[25]

Apparently, a taxpayer may enjoy preferential tax treatment simply by declaring some sort of public purpose in a deed granting an easement or in the restrictive covenant regarding a particular parcel of land. Any challenge to such preferential treatment may require a landowner to prove the public purpose as one worthy of conferring preferential tax treatment. In a case in which the landowner's deed restrictions limited the resale value to the initial purchase price plus consumer price index increases to ensure the availability of affordable housing in the area, the Tax Court would not grant an assessment reduction based on the restrictions until remand.[26] This case is valuable for noting the similarities between easements in gross (specific to the easement holder) and restrictive covenants (that are to "run with the land" forever).

Like some states, New Jersey has used innovative measures, such as the transfer of development rights, to guard against overdevelopment of sensitive areas, as in the case of the 6 million acres of the Pinelands National Reserve. New Jersey authorizes the municipalities in the reserve to prepare an ordinance managing growth by designating "sending" zones and "receiving" zones, encouraging "the transfer of development potential from areas requiring special protection (farmland, woodland, floodplain, aquifer recharge area, natural habitats, recreation or parkland, or land that has unique aesthetic, architectural, or historic value) to areas that can absorb increased development without substantial adverse impact."[27] Each municipality must prepare a report on the feasibility of such a project. In particular, each municipality must assess the development market potential of the receiving zone(s) and seek approval of the ordinance from the county planning board, the Pinelands Commission, and the county's agriculture development board. Within three, six, and twelve years of passage of a growth management ordinance establishing sending and receiving zones, the municipalities are required to review their performance to determine if sufficient percentages of the development potential have been transferred or else repeal the ordinance.

Under the New Jersey Pinelands Protection Act, farmers are limited in the use of their property through a recorded deed restriction.[28] In exchange, the property owner could receive transferable development credits. Transferable development credits allow the landowner to sell off the subdivision or development rights that have been now restricted on his or her own parcel. The credits are then transferred to another parcel seeking to be developed beyond that allowed by existing ordinances. Thus, the landowner transferring credits is not financially penalized for the imposition of land use restrictions on his or her land. In *Gardner v. New Jersey Pinelands Commission*, this restriction was challenged.[29] A farmer landowner argued the legislation effected a constitutional taking, or in the alternative, an illegal "exaction" requiring Pinelands farmers to pay the costs of zoning benefits for the public at large. If true, a governmental taking action would require the government unit enforcing the restrictions to pay the landowner for the value of the land rights rendered useless. This is a balancing act, for in the process of enforcing powers for the good of the state, a government cannot be required to pay for each and every action, or it would be stymied from ever acting. The state's supreme court upheld the legislation for a number of reasons. First, it ruled that the act "advances a valid public purpose . . . by its measures to safeguard the environment and protect the water supply by severely limiting development," and thus was an appropriate use of the state's police power for preserving the health, safety, and welfare of the municipality and its inhabitants, including the farmer. The court also found that the uniform land use restrictions at issue and several interrelated federal and state statutes comprised a Pinelands comprehensive management plan, aimed at furthering the "continuation and expansion of agricultural and horticultural uses" of lands within the reserve. Finally, the court noted that farmlands in the case were located within a region in which the owner could sell development credits for a high price. This, the court argued, coupled with the agricultural productivity of the land, did not destroy all beneficial use of the property and thus was not a constitutional taking and did not require the government to pay compensation to the farmer.

Cases involving the common law of easements are mixed and only serve to highlight the need for statutory protection, such as that offered by the UCEA, to ensure the long-term efficacy of conservation easements in New Jersey. The state's supreme court has implied the permanency of easements by declaring that mere nonuse was insufficient to destroy the easement holder's rights and hence the easement.[30] To establish that an easement has been abandoned, the court stated that the owner of the benefited parcel must either present clear and convincing evidence of the easement holder's intention to relinquish the easement or must prove that the owner's own conduct, allowed by the easement holder, was adverse to the easement's existence. Although acknowledging the court's ruling in Baumgartner, as well as the rule that an ambiguous easement "is to be construed most strongly against the grantor," the appellate court has found clear and convincing evidence that an easement was abandoned in a case where the easement holder had built a structure rendering the continuation of the easement impracticable. Yet, the courts have stressed where uncertainty about the scope of the grant exists, "the surrounding circumstances, including the physical conditions and character of the servient tenement, and the requirements of the grantee, play a significant role in the determination of the controlling intent."[31] The court went further than it needed to in reaching its conclusion by recognizing the doctrine of changed conditions as a broad-based rule, extending beyond its initial applications to neighborhood subdivision plans!

Of concern is the case of *Kline v. Bernardsville Assn., Inc.,* in which the appellate court (court of first appeal) advocated a "flexible approach" toward modifying easements, an approach based "in large part on the doctrine of relative hardship regarding petitions to the court for an injunction (compelling or blocking an action by another party)."[32] A court may compel or allow relocation of an easement without consent of the holder, the court reasoned, as "an extraordinary remedy . . . grounded in a strong showing of necessity . . . if the modification is minor and the parties' essential rights are fully preserved." The case cites *Kruvant v. 12-22 Woodland Avenue Corporation,* which confirmed the validity of an ancient easement by prescription (one gained by practice over time) to cross land to fish, hunt, and ride, yet allows the burdened parcel of land to adjust the course of the easement as long as "the same convenience is afforded the dominant owner under similar conditions."[33] Finally, in *Eggleston v. Fox*, the court determined that the easement was in fact a "terminable" one, much like a fee simple determinable (where landowner enjoys all rights to the property, but for a defined period of time), one that "may likewise be created for a fixed term or for the accomplishment for a specific purpose."[34] There, because the municipal easement holder had never used the easement and, moreover, indicated it never could because of circumstances on surrounding lands, the court ruled that this owner of the benefited parcel of land terminated its own "easement."

Pennsylvania

As of early 1999, no form of the UCEA or state enabling legislation had been passed in Pennsylvania. There is need for a form of the UCEA in the state, however, for treatment of traditional easements by the Pennsylvania courts shows that case law offers uncertain protection at best for conservation easements. Despite intense lobbying by the Pennsylvania Land Trust Alliance (PaLTA), efforts to pass bills based on the UCEA have been fruitless because of opposition from coal and utility industry groups.[35] In an attempt to preempt easements, the coal industry, especially strong in the state, insists that landowners be notified regarding their ability to create easements on land under which they may not own the mineral rights.[36] These notifications serve an additional purpose, reminding landowners still owning mineral rights under the land that they can sell such rights.

Despite the lack of legislation to enable easements and the threat that the possibility of federal tax law changes presents, land trusts in the state nevertheless continue to promote conservation easements as a land protection tool. Many of these early easements were created as tax shelters for politically connected donors to well-funded conservancies. The earliest easements, created in the western half of the state in the 1970s, were primarily for scenic purposes, done without any of the current requirements easements to permit public access that many current easements contain. In several instances, easements were placed over large areas, resulting in large tax exemptions, yet carving out smaller parcels of land inside the borders to allow for the placement of homes. Most of the small parcels were created before, but some were created even after the easement was executed; because they are specifically excluded from the easement, these parcels were hence excluded from any land use restrictions. Surprisingly, however, challenges to such cases so far have been rare. A notable exception was a case in which the IRS unsuccessfully attempted not only to audit the donor of an easement but also to revoke the tax-exempt status of the Western Pennsylvania Conservancy.[37]

The appellate court has endorsed the importance of conservation in two unreported rulings in eastern Pennsylvania involving the French & Pickering Creeks Conservation Trust, Inc.[38] In 1992, the court upheld the validity of an easement that permitted only one structure, the existing house, upon property that the Trust owned. The petitioner had proposed buying the property and building a second residence to be used by an agricultural tenant and asked the court to alter the easement language. In another case, the trust owned property divided into two parcels by a road; it created a single easement that differentiated between the two parcels, permitting a single-family residence on one parcel and a structure for farming on the other. The trust sold the property to the Natale family, who informed the trust that they intended to build a house on the parcel where residential construction was not permitted under the easement. In court, the trust sought to prevent construction based on the existing easement language. The court ruled against the trust, finding that the restriction against construction was in the nature of a servitude (a permanent restriction that follows ownership of the land), a burden to alienability (that is, to the right to freely transfer the land), and therefore against public policy. The trust appealed to the Pennsylvania Superior Court, the state's first level court of appeals, but before a court decision was reached, the Natales built the house. Although the appellate court reversed the trial court in 1995, ruling in favor of the original easement language, efforts by the trust to get the house removed have not been successful.

Such a case points out the need for the added shield of an easement statute. The treatment of traditional easements by the Pennsylvania appeals courts shows that case law offers uncertain survival for conservation easements. In 1977, the state supreme court found that an easement may create an agreement to use land as a park for use of the dominant tenement and acknowledged that, for all practical purposes, such an interest limits the servient tenement to the same use. The court reasoned that other potential, although remote, uses might be contrived that are not inconsistent with the easement's goals.[39] The Commonwealth Court, the court of first appeal for state agency matters, has authorized the conversion of an unused rail line for trail use.[40] The court based its ruling on the Interstate Commerce Commission's decision that such nonuse is not actual "abandonment" of the eased railway triggering the fee owner's reversionary rights, given that the National Trail Systems Act envisions future reactivation of railways.

Some cases do stress that easements created by a grant (via sale or gift) or a reservation (by setting aside the limited rights to the easement within a legal document transferring the whole of the property rights), rather than by implication (inferred from behavior of the parties) or prescription (created by long-term, obvious use of one party without opposition by the other) must be construed in favor of the easement holder. The notice of the existence of such an easement is derived from the duty in Pennsylvania to research the chain of title to the property in question; that is, let the buyer beware.[41]

Nevertheless, those same courts still give credence to the common-law notion that an easement in gross is a purely "personal right" that is not assignable to another person and does not run with the land forever.[42] Many other jurisdictions around the nation have modified such a notion, particularly in cases where the grantor obviously meant to create an assignable (transferable) easement, even though there existed no adjacent parcel to receive the benefit of the created easement. Without statutory protection, then, the status of conservation easements is left open to the whims of the courts.

For example, the Pennsylvania appellate courts have stated that mere nonuse of the easement is not sufficient to establish abandonment by the holder. Although they have argued that termination must be clearly demonstrated by an easement holder, the courts have, however, allowed for the possibility that where an easement was created for a particular purpose, evidence that the purpose had already been fulfilled or could no longer be fulfilled is relevant to the decision to extinguish it.[43] The state supreme court has also ruled that abandonment can be found where intent is coupled with circumstances that make use of the easement no longer possible.[44]

Often, the higher state courts in Pennsylvania construe easement stipulations narrowly when the original easement language is unambiguous and the context clearly shows that the grantor meant for the grantee to enjoy only certain specified rights.[45] Thus, citing the principle that doubts about land use restrictions are to be resolved in favor of the free use of land, the Pennsylvania Superior Court has in one case refused to find constructive ("let the buyer beware") notice of subdivision land use restrictions to a subsequent buyer even within an existing subdivision plan.[46]

Pennsylvania does have some useful statutes promoting agricultural conservation easements and offering reduced tax assessments for term agreements that try to preserve forest and agricultural lands and open space. In an effort to "broaden the existing methods by which the Commonwealth may preserve land in or acquire land for open space uses," the legislature authorizes the commonwealth to acquire the fee title (full title, at least to surface rights) to such real property with the consent of the landowner. In an attempt to keep land in private ownership and to lessen the state's costs of holding easements, the legislation requires that all such property "shall be offered for resale . . . within two years . . . subject to restrictive covenants or easements limiting the land to such open space uses . . . in accordance with the land use plan established. . . . "[47]

These statutes are all designed to protect a variety of resources, such as water and watersheds, natural or scenic resources, forests and timberlands, existing or planned parks, wildlife preserves, nature reserves, recreation sites, and historic, geologic, or botanical sites. They are also designed "to promote sound, cohesive, and efficient land development by preserving open spaces between communities." Unfortunately, the procedural requirements under this statute can be cumbersome, and many have not been followed in the 1990s.

State agencies and counties must submit a "resource, recreation, and land use plan" to the state planning board or county planning commission and have it approved before acquiring any real property interests. After designating the property to be acquired, a state agency must hold a public hearing, giving notice to all affected landowners and municipalities and an opportunity to present evidence either for or against the proposal. The commonwealth may only acquire land from willing landowners and with the consent of the local government units in which the proposed acquisition is situated.

If the state successfully acquires an easement on a property, the private fee holder's tax assessment is to be reduced "to reflect any change in market value of the property which may result from the acquisition of open space property interests."[48] The same provision applies in cases where state owns the whole fee interest and conveys it subject to easement restrictions.

Under this statute, open-space property held by the state or counties is to be completely tax exempt. In an effort to placate local governments that claim that more publicly owned property interests reduce the amount of tax revenue, the state makes payments in lieu of tax to the local governing units on a per acre basis.[49]

A shift in the political climate in Pennsylvania has led to the gradual decline in the state's willingness and ability to purchase fee title. State agencies used nonprofit land trusts as straw parties to acquire much of the state's park, forest, and game lands in the past, but that has been severely curtailed of late. Since 1995, the commonwealth's acquisition of natural and recreational lands was funded by the Keystone Fund, financed by monies raised from the issuance of a state bond. Until 1995, the Department of Environmental Resources, and its predecessor, the Department of Conservation and Natural Resources, were given authority to award money from the fund to municipalities and land trusts to purchase fee title or easements. The grant process is competitive, and unfortunately, awards tend to land with politically connected conservancies and municipalities.

Those receiving grants incur expenses. Recipients must raise 50 percent of the grant themselves and, of course, must set aside money and staff time to monitor easement restrictions for violations. Even land trusts make payments in lieu of property taxes; otherwise, they must seek tax exemption for eased properties on a county-by-county basis. Increasingly, however, land trusts prefer the costs of holding an easement to the costs of owning and managing the entire fee. These costs affect the ability of a land trust to preserve land. As of 1999, without reauthorization or another source of funding, the Keystone Fund is financed solely through the realty transfer tax, severely diminishing its size and hence its ability to fund land acquisition. Consequently, land trusts are forced to look to private contributions and foundations more heavily for funds.

Agriculture is the principal industry in Pennsylvania, followed by tourism. Some of the richest agricultural land in the nation sits in the Lancaster and Lehigh Valleys of south-central and east-central Pennsylvania. As farmland was threatened by development associated with the demands of Philadelphia residents, and even those of New York City, the legislature responded with the Agricultural Area Security Act of 1981, which recognized the importance of agricultural lands.[50] This legislation described agricultural lands "as valued natural and ecological resources which provide needed open spaces for clean air, as well as for aesthetic purposes." Its stated purposes were (1) encouraging "landowners to make a long-term commitment to agriculture by offering them financial incentives," (2) protecting "farming operations ... from incompatible non-farm uses that may render farming impracticable," (3) ensuring "permanent conservation of productive agricultural lands to protect the agricultural economy of [the] Commonwealth," and (4) providing "compensation to landowners in exchange for their relinquishment of the right to develop their private property."

Revisions to the act in 1989 created a way for the counties and the commonwealth, either individually or jointly, to purchase agricultural conservation easements.[51] The framework of this purchase program is flexible in theory but complicated in practice. One or more landowners can ask their local governing unit to designate an agricultural security area (ASA). In response, a county or municipality must formulate a program for an ASA by examining the quality of the farmland in the proposed area.[52] Such programs must be approved by the Court of Common Pleas in which such land "or the major part thereof lies" before they can take effect.[53] The local government then sets up an advisory committee consisting of active farmers, a citizen, and a local government official who will work with the planning commission for that area. The committee will review the proposals for the ASA and applications for inclusion and will suggest modifications. Land may be added to or removed from the ASA at a later time.

Any landowner within an ASA can apply to the relevant local government unit to include any productive farmland or timberland composing of 250 acres or more. All applications are considered at a public hearing. The planning commission may submit a report on the effects that such an application would have on the local government's planning policies and objectives. At the hearing, the municipality in which the land is located, adjacent municipalities, and landowners either "adjacent or near to" the proposed area are all considered a "party in interest"; each may lodge objections to either the application for inclusion of or the composition of an ASA. If the applicant succeeds in winning the county board's recommendation, the county recommendation then goes to the state.

Pennsylvania's Agricultural Land Preservation Board, representing state agencies, counties, farmers, and builders, has broad powers to further the act's purpose to:

1. adopt rules and regulations pursuant to the act;
2. approve a county's program;
3. approve a county's recommended easement purchases;
4. appoint its general real estate appraiser;
5. make its own purchases or joint purchases of easements within agricultural security areas;
6. legally record easement deeds and to maintain records;
7. furnish the general assembly an annual report of agricultural security area and agricultural conservation easements;
8. borrow monies and issue bonds for the Agricultural Conservation Easement Purchase Fund, to allocate monies requested by counties to buy easements, to reimburse nonprofits for expenses of acquiring and transferring easements to the Commonwealth or its counties, to retire debt from the Agricultural Conservation Purchase Sinking Fund; and
9. formulate procedures regarding all the above.

Only if the state board approves the county's recommendation (or its own) can an easement be created and conveyed.

There are additional limitations under the act. The purchase price of the easement is limited to the difference between the nonagricultural and the agricultural value of the land at the time of purchase, as valued by the state's or county's certified appraiser, and cannot exceed $10,000 per acre. Easements are all perpetual and may not be conveyed in whole or in part for twenty-five years, and then only with notice to the county board of the buyer's name and address subject to the easement. Municipalities and political subdivisions containing agricultural security areas are prohibited from enacting ordinances that unreasonably restrict farm practices unless such practices involve a danger to public health or safety.[54]

Finally, any entity seeking to exercise eminent domain (that is, to condemn land to another potential public purpose) within an agricultural security area must first obtain permission from the Agricultural Security Area Advisory

Committee and local governments. This requirement has been challenged, albeit only procedurally. The Commonwealth Court denied the petition of a school district within an ASA to condemn land for a new school building because the district presented no evidence that there were no reasonable alternatives.[55]

There are several benefits to landowners enrolling their land in an ASA. The first is that the restricted farmland value is multiplied by the established common level ratio of the county to determine the encumbered land's assessment and that such figures cannot be changed until a countywide reassessment is performed. The second is that land is not prohibited from qualifying for other preferential tax assessments under other laws.[56] The designations farmland, forestland, and open-space land describe tracts in common ownership of at least 20, 25, and 10 acres, respectively, used for their named purposes. Changing the use of land designated in the covenant is a breach for which the landowner or his or her successors and/or buyers must pay damages to the county. Damages are essentially the tax difference they saved plus 5 percent compounded interest from the date of forming the agreement to the date of breach or five years, whichever is shorter. Therefore, incentives exist for participation by property owners, and conservation stands to gain if they succeed in obtaining protection.

There are some major flaws to the law, however. To start with, the state's extractive industries are accorded considerable deference. Even though coal, oil, and gas exploration, development, storage, or removal is fully permitted by the statute, counties purchasing easements are required to compensate owners of "surface-mineable coal that will be affected or disturbed by" an easement. Without this compensation, the state board may disapprove a county's recommendation to establish an ASA. Cellular communication towers may also lease half an acre of the eased lands.

In addition, the law contains statutory language that could encourage tearing down of the easements' durability. After twenty-five years, if the land encumbered with an easement "is no longer viable agricultural land, the Commonwealth, subject to the approval of the state Board, . . . and the county board, may sell . . . the agricultural conservation easement to the record owner of the farmland." The question of who determines viability is not addressed, although *viable* is defined as "suitable for agricultural production and which will continue to be economically feasible for such use if real estate taxes, farm use restrictions, and speculative activities are limited to levels approximating those in commercial agricultural areas not influenced by the proximity of urban and related nonagricultural development."

The statute permits a landowner or the landowner's family to create subdivision for constructing the principal residence. In fact, a county's program may allow landowners to subdivide encumbered parcels, yet the statute offers no guidelines other than a prohibition that the farmland's "economic viability" may not be harmed. After acceptance of the program by the state board, requests for subdivision by landowners must be approved if within the parameters of the county's program.

Cases interpreting possible agreement violations in programs pursuant to "covenants preserving land uses" found within the laws governing counties have mostly been heard in Pennsylvania's Commonwealth Court.[57] They have nonetheless so far been inconsistent and riddled with procedural difficulties. First, consider cases in which the landowner or taxpayer lost. In 1981, the court found a landowner had contravened the statute when she built a single-family residence for herself. Despite the appellant arguing that the land remained in active farming and open space and that the structure did not detract from its character because it was located in a wooded section, the court maintained, "To interpret the definitions as the appellants urge would not only fly in the face of the covenant, it would also undermine the purpose of the Act." The court ordering rollback taxes to be paid, finding that the landowner had violated the agreement.[58]

Another, *Deigendesch v. County of Bucks,* is actually two cases.[59] The first case in that state Supreme Court ruling is *Bucks County Board of Assessment Appeals v. Feeney's Nursery, Inc.* There, the party selling the property to Feeney's Nursery made an agreement with the county and got reduced taxes, later conveying some 5 acres to Feeney's Nursery. The assessment board found a breach of original agreement with the county in that the land under agreement was no longer in common ownership, a statutory requirement, and assessed rollback taxes. Statutes providing exemptions from taxation are strictly construed against the taxpayer, the court ruled, and so the taxpayer should not be able to subdivide eased land into portions that would not alone qualify for the minimum acreage required under Act 15. The court noted, however, that the landowner therein did not exercise an option available under Pennsylvania's Farmland and Forest Land Assessment Act of 1974.[60] The act allows a landowner receiving preferential tax treatment to split off up to 2 acres annually up to a maximum total of 10 acres as long as the party obtaining the acreage lives on and uses it for residential, agricultural, or forest uses.[61] In the second case, *Deigendesch,* a father covenanted for restrictions on all his land to the county, and after his death, the mother willed chunks of it to their children. Without mentioning that no actual change in usage of the land had occurred, the assessment board found a breach based solely on the subdivision to the children and assessed rollback taxes. No ruling was made on the underlying issue of whether gift to one's own children (if otherwise within the parameters) triggers the violation, yet, from the joining of the two cases, it is obvious that the court would have reached the same result.

Consider the differing results reached in the following cases where the landowner or taxpayer won. Land granted a lower tax assessment when originally held in common by owners who contracted to keep it as open space was judged not in violation when one of the parties conveyed his interest to the other as long as it remained as open space, according to *Revenue Appeals Board of Northampton v. Fuisz*.[62] Alternatively, in *Appeal of Exton Development, Ltd.*, a developer covenanted for 271 acres of open space, maintained as three separate tracts on the tax rolls.[63] Four acres of one parcel were taxed separately due to buildings existing on them; 3 of the 4 acres were conveyed out and *then* given a variance to operate as restaurant and motel. The court had to stretch to reach their conclusion: Although the developer never specifically excluded the acres on which the structures were located, the court found that because those acres never received special tax treatment, they were not really part of the original agreement, and thus no breach occurred, despite the subdivision.

More fair, yet no less confusing, is the ruling in *Cook v. Pennsylvania Dept. of Agriculture*.[64] Landowners who granted an easement jointly to the county and state requested subdivision of their parcel, and the county board deferred to the state's Agricultural Land Preservation Board for a decision. The state board decided "not to support" the subdivision because it was "not in the interest of farmland preservation." The court set aside the board's decision, remanded the decision, and sent it back to the board for reconsideration, in part because the state board did not answer the county board's question of whether the acreage in question was "an economically viable farm" under the Agricultural Area Security Law, as required. It also insisted the state and county act jointly so that "landowners who have cooperated with the easement program do "not have to deal with such a bureaucratic dilemma."

The only distinguishing factor one can deduce from these cases is that the courts do not seem to find a breach where the restricted parcel did *not* receive preferential tax treatment before subdivision occurred and do find a breach where it *did* receive preferential tax treatment before subdivision occurred. Thus, landowners would be wise to parcel out land before forming a covenant and seeking tax reduction, as the fee owners in the scenic easement cases mentioned above have done.

The case most damaging to conservation aims is *Lenzi v. Agricultural Land Preservation Board*, in which the Commonwealth Court actually contradicts itself.[65] According to the Agricultural Area Security Law process, which the court profusely cites, a local government unit considering whether to establish an ASA must give notice to affected municipalities, landowners, and neighbors; thereafter, parties aggrieved by the designation are to address their appeal to the Court of Common Pleas. In this case, the petitioner, a neighboring landowner who was not involved in the establishment of the ASA, later objected to the county board's decision to purchase an easement within the established area. The court itself states that by the time the county "recommends such a purchase to the state Board, the public has already had ample notice and the opportunity to be heard on the issue of whether the land in question meets the criteria of the law and regulations and furthers the purpose of the legislature."

Nevertheless, the court found that the General Assembly's decision to afford neighboring landowners notice of designation gives them a direct interest and thus standing to intervene *anytime* an easement purchase is being contemplated by the county or the state. Therefore, the court reasoned, the state board's failure to notify Lenzi of its hearing on the addition of land to an existing ASA was a violation of Pennsylvania's Administrative Agency Law, rendering its decision invalid.

The results in the above cases display why it is better in Pennsylvania not to get the state involved in alienation of property, unless its involvement is administering the UCEA. To pass the model act would give Pennsylvania landowners, charitable trusts, and government bodies a clearer assurance that their intentions would be upheld in the years to come.

Virgin Islands

In terms of specific real property legislation regarding conservation servitudes, the Virgin Islands has only its Solar and Wind Energy Systems Law.[66] This act requires the setting aside of easements to ensure the receipt of sunlight and wind for each parcel within a subdivision development.

The only other relevant land use law affecting the Virgin Islands is the federal Coastal Zone Management Act of 1972, administered by the Office of Ocean and Coastal Resource Management of the U.S. Department of Commerce.[67] In the introduction, the U.S. Congress finds that "the increasing and competing demands upon the lands and water of our coastal zone occasioned by population growth and economic development, including requirements for industry, commerce, residential development, recreation, extraction of mineral resources and fossil fuels, transportation and navigation, waste disposal, and harvesting of fish, shellfish . . . have resulted in the loss of living marine resources . . . permanent and adverse changes to ecological systems, decreasing open space for public use, and shoreline erosion." The introduction continues to say that the national policy is to "encourage and assist the states to exercise effectively their responsibilities . . . through . . . implementation of management programs to achieve wise use of the land and water resources of the coastal zone, giving full consideration to ecological, cultural, historic, and esthetic values as well as the needs for compatible economic development," and requires "the management of coastal development to minimize the loss of life and property caused by improper development. . . ." Coastal zones include islands, intertidal areas, salt marshes, wetlands, beaches, and the waters therein and thereunder.

The act designates a Coastal Zone Management Commission to oversee the activities of the states and protectorates (such as the Virgin Islands) regarding land use and resource management within the coastal zones, and the secretary of commerce promulgates rules and regulations for execution of the law. Matching "improvement" grants are available from the secretary once a state has designed a management program that (1) defines permissible land and water uses, (2) constructs a planning process for the protection of public coastal areas, (3) forms procedures to designate specific areas in need of preservation or restoration, and, (4) provides authority for state review and enforcement of land and water uses. Public hearings on the program are to be held, with notification to federal and state agencies, local government units and port authorities, and interested private and public parties to participate. Local zoning ordinances must be considered for conflicts. Grants may be used to administer regulations controlling development, for acquisition of lands and waters in fee simple or lesser interest (including by condemnation "when necessary to achieve conformance with the management program") or to complete construction projects for paths, parks, historic building rehabilitation, and so forth. "Enhancement" grants may also be made for purposes such as "eliminating development in high-hazard areas," "attaining increased opportunities for public access," assessing "cumulative and secondary impacts of coastal growth and development" including "individual uses and activities," and adopting procedures regarding "the siting of energy facilities and Government facilities." After the secretary's final approval of a management program, an applicant for any federal permit or license affecting land, water, or natural resource use within the coastal zone must certify how its proposed activities will comply with and be conducted within the enforceable policies of the program.

Conclusion

Based on the statutory and case law of conservation easements and related land use tools in the Third Federal Circuit states, Delaware's laws are in totality most favorable to private and state land preservation. They grant the most incentives for landowners who cede restrictions on development of their property to the public as well as to provide the best chance of an easement or other conservation servitude having a long life (see Table 8.1). This situation is somewhat ironic, yet nonetheless appropriate, because Delaware may be the state with the least open space left to conserve.

Table 8.1. Comparison of Statutory Language and Terminology in the Third Federal Circuit

Comparison of Statutory Language	UCEA	Pennsylvania	New Jersey	Delaware	Virginia
Description of Interest					
Nonpossessory interest	X		(X)		
Easement	X	X	X	X	X
Restriction	X	X	X	X	
Equitable servitude	X			X	
Covenant	X	X	X	X	
Articles of dedication					
Condition			X	X	
Lesser interest in land permitted		X	X	X	
Incorporeal right		X	X		
Easement of view					X
Easement in structures					X
Obligation					
Affirmative duty	X				X
Negative duty (limitations/restrictions)	X	X	X	X	X
Holder's access to ensure compliance				X	X
Public use permitted by contract				X	X
Management to preserve, maintain, or enhance				X	X
Protected Subject Matter					
Natural values	X	X	X	X	X
Natural beauty					X
Scenic values	X	X	X	X	X
Open-space values	X	X	X	X	X
Wetland areas			X	X	X
Farmland		X	X	X	
Coastal or beach areas		X			X
Agricultural resources	X	X	X	X	
Wooded condition			X	X	
Habitat for fish			X	X	X
Habitat for plants		X	X	X	
Habitat for wildlife			X	X	X
Forest resources	X	X	X	X	
Parks and recreational resources	X	X	X	X	X
Natural resources	X	X	X	X	X
Natural areas			X	X	X
Geological resources		X	X	X	
Natural diversity				X	
Biological or ecological resources				X	X
Scenic resources		X	X		X
Archeological resources				X	X
Horticultural resources			X		
Rock or subsurface mineral resources			X		
Botanical resources		X	X		
Silvicultural resources		X			
Soil or shoreline resources		X	X		X
Bodies of water, waterways, or reservoirs			X	X	X

Comparison of Statutory Language	UCEA	Pennsylvania	New Jersey	Delaware	Virginia
Aesthetic or visual values		X	X	X	X
Audible effect					X
Atmospheric effect (light, wind)					X
Air quality	X	X		X	(X)
Water quality	X	X	X	X	X
Public access		X	X	X	
Public health				X	
Historical aspects	X	X	X	X	X
Architectural aspects	X	X	X	X	X
Facade/external appearance			X		
Cultural aspects	X	X	X	X	X
Historical value on designated registers			X		
Cultural heritage					X
Structures					
Permissible Conservation Easement Holder					
Authorized governmental body	X	X	X	X	X
Charitable corporation	X	X	X	X	
Charitable association	X	X		X	
Charitable trust	X	X	X	X	
Authorized tax-exempt section 501(c) charitable organization		X	X	X	X
Organization				X	
Permissible Third-Party Enforcer					
Governmental body	X	X	X	X	X
Charitable corporation	X	X	X	X	X
Charitable association	X	X		X	
Charitable trust	X	X	X	X	
Beneficiary					X
Real property owner	X			X	
Conservation easement holder	X	X	X	X	X
Authorized third party	X			X	
Person authorized by law	X			X	
Legal and equitable principles unaffected	X	X	X	X	
Representatives, heirs, and assigns		X		X	X
Creation, Conveyance, Acceptance, Duration					
Same as other easements	X	X	X	X	
Same as other interests in land			X	X	
Holder's acceptance prerequisite to enforcement	X	X		X	
Recordation of acceptance prerequisite to enforcement	X	X	X	X	
Prior notice to or adjacent municipalities and landowners		X			X
Government body to publicly adopt development plan prior to creation		X	X	X	X
Prioritize public preservation by use of ranking system or scientific principles				X	

(continues)

Table 8.1. Continued

Comparison of Statutory Language	UCEA	Pennsylvania	New Jersey	Delaware	Virginia
Compensation to be provided to owners of surface-mineable coal		X			
Consideration of zoning conflicts				X	X
Notify assessor			X		
Duration unlimited in some instances	X	(X)		(X)	
Duration for life of another					
Duration for owner's life					
Duration as stated or a specific period	X	X	X	X	X
Written consent of subsurface right required		X			
Court or county of record approval required in some instances		X			
Minimum acreage in some instances		X			
Fee simple (in some instances)		(X)		(X)	(X)
Acquisition by donation		X	X	X	X
Acquisition by purchase		X	X	X	X
Cancel after period of ten years if not enforced and tax repaid				X	X
Acquisition by eminent domain		X	X	X	X
Enforcement					
Action at law		(X)	(X)	(X)	(X)
Injunction		(X)	(X)	X	(X)
Equitable action		(X)	(X)	X	(X)
Civil penalties		X	X	X	
Specifically enforceable				X	
Review by government body prior to termination and recordation of release		X	X	X	
Municipal review of ordinances or plans after period to determine validity		X	X		
Superior Interests					
Existing interests absent written consent	X	X			
Surrounding coal mining operations		X			
Surrounding coal transportation					
Surrounding oil and gas operations		X			
Cellular phone towers permitted to acquire or lease portion of property		X			
Innocent bona fide purchaser protected					
Subdivision permitted with approval of government body		X			
Eminent domain not impaired			X	X	
Doctrine of changed conditions				X	
Defenses Specifically Eliminated					
Not appurtenant	X			X	
Assignability	X	(X)	(X)	X	
Not recognized by common law	X	(X)		X	
Imposes a negative burden	X	(X)		X	

Comparison of Statutory Language	UCEA	Pennsylvania	New Jersey	Delaware	Virginia
Imposes affirmative obligations	X	(X)		X	
Benefit does not touch/concern real property	X	(X)	(X)	X	
No privity of estate	X	(X)	(X)	X	
No privity of contract	X	(X)	(X)	X	
Frustration of purpose					
Nontermination for violation of conservation easement terms					
Applicability of Statute					
Interests created after effective date of statute	X	X	X	X	
Permissible interests created before effective date	X	X	X	X	
Does not invalidate other lawful interest	X	X	X	X	
Only in counties over 200,000 people					
In approving county/municipality		X			
Uniformity of Application and Construction					
Applied to effectuate uniform law	X				
Construed to effectuate uniform law	X				
Tax Valuation					
Taxable at eased value for tax-exempt organizations		X	X	X	X
Full tax emeption			X	X	
Public body tax exemption		X		X	X
Credit for transfer of development rights			X	X	

Note: Items marked (X) are not addressed fully or directly in legislation or court cases.

Although New Jersey has passed conservation easement enabling legislation, there is little doubt that it, along with Pennsylvania, would benefit from passage of the UCEA or a version that addresses issues current law does not. For Pennsylvania and New Jersey, passage of the UCEA would work to both clear up inconsistencies in state case law and to shore up federal tax legislation benefiting those who contract for easements on their land.

Notes

1. 7 Del. C. §6901 et seq., effective July 18, 1996.
2. As indicated in the comment to the main volume of the 1981 model UCEA.
3. *Richard Paul, Inc. v. Union Improvement Co.,* 91 A.2d 49 (De. 1952).
4. *Woods v. Maicey,* 148 A.2d 544 (1959).

5. *Rivas & Rivas, Inc. v. River Road Swimming Club,* 180 A.2d 282 (Del. Ch. 1962)
6. *Guy v. State,* 438 A.2d 1250 (Del. Super. 1981).
7. *Edgell v. Divver,* 402 A.2d 395 (Del. Ch. 1979).
8. 7 Del. § 7501 et seq.
9. Four members of whom "shall be persons who have been active or have shown an interest in preserving open space."
10. Twenty-First Century Fund Investments Act, 29 Del. c. § 6102A.
11. Delaware Agricultural Lands Preservation Act, 3 Del. C. § 901 et seq.
12. The land may not fall within a subdivision plan.
13. N.J.S.A. § 13: 8B-1 et seq.
14. Such as what obligations may be imposed upon the burdened estate or the easement holder, whether the rule requiring that the easement restrictions result in benefit to particular land (touch and concern property) is abolished, and whether an easement will be enforceable in the future once it is passed beyond the original parties to the agreement.
15. N.J.S.A. § 13: 8B-1 et seq.
16. N.J.S.A. § 13: 8A-1 et seq.
17. N.J.S.A. § 54: 4-23.1 et seq.
18. N.J.S.A. § 54: 4-3.61 et seq.
19. N.J.S.A. § 54: 4-23.1 et seq.
20. *The Federal Tax Law of Conservation Easements* published by the Land Trust Alliance.
21. I.R.C. § 2301(c)(3).
22. *Village of Ridgewood v. The Bolger Foundation,* 517 A.2d 135 (1986).
23. 6 N.J. Tax 391 (1984).
24. 69 N.J. Super. 514 (App. Div. 1961).
25. 86 N.J. Super. 492 (App. Div. 1965).
26. See *Prowitz v. Ridgefield Park Village,* 568 A.2d 114 (N.J. Super. 1989).
27. As in N.J.S.A. § 40: 55D-113 et seq., a demonstration act regarding Burlington County, within the reserve. Incentives are created for property owners in one area, a sending zone, to sell the development potential of their land to developers in another area, the receiving zone. This enables them to increase the amount of development otherwise permitted by zoning ordinances.
28. The Pinelands National Reserve and the New Jersey Pinelands Protection Act, N.J.S.A. § 13: 18A-1 to 29.
29. 593 A.2d 251 (N.J. 1991).
30. *Faircloth v. Baumgartner,* 84 A.2d 545 (1951).
31. *Leasehold Estates, Inc. v. Fulbro Holding Co.,* 136 A.2d 423 (N.J. Super. 1958) (citing *Hyland v. Fonda,* 129 A.2d 899 (N.J. Super, App. Div. 1957)). (See also *Boss v. Rockland Elec. Co.,* 468 A.2d 1055 (N.J. 1983), in which the state supreme court sent the case to the cognate administrative tribunal for a ruling on disputed factual issues because it found the language of an easement to be ambiguous and so to be looked at in context.)
32. 631 A.2d 1263 (N.J. Super. App. Div. 1993).

33. 350 A.2d 102 (N.J. 1975), citing Thompson on Real Property, § 440 (1961 Replacement).
34. 232 A.2d 670 (N.J. Super. 1967).
35. PaLTA has been instrumental in efforts to get enabling legislation passed to provide a statutory basis for conservation easements held by private nonprofit organizations. The following bills have been prepared for introduction in the Pennsylvania House of Representatives since 1991: H. B. 176, Printer's No. 182, Session of 1991, referred to Committee on Conservation on January 30, 1991; H. B. 1818, Printer's No. 2179, Session of 1993, referred to Committee on Conservation on June 21, 1993; and H. B. 1836, Printer's No. 2197, Session of 1993, referred to Committee on Conservation; H. B. 2919, Printer's No. 4065, Session of 1998, referred to Committee on Agricultural and Rural Affairs on November 10, 1998. PaLTA is an association for land trusts operating in the state. PaLTA formally organized in 1991 to facilitate the cooperative efforts of land trusts across the state and to benefit land conservation by working to establish sound state policies and laws.
36. Lobbying for stipulation has resulted in its killing the most recent PaLTA bills.
37. *McLennan v. United States,* 994 F. 2d 839 (Fed. Cir. 1993).
38. The author has confirmed the outcomes of the cases with the attorney who handled these cases for the French & Pickering Creeks Trust, Inc.
39. *Reed v. Reese,* 374 A2d. 665 (1977).
40. *Burnier v. Dept. of Env. Resources,* 611 A.2d 1366 (1992).
41. *Southall v. Humbert,* 685 A.2d 574 (Pa. Super. 1996); *Ozehoski v. Scranton Spring Brook Water Service Co.,* 43 A.2d 601 (Pa. Super. 1945).
42. *Southall v. Humbert,* 685 A.2d 574 (Pa. Super. 1996).
43. *Iorfida v. Mary Robert Realty Co., Inc.,* 539 A.2d 383 (Pa. Super. 1988).
44. *Piper v. Mowris,* 351 A.2d 635 (1976).
45. *Zettlemoyer v. Transcontinental Pipe,* 657 A.2d 920 (Pa. 1995); *Sigal v. Manufacturers Light & Heat Co.,* 299 A.2d 646 (Pa. 1973).
46. *Burns v. Baumgardner,* 449 A.2d 590 (1982). This decision contravenes earlier state supreme court rulings in *Vogel v. Haas,* 322 A.2d 107 (1974), and *Brodt v. Brown,* 172 A.2d 152 (1961), and goes against the principle of inquiry notice, that is, that the buyer should learn of deed restrictions by researching the recorded deeds in the chain of title.
47. 32 P.S. § 5001 et seq., Open Space Lands Acquisition and Preservation.
48. 32. P.S. A7 § 5001 et seq.
49. Such agreements formed are governed by 16 P. S. A711941 et seq., Covenants Preserving Land Uses.
50. 3 P.S. § 901 et seq. (regulations pursuant issued by the secretary of agriculture found in 7 Pa. Code § 138.1 et seq.). As of 1994, there were 614 ASAs in sixty-two counties across Pennsylvania. Included in these ASAs were 23,128 farms and over 2.4 million acres of land.
51. The 1989 amendments to Act 43 were spurred by Pennsylvanians "who took action to assure that the Commonwealth's productive farmlands would be protected for future generations by approving a $100 million bond issue to fund the

Pennsylvania Agricultural Conservation Easement Purchase Program." J. A. Gustanski, *Protecting Unique Land Resources: Tools, Techniques and Tax Advantages. A Handbook for Pennsylvania Landowners* (Mt. Wolf, Penn.: 4Ever Land Conservation Association, 1997), p. 59.

52. Examples are soil productivity, the likelihood that the land will be converted to nonagricultural use, the location adjacent to other farmlands, and whether lands are managed under approved soil conservation and nutrient control practices.

53. Per 16 P.S. § 11943.

54. Such as nuisance laws, where the farm practice came before the land ownership of the party to whom the behavior is considered a nuisance.

55. In *Northwestern Lehigh School District v. Commonwealth Agricultural Lands Condemnation Approval Board*, 578 A.2d 614 (1990).

56. Additional provisions on covenants preserving land uses is found within the laws governing counties in Pennsylvania, 16 P.S. § 11944.

57. 16 P.S. § 11941 et seq., commonly referred to as Act 15.

58. *Appeal of Pfirrmann* 437 A.2d, 1336 (Pa. Commw. 1981).

59. *Deigendesch v. County of Bucks*, 482 A.2d 228 (Pa. 1984).

60. 72 P.S. § 5490.6.

61. 72 P.S. § 5490.6.

62. 563 A.2d 981 (Pa. Commw. 1989).

63. 494 A.2d 34 (Pa. Commw. 1985).

64. 646 A.2d 598, (Pa. Commw. 1994).

65. 602 A.2d 396 (Pa. Commw. 1992).

66. 72 P.S. 5490.6.

67. 16 U.S.C. 1450 et seq., the Coastal Zone Management Act.

Chapter 9

🦋 🦋

Enforcement Problems with Successor Grantors

Dennis G. Collins

The Wildlands Conservancy has been actively preserving land since 1973. It strongly believes that conservation easements are a very effective tool for land preservation. In many cases, the conservancy would prefer to hold an easement on a property rather than owning the property outright. All the concerns of ownership and management remain with the landowner. The conservancy looks at ownership as more burdensome than holding an easement, and unless there is some compelling reason to hold title, such as a rare or threatened species or habitat, conservation easements are preferable.

Most conservation easements have not been a problem for the Wildlands Conservancy. They are monitored regularly, and the landowners are met with as a matter of course. Occasionally, however, problems arise. Sometimes these can be solved in a friendly, amiable manner, but one bad experience shows how important it is to be as exact as possible in the language of an easement and how difficult it can be to monitor and enforce an easement against an uncooperative landowner. The conservancy has had one such experience, described here, from which it has learned much.

The grantor executed a conservation easement in anticipation of selling 35.34 acres of land, located in Albany Township, Berks County, Pennsylvania (Figure 9.1). He donated the easement to Wildlands Conservancy in December 1990. Prior to the grantor's purchase of the property, it had been subdivided into five lots, bisected by a state highway. The south tract, containing two lots, occupies 13.18 acres and includes a small stream, wetlands, woods, and pasture. On the property is a barn. The north tract, containing three lots, occupies 22.16 acres, the bulk of which is farmland and wetland bisected a substantial stream and a tributary. This tract contains a single-family dwelling and several small outbuildings.

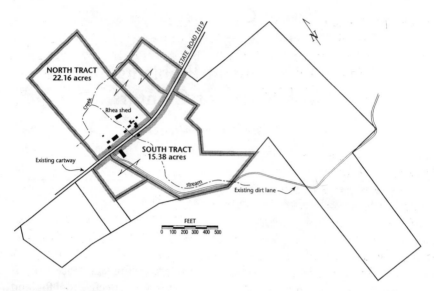

Figure 9.1. North and South tract plan.
Source: Dennis Collins, Wildlands Conservancy
Redrawn: Cartography Lab, University of Minnesota

The grantor, familiar with the concept of conservation easements from public meetings and conversations with conservancy staff, expressed a strong interest in keeping the property as open space and preventing further subdivision. He was particularly concerned with protecting the wetlands and two streams located on the property.

The grantor had originally intended to live on the property, in the dwelling on the north tract. Instead, when he decided to sell, he executed a conservation easement and accompanying conservation plan (see appendix B, p. 516); the conservation plan is incorporated by reference into the easement. The easement covered both tracts, as the grantor did not want to create separate easements and both the grantor and the conservancy believed one easement would be sufficient.

After considerable negotiation, the terms of the easement were agreed upon. The easement contained several key restrictions. A single-family dwelling could be built on either lot 1 or lot 2 of the south tract, but not on both. If the barn was converted to a dwelling, then no further dwellings could be erected. The grantor retained the right to build a pond or swimming pool on both the north and south tracts, giving the grantee, Wildlands Conservancy, the right to require and approve site and building plans. The plan made specific provisions for keeping livestock and domestic animals, locating the permitted swimming pools, and bridging or fording the streams.

The conservancy is aware that the grantor took a tax deduction for the value of the easement, but does not know the exact amount of the deduction. The property was subject to a mortgage at the time the easement was executed, and the mortgagee was willing to subrogate its interest to the easement.

The South Tract

Two years after the easement was negotiated, the grantor sought to change a provision in the conservation plan so as to sell the property. The conservation plan stipulated that no more than four horses were to be kept on the north and south tracts combined. Mr. Brown, a prospective buyer of the south tract, refused to purchase the south tract until the stipulation was modified to allow horses on both tracts. He was concerned that if he purchased the south tract, a buyer might purchase the north tract and put the maximum number of allowed horses on that tract before he, Brown, acquired any horses to be kept on the south tract, thus preempting his right to keep horses. After negotiation, Wildlands Conservancy agreed to amend the conservation plan and allow one horse per 8 acres of land, thus dividing the permissible number of horses between each buyer while preserving the intent of the grantor to restrict the total number of horses. This amendment was signed by the grantor, the conservancy, and Brown. The amendment was filed in the Berks County land records. Because the purposes of the easement had not been changed, the conservancy argued that the tax deduction taken by the grantor for the donation of the easement was not at risk.

The next problem arose after Brown completed purchase of the south tract. The conservation plan prohibited any earth disturbance within fifty feet of the streams or wetlands. Brown stated that these restrictions, combined with the local zoning setback regulation, precluded him from building a permitted pond on his property. Once again the conservancy agreed to negotiate. Eventually, a modest intrusion into the wetland area was allowed, mostly because it was agreed between the parties that any wetlands disturbed during the pond's construction would revert to wetlands almost immediately. In addition, the construction would actually create a small amount of additional wetlands. The conservancy could see no damage to the intent of the easement, and permitted Brown to build his pond without any amendment to the easement.

Although these problems required extended discussions with the grantor, they were relatively simple to resolve. In the initial discussions concerning the easement, the grantor wanted to be very restrictive in how the land could be used. After donating the easement, when he found that the restrictions inhibited his ability to sell the property, he changed his mind, wanting Wildlands Conservancy to relax some of the restrictions. It took considerable negotiation to keep many of them. As he had already taken a tax deduction for the donation, he was cautioned that there could be a financial penalty to him in relaxing the restrictions to obtain a quick sale.

In early 1997, Brown placed the south tract on the market, stating that the property was subject to a conservation easement. The conservancy, as holder of the easement, received a number of inquiries asking for a clarification of the land use restrictions contained in the easement. It was asked on numerous occasions if these restrictions could be changed. When told that changes were not possible, several callers became agitated, asserting that such a position was unfair to any potential buyer. One such caller wanted to know if the barn could be used as both residence and artist's studio. When told that the easement would not allow any commercial sales from the studio, he lost interest in the property.

After the property had been on the market for several months, Brown called the conservancy to say that he regretted ever having bought the property because the easement made it impossible to sell. In frustration, he put the property up for auction. The auction advertisements did not mention the conservation easement. The conservancy contacted the auctioneer to ensure that he was aware of its existence. In fact, the auctioneer did know about the easement but he did not know what it meant in terms of restrictions on the prospective uses of the property. The conservancy urged the auctioneer to review the restrictions and to announce them prior to the start of bidding on the property. At auction, the property failed to sell, as no bids met the reserve price, and as of June 1998, the property remained unsold.

The North Tract

Ms. Jones and her husband, Mr. Jennings, acquired the north tract in 1994. The conservancy was not notified by the grantor that he had sold this tract. By chance, a member of the conservancy staff drove by the property some months after Jones had purchased it and noted that a barn had been constructed on the property. The barn was being used to house a number of rheas, a large ratite bird relative to the ostrich. Jones was raising these bird for commercial purposes, selling both living birds and rhea meat (Photograph 9.2).

The easement prohibits any commercial or industrial activities on the property, and, as Brown had previously discovered on the south tract, construction within fifty feet of a stream or wetland. The easement also requires the landowner to obtain conservancy approval for the site location and building plans for any construction. In addition, the easement requires the

Photograph 9.1. Barn and rhea enclosure constructed on the North tract without notification.
Photo credit: Diane Matthews-Gehringer, Wildlands Conservancy

Photograph 9.2. Rheas and barn enclosure.
Photo credit: Diane Matthews-Gehringer, Wildlands Conservancy

landowners to erect fences to prevent any domestic animals from entering any wetland area or stream. No animal waste of any kind was permitted to enter the larger stream on the property. Upon reviewing the conditions of the easement and inspecting the property, the conservancy determined that several violations of the easement had occurred.

The conservancy informed Jones of the violations. She stated that she was unaware of any restrictions on her activities, even though the easement had been recorded in the county land records and should certainly have been known to her at the time of her settlement on the property.

The first, and perhaps most egregious, violation of the easement concerned the barn. The building was sizable, approximately fifteen by forty feet, and substantially constructed. The conservancy pointed out that no such construction was allowed without site plan and building plan approval by the conservancy. Jones responded that the barn was only a temporary structure, resting on the ground without a foundation, and thus she did not need a building permit from the conservancy or even the township. The conservancy suggested that the building be removed. The second violation concerned the operation of a commercial business. Jones responded that every farm was in essence a commercial business and thus hers was not unique. She pointed out that the conservancy was actively trying to save farms for farming. Correcting the remaining violations became a function of negotiating solutions to these two problems.

Jones then informed the conservancy that she contemplated replacing some of the outbuildings on the property with larger ones, expanding the single-family dwelling and installing both a pond and a swimming pool. She refused to accept the conservancy's assertion that she would need approval. At that point, the conservancy sought legal counsel to enforce the easement on the property, to require Jones to correct the violations she had already made, and to require her to live up to the terms of the easement. Jones was put on notice that the conservancy intended to take whatever action was necessary to enforce the easement.

Jones then consulted her own counsel, who informed the conservancy that the easement was of no standing, although he could not substantiate that claim.[1] Lengthy negotiation ensued between Jones and the conservancy. The conservancy formally requested that Jones remove the barn, cease commercial operations, and curtail plans for replacing existing structures with larger ones. In exchange, the conservancy offered to drop any objection to enlargement of the existing dwelling and installing either a swimming pool or pond.

The conservancy noted, with reference to the file when the easement was originally created, that one of the purposes of the easement was to limit the number of horses allowed on the property. The reason for this was apparent.

Too many animals confined on small areas, such as a corral or pen, denude the soil of its plant cover, decrease the rate at which water is absorbed into the ground, and increase the rate at which water flows overland, carrying sediment and animal waste into adjacent wetlands and streams. This situation was occurring on Jones's property where the birds were penned. They continually scratch the ground and had removed almost all the ground cover. The conservancy objected to such damage by these birds in the same way that it had anticipated such damage by horses.

Jones completely rejected the conservancy's offers, claiming that she had invested heavily in the barn and in her stock of birds. No counteroffer was made. The conservancy offered to agree to modify certain other restrictions, allowing the present dwelling to be enlarged, allowing the replacement of outbuildings to be on a square foot for square foot basis, and allowing such replacements to be erected in locations other than the original locations. These offers were also rejected. In addition, the conservancy met with the original grantor of the easement to discuss possible compromises and amendments, but by this time the grantor wanted no further part in the whole matter.

Almost two years of negotiations, accompanied by threats of court action on both sides, resulted in a compromise. The agreement was filed in the land records and thus is a fully legal document, and it essentially sets forth the terms under which both parties will operate. The agreement was preceded by the following preamble:

> WHEREAS, certain questions have arisen regarding the interpretation and application of the Conservation Easement to the Successor Grantor's use and enjoyment of the Successor Grantor's property; and WHEREAS, the parties desire to conform and clarify the interpretation and application of the Conservation Easement with respect to the Successor Grantor's property, NOW, THEREFORE . . . THE PARTIES AGREE AS FOLLOWS:

Jones was permitted to expand the present dwelling and its terrace. These improvements could not increase the total square footage of the dwelling and terrace by more than 50 percent.[2] Jones could construct a swimming pool, not to exceed 600 square feet, or a pond, but not both. She could continue to raise birds or animals, but could not denude more than a half acre of land. The existing barn was allowed to remain, and Jones could erect two small temporary structures, totaling no more than 450 square feet, to provide shelter for livestock other than birds. Jones could continue to sell birds for breeding purposes, but had to cease slaughtering and processing any animal or bird products on the property. In addition, the conservancy reserved the right to approve any new structures.

The agreement was considered by the conservancy to be less than desirable, because Jones apparently achieved most of her goals, but the results are probably the best that could be obtained without court action. The conservancy did not wish to incur further costs by having the proceedings drawn out further.

Although the conservancy did have adequate resources to pursue further action, due to a contribution made to its conservation easement monitoring and enforcement fund by the original grantor, but following the advice of counsel, it decided to accept what it could without resort to the courts. The conservancy spent almost $3,000 in attorney's fees, in addition to more than $2,000 in staff time to resolve the conflicts. This equaled the amount contributed by the original grantor.

The lack of conservation easement enabling legislation in Pennsylvania was a prime consideration in the conservancy's decision. Absent such legislation, the burden of proof was on the conservancy to prove that Jones had violated the easement. With such legislation, the burden would have shifted to Jones to prove that she was not in violation. Despite several previous favorable court rulings in Pennsylvania upholding the validity of conservation easements, the conservancy did not have enough confidence in the wording of this particular easement to risk losing in court.[3] Such a loss would not only have been a blow to the conservancy, but might have resulted in an unfavorable precedent for contesting conservation easements in Pennsylvania by the conservancy and other similar organizations.

Conclusion

Because this was one of the very first easements drafted by Wildlands Conservancy, the staff sought advice from other land trusts. Despite this, and with hindsight, the easement contained a number of ambiguities and loopholes that had to be addressed at considerable time and expense in the course of seeking enforcement of the easement after its recordation. The conservancy tried to meet goals that could be seen as too specific and that could have been addressed in more general terms. It tried to anticipate some problems but clearly did not anticipate others. As a result, the conservancy has developed a much better basic easement document, one more closely modeled after the easement published in the *Conservation Easement Handbook* of the Land Trust Alliance.[4]

The problems associated with this easement were an object lesson for the conservancy, not only in the diligent drafting of easement language, but also to the conservancy's philosophy as to what should be included in a conservation easement. Since this easement was drafted, attention to the exactness of both language and intent has been strengthened, and the conservancy is less likely to try to micromanage land use through a conservation easement. Neither landowners nor the conservancy can anticipate every potential use of a property, and the conservancy negotiations with landowners now always included discussion as to the ability of the conservancy to monitor and enforce easement terms that may be seen as too restrictive.

Absent a conservation easement enabling statute in Pennsylvania, the problems of enforcement are much more difficult. Without such a statute, the burden of proof is placed on the holder of the easement, whereas easement enabling legislation such as is in place in forty-five other states places all the burden of proof on the grantor. Without such a statute, a judge can rely on the common law and may well conclude that certain restrictions in an easement are too burdensome for a landowner (particularly a successor owner). The court could then negate the restrictions. Thus, in Pennsylvania, land trusts must be very careful how they craft easement restrictions. Although the original grantor may want very tight restrictions, the danger is that a court might find them too burdensome on successor owners. Since 1990, there have been several attempts by the Pennsylvania Land Trust Association, in alliance with the land trust community of the commonwealth, to obtain the passage of such enabling legislation, but as yet, there has been no success.

Notes

1. Pennsylvania is one of only two states that has no statutory basis authorizing conservation easements in gross to be held by other than certain governmental agencies. This became a key factor in the resulting negotiations. The conservancy's counsel was reluctant to use the courts to enforce the easement, stating that without such legislation, in the possible selection of a judge who might look unfavorably upon any restrictions on a landowner's rights, and in the possible interpretation of certain language in the easement and conservation plan to be ambiguous, negotiation was by far the most preferable course of action. But note also that there have been favorable court decisions in the state upholding conservation easements.

2. The conservancy actually measured the buildings to determine the basis for expansion.

3. Janet Diehl and Thomas S. Barrett. *The Conservation Easement Handbook: Managing Land Conservation and Historic Preservation Easement Programs.* (San Francisco: Trust for Public Land and the Land Trust Exchange with the Public Resource Foundation, 1988).

4. Diehl and Barrett, *The Conservation Easement Handbook.*

Chapter 10

❧ ❧

Saving Agricultural Land with Conservation Easements in Lancaster County, Pennsylvania

Tom Daniels

Between 1980 and 1990, Pennsylvania lost more than 900,000 acres of farmland, comprising 10 percent of the farmland base, to other uses. Thirty-two percent of this land was classified as prime or unique farmland. In the loss of prime farmland, Pennsylvania ranked twelfth nationally.[1] Lancaster County is Pennsylvania's leading agricultural county, producing about one-sixth of the state's farm output. The combination of the county's excellent soils, a strong farming ethic, and the presence of Amish and Mennonite sects with close ties to the land has resulted in a successful farm economy. Even so, the county has 460,000 inhabitants and faces the challenge of balancing economic and population growth with an important farming sector that also provides abundant open space.

Two driving forces compel farmland protection: sprawling development and farmland usually being worth more for building sites. In response, Lancaster County has forged a public–private effort to plan for the protection of farmland and to preserve farmland through the acquisition of conservation easements. The Lancaster County experience illustrates that conservation easements can achieve public growth controls and at the same time help landowners meet financial and family goals. Landowners sell or donate conservation easements for financial benefits, as a way to transfer the farm to the next generation, and often from a strong desire to see the land they love remain in farm use.

Protecting farmland is complex. Not only does it involve individual farmers and their families, but it also encompasses a broad range of interwoven economic, social, and environmental issues. Farming requires a large investment in land and equipment for a rather low rate of return. Many farmers view land as a current bank account, a future retirement plan, and an insurance policy rolled into one. Although most farmers love their land and their lifestyle, they are well aware of its value as lots for residential and commercial construction. The choices most farmers eventually face are (1) sell the farm for development and hope for top dollar, (2) pass the farm on to a family member, or (3) sell to another farmer. Conservation easements can make the second and third choices financially competitive with selling the farm for development and are emotionally more satisfying to most landowners.

Across the nation, Americans tend to take farmland for granted, perhaps because they spend a smaller percentage of their disposable income on food than any other nation.[2] Nonfarmers place a high value on the open space and wildlife habitat that farms provide but often do not appreciate the odors, dust, noise, slow moving machinery on roads, and chemicals associated with modern farming practices. The United States loses about 1 million acres of farmland to nonfarm development each year.[3] Losses have been most dramatic in metropolitan counties and metro-adjacent counties as people seek open space with the convenience of short travel times to work and urban amenities. These counties produce about 56 percent of the nation's total farm output and more than half of the nation's fruits, vegetables, and dairy products.[4] Continuing urban, suburban, and exurban growth will continue to put pressure on farmland in these counties. Conservation easements are a tool that has shown promise in both slowing the rate of farmland conversion and as a supplement to countywide growth management efforts.[5]

There are several ways to protect farms and farmland from sprawling urban and suburban development. Obviously, no one technique can insulate farmland from all the threats, particularly as farmers age and urban and suburban areas expand. The most successful farmland and open-space programs in the nation combine a number of techniques that complement each other. Most include conservation easements, a tool that has grown in popularity since the 1970s.[6] Recent research indicates that approximately 51 percent of the nation's land trusts include the protection of farmland in their land protection efforts.[7] Similarly, in 1994, the Land Trust Alliance reported that more than sixty land trusts, including those concerned almost exclusively with farmland protection, named acquiring easements on farmland as a priority.[8] Several local and regional land trusts across the United States hold farmland preservation as their primary goal, including Marin Agricultural Land Trust (California), Lancaster Farmland Trust (Pennsylvania), Colorado Cattlemen's Land Trust, Montana Land Reliance, and the nationwide American Farmland Trust.

Although many land trusts rely on the donation of easements or bargain sales, sixteen states, mainly in the Northeast, and a few dozen county and municipal governments have established programs to purchase agricultural conservation easements (PACE); see Table 10.1.[9] To date, PACE programs have received over $800 million in public funds and preserved over 400,000 acres of farmland.[10] Federal grants to state and local governments for purchases of conservation easements began in 1996 when Congress appropriated $35 million to make grants to state and local governments for the purchase of conservation easements.[11]

Table 10.1. States with PACE Programs

State	Year Enacted and Statute	Short Title(s)
Arizona	Ariz. Rev. Stat. Ann. § 11-935.01 and Ariz. Rev. Stat. Ann. §§ 9-464–464.01	Open-space land acquisition Open-space conservation
California	1995; Cal. Pub. Res. Code §§ 10200–10277 Cal. Pub. Res. Code §§ 31150–31156	Agricultural Land Stewardship Program Act of 1995 Preservation of agricultural land (h)
Colorado[a]	1994; Colo. Rev. Stat. §§ 38-30.5-101–38-30.5-110	Conservation easements
Connecticut	1978; Conn. Gen. Stat. §§ 22-26aa–26jj Conn. Gen. Stat. sec. 7-131q	Agricultural lands Agricultural Land Preservation Fund
Delaware	1991; Del. Code Ann. tit. 3, §§ 901–930	Delaware Agricultural Land Preservation Act
Kentucky	1994; Ky. Rev. Stat. Ann. §§ 262.900–262.920	Agricultural conservation easement
Maine	1987, and revised 1993; Me. Rev. Stat. Ann. tit. 5, §§ 6200–6210	Land for Maine's Future
Maryland	1977; Md. Code Ann., Agric. §§ 2-501–2-516 Md. Code Ann., State Fin. & Proc. § 5-408	Maryland Agricultural Land Preservation Foundation Purchase of Agricultural Conservation Easements
Massachusetts	1977; M.G.L. Chapter 184, Section 31	
Michigan	1994; Mich. Comp. Laws §§ 36101–36117	Farmland and Open Space Preservation
New Hampshire	1979, N.H. Rev. Stat. Ann. §§ 432.18–432.31a	Purchase of Agricultural Conservation Easement Trust Fund
New Jersey	1983; N.J. Rev. Stat. §§ 4:1C-1–55	Agricultural Development and Farmland Preservation Act
New York[a]	N.Y. Gen. Mun. Law § 247	Acquisition of open spaces and areas

State	Year Enacted and Statute	Short Title(s)
New York[a]	N.Y. State Fin. Law § 87	Farmland protection trust fund
	N.Y. State Fin. Law § 92-s	Environmental protection fund
Pittsfield	1996	County-level farmland pro-
Southampton	1980	tection programs implemented
Southold	1986	through various means,
Suffolk	1975	including municipal bonds and property tax increases
North Carolina[a]		
Forsyth	1984	Implemented at county level through budget reserve
Pennsylvania	1988; 3 Pa. Cons. Stat. §§ 901–915, and;	Agricultural Area Security Law
	3 Pa. Cons. Stat. §§ 1201–1208, Section 7.3	Agricultural land conserva- tion assistance grant program
Rhode Island	1981	
Vermont	1987; Vt. Stat. Ann. tit. 6, §§ 31–33	Ag Land Development, Rights Acquisition Program
	Vt. Stat. Ann. tit. 15, §§ 301–325	Vermont Housing and Con- servation Trust Fund Act
	Vt. Stat. Ann. tit. 10, §§ 6301–6309	Acquisition of Interests in Land by Public Agencies
Virginia*		
Virginia Beach	1995	County-level program imple- mented through contribu- tions from increase in prop- erty tax and cellular phone tax
Washington[a]	1982; Wash. Rev. Code §§ 84.34.010– 84.34.922	Open space, agricultural, timber lands–current use– conservation futures
King Co.	1979	County-level farmland pro-
San Juan Co.	1990	tection programs implemented through municipal bonds and real estate transfer tax
West Virginia	1990; W. Va. Code §§ 8-24-72–78 (1990)	Farmland preservation program
Wisconsin[a]		
Town of Dunn	1996	Township program funded by property tax increase

[a]Denotes local or regional level PACE programs only.

Sources: Miscellaneous state statutes and American Farmland Trust Fact Sheet, March 1998; *Farmland Preservation Report* (unpublished data).

Because conservation easements depend on variations in state enabling laws, how they are used varies from state to state and even within a state. For example, land trusts often draft easements that vary from farm to farm to reflect individual properties and individual landowner circumstances. Governments tend to use a "one size fits all" easement document. Still, the fundamental purpose of a conservation easement is to protect existing agricultural and open-space uses. A conservation easement is, as numerous legal scholars have pointed out, a negative easement in gross and cannot impose an affirmative obligation on the landowner.[12] For that reason, an easement can restrict an owner's use of the land; it cannot require the property to be actively farmed. Consequently, routine agricultural practices are permitted as long as they comply with local zoning regulations and with state and federal laws. Most agricultural conservation easements do not limit crops grown, livestock maintenance, or construction of agricultural structures, and they frequently provide for the building of an additional house for persons involved in the farm operation. Such easements also often allow for part-time "rural enterprises" to encourage additional sources of on-farm income. Public access is not normally allowed, nor is the dumping of garbage or removal of soil.[13] With many publicly funded PACE programs, a soil conservation plan is required.[14] Occasionally, an easement may be seen by a landowner as a tool to ensure that certain land use activities are or are not carried out, but special requests on restrictions should be carefully weighed against difficulties that may arise on long-term monitoring, the ability to enforce, and conservation goals. For example, a few land trusts have attempted to require organic farming methods on farmland protected by an easement. By placing such restrictions within an easement, the land trusts have placed a heavy burden on themselves for monitoring and enforcement over time.

Conservation Easements and Community Growth Management Efforts

A successful farmland protection program possesses the following goals:

1. Protecting a "critical mass" of farmland, a sufficient base of farmland to enable farm-related supply, processing, and transportation businesses to survive and keep agricultural operations alive[15]
2. Maintaining affordable land prices to allow existing farmers to expand their operations and new farmers to acquire land and begin operations
3. Creating a reliable land protection program, keeping land in farm use or available for farm use, over the long term
4. Ensuring that the benefits of farmland protection are delivered at a reasonable cost[16]

Such a program will include the following elements:

1. The political support of elected officials and the general public
2. Comprehensive planning at all levels of local government, including restrictive agricultural zoning that permits only low-density residential and limited commercial and industrial development in the countryside
3. Statutory provisions allowing landowners to sell or donate conservation easements to a land trust or the local or state government
4. Statutory preferential real property taxes for commercial farmers
5. State right-to-farm statutes aimed at protecting farmers against nuisance suits for standard farming practices
6. Statutory protection for farmers against eminent domain
7. Growth boundaries drawn around urban and village areas to prevent sewer and water lines from being extended into farming areas
8. Rural residential zones on lower-quality soils and in locations that will not interfere with commercial farming

Lancaster County, Pennsylvania

Lancaster County covers 603,000 acres of southeast Pennsylvania about sixty miles west of Philadelphia and contains some of the most productive land in the nation. Prime farmland, class I and II soils, cover more than 50 percent of the county, and almost two-thirds of the county, 388,000 acres, is farmed.[17] In this county, 4,700 farms, with an average size of 86 acres, raise cattle, poultry, and hogs; produce milk; and grow hay, corn, soybeans, wheat, tobacco, and vegetables.[18] In 1997, these farms sold over $800 million in farm products, making Lancaster County the leading agricultural county in Pennsylvania and in the entire northeastern United States.[19]

The strength of the county's farm economy, along with a thriving tourist industry largely driven by the attraction of its spacious farmlands and Plain Sect community, strongly suggests a county farmland protection program aimed at maintaining a working rural landscape. Approximately 30 percent of the county's farmers belong to the Plain Sect community: Amish, Mennonite, and Brethren. Lancaster County is the heart of the Pennsylvania Dutch country. There is a strong connection between Plain people's religious beliefs and farming as a way of life. Selling land for development is rare among the Plain Sect farmers. Moreover, the Amish increased their farm holdings in the 1990s, which has helped to stabilize the farmland base and curb the spread of non-farm residences in the countryside. The county's tourist industry, which is in no small way influenced by the presence of the Plain Sect and their strong commitment to agriculture, brings an estimated 5 million visitors each year and $500 million in annual revenues.

Given its proximity to Philadelphia, its natural beauty, and its rolling fertile farmlands, Lancaster County has continued to retain native residents and attract urban refugees. Development pressures in Lancaster County have been consistently on the rise. Between 1950 and 1980, the county population increased by 127,000 people, an increase of 48 percent.[20] In April 1994, *U.S. News & World Report* named Lancaster County as one of the ten booming areas of the United States.[21] In 1997, over 450,000 people lived in the county. Projections for the year 2020 show an increase to 600,000 people.[22] Local government officials are faced with the same commercial, industrial, and residential growth pressures that have occurred in metropolitan areas throughout the United States.

The visible loss of farmland and open space together with serious traffic congestion have convinced many county inhabitants that managing growth is essential if the farming landscape, and the quality of life it provides, is to be sustained.[23] A March 1995 poll by the *Lancaster New Era* found that farmland preservation was the second priority among county residents, taking a backseat only to crime and just ahead of traffic congestion.[24]

Using Conservation Easements Strategically to Manage Growth

By early 1998, Lancaster County ranked first in the nation among counties in the number of easements acquired (330) and second in the number of acres preserved, 28,000, behind Montgomery County, Maryland.[25] Lancaster County has achieved this distinction in large part through the county government's pursuit of a four-part strategy of acquisition of conservation easements:

1. Creating a public–private partnership between the county government and the private, nonprofit Lancaster Farmland Trust
2. Acquiring easements to protect large contiguous blocks of preserved farmland
3. Acquiring easements that form portions of the urban and village growth boundaries
4. Acquiring easements to enhance existing agricultural zoning[26]

Public–Private Partnership

Historical Setting

Lancaster County purchased its first agricultural conservation easement in 1983.[27] Initially, the county established its easement purchase program under Pennsylvania's Act 442 of 1968 and the Agricultural Security Areas Act of

1981, also known as Act 43.[28] Among other things, this act gave counties the authority to enact easement purchase programs, but provided no funding. In forming the first farmland preservation program, funded exclusively by the county, Lancaster County marked its statewide leadership role in the preservation of agricultural lands. The county, however, could only purchase easements on farms enrolled in an agricultural security area (ASA) or agricultural district. This regulation has meant that the county government has the potential to purchase easements on the 125,000 acres enrolled in security areas, out of 388,000 acres in farm use in the county.

Spearheaded by a group of farmers and community leaders who recognized the limitations of the ASA legislation and the fiscal limitations of purchasing easements on all lands worthy of such protection, the Lancaster Farmland Trust (LFT) was formed in 1988 to supplement the county program. As with most land trusts across the nation, LFT is a private, nonprofit land conservation organization. It achieves its goals of permanently preserving farmland by accepting donations of conservation easements, arranging for testamentary gifts of land and easements, making bargain sale easement purchases, and securing options to acquire easements.

In 1987, voters in Pennsylvania acted to ensure that the commonwealth's productive farmlands would be protected for future generations by approving a $100 million bond issue to fund the Pennsylvania PACE program. This program extended the effectiveness of Act 43, amending it to include both matching grant funds and criteria for those counties wanting to establish a farmland preservation program. Having the advantage of a program already in place, Lancaster was the first county to receive funds through the newly formed PACE program.[29] In 1997, the county received its first federal funds, $305,947, for purchasing easements from the 1996 farm bill.[30]

Forming a Unique Public–Private Partnership

In 1990, the county Agricultural Preserve Board and the LFT entered a cooperative agreement to coordinate their farmland preservation efforts.[31] The benefits of the agreement have mutually served both organizations in their efforts to protect Lancaster's farmland. The county possesses substantial funds, averaging about $4 million a year through the 1990s, while as a private organization; the LFT possesses the agility to act quickly. In addition, the Amish and Plain Mennonite farmers will work with the LFT, but they will not yet accept public funds for easements. Furthermore, under the act, the county program is limited to acquisition of easements in established ASAs, which currently cover only one-third of the county's farmland.[32] The Farmland Trust has no such limitations on where it can acquire easements. To date, this agreement, now used in several other counties in Pennsylvania, has yielded significant results. Three farms have been jointly preserved in Lancaster County, including the farm where much of the movie *Witness* was filmed. On two occasions, the LFT stepped in and acquired easements on critical farms for the Preserve Board, which later purchased the easements from the LFT. In addition, the Preserve Board and the LFT staff share information on easement prospects, and a joint board meeting is held once a year to review progress.

The easement programs of Lancaster County and the LFT complement each other both on the ground and in public relations. As of early 1998, the Preserve Board possessed 250 easements on 23,000 acres, some of which were held jointly with the commonwealth through the PACE program, whereas the LFT held 80 easements on 5,227 acres. In several places, easements owned by the Preserve Board are adjacent to easements held by the LFT, contributing to the creation of large blocks of protected land.

Creating Large Contiguous Blocks of Preserved Farmland

The Agricultural Preserve Board follows a strategy of purchasing easements to create large contiguous blocks of preserved farmland. This strategy serves several purposes. First, a block of preserved farmland helps to keep nonfarm development at a distance. Farmers can operate without much fear of complaints or threats of lawsuits from nonfarm neighbors over standard farming practices. Second, the large-block practice helps to achieve a critical mass of land necessary to support farm support businesses and to maintain agriculture for the long term. Third, blocks of protected land should serve to minimize sprawl into the countryside and to direct nonfarm development toward areas where appropriate public services, particularly sewer and water, exist.

In an effort to implement this strategy, the Agricultural Preserve Board, as mandated under terms of the PACE program, uses a system to rank applications from landowners wishing to sell an easement.[33] One of the criteria gives added weight to applicant farms either next to land already protected by a conservation easement or next to another applicant farm. Consequently, nearly three-fourths of the farmland that the Preserve Board has preserved is contiguous to, or within half a mile of, another protected farm. The Preserve Board and the LFT have created several large blocks of protected farmland. Three involve blocks of land that are over 1,200 acres in size and another ten involve blocks of land that exceed 300 acres. These large areas of protected land are especially significant because the average Lancaster farm is only 86 acres. In 1998, the Preserve Board had over 200 applications on file, many from farmers located close or adjacent to existing preserved farms.

The availability of land for easement acquisition, whether by purchase or donation, is strictly voluntary. This fact creates two difficulties in achieving the creation of the large blocks of protected lands. First, some landowners will choose not to participate. Second, especially when an easement program is new, a number of widely separated farms may be initially preserved. The county or land trust is gambling that a large block can be created over time. If the gamble fails, isolated farms can end up as islands of preserved farmland.

Under Act 43, after a county- or state-purchased easement has been in effect for twenty-five years, a landowner may apply to buy out of the easement, at its appreciated value.[34] To receive permission to end an easement in this way, however, the landowner must prove that surrounding development has rendered the land no longer economically viable for farming. If a particular preserved farm is part of a larger block of preserved farms, though, any future landowner will be hard put to make a convincing case to buy back the easement.

Acquiring Conservation Easements to Help Create Urban or Village Growth Boundaries

Lancaster County is the only jurisdiction in the nation using conservation easements to help create urban or village growth boundaries (Figure 10.1).[35] Twenty growth boundaries between rural townships and boroughs have been created since 1993. These growth boundaries have been designed to both promote more compact and cost-effective development and to discourage sprawl onto productive farmland.[36]

These growth boundaries may change over time, but will probably not be allowed to expand at the expense of the preserved farms as long as the pre-

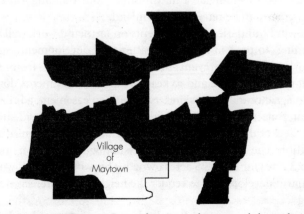

Figure 10.1. Lancaster County, Pennsylvania—urban growth boundaries.
Source: Tom Daniels

served farms are in a contiguous block, such as around Maytown in Figure 10.1. Utilities, such as public sewer and water lines, may be extended through a preserved farm, which, in practice, could result in nonfarm development leaping over the growth boundary and sprawling into the countryside. Existing zoning along with the presence of a growth boundary, however, should prevent such sprawl. In Figure 10.1, for example, only one 2-acre building lot per 25 acres is permitted. In this case, although some nonfarm residential development could occur in the countryside, the number of allowable houses would probably be too low to justify the expense of extending sewer and water lines.

Farm easement sale applications receive greater priority if they are located close to development along a growth boundary. Figure 10.1 shows the preservation of several farms along the growth boundary of Maytown. Maytown can expand in only one direction and not out into prime farming areas. In this way, the easements and growth boundary work together to curb sprawl and channel development into appropriate locations.

Acquiring Conservation Easements to Strengthen Agricultural Zoning

Agricultural zoning, which separates farms from conflicting nonfarm uses, is the first line of defense in farmland protection.[37] Most agricultural zoning allows for some nonfarm residences, although limitations are set for proximity to existing farms so as not to clash with farm operations. Some 320,000 acres, covering 54 percent of Lancaster County, are zoned for agriculture. Across the county, agricultural zoning generally allows one building lot of up to 2 acres for every 25 acres owned.[38] Hence, a landowner with 100 acres would be allowed to subdivide a maximum of four building lots covering 8 acres, with 92 acres to be retained as farmland.

Both growth boundaries and easements on farmland work well with agricultural zoning to prevent sprawling patterns of development. Agricultural zoning works both to prevent nonfarm development from sprawling throughout the countryside and to keep the costs of easements down. When a farm in an agricultural zone is preserved with an easement, adjoining farmland in that zone cannot be subdivided into dozens of residential lots to exploit the view of the preserved farm next door and cause conflicts with the farm operation. The adjoining farm can be subdivided based on one building lot of up to 2 acres for every 25 acres owned. This would probably not be sufficient nonfarm development to render the neighboring preserved farm unfit for farming.

As more tracts in agriculturally zoned areas are protected with conservation easements, the less likely it is that requests for rezoning will be granted on remaining agricultural land, especially in areas distant from public sewer and water.

Agricultural zoning tends to hold down the cost of conservation easements by reducing the development potential of a farm property.[39] The easement value is determined by an appraiser who estimates the current market value of the farm (also known as the before-easement value) and the value of the farm restricted to agriculture (or the after-easement value). The difference between the two values is the easement value itself. The market value of land zoned for agriculture is distinctly less than the value of land zoned for rural residential development. In 1997, the county paid approximately $2,000 an acre for easements. By comparison, to the east in Chester County, Pennsylvania, where there is almost no agricultural zoning, the average easement price was about $6,000 an acre.

In estimating the market value of land zoned for agriculture, the appraiser must determine the likelihood of a zoning change that would allow more development on the property in the near future.[40] For farmland beyond half a mile of public sewer and water, the likelihood of any rezoning in Lancaster County is remote.

Voluntary agricultural districts, or ASAs, currently cover 125,000 acres in the county and provide a further complement to agricultural zoning. Within the ASAs land is predominantly zoned for agriculture, and the state's right-to-farm law gives landowners some protection against eminent domain actions as well as making participating farms eligible for the PACE program.[41] ASAs are nonregulatory, however; they impose no restrictions on farmers. Land in an ASA need not be zoned for agriculture. Land in an ASA may be developed according to the local zoning.

Landowner Benefits from Selling or Donating a Conservation Easement

Financial Benefits from Selling

The most obvious benefit from the sale of a conservation easement is that the landowner receives a cash payment in return for the restrictions placed on the use of the farmland. The landowner retains ownership of the farm, which can be sold or passed on to heirs. The landowner can use the cash to buy down debt, reinvest in the farm operation, pay bills, or plan for a retirement. In addition, the value of the property is reduced in determining the value of an estate for federal estate tax purposes. There are no property tax benefits from selling or donating easements in Pennsylvania.

The cash payment for an easement is taxed as a capital gain. As of 1998, capital gains on property held for more than one year was 20 percent. In 2001, the rate on property held five or more years drops to 18 percent. In short, capital gains are taxed at a lower rate than ordinary income.

In addition, because the easement is taxed as a capital gain, by both the federal government and the state of Pennsylvania, the easement seller can deduct the basis in the farm from the easement payment.[42]

Easement Sale Example
250-Acre Farm:

$750,000	Appraised fair market value of farm
– $500,000	Appraised value restricted to farming or open space
$250,000	Appraised easement value and cash paid to landowner
– $170,000	Landowner's basis in farm
$80,000	Landowner's taxable capital gain

Capital gains tax due at 20 percent federal and 2.8 percent state = $18,240
Landowner's net return from easement sale = $231,760

The deductibility of the basis is especially attractive for young farmers who have recently purchased a farm and have a high basis. If the basis equals or exceeds the easement payment, the landowner can deduct the entire easement payment *and owe no federal capital gains taxes.*[43]

Both the Lancaster County Preserve Board and the LFT have the flexibility to make cash payments for easements in one lump sum or in installments spread out up to five years. The landowners generally receive 5 percent interest rate on the unpaid installments. Older farmers with a small basis often face a substantial capital gains tax bill from selling an easement. To avoid this, the Preserve Board sponsored a private letter ruling to get a determination from the IRS on the use of an easement payment in a "like-kind exchange."[44] Strictly speaking, a like-kind exchange allows for the exchange of real estate involved in business, trade, or investment and the deferral of any capital gains taxes that might be due.[45] The IRS first ruled that an easement is an interest in real estate and can be used in a like-kind exchange, and, second, the easement can be used to acquire any real estate involved in business, trade, or investment, such as more farmland or rental apartments.[46]

The most obvious use of the like-kind exchange is for the landowner to use the easement money to acquire additional farmland. Since the letter ruling, like-kind exchanges of this nature have been used several times in Lancaster County, throughout Pennsylvania, and in Delaware, New Jersey, and Vermont. Some older farmers, however, are not looking to expand their operations. Instead, they are planning to retire. Some of these farmers used the like-kind exchange provision to acquire rental units to give them an income stream for the future. One creative landowner used the like-kind exchange process to avoid the common situation in which parents leave a farm to several children and the farm is sold for development because one or more of the children wants to be "cashed out." He sold an easement, then through the like-kind exchange process acquired rental townhouses and sold the farm at a preferential price to his son who was already farming the property. Through imaginative use of the like-kind exchange, all children are now able to receive a legacy from their father: The farm was passed intact to the next generation, and the other children will receive the townhouses through their father's will.[47]

Financial Benefits from Donating

Donating an easement to a government agency or a qualified nonprofit 501(c)(3) organization makes financial sense for landowners who are in the highest income tax brackets or who possess estates worth over $2 million. A landowner can use the value of the easement to offset income up to a maximum of 30 percent of adjusted gross income in a particular year and can spread such offsets over a period of six successive years. One problem faced by retirees and farmers, with a small adjusted gross income and a large easement value, is that any portion of the deduction that a landowner cannot use over the six-year period will be lost.

Easement Donation Example[48]
200-Acre Farm

$600,000	Appraised fair market value
– $360,000	Appraised value restricted to farming or open space
$240,000	Appraised easement value

Landowner's adjusted gross income = $100,000

30 percent of adjusted gross income is the maximum deduction for one year, but the landowner can spread out the deductions up to six years.

$30,000 = maximum one-year deduction

$30,000 × 6.= maximum deduction over six years (assuming a constant adjusted gross income of $100,000 a year)

Total income tax savings ~ $55,000

Note: The landowner is able to use only $180,000 of the $240,000 donation. The remaining $60,000 donation is lost

In addition to income tax benefits, there are two potential estate tax benefits from donating a conservation easement to qualifying farmland. First, the value of the farm is reduced for estate tax purposes, just as with the sale of an easement. Estate taxes fall on individual estates worth over $625,000 in 1998. This unified credit threshold will rise to $1 million in 2007. Estate taxes start at a rate of 37 percent, rising to as much as 55 percent on estates worth $3 million. Second, Congress revised the IRS Code in 1997 to allow farmland owners within 25 miles of a metropolitan area who donated conservation easements to further reduce the value of their taxable estate.[49] Farm heirs may deduct an additional 40 percent off the value of the estate should the easement reduce the market value of the farm property by 30 percent or more.[50]

Estate Value Exclusion[51]

$1,000,000	Fair market value
− $700,000	Restricted agricultural value
$300,000	Easement value (30 percent diminution in value)

For estate tax value,
$700,000 - $280,000 (40 percent of $700,000) = **$420,000 farm estate tax value**

Should the easement reduce the value of the farm less than 30 percent, the 40 percent exclusion is reduced by 2 percent for each 1 percent short of the 30 percent level. For example, suppose a farmer owning land with a market value of $1 million donates an easement appraised at $200,000. The value of the farm is now $800,000, or 20 percent less than previously. The extra estate exclusion is 20 percent of $800,000, or $160,000. The total exclusion is the easement value plus the extra exclusion, or $360,000. The federal estate tax begins at 37 percent, so this would mean savings of at least $133,200.

These tax benefits pass on to heirs who continue to hold the farm property. Congress allows the landowner's executor to donate an easement, and reduce the estate value, after the landowner dies.

A Performance Evaluation of Lancaster County's Farmland Protection Efforts

In Lancaster County, both the public and private easement programs have made substantial progress toward protecting a "critical mass" of farmland. Together they have established large blocks of preserved land and have formed portions of established growth boundaries. These preservation strategies have served to reduce conversion pressures on farmland by promoting development that is more compact while simultaneously discouraging the extension of public sewer and water lines into productive farming areas. Over 28,000 acres of farmland have been preserved since 1983, and the rate of conversion has slowed from about 3,000 acres annually throughout the 1980s to about 1,500 acres a year in the 1990s.

To look at only the amount of farmland under easements in Lancaster County as an indicator of farmland preservation is somewhat misleading.

Strategies employed by individual farmers, the Lancaster County Agricultural Preserve Board, the LTA, and numerous local governments complement each other to create a sense of security for farmers and a sense of permanence for farmland. Often the knowledge that a neighboring farmer has encumbered the property with an easement, preserving it as a farm, will convince other farmers to remain in farming. This situation can be called the permanence syndrome, the opposite of the impermanence syndrome in which farmers reduce investment in their farms as they perceive the inevitable approach of development. The combination of ASAs and agricultural zoning serves to further strengthen the perception of permanence. Although it is possible for a township to rezone farmland in an ASA to a nonfarm use, most townships appear reluctant to allow such rezonings. Perhaps it is this sense of security that has led to the protection of over 330 farms in Lancaster County.

There are, however, some shortcomings to the Lancaster County program. First, only a relatively few landowners will receive easement payments because of limited funds. In addition, the payment benefits primarily the current generation, not future landowners. Second, in Pennsylvania, there are yet no property tax advantages to landowners for selling an easement. Farmland owners in Pennsylvania may qualify for use-value assessment, which results in the land being taxed at its agricultural use value rather than at its fair market value as development property. Although this generally keeps farm property taxes low, taxes are increasingly a determining factor in whether or not a landowner will continue to farm. Third, because of the voluntary nature of the easement programs, there is always a possibility that key properties will not be protected because the owners wish to hold out for eventual development.

Prices for farmland in Lancaster County continue to be high, averaging $5,000 to $6,000 an acre, creating difficulties not only for new farmers but also for existing farmers who wish to expand.[52] To date, the integrated package of agricultural zoning, ASAs, conservation easements (purchased and donated), and urban growth boundaries have served as a reliable farmland protection program. The real test will come in 2020, when an additional 150,000 people are expected to live in Lancaster County. The cost of farmland protection has been reasonable. Zoning and urban growth boundaries are low-cost techniques, and even easement purchases averaging $2,000 an acre appear to be good long-term investments, especially compared with easement costs in suburban Philadelphia counties, which average over $5,000 an acre.[53]

If farmland in Lancaster County is to be protected through the purchase of conservation easements, continued public support and funding is crucial. The general public and public officials are faced with essentially two choices. They can choose to invest in conservation easements and strive to maintain a viable farm economy and attractive rural landscape, forcing growth to concentrate in and around existing settlement centers. The other choice is to allow farmland to be developed and to spend substantial public funds on new roads, schools, sewer, and water lines required to service a sprawling settlement pattern.

The success of any farmland protection depends on farmland owners. In Lancaster County, landowners have demonstrated a strong commitment to remain in farming. This commitment is in part due to the presence of the Plain Sect community for whom farming is an integral part of their religion and culture, and partly because farmers perceive an opportunity to make a living in farming. Nevertheless, should the economics of farming become less attractive and the lure of development dollars rise, greater pressures will surely be brought to bear on agricultural zones. In such a scenario, public offers to purchase development rights might not be competitive with non-farm offers.

Notes

1. Julie Ann Gustanski, *Protecting Unique Land Resources: Tools, Techniques and Tax Advantages,* (Mt. Wolf, Penn.: 4Ever Land Conservation Associates, 1997).
2. Tom Daniels and D. Bowers, *Holding Our Ground: Protecting America's Farms and Farmland* (Washington, D.C.: Island Press, 1997), p. 10.
3. *Holding Our Ground,* p. 9.
4. *Holding Our Ground,* p. 10.
5. Growth management is generally considered a state, regional, county, or municipal government program to control the timing, location, type, and design of land development.
6. *Holding Our Ground,* p. 146.
7. J. A. Gustanski, data from unpublished research surveys conducted July 1996 through October 1997, orally reported in "The Issue of Private Lands: Land Trusts Mastering the Art of Innovation," paper presented at "Who Owns America II?" Conference, University of Wisconsin, Land Tenure Center, June 1998.
8. *Farmland Preservation Report* 4, no. 10 (July 1994).
9. A bargain sale occurs when a landowner sells an easement for less than the appraised value of the easement. The landowner in effect donates part of the easement value. PACE programs pay farmers to keep their land available for agriculture. Landowners sell an agricultural conservation easement to a qualified government agency or private conservation organization. Landowners retain full ownership and use of their land for agricultural purposes. PACE programs do not give government agencies the right to develop land. Development rights are essentially extinguished in exchange for compensation. PACE is also known as purchase of development rights (PDR) and as agricultural preservation restriction (APR) in Massachusetts.
10. Statistics from the American Farmland Trust, March 1998, and Farmland Preservation Report (unpublished data).

11. Section 388 of the Federal Agriculture Improvement and Reform Act of 1996.
12. A negative easement in effect tells a landowner what he or she cannot do with the land. An easement cannot require the landowner to raise certain crops as this that would impose what is referred to in legal parlance as an "affirmative obligation."
13. In an easement donation, a landowner may allow public access to show that the easement provides a public benefit and hence the value of the easement is tax deductible. Public access, however, is rarely required for an easement sale. Moreover, farmland is usually not accessible to the public, whether an easement is sold or donated.
14. The purpose of a soil conservation plan is to promote good management of preserved land.
15. A "critical mass" of farms and farmland will vary according to the type of agriculture. In general, as of the late 1990s, critical mass for a county is about $50 million in gross farm sales and 100,000 acres in farm use.
16. Thomas L. Daniels, "Policies to Preserve Prime Farmland in the USA: A Comment," *Journal of Rural Studies* 6, no. 3 (1990): 331–336.
17. Natural Resources Conservation Service, *Soil Survey of Lancaster County, Pennsylvania* (Washington, D.C.: U.S. Department of Agriculture, 1985); U.S. Department of Agriculture, *1992 Census of Agriculture* (Washington, D.C.: U.S. Department of Agriculture, 1992).
18. *1992 Census of Agriculture.*
19. Figures from the Lancaster County Chamber of Commerce, 1998.
20. United States Census statistics.
21. "America's New Boomtowns," *U.S. News & World Report,* April 11, 1994, pp. 62–69.
22. Lancaster County Planning Commission, 1998.
23. In the 1980s, Lancaster County lost farmland at a rate of about 3,000 acres per year.
24. "Life in Lancaster County," *Lancaster New Era,* March 21, 1995, p. 1.
25. These figures include both the Lancaster County Agricultural Preserve Board (250 easements and 23,000 acres preserved) and the private Lancaster Farmland Trust, as of June 1998 (85 easements and 5,412 acres preserved).
26. In Pennsylvania, sections 604(3) and 603 of the Municipal Planning Code requires municipalities to zone for the protection of prime agriculture and farmland. In fact, some counties have widely adopted various forms of agricultural zoning ordinances, and the State Court has upheld both fixed area based allocation and sliding scale area based agricultural zoning ordinances against claims that they deprived landowners of property without substantive due process. *Boundary Drive Associates v. Shrewsbury Township Board of Supervisors,* 507 Pa. 481, 491 A. 2d. 86 (Pa. 1985); J. A. Gustanski, *Protecting Unique Land Resources: Tools, Techniques and Tax Advantages for Pennsylvania Landowners,* (Mt. Wolf, Penn.: 4Ever Land Conservation Associates, 1997).
    Agricultural zoning is a form of local land use regulation Such ordinances are designed to protect the agricultural land base by limiting nonfarm uses, prohibiting high-density development, requiring houses to be built on small lots and

restricting subdivision of land into parcels that are too small to farm. Agricultural zoning can take many forms. Exclusive agriculture zoning acts to prohibit non-farm residences and most nonagricultural activities; exceptions are made for parcels that are not suitable for farming. Large lot zoning requires a certain number of acres for every nonfarm dwelling (i.e., 20-acre house lots). Variation in acreage is found across the United States. Under sliding scale zoning, the number of dwellings permitted varies with the size of the tract. Owners of smaller parcels are allowed to divide their land into more lots on a per-acre basis than owners of larger parcels. Area or density-based zoning establishes a formula for the number of nonfarm dwellings permitted per acre, but houses are generally built on small lots. Fixed area–based zoning specifies a certain number of acres per unit.

27. In 1980, the Lancaster County Commissioners created the Agricultural Preserve Board. The nine-member board includes at least four farmers, a county commissioner, a township supervisor, a member from the building industry, and two at-large members.

28. 3 Pa. Cons. Stat. §§ 901–915. Short title "Agricultural Area Security Law" Agricultural Area Security Act of 1981, P.L. 128, No. 43, with amendments.

29. The county easement program began receiving additional funds in 1989 from the statewide PACE program.

30. Under the Federal Farmland Protection Program, section 388 of the Federal Agriculture Improvement and Reform Act of 1996.

31. See *Holding Our Ground*, pp. 293–294.

32. See Agricultural Area Security Law, note 28.

33. 3 Pa. Cons. Stat. 914.

34. See note 26.

35. A growth boundary is drawn around a city or village with the aim of providing enough buildable land for the next twenty years within the boundary, and urban services—particularly public sewer and water—will not be extended beyond the boundary.

36. See Lancaster County Planning Commission, Urban Growth Boundary Map.

37. Sections 604(3) and 605 of the Pennsylvania Municipalities Planning Code give authority to municipalities for zoning.

38. Thirty-nine of the county's forty-one townships have zoned land for agricultural use.

39. The cash value of an easement is based on the difference between the sale price of farms without easements and the sale price of farms with easements, a price that reflects the restricted agricultural value of the farm.

40. According to standard appraisal practice.

41. See 3 Pa. Cons. Stat. §§ 901–915.

42. Basis is what a landowner paid for the property plus improvements minus depreciation. Basis in both land and buildings can be deducted (see Revenue Ruling 77-414). If the easement payment is $250,000 and the basis is $170,000, the taxable gain is $80,000 and the federal capital gains tax due is $16,000 (20 percent of $80,000). State capital gains tax also applies.

43. The help of an experienced accountant is always recommended in determining a landowner's basis.
44. Section 1031 of the IRS Code.
45. IRS Letter Rulings 92-15049 and 92-32030.
46. IRS Letter Rulings 92-15049 and 92-32030.
47. The service of an attorney experienced in section 1031 exchanges is essential. If the exchange property remains in the landowner's estate and then passes to heirs, the heirs will receive a stepped-up basis on the property and there may be no capital gains or estate taxes due, depending on the value of the landowner's overall estate.
48. This is for illustration only. Consultation with an attorney is strongly recommended.
49. American Farm and Ranch Protection Act, § 508 of P.L. 105-34, the Taxpayer Relief Act of 1997; see also J. A. Gustanski, *Protecting Unique Land Resources,* pp. 22–24.
50. Section 2031(c) of the IRS Code.
51. See Agricultural Area Security Law, note 28.
52. Lancaster County Agricultural Preserve Board, *1997 Farm Sales Analysis,* March 1998.
53. Bucks, Chester, Montgomery, and Delaware Counties in "suburban" Philadelphia area.

Chapter 11

🎗 🍂

Conservation Easements in the Fourth Federal Circuit

*T. Heyward Carter Jr., W. Leighton Lord III,
and Chalmers W. Poston Jr.*

The states in the Fourth Federal Circuit are all common-law jurisdictions and thus have a historic similarity in their treatment of real property (Figure 11.1). Despite such similarity, however, they have enacted statutes enabling conservation easements, or similar agreements, that are as varied as the natural landscapes of the region. Table 11.1 reflects the differences in terminology applied to easements and how they protect various lands throughout the circuit. Although South Carolina, Virginia, and West Virginia have enacted versions of the Uniform Conservation Easement Act (UCEA), each state has modified it to some extent and have enacted other conservation-related legislation specific to its needs.

South Carolina has adopted the UCEA with the fewest modifications. To augment this conservation easement legislation, the South Carolina General Assembly has also enacted the Scenic Rivers Program and the Heritage Trust Program. On the other hand, Virginia and West Virginia have made substantial modifications to the version of the UCEA adopted in each state. Virginia and West Virginia have also augmented the conservation easement legislation with additional legislation aimed at preserving the natural environment. Prior to the enactment of the Virginia Conservation Easement Act, the General Assembly of the Commonwealth of Virginia enacted the Open Space Land Act. Following the adoption of the Conservation and Preservation Easement Act in West Virginia, West Virginia enacted the West Virginia Stream Partners Program. Table 11.2 gives a comparison of laws as they pertain to what conservation easements are to protect within respective states.

Although Maryland and North Carolina have not enacted the UCEA; each has enacted legislation that allows for land protection. Maryland has long been an activist state at the forefront of the land protection movement and

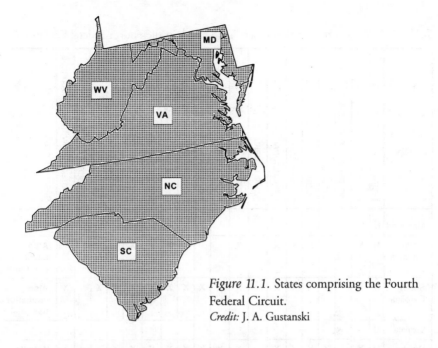

Figure 11.1. States comprising the Fourth Federal Circuit.
Credit: J. A. Gustanski

Table 11.1. How Conservation Easements Protect Land in the Fourth Federal Circuit

State	UCEA	Negative Rights	Affirmative Rights	Holder's Right of Access	Non-Possessory Interest	Restriction	Easement	Covenant	Condition	Equitable Servitude	Interest in Land	Incorporeal Right	Interest in Property	Contractual Right
Maryland	N	X				X	X	X	X			X		
North Carolina	N	X				X	X	X	X		X			
South Carolina	U	X	X		X	X	X	X		X				
Virginia	U	X	X		X		X							
West Virginia	U	X	X		X	X	X	X		X				

U = Conservation easement legislation directly influenced by UCEA.
N = Conservation easement legislation absent or not influenced by UCEA.

Table 11.2. What Conservation Easements Protect in the Fourth Federal Circuit

STATE	UCEA	HOLDER'S PURPOSES	HOLDER'S PURPOSES ARE:	NATURAL	SCENIC	OPEN SPACE	AGRICULTURAL	SILVICULTURAL	FOREST	RECREATIONAL	AIR QUALITY	WATER QUALITY/WATER AREA	HISTORICAL	ARCHITECTURAL	ARCHEOLOGICAL	PALEONTOLOGICAL	CULTURAL	CONSERVATION OF LAND	PROTECTING NATURAL RESOURCES	SPECIAL NOTES
Maryland	N																			Silent
North Carolina	N	X		X	X	X	X		X				X	X	X					Also horticulture and farming
South Carolina	U	X		X	X	X	X		X	X	X	X	X	X	X		X		X	Also educational use
Virginia	U																			
West Virginia	U	X		X	X	X	X		X	X	X	X	X	X	X		X		X	Wildlife

U = Conservation easement legislation directly influenced by UCEA.
N = Conservation easement legislation absent or not influenced by UCEA.

has many unique programs designed to encourage land protection. The Maryland statutory scheme allows for the creation of conservation easements and tax credits, but Maryland has also enacted governmental programs such as the Wildland and Open Area Act, the Heritage Conservation Fund, and the Rural Legacy Program, each of which has a goal of preserving the natural environment.

North Carolina has not officially adopted the UCEA, but it has embraced the major components of the UCEA through the Conservation and Historic Preservation Agreements Act. Although labeled "agreements" in the North Carolina Act, North Carolina allows for the creation of comprehensive instruments to protect both the natural environment and points of historical significance.

Thus, states of the Fourth Federal Circuit have not adopted the UCEA unanimously, and those that have have modified the act to varying degrees. Nonetheless, each offers extensive opportunities to protect land of natural or historical significance (see Table 11.2). Although the Fourth Federal Circuit represents diversity in the approaches to protecting land, the central theme in

the circuit is legislative support for conservation by offering extensive opportunities and benefits for land protection.

Maryland

Maryland legislature has been in the forefront of the land protection movement. Maryland, a densely populated state with an abundance of natural
resources, has long had a stated governmental policy of encouraging the
preservation of wildland and open spaces. Although Maryland has not
adopted the UCEA, the major components in the act, allowing conservation
easements and permitting them to qualify for property tax credits, are part of
Maryland's statutory scheme. In addition, Maryland has enacted governmental programs such as the Wildland and Open Areas Act, the Heritage Conservation Fund, and Rural Legacy Land Program, all with the goal of preserving
natural areas.

Conservation Easements in General

Since 1957, Maryland has permitted the creation and enforcement of private
conservation easements.[1] The statute allows landowners to create and enforce conservation easements to preserve water or land areas by restricting
building, signage, dumping, dredging, removal of vegetation, and other acts
that interfere with the preservation of land areas or the structures built on
them. As with other easements on real property, conservation easements must
be executed in a manner similar to the execution of deeds or wills. Extinguishment or release occurs in the same manner as well.

   If the grant clearly indicates the maker's intention to allow public use of
any property to preserve the agricultural, historical, or environmental qualities of the property, but fails to specify a donee or specifies a donee that is not
legally capable of accepting such an interest, the grant passes to the Maryland
Agricultural Land Preservation Foundation, the Maryland Historical Trust,
or the Maryland Environmental Trust.

   Although Maryland allows conservation easements to be created, it has
only allowed property tax credits for such easements since July 1, 1991. Moreover, a property tax credit is only allowed if the conservation easement is certified by the Maryland Environmental Trust as encumbering "conservation
land," subject to a perpetual easement that is held be a land trust—essentially,
a qualified conservation organization exempt from federal taxation under
Internal Revenue Code section 501(c)(3)—or subject to an agreement to sell
to a government agency, and if the property tax credit has been granted by the
governing body of the local county or city where the property is located.[2]
Conservation land is defined as land used to assist (1) in preserving of a natural area, (2) in environmental education, (3) in generally promoting conser-

vation, or (4) in maintaining a natural area for public use or a sanctuary for wildlife.[3] Each governing body of a county may also specify the amount and duration of the property tax credit. Notably, every five years, the Maryland Environmental Trust must renew in writing the certificate that qualifies conservation land.[4]

Government-Sponsored Programs

Wildland and Open Areas Act. As far back as 1957, Maryland enacted the Wildland and Open Areas Act with the stated purpose "to secure for the people of present and future generations the benefits of an enduring resource of State wildlands."[5] The act established a state wildlands preservation system, allowing public funds to be spent to acquire open space and wildlands. The act also allows the Department of Natural Resources to accept gifts, purchase conservation or scenic easements, and purchase fee interests in the name of the state. In addition, the act allows the purchase of recreational access easements by local governments.

Maryland Environmental Trust. Also established in 1957, the Maryland Environmental Trust was created to conserve the aesthetic, natural, health and welfare, scenic, and cultural qualities of the environment, including land, water, air, wildlife, scenic qualities, and open space and to promote continuing interest in and the study of these matters.[6] Managed by a fifteen-person board of directors, the trust can acquire and hold real property and is charged with certifying that real property subject to a conservation easement is eligible for a property tax deduction.

In addition, the Maryland Environmental Trust administers a Land Trust Grant Fund, a revolving fund making grants to land trusts to encourage the preservation and protection of open space and natural areas in the state.[7] Although not a requirement in making grants, the trust is to consider the amount of funds contributed as a match by a land trust and the amount of funds contributed by other parties.[8] Generally, the trust requires the granting of a conservation easement or reversionary interest in favor of the trust as a condition of the grant, and grants must be repaid to the trust upon subsequent sale or transfer of the property.[9]

Heritage Conservation Fund. Established in 1986, the Heritage Conservation Fund enables the state to acquire fee title or other interests, including conservation easements in wetlands, wilderness areas, scenic areas, and unique ecological areas.[10] General funds of the state, under the control of the Department of Natural Resources, together with special bond authorization may be used to acquire and manage suitable lands.

Rural Legacy Land Program. A new tool in the Maryland land preservation-ists' toolbox is the Rural Legacy Land Program, which is intended to dramat-ically increase the pace of land conservation. The mission of the program is to protect "rural legacy areas," defined as regions "rich in a multiple of agri-cultural, forestry, natural and cultural resources."[11] Its goals are to protect large contiguous tracts of land and other strategic areas from sprawl and development and to enhance natural resource, agricultural, forestry, and environmental protection through cooperative efforts among the state gov-ernments, local governments, and land trusts. Of note, under this program, state or local condemnation authority may not be used to acquire real prop-erty interests. Funds may be used to protect historic sites or significant arche-ological areas that otherwise meet the goals of the program only if the spon-sor is acquiring the fee title through purchase.

Through the Rural Legacy Land Program, the state provides funds to both local governments and land trusts to acquire interests in real property, includ-ing easements, in designated rural legacy areas. A board of directors com-posed of representatives of government, conservation organizations, and pri-vate industry has the responsibility of designating rural legacy areas. The Department of Natural Resources provide staff for the Rural Legacy Land Program with assistance from the Department of Agriculture and the Office of Planning. Sponsors, one or more local governments, or land trusts endorsed by local governments may make application to the Rural Legacy Land Program for grants. The application requires detailed information, including a description of the area, an identification of existing protected lands, the anticipated level of initial landowner participation in the program, and the proposed grant amount. A rural legacy plan outlining future man-agement must also be completed.

The board of directors considers applications based on criteria such as (1) the significance of the agricultural, forestry, and natural resources proposed for protection; (2) the degree of threat to the resources and character of the area, as reflected by patterns and trends of development and landscape mod-ifications in and surrounding the area; (3) the significance and extent of the cultural resources proposed for protection through fee simple purchases; (4) the economic value of resource-based industries or services proposed for pro-tection through land conservation; (5) the strength and quality of partner-ships created for land conservation among federal, state, and local govern-ments and land trusts; and (6) the sponsor's ability to carry out the proposed rural legacy plan.[12] The Maryland Legislature has provided $71.3 million for the Rural Legacy Land Program for fiscal years 1998 through 2002. Of this, $23 million will come from general obligation bonds, $18.3 million from a scheduled 10 percent increase in the existing real estate transfer tax revenue for open space available to Program Open Space, and $30 million from the stateside land acquisition budget of Program Open Space.

In June 1998, the board of directors of the Rural Legacy Land Program designated 2,700 acres as rural legacy areas and secured over $8.250 million from the state to purchase conservation easements. This program is expected to protect up to 200,000 acres by 2011.

Conclusion

Maryland has long recognized the public good accomplished through land preservation and has enacted various programs to accomplish its conservation-related policies since 1957. Maryland has provided for the beneficial creation of conservation easements and has established programs that encourage the state, local governments, conservation organizations, and individuals to acquire conservation land and to work with landowners to meet conservation policy goals.

North Carolina

North Carolina has not officially adopted the provisions of the UCEA. Nonetheless, it has embraced many of its major components through the Conservation and Historic Preservation Agreement Act designed to encourage and facilitate conservation easements. In addition, the legislature has established a Conservation Grant Fund to further promote the use of conservation easements.

Conservation and Historic Preservation Agreement Act

In North Carolina, the main act dealing with conservation easements is the Conservation and Historic Preservation Agreement Act.[13] Rather than label the interests created as a "conservation easement," North Carolina designates such interests as "conservation agreements." A conservation agreement refers to a right, whether or not stated in the form of a restriction, reservation, easement, covenant, or condition, in any deed, will, or other instrument executed by or on behalf of (1) the owner of the land or improvement on the land or (2) the state as owner through a taking. The General Statutes of North Carolina section 121-35(1) describes such conservation agreements as serving the purpose of retaining land or water areas in their natural, scenic, or open condition or in agriculture, horticultural, farming, or forest use and forbids or limits activities such as placing structures on the land and dumping wastes and any activities that affect the natural drainage.

In addition to conservation agreements, the act allows landowners to create a preservation agreement. Preservation agreements are instruments, whether or not stated in the form of a restriction, reservation, easement, covenant, condition, or otherwise, in any deed, will, or other instrument executed by or on behalf of the owner of the land, or any order of taking, appropriate to preserving a structure or a site of historical significant for its architecture, archaeology, or historical associations.[14] Preservation agreements are defined to forbid or limit (1) alteration in features of a structure, (2) changes in appearance or condition of a site, (3) use not historically appropriate, or (4) things generally detrimental to preservation.[15]

North Carolina specifies that entities able to accept and maintain both conservation and preservation agreements are: (1) public bodies of the state, which include the state and its agencies, local governments such as cities, counties, and districts, and municipal and public corporations; (2) any agency, department, or instrumentality of the United States; (3) any non-profit corporation or trust; and (4) any private corporation or business entity whose purposes include any of those listed in N.C. General Statutes section 121-35 (3) and (4).[16]

All agreements falling within the terms and conditions of the act must comply with N.C. General Statutes section 121-36. The act, however, cannot be construed as making any restriction, easement, covenant, or condition not complying with the act unenforceable. In addition, the act specifically states that in no way does the act diminish the eminent domain power of any entity authorized with such power.

Furthermore, the act offers a broad statutory method for creating agreements. Section 121-37 states that "any holder may, in any manner, acquire, receive or become a party of the Agreements." Thus, any legal entity that can hold agreements can create and acquire agreement in virtually any manner desired. Section 121-38(b) states that the agreements are interests in land and can be acquired by any holder in the same manner as other interests in land. Table 11.3 reflects on the differences applied to the eligibility of holders by states of the Fourth Federal Circuit.

Like the Uniform Act, the act also includes a section to guarantee the validity of any agreements from common-law defenses that could affect the use of easements for conservation or preservation. Section 121-38 states that the agreements shall not be found unenforceable because of lack or privity of estate or contract, lack of benefit to particular land or person, and the assignability of the benefits to another holder.[17]

North Carolina allows considerable flexibility in the duration of agreements. Section 121-38(c) and (d) allows them to be perpetual or for a period of time if stipulated in the agreement. The agreements may impose present, future, or continuing obligations on the parties to the agreement or their successors. See Table 11.4 for a comparative review of the terminology as it affects the issue of duration across the Fourth Federal Circuit states.

Table 11.3. Who May Hold Conservation Easements in the Fourth Federal Circuit

STATE	UCEA	GOVERNMENT	CHARITABLE TRUST	CHARITABLE ASSOCIATON	CHARITABLE CORPORATION	SECTION 501 (c)(3) TAX-EXEMPT ORGANIZATION	SPECIAL NOTES
Maryland	N						
North Carolina	N	X	X		X		**Also, private corporation or business**
South Carolina	U	X	X	X	X[a]		**[a] Charitable not-for-profit or educational organization**
Virginia	U	X	X	X	X	X	**Implied but not stated**
West Virginia	U	X	X	X	X	X	

U = Conservation easement legislation directly influenced by UCEA.
N = Conservation easement legislation absent or not influenced by UCEA.

All holders of agreements possess the right to enforce the terms specified in the agreements by either injunction or other equitable relief administered by the North Carolina courts. Damages or other monetary relief may be awarded to the holder, the grantor, or his or her successors for violating any of the obligations mentioned in an agreement. Accordingly, section 121-39(b) allows representatives of the holder to gain access to the encumbered land or improvement in a reasonable manner and at reasonable times to ensure compliance.

North Carolina offers tax advantages for any landowner creating an agreement. Real property subject to an agreement is to be assessed at the true value of land or improvement reduced by any reduction in value caused by the agreement. *Rainbow Springs Partnership v. County of Macon* addressed the issue of calculating the assessed value of land encumbered with a conservation easement.[18] The case involved 2,252.2 acres owned by a partnership that conveyed a conservation easement on a portion of the land to The Nature Conservancy. The court stated that the true value of the property was its market value, as that term is defined in the state's General Statutes section 105-283, before the easement was created. In the court's determination, the highest and best use of the land was for a hunt club and not development, as argued by plaintiffs. The assessed value was thus the market value less the

Table 11.4. Duration of Conservation Easements in the Fourth Federal Circuit

State	Perpetual by Default	Term by Default	Silent
Maryland			X
North Carolina	Not available	Not available	
South Carolina	X		
Virginia	X		
West Virginia		25 years	

reduction caused by the easement. As shown in *Rainbow Springs,* calculating the assessed value of a property that materially affects the benefit derived by a landowner granting the agreement is based on expert valuation. Perhaps an appropriate course of action is for the parties concerned in agreements and the state to agree on the market values prior to creating and conveying any easements to avoid such litigation.

To enhance the enforceability of conservation agreements, North Carolina requires that conservation agreements be recorded in the office of the Register of Deeds in the county where the agreements are created. Actions that affect the agreement, such as termination, must also be recorded.

Conservation Easements Program

North Carolina has also enacted a Conservation Easement Program. In 1997, the legislature authorized the Department of Environment and Natural Resources to (1) create a "statewide network of protected natural areas, riparian buffers, and greenways" and to promote its public use by encouraging and facilitating conservation easements and (2) support the efforts of nonprofit land trusts participating in land and water conservation.[19] The nonregulatory program uses conservation tax credits to facilitate initiatives aimed at protecting land through conservation easements, including those agreements created under the Conservation and Historic Preservation Agreement Act.

Conservation Grant Fund

The General Statutes of North Carolina section 113A-232, enacted in 1997, creates a Conservation Grant Fund within the Department of Environment and Natural Resources. The purpose of the fund is to stimulate the use of conservation easements to improve the capability of private non-profit land trusts to successfully accomplish conservation projects, to better equip real estate related professionals to pursue opportunities for conservation, to increase citizen participation in land and water conservation, and to provide an opportunity to leverage private and other public monies for conservation easements.

Appropriations from the General Assembly together with other public and private sources will finance the fund. For land to be eligible for a grant from the Fund, it must (1) possess, or is likely to possess, ecological value; (2) be reasonably restorable; and (3) qualify for tax credits. To receive a grant through the fund, a private nonprofit land trust organization must qualify under both sections 105-13.34 and 105-15.12 and be a section 501(c)(3) charity under the Internal Revenue Code.

A grant from the fund cannot be used by land trusts to pay the purchase price for any interest in land but only to reimburse transaction costs incurred in donating conservation easements and then only if (1) an individual or a corporation is unable to pay the costs or earns insufficient taxable income to allow them to be included in the donated value or (2) an individual or a corporation possessed insufficient tax burdens to allow the costs to be offset by the value of tax credits by charitable deductions, management support, monitoring costs, educational information on conservation, stewardship of land, additional transaction costs such as legal fees, closing costs, and title costs, and administration costs for short-term growth or for building capacity.

The department is empowered to establish procedures and criteria for awarding grants and administers the fund. The secretary of the department has final decision-making authority on awarding the grants.

Conclusion

Although North Carolina has not adopted the UCEA per se, the programs in place incorporate the major provisions of the act and allow conservation or preservation agreements to be created.

South Carolina

With few modifications, South Carolina adopted the UCEA as the South Carolina Conservation Easement Act of 1991 and incorporated it into Chapter 8, Title 27 of the 1976 Code.[20] The state possesses two other programs that similarly protect property. The Scenic Rivers Program encourages riparian landowners to voluntarily donate land or conservation easements to protect lands in the catchment area of six designated river corridors within the state.

The Heritage Trust Program is designed to inventory and subsequently manage unique and outstanding natural or cultural areas and features in South Carolina.

South Carolina Conservation Easement Act of 1991

Only minor variances exist between the UCEA and the South Carolina Conservation Easement Act of 1991.[21] The primary differences are that South Carolina's legislation includes a provision dealing with the conveyance of easements to governmental bodies and a provision that requires the easement to be recorded in the local register of deeds before any rights pass to a holder. Unless unconstitutional, its provisions apply to those real property interests created before the effective date of the act that would have been enforceable if created after May 27, 1991. The official comments to the UCEA have not been adopted.

Scenic Rivers Program

South Carolina has also established two programs to promote land protection—in line with the objectives of the conservation easement legislation. In 1974, the South Carolina General Assembly created the Scenic Rivers Program to protect designated scenic rivers across the state.[22] South Carolina's Scenic Rivers Program encourages riparian landowners within specific river corridors to voluntarily contribute fee title or conservation easements to the state. The state updated its Scenic Rivers Program when it enacted the Scenic Rivers Act of 1989. The act maintains the voluntary aspects of the 1974 legislation and, at the same time, tries to encourage broader landowner participation by creating a Scenic Rivers Trust Fund that provides more options for landowners interested in protecting their land. Prior to this legislation, landowners registered their land with the state, signed a memorandum of agreement with the state, and donated or sold a conservation easement or donated the title to the state. The Scenic Rivers Act of 1989 provides significant income and property tax incentives. A landowner who donates a conservation easement to the state receives (1) a state income tax deduction equal to the fair market value of the easement and (2) complete exemption from real property taxes due on the land covered by the easement.

Heritage Trust Program

In 1976, the General Assembly enacted the South Carolina Heritage Trust Program. The act was revised in 1993 and codified at S.C. Code sections 51-17-10 to 150 (Supp. 1997). The purpose of the Heritage Trust Program is to take inventory and subsequently manage unique and outstanding natural or cultural areas and features in South Carolina. Property owners of such areas and features may establish a heritage preserve by donating the fee title, a conservation easement, or an open-space easement to the state Department of Natural Resources. Landowners must also sign a Dedication Agreement regarding use of the property. In a private letter ruling, the IRS has found donations to the Heritage Trust Program to be qualifying donations under Internal Revenue Code section 170(h).

Case Law

There are currently no reported cases interpreting any provision of the South Carolina Conservation Act of 1991, the Scenic Rivers Act of 1989, or the Heritage Trust Program.

Conclusion

In addition to adopting statewide conservation easement enabling legislation, South Carolina has established two programs that serve to complement and further land protection efforts by encouraging individual landowners to create and convey conservation easements. Although the state may become the holder of the easement under certain circumstances, the plethora of active conservation organizations illustrates the dynamic and growing role being played by nongovernmental groups.

Virginia

Virginia's Conservation Easement Act was enacted by the General Assembly of the Commonwealth of Virginia in 1988.[23] Although the General Assembly substantially adopted the major provisions of the UCEA, several modifications were made. The official comments to the UCEA have not been adopted.

Open Space Land Act

The Open Space Land Act, enacted in 1966, was the first Virginia statute to provide for the creation of easements in Virginia.[24] The act authorizes any state agency having authority to acquire land for a public use, any county or municipality, any park authority, any public recreational facilities authority, any soil and water conservation district, or the Virginia Recreational Facilities Authority to acquire interests in land to preserve open space. These public bodies can acquire interests in various ways, but they must be acquired for a period of at least five years and must preserve open space by (1) protecting natural, historic, or scenic resources, including wetlands; (2) creating or preserving land for recreational purposes in an urban area; and (3) assisting in community development.

The Open Space Land Act is important to remember because the Virginia General Assembly has stated that if other provisions of the Virginia Conservation Easement laws are inconsistent with the Open Space Land Act, then the provision of the Open Space Land Act will control.

The Recreational Facilities Authority has specific powers necessary or convenient to carry out the purposes of the Open Space Land Act, including the authority to designate and use any real property in which it possesses an interest to provide and preserve open space. Thus, this public body can accept public funds, borrow money and make loans, and make contracts. It may demolish or dispose of structures considered detrimental to open-space purposes. It can also acquire a range of real property interests to maintain open-space lands. The Recreational Facilities Authority may acquire unrestricted fee simple title, fee simple title with a reservation of agricultural or timber rights, or easements in gross or other interests in real property, for example. None of these interests may be owned for fewer than five years. To appease agricultural interests, Virginia charged the authority with making special effort to maintain agricultural and timber uses of the acquired property.

The Recreational Facilities Authority has the authority to convey or lease open-space land. It is limited, however. Any interests acquired under this act will not be converted or diverted from open-space land unless such action is determined essential to the orderly development and growth of the locality where the land is located. In addition, the use to which it is converted must be in accordance with the current official comprehensive plan for the locality. Moreover, if land is converted or diverted, the authority must acquire other real property nearby having similar fair market value or greater value as permanent open-space land and having equivalent utility as the converted land. The authority has the affirmative duty to ensure that the substituted property will be subject to the provision of the act. The Recreational Facilities Authority is little used and considered by most as an avenue of last resort.

Virginia Conservation Easement Act

The Virginia Conservation Easement Act, enacted in 1988, begins with a substantial adoption of the definitions in the UCEA.[25] The General Assembly, however, specifically stated that a conservation easement, whether easement appurtenant or in gross, acquired through gift, purchase, devise, or bequest, is a nonpossessory interest in real property.

The Virginia act specifically requires an easement holder, other than a nonpublic body, to be a charitable corporation, charitable association, or charitable trust that is exempt from taxation under 26 U.S.C. section 501(c)(3). The charitable entity must also have certain primary purposes or powers, including those listed in the UCEA but excluding scenic and cultural values. Hence, Virginia defines a charitable entity able to acquire and hold conservation easement much more narrowly than the UCEA.

In addition, Virginia strictly defines those public bodies that can acquire conservation easements. Only state agencies having authority to acquire land for a public use, counties or municipalities, park authorities, public recreational facilities authorities, soil and water conservation districts, and the Virginia Recreational Facilities Authority may hold conservation easements. The Virginia act contains the same language as the UCEA concerning third-party right of enforcement.

Virginia's act states that a qualified charity or public body may acquire a conservation easement by gift, purchase, devise, or bequest. The act retains other language found in the UCEA (1) allowing a conservation easement to be created, conveyed, recorded, assigned, released, modified, terminated, or otherwise altered or affected in the same manner as other easements and (2) stipulating that no right or duty in favor of or against either a charitable entity, public body, or person having a third-party right of enforcement arises until the conservation easement has been accepted by the holder and the acceptance has been recorded. Table 11.5 identifies how states of this circuit have addressed third-party rights of enforcement.

Like the UCEA, the language of the act stipulates that the easement will be perpetual unless a contrary intent is specified in the instrument creating the easement. For an easement to be perpetual, however, the act requires that (1) the charitable entity acquiring the easement be a section 501(c)(3) charity, organized for the purposes stipulated in the Act and possessing the specified powers and (2) the charitable entity must have had a principal office in Vir-

Table 11.5. Third-Party Enforcement Rights in the Fourth Federal Circuit

STATE	UCEA	THIRD-PARTY ENFORCEMENT	NO STATUTORY REFERENCE
Maryland	N		X
North Carolina	N		X
South Carolina	U	X	
Virginia	U	X	
West Virginia	U	X	

U = Conservation easement legislation directly influenced by UCEA.
N = Conservation easement legislation absent or not influenced by UCEA.

ginia for at least five years (see also Table 11.2). This requirement was intended to prevent an easement being granted to a "fly-by-night" organization that would accept an easement and then not be around to enforce the easement.

Virginia's act states that an interest in real property existing at the time the easement is created cannot be impaired unless the owner of the interest is either (1) a party to the easement or (2) consents to the easement in writing. The requirement that the consent be in writing differs from the UCEA, which simply requires consent. Another requirement falling outside the UCEA is that no conservation easement is valid and enforceable in Virginia unless the limitations or obligations described in the easement conform in all respects to the comprehensive plan in place at the time the easement was created. Hence, a drafter of an easement must be certain that the restrictions on land use are not inconsistent with the general land use plan for the area in which the real property burdened by the conservation easement is located. Virginia intended for this section to facilitate comprehensive land use planning.

Virginia's act adheres to the language found in the UCEA and states that the creation of a conservation easement does not impact the power of a court to modify or terminate an easement in accordance with principles of law and equity or in any way limit the power of eminent domain. Table 11.6 shows how state enabling laws in the Fourth Federal Circuit have addressed issues pertaining to termination, modification, assignability, and release of a conservation easement.

Under the Virginia act, if the conservation easement is perpetual, the interest of a qualifying charitable entity, public body, or the holder of a third-party right of enforcement is not subject to state or local taxation, and the owner of the fee cannot be taxed for those interests either. Virginia is one of the few states whose statutory language specifically identifies that land subject to a perpetual conservation easement is to be taxed in accordance with its use. Those lands subject to a perpetual conservation easement created under the Virginia Conservation Easement Act or the Open Space Land Act, devoted to open-space use as defined in Va. Code Ann. section 58.1-3230, and located in a county, city, or town that assesses and taxes land pursuant to Va. Code Ann. section 58.1-3231 or section 58.1-3232 will be assessed as open space and taxed accordingly, if the land qualifies at the time the easement is created. If the conservation easement exists prior to a county, city, or town enacting such a policy, the conservation easement will qualify for the assessment. In addition, once the easement qualifies for land use assessment, the easement will continue to qualify as long as the county, city, or town employs such a policy.[26]

Unlike the UCEA, Virginia requires that the party responsible for recording an easement created after July 1, 1988, mail certified copies of the instru-

Table 11.6. Permissible Terminations, Modifications, and Assignment of Conservation Easements in the Fourth Federal Circuit

STATE	UCEA	RELEASED	TERMINATED	TERMINATION BY COURT (UNDER THE PRINCIPLES OF LAW AND EQUITY)	TERMINATION BY TAKING	ABANDONED	TERMINATED BY MERGER	MODIFIED	MODIFIED BY COURT	ASSIGNABLE	SPECIAL NOTES
Maryland	N	X	X							X	
North Carolina	N	X	X		X					X	
South Carolina	U	X	X	X				X	X	X	
Virginia	U	X	X	X	X			X	X	X	**Compensation required**
West Virginia	U	X	X	Xª				X	Xª	X	**ªIf consistent with public policy**

U = Conservation easement legislation directly influenced by UCEA.
N = Conservation easement legislation absent or not influenced by UCEA.

ment conveying the easement, together with notice as to when and where the easement was recorded, (1) to the local jurisdiction in which the real property subject to the easement is located, (2) to the attorney general of the Commonwealth of Virginia, (3) to the Virginia Outdoors Foundation, and (4) to any public body named in the instrument conveying the easement. Once the easement is recorded, certified copies of recorded documents must again be mailed to all parties. If lands that are part of a historic landmark, as certified by the U.S. government or the Virginia Historic Landmarks Board, are the subject of a conservation easement, all required notices described above must also be sent to the Historic Landmarks Board.

Virginia expands upon the UCEA listing of parties able to bring an action to enforce a conservation easement and requires that the third-party right of enforcement must have standing. Those agencies and/or bodies include (1) an owner of an interest in real property burdened by the easement; (2) the charitable entity or public body holding the easement; (3) a person having an express third-party right of enforcement; (4) the Attorney General of the commonwealth; (5) the Virginia Outdoors Foundation; (6) the Virginia Historic Landmarks Board; (7) the local government in which the real property is located; or (8) any other governmental agency or person with standing under other statutes or common law.

Virginia has adopted Section 4 of the UCEA, ensuring the validity of conservation easements regardless of how the common law treats them. The act removes the common-law problems associated with such easements, such as the imposition of a negative burden, that could render an easement void.

Section 10.1-1015 of the Virginia act stipulates that when a charitable organization holding an easement ceases to exist, both the easement and the right to enforce the easement will vest in the Virginia Outdoors Foundation unless the instrument creating the easement provides for transfer to another entity. Such language both requires grantors to consider alternative provisions in the event that a land trust is dissolved and conservation easements to make explicit provisions. In the absence of any provisions, the state acquires the easement. Any successor charitable organization must be a section 501(c)(3) charity and with a principal place of business in Virginia for five years; otherwise the easement will not be deemed perpetual. The Virginia Outdoors Foundation may either (1) retain such easements or (2) convey such easements to another public body or a charitable organization that it deems most appropriate to hold and enforce the easement. Virginia takes a clear stance and regards easements as an important instrument of public policy. By providing a default plan that offers assurance that easements will continue in the event the original holder cannot fulfill his or her obligations, the law clarifies this stance.

The act offers an express method for creating and enforcing conservation easements. It does not provide the sole means by which such easements can be acquired or enforced in the state, however. Thus, the stipulations in the act are not intended to affect the power of a public body under any other statute, including the power of the Virginia Outdoors Foundation and the Historic Landmarks Board, to acquire and hold conservation easements under other statutes, nor do they affect the terms of any other easements held by any public body.

Virginia has not adopted section 5 of the UCEA, a section designed to establish or confirm the validity of (1) any interest complying with the Uniform Act created after the effective date of the UCEA, (2) any interest created before the effective date of the UCEA that would have been enforceable had it been created after the act, and (3) any conservation or preservation easement or covenant, equitable servitude, restriction, or easement enforceable under another law. Virginia has adopted a provision equivalent to item three, however; the statute does not refer to the real property interests created before the act was passed. An interest created prior to the passage of the act, although meeting the requirements described in the statute, probably cannot look to the act for validity. In addition, the real property interest created under the Virginia act should be labeled a conservation easement because the UCEA section that gives validity to other named interests was not adopted.

Virginia Outdoors Foundation

The Virginia General Assembly established the Virginia Outdoors Foundation, a public entity managed by trustees, in 1997. Its purposes are to promote open-space preservation and to encourage private donations of money, securities, land, or other property to the commonwealth to preserve the natural, scenic, historic, scientific, open-space, and recreational areas of Virginia. The foundation can perform any lawful acts to carry out its purpose, and it possesses the power to acquire, hold, and manage property, to make contracts, and to promulgate regulations.

Open-Space Lands Preservation Trust Fund

The Virginia act also established a special nonreverting trust fund in the state treasury, the Open-Space Lands Preservation Trust Fund. The fund is administered by the Virginia Outdoors Foundation solely for the purpose of providing grants to persons conveying conservation easements on agricultural, forestry, or other open-space land under the conditions outlined in the Open-Space Land Act and the Virginia Conservation Easement Act. The purpose of the grants are to aid the grantors of conservation easements with the costs associated with creating and conveying such easements, including the legal costs, the appraisal costs, or all or part of the value of the easement. To be eligible for a grant, the conservation easement must be perpetual and conveyed to the foundation and a local coholder. If, after the easement is created, the local coholder ceases to exist, the easement will vest solely with the foundation, and the foundation must seek another local coholder within two years.

To develop criteria for awarding the grants, Virginia created six regional, open-space preservation advisory boards. Each board consists of nine members and is appointed by the Virginia governor. Advisory boards are composed of the following residents of the region: a local government officer, a representative from a charitable entity meeting the definition of a conservation easement holder under the Virginia Conservation Easement Act, a representative from a sportsman's organization, the elected officer of a soil and water conservation district, two farmers, and one representative from each of the region's tourism, forestry, and real estate industries. The board examines grant applications to identify those that will provide the greatest open-space preservation benefits. Their decision is reflected in the recommendation made to the foundation.

All gifts, devises, or bequests, whether personal or real property, along with the income derived from them accepted by the foundation are classed as gifts to the commonwealth and are exempt from all state and local tax laws.

Virginia's Historic Landmarks Board is vested with the power to acquire, by purchase or gift, designated landmarks and sites or easements or interests therein. When the board acquires partial interests, including an easement, they are to be recorded, and local taxation of the property shall reflect any resulting change in market value.

Conclusion

The Commonwealth of Virginia has both an expansive statutory foundation and programs in place to promote conservation easements and to facilitate their creation. The Virginia statute favors granting the easement to the commonwealth via the Virginia Outdoors Foundation. Consequently, the vast majority of the over 100,000 acres under conservation easement in Virginia have been granted to the Virginia Outdoors Foundation. Yet, there are also opportunities for grantors to designate an appropriate private nonprofit entity. Overall, Virginia offers a comprehensive system of preserving the environment through the promotion and use of conservation easements.

West Virginia

In 1995, West Virginia adopted the Conservation and Preservation Easements Act.[27] Although this statute adopted the major provisions of the UCEA, several modifications were made, and the official comments were not adopted. West Virginia has also enacted the West Virginia Stream Partners Program Act to encourage citizens to work in partnership with the state to protect West Virginia's rivers and streams.[28]

The Conservation and Preservation Easements Act

As the title of the Conservation and Preservation Easements Act indicates, West Virginia groups preservation easements and conservation easements together and expands the definition of conservation easements in the UCEA, stating that a conservation easement is a nonpossessory interest in real property, "whether appurtenant or in gross."[29] The statute also requires that a conservation easement be for the public benefit.[30]

As in the other states in the Fourth Federal Circuit, the act states that only charitable corporations, charitable associations, or charitable trusts registered with the West Virginia secretary of state and exempt from taxation pursuant to Internal Revenue Code section 501(c)(3) may hold a conservation easement. Furthermore, these organizations must exist for the purposes listed in the UCEA, although expanded to include protecting the agricultural value of real property, protecting wildlife, and maintaining or enhancing land qual-ity.[31] Thus, in West Virginia, any charitable entity holding a conservation easement must be tax exempt, a stricter requirement that than the UCEA.

The method of creating conservation easements roughly follows the UCEA, although West Virginia requires that an easement be created for a minimum period of twenty-five years.[32] The Conservation and Preservation Easements Act also includes language stating that conservation easements be liberally construed in favor of the grants contained therein to effect the purposes of the easement, language that might have ramifications in any judicial action. The statute also notes that holders of all easements, other than regulated public utilities, cannot institute eminent domain or condemnation proceeding affect-ing the property without acquiring the entire fee interest in the property. Finally, an easement must be recorded within sixty days of its effective date.[33]

West Virginia Stream Partners Program

In 1996, West Virginia enacted the West Virginia Stream Partners Program Act[34] to encourage citizen participation in protecting, restoring, and using the state's rivers and streams to safeguard the public health, to ensure their con-tinued use for recreation and commerce, and to protect wildlife habitat. Under the act, the legislature may appropriate money from the general rev-enue to groups dedicated to protecting West Virginia's rivers to purchase ease-ments or fee simple interests in property. Any group receiving a grant, which cannot exceed $5,000, must provide matching funds equal to, or exceeding, 20 percent of the grant.

Conclusion

Both the Conservation and Preservation Easements Act and the West Virginia Stream Partners Program provide the citizens of West Virginia with statutory vehicles for protecting property through conservation easements. Generally following the UCEA, the Conservation and Preservation Easements Act does expand the definition of some terms, which can be quite significant.

Conclusion

As discussed above, the land conservation movement has taken hold in the states in the Fourth Federal Circuit; South Carolina, Virginia, and West Vir-ginia have all enacted versions of the UCEA, and Maryland and North Car-olina have, in essence, enacted most of its major provisions. Unfortunately, the laws in the various states reflect programs and goals unique to each state and its culture. Consequently, the issues and problems associated with con-servation easements from both real property and tax law perspectives vary widely among the states.

Due to this diversity, uncovering a central theme of land protection in the Fourth Federal Circuit is difficult. Nonetheless, at least two trends appear. First, each state in this circuit, whether through adoption of the UCEA or similar legislation, has embraced land conservation and enabled such through statutory authority. Second, each state has tailor fit the statutory scheme to balance diverse interests existing in a particular state. For instance, Virginia balanced the interests of agriculture and land preservation by allowing agricultural activities on land protected by a conservation easement. Such balancing policies have enabled the states to enact functional land preservation programs beneficial to the diverse interests of a state.

In sum, the Fourth Federal Circuit offers an example of a geographically diverse region enacting land preservation programs fit to the interests of the individual states. Regardless of this diverse, individualized approach to land preservation, however, the circuit as a whole has certainly embraced the land conservation movement.

Notes

1. MD RP Code Ann. § 2-118.
2. MD TP Code Ann. § 9-220.
3. MD TP Code Ann. § 9-220.
4. MD TP Code Ann. § 9-220.
5. MD NR Code Ann. § 5-1203(a).
6. MD NR Code Ann. § 3-201.
7. MD NR Code Ann. § 3-2A-02.
8. MD NR Code Ann. § 3-2A-07. At least 15 percent or an agreement to resell the property to the state or a local governing body is required.
9. MD NR Code Ann. § 3-2A-08.
10. MD NR Code Ann. § 5-1502.
11. MD NR Code Ann. § 5-9A-02(h).
12. See MD NR Code Ann. § 5-9A-05 for complete criteria.
13. N.C. Gen. Stat. § 121-34, et. seq.
14. N.C. Gen. Stat. § 121-35(3).
15. N.C. Gen. Stat. § 121-35(3).
16. N.C. Gen. Stat. § 121-35(2).
17. N.C. Gen. Stat. § 121-38.
18. 339 S.E.2d 681 (N.C. Ct. App. 1986).
19. N.C. Gen. Stat. § 113A-230, et. seq.
20. Chapter 8, Title 27 of the 1976 Code. as §§ 27-8-10 to 80 (Supp. 1997).
21. Effective as of May 27, 1991.
22. See S.C. Code Ann. § 49-29-20 et seq. The General Assembly has currently designated six river corridors as qualifying corridors under the act.
23. Title 10.1 of the Virginia Code Annotated as §§ 10.1-1009–10.1016.
24. Va. Code Ann. §10.1-1700 et. seq. (Michie 1993).

25. Va. Code Ann. §10.1-1009 et. seq. (Michie 1993).
26. Va. Code Ann. §10.1-1011.
27. Incorporated as § 20-12-1–8 of the West Virginia Code.
28. W.Va. Code § 20-13-1 et seq.
29. W.Va. Code § 20-12-3(a).
30. W.Va. Code § 2-12-3(a).
31. W.Va. Code § 2-12-3(b).
32. W.Va. Code § 20-12-4(c).
33. W.Va. Code § 20-12-6(b).
34. W.Va. Code § 20-13-2.

Chapter 12

❧ ❧

Applicability of South Carolina's Conservation Easement Legislation to Implementation of Landscape Conservation in the ACE Basin

Sharon E. Richardson

South Carolina's Conservation Easement Act of 1991[1] provides the legal foundation that has enabled conservation organizations, working with federal and state government entities and, most importantly, private landowners to protect over 80,460 acres of biologically diverse land within coastal South Carolina. In South Carolina, federal income and estate tax relief provides government incentives for voluntary conservation easements. There are very few additional local- or state-initiated incentive programs. Land conservation has been very successful, however, especially along the coast of South Carolina, despite the absence of government incentive programs.

This success can be measured on many different levels. Most importantly is a positive cumulative effect of landscape-level preservation accomplished through the collective efforts of landowners and conservation organizations. Although fee simple acquisition by government entities has been a strong component in the protection of natural resources, the ability to use conservation easements as a voluntary technique has provided much of the momentum and enthusiasm for conservation in the landowner community. Success can also be considered on an organizational level. The cooperative relationship between conservation organizations and government agencies in South Carolina reflects a deep commitment to protecting regional resources, with minimal interorganizational strife and competition. Finally, success can be measured in the ability to replicate a successful model from one major coastal watershed to four other coastal watersheds, despite political, geographic, and demographic differences. These successes can largely be attributed to the deep land ethic of landowners and conservation organizations that reflects a reverence for the history of the landscape, compounded by a growing concern with increasing development pressures along a fragile and beautiful coast.

ACE Basin Model

The collective conservation efforts that occur in the ACE basin (Figure 12.1) are one of South Carolina's most successful examples of conservation easements. This 350,000-acre region, 35 miles southwest of Charleston, is within the coastal watersheds of the Ashepoo, Combahee, and Edisto Rivers (ACE).[2] Located in the coastal plain, South Carolina's "Lowcountry," the ACE basin includes the St. Helena Sound estuary, one of the largest remaining undeveloped forest and wetland ecosystems along the Atlantic coast. The ACE basin contains exceptional habitat diversity, including 91,000 acres of salt, brackish, and freshwater tidal and nontidal marshes; 26,000 acres of the estuarine impoundments; over 50,000 acres of bottomland and hardwood forests; and extensive forested uplands. A minor component of the landscape is in residential and commercial use, and only a small portion is still in active agricultural cultivation. Habitat diversity directly corresponds to that of the wildlife.

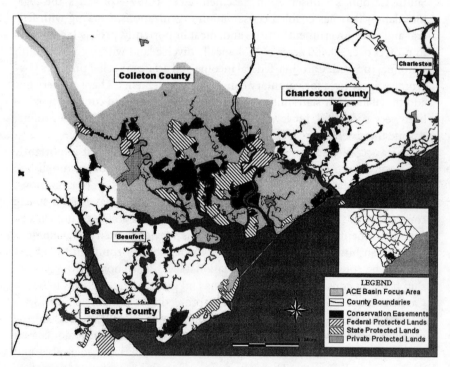

Figure 12.1. ACE basin region, South Carolina.
Source: Lowcountry Open Land Trust
Credit: Christopher Walters (1999)

Table 12.1. Federally Listed or Endangered Species in the ACE Basin[a]

Speicies	Status	Ecosystem	Habitats
American alligator	Threatened	Estuarine	Low-salinity brackish marshes; impoundments
Atlantic loggerhead turtle	Threatened	Marine, estuarine	Offshore waters; St. Helena Sound; nest on beach
Finback whale	Endangered	Marine	Open waters
Shortnose sturgeon	Endangered	Estuarine	Estuarine rivers
Southern bald eagle	Endangered	Estuarine, palustrine, upland	Estuarine rivers, impoundments; associated uplands
West Indian manatee	Endangered	Marine	Estuarine rivers
Wood stork	Endangered	Estuarine, palustrine	Estuarine impoundments; intertidal flats; forested scrub-shrub wetlands

[a] Table compiled by J. A. Gustanski, sources of information include: National Oceanic and Atmospheric Administration Costal Services Center; South Carolina Department of Natural Resources Marine Resources Division.

The ACE basin supports over 1,500 species of plants and animals, nine of which are federally listed as threatened or endangered (Table 12.1). In addition, 500 species of birds use a variety of habitats in the ACE basin for breeding, wintering, roosting, and feeding grounds, including numerous migratory neotropical bird species. Nearly 30 percent of the nesting population of bald eagles in South Carolina nest in the ACE basin, and it has been identified as an essential component in the U.S. Fish and Wildlife Service bald eagle recovery plan.

Threats

Like most threatened landscapes in America, the integrity of the ACE basin is threatened by increasing development pressures and insufficient public policy safeguards, compounded by a lack of intergovernmental coordination. Four counties—Beaufort, Colleton, Hampton, and Charleston—have jurisdiction over the ACE basin. Most of the land use decisions are determined on a county-by-county basis, and the development pressures, economies, and demographic characteristics of the three counties differ dramatically from one another.

Shared by the counties is the insufficiency of the existing county land use plans and the development restrictions to provide significant protection for the integrity of the natural landscape and the rich biological diversity within the ACE basin. Beaufort and Charleston Counties, however, are both in the process of revising comprehensive plans and development ordinances. Both counties have recommended higher levels of regulations to protect the resources within the ACE basin, with Beaufort County trying to implement strong watershed level–based protection mechanisms. Both counties are also exploring the use of purchase of development rights and transfer of development right programs to redirect growth and infrastructure investment to specific growth areas, thereby alleviating development pressures in sensitive areas of the counties. Colleton and Hampton Counties have the least restrictive land use regulations in the ACE basin. Recent efforts to implement a countywide comprehensive plan in Colleton County were abandoned due to local political pressures to prevent government intervention in land use decisions. In addition to the political and regulatory threats to the landscape are potential threats associated with traditional uses, such as agriculture and forestry activities. A large portion of the ACE basin is in active timber production. With changing forestry markets are changing pressures on the forest communities, including bottomland hardwood swamps. Although best management practices are recommended within the industry, there are few guarantees, short of strong conservation easements, that would prevent extensive clear-cutting of long-standing forest communities. Given the history of land use in the ACE basin, there is an irony in land conservation and land management.

Historical Land Uses

Currently, the ACE basin is characterized as predominantly natural. Although the ACE basin represents a uniquely undisturbed natural habitat, it has been manipulated and managed for centuries. Records from the late seventeenth century indicate that settlers received grants from the Lords' proprietors (those individuals first granted title to land in the Carolinas by the British crown) in the ACE basin. The landscape is defined by a limited amount of fertile land surrounded by tidally influenced creeks and waterways, with enough distance from the ocean to achieve freshwater habitats. With limited prospects for income other than trade, settlers began to redefine the landscape through the construction of extensive banks, irrigation systems, dikes, canals, and dams that provided the foundation for a thriving agricultural economy based on rice cultivation. At the peak of the rice culture empire in the 1860s, 96 percent of the entire nation's production of rice was in the impounded rice fields of coastal South Carolina. In the ACE basin, more than 26,000 acres of floodplain forests were converted to rice cultivation. The rice plantation culture of the ACE basin produced a working landscape unparalleled in the Southeast.

Following the Civil War, the use of the plantation for agriculture and rice cultivation was replaced by management strategies for wildlife and recreational hunting activities. In fact, it is the remnants of the successful manipulation by humans to create and sustain a thriving rice culture that provide much of the critical habitat now valued for wildlife and biological diversity. In the areas where historic impoundments had not been maintained or restored, the habitat has naturally changed back to floodplain swamp. The combination of habitat, both managed and unmanaged, provides a landscape that is uniquely abundant in habitat types with a corresponding rich biodiversity. Today, over 26,000 acres of diked impoundments have survived the collapse of the rice culture (Photograph 12.1). Diked marshes are managed primarily to attract wintering waterfowl. Uplands are managed in varying degrees for timber production, bobwhite quail, wild turkey, mourning dove,

Photograph 12.1. Aerial view of impounded rice fields on a portion of Lavington Plantation on the Ashepoo River protected by fifth-generation landowners.
Source: Lowcountry Open Land Trust
Credit: B.J. Richardson (1997)

and white-tailed deer. Significant portions are left unmanaged, and the combination of habitats provides ecological diversity. The impounded marsh and open water habitat and the continued management of the water control structures allow for extensive manipulation of water and plant life to encourage and sustain migrating waterfowl and numerous other avian species. The historic manipulation of water did not compromise the fertile waterways of the estuary system, and other traditional uses such as shrimping remain important to the coastal economy.

Despite the change in management regimes, from agriculture to recreational hunting, the historic land ownership patterns of large-tract plantations that has remained intact essentially since the late seventeenth century has probably provided the best form of protection to the natural resources of the ACE basin. There are approximately forty to fifty principal ownership blocks ranging from 1,000 acres to 12,000 acres in size, including twenty-five landowners with large plantations along the rivers. A connection to the heritage that defines the South perpetuates a stewardship ethic and an obligation to retain these connections for future generations. These factors foster the opportunities for voluntary land conservation through conservation easements. The ability to use legally binding restrictions, without requiring government intervention, has great appeal to landowners who associate the federal government with the loss of a thriving agricultural economy.

Land ownership patterns have shifted in other coastal regions and have worked against conservation efforts. Similar land ownership patterns have facilitated extensive land use alterations, as large tracts of land once held in private family ownership are sold to golf course communities and other large residential subdivision projects that appeal to an increasing market of migrating retirees. With the Department of Commerce projecting that over half of the U.S. population is expected to live within fifty miles of the coasts by 2030, the need to convert natural habitat to support that development will only escalate unless protection is secured now.[3]

An Organizational Context for Conservation

The boundaries of the ACE basin were informally defined by the Atlantic Coast Joint Venture as part of the North American Waterfowl Management Plan. In 1986, the North American Waterfowl Management Plan[4] identified the ACE basin as a flagship project of the U.S. Atlantic Coast Joint Venture. The policy guidelines promote overall biological diversity through the preservation of diverse habitats that support many species other than waterfowl, primarily associated with historic impounded of rice fields. In 1988, a task force composed of private landowners, including private industry, government entities, and nonprofit conservation organizations, was formed to coordinate protection efforts within the basin. The original task force members included private landowners, Ducks Unlimited, The Nature Conservancy, the U.S. Fish and Wildlife Service, and South Carolina Department of Natural Resources.

Task force members were very effective in working collaboratively to identify and protect key properties through a variety of techniques and designations.[5] By 1995, state and federal government entities had purchased 49,319 acres within the 350,000-acre watershed. Purchases were often facilitated with assistance from the Nature Conservancy, Ducks Unlimited, or both. Again, though, the conservation motivation of the landowner is often the key component to a successful conservation strategy. Another component is the ability to provide for public access to the land and water resources, which can be more easily accomplished on land that has been acquired and is in government ownership.

With sufficient lands in protection through acquisition, other landowners quickly appreciated the opportunity to contribute to the conservation efforts without selling their land. In 1991, Ted Turner donated the original conservation easement on Hope Plantation, which helped generate a domino effect with surrounding landowners. In ten years, Ducks Unlimited has worked with twenty-two families to negotiate conservation easements that protect nearly 30,000 acres of habitat in the ACE basin. The Nature Conservancy has designed conservation easements on approximately 6,000 acres, including Hope Plantation (Table 12.2).

Table 12.2. Conservation Easements in the Ace Basin

Property	Acres	Easements Held by[a]
Botany Bay Island	493	TNC
Hope Pantation	5,232	TNC
Willtown Bluff	1,000	TNC
Church Trct	326	DU
Cheeha-Combahee	12,350	DU
Walnut Grove	635	DU
Godfrey Tract	155	DU
McMillan Tract	20	DU
Pon Pon	3,249	DU
Ashepoo	5,240	DU
Fenwick Island	4,183	DU
Combahee	1,204	LOLT

(*continues*)

Table 12.2. Continued

Property	Acres	Easements Held by[a]
Musselboro Island	953	DU
Oak Island	396	LOLT
Little Palmetto Island	41	DU
Prospect Hill	87	LOLT
Rose Hill	1,000	TNC
Plum Hill	945	LOLT
Auld Brass	138	TNC
Parkers Ferry	185	BCOLT
Tomotley	771	BCOLT
Ivan hoe	59	LOLT
Lavington Plantation	2,324	LOLT
Paul and Dalton	2,122	LOLT
Airy Hall Plantation	1,062	LOLT
South Fenwick Island	328	DU
McCollum Tract	33	LOLT
Shell Point	45	LOLT
Slann Island	333	LOLT
Tilt Tract	80	LOLT
Jehossee Farm	484	TNC
Great Swamp Tract	415	TNC
Racoon Island	121	DU
Borders Island	1,724	DU
Prescott Plantation	317	DU
TOTAL	48,050	

[a] TNC: The Nature Conservancy; DU: Ducks Unlimited; LOLT: Lowcountry Open Land Trust; BCOLT: Beaufort County Open Land Trust
Sources: National Oceanic and Atmospheric Administration Coastal Services Center, South Carolina Department of Natural Resources Marine Resources Division, The Nature Conservancy, and Ducks Unlimited.
Compiled by J. A. Gustanski (1998); revised April 1999 with assistance from Sharon Richardson.

Each conservation easement in the ACE basin is specific to the protection needs of a particular parcel of land. Terms of the easement are specific and detailed and include documentation such as maps, photographs, and biological inventories. In general, these easements limit subdivision of the properties while allowing for continuation of traditional uses such as hunting, fishing, agriculture, wildlife management, and the harvesting of forest products.

Additional organizations recognized for their demonstrated successes in protection efforts, including the Lowcountry Open Land Trust, the Nemours Plantation Wildlife Foundation, and Westvaco, have since been added to the task force. The Nemours Plantation Wildlife Foundation, a nonprofit research foundation established by the late Eugene duPont III, protects 9,800 acres of land within the Beaufort County portion of the ACE basin. The Lowcountry Open Lands Trust, a regional land trust headquartered in Charleston, has designed voluntary conservation easements for thirteen families in the ACE basin to protect 8,693 acres. Westvaco has been a leader in the forest products industry and has endorsed the ACE basin since its inception, signing a memorandum of understanding for protection on corporate holdings. The collective efforts of the participating partners have achieved permanent protection of 130,224 acres, or 37 percent of the basin, using various conservation tools. The protection of individual tracts has resulted in the landscape-level protection of large contiguous areas characteristic of the whole spectrum of habitat types. The collective efforts continue to serve as incentive to surrounding landowners to contribute to the successes of the region.

The task force model has been replicated in four other coastal focus areas that cover the coast of South Carolina from the Georgia border to Myrtle Beach. The state and federal government and nongovernment organizations participate in each task force, but the leadership is generated by the landowners that serve on the task forces. The landowners define the tone, strategy, and priorities for land conservation and typically serve as liaisons with the landowner community. The government entities provide leadership through acquisition and protection projects, including South Carolina wildlife management areas and U.S. Fish and Wildlife Service National Wildlife Refuges. In addition, the government entities such as the U.S. Fish and Wildlife Service Coastal Program have the resources to provide technical support through computer analysis, mapping, and ecological assessments.

The conservation organizations provide leadership in landowner education and in assisting landowners through the conservation easement process. Ducks Unlimited and the Nature Conservancy offer a national perspective to regional protection efforts and provide extensive resources in terms of waterfowl management recommendations and habitat preservation for rare and endangered species and ecosystems. The national organizations also have the organizational capacity to be more active in acquisition projects. Ducks Unlimited and the Nature Conservancy have been instrumental in the purchase and protection of many critical lands in the ACE basin.

In addition, several land trusts, including the Beaufort County Open Land

Trust, the Edisto Island Open Land Trust, and the Lowcountry Open Land Trust, has been organized in different coastal communities. The Beaufort County Open Land Trust has accepted the early conservation easements of 1,635 acres in the ACE basin. Of the coastal land trusts, the Lowcountry Open Land Trust is the only land trust with a regional scope and demonstrated successes in each of the five coastal focus areas; members serve on all five coastal task forces.

Task forces provide an informal opportunity for participating members to analyze watershed resources, threats, and land ownership characteristics; evaluate and prioritize land protection strategies; and implement conservation. The forum also provides an opportunity for conservation organizations to share resources and a support network. The conservation organizations have different missions and are therefore interested in different types of properties. In addition, each organization appeals to different types of landowners, because relationships are the driving force behind the decisions of the landowners who donate easements. Often landowners who are private about their family and land affairs seek out the Lowcountry Open Land Trust because its board of trustees is composed of local landowners, many of whom have donated conservation easements. Other landowners who have specific management issues are interested in the resources available from the national organizations. The conservation organizations refer landowners to other appropriate conservation organizations to ensure that the particular perpetual relationship meets the needs of the landowner and the resource. The overall perspective shared by the organizations seems to appeal to landowners, and the opportunity to have a choice increases the comfort level of the landowners considering a permanent protection. In addition, the organizations often serve as secondary holders to easements designed by the other organizations. This cooperative relationship strengthens the conservation efforts of each individual entity. The strength and commitment of the partnership approach to conservation has been working well since 1988. Without a cohesive task force, the protection efforts would have been minimal.

Success

The success of the ACE basin belongs with the landowners who have taken the initiative to preserve a heritage unique to the Lowcountry, protecting remnants of cultures that have long since been abandoned but that represent the fabric of the region and the nation (Photograph 12.2). The land ethic of the landowners in the ACE basin is not driven by intense development pressures, nor is it driven by innovative public policies that encourage landowners. Without the intense development pressures, the diminishment in the fair market value is not always a driving financial consideration. It is the opportunity to protect and promote a land legacy, on their own initiative, without government intervention, that provides a winning combination to landowners who value their connection with the land. The example set by landowners in the ACE basin has driven the successes in other coastal focus areas where development pressures are more intense. The commitment of the landowners is further evidenced by the lack of legal challenges to the conservation easements. Land has changed hands, but given the critical mass for conservation achieved in the ACE basin, there is a high demand among conservation buyers for protected land.

The forces are in place for a conservation effort to sustain itself in perpetuity. The uses that enable the landowner to generate sufficient revenues to manage the land are retained. Opportunities for new sources of income through ecologically sensitive activities are also retained, thereby providing some entrepreneurial flexibility that often appeals to conservation-minded landowners. The threats of converting the natural landscape to an impervious surface associated with extensive residential, commercial, or industrial uses are permanently eliminated. Moreover, a land legacy is defined for the

Photograph 12.2. Arthur Whaley guides author on tour of his boyhood home, South Fenwick Island, now protected in partnerhsip with Lowcountry Open Land Trust and Ducks Unlimited.
Source: Lowcountry Open Land Trust
Credit: B. J. Richardson (1996)

future. The initiative and momentum that have sustained the success of the ACE basin have been driven by the commitment to the land, the diversity of resources, the traditional uses of hunting and fishing, and a commitment to the community. The ACE basin is an outstanding example of how government, nonprofit conservation groups, and private landowners can unite to protect important natural resources. Traditional uses, which provide economic benefits, mesh with maintaining the ecological integrity of this area. Private property rights have been preserved in a manner that will benefit individual landowners and the greater public. This commitment, combined with South Carolina's sound legal foundation, has empowered perpetual protection not only in the ACE basin but throughout coastal South Carolina. This is truly a landowner legacy.[6]

Notes

1. South Carolina Conservation Easement Act of 1991 incorporated into Chapter 8, Title 27 of the 1976 Code as §§ 27-8-10–80 (Supp. 1997).
2. In 1992, the ACE basin was added to the National Estuarine Research Reserve System, consistent with the provisions of section 315 of the Coastal Zone Management Act, 16 U.S.C. 1461.
3. Thomas J. Culliton, M. A. Warren, T. R. Goodspeed, D. G. Remer, C. M. Blackwell, and J. J. McDonough III. *Fifty Years of Population Change along the Nation's Coasts, 1960–2010* (Rockville, Md.: U.S. Department of Commerce, National Oceanic and Atmospheric Administration, 1990).
4. The North American Waterfowl Management Plan is a policy document between Canada and the United States. Its purpose is to provide a set of guidelines to manage and improve waterfowl populations by protecting wetland and upland habitat critical to the life stages of migrating waterfowl.
5. Techniques used include acquisition, federal and state designations such as the ACE Basin National Wildlife Refuge (11,019 acres) and the designation of the ACE Basin National Estuarine Reserve (11,942 acres), and working with private landowners to facilitate the donation of critical lands, including the Donnelly Wildlife Management Area (8,048 acres).
6. Over 80,460 acres have been protected in coastal South Carolina.

Chapter 13

❦ ❧

Use of Conservation Easements to Protect the Scenic and Natural Character of the Blue Ridge Parkway: A Case Study

Charles E. Roe

The Blue Ridge Parkway, part of the national park system, is the nation's premiere scenic "motor road." The 469-mile-long roadway connects Shenandoah National Park in western Virginia to the Great Smoky Mountains National Park in southwestern North Carolina, following the crest of the Blue Ridge Mountains escarpment (Figure 13.1). In some locations, the mountain escarpment, or "front," rises dramatically more than 3,000 feet above the adjacent Piedmont lowlands. From the parkway, motorists are afforded magnificent views, not only of nearby lush southern Appalachian forests, rock cliffs, and mountainsides, but also of distant valleys and Piedmont foothills. The parkway "connects" dozens of natural areas and rare species habitats that are ranked by state and national agencies as important nature reserves.

More people visit the Blue Ridge Parkway, the nation's oldest and longest public parkway, than any other unit of the national parks system.[1] Twenty million people travel the parkway each year, contributing over $2 billion to the regional economy and adding more than $100 million in state and local taxes.[2] The continued popularity of the Blue Ridge Parkway is considered vital to the economy of the region.

This connection to the economy is especially true in North Carolina, where tourism is the state's second largest income-producing industry and the parkway is the top tourist attraction. The North Carolina portion of this road, some 270 miles, has been designated an All American Highway. The state's tourism industry has promoted numerous side loop routes from the parkway carrying visitors to other regional attractions such as local craft and artisan centers, historic sites, and other parks.

Blue Ridge Parkway Corridor

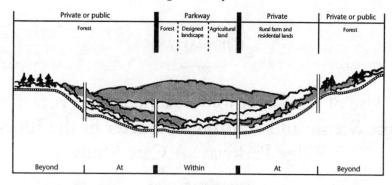

Inventory of Resource and Visitor Experience Components

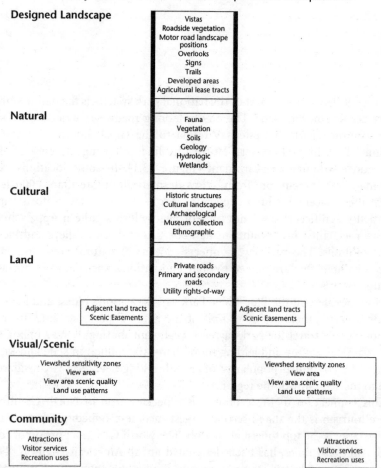

Figure 13.1. Blue Ridge Parkway corridor and inventory of resource and visitor experience components.

Source: Chuck Roe, CTNC (courtesy of National Park Service, Draft Plan)
Credit: Cartography Lab, University of Minnesota

Brief History

Congress authorized the Blue Ridge Parkway in 1936 as part of the federal public works program during the Great Depression to stimulate the stagnant economies of western Virginia and North Carolina. Although part of a federal program, the two states were responsible for acquiring much of the land necessary for the road right-of-way. Throughout the 1930s and 1940s, these lands were transferred to the National Park Service, the agency responsible for constructing the parkway. The original design for the parkway called for the government to acquire fee title to lands averaging 100 acres per roadway mile and to place scenic easements on an additional 25 acres per roadway mile. (These acreages, however, were often not achievable, and for the most part, substantially fewer scenic easements were acquired.) In some locations, larger park and recreational areas were established along the parkway, such as the Peaks of Otter and Rocky Knob in Virginia and Doughton Park, Julian Price Park, Linville Falls, Crabtree Meadows, Craggy Gardens, and Mount Pisgah in North Carolina. Aside from these larger parks and recreation areas, however, the parkway's publicly owned right-of-way averages just 800 feet wide and is as narrow as 200 feet in some locations. Some sections of the parkway route were not acquired and constructed until the 1950s and 1960s, and the last segment at Grandfather Mountain was finally completed in the early 1980s. The National Park Service now owns and manages a total of 81,565 acres in parkway lands.[3]

Although national forestlands bound 190 of the parkway's 469 miles on both sides, most of the lands within view of those traveling the parkway are in private ownership. Until recently, most of the privately owned lands next to the parkway remained in forests or farmsteads. The scenic beauty of this mountain roadway, however, is threatened by increasing residential and commercial development along many sections of the parkway (Photograph 13.1). Construction of residential subdivisions, vacation resorts, and commercial stores on lands adjacent to the parkway has increased. In many cases, these developments replace the beautiful pastoral and forested landscapes characteristic of the southern Appalachians. Neighboring farms and forests are being eliminated in numerous locations, particularly in southwestern Virginia and near Boone and Blowing Rock, Asheville, and Maggie Valley in North Carolina. Development along the parkway imperils the very reasons so many visitors from around the nation and world come to enjoy it.

Only fifteen of the twenty-nine counties through which the Blue Ridge Parkway passes have adopted any form of local land use zoning controls, and those controls that do exist are modest in their restrictions. Such inattention to regulating development of land near the parkway stems from traditional distrust of government and lack of knowledge about the importance and

Photograph 13.1. Parkway scene of mountain ridges.
File photo: Courtesy of National Park Service

fragility of the scenic resources in the parkway's corridor. One current emphasis by the parkway's planning and resource staff is to educate local community leaders. This process has been assisted by recent completion of studies that prioritize tracts near the parkway for their scenic importance.

Using computer analysis and mapping lands visible from the parkway prepared by the North Carolina State University School of Design, National Park Service staff has identified those tracts of greatest importance to maintaining the scenic character of the parkway. These tracts are currently being ranked according to their scenic values.

Conservation Easements and the Parkway

Conservation easements are legal restrictions that permanently limit a property's uses so as to protect its conservation values. An easement is tailored to protect the natural or open-space character of land while meeting the personal and financial needs of the landowner. The easement is conveyed by the landowner by sale or donation to a qualified public agency or private conservation organization and is made a permanent part of the property deed. Future owners are bound by the easement's terms. In some cases, an easement may apply to just a portion of a property and may allow rights for limited building even on land under the easement. The holder of the easement is responsible for enforcing its terms and restrictions. Donations of conservation easements are encouraged by federal and state tax laws that award income tax deductions and credits, lower estate and inheritance taxes, and minimize property taxes on land affected by easements.

Some of the first uses of conservation easements in America were associated with the Blue Ridge Parkway. When the parkway was established, scenic easements were acquired by Virginia and North Carolina, prohibiting nonagricultural or commercial development on more than 2,000 acres of private land immediately adjacent to the publicly owned right-of-way. Approximately 215 acres of land in Virginia and another 809 acres in North Carolina are still protected under these scenic easements. The rest of the easements originally acquired during the creation of the parkway were later exchanged or the land was later acquired in fee.[4]

The first conservation easements acquired in the 1930s and 1940s were simple "short form" agreements and were often vaguely written and poorly understood by the original sellers or successive owners. Generally, the early conservation easements served to maintain land neighboring the parkway in forest or agricultural uses. The National Park Service has experienced numerous misunderstandings and conflicts with subsequent owners, and those difficulties have created a sense of apprehension about the use of conservation easements by park administrators and private landowners.[5] Nevertheless, the National Park Service's 1994 Land Protection Plan for the Blue Ridge Parkway recommended that the federal government acquire conservation easements on an additional 5,550 acres of land adjacent to the parkway, primarily to control and reduce land uses that are inconsistent or incompatible with the parkway's scenic vistas.[6]

The Role of the Conservation Trust for North Carolina

The Conservation Trust for North Carolina (CTNC) is a nonprofit, private land trust dedicated to helping save natural and rural resources throughout the state, either through direct actions or by aiding a network of local land trusts.[7] In 1996, the CTNC responded to requests from administrators of the Blue Ridge Parkway and North Carolina's Year of the Mountains state commission to assume a leadership role in protecting the parkway's scenic and natural corridor. This effort involves numerous actors.

The chair of the Year of the Mountains state commission, Hugh Morton, had previously placed conservation easements on 2,000 acres of his beautiful and ecologically unique Grandfather Mountain next to the parkway's famous Linn Cove Viaduct bridge and Tanawha hiking trail. He had donated these easements to the Nature Conservancy.

The CTNC and the Year of the Mountains commission initiated a public fundraising campaign in late 1996. By early 1998, the CTNC had received more than $1.3 million in contributions from nearly 400 individuals, private corporations, and foundations. The funds are being used to purchase land and conservation easements on key tracts of land adjacent to the parkway. In addition, U.S. senators from North Carolina obtained appropriations of $750,000 for the National Park Service to purchase conservation easements along the parkway in that state. The governor of North Carolina requested the state legislature to appropriate $2 million to acquire the fee title or easements on land parcels next to the parkway, and the North Carolina Department of Transportation committed an additional $2 million to purchase land in the parkway corridor. The CTNC is also negotiating with individual landowners and accepting donations of conservation easements.

The land protection project was launched in 1996 when the city of Asheville conveyed a conservation easement over more than 17,000 acres to the CTNC. The easement covers the North Fork and Bee Tree watersheds, the primary source of drinking water for Asheville, and affords a beautiful mountain panorama along fifteen miles of the parkway between Mount Mitchell (the highest peak in the eastern United States) and Craggy Gardens. Reaching elevations of 6,800 feet, the watershed is visible to travelers along Interstate Highway 40 as the dramatic mountain backdrop north of Montreat and Black Mountain. The terms of the easement maintain the character of the mountainside, which can only be used as a catchment for the water supply of Asheville or as public parkland. The easement prohibits any timber cutting on the mountain slopes from the summits down to 3,600 feet, yet permits selective tree cutting in the lower slopes near the municipal water reservoirs. Future subdivision and development is prohibited. In addition, the easement specifically states that rare species and significant natural areas must be protected. This landmark easement has prompted other municipalities in both North Carolina and Virginia to consider creating conservation easements on their watersheds and parklands adjacent to the parkway, although no easements have been completed to date.

The CTNC has begun to purchase critical tracts next to the parkway in locations most threatened by intensive residential or commercial development. In 1997, the CTNC purchased an abandoned farmstead of 48 acres near Blowing Rock, in a locality where purchase prices have soared in some locations to as much as $26,000 per acre, for $470,000 with privately raised funds (Photograph 13.2). A ridge separates this farm, which is a classic example of the parkway's rural landscape, from a residential subdivision. The CTNC purchase thwarted the plans of adjacent landowners who had hoped to buy the old farm and develop it for residential or commercial purposes, such as a horse stable and dozens of vacation cabins. The CTNC subsequently divided the property. Twelve acres on which a conservation easement was placed were sold to a conservation-minded individual restricted to constructing a single

Photograph 13.2. Critcher Farm: CTNC purchased and placed conservation easements on land before resale for farming to private buyer.
File photo: CTNC

new home and barn, in a "traditional" or "vernacular" style, and to using the land for livestock grazing, haying, or row crops only. The CTNC demolished and removed the existing derelict structures and conveyed a conservation easement on the other 35 acres to the National Park Service, prohibiting any structures and permitting only grazing or haying. The CTNC then sold the underlying title to these 35 acres to the owners of the other 12 acres. Thus, the land is ensured to continue to be used as a functioning farm.

In addition, in 1997, Sterling Carroll, a businessman from Boone, North Carolina, donated a conservation easement to the CTNC that gave it authority over all future forest management on the 234-acre tract. Designed to protect the forested mountainside below the parkway's Grand View Overlook near Deep Gap, east of Boone, in one of the more intensively developing areas of the parkway corridor, Carroll intended for this easement to become a model for other private landowners. This easement restricts future development to the construction of up to two new homes on lower elevation sites not visible from the parkway.

The CTNC's project representatives are currently working with other owners of land near the parkway who have expressed interests in donating easements that will preserve the forests or meadows (Photograph 13.3). One landowner has donated an easement over 69 acres adjacent to the parkway's Moses Cone Park, which protects a forested natural area and restricts future

Photograph 13.3. Blue Ridge Parkway through farm meadows.
File photo: Courtesy of National Park Service

development to building and maintaining two homesites on the lower slopes. Another is donating an easement over her 3-acre parcel on the slopes above a lake in the parkway's Julian Price Park. In addition, the CTNC has made purchase offers on land and easements over several large tracts that would connect the parkway to Stone Mountain State Park.

The CTNC presents public seminars to educate the public about the threats to the continued beauty of the parkway and to explain conservation easements and the tax reductions that may result from their donation. The seminars explain how conservation easements may be individually designed and written to satisfy a variety of conditions and future uses. Some easements may reserve forestland as nature preserves; others will allow existing uses such as timber management, livestock grazing, or active farming to continue according to "best management" practices; and yet others will allow construction of a few new homes, but in sites least noticeable to the parkway visitor and in keeping with the characteristics of traditional mountain residences.

The CTNC is not alone in helping to protect the parkway. Other private land conservation organizations have also become involved in the efforts. In Virginia, the private Western Virginia Land Trust and Valley Conservation Council along with the Virginia Outdoors Foundation, a public agency, are attempting to acquire conservation easements near the parkway. In North Carolina, the Southern Appalachian Highlands Conservancy has acquired easements over 103 acres near the parkway. National organizations including the Conservation Fund, Trust for Public Land, and the Nature Conservancy have also become active in land acquisition efforts that benefit the parkway. The CTNC has forged agreements among many of the private land conservation organizations and has organized a planning forum among them to help encourage cooperation and collaborating.

Conclusion

The CTNC is currently involved in discussions with owners of numerous tracts who have expressed interests in ceding conservation easements over their land. The future progress of this long-term project will be instrumental in examining the practical uses of conservation easements to protect public lands and linear parkways. It will help evaluate the effectiveness of easements with various types of use restrictions, analyze land values affected by various types of easements, and assess satisfaction of the future owners of land affected by easements. Moreover, it will employ easements in conservation-oriented development designs and help determine long-term costs for easement monitoring and stewardship. The Blue Ridge Parkway scenic corridor protection project will become a national model in the future.

Notes

1. Blue Ridge Parkway 1987–1996 visitation records.
2. Gene Brothers and Rachel J. C. Chen. *Economic Impact of Travel to the Blue Ridge Parkway, Virginia and North Carolina* (Raleigh, N.C.: Department of Parks, Recreation and Tourism Management, North Carolina State University, 1995–96).
3. Blue Ridge Parkway 1996 Lands Records.
4. Blue Ridge Parkway 1996 Lands Records.
5. Blue Ridge Parkway 1996 Lands Records.
6. U.S. Department of the Interior, National Park Service, *Blue Ridge Parkway Land Protection Plan* (Asheville, N.C.: National Park Service, Nov. 1994).
7. The CTNC was established in 1991 and is dedicated to conserving land and water resources throughout North Carolina through direct action and by helping communities, private land trusts, and landowners protect lands important to them for their natural, scenic, historic, and recreational values.

Chapter 14

❦ ❧

Grannybelle Woods Conservation Easement

Randolph Y. Brown

Like many who visit the Great Smoky Mountains National Park and the foothills region of eastern Tennessee, Kerwin Stallings decided that the area was a good place to spend his retirement. In 1987, after completing a thirty-year career as an economist in New York City, he and his wife, Vera, loaded up their Greenwich Village belongings in the truck and moved to Blount County, Tennessee. The Stallings purchased 200 acres of two overgrown farms in the steep "knobs" or foothills near Maryville, Tennessee, just west of the national park. They named their property Grannybelle Woods after Belle Walker Everett, former owner of some of the land and a noted local personality.[1] The Stallings's plan was to establish an economically viable hobby farm in an environmentally sensitive manner.

Their object was threefold. First, they wanted to return the gently sloping abandoned fields in the valley, locally referred to as hollows, to pasture and some low-intensity arable farming, mostly corn. Second, they wanted to create a country estate, an environment suitable for walking and horseback riding. Third, they wanted to preserve the erosion-prone knobs. The Stallings' decided to sell 80 acres on the major knobs in eleven tracts, between 5 and 10 acres in size, interspersed throughout the farm (Figure 14.1).

After deciding which parts of the property were best suited for agriculture and where the road and utilities (to be built underground) were to be located, the Stallings and their attorney developed strict restrictions or covenants for the eleven lots. They restricted they amount of area on each lot that could be cleared for a house, lawn, and garden. In addition, they imposed very strong controls on what may be visible from the narrow lanes that wind through Grannybelle Woods. The result to the casual visitor or evening walker is that Grannybelle Woods appears to be a historic

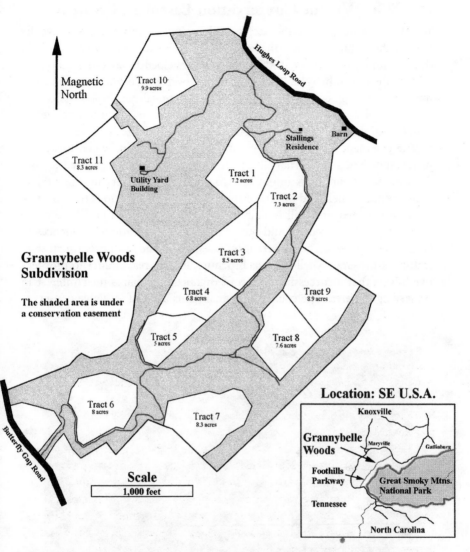

Figure 14.1. Grannybelle Woods subdivision with regional location inset.
Credit: Randy Brown

Appalachian farm with well-maintained meadows in the hollows and quiet woods on the knobs. The residents of the woods are not the only ones to use the country lanes for hiking. With permission from the Stallings, folks from surrounding areas come to the area for quiet walks.

Why Was the Conservation Easement Created?

To ensure protection of the scenic and ecological values of Grannybelle Woods, the Stallings came to the Foothills Land Conservancy in 1991, early in their planning process. First, the conservancy helped to lay out the boundaries of the lots to be sold. Because there are twelve properties and two easement preservation categories, the job proved to be fairly complex. Once this was accomplished, the conservancy worked with the landowners to refine the language of the easement on the 120 acres retained by the Stallings.

The easement on the land the Stallings were to retain, which was completed and signed in February 1993 after the conservancy had hired its first professional employee, is important. In addition to preserving the land, it reassures the owners and buyers of the eleven lots on the knobs that the area around their property will remain as it is (Photograph 14.1). Without the easement a future owner could put as many as 200 additional residences in Grannybelle Woods. The conservation easement, is the most prominent sales feature of the Grannybelle Woods brochure. It gives reassurance to prospective buyers that a successful nonprofit organization shares their interest in preserving the area. The conservancy maintains a list of available conserva-

Photograph 14.1. Grannybelle Woods.
Photo credit: Randy Brown (1998)

tion properties in the region, which includes Grannybelle Woods. Frequent telephone and e-mail requests from visitors seeking land with conservation value in the region attest to the attraction of the area and the demand for protected land.[2]

Who Were the Legal Parties Involved?

The owners of Grannybelle Woods are Kerwin (now deceased) and Vera Stallings, formerly of New York City. They became familiar with the foothills of east Tennessee during visits to the Great Smoky Mountains National Park. In addition, their daughter attended Maryville College, so they came to know the area well before deciding where to relocate when Kerwin retired.

The Foothills Land Conservancy was founded in 1985 by a group of citizens concerned about the increasing loss of forest and open space in the foothills of the Smoky Mountains. In 1992, the conservancy, led by a volunteer board of directors, opened its office with full-time staff headed by an executive director in Maryville, Tennessee. To date, the Foothills Land Conservancy has been involved in fourteen projects and has protected more than 8,700 acres. Conservation tools include the use of donated conservation easements, donations of land in fee, fee simple purchases, bequests, revocable trusts, and green or conservation developments. The Foothills Land Conservancy has protected more than 900 acres of farm and forest land using conservation easements.

The conservancy is in the process of acquiring several strategic parcels of land to create a buffer zone between the Great Smoky Mountains National Park and the suburban sprawl of the greater Knoxville metropolitan area. In 1995, the Foothills Land Conservancy completed the first such buffer zone project. To purchase the 4,700 acres along the park boundary threatened by commercial development, the conservancy raised $1.2 million. Contributions made to the project came from more than 3,500 individuals, businesses, foundations, and civic and outdoor groups located in thirty-five states. The conservancy gave 400 acres along Abrams Creek, one of the largest and most productive streams in the park and home to two endangered fish species, to the National Park Service. The remaining 4,300 acres were donated to the Tennessee Wildlife Resources Agency to establish the first unit of the Foothills Wildlife Management Area (WMA).[3] In 1997, the conservancy completed its second buffer zone project, raising more than $500,000 to purchase an additional 1,516 acres adjoining the Foothills WMA. The conservancy is in the process of transferring this tract to the Tennessee Wildlife Resources Agency for inclusion in the Foothills WMA.

The conservancy's long-range plans call for the establishment of several more wildlife units along the northern boundary of the national park. These large tracts of land provide both critical autumn feeding grounds for black bears and many other species of wildlife and much needed public space for hiking, biking, bird watching, hunting, and camping.[4]

What Did the Conservation Easement Say?

To ensure the permanence of Grannybelle Woods's idyllic setting, the owners granted a conservation easement on the 120 acres they intended to retain. The easement is fairly complex because the terrain is diverse and the Stallings wanted to maintain and improve the hollows in pasture and gardens. They did this not so much for agricultural as aesthetic reasons, wanting to re-create the bucolic experience once prevalent in the hollows of the southern Appalachians by permitting a mix of forest and traditional agriculture instead of monotonous second-growth forest.

The protective covenants of Grannybelle Woods that apply to individual lots allow all property owners unrestricted access to the "parkland," the land under the conservation easement. The easement has two protection categories, farmland and woodland, both of which preclude further subdivision or development. The land area covered by these categories was surveyed as a part of the initial subdivision, making them easy to identify both on baseline report maps and in the field. Areas designated as farmland are the hollow floors that lie along the two miles of gravel road that winds through the subdivision. In several places, the previous owners had not maintained the pastures and garden areas, and they were overgrown with briars and Virginia pines. The easement allows the Stallings to reclaim these areas and maintain them as pasture or garden.

Commercial forestry is not permitted in the woodland areas that cover the bulk of the 120 acres. Residents of Grannybelle Woods may cut dead trees for personal firewood use, and other tree cutting is allowed for safety purposes.[5]

What Are the Consequences So Far?

Since the easement was signed, the owners have sold all but two of the tracts, tracts 4 and 6. One tract has been sold twice. Grannybelle Woods has turned out just as the Stallings planned. Kerwin Stallings died in 1997 but Vera continues to manage Grannybelle with relish. She has a comfortable country estate and her daughter has decided to build on a tract near Vera's home. In the summer of 1998, Vera and one of the other property owners began growing pumpkins to sell during the busy fall tourist season. The parkland area is used to support one resident's horse, and many local residents venture to Grannybelle Woods to walk. It has turned out to be a successful subdivision for the owner, the residents, tourists, nearby neighbors, and a host of wildlife, including wild turkey and an occasional black bear.

Grannybelle Woods has also had a positive effect on the Great Smoky Mountains National Park. Lying just below the Foothills Parkway, a mountaintop scenic highway managed by the National Park Service, Grannybelle Woods provides a continuous block of forested land, surrounded by the ever-increasing suburban sprawl.

In addition, the Grannybelle Woods easement received a great deal of media attention. As a result, landowners and developers in the region have started to take an interest in the concept of mixing conservation and development. This has led the Foothills Land Conservancy to become involved in four other easements related to "sustainable" developments in the foothills of the Smoky Mountains.

How Is the Easement Enforced?

The Grannybelle Woods easement is enforced just as any other easement—annually—to help ensure that the terms of the easement are not violated. The Stallings (now just Vera) have remained strong financial and vocal supporters of the Foothills Land Conservancy. Usually, successors require some "supervision" in the early days of their ownership of a protected property. By in large, most easement violations occur at the hand of successors to the grantor who either do not fully understand the terms or want to break them regardless; new owners have to be "brought along" to accept and maintain the terms.

What Were the Financial Considerations Involved?

The easement on Grannybelle Woods was donated to the Foothills Land Conservancy, but there were some financial concerns for both parties. The Stallings's primary concern was to design the subdivision and easement to balance the financial returns with their desire to conserve the bulk of the property. They are very happy with the outcome.

At the time, the conservancy was in its infancy, which resulted in concerns over hiring staff and the expenses incurred in the process of documenting the easement, including legal review of the easement and creation of the baseline report. These concerns were quickly overcome, however.[6] In fact, the widespread publicity about the Grannybelle Woods easement launched the Foothills Land Conservancy on the path to protecting more than 8,000 acres in the next five years.

Difficulties and Uniqueness

Grannybelle Woods was the first easement that the Foothills Land Conservancy completed and the first that involved a related development. It has been a great success and a model for several other similar projects in the region because the "fathers" of the project, Kerwin Stallings, and the conservancy president at the time, Rick Everett, both brought unique gifts to the project. Kerwin Stallings was a thoughtful man and conscientious developer. Everett was and is a dedicated environmentalist and professional surveyor. Together, they created a truly successful, just-plain-comfortable, community while preserving 90 percent of the area as either forest or farmland. The easement protects 120 of 200 acres, but perhaps the key to making Grannybelle Woods a successful conservation effort lies as much in the subdivision restrictions, protecting as much as 60 acres of the land sold, as in the easement. These restrictions preclude the deforestation and "lawning" of most of the area of each tract and any development or alteration of the areas in sight of the parkland.

Grannybelle Woods, with its enlightened design and conservation easement, has become a model for "green" or sustainable development in the foothills of the Smoky Mountains. It has proved beyond a shadow of a doubt that landowners can enjoy a return from their property while maintaining its scenic, ecological, and agricultural values.

Notes

1. Noted for community involvement, fund-raising for Gideon Bibles, caring for needy children, and a long life. A neighbor just told me she was "a favorite of everybody for just about everything."
2. A conservation is a buyer who seeks to purchase a tract of land with the intention of preserving and/or improving its conservation or environmental values.
3. The Foothills WMA is a 5,800-acre tract purchased by the Foothills Land Conservancy and donated to the Tennessee Wildlife Resources Agency. It shares about a mile of boundary with the Great Smoky Mountains National Park. The Tennessee Wildlife Resources Agency manages the Foothills WMA, as it does all its WMAs—for maximum wildlife production and for hunting and fishing. The Foothills WMA management plan requires careful monitoring and management of the black bear population. (The bear population of the southern Appalachians fluctuates dramatically, depending on the mast crop.) When the bear population is high, bear hunting is allowed on the WMA. When the population is low, bear hunting may be banned. The overriding mission of the Foothills WMA is to preserve a healthy bear population for generations to come.
4. It is one of the most pressing problems we have: growing residential and tourist populations and rapidly shrinking wild public spaces. The Smoky Mountains and their foothills are subject to the longest ongoing black bear habitat use study in the world. In 1972, the principal researcher, Dr. Mike Pelton, first brought attention to the need for fall and spring feeding areas outside currently established preserves. He currently serves on the board of the directors of the Foothills Land Conservancy.

5. Sample language may be helpful for anyone with similar concerns. The following comes from our easement template:

> (f) The cutting down or other destruction or removal of any trees, shrubs or herbs,
>
> live or dead or standing or fallen, except as follows:
>
> (1) the cutting down or removal of trees or other vegetation necessary to control or prevent hazard along established trails and roadways, described in Exhibit B;
>
> (2) with prior notification and approval of Grantee, the cutting, removal, or use of chemical agents in the control of non-indigenous plant species; such actions shall be in compliance with all applicable state and federal law;
>
> (3) the cutting of dead standing or fallen trees for personal firewood use by Grantor or his assignees.

6. Although the Foothills Land Conservancy did receive a substantial challenge grant from a regional foundation at about the same time, the key is, was, and always will be (to me at least) to get recognition for actually doing projects, protecting land, and getting the job done. Do that and the money will follow. The foundation grant was limited to a one-to-one match for donation from the public. The way to raise money is to do your job—not talk or plan forever—and make sure the public hears about it.

Chapter 15

🎗 🎗

Conservation Easements in the Fifth and Eleventh Federal Circuits

Beth Davis, Laurie Fowler,
Scott Hitch, and Hans Neuhauser

For the most part, the states in the Fifth and Eleventh Federal Circuits have adopted the provisions of the Uniform Conservation Easement Act (UCEA). The omission of a particular provision, however, such as Louisiana's omission of the provision validating easements when not appurtenant to real property, seriously undermine the statute's effectiveness in preserving land. By contrast, some states add statutory language increasing the attractiveness of conservation easements to potential grantors and grantees. For example, both Florida and Georgia limit the liability of easements, and Mississippi treats merger, capital improvements, and rights of enforcement. This chapter explores these provisions in detail.

Alabama

Enacted in 1997, Alabama's Conservation Easement Act draws largely on the UCEA, although several added provisions substantially weaken the state statute. Most importantly is that the act limits the term of easements for which no express term is stated to "the lesser of 30 years or the life of the grantor, or upon the sale of the property by the grantor."[1] Thus, in Alabama, it is imperative that the language of the easement explicitly states the perpetual nature of the encumbrance. Easements that do not expressly state perpetuity as a condition may be terminated. Table 15.1 reflects on how other states in the two southern circuits have addressed this issue.

The Alabama legislature added language to UCEA section 2(a) prohibiting any governmental body from expanding or creating conservation easements by eminent domain.[2] The government cannot force a landowner to sell or donate a conservation easement; a willing grantor is required. On the other hand, the Alabama statute states:

> Nothing in this act shall be construed to impair or diminish in any way the rights of any person, entity, or governmental body authorized by the laws of this state or under federal law to acquire property interests through the exercise of eminent domain or condemnation. A conservation easement may be condemned or appropriated through eminent domain in the same manner as any other property interest.[3]

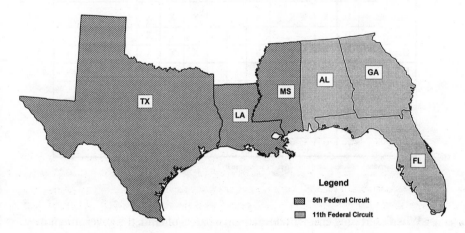

Figure 15.1. States comprising the Fifth and Eleventh Federal Circuits.
Credit: J. A. Gustanski

Table 15.1. Duration of Conservation Easements in the Fifth and Eleventh Federal Circuits

State	Perpetual Mandatory	Perpetual by Default	Term by Default	Silent
Alabama			X	
Florida	X			
Georgia		X		
Louisiana		X		
Mississippi		X		
Texas		X		

Table 15.2. Permissible Terminations, Modifications, and Assignment of Conservation Easements in the Fifth and Eleventh Federal Circuits

STATE	UCEA	RELEASED	TERMINATION BY COURT (UNDER THE PRINCIPLES OF LAW AND EQUITY)	TERMINATION BY TAKING	ABANDONED	TERMINATED BY MERGER	MODIFIED	MODIFIED BY COURT	ASSIGNABLE	SPECIAL NOTES
Alabama	U	X	X	X			X	X	X	
Florida	U								X	
Georgia	U	X	X	X			X	X	X	
Louisiana	U	X	X				X	O	X	
Mississippi	U			X[a]	N			X[a]	X	[a] Land trust is compensated for the value of the conservation easement.
Texas	U	X	X	X			X	X	X	

U = Conservation easement legislation diversity influenced by UCEA.

When exercising eminent domain on a parcel of land, the government may also terminate the conservation easement on that parcel as long as the easement holder as well as the landowner are reasonably compensated. Therefore, although section 2(a) prohibits the state government from *creating* conservation easements through eminent domain, the state can use its eminent domain power to *terminate* an easement. In Table 15.2, statutory provisions of enabling legislation from the Fifth and Eleventh Federal Circuits pertaining to issues of termination, assignability, and modification of easements are compared. The statute also adds language requiring that consent must be obtained from mineral right owners before a conservation easement is created and conveyed.

The Alabama act omits several important provisions of the UCEA. For example, it does not include language that makes the statute applicable to interests created after the effective date of the act.[4] The Alabama act thus requires that instruments creating conservation easements specifically state that they are conservation easements for the act to apply. An instrument that describes the interest created as a "conservation servitude" would not qualify as a conservation easement in the Alabama act.[5]

The Alabama act is not retroactive; the legislature omitted the provisions in UCEA section 5(b). Instead, Alabama replaces that subsection with language that merely specifies that the act will not invalidate other restrictions, including previous conservation easements. Hence, an instrument created before the act was adopted, although claiming to be a conservation easement, is not necessarily entitled to the protection of the act. Such an omission limits the effectiveness of Alabama's law because it restricts the number of easements protected under the act.[6] Table 15.3 illustrates and compares the terminology used for easements across the Fifth and Eleventh Federal Circuit states.

Although it passed unanimously in both the Alabama House and the Alabama Senate, the governor nearly vetoed the Alabama Conservation Easement Act. According to Cathy Stiles Cooley of the Alabama Nature Conser-

Table 15.3. What Conservation Easements Protect in the Fifth and Eleventh Federal Circuits

STATE	UCEA	HOLDER'S PURPOSES	HOLDER'S PURPOSES ARE:	NATURAL	SCENIC	OPEN-SPACE	AGRICULTURAL	SILVICULTURAL	FOREST	RECREATIONAL	AIR QUALITY	WATER QUALITY/WATER	HISTORICAL	ARCHITECTURAL	ARCHAEOLOGICAL	PALEONTOLOGICAL	CULTURAL	CONSERVATION OF LAND	PROTECTING NATURAL RESOURCES	SPECIAL NOTES
Alabama	U	X		X	X	X	X	X	X	X	X	X	X	X	X	X	X	X		X	
Florida	U	X		X	X	X	X			X	X	X	X	X	X	X		X		X	
Georgia	U	X		X	X	X	X			X	X	X	X	X	X	X		X		X	
Louisiana	U	X		X	X	X	X			X	X	X	X	X	X	X		X		X	Also immovable property and unimproved immovable property
Mississippi	U	X		X	X	X	X			X	X	X	X	X	X	X		X		X	Also property available for educational use
Texas	U		X	X	X	X	X			X	X	X	X	X	X	X		X		X	Created or empowered to

U = Conservation easement legislation diversity influenced by UCEA.

vancy, it was a "blessed miracle" that the act passed at all because of the extreme paranoia regarding the environmental impact of the statute on the timber industry.[7] In fact, the provision limiting the term for the easements that do not specify that they are perpetual was inserted at the insistence of a few senators and companies fearing "management from the grave." Careful drafting is the key to overcoming this obstacle. Stiles Cooley and her colleagues championed the bill for over ten years before it was finally enacted.

Florida

Florida enacted the entire UCEA in 1986, adding one section with a series of subsections different from the federal act.[8] Though several of these subsections enhance the attractiveness of easements, others are confusing and work at cross purposes. For example, the act provides that

> conservation easements are perpetual, undivided interests in property and may be created, stated in the form of a restriction, easement, covenant, or condition in any deed, will, or other instrument executed by or on behalf of the owner of the property, or in any order of taking.[9]

In Table 15.4, various forms of restrictions used across the states are indexed. As can be seen, Florida, a state that has largely adopted the Massachusetts model, exhibits only minor variation compared with other states of the region.

All conservation easements are apparently perpetual, yet some instruments creating and conveying conservation easement in Florida include language declaring that the easement may be terminated upon agreement of the parties. Such wording would seem to disqualify these easements from tax advantages provided under state statute and the UCEA. Thus, if a potential donor of a conservation easement is reluctant to agree to the permanence of the instrument, then a different instrument should be used and a different legal relationship should be created between the parties involved. To compound this problem, the Florida statute adds that "a conservation easement may be released by the holder of the easement to the holder of the fee even though the holder of the fee may not be a governmental body or a charitable corporation or trust."[10] This provision allows a statutory way out of a perpetual easement for the landowner. The easement is terminated upon the release to the owner of the underlying fee title because the easement interest merges into the fee interest when both are owned by the same party. On its face, it appears that Florida's section 4 jeopardizes the likelihood that easements would receive federal tax benefits. One way to ensure that a conservation

Table 15.4. How Conservation Easements Protect Land in the Fifth and Eleventh Federal Circuits

STATE	UCEA	NEGATIVE RIGHTS	AFFIRMATIVE RIGHTS	HOLDER'S RIGHT OF ACCESS	NONPOSSESSORY INTEREST	RESTRICTION	EASEMENT	COVENANT	CONDITION	EQUITABLE SERVITUDE	INTEREST IN LAND	INCORPOREAL RIGHT	INTEREST IN PROPERTY	CONTRACTUAL RIGHT	SPECIAL NOTES
Alabama	U	X	X		X	X	X	X		X					
Florida	U	X	X			X	X	X	X						Massachusetts model
Georgia	U	X	X		X	X	X	X		X					
Louisiana	U	X	X		X^a	X		X		X					^a Nonpossessory interest in immovable property
Mississippi	U	X	X		X	X	X	X		X					
Texas	U	X	X		X	X	X	X		X					

U = Conservation easement legislation diversity influenced by UCEA.

easement cannot be terminated in such a manner is to include language in the easement itself restricting its transfer to a designated or qualified third party.

Other discrepancies between the Florida statute and the UCEA are more benign. Florida provides that an easement "shall not be unassignable to other governmental bodies or agencies, charitable organizations, or trusts authorized to acquire such easements, for lack of benefit to dominant estate."[11] This language voids the common-law requirement that an easement must benefit land in some way be transferrable. Thus, the grantee of an easement can assign the easement to another entity if for some reason the grantee can not maintain it. A land trust not having the money to monitor the conditions of an easement or in the process of dissolving, for example, may assign the easement to another grantee.

In Florida, easements may be enforced "by injunction or proceeding in equity or at law, and shall entitle the easement holder to enter the land in a reasonable manner and at reasonable times to assure compliance,"[12] actions that are not specifically authorized in the UCEA. Holders of easements may monitor them to ensure that the land use restrictions are being observed, and the fee title landowner may not deny access for such purposes. The holder may sue for an injunction to stop easement violations that may have occurred or to prevent proposals that are incompatible with the easement terms.

Florida also adds the following to the UCEA: "Recording of the conservation easement shall be notice to the property appraiser and tax collector of the county of the conveyance of the conservation easement."[13] Such language requires that those involved in assessing and appraising land take account of the easement in their valuation procedures. Florida's language in this regard could be stronger, perhaps similar to the language in Georgia's statute. The Florida act does not require any action on the part of appraisers and assessors when easements are created and thus does not suggest that a landowner creating an easement is entitled to a reevaluation of the property.[14]

Florida's act also includes language that limits the liability of organizations holding easements in the state: "The ownership or attempted enforcement of rights held by the holder of an easement does not subject the holder to any liability for any damage or injury that may be suffered by any person on the property or as a result of the condition of the property encumbered by a conservation easement."[15] This insulation from liability makes the position of grantee infinitely more appealing. As shown in Table 15.5, all states across the region provide for enforcement of third-party rights.

Peter Foder of Florida's Department of Environmental Protection states that the state's conservation easement policy is currently under revision.[16] At present, the state spends $300 million per year acquiring land, the largest public and acquisition program in the country. Some legislators feel that easements should be used more frequently, thereby allowing land to stay in private ownership, yet flaws in the Florida act frustrate the effectiveness of the

Table 15.5. Third-Party Enforcement Rights in the Fifth and Eleventh Federal Circuits

STATE	UCEA	THIRD-PARTY ENFORCEMENT
Alabama	U	X
Florida	U	X
Georgia	U	X
Louisiana	U	X
Mississippi	U	X
Texas	U	X

U = Conservation easement legislation diversity influenced by UCEA.

conservation easement as a land preservation tool. Clearly, the intent is that easements created under the act should be permanent and that term easements are discouraged. The statute allows an easement to be released back to the owner in fee, however, which is in direct conflict with the federal provisions requiring perpetuity and which, according to Foder, defeats the purpose of the easement.

Georgia

Georgia's Uniform Conservation Easement Act was enacted in 1992.[8] For the most part, the state treats conservation easements the same as other easements, except that they may not be created or expanded by condemnation.[19] Several additions to the UCEA language enhance the Georgia statute.

Perhaps most important is the act's directive to county tax assessors. It provides that conservation easements be

> recorded in the office of the clerk of the superior court in the county where the land is located. Such recording shall be notice to the board of tax assessors of such county of the conveyance of the conservation easement and shall entitle the owner to a reevaluation of the encumbered real property so as to reflect the existence of the encumbrance on the next succeeding tax digest of the county. Any owner who records a conservation easement and who is aggrieved by a revaluation or lack thereof under this Code section may appeal to the board of equalization and may appeal from the decision of the board of equalization in accordance with Code Section 48-5-311.[20]

Thus, the Georgia act contains language that more directly signals the tax appraiser to reevaluate land subject to a conservation easement than does the Florida statute. The language highlights that a prospective grantor may acquire property tax relief and provides means for landowners to appeal an unfavorable tax assessment. Conservationists in the state advocate an even more aggressive treatment of the property tax issue by the legislature.

In theory, assessment should reduce property taxes to reflect the burden of the easement. There is, however, no express assurance in the act that the assessment will not be higher, which is particularly true if the land has not been evaluated recently and land values in the area have appreciated substantially in intervening years. Under this scenario, even with an easement the land may have a higher value than under previous valuation. Also, some assessors report that even when the value of land with an easement did decrease, the value of surrounding parcels has increased. If a landowner owns these adjacent parcels, the tax benefits of the easement-encumbered parcel are nullified by the corresponding tax increase of the other parcels. In effect, this situation jeopardizes the tax incentives for landowners considering an easement.

As in Florida, Georgia's statute removes the easement holder from any liability associated with the land, thus encouraging the creation of easements.[21] The act states that "the ownership or attempted enforcement of rights held by the holder of an easement shall not subject such holder to any liability for any damage or injury that may be suffered by any person on the property or as a result of the condition of such property encumbered by a conservation easement."[22]

Also helpful is Georgia's requirement that easement holders must be a party to any proceedings held to determine appropriate licenses or permits for construction or demolition activities that might occur on the property.[23] Such a provision gives the grantee the necessary standing to take part in proceedings involving activities that would be inconsistent with the easement conditions.

Louisiana

The Louisiana Conservation Servitude Act, enacted in 1987, omits several provisions of the UCEA, and thus its effectiveness is substantially weakened.[24] For example, the statute omits the UCEA language validating conservation easements although not appurtenant to a real property interest or lacking privity of estate or contract. The omission of these validations probably occurred because they identify characteristics that invalidate an easement, and Louisiana's statute describes conservation easements as servitudes.[24] The "touch and concern" and privity requirements, however, are traditional defenses against creating servitudes and should therefore be specifically disallowed.

A less significant omission on Louisiana's part is that of UCEA section 3(b): "This Act does not affect the power of a court to modify or terminate a conservation easement in accordance with the principles of law and equity."[25] Even without such power, the courts may modify or terminate conservation easements using the doctrine of changed conditions.

Louisiana adds to UCEA section 6 that "this Chapter shall not be applied or construed to allow or permit the holder or owner of such servitude to obstruct or in any way impede the construction, operation, or maintenance of needed public utility facilities as provided by law on the effective date of this Chapter."[26] By incorporating this language, Louisiana gives precedence to public facilities over conservation servitudes, which directly contradicts Mississippi law expressly restricting capital improvements on land protected by an easement.

According to Skipper Dickson of the Tensas Conservancy Coalition, conservation servitudes are a new phenomenon in Louisiana and therefore are not yet widely used.[27] In addition, conservation easements in the state may possess limited attractiveness to landowners because relatively low land values do not entitle them to substantial property tax breaks.

Mississippi

The Mississippi Conservation Easement Act of 1986 has added three key provisions to the UCEA that strengthen it significantly.[28] For example, Mississippi added to UCEA section 2 that "a conservation easement shall continue to be effective and shall not be extinguished if the easement holder is or becomes the owner in fee of the subject property."[29] Contrast this provision with Florida's "escape clause." In Mississippi, then, a conservation easement is not extinguished if the easement holder acquires fee title to the land on which an easement exists. This provision has an obvious advantage: A land trust may acquire the fee to a parcel of land on which it holds an easement without terminating the easement.

Mississippi has increased the likelihood that land use restrictions described in conservation easement documents will be enforced by allowing "the Attorney General of the state of Mississippi; and The Mississippi Department of Wildlife Conservation," to bring a civil action to enforce the terms of a conservation easement.[30] This provision allows cash-strapped land trusts to form partnerships with better financed public agencies to ensure that an easement is enforced.

Mississippi provides that whenever any conservation easement is conveyed and recorded, the clerk of the court must mail certified copies and notice of the date and place of recording to the attorney general and the Department of Wildlife Conservation. Such a requirement must be included as a provision in the deed of conservation easement. In addition, the holder of any conservation easement created prior to the date of the act who wished to qualify for the benefits provided by the act was required to provide similar notice to the attorney general and the Department of Wildlife Conservation within a year after the act went into effect.[31] These provisions ensure that the attorney general and the Department of Wildlife are notified that a conservation easement, which they may be required to enforce, has been created. An additional benefit of these provisions is that they effectively create a centralized database of all the conservation easements in the state. Finally, the notice provisions allowed those landowners who placed conservation easements on their property before the act was passed to gain the benefits of this act retroactively.

The Mississippi statute also provides that public money shall *not* be expended for capital improvements on any real property upon which a conservation easement has been granted. There are, however, two categories of exceptions.[32] The first exception arises if the conservation easement is perpetual, if a governmental body holds the easement, and if the capital improvements are solely for the use and benefit of the holder.[33] The government may not, for example, install a sewage pipe along the banks of a river where a perpetual conservation easement exists unless the government holds the easement and unless it can be shown the proposed improvements are solely for the use and benefit of the public. The second exception applies to "Mississippi Landmarks" and properties entered in the National Register of Historic Places.[34]

Mississippi has expanded those provisions of the UCEA that limit the definition of "holder" of conservation easements to charitable corporations, charitable associations, or charitable trusts. In Mississippi, holders may include private, nonprofit, or educational corporations, associations, or trusts.[36] Therefore, virtually any organization may accept a conservation easement in the state. For the grantor to be eligible for federal income tax benefits, however, the grantee must meet the requirements of "a qualified organization" under the federal tax code. Table 15.6 indicates that all states across the two judicial circuits allow for the holding of conservation interests by nonprofit organizations, government agencies, and other charitable organi-

Table 15.6. Who May Hold Conservation Easements in the Fifth and Eleventh Federal Circuits

STATE	UCEA	GOVERNMENT	CHARITABLE TRUSTS	CHARITABLE ASSOCIATIONS	CHARITABLE CORPORATIONS	SECTION 501 (C)(3) TAX-EXEMPT CORPORATION	SPECIAL NOTES
Alabama	U	X	X	X	X		
Florida	U	X	X		X		
Georgia	U	X	X	X	X		
Louisiana	U	X	X	X	X		
Mississippi	U	X	X	X	X		Private, nonprofit, charitable, or educational organization
Texas	U	X	X	X	X		

U = Conservation easement legislation diversity influenced by UCEA.

zations, although Mississippi is the most flexible in allowing "private, non-profit, charitable, or educational organization[s]" as well.

The Mississippi statute omits UCEA language allowing a conservation easement to be "released, modified, terminated, or otherwise altered or affected" in the same method and manner as other easements. Thus, easements may be exempt from the traditional easement methods of modification and termination because the statute does not expressly refer to them.[37]

T. Logan Russell of the Delta Environmental Land Trust Association said that the principal impediment to the use of conservation easements in Mississippi is not the statute, but rather the economics of easements.[38] He explained that people will not encumber land unless they receive adequate financial reward for doing so. Russell suggests that the American Farm and Ranch Protection Act, which Congress passed in 1998, will encourage the use of easements by providing greater tax incentives.

Texas

Enacted in 1983, the Texas Conservation Easements Act is unique in imposing a penalty on landowners who terminate a conservation easement. The act states:

> If a land that has been subject to a conservation easement is no longer subject to such easement, an additional tax is imposed on the land equal to the difference, if any, between the taxes imposed on the land for each of the five years preceding the year in which the easement terminates and the taxes that would have been imposed had the land not been subject to a conservation easement in each of those years, plus interest at an annual rate of seven percent calculated from the dates on which the differences would have become due.[39]

This penalty on easement termination can be perceived as positive for land trusts and conservation interests by discouraging termination. Audry Martin of the Valley Land Trust says the rollback provision is harmful to conservation easements in Texas because the tax penalty for terminating an easement discourages a landowner from ever creating one.[39] She views it as a penalty for ever accepting the reduced tax rate.

Edward Fritz of the Natural Area Preservation Association believes that one of the largest impediments to the use of conservation easements is the reluctance of county tax appraisers to reevaluate land burdened by easements.[40] He advocates language in the statute specifying that land burdened by a conservation easement must receive a tax reduction.

Conclusion

In the Fifth and Eleventh Federal Circuits a common and major impediment to conservation easement is the lack of property tax relief afforded by the various state statutes, a problem reiterated by conservationists in Georgia, Texas, Mississippi, and Louisiana. Although the Georgia statute goes the farthest by providing that a conservation easement may trigger a property evaluation, even that statute does not ensure property tax relief. One way the states might rectify this situation is to require the local governments' property tax assessment to incorporate or at least take into consideration the property owner's independent appraisal conducted for IRS purposes. This method would help avoid the problem that arises when the county appraiser, basing the reevaluation on a historical assessment, comes up with a higher value than the landowner anticipates. Another option would be for states to guarantee property tax reductions at a specified rate if conservation easements meet certain requirements. The states could then pay the local government, which otherwise would be losing tax revenues, the amount they would otherwise be receiving for a defined period. Then, when the period ends and the state ceases to guarantee the reduction, the tax could be reinstated reflecting the lower property value.

Notes

1. AL § 2(c).
2. AL § 2(a). "A conservation easement may not be created or expanded under this act by any state, county, or local governmental body through the exercise of the power of eminent domain."
3. AL § 2(e).
4. UCEA § 5(a).
5. AL § 5(a).
6. See note 5.
7. Personal correspondence between Beth Davis and Cathy Stiles Cooley, 1998.
8. Fla. Stat. § 704.06 (1996).
9. Fla. Stat. (2). The "in any order of taking" language is later limited in the statute to the express statement that the government may not create a conservation easement by eminent domain.
10. Ibid.
11. Ibid.
12. Fla. Stat. (4).
13. Fla. Stat. (7).
14. GA § 44-10-8.
15. Fla. Stat. (10).
16. Telephone conference between Beth Davis and Peter Fodor, 1998.
17. GA § 44-10-1 et seq.
18. GA § 44-10-3(a).

19. GA § 44-10-8.
20. GA § 44-10-3(e).
21. Ibid.
22. GA § 44-10-3(e).
23. La. R.S. 9:1272 (1997).
24. La. R.S. 9:1272 (1997).
25. La. R.S. 9:1272 (1997).
26. LA § 9:1276(c).
27. Personal conversation between Beth Davis and Skipper Dickson, 1998.
28. Miss. Code Ann. § 89.19-1 (1996).
29. Miss. Code Ann. § 89-19-5 (5).
30. Miss. Code Ann. § 89-19-7(d) and (e).
31. Miss. Code Ann. § 89-19-15.
32. Miss. Code Ann. § 89-19-11.
33. Ibid.
34. Mississippi Landmarks are defined by the Antiquities Law of Mississippi section 39-7-1 et seq., Mississippi Code of 1972.
35. UCEA § 1, (2)(ii); Miss. Code Ann. § 89-19-3 (2)(b).
36. UCEA § 2 (a); Miss. Code Ann. § 89-19-5 (1). This omission may not be relevant when viewed in conjunction with Miss. Code Ann. § 89-19-7 (7), which reserves the power of the court to modify or terminate an easement according to the laws of equity. This provision could be helpful because there are many ways to terminate an easement in common law, and by omitting this language, methods that are not expressly mentioned in the statute might not be applied to conservation easements. By omitting such language, the legislatures may have restricted the ability of the courts to terminate easements under traditional doctrines, such as the "doctrine of changed conditions." Because such doctrines stem from traditional judicial principles and because the statute does not expressly rule them out, however, the effect may be negligible.
37. Personal correspondence between Beth Davis and T. Logan Russell, 1998.
38. Tex. Nat. Res. Code § 183.002(f).
39. Personal conservation between Beth Davis and Audry Martin, 1998.
40. Personal conversation between Beth Davis and Edward Fritz, 1998.

Chapter 16

꙰ ꙰

Acacia Protecting Texas Hill Country

David Bezanson

The state of Texas is remarkable for its natural diversity as well as for Texans' enthusiasm for nature and outdoor recreation. Yet despite Texans' love of the outdoors, Texas contains relatively little public land under management for wildlife conservation. Most public parks and wildlife areas are concentrated in a few parts of the state (notably west Texas and the Gulf coast). In much of Texas, the burdens of land and wildlife conservation fall largely on the shoulders of private landowners. Consequently, institutions and incentives that encourage private conservation are extremely important in Texas.

Urban development has transformed the character and landscape of Texas in recent decades. The state's population has doubled since 1960, with dramatic growth occurring around Austin, Houston, Dallas–Fort Worth, San Antonio, El Paso, McAllen, Brownsville, Killeen, and other urban areas.[1] According to the *Dallas Morning News,* "During the same time period, the percentage of Texans who own or manage farming and ranching operations has steadily decreased."[2] These realities are reshaping patterns of land ownership in Texas as well as the growing economic importance of hunting and other recreational activities. Many landowners, whether they manage long-held properties or recently acquired ones, are seeking new ways to balance production and conservation.

Today's landowners inherit rural landscapes greatly modified by agriculture and industry. East Texas today is a mosaic of pine plantations, small ranches, towns, and cities. North-central Texas, the coastal plain, the Panhandle, and other parts of the state are dominated by intensive agriculture, with tens of millions of farmed acres. Cattle ranching is economically important in almost every Texas county. Each of the industries that have supported the region's wealth—cotton, corn and wheat, cattle, wool and mohair, oil, technology—has left imprints on the land.

A century of cattle, sheep, and goat ranching has greatly altered the vegetation of the Edwards Plateau of central Texas, or Texas hill country, which is now under further threat from urbanization, rural subdivision, and development (Figure 16.1). Originally an open grassland of native bluestem grasses and live oaks, the upland ranch country of the Edwards Plateau is now infested with invasive brush species such as Ashe juniper, mesquite, and exotic grasses such as King Ranch bluestem. Range conditions have deteriorated severely in some parts of the plateau. Landowners and conservation organizations often must conduct restoration and management activities, including prescribed burning and brush control, to reestablish range productivity.

Hills and canyons of the Edwards Plateau area are becoming choice locations for residential development, especially around the expanding metropolitan centers of Austin and San Antonio. These slopes and canyons are also of unique ecological importance, containing hardwood trees and other native plants that have become scarce in the uplands and more accessible areas due

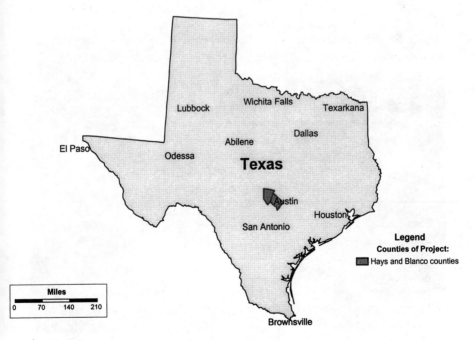

Figure 16.1. Texas and regional perspective.
Credit: J. A. Gustanski

to livestock grazing, browsing by white-tailed deer, fire, drought, or long-term climatological changes. The canyons also contain mature Ashe junipers, which provide the preferred nesting habitat of the golden-cheeked warbler, an endangered songbird.

Water quality and water conservation are important political issues in central Texas. The Edwards Plateau contains limestone aquifers that supply drinking water to San Antonio and other cities; development in slope areas impacts groundwater quality. Because of the ecological significance of the land and aquifers, private landowners in the hill country have faced numerous regulatory constraints, from the federal Endangered Species Act to municipal ordinances restricting development. In general, these constraints have not deterred growth and development in the region, but have created a charged political climate in which regulatory authorities and environmentalists have been accused of discouraging private conservation. After spearheading several public land conservation efforts around Austin, groups such as The Nature Conservancy are pursuing land conservation projects that emphasize private stewardship.

In 1994, Nancy Powell Moore, a Houston philanthropist, acquired a 158-acre ranch in Hays and Blanco Counties near Austin, with the intent of restor-

Photograph 16.1. Acacia-protected Texas hill country.
Photo credit: David Bezanson.

ing its resource values and the integrity of its natural landscapes (Photograph 16.1). Moore's property fronts the Pedernales River (made famous by President Lyndon B. Johnson, whose nearby ranch is now a national park). The Pedernales valley is urbanizing as Austin and other hill country towns grow together. The rapidly escalating land values in the area (land with river or lake frontage can range from $10,000 to $50,000 per acre) make agriculture and wildlife management increasingly nonviable options for landowners.

With extensive frontage on the Pedernales and several scenic canyons on the property, Moore's ranch was a prime candidate for breakup into "ranchettes" of 5 to 15 acres. Moore decided that she was not interested in subdivision. "That's not my business," she said. "If I buy something, I want to keep it forever."[3]

Moore sought partners to help her protect the property. She became interested in the concept of conservation easements after reading information from The Nature Conservancy, but like many landowners, she was initially hesitant about working with strangers and embracing a new idea. In taking such a step, Moore said, "Trust is everything."[4]

Conservation easements are not completely new to Texas—they were first authorized by the state legislature in 1982—yet at best the concept has caught on slowly and is still unfamiliar territory to a number of Texas's 254 appraisal districts. In 1994, only a handful of land trust organizations existed in Texas to receive conservation easements, and Moore did not personally know anyone involved with a land trust other than the Nature Conservancy. Fortunately, The Nature Conservancy and Texas Parks and Wildlife Department staff referred her to a trust, the Natural Area Preservation Association (NAPA), which accepts land or conservation easements on property containing native habitat. NAPA currently owns or manages about 4,000 acres around the state, mostly in east and north Texas.[5]

After Moore met with NAPA's officers, NAPA introduced Moore to other landowners who had granted easements or decided to manage land for conservation. Moore also talked to J. David Bamberger, a retired businessperson who had purchased a nearby ranch and painstakingly restored its range vegetation. Bamberger credits his efforts with restoring several natural springs on the property that had dried up, choked by juniper and other invasive species of brush.[6]

The landowners' enthusiasm and dedication, as well as the land trust's respect for their wishes, impressed Moore. "[The preserves] were all very different," Moore said, "but that was fine; they were all about the same thing: protection of Texas's varied environment."[7] After deciding that NAPA's goals were compatible with hers, Moore granted a conservation easement on her property to NAPA in 1996.

Moore's ranch, now named Acacia, contains many of the unique and special features of the hill country (see Photograph 16.1). Part grazing land, the property descends 150 to 200 feet to rugged spring-fed canyons that flow into the Pedernales River. Large bald cypress and pecan groves that survive semi-annual scouring floods that occasionally send thirty-foot walls of water down the Pedernales canyon line the river. The smaller canyons contain perennial creeks lined with bald cypress, sycamore, and elm trees as well as scarce understory trees such as rough-leaf dogwood, Texas ash, and black cherry. The creeks sustain water-loving plants, including the chatterbox orchid and maidenhair fern.

Part of the property that Moore bought also carries with it an easement granting access to Deadman's Hole, a collapsed sinkhole with a waterfall and swimming hole located on a nearby property. The easement is open to landowners, including Moore, who share ownership of the canyon of Deadman's Creek.

Moore and NAPA wrote the provisions of her conservation easement to protect the unique natural features of the property, while allowing Moore and her family to build residential structures.[8] The easement permanently prohibits any removal of topsoil, sand, rock, or gravel except for construction and maintenance of permitted improvements; other language disallows removal of native trees (other than young Ashe junipers, which are considered invasive) except for permitted activities. The easement also prohibits destruction to wildlife and plants (except Ashe juniper) by motorized vehicles and prohibits hunting of native animals except in the event of disease or overpopulation. Culling of white-tailed deer may occur on the property if animal density threatens the native vegetation.[9]

In the easement, Moore reserved the right to build an agreed-upon number of structures, access roads, and related infrastructure, but stipulated that the structures will be located on an upland site rather than a sensitive canyon or slope area. The easement also restricts the aggregate footprint area of all structures on the property. Agricultural activities that are consistent with the stated purposes of the easement are allowed. No activity permitted by the easement is likely to conflict with the easement's primary goal: to preserve the property in perpetuity "as a natural and ecological resource and as habitat for native animals and plants."

Stewardship committees manage NAPA's preserves. Each committee consists of the landowner and a few volunteers chosen by the landowner and NAPA. This committee manages the property under the terms of the easement and, when necessary, helps to bring in additional labor and expertise. Moore's committee has met twice a year since 1996. Committee meetings are a combination of business and pleasure, usually including a site visit and dinner before the business meeting, in which management activities and modifications to the property are discussed.

When Moore bought Acacia, the upland part of the property was leased for grazing to qualify for agricultural property tax exemption, which reduced the tax valuation to a fraction of market value. Range conditions had been impoverished by overgrazing (like many Edwards Plateau ranches), and Natural Resource Conservation Service (NRCS) personnel recommended either removing the cattle or reducing animal density, which the leaseholder refused to agree to.

Fortunately, in 1995, the Texas legislature authorized a tax exemption for wildlife management, available to holders of the agricultural exemption.[10] Tired of arguing with the leaseholder about animal density, Moore terminated the grazing lease and applied for the wildlife management exemption, which requires qualifying landowners to conduct extensive improvements to benefit wildlife. These activities may include habitat enhancement; erosion control; predator control; creation of supplemental food, water, or shelter; and population censuses.

To qualify for the exemption, Moore invited volunteer teams to conduct annual bird surveys and monitor nesting by endangered golden-cheeked warblers on the property. Friends cleared acres of Ashe juniper and stacked piles of dead brush to protect plant seedlings and to block erosion. Family members and friends have built nesting boxes for wood ducks and songbirds.

For a bigger erosion control project, Moore received free advice from NRCS personnel and from Beyrl Armstrong, a land management consultant who assists hill country landowners in working with regulatory restrictions and other problems. Bamberger helped Moore contact Americorps volunteers from Austin. For a minimal stipend, the Americorps volunteers—mostly high school or college-aged students—planned and built (with Armstrong's help) a geofabric and rock-and-gravel chute to redirect an erosive gully that threatened to wash out a ranch road.

The Americorps team also designed and constructed a 1,000-gallon water catchment project to benefit wildlife. The catchment area of the project catches rainwater and directs it into a fiberglass tank. It proved worthy during a summer drought in 1998. "It stayed essentially full through the drought," Armstrong said. "It could provide the majority of water for a household." Americorps students also constructed a nature trail that blocks erosion on a steep slope.[11]

The importance of Acacia for conservation has allowed Moore to draw on an unusual amount of volunteer labor. Management of the property has benefited from the expertise of a wildlife biologist with the state Parks and Wildlife Department, who has donated her time to serve on the committee and oversee a wildlife surveillance project. Armstrong and bird expert John Gee, both neighbors, donated time to conduct monitoring activities. Austin birders come to record residents and migrants several times a year.

Moore has encouraged other landowners to become involved in wildlife activities, using the tax benefit as an incentive to promote cooperative management. The idea of a wildlife management cooperative was attractive to some of the holders of adjacent 5-acre canyon lots, as their tracts are too small for agricultural or large-scale management activities that would allow them to qualify for tax exemptions. These tracts previously held an agricultural exemption in common with the land that Moore bought and thus were eligible for the switch. Moore eventually hopes to bring in all the landowners that share the canyon of Deadman's Creek and thus reunite the area, once a single ranch, under a single management plan.

In acquiring the property, Moore learned of a restrictive covenant on the old ranch, including her ranch and other tracts along Deadman's Canyon, by former owners at the time of a previous subdivision in 1981. Recognizing the uniqueness of their land, previous owners James and Leta Hurlbut placed deed restrictions on the canyon property prohibiting mobile homes, Quonset structures, campers, trailers, junkyards, swine farms or commercial feed lots, nonagricultural commercial activities, or subdivision into tracts smaller than 5 acres. These restrictions—sort of a protolandscape ordinance—apply to Moore and most of her neighbors and probably help to limit construction in the sensitive canyon areas. Therefore, with her conservation easement, Moore is carrying out the Hurlbuts's wishes, too.

Moore has sought conservation buyers to buy the valuable tracts around her, especially the undivided tracts that share parts of the canyon of Deadman's Creek. Nevertheless, the growth of resort communities and subdivision of family ranches is creating a patchwork of small land holdings that will make protecting the area's natural values more difficult. The same forces of urban encroachment and subdivision are ongoing in many parts of Texas. In the process, many landowners feel that the attractive qualities of rural central Texas are being lost.

Texas landowners face a threatening future shaped by urban development, increasingly marginal returns from agricultural activities, and crippling estate taxes. Land ownership in rural areas of Texas, including the hill country, is increasingly dominated by retired or second-home owners from the cities. The large family ranching operations that once dominated central and west Texas, surviving until the present day, are now being broken up into suburban or ranchette subdivisions, particularly in scenic parts of the hill country and west Texas.

New conservation strategies are being tailored to exploit these trends. For example, the wildlife management tax valuation provides an incentive for a new kind of low-density subdivision. In a handful of new subdivisions in the hill country, homeowners are voluntarily forming cooperatives and contracting with companies like Armstrong's to conduct wildlife management activities on areas of the subdivision that are reserved as open space. Like Moore's neighbors, members of these cooperatives are able to qualify for the lower valuation and realize substantial tax benefits despite the small size of their individual holdings. The resulting low-density development is attractive to some county governments in the hill country, because it attracts growth while protecting the wildlife and rural character, the basis of local tourism.

Around Austin, concern over watershed protection has led city officials and planners to look for unusual ways to control suburban sprawl. In 1998, Austin voters approved $60 million in bonds to purchase and preserve undeveloped ranchland in watersheds that drain into the city or the nearby Edwards Aquifer.[12] Much of this purchase, supervised by the city and the Nature Conservancy, will be accomplished through resale of the land with conservation easements.

Large conservation efforts, however, are likely to remain tied to Austin and other cities. Conserving land and wildlife through private ownership is a tradition among Texas landowners, but many Texans mistrust the idea of coordinated planning for conservation, particularly if governments are involved. In the early 1990s, the threatened regulation of private land under the Endangered Species Act to protect songbirds, as well as the creation of a regulatory authority to conserve water in the Edwards Aquifer, triggered protests from landowner groups in central Texas. Since then, "private property" interests and some public officials have discouraged and criticized new regulation of private land.

In the meantime, as growth continues and land prices push higher, private conservation efforts have accelerated. Many landowners, motivated by the conviction that rural Texas is slipping away, have chosen voluntarily to place their land under protection. Many, such as businessperson Roland Baird Jr., are motivated by values rooted in the culture of this conservative state. Baird's late mother, Faye Baird, donated the conservation easement on their family ranch near the Pedernales to ensure preservation of the ranch as she had known it.

Today, Roland Baird maintains a small number of cattle (primarily as pets) on upland pasture, which has been liberated from Ashe juniper by extensive clearing and light grazing. Wire fences protect "enclosures" of native vegetation from overbrowsing by deer. The canyons of the ranch shelter native hardwood species, including cherry and oak trees. The conservation easement, held by NAPA, adorns the wall of the ranch house.

In addition to NAPA, Texas now has more than a dozen active land trusts, most established since 1982. Several land trusts have formed to address conservation needs in specific parts of the state, including the Valley Land Fund in south Texas and the Katy Prairie Conservancy in Houston. Statewide, the Nature Conservancy has led region-based conservation projects and preserved many important sites through ownership, conservation easements, and transfer to other management entities. All together, private groups or citizens have protected more than 250,000 acres in Texas. Most of that land has been set aside to protect wildlife or native habitat.

As urban sprawl changes the character of Texas, private conservation will continue to be vital for preserving the wildlife that Texans value so highly. Private hunting leases generate $170 million annually, and hunting is an economic mainstay of many rural counties.[13] Hunters spent $1.3 billion to hunt in Texas in 1996.[14]

After the Shields family donated their property near Dallas to NAPA in 1996, they noticed more wildlife on their preserve. "As southwest Dallas grows and development becomes more intense," said Polly Shields, "that only makes [preserving habitat] more important."[15]

Her mother, Wilma Shields, began buying land behind her house— located just off an interstate highway in a Dallas suburb—in the 1980s to protect her backyard view and creek from developers. She fought off an attempt by the county to seize the land and other attempts to develop it. Had she chosen to sell the land, it would have been extremely valuable as development property.

Instead, Shields dedicated the land to a different purpose: honoring her mother's memory by establishing the Veda Farrington Preserve, 315 acres of prairie, hilltop views, and oak and pecan groves that will never be cleared to build tract houses or freeways. The land is greatly devalued with the conservation easement, which suits Wilma and Polly Shields just fine. "We plan to keep it that way," said Polly Shields. "We want to do whatever we can to protect what is already there."

For the Shields, protection will probably involve little active management, although control of Ashe juniper is likely to be an ongoing task. After years of alteration, it will take a while for range plants to regenerate, a struggle faced by dozens of property owners around the state.

Continued effort and sacrifice by landowners will be essential to preserve the natural ecosystems, wildlife, and rural character of Texas. In preserving their lands, Moore, Shields, and dozens of others are making valuable contributions, ensuring that their children and grandchildren will see the landscapes and wildlife that Texans enjoy today.

Notes

1. According to the U.S. Census Bureau, the 1960 population of Texas was 9,579,677; the bureau's estimated population of Texas in 1997 was 19,439,000. During the same period, the population of just the Austin–San Antonio area grew from roughly 1 million to an estimated 2.4 million. Much of this growth has involved formerly rural areas. U.S. Census Bureau, Internet: www.census.gov/, 1997.

2. Dallas Morning News, *1994-95 Texas Almanac and State Industrial Guide* (Dallas: Dallas Morning News, 1993).

3. Personal communication, May 1998.

4. Ibid.

5. NAPA, a private, volunteer, land trust corporation dedicated to preserving area of land in natural condition in Texas, was incorporated in 1982. Its bylaws state that the organization's purpose, in part, is "to preserve significant natural areas for wildlife protection and to advise and help people to preserve ecosystems and protect wildlife by educating citizens, including landowners, about the values and methods of preservation . . . by owning and protecting natural areas."

6. Personal communication, May 1998.

7. Ibid.

8. Covenants of the easement state that

> "The uses of the Protected Property will be confined to activities that are consistent with the goals enunciated in this Dedication of Conservation Easement or in Section 170(h) of the Internal Revenue Code or that are expressly permitted in this Dedication of Conservation Easement. . . . The following structures and activities are allowed: roofed shelters for camping, picnicking or nature study; two houses and future additions; recreation facilities; kitchen gardens for personal use; storage sheds; barns/garages; firewood sheds; outhouses; sauna/bath houses; greenhouses; workshops; propane tanks; water storage tanks; plumbing; electrical service; power generators; water wells and water pumps; and vehicle parking. Grantor may provide utilities including water, domestic waste disposal, overhead electricity, and telephone lines to and from the above-mentioned structures. . . . In connection with the proposed "two houses and future additions" permitted in paragraph 2 above, Grantor makes the following stipulation. Grantor has delivered to Grantee a plat of the Protected Property with elevation contours marked on it delineating 20 feet elevation increments. On this plat, Grantor has crosshatched the area which extends downward from the 840 foot elevation contour line to the centerlines of Live Oak Creek, Deadman's Creek and Perch Creek. . . . Grantor understands and agrees

that this crosshatched area will not be utilized as the site for the "two houses and future addition." The size and location of the structures described . . . above shall be determined by Grantor keeping in mind the goals enunciated in this Dedication of Conservation Easement. Furthermore, Grantor stipulates that the aggregate footprint area of all these structures shall not exceed 6 acres. (Hays County Deed Records, Vol. 1279, p. 292.)

9. The easement states:

There shall be no hunting, killing, trapping or taking of animals except to correct an imbalance, or to remove domestic animals or diseased animals. Any intended taking or capture of animals must be approved by the hereinafter described Stewardship Committee after consultation with state or federal agencies having wildlife and/or plant life under their jurisdiction.

This language was written to allow culling of deer in the event of overpopulation. The easement also provides that

There shall be no removal, destruction or cutting of trees except as follows: (i) as necessary in the construction of and participation in allowable activities other than activities specified in paragraph 7 above [removal of topsoil, sand, gravel, rock, etc.], (ii) Chinese tallow and other exotic plants, and (iii) juniper having trunks below 10 inches in diameter, breast height.

10. Texas Tax Code Ann. 23.51 (Vernon 1992 and Supp. 1998).
11. Personal communication with Moore, May 1998.
12. Nature Conservancy of Texas, personal communication, 1998.
13. Dallas Morning News, *1994-95 Texas Almanac and State Industrial Guide*.
14. Texas Parks and Wildlife Department, personal communication, 1998.
15. Personal communication, November 1998.

Chapter 17

Conservation Easements in the Sixth Federal Circuit

John F. Rohe

The Sixth Circuit Court of Appeals of the federal judicial system is composed of Kentucky, Michigan, Ohio, and Tennessee (Figure 17.1). All four states have one thing in common: Each has a unique conservation easement statute. Amid differences in terminology, the statutes provide a mechanism to protect natural and cultural resources. Semantic distinctions from one state to the next may result from the relative novelty of conservation easements to the traditional body of real property law. Accordingly, differences in terminology could often be matters of form rather than substance.

Kentucky

Kentucky has explicitly adopted the Uniform Conservation Easement Act (UCEA) with only minor grammatical adjustments. For example, the UCEA states: "a conservation easement is unlimited in duration." The Kentucky legislature, with a flair for temporal accuracy, modified this provision as follows: "a conservation easement shall be unlimited in duration."[1] Similarly, the UCEA states: "An interest in real property . . . is not impaired." Kentucky, however, prefers: "An interest in real property . . . shall not be impaired."[2] These minor adjustments in tense should have no substantive impact, particularly because both the Kentucky statute and the UCEA "shall be applied and construed to effectuate its general purpose to make uniform laws with respect to conservation easements among the states enacting them."[3]

In the Sixth Federal Circuit, Kentucky holds a distinction in conservation easement law. It is the only state in which mining lobbyists have left their mark indelibly etched on the conservation easement terrain. Fearing the interests protected by conservation easement laws might interfere with inter-

263

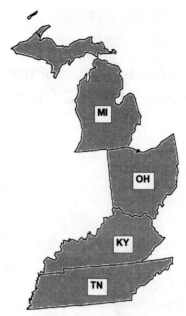

Figure 17.1. States comprising the Sixth Federal Circuit.
Credit: J. A. Gustanski

ests of the mining industry, Kentucky Revised Statutes Annotated section 382.850 states:

> (1) A conservation easement shall not be transferred by the owners of property in which there are outstanding subsurface rights without the prior written consent of the owners of the subsurface rights.

> (2) A conservation easement shall not operate to limit, preclude, delete or require waivers for the conduct of coal mining operations, including the transportation of coal, upon any part or all of adjacent or surrounding properties . . . .

Kentucky holds a unique distinction in affording subsurface property owners a hand in above-surface interests. Thus, substantive above-ground interests can paradoxically depend on whether the conflicting claim resides above or below ground level, which could lead to peculiar claims. For example, the approval of a below-ground basement tenant could be required to approve an above-ground historic easement, yet consent of the first-floor tenant might, interestingly, be unnecessary.

Michigan

Conservation easements were used by conservancies and land trusts in Michigan long before the state's Conservation and Historic Preservation Easement Act[4] became effective in 1995. They were commonly assumed to be legal, and their validity was not challenged in reported case law. Although certain jurisdictions have not recognized easements in gross,[5] Michigan courts have. Because a conservation easement is generally not an appurtenant easement, prior to the adoption of Michigan Conservation and Historic Preservation Easement Act, practitioners considered them to be easements in gross. In 1923, the Michigan Supreme Court contrasted easements in gross with easements appurtenant in *Smith v. Dennedy*[6]:

> Under the rule that there can be no easement without a distinct dominant tenement, it is said that there can, in strictness, be no such thing as an easement in gross. But there is a class of rights which one may have in another's land without their being exercised in connection with the occupancy of other lands, and they are therefore called rights or easement in gross, and in such cases, the burden rests upon one piece of land in favor of a person or an individual; the principal distinction between an easement proper, that is an easement appurtenant, and a right in gross is found in the fact that in the first there is and in the second there is not a dominant tenement.

Easements in gross, however, were known to arise commonly in connection with utility companies and railroads.[7] Admittedly, before Michigan's enabling legislation for conservation easements, land trusts did not possess explicit legal authority for a conservation easement. The uncertainty provided interesting fodder for intellectual consumption at land trust meetings, but never materialized in a reported case. The 1995 statute silenced any possible claim of invalidity.

Although Michigan did not explicitly adopt the UCEA, the state's legislative scheme essentially upholds interests protected by it. As Michigan is a race-notice state,[8] the statute explicitly protects the rights of a "bona fide purchaser for value without actual notice."[9]

Unlike Tennessee, the Michigan Conservation and Historic Preservation Easement Act does not, by its terms, authorize a reduction in ad valorem taxes due to the conservation easement. The Michigan Tax Tribunal has, however, ruled, in a case of first impression, that eased lands are to be taxed at their eased value.[10]

Michigan land trusts have experienced a surge in popularity. Of the state's thirty-eight land trusts, twenty-two were formed after 1987,[11] an impressive increase of 237 percent in approximately one decade.

According to a 1998 survey by Michigan Outdoors Habitat Brokerage, Inc.,[12] the nineteen Michigan conservancies that responded have protected a total of 40,947 acres. Forty-three percent of the sheltered land is characterized as wooded. Wetlands and open space also draw the attention of Michigan conservationists. Other than federal and state lands, the Michigan chapter of the Nature Conservancy holds the largest slice of Michigan's conservation pie with 15,712 acres. The Little Traverse Conservancy ranked second with 9,884 acres (now 11,000), and the Michigan Nature Association was third with 5,699. These figures do not include in partnership "assists" with public agencies. For example, The Nature Conservancy has "assists" exceeding 50,000 acres.

Partnerships and "assists" have recently expanded the traditional role of conservancies. For example, the Little Traverse Conservancy has joined with local units of government in partnership "assists" to secure state and federal funding for parks and nature preserves by lending grant-writing expertise to well-intentioned members of local boards. In Cedarville, The Nature Conservancy's expertise has empowered the chamber of commerce to appreciate and respect the foundational role of a natural resource base for a healthy economy. Similarly, the Grand Traverse Regional Land Conservancy has provided expertise in a "community visioning" project to guide urban planning.

Land conservancies have enabled members of the State Bar of Michigan to provide legal expertise and to form gratifying relationships in the conservation community. Bar members regularly offer services to land conservancies at reduced or nonexistent fees. Unfortunately, these services do not qualify as pro bono under the guidelines adopted by the State Bar of Michigan Representative Assembly on April 28, 1990. The pro bono guidelines encourage bar members to "participate in the direct delivery of pro bono legal services to the poor," yet the definition of "poor" narrowly includes only one species in a biodiverse setting. Assisting a poverty-stricken family is a worthy and commendable effort, but why is lending a helping hand to impoverished ecosystems beyond the pale? Endangered trees will continue to have limited standing unless the pro bono standards are expanded to include legal services contributed to conservancies.

Interested lawyers can help the conservation movement now in the following ways:

- Assisting with the formation of a conservancy, typically a Michigan nonprofit corporation, and thus creating links among real estate professionals, the title industry, business interests, conservationists, environmentalists, and the community at large.

- Serving on the board of directors of a local conservancy.
- Assisting in land donations to establish nature preserves or conservation easements (see Appendix 17A).
- Conducting seminars with local conservancies or The Nature Conservancy on protection measures for natural amenities, open space, and farmland. The conservancies will help by providing suitable information and topics for conferences.
- Arranging conferences on conservation easements for civic-minded real estate professionals.
- Offering advice on tax benefits available through land conservation, such as reducing real property tax assessments,[13] obtaining charitable income tax deductions, and minimizing or eliminating estate taxes.
- Learning about the natural history of a region and understanding why clients, as prospective donors, may derive a good night's sleep from leaving a legacy of not only natural land, but also of a conservation ethic.
- Becoming familiar with opportunities for enlightened self-interest arising from the estate, property, and income tax benefits of land conservation.
- Developing expertise in conservation easements and offering legal services at reduced rates to land conservancies for counseling prospective donors.

Ohio

The Ohio legislation is unique in its descriptive terminology, which bespeaks the importance of promoting standardized nationwide terminology. To ensure that all semantic bases are covered, the Ohio statute variously describes the conservation easement by invoking each of the following terms: an easement, a restriction, a covenant, articles of dedication, a condition, an interest in land, and an incorporeal right. By way of contrast, the UCEA uses the following terminology: nonpossessory interest, easement, restriction, equitable servitude, and covenant.

In defining the protected subject matter, Ohio also distinguishes itself with the most comprehensive terminology. The protected subject matter in Ohio includes natural values, scenic values, open-space values, wetland area, agricultural resources, wooded condition, habitat for fish, habitat for plants, habitat for wildlife, forest resources, archeological resources, horticultural resources, and silvicultural resources. Ohio does not, however, provide for the protection of history or culture other than archeological resources.

Ohio is the only state specifically authorizing the conservation easement holder's access to the eased property for monitoring compliance with the terms of the conservation easement. Generally, the right to monitor is established by the terms of the conservation easement, rather than by statute.

Also, Ohio is the only state not to specifically authorize an affirmative duty on the part of the eased property owner. The statute permits limitations or restrictions on the use of land, but is silent as to affirmative duties. There is a difference between negative duties, such as limitations and restrictions, and affirmative responsibilities, such as active protection and restoration. These differences become significant to a conservation easement whenever threats to a conserved habitat require assertive safeguards. The Ohio statute does not, in any event, prohibit the donor from agreeing to assume affirmative responsibilities.

Tennessee

Conservation easements remained suspect under Tennessee's 1973 Protective Easements statute. This situation changed in 1981. A review of the 1973 act lends appreciation to just how far conservation easements have come in Tennessee.

The 1973 apprehension over conservation easements was betrayed by several statutory provisions. Historic easements and structures applied only in counties having a population of at least 200,000 people because of a legislative finding that redevelopment pressures are greater on historic structures in heavily urbanized areas.[14] Did historic structures in Tennessee small towns reside beyond the pale? Or did they not merit protection?

Under the 1973 statute, only public bodies[15] in Tennessee were statutorily authorized to hold conservation easements.[16] A beneficiary could, however, have enforced the terms of the easement.

The protected interest in Tennessee's 1973 statute was described as an easement, as an interest in land, and as an easement of view. It authorized the imposition of both an affirmative and a negative duty.

Prior to 1981, Tennessee was the only state in the Sixth Federal Circuit to call for the termination of a conservation easement after a specified number of years. The public body in Tennessee was obligated to cancel the easement if, after a period of at least ten years, the planning commission having jurisdiction and the governmental holder concurred that the public interest would have been better served by the cancellation.[17]

Tennessee was also the only jurisdiction to oxymoronically characterize a "scenic easement" as a "surrender by the owner of the easement to a public body . . . in fee simple."[18] An easement is, by definition, not fee simple.

Tennessee turned a sharp corner under its Conservation Easement Act of 1981.[19] This legislation provided broad protection for the state's land, water, geological, biological, historical, architectural, archeological, cultural, and scenic resources.[20] It is specifically enforceable by not only the holder of the conservation easement, but also by a beneficiary.[21] The statute provides for both negative and affirmative responsibilities. Under the conservation easement, the land owner could be obligated to provide for management of the servient land, structures, or features. These responsibilities can be intended to not only preserve and maintain the land, but also to enhance the present condition, use, or natural beauty of the land.[22] Under the 1981 legislation, conservation easements can also protect the facade and external appearance of structures.[23] And tax-exempt organizations, in addition to public bodies, are also statutorily entitled to hold conservation easements.[24]

Tennessee has a unique provision authorizing conservation easements to contain public use clauses.[25] Furthermore, even in the absence of express provisions authorizing entry to monitor the land, the conservation easement holder has a statutory right of entry at reasonable times for inspection purposes.[26]

Under the 1981 legislation, conservation easements may not be acquired by eminent domain unless the easement is necessary to accomplish a specific statutorily authorized public project. In addition, private nonprofit organizations have no right to acquire conservation easements by eminent domain, even if they otherwise have such power. Enabling legislation in the 1981 Conservation Easement Act authorizes public bodies to appropriate or borrow funds and to acquire grants or give security in connection with the acquisition of conservation easements.[27]

As in other states, Tennessee has eliminated certain defenses to conservation easements, such as privity of estate or contract, lack of benefit, or nonappurtenance to the servient land. It even provides that a conservation easement is not automatically extinguished because of a violation of its terms or frustration of its purposes.[28]

The value of the conservation easement in Tennessee is deducted from the assessment for taxation purposes. The tax exemption even applies to conservation easements in structures limited to a specific number of years. The tax exemption will continue during the life of the conservation easement.[29]

Terminology

Table 17.1 contrasts differing terminology in the conservation easement statutes of the Sixth Federal Circuit. There is little uniformity; thus, the description of the real property interest protected by the conservation easement is variously referred to as a nonpossessory interest, easement, restriction, equitable servitude, covenant, articles of dedication, condition, interest in land, incorporeal right, and easement of view. One develops a sense that the chosen terminology is often a matter of preference rather than substance. The same essential real estate interest is seemingly subject to protection in the state statutes, only the terminology differs.

Table 17.1. Comparison of Statutory Language and Terminology in the Sixth Federal Circuit

Comparison of Statutory Language	UCEA	Kentucky	Michigan	Ohio	Tennessee
Description of Interest					
Nonpossessory interest	X	X			
Easement	X	X	X	X	X
Restriction	X	X	X	X	X
Equitable servitude	X	X			
Covenant	X	X	X	X	
Articles of dedication				X	
Condition				X	
Interest in land			X	X	X
Incorporeal right			X	X	
Easement of view					X
Easement in structures					X
Obligation					
Affirmative duty	X	X	X		X
Negative duty (limitations/restrictions)	X	X	X	X	X
Holder's access to ensure compliance				X	X
Public use permitted by contract					X
Management to preserve, maintain, or enhance					X
Protected Subject Matter					
Natural values	X	X	X	X	X
Natural beauty					X
Scenic values	X	X	X	X	X
Open-space values	X	X	X	X	X
Wetland area				X	
Agricultural resources	X	X	X	X	
Wooded condition				X	
Habitat for fish				X	
Habitat for plants				X	
Habitat for wildlife				X	
Forest resources	X	X	X	X	
Recreational resources	X	X			
Natural resources	X	X			
Natural area					X
Geological resources					X
Natural diversity					X
Biological resources					X
Scenic resources					X
Archeological resources				X	X
Horticultural resources				X	
Silvicultural resources				X	
Visual effect					X
Audible effect					X
Atmospheric effect					X
Air quality	X	X			
Water quality	X	X	X		
Historical aspects	X	X	X		X
Architectural aspects	X	X	X		X
Facade/external appearance					X

Comparison of Statutory Language	UCEA	Kentucky	Michigan	Ohio	Tennessee
Cultural aspects	X	X	X		X
Historical value on designated registers			X		X
Cultural heritage					X
Structures					X
Permissible Conservation Easement Holder					
Authorized governmental body	X	X	X	X	X
Charitable corporation	X	X	X		
Charitable association	X	X	X		
Charitable trust	X	X	X		
Authorized tax-exempt section 501(c) charitable organization				X	X
Organization					X
Permissible Third-Party Enforcer					
Governmental body	X	X			
Charitable corporation	X	X			
Charitable association	X	X			
Charitable trust	X	X			
Beneficiary					X
Real property owner	X	X			
Conservation easement holder	X	X			
Authorized third party	X	X			
Person authorized by law	X	X			
Legal and equitable principles unaffected	X	X			
Representatives, heirs, and assigns					X
Creation, Conveyance, Acceptance, Duration					
Same as other easements	X	X			
Same as other interests in land				X	
Holder's acceptance prerequisite to enforcement	X	X			
Recordation of acceptance prerequisite to enforcement	X	X			
Notify assessor					X
Duration unlimited	X	X			
Duration for life of another					X
Duration for owner's life					X
Duration as stated	X	X			X
Written consent of subsurface right required		X			
Fee simple					X
Acquisition by donation					X
Acquisition by purchase					X
Cancel after ten years if not needed and tax repaid					X
Enforcement					
Action at law			X		
Equitable action			X		X
Civil action				X	
Specifically enforceable					X

(*continues*)

271

Table 17.1. Continued

Comparison of Statutory Language	UCEA	Kentucky	Michigan	Ohio	Tennessee
Superior Interests					
Existing interests absent written consent	X	X			
Surrounding coal mining operations		X			
Surrounding coal transportation		X			
Innocent bona fide purchaser protected				X	
Eminent domain not impaired		X			
Defenses Specifically Eliminated					
Not appurtenant	X	X			X
Assignability	X	X	X	X	
Not recognized by common law	X	X			
Imposes a negative burden	X	X	X		X
Imposes affirmative obligations	X	X	X		X
Benefit does not touch/concern real property	X	X	X	X	X
No privity of estate	X	X	X	X	X
No privity of contract	X	X	X	X	X
Frustration of purpose					X
Nontermination for violation of conservation easement terms					X
Applicability of Statute					
Interests created after effective date of statute	X	X			X
Permissible interests created before effective date	X	X	X		
Does not invalidate other lawful interest	X	X	X	X	X
Only in counties over 200,000 people					X
In approving county/municipality					X
Uniformity of Application and Construction					
Applied to effectuate uniform law	X	X			
Construed to effectuate uniform law	X	X			
Tax Valuation					
Taxable at eased value for tax-exempt organizations					X
Public body tax exemption					X

Protected Subject Matter

The protected subject matter can be divided into four basic categories: biological habitat, aesthetic amenities, resource base, and cultural values. The terminology differs slightly. A protected biological habitat is variously described as natural values, wetland area, wooded condition, habitat for fish, habitat for plants, biological resources, habitat for wildlife, natural diversity, natural heritage, and natural area. Aesthetic amenities include the following descriptive terms: scenic values, scenic resources, open-space values, visual effect, natural beauty, and audible effect. In protecting a resource base, the legislatures adopt the following exemplary terminology: agricultural resources, recreational resources, geological resources, natural resources, horticultural resources, silvicultural resources, atmospheric effect, air quality, and water quality. Finally, protected cultural values include the following words and phrases: archeological resources, historic aspects, cultural resources, architectural aspects, appearance of the structure, facade/external appearance, cultural aspects, and historic values on designated registers.

Table 17.1 depicts the terminology adopted by each of the states. In general, all four states protect certain aspects of biological habitat, aesthetic amenities, resource bases, and cultural values.

Holders

All Sixth Federal Circuit jurisdictions authorize designated tax-exempt entities to hold conservation easements. Only Kentucky, however, joins the UCEA in empowering certain nonbeneficiary third parties to enforce the terms of a conservation easement.

Conveyancing

In all four jurisdictions, conservation easements appear to be created, conveyed, and accepted in accordance with customary standards established for real estate transactions by the state's conveyancing laws.

Duration

In general, conservation easements can be of a perpetual duration, but only the UCEA and Kentucky explicitly say so. Tennessee had a peculiar cancellation provision after ten years, but this limitation does not appear in Tennessee's Conservation Easement Act of 1981.

Defenses

All four jurisdictions join the UCEA in explicitly eliminating certain common-law defenses to the enforcement of a conservation easement. The eliminated defenses include nonappurtenance, assignability, nonrecognition at common law, the imposition of a negative burden or affirmative obligations, the benefit does not touch or concern real property, and the lack of privity of a state or of contract.

Conclusion

Philanthropic conservationists and conservancies now have ample room to thrive in the statutory framework established by all four states in the Sixth

Federal Circuit. The priority afforded subsurface interests in Kentucky could present a threat to eased land. Tennessee, which limited conservation easement holders to defined public bodies and provided a mechanism for cancellation after ten years, adopted a more progressive statute in 1981.

Notes

1. KRS 382.810(3).
2. KRS 382.810(4).
3. KRS 382.860 and UCEA section 4.
4. MCL 324.2140 et seq.; MSA 13A.2140 et seq.
5. See generally, Comment *Assignability of Easement in Gross,* 32 Yale L. J. 813 (1922–1923).
6. *Smith v. Dennedy,* 224 Mich 378; 381, 194 N.W. 998, 998-999 (1923).
7. *Johnston v. Michigan Consolidated Gas Co.,* 337 Mich. 572; 60 N.W. 2d. 464 (1953); *Stockdale v. Yerden,* 220 Mich. 444; 190 N.W. 225 (1922). Michigan Land Title Standard 14.2.
8. MCL 565.29; MSA 26.547.
9. MCL 324.2142; MSA 13A.2142.
10. *Indian Garden Group v. Resort Twp.,* Michigan Tax Tribunal Docket No. 157,543.
11. The Nature Conservancy, *Michigan Land Trust Directory.* East Lansing, Mich.: The Nature Conservancy, 1998.
12. *Private Land Protection in Michigan, 1998.* Traverse City, Mich.: Michigan Outdoor Habitat Brokerage, 1998. This study was funded through charitable grants from several foundations.
13. *Indian Garden Group v. Resort Twp.,* Michigan Tax Tribunal Docket No. 157,543.
14. TCA 11-15-106.
15. A "public body" is defined as "the state, counties, municipalities, metropolitan governments, the historic commission of any state, county, municipal, or metropolitan government and park or recreation authorities." TCA 11-15-102(2).
16. TCA 11-15-101 and TCA 11-15-102(2).
17. TCA 11-15-108.
18. TCA 11-15-102(3)(B)(i).
19. Tenn. Code Ann. § 66-9-301–309.
20. Tenn. Code Ann. § 66-9-302.
21. Tenn. Code Ann. § 66-9-303(1)(A)(ii).
22. Tenn. Code Ann. § 66-9-303(1)(A)(iii).
23. Tenn. Code Ann. § 66-9-303(1)(B).
24. Tenn. Code Ann. §§ 66-9-303(2) and 66-9-305(a).
25. Tenn. Code Ann. § 66-9-304(b).
26. Tenn. Code Ann. § 66-9-304(c).
27. Tenn. Code Ann. § 66-9-305.
28. Tenn. Code Ann. § 66-9-306.
29. Tenn. Code Ann. § 66-9-308.

Appendix 17A

❧ ❧

Michigan Model Conservation Easement

Conservation Easement

(NOTE TO USER: Please delete the indented "Explanation" sections from the final copy to be signed by the Donor and the Conservancy.)

DATE: _____

DONOR: _____ , husband and wife

CONSERVANCY: (Conservancy/Organization Name and Address)

> EXPLANATION: The words "Grantor" and "Grantee" are commonly used in conveyancing forms. These words could appear in a warranty deed as well as in a quit claim deed. The words "Donor" and "Conservancy" similarly offer no insight into whether this is a conveyance with or without warranties. The term "Donor" may be preferable to "Grantor" since it more accurately captures the nature of the gift. On the other hand, the term "Donee" seems legalistic or cumbersome. Therefore this form identifies the recipient of the easement as the "Conservancy." The term "Donor" is used in its singular form in the agreement. Although the singular convention might seem awkward for husband and wife donors, any of the alternatives also have disadvantages. A plural convention would probably be more offensive for a singular donor. The use of one agreement form for a single donor and a separate form for multiple donors has administrative difficulties. The form will inevitably undergo revision in the future. Particular attention will then be required to assure all eventual changes are incorporated in both forms. There is also a risk of accidentally substituting a plural for a singular form. What started out as a multiple, may eventually become a single, donor (or vice versa) before signing. Since each of the agreements will be separately word-processed, it would be tedious to assure that all word-processed changes follow through the substitution of one form for another. In balance, the semantic disadvantages of the singular "Donor" convention seem to be outweighed by the advantages.

PROPERTY: In Township, County, Michigan:

> **EXPLANATION:** The full legal description should be inserted here. A street address will not suffice. The legal description will commonly be derived from a prior deed, a title commitment, or a survey.

CONVEYANCE: The Donor conveys and warrants to the Conservancy a perpetual Conservation Easement over the Property. The scope of this Conservation Easement is set forth in this agreement. This conveyance is a gift from the Donor to the Conservancy.

> **EXPLANATION:** The Conservation Easement must be perpetual in order to be tax-deductible. The preceding provision includes a warranty of title. A quit claim would also be sufficient to convey title and for tax deductibility, but it lacks the Donor's assurance of ownership. Under a quit claim the Conservancy could not require the Donor to satisfy an existing mortgage. The Donor represents "fee title" ownership in a subsequent provision. In some cases, the Conservancy may require a warranty of title. The statutory warranty deed form uses the phrase "conveys and warrants." Alternatively, the statutory quit claim simply defines the conveyance as a "quit claim." The word "conveys" invokes principles of "conveyancing" laws, albeit without warranties. The word "quitclaim" sounds less respectful of the Donor's intent than the word "convey." If a conveyance is to be without warranties of title, the word "convey" is preferred to the words "quit claim."

CONSERVATION VALUES: The Property possesses natural, scenic, open space, scientific, biological and ecological values of prominent importance to the Donor, the Conservancy and the public. These values are referred to as the "Conservation Values" in this easement.

> **EXPLANATION:** Conservation easements traditionally set forth a broad range of "conservation values." These conservation values appear in subsequent portions of the easement to prescribe the rights and responsibilities of the parties. The conservation values are also specifically explained to meet the criteria for tax purposes.

Purpose of this Conservation Easement:
A. The Donor is the fee simple title owner of the Property, and is committed to preserving the Conservation Values of the Property. This Conservation

Easement assures that the Property will be perpetually preserved in its predominately (natural, scenic, historic, agricultural, forested, open space) condition. Any use of the Property which may impair or interfere with the Conservation Values are expressly prohibited. Donor agrees to confine use of the Property to activities consistent with the purposes of this easement and preservation of the Conservation Values.

> EXPLANATION: This paragraph sets forth generic conservation values. It is patterned after the conservation purposes set forth in IRC Section 170(h). The generic conservation values in the preceding paragraph are followed by more specific references.

B. The Conservancy is a tax-exempt, nonprofit Michigan corporation qualified under Internal Revenue Code Sections 501(c)(3) and 170(h)(3) and 170(h)(4)(ii) and (iii); the Conservation and Historic Preservation Easement Act, MCL 324.2140 et seq. The Conservancy protects natural habitats of fish, wildlife, plants or similar ecosystems. The Conservancy also preserves open spaces, including farms and forests, where such preservation is for the scenic enjoyment of the general public or pursuant to clearly delineated governmental conservation policies and where it will yield a significant public benefit.

> EXPLANATION: The conservancy should confirm that it is, in fact, qualified under the cited statutes.

C. The Property has the following specific Conservation Values:
   • Significant natural habitat in which fish, wildlife, plants or a similar ecosystem thrive in a natural state.
   • Habitat for rare, endangered or threatened species of animal, fish or plants.
   • Natural areas which represent high quality examples of terrestrial or aquatic community.
   • It consists entirely of "prime farmland" and "farmland of local importance" as classified by the U.S. Department of Agriculture and the Soil Conservation Service.
   • A natural area which contributes to the ecological viability of a local, state or national park, nature preserve, wildlife refuge, wilderness area or other similar conservation area.
   • It is preserved pursuant to a clearly delineated federal, state or local conservation policy and yields a significant public benefit. The following legislation establishes relevant public policies: the Water Pollution Control Act of 1972, 33 USC 404 et seq.; the Coastal Zone Management Act, 16 USC §1451 et seq.; the Michigan Shorelands Protection and

Management Act of 1970, MCL 324.32301 et seq.; the Goemaere-Anderson Wetland Protection Act of 1979, MCL 324.30301 et seq.; the Inland Lakes and Streams Act, MCL 324.30101 et seq.; the Great Lakes Submerged Lands Act, MCL 324.32501 et seq.; the Michigan Farmland and Open Space Preservation Act of 1974, MCL 324.36101 et seq.; the Natural Rivers Act, MCL 324.30501 et seq.; the Conservation and Historic Preservation Easement Act, MCL 324.2140 et seq.; the Conservation and Historic Preservation Easement Act, MCL 324.2140 et seq.; and the _____ .

EXPLANATION: Any other legislation or local ordinance should be mentioned in the blank. There may, for example, be a local wetlands ordinance.

- A scenic landscape and natural character which would be impaired by a modification of the Property.
- A scenic panorama visible to the public from publicly accessible sites which would be adversely affected by modifications of the natural habitat.
- Relief from urban closeness.
- Harmonious variety of shapes and textures for the scenic enjoyment of the public.
- The governmental agency has endorsed the proposed scenic view of the Property under a landscape inventory, pursuant to a review process.
- Valued wetlands, as described in Goemaere-Anderson Wetland Protection Act of 1979; MCL 324.30301 et seq.
- Sustainable habitat for biodiverse vegetation, birds, fish, and terrestrial animals.
- A diversity of plant and animal life in an unusually broad range of habitats for property of its size.
- A natural habitat for the endangered or threatened _____ .
- Proximity to the following conserved properties which similarly preserve the existing natural habitat. . . .

EXPLANATION: List other conserved properties, such as nature preserves, state land, parks, eased properties, etc.

- Preservation of the Property enables the Donor to integrate the Conservation Values with other neighboring lands.
- The _____ office has recognized the importance of the Property as an ecological and scenic resource, by designating this and other land as a _____ .

- Prominent visibility to the public from _____, and if preserved in its natural state it will enhance tourism.
- Biological integrity of other land in the vicinity has been modified by intense urbanization, and the trend is expected to continue.

  There is a reasonable possibility that the Conservancy may acquire other valuable property rights in other nearby properties to expand the Conservation Values preserved by this Conservation Easement.

EXPLANATION: As distinguished from the generic conservation values, the preceding list sets forth specific reference points for the Conservation Easement. To some extent it may parallel the baseline information. Treasury Regulation 1.170A-14(d) identifies essentially four "conservation purposes," only two of which are generally relevant to conservation easements. One of the other two requires the property to be open to the general public and the other pertains to historically important land or certified historical structures. The two relevant provisions read as follows:

(ii) Protection of a relatively natural habitat of fish, wildlife or plants, or similar ecosystem, within the meaning of paragraph (d)(3) of this section,

(iii) The preservation of certain open space (including farmland and forest land) within the meaning of paragraph (d)(4) of this section,

The specific conservation purposes should be enumerated. Furthermore, baseline information will likely be prepared at approximately the same time. The preceding exhaustive list of conservation purposes is intended to be word-processed with the expectation that only a handful of the specific paragraphs will actually be used in any particular conservation easement agreement. The preceding list is prepared on the theory that it's easier to word-process out (i.e. delete) revisions than to word-process them in from somewhere else. The preceding list specifically excludes conservation purposes found in the regulations for outdoor recreation of the general public, since these provisions would be more applicable to nature preserves than to eased property. A number of the provisions have been copied directly out of the Treasury Regulations. For example, the somewhat awkward "relief from urban closeness" is "IRS-ese" from the Treasury Regulations.

D. Specific Conservation Values of the Property have been documented in a natural resource inventory signed by the Donor and Conservancy. This "Baseline Documentation" consists of maps, a depiction of all existing man-made modifications, prominent vegetation, identification of flora and fauna, land use history, distinct natural features, and photographs. The parties acknowledge that this natural resources inventory (the Baseline Documentation) is an accurate representation of the Property at the time of this donation.

> **EXPLANATION:** Treasury Regulation 1.170A-14(g)(5)(i) requires Baseline Documentation for an allowable tax deduction. The documentation must establish the condition of the property at the time of the gift. Both parties must sign a statement substantially in the following form: "This natural resources inventory is an accurate representation of (the protected Property) at the time of the transfer." It's not necessary for the Baseline Documentation to be incorporated into the conservation easement. The preceding provision contains the essential language from the Treasury Regulations. This assures that the requirement of a signed statement will not be overlooked or accidentally discarded. Notwithstanding this provision, it is still advisable for both parties to sign the Baseline Documentation.

The Parties Agree to the Following Terms of this Conservation Agreement:

1. **PROHIBITED ACTIONS.** Any activity on or use of the Property inconsistent with the purposes of this Conservation Easement or detrimental to the Conservation Values is expressly prohibited. By way of example, the following activities and uses are explicitly prohibited:
   a. <u>Division.</u> Any division or subdivision of the Property is prohibited.

   > **EXPLANATION:** Any exceptions to the prohibition against subdividing should be noted here.

   b. <u>Commercial Activities.</u> Commercial or industrial activity is prohibited.

   > **EXPLANATION:** Any exceptions, such as a small business activity taking place out of a home or existing building and that does not require additional structures beyond the modifications authorized in this easement should be noted here.

c. Construction. The placement or construction of any man-made modification, such as buildings, structures, fences, roads and parking lots is prohibited.

EXPLANATION: Any exceptions to the prohibition against construction should be noted here.

d. Cutting Vegetation. Any cutting of trees or vegetation is prohibited.

EXPLANATION: Any exceptions to the prohibition against cutting vegetation should be noted here.

e. Land Surface Alteration. Any mining or alteration of the surface of the land is prohibited.
f. Dumping. Waste and unsightly or offensive materials is not allowed and may not be accumulated on the Property.
g. Water Courses. Natural water courses, lake shores, wetlands, or other water bodies may not be altered.
h. Off-Road Vehicles. Motorized off-road vehicles, such as snowmobiles, dune buggies, all terrain vehicles and motorcycles may not be operated on the Property.
i. Billboards. Billboards and signs are prohibited. A sign may, however, be displayed to state:
   • The name and address of the Property.
   • The owner's name.
   • The area protected by this Conservation Easement.
   • Prohibition of any unauthorized entry or use.
   • An advertisement for the sale or rent of the Property.

2. **RIGHTS OF THE CONSERVANCY.** The Donor confers the following rights upon the Conservancy to perpetually maintain the Conservation Values of the Property:
   a. Right to Enter. The Conservancy has the right to enter the Property at reasonable times to monitor or to enforce compliance with this Conservation Easement. The Conservancy may not, however, unreasonably interfere with the Donor's use and quiet enjoyment of the Property. The Conservancy has no right to permit others to enter the Property. **The general public is not granted access to the Property under this Conservation Easement.**
   b. Right to Preserve. The Conservancy has the right to prevent any activity on or use of the Property that is inconsistent with the purposes of this easement.
   c. Right to Require Restoration. The Conservancy has the right to require restoration of the areas or features of the Property which are damaged by activity inconsistent with this Conservation Easement.
   d. Signs. The Conservancy has the right to place signs on the Property which

identify the land as being protected by this Conservation Easement. The number and location of any signs are subject to Donor's approval.

3. **PERMITTED USES.** Donor retains all ownership rights which are not expressly restricted by this Conservation Easement. In particular, the following rights are reserved:

   a. Right to Convey. The Donor retains the right to sell, mortgage, bequeath or donate the Property. Any conveyance will remain subject to the terms of this Conservation Easement and the subsequent owner will be bound by all obligations in this agreement.

   b. Right to Maintain and Replace Existing Structures. The Donor retains the right to maintain, renovate and replace the existing structure(s) as noted in the baseline documentation in substantially the same location and size. Any expansion or replacement may not substantially alter the character or function of the structure.

   c. Right to Add Designated Structures or Uses. The Donor retains the right to add the following structures, modifications or uses to the Property without notifying the Conservancy.

      * _____
      * _____

   EXPLANATION: The Donor may wish to add specified structures to the Property that should be listed here. Examples of specified structures or uses are: * Accessory, nonresidential structures within the designated Residential Area * One dock not to exceed ___ feet in length * Access drives and footpaths * Agricultural uses. **If there are no additional uses or structures, then this paragraph should be deleted in its entirety.**

4. **CONSERVANCY REMEDIES.** This section addresses cumulative remedies of the Conservancy and limitations on these remedies.

   a. Delay in Enforcement. A delay in enforcement shall not be construed as a waiver of the Conservancy's right to eventually enforce the terms of this Conservation Easement.

   b. Acts Beyond Donor's Control. The Conservancy may not bring an action against the Donor for modifications to the Property resulting from causes beyond the Donor's control. Examples are: unintentional fires, storms, natural earth movement, trespassers or even a Donor's well-intentioned actions in response to an emergency resulting in changes to the Property. The Donor has no responsibility under this Conservation Easement for such unintended modifications.

   c. Notice and Demand. If the Conservancy determines that the Donor is in violation of this Conservation Easement, or that a violation is threatened, the Conservancy may provide written notice to the Donor unless the violation constitutes immediate and irreparable harm. The written notice will identify the violation and request corrective action to cure the violation or to restore the Property.

d. Failure to Act. If, for a 28 day period after written notice, the Donor continues violating this Conservation Easement, or if the Donor does not abate the violation and implement corrective measures requested by the Conservancy, the Conservancy may bring an action in law or in equity to enforce the terms of this Conservation Easement. The Conservancy is also entitled to enjoin the violation through injunctive relief, seek specific performance, declaratory relief, restitution, reimbursement of expenses, or an order compelling restoration of the Property. If the court determines that the Donor has failed to comply with this Conservation Easement, then the Donor also agrees to reimburse all reasonable costs and attorney fees incurred by the Conservancy.

e. Unreasonable Litigation. If the Conservancy initiates litigation against the Donor to enforce this Conservation Easement, and if the court determines that the litigation was without reasonable cause or in bad faith, then the court may require the Conservancy to reimburse the Donor's reasonable costs and attorney fees in defending the action.

f. Donor's Absence. If the Conservancy determines that this Conservation Easement is, or is expected to be, violated, the Conservancy will make good-faith efforts to notify the Donor. If, through reasonable efforts, the Donor cannot be notified, and if the Conservancy determines that circumstances justify prompt action to mitigate or prevent impairment of the Conservation Values, then the Conservancy may pursue its lawful remedies without prior notice and without awaiting the Donor's opportunity to cure. The Donor agrees to reimburse all costs associated with this effort.

g. Actual or Threatened Non-Compliance. Donor acknowledges that actual or threatened events of non-compliance under the Conservation Easement constitute immediate and irreparable harm. The Conservancy is entitled to invoke the equitable jurisdiction of the court to enforce this Conservation Easement.

h. Cumulative Remedies. The preceding remedies of the Conservancy are cumulative. Any, or all, of the remedies may be invoked by the Conservancy if there is an actual or threatened violation of this Conservation Easement.

5. **OWNERSHIP COSTS AND LIABILITIES.** In accepting this Easement, the Conservancy shall have no liability or other obligation for costs, liabilities, taxes or insurance of any kind related to the Property. The Conservancy, its members, directors, officers, employees and agents have no liability arising from injury or death to any person or physical damage to any property on the Property. The Donor agrees to defend the Conservancy against such claims and to indemnify the Conservancy against all costs and liabilities relating to such claims during the tenure of the

Donor's ownership of the Property. Subsequent owners of the Property will similarly defend and indemnify the Conservancy for any claims arising during the tenure of their ownership.

6. **CESSATION OF EXISTENCE.** If the Conservancy shall cease to exist or if it fails to be "a qualified organization" for purposes of Internal Revenue Code Section 170(h)(3), or if the Conservancy is no longer authorized to acquire and hold conservation easements, then this Conservation Easement shall become vested in another entity. This entity shall be a "qualified organization" for purposes of Internal Revenue Code Section 170(h)(3). The Conservancy's rights and responsibilities shall be assigned to the following named entities in the following sequence:

   (1) _____
   (2) _____
   (3) Any other entity having similar conservation purposes to which such rights may be awarded under the *cy pres* doctrine.

   EXPLANATION: The preceding has been referred to as the "Executory Limitation" in the existing Land Trust Alliance Model Conservation Easement. As a practical matter, the doctrine of *cy pres* would govern the eventual disposition of charitable gifts, whether we say so or not. This doctrine would require the conservation Easement to be given to another similar entity if the conservancy is no longer viable. If the conservancy is no longer viable, then what is the likelihood of another existing conservancy surviving?

7. **TERMINATION.** This Conservation Easement may be extinguished only by an unexpected change in condition which causes it to be impossible to fulfill the Conservation Easement's purposes, or by exercise of eminent domain.

   a. <u>Unexpected Change in Conditions.</u> If subsequent circumstances render the purposes of this Conservation Easement impossible to fulfill, then this Conservation Easement may be partially or entirely terminated only by judicial proceedings. The Conservancy will then be entitled to compensation in accordance with the provisions of IRC Treasury Regulations Section 1.170A-14(g)(6)(ii).

   b. <u>Eminent Domain.</u> If the Property is taken, in whole or in part, by power of eminent domain, then the Conservancy will be entitled to compensation by the same method as is set forth in IRC Treasury Regulations Section 1.170A-14(g)(6)(ii).

8. **LIBERAL CONSTRUCTION.** This Conservation Easement shall be liberally construed in favor of maintaining the Conservation Values of the Property and in accordance with the Conservation and Historic Preservation Easement Act; MCL 324.2140 et seq.

9. **NOTICES.** For purposes of this agreement, notices may be provided to either party by personal delivery or by mailing a written notice to that party (at the address shown at the top of this agreement, or at last known address of a party) by First Class mail. Service will be complete upon depositing the properly addressed notice with the U.S. Postal Service with sufficient postage.

   EXPLANATION: The certainty that the notice has been received would be greater with certified mail; however, this is far less conciliatory than first class. Since the mail may be used to notify the Donor, or successors, of a possible (perhaps merely suspected) violation, there may be good reason to minimize the possibility of an adversarial posture. Therefore, this form contemplates personal delivery or First Class mail. There is certainly no prohibition against Certified Mail, which would be recommended if a hostile relationship is inevitable.

10. **SEVERABILITY.** If any portion of this Conservation Easement is determined to be invalid, the remaining provisions will remain in force.

11. **SUCCESSORS.** This Conservation Easement is binding upon, and inures to the benefit of, the Donor's and the Conservancy's successors in interest. All subsequent owners of the property are bound to all provisions of this conservation easement to the same extent as the current property owner.

12. **TERMINATION OF RIGHTS AND OBLIGATIONS.** A party's future rights and obligations under this easement terminate upon transfer of that party's interest in the Property. Liability for acts or omissions occurring prior to transfer will survive the transfer.

13. **MICHIGAN LAW.** This Conservation Easement will be construed in accordance with Michigan Law.

14. **ENTIRE AGREEMENT.** This Conservation Easement sets forth the entire agreement of the parties. It is intended to supersede all prior discussions or understandings.

WITNESSES: DONOR:
(*print/type names under signatures)

*_____   *_____

*_____   *_____

STATE OF MICHIGAN

COUNTY OF _____

Acknowledged before me on _____, 19____, by

_____

Notary Public, _____ County, Michigan.
My commission expires: _____

WITNESSES:

NAME OF YOUR CONSERVANCY, a Michigan nonprofit corporation

(*print/type names under signatures)

*_____   By: _____

Its:

*_____

STATE OF MICHIGAN

COUNTY OF _____

Acknowledged before me on _____, 19____, by

_____

known to me to be the _____ of the NAME OF
YOUR CONSERVANCY, a Michigan nonprofit corporation.

Notary Public, _____ County, Michigan.

My commission expires: _____

PREPARED BY: Name and address of the person preparing the document.

_____

_____

_____

_____

Chapter 18

🐦 🐦

Mackinaw Headlands: A Model in Public–Private Partnerships

Linda J. Mead

In the north country of Michigan, where Lakes Huron and Michigan come together at the Straits of Mackinaw, 600 acres of primeval forest will remain as it was in the days of the Ice Age, thanks to the foresight of a public–private partnership led by the Little Traverse Conservancy and the McCormick Foundation (Figure 18.1). Back in the late 1800s when Cyrus McCormick invented the mechanical reaper that began an agricultural revolution, he could not have visualized how development pressures would threaten these lands in Michigan that his family eventually came to own. His legacy of stewardship in working with and caring for the land, however, was made clearly evident over a hundred years later when members of the McCormick family made a commitment to preservation of this critical parcel.

Cyrus's grandson, Roger, purchased this pristine forest with plans to create a magnificent family resort. With glorious sunset views from the bluffs and two miles of frontage on the historic Straits of Mackinaw in the Headlands area, Roger envisioned his private retreat to include a mansion, a swimming pool, and a guesthouse, among other amenities. His dream came to a halt when he passed away before its completion, at which time the land was bequeathed to a family foundation. The structures that had already been built on the property were put to use over the next few years as a conference center, primarily for nonprofit groups. A unique premedical school program for Native Americans was conducted at the site. In the mid-1990s, however, the foundation no longer had an interest in the land and began to make discrete inquiries about placing the property on the real estate market.

The village of Mackinaw, a small rural community of just over 800 people, became concerned about how they might be affected if this 600-acre parcel on the western city limits were to be developed. As a second-home resort area

Figure 18.1. Headlands and straits of Mackinaw
Source: Tom Bailey, Little Traverse Conservancy

that some consider the Cape Cod of the Midwest, the surrounding region had been booming with new commercial development. Joe Duff, the village manager, became the catalyst for the preservation process that would follow.

Duff contacted the McCormick Foundation and the Little Traverse Conservancy, a regional nonprofit land conservation organization, to see if there was a better alternative that development for this land. Tom Bailey, executive director of the conservancy, had been in contact over recent years with Michael Kennedy, the attorney for the foundation.[1] Kennedy was a local resident who had an ongoing interest in the community. From the beginning, Kennedy made it clear that the property could not be considered for a gift, but that the foundation's trustees would be willing to work toward a solution that would preserve the land and benefit all parties.

Bailey knew immediately that this project was key for the conservancy. The ancient forest that covers this large parcel of land in the Mackinaw Headlands with significant lake frontage serves as habitat for several endangered species (Photograph 18.1). The mixed deciduous and conifer forest, the upland hardwoods, the beach ridges, and limestone outcroppings all provide excellent

Photograph 18.1. Headlands with Mackinaw City and Mackinaw Bridge in background.
Photo credit: Tom Bailey, Little Traverse Conservancy

habitat for migratory raptors. Funded from royalties generated by oil and gas leases on state lands, the trust provides grants to local governments to support the acquisition of conservation and recreational lands. It was the first of its kind in the nation. Little Traverse Conservancy has helped local governments access this fund for ten different projects, with a total value of almost $19 million.

Little Traverse Conservancy acted as the coordinator to bring together the necessary parties: the foundation, the town, the trust, and ultimately the county as the recipient of the property. As in many successful land transactions, it was the personal commitment of individuals that made a difference throughout the negotiation process. Before any formal action to place preservation in motion could be taken, however, the town had to go through the process of debating the merits of preserving this land at public hearings.

Taking the land off the tax rolls and the loss of potential jobs that might be generated from the development of this property were key arguments used by those who felt that there was enough public open space and that the town should back away from the acquisition. Local conservationists argued the merits of preservation and eventually won the support of the town council, who voted overwhelmingly to proceed. Throughout the debates, the conservancy maintained its role as impartial facilitator and adviser, leaving the town to make the decision that was in their own citizens' best interests.

With town approval secured, the conservancy assisted with the grant application process to ensure 75 percent of the $5.5 million purchase price from the Natural Resources Trust Fund. The fund generates $15–20 million per year to be used throughout the state for land acquisitions; this project was rated the trust's top scorer of the year.

With the bulk of funding in hand, the McCormick Foundation now offered another challenge to the conservationists: If significant local dollars could be raised as part of the purchase, the foundation would consider a bargain sale. What a wonderful opportunity for a fundraiser! Tom Bailey of the Little Traverse Conservancy contacted the Harold C. Schott Foundation with this unique opportunity to leverage substantial public funds enabling the preservation of significant Mackinaw Headlands property. Although the Schott Foundation had never been involved in land acquisition grants, they realized the importance of this donation and awarded a $200,000 grant that secured the bargain sale agreement.

Due to the scope of the project, the town was concerned about the ongoing stewardship costs of owning the property. Again, Bailey was able to use his contacts to offer a solution. Jim Tamlyn, chair of the Emmet County Commissioners, and Lyn Johnson, county controller, were key in securing the county's commitment to become owner and steward of the preserved property as the newest addition to the county park system.

There was only one more item to complete before the deal could be consummated. Although the state required that the land be used only for the open-space and recreational purposes allowable under the trust charter, the local community felt that adding another level of protection would best ensure that the land would remain in its natural condition for all time. The McCormick Foundation worked with the Little Traverse Conservancy to identify terms of a conservation easement to be held by the conservancy. Based on the Michigan model conservation easement (see Appendix 17.1), the legally recorded document permits recreational trails and, most important, limits the land to uses consistent with its conservation values. The Michigan model conservation easement is similar to the standard easement adopted by the Land Trust Alliance, except that it is written in plain, simple English easily understood by those unfamiliar with legal documents, and it has been further adapted to Michigan law. In addition to all parties' agreement to the terms of the easement, the McCormick Foundation generously offered donation of a substantial endowment to fund the conservancy's monitoring and stewardship responsibilities.

Finally, after two years of creative thinking, hard work, town debates, and partnership agreements, the deal was settled. At the settlement table, the village of Mackinaw in a bargain sale purchased the property from the McCormick Foundation. The state trust and the Schott Foundation provided funds for the acquisition. The village then donated a conservation easement to the Little Traverse Conservancy and subsequently transferred the property to Emmett County.

Everyone in attendance—the town council, the trustees of the McCormick Foundation, the Little Traverse Conservancy, and county officials—joined together to celebrate a win-win situation for all involved. The personal satisfaction of the many players who contributed to this conservation success is best summed up by Bailey: "Driving home, I just had to pull off the road by the side of the property and walk into the woods. I was overwhelmed by the knowledge that we did it—we saved the property so that it could be managed by Mother Nature for all time."[2]

The McCormick Foundation received substantial value for divesting their property and at the same time was able to leave something of unique significance to the community. The Michigan Natural Resources Trust Fund set precedent, as this was the first time in its twenty-year history that lands had been protected using a conservation easement to a private conservancy. Funders were happy to leverage their money, and the conservancy advanced its goals for preservation of the region. Moreover, local residents can continue to enjoy the scenic beauty and recreational use of these 600 acres without negative impacts on their community from traffic, schools, and related development activities. Perhaps happiest of all are the raptors and songbirds that continue to fly over this primeval forest, finding a place to rest on their migratory route.

Notes

1. Tom Bailey provided the background information for this chapter. Linda Mead interviewed him in July 1998. He has served as the executive director of the Little Traverse Conservancy since late 1984. During this time, the conservancy has successfully completed over 150 land conservation projects protecting land valued at over $30 million. Bailey received a gubernatorial appointment to the Michigan Water Resources Commission and subsequently the Technical Advisory Board of the Michigan Great Lakes Protection Fund. He holds B.S. in park and recreation resources from Michigan State University and pursued graduate study at that university in land use, resource economics, and environmental law. He spent six years with the Michigan Department of Natural Resources, administering grants for water pollution control and regulating hazardous wastes. He has been a National Park ranger, a lobbyist and citizen representative for various conservation groups, and a fishing guide.
2. Personal communication, July 1998.

Chapter 19

❧ ❧

Conservation Easements in the Seventh and Eighth Federal Circuits

Brian Ohm, Matthew B. Cobb, Julie Ann Gustanski, and Larry E. Meuwissen

The Seventh and Eighth Federal Circuits of the United States include ten states that comprise much of the country's productive farmland. The Seventh Federal Circuit, which includes Illinois, Indiana, and Wisconsin, is located between the Ohio River and the Great Lakes (Figure 19.1). The Eighth Circuit, consisting of Arkansas, Iowa, Minnesota, Missouri, Nebraska, North Dakota, and South Dakota represents a large portion of those lands acquired from France in the Louisiana Purchase and constitutes a major part of the Missouri and Mississippi Rivers watersheds.

The border between Minnesota and the Dakotas is formed by the Red River of the North, which flows northward to Lake Winnipeg in the Canadian province of Manitoba; its waters ultimately flow into Hudson Bay. In addition to its famed 10,000 lakes, Minnesota has a third major continental divide in the region of Lake Superior for the St. Lawrence watershed that empties to the North Atlantic. With these abundant natural and water resources and rich soils, the states of the Seventh and Eighth Federal Circuits are well-suited for agriculture and are also traversed by major flyways for migratory birds. The western plains in Nebraska and the Dakotas, once home to vast herds of buffalo, now produce much of the nation's grain. The Ohio, Missouri, and Mississippi Rivers have been made navigable for much of their length and provide access to world markets for the products of this region.

The aboriginal Americans who occupied these lands had a rich tradition of conservation that survives today, despite the march of European civilization. This tradition together with the natural and manufactured geographical elements and, surely, the economic dependence on agriculture have all contributed significantly to maintaining and promoting positive local and

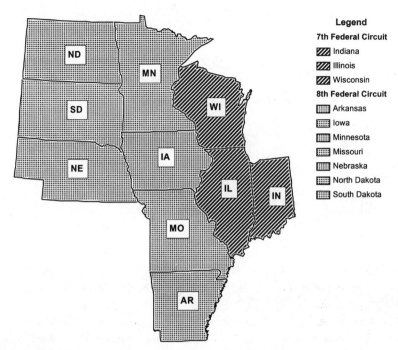

Legend

7th Federal Circuit

▨ Indiana
▨ Illinois
▨ Wisconsin

8th Federal Circuit

▦ Arkansas
▦ Iowa
▦ Minnesota
▦ Missouri
▦ Nebraska
▦ North Dakota
▦ South Dakota

Figure 19.1. States comprising the Seventh and Eighth Federal Circuits.
Credit: J. A. Gustanski

regional attitudes toward conservation measures among citizens and governments in the region.

Every state, with the exception of North Dakota, has enacted legislation of some kind providing for the creation of conservation easements. Table 19.1 compares the statutory language for these states. Indiana, Minnesota, South Dakota, and Wisconsin have adopted the language from the Uniform Conservation Easement Act (UCEA), whereas Arkansas, Illinois, Iowa, Missouri, and Nebraska have drafted their own versions of legislation. The two circuits under examination in this chapter cover an enormous amount of land with varied terrain, vegetation, and animal life. Many of the states are reliant on agriculture, yet several states—Illinois, Wisconsin, Minnesota, and Missouri—also have large and growing urban areas.

Across this region, is also great variation in both land trust activity and the number of land trusts in the various states that take advantage of the available legislation. Wisconsin, for example, has a long history of the use of conservation easements and a strong and growing land trust movement. According to the 1998 National Land Trust Census, Wisconsin land trusts had 5,141

Table 19.1. Comparison of Statutory Language and Terminology in the Seventh and Eighth Federal Circuits

Comparison of Statutory Language	UCEA	Illinois	Indiana	Wisconsin	Arkansas	Iowa	Minnesota	Missouri	Nebraska	North Dakota	South Dakota
Description of Interest											
Nonpossessory interest	X		X	X	X		X				X
Easement	X	X	X	X	X	X	X	X	X		X
Restriction	X	X	X	X	X	X	X		X		X
Equitable servitude	X	X	X	X	X	X	X		X		
Covenant	X	X	X	X	X		X	X	X		X
Conservation right	X										
Preservation restriction	X										
Obligation											
Affirmative duty	X	X	X	X	X		X	X	X		X
Negative duty (limitations/restrictions)	X	X	X	X	X		X	X	X		X
Protected Subject Matter											
Natural values	X	X	X	X	X		X		X		X
Scenic values	X	X	X	X	X	X	X	X	X		X
Open-space values	X	X	X	X	X		X	X	X		X
Agricultural use	X		X	X	X		X		X		X
Forest use	X	X	X	X	X	X	X		X		X
Recreational use	X		X	X	X	X	X		X		X
Open-space use	X	X	X	X	X		X	X	X		X
Natural resources	X	X	X	X	X	X	X	X	X		X
Air quality	X		X	X	X		X		X		X
Water quality	X		X	X	X		X	X	X		X
Historical aspects	X	X	X	X	X		X	X	X		X
Architectural aspects	X	X	X	X	X		X	X	X		X
Archeological aspects	X	X	X	X	X		X	X	X		X
Cultural aspects	X	X	X	X	X		X		X		X
Human burial sites				X							
Fish habitat		X			X		X				
Plant habitat		X									
Wildlife habitat		X				X		X	X		
Paleontological						X		X			X
Riparian lands						X					
Wetlands						X		X			

Permissible Conservation Easement Holder												
Governmental body	X	X	X	X	X	X	X	X	X	X	X	X
Charitable corporation	X	X	X	X	X	X	X	X	X	X	X	X
Charitable association	X		X	X	X	X		X	X		X	X
Charitable trust	X	X	X	X	X	X	X			X		X
Private nonprofit orgnization that provides for transfer to public body or another nonprofit upon dissolution					X	X						
Permissible Third-Party Enforcer												
Governmental body	X	X	X	X	X	X	X	X	X	X	X	X
Charitable corporation	X	X	X	X	X	X	X	X	X	X	X	X
Charitable association	X		X	X	X	X		X	X		X	X
Charitable trust	X		X	X	X	X		X	X		X	X
Real property owner	X	X		X	X	X		X	X			X
Easement holder	X	X		X	X	X		X	X			X
Authorized third party	X			X	X	X		X	X			X
Legal and equitable principles unaffected	X			X	X	X		X	X			X
Any property owner within 500 feet		X				X					X	X
Creation, Conveyance, Acceptance, Duration												
Same as other easements	X			X	X	X		X	X		X	X
Holder's acceptance prerequisite to enforcement	X	X		X	X	X		X	X		X	X
Recordation of acceptance prerequisite to enforcement	X	X		X		X		X	X			X
Duration unlimited	X			X	X	X		X	X		X	X
Duration as stated	X			X	X	X		X	X		X	X
Termination by change of circumstances renders it no longer beneficial to the public	X							X			X	
Release by holder				X	X	X					X	
Termination by agreement of grantor and grantee			X									
Copy to state Department of Natural Resources	X											

(continues)

Table 19.1. Continued

Comparison of Statutory Language	UCEA	Illinois	Indiana	Wisconsin	Arkansas	Iowa	Minnesota	Missouri	Nebraska	North Dakota	South Dakota
Enforcement											
Injunction		X									X
Specific performance		X									
Damages		X									
Punitive damages		X									
Defenses Spefically Eliminated											
Not appurtenant	X		X	X	X		X				X
Assignability	X	X	X	X	X		X		X		X
Not recognized by common law	X		X	X	X		X				X
Imposes a negative burden	X		X	X	X		X				X
Imposes affirmative obligations	X		X	X	X		X				X
Benefit does not touch/concern real property	X	X	X	X	X		X		X		X
No privity of estate	X	X	X	X	X		X		X		X
No privity of contract	X	X	X	X	X		X		X		X
Marketable title act				X							X
Applicability of Statute											
Interests created after effective date of statute	X		X	X	X		X		X		X
Permissible interests created before effective date	X		X	X	X		X		X		X
Does not invalidate other lawful interest	X		X	X	X		X		X		X
Uniformity of Application and Construction											
Applied to effectuate uniform law	X		X	X							
Construed to effectuate uniform law	X		X	X							
Tax Valuation											
Tax at eased value			X	X			X	X	X		
Reduced valuation for parcels yielding a public benefit		X									

acres under easement.[1] In Indiana, the use of conservation easements is still in its infancy. The 1998 National Land Trust Census reflects this, reporting only 209 acres under easement in Indiana. Illinois, which has a very strong conservation easement law and moderate level of land trust activity, only has 3,498 acres under easement. The other states tend to have fewer active land trusts, with organizations such as The Nature Conservancy and the Trust for Public Land taking primary roles in land conservation activities.

The Seventh Circuit

The Seventh Federal Circuit includes Illinois, Indiana, and Wisconsin. All states in this Seventh Circuit have adopted some form of conservation easement enabling legislation. Indiana and Wisconsin have adopted the UCEA. Although Illinois has not adopted the UCEA, it has adopted several different laws concerning conservation easements.

Illinois

The main conservation easement law in Illinois is "the Real Property Conservation Rights Act,[2] adopted in 1977. The act has a strong orientation toward preservation of historic resources as well as natural resource conservation.[3] The act establishes the statutory concept of a "conservation right," which encompasses any instrument (easements, covenants, conditions) appropriate to preserving cultural, historic, and natural resources. Practitioners treat the conservation right as interchangeable with the concept of conservation easements.[4]

Although different from the UCEA in its verbiage, the Real Property Conservation Rights Act is similar in its purpose. Both acts enable the attachment to real property of durable restrictions and affirmative obligations to protect natural and historic resources. Both acts also remove some of the common-law impediments to the use of conservation easements. The general requirements for creating a conservation easement are also similar under both acts.

The Real Property Conservation Rights Act, however, also includes a number of unique provisions. For example, it includes a broader enforcement provision than the UCEA. The Real Property Conservation Rights Act provides that injunctive relief, specific performance, or damages in circuit court may enforce a conservation right by any of the following:

(a) the state of Illinois or any unit of local government;

(b) any not-for-profit corporation or trust which owns the conservation right;

(c) the owner of any real property abutting or within 500 feet of the real property subject to the conservation right.

These enforcement provisions are much stronger than the enforcement provisions under the UCEA. For example, under UCEA, for example, the conservation easement document can give a third-party enforcement right to a governmental body or a charitable corporation, association, or trust. Under the Real Property Conservation Rights Act, a neighbor located within 500 feet has the right to bring an enforcement action as a matter of law and is not dependent on having that right specified in the conservation easement document.

The Real Property Conservation Rights Act also provides that "any owner of property subject to a conservation right who willfully violates any term of such conservation right may, in the court's discretion, be held liable for punitive damages in an amount equal to the value of the real property subject thereto."[5] The UCEA says nothing about punitive damages.

The Real Property Conservation Rights Act also requires that, after the instrument creating the conservation right is recorded with the county registrar of titles, the registrar must mail a copy of the conservation right to the Illinois Department of Natural Resources. The registrar is also required to do likewise for instruments filed releasing conservation rights.[6]

Illinois law also includes a number of provisions for the reduction of property taxes due to conservation easements created under the Real Property Conservation Rights Act. Under the Illinois Property Tax Code, properties encumbered in perpetuity by a conservation easement must be assessed at 8 1/3 percent of its fair market value.[7] To qualify for this special property tax treatment, the conservation easement must yield a public benefit. The Illinois Department of Natural Resources makes the determination of public benefit for compliance with a list of statutory criteria. These criteria include land that is protected in perpetuity for public access to outdoor recreation and educational opportunities; land contributing to the ecological viability of park and conservation areas that are publicly owned or otherwise protected; and land included in federal, state, regional, or local plans for wildlife habitat, open space, protection or restoration of lakes and streams, or the protection of scenic areas.[8] These provisions apply everywhere in Illinois except Cook County, where Chicago is located.

If a conservation easement is terminated, the law provides for a recapture of the taxes that would have been due for the ten preceding years.[9] Other provisions of the Illinois Property Tax Code allow for property tax reductions for other classifications of land use, such as agricultural and open space, that may benefit property owners whose land is encumbered by a conservation easement.[10]

Finally, Illinois has additional laws, such as the Illinois Conservation Enhancement Act,[11] that promote the use of conservation easements. This act, which became effective in 1988, provides a fairly standard definition of "conservation easement" as opposed to a "conservation right."[12] It provides that a "conservation easement may be released at any time by mutual consent of the parties."[13] Conservation easements under the Illinois Conservation Enhancement Act are a major component of the Save Illinois Topsoil Program in which the state pays for conservation easements to address soil erosion and water-quality concerns.[14]

Indiana

Indiana adopted the UCEA in 1984.[15] The Indiana law follows the UCEA almost verbatim, but with two additional provisions. The first addition relates to actions to modify or terminate conservation easements, which appears in subsection 3(b) of the UCEA. That subsection UCEA states that the act "does not affect the power of a court to modify or terminate a conservation easement in accordance with the principles of law and equity." The Indiana law adds the phrase "or the termination of a conservation easement by agreement of the grantor and grantee"[16] to that subsection.

This phrase adds some uncertainty to the term of a conservation easement. The UCEA and the Indiana law provide that the term of a conservation easement is unlimited in duration unless the document creating the easement provides otherwise.[17] For example, the document creating the easement could state that it will terminate after a specific number of years or that it will terminate based on certain conditions or that it will terminate based on the agreement of the grantor and grantee. The additional phrase in the Indiana law, however, allows the document creating the easement to say one thing and the grantor and grantee to act differently.

It remains to be seen whether this additional provision will be subject to abuse. The potential for abuse could arise if, for example, someone donates a conservation easement to a qualified organization to take advantage of the income tax benefits. The easement document states that the easement is to last in perpetuity. The grantor qualifies for the charitable deduction for income tax purposes in accordance with the rules of the Internal Revenue Service. A year after taking the charitable deduction, however, the grantor and grantee agree to terminate the conservation easement and never report the action to the Internal Revenue Service. The grantor then develops the land, getting both the charitable deduction and the profit from developing the land.

The second provision that appears in the Indiana law but that does not appear in the UCEA is the provision that "real property subject to a conservation easement shall be assessed and taxed on a basis that reflects the easement."[18] This provision is in fact unique among enabling legislation across the United States and is not currently addressed by the majority of the state laws.

Wisconsin

Wisconsin was the first state in the nation to adopt the UCEA.[19] The law became effective in 1982, but the widespread use of conservation easements in Wisconsin, primarily in the form of scenic easements, goes back to the early 1950s. Wisconsin has long been "the pioneer state in the establishment of a program of scenic easements."[20] Wisconsin's scenic easement programs became models for the development and use of conservation easements elsewhere in the country.

In the early 1950s, the Wisconsin Highway Commission (now the Department of Transportation) embarked on a program of acquiring scenic easements along highways in certain scenic areas of the state. The most extensive area of acquisitions occurred along the entire length of the Mississippi River along Wisconsin's western border. These acquisitions were part of the Great River Road parkway project initially planned by the federal government in the 1930s. The state acquired the easements primarily through negotiations with property owners. Some acquisitions, however, could only occur through the use of eminent domain. The Wisconsin Supreme Court has upheld as constitutional the state's acquisition of scenic easements through the power of eminent domain.[21] According to the court, the public enjoyment of scenic beauty is a public use for which a limited interest in property could be "taken" through the use of scenic easements.

In light of this history, it is not surprising that Wisconsin was the first state to adopt the UCEA. What perhaps is surprising is that Wisconsin had not developed a general conservation easement law similar to the UCEA prior to the 1980s. Wisconsin's version includes a number of grammatical refinements to the UCEA and really deviates from it in only two areas.

First, Wisconsin's law provides that conservation easements can also be used to preserve human burial sites. The laws of 1985 as part of a comprehensive burial sites preservation law added this provision.[22] To the extent it was not clear, this addition clarifies the use of conservation easements to preserve burial sites.

Second, Wisconsin's law, as codified in the statutes, omits two of the three subsections in section 5 of the UCEA, which outline the classes of interest to which the UCEA might be made applicable. The Wisconsin statutes only state that the conservation easement law does not invalidate any interest created before or after adoption of the law that do not comply with the law but that are otherwise enforceable under the statutory and case laws of Wisconsin. This provision appears in subsection c of section 5 in the UCEA.

The law that created this section of the statutes, however, included the missing subsections a and b of section 5 in the UCEA.[23] These subsections extend the applicability of the conservation easement law to interests created after the adoption of the Wisconsin law that comply with the Wisconsin law in form and purpose and to interests created before the law's passage. The official version of the Wisconsin statutes published by the revisor of Statutes includes the interpretive notes of the revisor that alert the reader to the language omitted from the statutes.

Separate from the UCEA is a provision in Wisconsin law governing the valuation of real estate for property tax purposes that requires assessors to "consider the effect on the value of the property" of conservation easements.[24] There is a perception in the state that local assessors are not recognizing conservation easements when they assess property. In part, this perception may be due to expectations that the placement of a conservation easement on property should result in a dramatic reduction in the value of property. One recent unpublished Wisconsin Court of Appeals court case illustrates this issue.[25] The property owners had federally imposed scenic easements along the St. Croix River, a National Wild and Scenic Riverway. The property owner challenged the property assessment, arguing that the scenic easements lowered the property value and that the property tax assessment should be reduced by 50 percent. The property owner based the claim on a letter from a realtor, which stated that the easements reduced the property's value by 50 to 90 percent of the town's assessed value. The Court of Appeals was not persuaded by the evidence and upheld the assessment.

Wisconsin's marketable title statutes also recognize conservation easements. Recognizing the perpetual nature of easements, the law provides that the forty-year statute of limitations period for actions to enforce easements does not apply to conservation easements.[26]

The Eighth Federal Circuit

The Eighth Federal Circuit includes Arkansas, Iowa, Minnesota, Missouri, Nebraska, North Dakota, and South Dakota. Minnesota and South Dakota have adopted the UCEA. North Dakota has not adopted a conservation easement law. The remaining states have adopted their own versions of conservation easement enabling legislation.

Arkansas

Arkansas has adopted non-UCEA–type enabling legislation. The statutes were passed into law by the Arkansas legislature in 1983, only two years after the UCEA was approved.[27] The relevant subchapter is referred to as the Conservation Easement Act.[28]

The second section of the Arkansas Conservation Easement Act provides the definitions section, and the wording is almost identical to the UCEA's definitions in section 1.[29] Subparagraphs (1), (2)(B), and (3) of Arkansas's legislation is a word-for-word adaptation of the UCEA regarding the definitions of "conservation easement," nongovernmental "holders" and "third-party right of enforcement." The slight difference relates to Arkansas's some-what more narrow definition of a governmental holder.

The "applicability and construction" section of Arkansas's enabling statute is based on UCEA's four classes of interest in "applicability."[30] Arkansas simply adds a fourth paragraph stating that

> this subchapter shall not be construed to imply that any restriction, easement, covenant, or condition which does not come within the purview of this subchapter shall, on account of any provisions hereof, be unenforceable. Nothing in this subchapter shall diminish the powers granted by any general or special law to acquire by purchase, gift, eminent domain, or otherwise and to use land for public purposes. Nothing in this subchapter shall be construed to repeal or diminish any of the powers, functions, or responsibilities of any state agency, county, first or second class city, or incorporated town.[31]

The next sections in Arkansas's legislation are very similar to the UCEA's related provisions. Arkansas separates the UCEA's section 2 on creation, conveyance, acceptance, and duration into four separate subsections, but, the language used in Arkansas is essentially the same language found in the UCEA.[32] The validity section of Arkansas's enabling legislation is found at Ark. Stat. Ann. 15-20-409, and the wording used is lifted directly from the UCEA's section 4 on validity. The judicial actions section is also modeled on UCEA section 3.[33]

The last section of Arkansas's Conservation Easement Act lays out the rules for the Arkansas Commemorative Commission's actions relating to conservation easements.[34] It essentially gives the director of the commission power to approve the creation, modification, or termination of a conservation easement held by the commission. In addition, it places the burden to determine whether an easement, held by the commission, or its continuance is in the public interest. Easements held by the commission may be terminated or modified, but only after a public hearing with adequate public notice.

The last section of the Arkansas statute is a substantive deviation from the UCEA. The Arkansas Conservation Easement Act also lacks section 6 of the UCEA on uniformity of application and construction.

Unfortunately, there has been a lack of active land trusts in Arkansas. Both The Nature Conservancy and the Trust for Public Land, however, have an interest in conservation projects in Arkansas.

Iowa

Iowa first adopted conservation easement legislation in 1971.[35] As originally enacted, the legislation permitted such easements to be held only by the state

Department of Natural Resources, county conservation boards, or cities and city agencies. A 1984 amendment permits private, nonprofit organizations to hold conservation easements.[36] The purposes for which the Iowa act permits conservation easements are

> to preserve scenic beauty, wildlife habitat, riparian lands, wet lands, or forests, promote outdoor recreation, or otherwise conserve for the benefit the natural beauty, natural resources, and public recreation facilities of the state.[37]

Notably missing from this list are agricultural, historical, architectural, archeological, or cultural purposes as provided in the UCEA. Given the Iowa statute's clear emphasis on natural and outdoor settings, the validity of an easement for any of these additional UCEA purposes is open to question. Even the inclusive group that may "otherwise conserve" refers first to "natural beauty" and "natural resources;" therefore, the phrase "public recreation facilities" is subject to a narrow interpretation in light of the preceding terms. Such interpretation is further supported by the previous reference to "outdoor recreation."

The statute's references to wildlife habitat, riparian lands, wetlands, and forests all precede, in the same sentence, the reference to promoting outdoor recreation. Clearly, a "conservation" easement would be allowed to *promote the use* of wetlands, wildlife areas, forests, and lake or river shores for hunting or fishing.[38] An easement to promote hang gliding off the scenic Mississippi River bluffs is also permitted by this act. But what about the mythical baseball field built in an Iowa cornfield as depicted in the movie *Field of Dreams*? Although it would obviously qualify as an outdoor recreation facility, it is not at all clear that if it did exist, a conservation easement could be created for the protection of either the diamond or the cornfield. The act arguably appears to be limited to natural, rather than manufactured, wonders.

Although Iowa's conservation easement act omits agricultural purposes, the state does provide for preservation of agricultural lands. Similar to Minnesota's Metropolitan Agricultural Preserves Act,[39] Iowa has a statutory scheme to "preserve the availability and use of agricultural land for agricultural production."[40] The Iowa Agricultural Preservation Act was enacted in 1979 and is not merely aimed at preserving agricultural lands in metropolitan areas. The Iowa act created a "county land preservation and use commission" in every county of the state and charged these commissions with the duty to inventory unincorporated lands and to develop "county land use plans" for such areas after holding at least one public hearing.[41] An owner may petition to have land (meeting certain minimum criteria relating to size and use) designated as an agricultural area under this act. The county land preservation commission is required to hold a public hearing prior to making the designation, and once made, the designation is effective for six years, after which the owner may unilaterally withdraw the designation.[42] Land so designated enjoys protection from special assessments and some protection from state regulations.[43]

The Iowa act also contains a unique provision[44] that provides immunity from nuisance actions. The Iowa Supreme Court recently held that provision to be "flagrantly unconstitutional." In *Bormann v. Board of Supervisors in and for Kossuth County,* several landowners of an aggregate 960 acres applied to the Kossuth County Board of Supervisors for establishment of an "agricultural area."[45] The board denied the application, finding that

> there are no present or foreseeable nonagricultural develop-
> ment pressures in the area for which the designation is
> requested. . .
>
> the nuisance protections provided [in the act] will have a direct
> and permanent impact on the existing and long-held private
> property rights of the adjacent property owners.

Two months later, however, the applicants tried again, and this time the board approved the agricultural area designation by a three to two vote, with the deciding vote being determined by a coin toss. Thereafter opponents of the designation brought a court action to challenge the board's action, alleging, among other things, that the designation was arbitrary, capricious, and deprived them of property without due process or just compensation under both the federal and Iowa constitutions. On appeal, although the complainants neither alleged nor proved the existence of any specific nuisance, the Iowa Supreme Court agreed, saying:

> the state cannot regulate property so as to insulate the users
> from potential private nuisance claims without providing just
> compensation to persons injured by the nuisance. . . . [46]
>
> When all the varnish is removed, the challenged statutory scheme
> amounts to a commandeering of valuable property rights with-
> out compensating the owners, and sacrificing those rights for the
> economic advantage of a few. In short, it appropriates valuable
> private property interests and awards them to strangers.[47]

In the same vein, Iowa courts should recognize that conservation easements do constitute valuable property interests. Although the Iowa Conservation Easement Act does not contain any enforcement provision like the UCEA, the rights must surely be enforceable by the holder of the easement, whether it is public or private.

Mark Ackelson of the Iowa Natural Heritage Foundation gives an interesting disquisition on the aligned efforts of land trusts in four states from the Seventh and Eighth Federal Circuits to protect the blufflands along the upper Mississippi in Case Study.

Minnesota

Minnesota's first attempt to promote conservation by legislation was through a property tax measure adopted in 1967 popularly known as the Green Acres Act.[48] Under this law, property owners have been able to retain agricultural classification for property (thus lower taxes) located in areas under development pressure from urban expansion. Unlike conservation easements, however, the measure does nothing to perpetuate conservation; it merely delays the development of urban farmland until the surrounding lands become so highly developed that the owner literally receives an offer he or she cannot refuse. When the property is converted to other use, the law provides for retroactive taxation at the higher classification for three years prior to conversion. The Minnesota courts have attempted to ensure that the benefit is reserved to those having true agricultural enterprises.[49]

In 1980, Minnesota adopted another measure calculated to protect farmlands from urban sprawl, the Metropolitan Agricultural Preserves Act.[50] In addition to the goal of equitable taxation, this act is aimed at providing

> [an] orderly means by which lands in the metropolitan area designated for long term agricultural use through the local and regional planning processes will be . . . protected from unreasonably restrictive local and state regulation of normal farm practices, protected from indiscriminate and disruptive taking of farmlands through eminent domain actions, protected from the imposition of unnecessary special assessments, and given such additional protection and benefits as are needed to maintain viable productive farm operations in the metropolitan area.[51]

Although this act does permit landowners to create recorded restrictive covenants to run with the land, it is limited in that the land must be devoted to agricultural use and be within the designated metropolitan area.[52] Before a landowner may make such a dedication, the local unit of government exercising planning and zoning authority for the land specified must certify the land as eligible for long-term dedication to agriculture. Expiration of the dedication may be initiated by either the local authority or the landowner. The statute charges the local authority with responsibility for enforcing the covenant. In *Madson v. Overby et al.*, a local resident successfully secured a writ of mandamus requiring the city of Lake Elmo to enforce a covenant against the owner of dedicated agricultural preserve land.[53] Because the owner was a district court judge in Washington County, where the land was located, a judge from another judicial district was assigned to hear the case. The trial court found that a February 23, 1983, restrictive covenant signed by the judge and his wife as part of their initial application for the agricultural preserve designation was violated by their commercial storage use on agricultural preserve land in violation of the Metropolitan Agricultural Preserves Act. The trial court ordered an alternative writ of mandamus directing the owner to terminate the unlawful commercial use.

Then, in 1985, the state of Minnesota joined a growing band of states by enacting the UCEA.[54] As one of the nation's leading agricultural states, Minnesota over the course of time has enacted a number of important pieces of legislation geared toward keeping Minnesota's farming tradition strong,[55] yet it is Minnesota's Conservation Easement Act of 1985 that provides the legal foundation that has enabled conservation organizations to protect tens of thousands of acres of privately owned lands across the state. As in other jurisdictions, the act provides for a broad range of "conservation easements" including

> natural, scenic, or open-space values of real property, assuring its availability for agricultural, forest, recreational, or open-space use, protecting natural resources, maintaining or enhancing air or water quality, or preserving the historical, architectural, archaeological, or cultural aspects of real property.[56]

In 1990, yet another piece of legislation was introduced in Minnesota allowing for the acquisition of conservation easements.[57] The conservation reserve program is administered by a board, in consultation with the commissioner of agriculture and the commissioner of natural resources. Through the program, land placed under protection must be based on its potential for fish and wildlife production, reducing erosion, and protecting water quality. Subdivision 3 of the act proscribes the guidelines under which conservation easements on eligible land may be acquired.[58] An interesting attribute of the conservation reserve program is that it allows for conservation easements to be "permanent or of limited duration."[59] There are specific conditions set forth regarding prescribing when an easement must be permanent and under what conditions a limited-term easement may be acquired.[60] In subdivision 4, the nature of the property rights acquired and prohibitions that must be covered by the conservation are identified.[61] Other important sections address issues of easement renewal, in the case of a limited or term easement, and discussion of enforcement and damages.[62]

Minnesota's Twin Cities in the Midst of Sprawl

Minnesota's population density is fifty-three people per square mile, making the overall risk to its diverse ecosystems high.[63] Population density has increased 8 percent between 1982 and 1992. During this same ten-year period the amount of developed land increased 11 percent. Minnesota has lost nearly all its original tallgrass prairie and oak savanna (Photograph 19.1). Half of Minnesota's wetlands have been lost since 1780. The state has eleven federally listed threatened and endangered species.[64] As a result of these burgeoning pressures on the state's land resources, their protection has become a high-priority item.

If a recent report published by the Sierra Club is to believed, land protection efforts in the heartland of Minnesota are perhaps just in time. The report ranks the metropolitan region of Minneapolis–St. Paul, eighth out of the thirty considered most threatened by "sprawl."[65] Addressing the issue head on, the *St. Paul Pioneer Press* published a six-day series dedicated to sprawl in the Twin Cities in November 1996. In the November 16, 1996, issue, staff writer Lynda McDonnell brought the issue directly to the masses, when she wrote:

> In the beginning, sprawl smelled.
>
> It was the 1950s, and the great migration of Minnesotans from city to suburb was on. Acre after acre of ranch homes for growing families bloomed on farm fields in Roseville, Bloomington, Brooklyn Center.

Photograph 19.1. Typical Minnesota landscape, agricultural fields with remnant tall grass prairie
Photo credit: J. A. Gustanski

The growth soon overwhelmed sewage treatment systems in Minneapolis and St. Paul. But developers were undeterred. They dug wells, routed sewage pipes to tanks buried in back yards and promised buyers that effluent would filter harmlessly into the soil.

In 1959, nature gave the lie to that easy promise. The state Health Department found half the wells in 39 communities contaminated by septic waste. The Federal Housing Administration threatened to refuse mortgage insurance for homes not tied into a central sewer system.

From that public health crisis came the political willpower to overcome municipal rivalries and, in 1967, formed the Metropolitan Council, a regional agency charged with guiding development of the entire region.

Thirty years later, the Twin Cities face another sprawl crisis. Like its precursor, this one is born of growth and prosperity— of Americans' love of cars and elbow room, of fresh starts and new houses. But unlike the sprawl of the 1950s, this one emits no odor and has no easy answers.

The Twin Cities have sprawled lavishly during the past two decades. With two down towns to grow from and no geographic barriers to inhibit its spread, the Minneapolis–St. Paul area has become the third most sprawled region among the nation's 25 largest urban areas.[66]

Between 1982 and 1992, Minnesota lost 2.3 million acres of farmland to development. Hennepin County, where Minneapolis is located, lost the greatest proportion by far: 29 percent. The rate of open space destroyed by development increased by almost 25 percent in the Minneapolis–St. Paul metro area overall.[67]

Although area residents are leaving the city core (population decreased by 3.3 percent in Minneapolis–St. Paul between 1990 and 1996), the suburbs have seen steady and significant expansion.[68] The number of people moving to the Twin Cities' surrounding areas rose 25 percent in the 1980s and another 16 percent in the early 1990s. In particular, nearby Wright and Sherburne Counties have experienced astounding growth. The number of households grew 52 percent in Sherburne County and 25 percent in Wright County from 1986 to 1996.[69]

Regional planners calculate the cost of all this low-density growth at $3.1 billion for new sewers and water systems alone, as the region's population rises by 650,000 by 2020. Planners at the Metropolitan Council estimate that taxpayers in the Twin Cities region could save $600 million in public infra-structure costs by concentrating development in the urban core.[70]

Through both its continuing legislative actions and projects aimed at addressing issues of sprawl, Minnesota is making a concerted effort to look forward and take innovative measures to contend with development and growth.[71] The November 20, 1998, issue of the *Minneapolis Star Tribune* featured "Counties Get Creative in Efforts to Preserve Open Space." The article deals with growth management in the Twin Cities and around the country and on the Green Corridor project led by 1000 Friends of Minnesota. The article includes brief descriptions of various land protection tools, including conservation easements and outlines the history of the Green Corridor work.[72]

Conservation Easements: Land Trusts and Land Protection

Although relatively recent to the land trust scene, the eight chapters of the Minnesota Land Trust have protected over 7,750 acres in thirty-nine Minnesota counties since 1993.[73] In addition, national land conservation organizations like the Trust for Public Land, The Nature Conservancy, and the American Farmland Trust have all had a presence in the state. The Nature Conservancy's Minnesota chapter boasts being involved in the protection of over 252,000 acres throughout the state. These lands have been protected using various preservation strategies, from outright purchase to conservation easements and voluntary agreements.[74]

More than ten years before Minnesota adopted the UCEA, John R. Flicker made predictions as to the use and popularity of conservation easements in Minnesota:

> It is important to understand that conservation easements are not intended to replace any existing land use tools, or to complicate numerous land titles by doing away with conventional fee simple transfers. The conservation easement is intended to be a limited, but valuable, tool in particular kinds of situations where existing methods are not adequate. It is a tool which is now available and which attorneys may expect to be seeing more and more in the future.[75]

Case Law

There has not yet been any case construing an easement created under Minnesota's UCEA, but the Minnesota Supreme Court previously considered a case involving a "conservation easement" created before the act.[76] In the *Bly* case, a conservation easement against Outlot B was required by the city council in March 1982 as a condition for approval of a plat for five lots for single-

family homes. It was apparently stipulated at that time that no building permits would issue for any of the lots until final granting and recording of the
easement. Presumably, the plat was recorded and it appears that the restrictions were included in the plat and in other recorded documents. In March
1984, the plaintiffs entered into a purchase agreement for one of the lots and
Outlot B. A formal grant of the required easement for Outlot B was submitted to the city about three months later. This document provided that Outlot
B shall be "preserved predominantly in its natural condition" and that "no
building . . . or other man-made structure shall be placed in the conservation
area without the prior written consent of the city." The sale of Outlot B to the
plaintiff was closed one day after this declaration was given to the city. The
buyer then sued, claiming fraud. The case was on appeal from an order that
had discharged a notice of *lis pendens* filed by the plaintiff in an effort to tie
up the other lots owned by the seller until litigation was resolved. Curiously,
the appellate court and all parties appear to have assumed that the grant was
at least permissible, even though Minnesota did not adopt the UCEA until
1985. One must assume that the action was resolved without any subsequent
appeal on the merits, as there is no further reported decision.

Missouri

Missouri got into the conservation easement game relatively early, enacting
its conservation easement enabling legislation in 1971,[77] ten years before the
National Conference of Commissioners on Uniform States Laws drafted the
UCEA. Thus, the Missouri legislation[78] is quite different from the UCEA. The
general assembly of the Missouri legislature felt that "rapid growth and random spread of urban development" necessitated protection of open spaces.[79]

Missouri's definition of who may hold an easement is similar to the UCEA,
with an added population requirement for counties and cities. Missouri's legislation says that, "the Missouri state park board, and any county having a
population in excess of two hundred thousand and any county adjoining, or
city not within but adjoining such county, may acquire . . . a conservation
easement."[80] The power to hold a conservation easement is also given to not-
for-profit organizations.[81] Section 67.910 specifically excludes purported
"second-class" counties, those counties having a population of more than
100,000 and less than 110,000, from holding conservation easements. The
reasoning behind this exclusion is not immediately clear. The UCEA simply
defines a "holder" as a government body empowered to hold an interest in
real property or a proper charitable organization.[82]

Missouri's definition of open space or open area differs slightly from the
UCEA. Both Missouri legislation and the UCEA share the goals of preserving
open space that protects natural, scenic, or open-space resources, parks or
recreation areas, archaeological sites, natural resources, and water supply and

quality. The main differences relate to Missouri's inclusion of a clause designed to aid state planning agencies in development plans and another clause to "promote orderly urban or suburban development"[83] and the UCEA's expansion of protection to land for "assuring its availability for agricultural . . . use."[84]

Unlike the UCEA, Missouri requires all county and municipal assessors and taxing authorities to take into account valuation of property with conservation easements.[85] Furthermore, Missouri's enabling law specifically authorizes the state park board, any county having a population in excess of 200,000 or any county adjoining, or a city not within but adjoining such county to accept monies from any agency, organization, or private person for the purposes of sections 67.870 to 67.910.[86]

The UCEA has several major sections that Missouri does not have: section 2 on creation, conveyance, acceptance, and duration; section 3 on judicial actions; section 4 on validity; section 5 on applicability; and, of course, section 6 on uniformity of application and construction.

The Ozark Regional Land Trust (ORLT) is an active land trust in Missouri that uses available legislation. It operates mainly in the Ozark bioregion encompassing much of southern Missouri, part of northern Arkansas, and the northeastern tip of Oklahoma. This unique area is rich with springs, rivers, lakes, caves, and hilly terrain. The ORLT uses several conservation tools in addition to conservation easements; the newest is their land stewardship registry. The ORLT says that this "is a non-binding land protection agreement for landowners wishing to express their good faith adherence to an ecological land ethic."[87]

Nebraska

Nebraska is another state in the Eighth Federal Circuit that has non-UCEA enabling legislation and a lack of active land trusts. Nebraska's legislation was adopted by their unicameral legislature in 1981, the same year that the UCEA was approved by the National Conference of Commissioners on Uniform State Laws.[88]

The first noticeable difference between the UCEA and Nebraska's legislation is in the title of Nebraska's enabling statute. Nebraska has a broad section encompassing both conservation and preservation easements called the Conservation and Preservation Easement Act.[89] The idea of preservation relates to historical, architectural, archeological, or cultural aspects of real property, whereas the conservation element relates to retaining or protecting property in its natural, scenic, or open condition.

The next difference is quite a bit more substantive than the first because it has approval requirements for conservation easements.[90] To minimize conflicts with land use planning, this section requires the "appropriate governing body" to approve each conservation or preservation easement. This approval comes after the governing body refers the proposal to the local planning commission with jurisdiction over the property and receives comments from the planning commission. There is a default provision that says if the planning commission fails to respond within sixty days, the easement is deemed approved by the planning commission.

The appropriate governing body may deny the proposed acquisition if the acquisition is not in the public interest when the easement is inconsistent with

> (a) a comprehensive plan for the area which had been officially adopted and was in force at the time of the conveyance, (b) any national, state, regional, or local program furthering conservation or preservation, or (c) any known proposal by a governmental body for use of the land.

This section gives latitude for governmental agencies to terminate a proposal for an easement under a subjective test.

The Nebraska law gives power to the court to modify or terminate an easement only if "the petitioner establishes that it is no longer in the public interest to hold the easement or that the easement no longer substantially achieves the conservation or preservation purpose for which it was created." This clause differs from the UCEA section 3 on judicial actions that, under subsection (a), simply lists the four categories of persons who may bring actions to enforce, modify, or terminate conservation easements. Subsection (b) of section 3 states that the UCEA does not effect the power of a court to modify or terminate a conservation easement in accordance with the principles of law and equity.

Nebraska does not address all the common-law defenses and problems associated with conservation easements.[91] Nebraska removes the possible common-law defenses relating to lack of privity of estate or of contract, lack of benefit to a dominant estate, or an account of the easement being assignable. This section does not address the additional problems the UCEA does, which has the additional declarations that a conservation easement is valid even though it is not appurtenant to an interest in real property, if it is not of a character that has been recognized traditionally at common law, if it imposes a negative burden, or if it imposes affirmative obligations upon the owner of an interest in the burdened property or upon the holder.

Another section of Nebraska's law reiterates the state's power to terminate an easement. The government's powers of eminent domain and condemnation take precedent over an easement, and the Conservation and Preservation Easement Act shall not interfere with these powers.

North Dakota

North Dakota is the only state in these two circuits that has not enacted legislation for the establishment of conservation easements. Perhaps an explanation for this lies is that North Dakota has been a frequent battleground over easements for waterfowl management rights owned by the federal government. As the district court noted:

> Much of the State of North Dakota, as well as parts of the Canadian Provinces of Manitoba, Saskatchewan, and Alberta, constitutes what marine biologists call the northeastern drift plain. As a prairie pothole region, each square mile of the drift plain is dotted by as many as seventy to eighty potholes, three to four feet deep, that retain water through July or August because of the soil's poor drainage capacity. These geographical attributes are of particular importance to certain migratory waterfowl that prefer these potholes as a habitat to raise their young because they provide isolated protection and a source of aquatic food.[92]

In *United States v. Albrecht*,[93] a prior owner had sold a perpetual easement to the state government in 1964 for the maintenance of land for a waterfowl production area. The easement had been a matter of record when the defendant acquired the property in 1967. The action was brought by the government to secure injunctive relief against ditching and drainage activities of the defendant. The defendant argued that the easement was invalid under North Dakota law or, if valid, it was merely "an easement in gross, not binding on the defendants as successors in title to the original grantors." The court did not consider whether North Dakota law permitted such easements. The court pointed instead to the federal law that

> authorizes the Secretary of the Interior to acquire ". . . small wetland and potholes areas, interests therein, and rights-of-way to provide access thereto."[94]

The court relied on the existence of a federal program under which the United States acquired contractual rights and held that "no rule may be applied which would not be wholly consistent with that program."[95]

This program has been the subject of a considerable amount of litigation since *Albrecht*.[96] In answer to growing frustration and antieasement sentiment on the part of landowners, the state of North Dakota enacted legislation in 1977 attempting to limit further acquisitions by the federal government. This legislation sought to make additional acquisitions subject to the approval of the board of county commissioners in the county where the land is located. It required the county agent in the affected county to prepare an impact analysis for the county board and required the Department of the Interior to reimburse the county for the cost of the analysis. It also permitted the affected land owner to negotiate the terms and duration of the lease or easement and put a ninety-nine-year cap on any government lease or easement.[97] The United States thereafter brought a declaratory judgment action in U.S. District Court in North Dakota seeking to have the North Dakota statutory limitations declared null and void. Following an adverse ruling, the state appealed to the Eighth Circuit Court of Appeals[98] and then to the United States Supreme Court.[99]

The Supreme Court agreed with the state only with respect to the state's argument that gubernatorial consent was required by section 3 of the Wetlands Act of 1961 prior to federal acquisition of the wetland easements. As a matter of fact, consents had been given by successive governors between 1961 and 1977. The Court held that once the consent had been given, it could not be revoked and that no state legislation could limit the ability of the United States to acquire easements pursuant to consent previously given. The Court also noted that the United States did not dispute the portion of the state law that permitted a landowner to negotiate the conditions of an easement and have the scope of the easement restricted to a specific legal description.[100] This critical point later resulted in the reversal of a criminal conviction for drainage activity in *United States v. Johansen*. In this decision, the Court criticized sharply the government's prosecution of the case and appeared to signal a new chapter in state and federal relations with respect to waterfowl management. Perhaps in time, North Dakota will enact conservation easement enabling legislation.

South Dakota

Although South Dakota adopted the UCEA in 1984, it had prior legislation for historical easements adopted in 1974. The 1974 measure defined "historic easement" as follows:

> any easement, restriction, covenant or condition running with the land, designated to preserve, maintain or enhance all or part of the existing state of places of historical, architectural, archaeological, paleontological or cultural significance.[101]

In recognition of its rich fossil deposits, the reference to paleontological interests is repeated in South Dakota's version of the UCEA.[102] In other respects, South Dakota's Conservation Easement Law tracks the UCEA.

There have not yet been any cases under the conservation easement act but there is an interesting case involving the Historic Preservation Act. In *Dono-*

van v. City of Deadwood, the owners of a commercial building in Deadwood known as the Treber Ice House applied for a demolition permit and were denied by the city.[103] Although the city claimed that the property was eligible for listing on the National and State Registers of Historic Places, the property was not listed and it was not within the city's "Historic District." Ultimately, the case did not turn on these facts, but rather on a legal determination that the city of Deadwood had improperly adopted the ordinance under which it denied the demolition permit at issue. The city admittedly had failed to follow the various procedural steps that the act prescribed prior to the adoption of a historic preservation ordinance. In addition to these procedural defects that invalidated the ordinance, the court noted that

> [nothing in the act authorizes] a commission to deny a demolition permit even if a property is historic. On the contrary, SDCL 1-19B-27 provides that historic properties may be demolished after 180 days notice given to the historic preservation commission and during that 180 day period, the commission may negotiate with the owner in an effort to find a means of preserving the property. However, at the conclusion of the 180 days, the owner of historic property may raze the property.

Of course one of the common problems with historic preservation and other involuntary measures for conservation and preservation is that they do restrict an owner's use and enjoyment of his or her property and, if it deprives the owner of reasonable economic use, it may result in a taking for public use. Nothing in the UCEA prohibits the acquisition of conservation easements by eminent domain, and South Dakota's 1974 legislation for historic preservation specifically authorizes acquisition by condemnation.[104] Voluntary creation is promoted through the incentives offered by the tax laws, and with the UCEA, states establish a means for judicial enforcement with standing vested in a number of interested parties.

Notes

1. 1998 National Land Trust Survey, Land Trust Alliance, Washington, D.C.
2. 765 ILCS 120/0.01–120/6.
3. Tobin M. Richter, 1983. "Conservation Rights in Illinois—Meshing Illinois Property Law with Federal Tax Deduction Requirements," *Illinois Bar Journal* 71, no. 7 (1983): 430–437.
4. George M. Covington, "Conservation Easements: A Win/Win for Preservationists and Real Estate Owners," *Illinois Bar Journal* 84, no.12 (1996): 629–633.
5. 765 ILCS 120/4.
6. 765 ILCS 120/5.

7. 35 ILCS 200/10-166.

8. 35 ILCS 200/10-167.

9. 35 ILCS 200/10-169.

10. George M. Covington, "Conservation Easements: A Win/Win for Preservationists and Real Estate Owners," *Illinois Bar Journal* 84, no. 12 (1996): 629–633.

11. 505 ILCS 35.

12. 505 ILCS 35/1-3(b).

13. Ibid.

14. 505 ILCS 35/2-1–2-5.

15. Ind. Code §§ 32-5-2.6-1–32-5-2.6-7.

16. Ind. Code § 32-5-2.6-3 Sec. 3(b).

17. Ind. Code § 32-5-2.6-2 Sec. 2(c).

18. Ind. Code § 32-5-2.6-7.

19. Wis. Stat. § 700.40.

20. *Kamrowski v. State,* 37 Wis.2d 195, 155 N.W.2d 125 (1967).

21. *Kamrowski v. State,* 31 Wis.2d 256, 142 N.W.2d 793 (1966).

22. 1985 Wis. Laws ch. 316.

23. 1981 Wis. Laws ch. 261, § 3.

24. Wis. Stat. § 70.32(1g).

25. *Bradac v. Farmington Town Board,* Nos. 94-1220, 94-1221, 1995 Wisc. App. LEXIS 234 (Wis. Ct. App. 1995) (unpublished opinion).

26. Wis. Stat. § 893.33(6m).

27. Arkansas Acts 1983, No. 567.

28. Ark. Stat. Ann. at 15-20-401 (1995).

29. Ark. Stat. Ann. at 15-20-402 and UCEA Section 1.

30. Ark. Stat. Ann. at 15-20-403 and UCEA Section 5.

31. Ark. Stat. Ann. at 15-20-403(d).

32. Ark. Stat. Ann. at 15-20-404 to 15-20-407.

33. Ark. Stat. Ann. at 15-20-409.

34. Ark. Stat. Ann. at 15-20-410.

35. Iowa Code 1971, § 111D.1 et seq. Since 1993, the act has been codified at Iowa Code §457A.1 et seq. The Iowa act expressly prohibits acquisition of conservation easements through eminent domain.

36. 84 Acts, ch. 1115, now Iowa Code § 457A.8.

37. § 457A.1.

38. In the case of *Linn County v. Kindred,* 373 N.W.2d 147 (Iowa App. 1985), the court considered an outright deed of land given to the County Conservation Board in 1965 for purposes of a wildlife refuge. Because of the county's admitted violations of its terms, including the failure to take action to prevent hunting in the area, the court held that the property reverted to the grantors heirs.

39. See notes 3, 4, and 5, and accompanying text.

40. Iowa Code § 352.1 et seq.

41. Iowa Code §§ 352.4 and 352.5.

42. Designation may be withdrawn after three years with approval of the county board. See Iowa Code § 352.9.

43. Iowa Code §§ 352.10 and 352.12. The latter section permits state rule-making agencies to adopt less restrictive rules provisions applicable to farms within designated agricultural areas than those applicable to other farms.

44. Iowa Code § 352.11.

45. *Bormann v. Board of Supervisors in and for Kossuth County,* 584 N.W.2d 309 (Iowa 1998).

46. Ibid.

47. Ibid.

48. Minn. Stats. § 273.111, also called the Minnesota Agricultural Property Tax Law. It is one example of Minnesota's frequently expressed dedication to "saving the family farm."

49. See, for example, *Barron v. Hennepin County,* 488 N.W.2d 290 (Minn. 1992); *Walthall v. County of Wadena,* 1985 Minn. Tax LEXIS 107 (Minn. Tax Court, 1985); *Haasken v. County of Carver,* 1994 Minn. Tax LEXIS 50 (Minn. Tax Court, 1994); *Eisinger, et al. v. County of Washington,* 1992 Minn. Tax LEXIS 104 (Minn. Tax Court, 1992).

50. Minn. Stats. §§ 473H.01–473H.17.

51. Minn. Stats. §§ 473H.01.

52. The minimum parcel size is 40 acres, although in some circumstances, a parcel as small as 20 acres may qualify if it is contiguous to other agricultural preserve land.

53. *Madson v. Overby et al.,* 425 N.W.2d 270 (Minn. App., 1988).

54. Minn. Stat. §§ 84C.01–.05, Conservation Easement Act.

55. Minn. Stat. § 394.25, "Forms of Control," Agricultural Protection Zoning Enabling law (1959 c. 559s 5; with revisions through 1990 c. 391 art. 8 s. 44); Minn. Stat. § 273.111, "Minnesota Agricultural Property Tax Law" (1967 c. 60 s. 1-13, with revisions to 1991); Minn. Stat. §§ 473H.01–.18, "Metropolitan agricultural preserves act," (1980 c. 566 s. 2); Minn. Stat. § 561.19, "Nuisance liability of agricultural operations," (1982 c. 533 s. 1; 1983 c. 182 s. 1); Minn. Stat. §§ 17.80–.84, "State agricultural land preservation and conservation policy" (1982 c. 512 s. 1).

56. Minn. Stats. § 84C.01.

57. Minn. Stats. § 103F.515, Conservation Reserve Program.

58. Minn. Stats. § 103F.515, Subd. 3.

59. Minn. Stats. § 103F.515, Subd. 3.

60. Minn. Stats. § 103F.515, Subd. 3.:

> An easement acquired on land for windbreak purposes, under subdivision 2, may be only of permanent duration. An easement of limited duration may not be acquired if it is for a period less than 20 years. The negotiation and acquisition of easements authorized by this section are exempt from the contractual provisions of chapters 16B and 16C. (b) The board may acquire, or accept by gift or donation, flowage easements when necessary for completion of wetland restoration projects.

61. Minn. Stats. § 103F.515, Subd. 4, Nature of property rights acquired: (a) A conservation easement must prohibit:

(1) alteration of wildlife habitat and other natural features, unless specifically approved by the board; (2) agricultural crop production, unless specifically approved by the board for wildlife management purposes; (3) grazing of livestock except, for agreements entered before the effective date of Laws 1990, chapter 391, grazing of livestock may be allowed only if approved by the board after consultation with the commissioner of natural resources, in the case of severe drought, or a local emergency declared under section 12.29; and (4) spraying with chemicals or mowing, except as necessary to comply with noxious weed control laws or emergency control of pests necessary to protect public health.

(b) A conservation easement is subject to the terms of the agreement provided in subdivision 5.

(c) A conservation easement must allow repairs, improvements, and inspections necessary to maintain public drainage systems provided the easement area is restored to the condition required by the terms of the conservation easement.

62. Minn. Stats. § 103F.515, Subd. 7; Subd. 9.

63. Census of Population and Housing (1990). Public Law (P.L.) 94–171. Data on CD-Rom, prepared by the Bureau of the Census. Washington, D.C.: U.S. Bureau of the Census, 1991.

64. Federally listed endangered species for Minnesota include:
Mammals: Gray wolf, *Canis lupus* (threatened).
Birds: American peregrine falcon, *Falco peregrinus anatum* (endangered); Bald eagle, *Haliaeetus leucocephalus* (threatened); Piping plover (Great Plains population), *Charadrius melodu* (threatened).
Clams (freshwater mussels, unionids): Higgins' eye pearlymussel, *Lampsilis higginsi* (endangered); Winged mapleleaf mussel; *Quadrula fragosa* (endangered).
Insects: Karner blue butterfly, *Lycaeides melissa samuelis* (endangered).
Plants: Leedy's roseroot, *Sedum integrifolium ssp. Leedyi* (threatened); Minnesota dwarf trout lily, *Erythronium propullans* (endangered); Praire bush-clover, *Lespedeza leptostachya* (threatened); Western praire fringed orchid, *Platanthera praeclara* (threatened).

65. 1998 Sierra Club Report, "The Dark Side of the American Dream: The Costs and Consequences of Suburban Sprawl"
Cities were ranked by a committee of Sierra Club suburban-sprawl experts. Selection criteria included trends in population and land-area growth for the urbanized areas as well as traffic congestion and open-space loss indicators. Sources include the U.S. Census Bureau, the Federal Highway Administration, the Texas Transportation Institute, and the American Farmland Trust. Other criteria, such as loss of important habitat and historical importance, were also taken into account. The committee ranked cities in three individual size categories: major

metropolitan areas with populations over 1 million, metropolitan areas with populations between 500,000 and 1 million, and metropolitan areas with populations from 200,000 to 500,000. The urban-area populations were determined by 1990 Urbanized Area data compiled by the U.S. Census Bureau.

66. *St. Paul Pioneer Press,* 16, November 1998, Lynda McDonnell, "Urban Sprawl: The Invisible Crisis," Special Series, pp. 1–3.

67. Census of Population and Housing (1990). Public Law (P.L.) 94–171. Data on CD-Rom, prepared by the Bureau of the Census. Washington, D.C.: U.S. Bureau of the Census, 1991.

68. Land Use Statistics and Profiles, Metropolitan Council, 1996.

69. Land Use Statistics and Profiles, Metropolitan Council, 1996.

70. The mission of the Metropolitan Council is to provide leadership in the effective planning of regional growth and redevelopment and in the delivery of quality regional services.

   The Metropolitan Council coordinates regional planning and guides development in the seven-county area through joint action with the public and private sectors. The council also operates regional services, including wastewater collection and treatment, transit, and the Metro HRA, an affordable-housing service that provides assistance to low-income families in the region. Created by the legislature in 1967, the council establishes policies for airports, regional parks, highways and transit, sewers, air and water quality, land use, and affordable housing and provides planning and technical assistance to communities in the Twin Cities region.

71. As part of continuing efforts in the Twin Cities region, the Metropolitan Council developed a Regional Blueprint at the directive of Minnesota Statute section 473.145. The law states:

   > The Metropolitan Council shall prepare and adopt . . . a comprehensive development guide for the metropolitan area. It shall consist of a compilation of policy statements, goals, standards, programs and maps prescribing guides for an orderly and economic development, public and private, of the metropolitan area. The comprehensive development guide shall recognize and encompass physical, social or economic needs of the metropolitan area.

   The Metropolitan Council's development guide, adopted in 1996 and mandated by the Minnesota legislature. The "Regional Blueprint for the Twin Cities Metropolitan Area" was adopted by the Metropolitan Council on December 19, 1996.

72. Jeffrey W. Peters, "Counties Get Creative in Efforts to Preserve Open Space." *Minneapolis Star Tribune,* November 20, 1998, p. 1B.

73. What is now known as the Minnesota Land Trust had its origins in the Washington County Land Trust founded in 1991. The Washington County Land Trust was created by conservation-minded citizens alarmed by the rapid loss of both agricultural and scenic space in the expanding county. The land trust expanded

its sights in 1993 to become a statewide organization, the Minnesota Land Trust. The eight chapters are the Central Minnesota Chapter (Todd, Stearns, Benton, Douglas, Morrison, Sherburne, Pope, Mille Lacs, Wright, Meeker, and Kandiyohi Counties); Headwaters Chapter (Beltrami, Cass, Clearwater, Hubbard, and Itasca Counties); Lake Superior Chapter (Cook County); West Metro Chapter (Hennepin, Carver, and Scott Counties); East Metro Chapter (Washington, Ramsey, Dakota, and Chisago Counties); Cannon River Chapter (LeSueur, Steele, and Rice Counties); Northern Blufflands Chapter (Goodhue and Wabasha Counties); and Southern Blufflands Chapter (Winona, Fillmore, and Houston Counties).

74. Minnesota Chapter of the Nature Conservancy, recent land statistics on protected lands.
75. John R. Flicker, "Conservation Easements," *Hennepin County Lawyer* (Jan.–Feb. 1976), 24–25.
76. *Bly v. Gensmer,* 386 N.W.2d 767 (Minn. App., 1986)
77. (l. 1971 H.B. 570).
78. Mo. Rev. Stat. 67.870 (1998).
79. Supra.
80. Mo. Rev. Stat. 67.880 (1998).
81. Mo. Rev. Stat. 67.890 (1998).
82. UCEA § 1(2)(i) and (ii).
83. Mo. Rev. Stat. 67.900(6) and (7) (1998).
84. UCEA § 1(1).
85. Mo. Rev. Stat. 67.895 (1998).
86. Mo. Rev. Stat. 67.905 (1998).
87. http://www.mrba.org/mrba.
88. Laws 1981, L.B.173.
89. R.R.S. Neb. at 76-2, 111 et seq. (1996).
90. R.R.S. Neb. at 76-2, 112 (1996).
91. R.R.S. Neb. at 76-2, 115.
92. *United States v. Johansen,* 93 F.3d 459, 461, n. 1 (8th Cir. 1996).
93. *United States v. Albrecht,* 364 F. Supp. 1349 (D. ND 1973).
94. 16 U.S.C. § 718d.
95. Citing *United States v. Little Lake Misere Land Company, Inc.,* 412 U.S. 580, at 602, 93 S. Ct. 2389, at 2402, 37 L. Ed. 2d 187 (1973).
96. See for example, *Werner v. United States,* 581 F.2d 168 (8th Cir., 1978) (landowners sought recession); *United States v. Welte,* 635 F. Supp. 388 (D. ND, 1982) (criminal enforcement under federal wetlands act for ditching property in violation of easement); *United States v. Vesterso,* 828 F.2d 1234 (8th Cir. 1987) (same, involving one of the plaintiffs in *Werner*).
97. The legislation applied to all easements in gross and thus would be a barrier to virtually all conservation easements.
98. *United States v. State of North Dakota,* 650 F.2d 911 (8th Cir. 1981).
99. *North Dakota V. United States,* 460 U.S. 300, 103 S. Ct. 1095, 75 L. Ed. 2d 77 (1983).

100. 460 U.S. at 317, 103 S. Ct. at 1105.
101. S.D. Codified Laws § 1-19B-16.
102. See S.D. Codified Laws §§ 1-19B-56–1-19B-60.
103. *Donovan v. City of Deadwood,* 538 N.W.2d 790 (1995).
104. S.D. Codified Laws § 1-19B-16.

Case Study

❦ ❧

The Iowa Natural Heritage Foundation and The Mississippi River Blufflands Alliance: Protecting Spectacular and Threatened Natural Resource Features in the Upper Midwest

Mark Ackelson

Introduction

The blufflands, whose dramatic features line some 400 miles of the upper Mississippi River, from the Twin Cities of Minnesota to the Quad Cities of Iowa and Illinois, are one of the most spectacular and threatened natural resources in the upper Midwest (Photograph 19.2). This region of twenty-three counties in four states is among the fastest-growing areas in the country (Figure 19.2).[1] The complexity of the region is reflected across its landscape. From its small farms and diverse communities to its rich archeological remains and natural resources to its spectacular views and fragile ecosystems, the fabric of the region is inextricably tied to the land. Issues related to river use have for decades concerned a multitude of public and private agencies with little attention given to the privately owned blufflands that line the river on both sides. Increased demand for residential sites on these blufflands, and the spectacular views of the river that are offered, are threatening to damage the bluffland resources.

Figure 19.2. The twenty-three county region comprising the Blufflands Alliance Project.

An Alliance is Formed

In 1991, four land trusts joined forces to establish the Mississippi River Blufflands Alliance (the Alliance). Initiated by the Iowa Natural Heritage Foundation (INHF) with major support from the McKnight Foundation, the Alliance includes INHF, the Natural Lands Institute, the Minnesota Land

Photograph 19.2. Dramatic features of the bluffland—bluffs with farm fields in the background.
Photo credit: John Ledger, Iowa Natural Heritage Foundation

Trust, and the Wisconsin Farmland Conservancy.[2] The Alliance formed to coordinate information and land protection strategies of the member land trusts on both sides of the Mississippi River and to encourage local participation in protecting the blufflands. While undertaking direct protection through conservation easements and fee acquisitions, the Alliance also works as a partner with communities throughout the region to explore other creative conservation tools to augment protection of the blufflands. The Alliance and its partners have come to recognize that their goal of protecting the blufflands can only be accomplished through strategic use of a combination of tools and an education program aimed at both landowners and local government officials.

As part of its work with the Blufflands Alliance, INHF and its partners have systematically contacted most of the landowners in the region personally.[3] This information together with natural and cultural resource data and information on public land ownership helped direct INHF to its initial priority sites.

INHF Using Conservation Easements to Protect Unique Bluffland Property

In 1996 INHF secured an option to purchase the partially wooded 320-acre Adams Mill Hollow property in Clayton County, Iowa, from Matt and Leonard Adams, who were the heirs to the property. Located near the Turkey River Mounds State Preserve, the bluffland property contained rare archeological features—a woman and a panther effigy. INHF wanted to use the project as an example of how the private sector could provide meaningful permanent protection and stewardship of a special site with minimal government help.

The Adams brothers needed an income from the property, their only major asset, to pay for nursing home and retirement expenses. Using a low-interest loan from The Conservation Fund, INHF purchased the property at fair market value. At the same time INHF began looking for a "conservation buyer"— an individual interested in acquiring the property to protect its natural and cultural features by purchasing the land in fee with a conservation easement already attached or to buy the land and convey a conservation easement back to the land trust. The low-interest loan gave INHF time to discuss these conservation strategies with several potential buyers. Recognizing the potential for problems with such a transaction, INHF spent considerable time assessing the motives and capacity of the potential buyers in its efforts to assure permanent protection. It took INHF over one year to close with the conservation buyer.[4]

Soon after acquiring the property, INHF began to compile detailed baseline inventories of the property in order to document the features that would be used to design the conservation easement.[5] In addition to conventional data collected for baseline inventories, INHF used a global positioning system to accurately locate site and boundary features, as well as geographical information system technology to map the resultant data.

To INHF's surprise, the inventory and preliminary legal review disclosed that the property contained a small 26-acre "in-holding" on the floodplain within the upper Mississippi River Wildlife and Fish Refuge. Paradoxically, the U.S. Fish and Wildlife Service had been trying to acquire this property to enable them to create a moist soil/wetlands management unit for the past 50 years. The U.S. Fish and Wildlife Service agreed to purchase this parcel at appraised value. Unfortunately, the sale took over two years to complete due to government funding limitations, boundary survey obstacles, and legal problems.

After several failed negotiations, the bulk of the property was eventually sold to a conservation buyer with an easement in place. The primary objectives of the conservation easement were to restrict development, limit grazing, and specify both forest and archeological resource management for the property.[6] With the easement in place, the property's market price was reduced, which required additional funding to bridge the gap between INHF's purchase price and the selling price. Grants obtained from the Iowa Department of Cultural Affairs, Office of the State Archeologist, the National Fish and Wildlife Foundation and other private donors collectively spanned this gap.[7]

Proceeds from the land sales to the U.S. Fish and Wildlife Service and the conservation buyer, along with other contributions, have been added to INHF's conservation easement monitoring and enforcement endowment fund. The purpose of the fund is to provide financial resources to cover long-term easement monitoring costs and potential legal fees in the event of a challenge to any of INHF's easements.

This project yielded not only the protection of a unique property, it offered an opportunity for community-wide involvement. College-age interns conducted baseline inventories and management planning, while various community nonprofit conservation and social service organizations carried out archeological and natural resource restoration work for INHF. This opportunity for exchange provided a meaningful educational experience for everyone involved, from the interns and resource professionals, to the Adams brothers themselves, who were able to share their love of the land and communicate the land's history with participants.

The completion of this project means that a significant natural and cultural resource area along the bluffs of the upper Mississippi River is protected. In addition, a model for future private stewardship and permanent land protection in this area has been created. Local governments were supportive of the actions because the property stayed on the tax rolls. Area citizens became more aware of the significance of the area through the involvement of young people. Most gratifying perhaps, is the fact that the project served to educate the public and the state legislatures about the role of land trusts in the protection of important lands. As a result, in 1998 the Iowa legislature created the Blufflands Protection Revolving Loan Program to provide no-interest loans for nonprofit conservation organizations to protect other important properties in the blufflands region of the upper Mississippi River and Loess Hills of western Iowa (Photograph 19.3).

Photograph 19.3. Upper Mississippi River and bluffland hills of western Iowa. *Photo credit:* John Ledger, Iowa Natural Heritage Foundation

Notes

1. According to Prof. Phil Lewis, University of Wisconsin, not by population but by urban sprawl. Personal comm., August 1998.
2. The Iowa Natural Heritage Foundation is a member-supported nonprofit organization that builds partnerships and educates Iowans to protect, preserve, and enhance Iowa's natural resources for future generations. INHF current priorities include permanent land protection, trail and greenway establishment, and the promotion of improved land management.

   The mission of the Minnesota Land Trust is to promote the protection and enhancement of open space in Minnesota. This includes farmland, wetlands, woodlands, bluff lands, wildlife habitat, and scenic areas. This is accomplished through direct conservation efforts, public education, and a number of community partnerships.

   The Wisconsin Farmland Conservancy (WFC) is a nonprofit 501 (c) (3) conservation organization. WFC's mission is to protect the character of the rural countryside—that mix of diversified farms, natural areas and forests, and small towns that makes rural Wisconsin a special place.

   WFC's program has three areas of focus: assisting landowners in private land protection efforts, working with local governments to establish land protection policies and programs, and helping farmers and rural communities to initiate environmentally sustainable economic development projects.
3. It should be noted that although this "paper" specifically discusses the efforts of INHF, these efforts parallel those of the other members of the Alliance.
4. Determining the motives and capacity of potential buyers while trying to assure permanent protection is time-consuming and often involves complex negotiations.
5. Baseline data needed for valuation purposes and to actually protect them in the easement language.
6. The easement was put on before the resale rather than counting on the subsequent owner donation back an easement to INHF to ensure there was full control of the future uses when the parcel was sold.
7. This was the first time the state archeologist had funded acquisition of a conservation easement even though it has been long recognized as an important protection tool.

Chapter 20

❧ ❧

A Farm and River Greenway on the St. Croix River: Standing Cedars Community Land Conservancy and Wisconsin Farmland Conservancy

Tom Quinn

In northwestern Wisconsin, a collaborative effort between farmers, land trusts, local community groups, and state agencies is working to establish a model "farm and river greenway" along the lower St. Croix River, near the community of Osceola[1] (Figure 20.1). The greenway protects several significant natural areas in the region using a variety of conservation tools. Lands throughout the greenway area have been purchased in fee and protected by conservation easements. Innovative strategies to help current farmers protect their land and to provide affordable land ownership opportunities for new farmers are also being used.

The lower St. Croix River in Polk County, designated a National Scenic River in 1972, is the border between the rapidly expanding metropolitan area of Minneapolis–St. Paul, Minnesota, and the still largely rural areas of northwestern Wisconsin (Photograph 20.1).[2] The river itself and the river bottom, ravines, and bluff faces provide spectacular scenic vistas and a diversity of habitats for trumpeter swans, bald eagles, great blue herons, migrating neotropical songbirds, waterfowl, and other species and plants, all within thirty miles of a major urban center.

Away from the river, agriculture and other rural land uses predominate, marked by Wisconsin's unique mix of modest-sized dairy farms, natural areas, forests, and small towns. Like so many rural areas across the United States, Polk County has been affected by the ever-tightening economic stress on family-sized farms. The average age of farmers is increasing, and fewer young people have the option of farming as a career choice.[3] As a consequence, people's livelihoods are shifting away from those traditionally based on land. In Polk County, for example, the rural farm population declined by

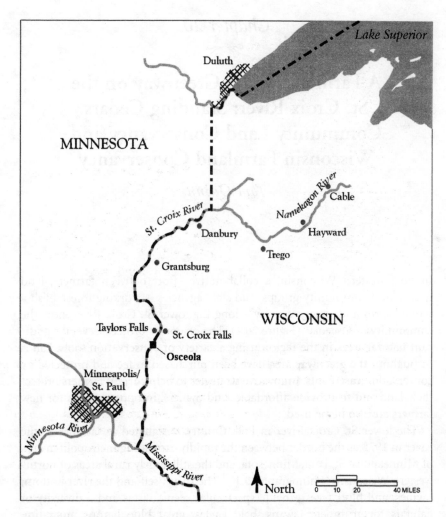

Figure 20.1. Map of Lower St. Croix River and Osceola.
Source: Tom Quinn, WFC

30 percent between 1980 and 1990,[4] which has had a dramatic impact on local economies throughout the area.

Access to this area of Wisconsin is limited to a few highways and narrow bridges, which has slowed its entry into the suburban sprawl experience that has occurred across the Twin Cities metropolitan region.[5] This situation is changing, though, and very quickly. One study by the American Farmland Trust identified this part of Wisconsin as one of the top fifty most threatened areas in the United States for conversion of farmland to residential develop-

Photograph 20.1. Winter waterfall on the Philadelphia community-supported agriculture farm property. *Source:* Tom Quinn, WFC

ment.[6] The Minnesota-Wisconsin Boundary Commission estimated that over sixty-one square miles of the Lower St. Croix watershed had been developed between 1973 and 1991.[7] From 1995 to 1999, over 7,000 acres of Polk County farmland had been converted to nonfarm uses. Between 1980 and 1990, the rural farming population in Polk County declined by over 30 percent.[8] With plans to build a new four-lane bridge and four-lane highway over the St. Croix River, it is expected that these land conversion trends will intensify in the near future.

Proposed Land Sale Spurs Action

The growing impact of what has become known as sprawl was brought home to Polk County in 1994, when one of the largest parcels of undeveloped land along the river was put on the market for residential development (Figure 20.2). The 1,120-acre Englewood property runs for 2.3 miles along the river and includes blufflands, upland forests, wetlands, and grasslands. The relatively pristine nature of the site and its diversity make it an ark for endangered species.

The property had been on the market in the past, although the owner was unable to find buyers willing to invest in such a large parcel on the Wisconsin side of the river. This time, however, the agent for the real estate firm indicated that several buyers were preparing to make purchase offers. The most likely scenario for future use of the land was a golf course development of 150 to 200 new homes, each with a starting price of $250,000.

By chance, at the time the property came on the market, the Wisconsin Farmland Conservancy and Philadelphia Farm, a local community-supported agriculture (CSA) farm, had just initiated a survey of area landowners to learn more about their interests in land protection.[9] Due to the clear impact and urgency brought on by the proposed Englewood sale, efforts quickly shifted toward protecting this property as the first step in building community support for land protection.

Not surprisingly, the biggest obstacle was the price of the land. The owner was willing to reduce the asking price for a conservation sale, but the price tag was still set at $1.7 million. Another substantial obstacle was the time frame for completing the purchase. The owner was only willing to provide a one-year purchase option.

The first step in acquiring the property was for the conservancy and Philadelphia Farm to identify a committee that would take responsibility for organizing the project. This committee included a number of high-profile community members, in part because of the important role fund-raising would play if the project were to be a success. Several members had both grant-writing experience and connections to potential major donors. A few committee members were also recruited from homeowners on the Minnesota side of the river who were concerned about protecting the view from their property.

Early on, it was decided that due to the size of the project and the need for active local responsibility for ongoing management, the project should be established as new land trust, the Standing Cedars Community Land Conservancy.[10] The members of the organizing committee served as the initial board for the new land trust. The new board also framed a mission for the new land trust that encompassed more than just protecting the Englewood property. Standing Cedars committed itself to establishing a "farm and river greenway" that could demonstrate a model for "protecting and restoring field and forest, and supporting community life along the Lower St. Croix River."[11]

At about the same time as the Englewood purchase was initiated, the staff of the Philadelphia Farm CSA, Rick Hall and Verna Kragnes, who provided much of the initial support for the Standing Cedars, were also beginning their own fund-raising effort to acquire and protect 300 acres of bluffland their farm wanted to purchase, two miles north of the Englewood property.[12] The Philadelphia Farm also possessed important natural features, including the approach to a forty-foot waterfall that drops into the river. Together, these two parcels would protect almost 1,500 acres of land and would provide a south and north anchor for a potential greenway along five miles of the St. Croix river.[13]

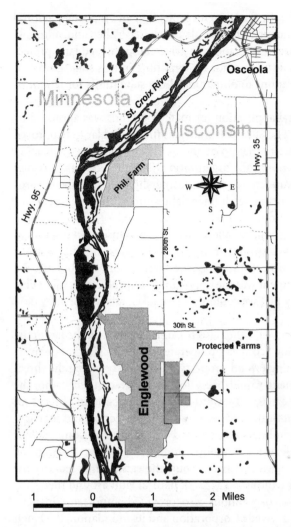

Figure 20.2. Map of farm and river greenway area.
Source: Tom Quinn, WFC

Raising Funds and Buying Land

As is typical of most large-scale projects, fund-raising was a collaborative effort. The diverse group of donors spanned the continuum from individuals to state government to private foundations and corporate organizations. The most essential partner was the Wisconsin Department of Natural Resources (DNR) Stewardship Fund, and one of the first steps taken was to ask for an informal assessment on whether the project fit their guidelines and priorities.

The stewardship fund was established by the state legislature in 1989 as way to provide funds for the permanent protection of important natural areas, either through easement or fee simple purchase.[14] The fund, administered through the DNR, was a milestone for privately sponsored land protection efforts in Wisconsin. It offered, for the first time in this state, a way for private nonprofit organizations to obtain matching state funds for land protection efforts.[15]

Standing Cedars' formal application for matching funds was approved by the DNR in August 1994. The $825,000 grant was the second largest approved by the stewardship fund up to that point and marked the largest partnership between the DNR and a nonprofit organization. The project was a banner model of the public–private conservation partnerships that are being promoted by the DNR as a way to stretch financial resources and to garner public support for land protection.

"It was an unusual situation," recalled Janet Beach Hanson, who serves as the nonprofit organization coordinator for the DNR. "Most small nonprofits don't come forward with projects this large. We went out on limb because the main thing for the Department was the opportunity to protect this incredible resource—an opportunity that we could not have taken advantage of by ourselves."[16]

The Beaver Valley Boy Scout Camp also became a partner in the land purchase. This small rustic Boy Scout camp operates on some 25 acres of riverfront surrounded by the Englewood property. Clearly recognizing the threat that residential development would bring to the future of their camp, the camp agreed to contribute $60,000 toward the land purchase. In observance of the camp's shared commitment to the long-term protection and management of the land, the Standing Cedars board included provisions in their bylaws that allowed the Beaver Valley Boy Scouts a permanent place on the board of directors of the new land trust. Thus, the camp gains security for their land and access to the thousand acres of natural land around them.

Local foundations and corporations also provided important financial support for the project. The Aveda Corporation and its foundation, the Hugh J. Andersen Foundation, and the McKnight Foundation were among the largest local contributors. National foundations such as Surdna, the National Fish and Wildlife Foundation, and Wildlife Forever also contributed funding support. Several of these foundations also made donations to protect the Philadelphia Farm.

Individual donors also played a major role. The Wisconsin side of the river had a fairly small potential donor base, but the area on the Minnesota side carried great promise. Much of the fund-raising efforts from individual donors focused on Minnesota homeowners whose viewshed would be destroyed by development across the river. In fact, one of these homeowners,

Bill Clapp, served as the initial board president and provided much of the leadership for identifying and approaching donors in the Minneapolis/St. Paul area. "I'm not much of a fundraiser," Clapp said, too modestly, "I just know a few friends who have money, and I ask them if they'll help."[17]

In the end, the help of individual donors proved crucial. With the purchase option deadline approaching and the land trust still short of its goal, the land trust board decided to ask the Conservation Fund for a bridge loan of $265,000 to allow the purchase to be completed.[18] The fund authorized the loan, but required financial guarantees to cover the loan amount. At that point, the land trust went back to the group of individual donors, who agreed to provide securities and cash for deposit in an escrow fund established at the River Bank in Osceola. With this support, the purchase of the land was completed in October 1996.

Ancillary fund-raising over the next year helped to pay off the loan from the Conservation Fund. In addition, in 1997, Philadelphia Farm completed purchase of their land north of the Englewood property, also with the help of a matching grant from the stewardship fund. Subsequent to acquisition of the property, the farm donated an easement on 331 acres to the land trust.[19] Once again, individual donors played a pivotal role in fund-raising, with members and supporters of the farm providing sizable contributions. The north and south anchors of a future greenway were now protected.

Developing a Management Plan: Community Involvement Holds the Key

One of the greatest challenges facing the new land trust was the need to manage the land that it now owned. Suddenly, this small land trust was responsible for managing a property larger than most of the state parks along the river. The terms of the DNR grant, as well as the land trust's own commitment to supporting the local community, required that the management plan provide for both considerable public access and the restoration of natural features and habitats.

The overall goal of the management plan was to protect and restore the natural features of the property, primarily oak savanna and native prairie. Public access would be allowed for activities such as hiking or cross-country skiing that did not negatively affect natural areas, but not allowed for activities such as mountain biking. The management plan would focus on providing the visitor with an opportunity to experience the area as it might have been in presettlement times. No new roads or motor vehicle access would be established to or through the area, and parking would be limited.

Responsibility for developing and implementing the land management plan for Standing Cedars has depended largely on the knowledge of Shawn Schottler, one of the trust's most committed supporters. Schottler is trained as an environmental chemist and works with the St. Croix Watershed Research Station, which is located directly across the river from Standing Cedars.[20] With Schottler's help, the trust has developed a plan that uses volunteers and interns to carry out most management activities.

The prairie restoration program is based on protecting local genotypes. All the prairie seeds are collected from native plants within thirty-five miles of the property. During the first year of restoration, 79 plant species were used, and during the second year, an additional 105 species were collected and reseeded. "The St. Croix valley is quickly losing its prairie remnants," Schottler pointed out, "and one of our goals is to provide a protected place where we can house the native plant genetics of our area."[21] He has continued to coordinate volunteers and interns for assistance with seed collection, brush cutting, controlled burns, fencing, and general maintenance of the property.

From the beginning, the trust's goal was to establish a management plan that encouraged local groups to take responsibility for monitoring the management practices that served their own goals and uses. For example, the cross-country ski club might take on ski trail maintenance or the local school could assist with the prairie restoration as part of an environmental curriculum.

One of the more interesting partnerships that have developed out of this voluntary management strategy involves access for public hunting. In Wisconsin, two recreational activities that dwarf all others in the level of interest in rural communities: following the fortunes of the Green Bay Packer football team and the annual ten-day deer hunting season.[22] Historically, farmers have allowed hunting on their land if requested, and informal understandings have developed between neighbors to allow hunting access on each other's land. There is also a general awareness among local landowners about the benefits that hunting provides in maintaining a balance in the deer population and avoiding deer damage to crops. In recent years, however, this cooperative system has suffered as urban buyers have begun purchasing large amounts of land for private hunting. In most cases, these landowners have denied or limited hunting access to neighbors.[23]

Over the years, the Englewood land had become a traditional hunting area for many members of the local community. When the Englewood property was put on the market, there was a general concern that access would be lost, particularly if it were developed as a golf course community. Even after the land was purchased by the land trust, there was a concern by local residents that the trust's emphasis on "environmental protection" could mean no hunting would be allowed.

The Standing Cedars board realized that hunting played an important management role and, more important, that hunting access had a meaningful purpose in connecting the property to the social and cultural life of the community. One of the first public meetings held by the trust was with the group of hunters who had been using the land for years. Instead of losing their access, the hunters were asked to take responsibility for managing access themselves through a system of permits so that those who had regularly hunted on the property retained first access. In exchange, hunters were asked to enforce the permit system and to keep records that would allow the game harvest and hunting pressure to be monitored. They were also asked to volunteer a certain number of hours each year to assist the land trust in carrying out various management projects, including habitat restoration. Over 130 hunters now participate in this program, and they provide over 80 percent of the volunteer hours for the management plan.

Farmland Protection in the Greenway

The second major aspect of Standing Cedars's mission, protecting farmland in the future greenway area, has also made some significant progress and has overcome some unanticipated obstacles. Paradoxically, one of the first obstacles was, in part, caused by the land trust's success in protecting so much land. In effect, by protecting the 1,300-acre Englewood property, the value of adjoining farms increased substantially. The expectations of farmers about the value of their land has been raised, and the choice between those who want to continue farming and those who seek the financial benefits a sale might bring has been sharpened.

One of the land trust's early goals was to demonstrate to farmers in the area that it was possible to protect farmland and, at the same time, protect the farmer's financial interests. Although the Wisconsin stewardship program provides matching funds to help purchase easements on natural areas, there is no state program to provide funding for permanently protecting or buying development rights on farmland. Instead, the land trust has begun to develop innovative options of its own. One of the most successful of these has involved a partnership between the proprietors of a small CSA farm in the greenway area, their urban customers, and the Wisconsin Farmland Conservancy.

Dan Guenther and Margaret Pennings have operated Common Harvest Farm since 1989, and it has become one of the Twin City area's most successful CSA farms. Each week during the growing season, they supply their 170 customer members with a steady supply of fresh vegetables and farm products. Every year, the farm allocates 10 percent of its production to low-income persons. This farming ideal, with its strong emphasis on a partnership between farmers and consumers to support food production, was compatible with Standing Cedars' emphasis on a partnership between community groups and the land trust to manage the natural area in the greenway.[24]

After renting land near the Twin Cities for seven years and being continually forced to move as development pressure increased, Common Harvest had come to settle on rented land near Osceola. Guenther and Pennings decided to stay in the area and looked at acquiring land for their operation for the first time. They faced the same problem encountered by many rural residents: Demand from an exurban population had pushed land prices beyond their reach. The solution was a creative partnership that allowed their customers to assist in purchasing and permanently protecting a new farm.

In the spring of 1997, they reached a purchase agreement with an older farmer to buy a small farm in the greenway area. The price, however, was much higher than its value as farmland. Together with the Wisconsin Farmland Conservancy, they developed a plan to ask the farm's customers to help make the purchase affordable.

"Most Americans don't own land," Pennings explained, "but all of us are intimately connected to the sun, the soil, and the plants that provide the food we eat. Why not ask the consumers of food to help share the costs of protecting the land on which their food is grown?"[25]

In June, CSA members received a letter from Guenther and Pennings and the Wisconsin Farmland Conservancy informing them about the opportunity for a farm purchase and inviting them to help. They were asked either to make contributions to the conservancy that could be used toward the purchase of a conservation easement on the farm or to provide a loan to Guenther and Pennings in the form of a prepaid annual share of food from the farm. This loan would be paid off over seven years.[26] The response was very positive. In only two months, CSA members had contributed over $40,000 toward the purchase of a conservation easement on the farm. Another $12,000 was provided in loans. The financing package for the farm purchase included a payment from the conservancy to obtain a conservation easement and the loan amount from the CSA members. The local bank agreed to allow the conservation easement to be placed in front of its mortgage, and the purchase was completed.[27]

The farm easement is held by the Wisconsin Farmland Conservancy. It protects the land from future development and establishes a "farmstead area" within which the CSA has the ability to operate farm-related enterprises and provide for seasonal housing of the student interns who are an integral part of the CSA apprenticeship model. The easement also provides a repurchase option for the conservancy in the event of a resale outside of the family. Since the farm purchase, the conservancy and Guenther and Pennings have developed a plan for implementing the repurchase agreement that will ensure that the farm remains affordable to a new CSA farmer in the future.[28]

At the farm's "christening" celebration, Guenther spoke about how the conservation easement was more than just a legal document. "Other than getting married and having children, this is the most important commitment we have ever made," he said. "We are wedding ourselves, on all sorts of levels—spiritual, emotional, social—to this place."[29]

Thoughts, Observations, and Actions Underway

The founders of Standing Cedars began by wanting to generate a community discussion about land protection and the economic and social value of maintaining rural character. As is often the case, this discussion was set aside in favor of a knuckle-biting effort to raise money, beat a deadline, and protect a very important property. The success of that effort, and the land trust's work to engage various community organizations in management activities, provides a model for how land protection can serve diverse community needs. Standing Cedars also affords an excellent model for the DNR's decision to allow nonprofit organizations to serve as partners in the stewardship fund.

Standing Cedars will undoubtedly face challenges in the future. Managing this very large natural area and providing public access will be a taxing responsibility, both financially and in terms of human resources. The present strategy of voluntary management and low-impact public access, in partnership with supportive organizations, seems to be working. Efforts to extend this strategy of voluntary management continue. In the summer of 1998, Standing Cedars and the Philadelphia Farm started a Youth Stewards program. The program offers training to teachers who want to integrate hands-on practice with classroom discussions in their environmental curriculum. The hope is that such a program can build enduring partnerships with local schools, a partnership that can provide both long-term stability and ongoing public outreach to the community. In its first year, this program included participation from eight school districts.[30]

The DNR also continues to provide valuable assistance to the land trust. The stewardship fund has provided an additional grant for habitat and natural area restoration projects. Portions of the Englewood site have now been designated by the DNR as a State Natural and Scientific Area. Such designation will provide an opportunity for special management assistance funds from the DNR, allow the trust to formally set aside the most fragile habitat areas for scientific study, and limit public access to them.[31] Another important effort includes some of the major donors. Several new donors are providing a dollar-for-dollar match to the trust for the purpose of establishing a permanent endowment fund that can support land management activities.

The other major challenge faced by the land trust comes from continued development pressure in the area. The Standing Cedars board recognizes that future protection efforts will need to involve assistance to landowners in developing protection plans that meet both their personal values and economic needs. The trust is exploring options for using a network of conservation buyers: individuals who are willing and able to purchase land that comes on the market and then provide permanent protection. One farm in the area has already been purchased in this manner. Strategies for assisting farmers and other landowners with development and implementation of conservation development plans are also being considered.[32]

Land use issues are becoming the focus of very heated discussions in rural Wisconsin towns and counties. The Standing Cedars board has recognized that the decisions that evolve out of such discussions will affect their mission and future strategies. Although the land trust itself has not played a direct role in local land use planning discussions, two members of the land trust board have served on the town planning committee. The trust, with the Wisconsin Farmland Conservancy as a partner, sees its role as one of providing local government with information on land protection options and programs that could be included in land use and zoning plans.

Standing Cedars has also continued to expand its direct land protection efforts. In 1998, the trust negotiated a purchase option on a 97-acre river bluff property adjacent to the north boundary of the Philadelphia Farm. This land will extend the trust's greenway protection area to the border of the village of Osceola. Fund-raising for this purchase will again include a mix of partners. The stewardship fund will provide matching funds to protect the most fragile habitat areas along the bluff ridge. The Fish and Wildlife Foundation has committed funding, and other foundations and individuals are expected to provide support. About half of this property is in agricultural use, and this portion will be sold to a local farm, at agricultural value, after an easement restricting development is in place.

The trust is also working with the Main Street Committee of Osceola to help facilitate the purchase of a prominent river bluff that is next to the village business district. The village has obtained a U.S. Department of Transportation grant to purchase the land and has asked the trust to assist in negotiating the purchase.[33] This purchase will provide the village with access to the area's most prominent view of the St. Croix river valley and provide significant benefits to the growing number of tourist-related businesses in the community. As awareness of the land trust spreads in the community, individual landowners are also beginning to explore donation of easements on their property, and, in 1998, the Wisconsin Farmland Conservancy protected another 157-acre farm in the area and Standing Cedars protected a 120-acre natural area, both with donated easements.

Dan McGuiness, president of Standing Cedars and former director of the Minnesota-Wisconsin Boundary Commission, views the growth of Standing Cedars in terms of both the amount of land protected and the mission of the trust. "Like most land trusts, we started out as a group of people who wanted to protect a special place that was being threatened," he observed. "Now we face both the challenge and opportunity of serving as a resource in the community's larger effort to protect its rural and small town character."[34]

Conclusion

The experience of Standing Cedars demonstrates some of the hidden benefits that land trusts can bring to a community. The process of building an organization, training board members in the nuts-and-bolts process of land protection, and exploring how the land protection tools available to land trusts provide a balance between public and private needs can all help build a base of citizens who have had firsthand experience at finding common ground on difficult issues. These citizens can bring a valuable resource to a community: the experience of working together to craft creative solutions to difficult problems. Land trusts can provide citizens and communities with the "space" to experiment with new ways of connecting their sense of community with their sense of place: ways of adding a spirit of democracy to the rights of private land ownership. It is their unique role in providing this special brand of community leadership, as much as the application of practical land protection tools and projects, that will define the success of land trusts as enduring community institutions in the future.

Notes

1. Key to the collaborative effect was the Wisconsin Farmland Conservancy, a nonprofit 501(c)(3) conservation organization. Its mission is to protect the character of the rural countryside, that mix of diversified farms, natural areas and forests, and small towns that makes rural Wisconsin a special place. The conservancy's program has three areas of focus: assisting landowners in private land protection efforts, working with local governments to establish land protection policies and programs, and helping farmers and rural communities to initiate environmentally sustainable economic development projects.

2. The Lower St. Croix River was designated as a wild and scenic river in 1972 (P.L. 92-560), under the authority of the National Wild and Scenic River Act (P.L. 92-542). State designation followed with the Wisconsin Lower St. Croix River Act (Chapter 197, Laws of Wisconsin, 1973).

3. William Saupe and Jennifer Eisenhauer, "The Wisconsin Family Farm Survey," in

Frederick Buttel, ed., *Status of Wisconsin Farming* (Madison: College of Agriculture and Life Sciences, University of Wisconsin–Madison, August 1994), pp. 30–43.

4. U.S. Census, 1990.

5. U.S. Census Bureau, OMB Bulletin 98-06, identified areas inclusive in the "Twin Cities Metro Region": Minneapolis–St. Paul MSA (MN–WI) as (1) Anoka County, Minn.; (2) Carver County; (3) Chisago County, Minn.; (4) Dakota County, Minn.; (5) Hennepin County, Minn.; (6) Isanti County, Minn.; (7) Ramsey County, Minn.; (8) Scott County, Minn.; (9) Sherburne County, Minn.; (10) Washington County, Minn.; (11) Wright County, Minn.; (12) Pierce County, Wisc.; (13) St. Croix County, Wisc.

6. American Farmland Trust, *Farming on the Edge*, (Dekalb: Center for Agriculture in the Environment, Northern Illinois University, March 1997). "Development" was defined as "the change in urban built-up land occurring within each of the 33,000 mapping units between 1982 and 1992."

7. Minnesota–Wisconsin Boundary Commission, Lower St. Croix River Stewardship Study, 1994. Analysis of land use based on aerial photographs from 1971 and 1974.

8. Between 1980 and 1990, Polk County's population grew by 7.5 percent. Since 1990, population has increased by another 11.7 percent. Land use and population projections are provided by the West Central Wisconsin Regional Planning Commission and Polk County Planning Office.

9. Community-supported agriculture farming is a term used to describe farms that develop a membership base of consumers who purchase an annual "share" in the production of the farm. CSA members typically make an annual payment prior to the start of the growing season and then receive a weekly delivery of farm products, depending on the season and the level of production. CSA farms generally engage their members in a variety of volunteer and educational activities. CSA farmers often describe their model as the fastest-growing segment of U.S. agriculture.

10. The phrase "Standing Cedars" was derived from the name used by native peoples and early settlers to identify the location of landmark cedar trees on a bend in the river.

11. Standing Cedars mission statement.

12. Philadelphia Farm is a CSA farm that also has a strong human services and community education commitment. The farm is incorporated as a 501(c)(3) nonprofit corporation.

13. The trust uses the term *farm and river greenway* to describe a model for land protection in the area of East Farmington Township, south of the village of Osceola, bordered by the St. Croix River (Standing Cedars map).

14. Warren Knowles–Gaylord Nelson Stewardship Fund, Wisconsin Statutes 23.0915.

15. The fund allocates dollars within several categories that include natural areas, habitat, lakeshore, and urban rivers. In most cases, the fund provides a 50 percent match of the appraised value of either the easement or the purchase value. The

nonprofit organization is required to provide a match, either in the form of cash or a donation by the landowner.

16. Personal comment, Janet Beach Hanson, September 1996.

17. Personal comment, Bill Clapp, October 1996.

18. The Conservation Fund is a national nonprofit organization that works with local governments and other nonprofit organizations to ensure long-term land protection. It has assisted in protecting 1.4 million acres in the United States. The fund also operates a loan fund that provides bridge financing for land and easement acquisition projects. The loan to Standing Cedars was a component of a program funded by the McKnight Foundation to support loans for projects in the Mississippi River basin.

19. The easement is held by Standing Cedars. Three separate areas of protection are identified: an agricultural area within which the right to farm is protected, a farmstead area within which farm or education-related buildings and residences may be constructed, and a natural area within which a management plan similar to the plan adopted for the Englewood property must be observed. The easement provides for shared management of the natural area with Standing Cedars.

20. The St. Croix Watershed Research Station is a project sponsored by the Science Museum of Minnesota to provide monitoring and research on environmental issues that affect the watershed of the St. Croix River.

21. Personal comment, Shawn Schottler, November 1998.

22. "I doubt there is any place that deer hunting involves as much ritual as it does in this state. One of every three Wisconsin males over the age of 12 hunts deer, and 46 percent of the state's households have at least one hunter in residence," said anthropologist Richard Nelson, quoted in "Deer to Our Culture," *Wisconsin Natural Resources*, 22, 2 (December 1998): 22.

23. "Deer to our Culture," *Wisconsin Natural Resources*.

24. Wisconsin Farmland Conservancy *Common Ground* III, no. 2 (fall 1997).

25. Wisconsin Farmland Conservancy, *Common Ground*.

26. The annual share cost for CSA members is $350. Members were asked to prepay their shares for up to seven years. Such prepayments allowed Guenther and Pennings to apply these funds toward their down payment and to pay these funds back using produce from the farm.

27. Guenther and Pennings obtained a bank mortgage to purchase the farm. Funds from the conservancy were used in the purchase to cover the difference between the market value of the property and the agricultural value after the easement was in place. The funds were provided at the real estate closing, and the easement was executed ahead of the mortgage.

28. The easement is held by the conservancy. It establishes a farmstead area within which the owners have the right to construct buildings that are related to the operation of the farm, and a farming area within which there can be no development and where strong protections are provided for natural areas and sustainable agricultural use. The easement has provisions that allow the conservancy to exercise a repurchase right in the event that the farm is sold outside of the immediate

family. Since the initial purchase, the parties have negotiated an additional agreement that is providing CSA members with an opportunity to make further contributions to be applied toward the conservancy's purchase of a substantial equity share in the farm from the owners. The goal is to allow the conservancy to repurchase the farm at its agricultural value and thus keep it affordable to a new CSA farmer.

29. Wisconsin Farmland Conservancy, *Common Ground.*
30. The Youth Stewards program is funded with a grant from the Wisconsin Community Service Board, which provides funding for programs that offer community service learning opportunities for young people.
31. The State Natural Area designation allows the state to provide special protection to lands that hold examples of native plant and animal life. These places protect hundreds of rare, endangered, and threatened species and allow for the opportunity to restrict public access and encourage scientific study.
32. The trust is discussing the potential for working with landowners who wish to protect their land, but who need to have some level of financial return. The trust recognizes that it will have limited financial resources to purchase easements, development rights, or fee simple ownership of land in the future. One solution is to work more proactively with landowners to design limited development options that provide for some development on a property, but also provide for a plan to protect the important natural or agricultural values permanently.
33. The village grant is through the Intermodal Surface Transportation Efficiency Act of 1991. This act broadened the Department of Transportation's focus to include transportation enhancement activities, including providing grants to local governments for the acquisition of scenic or historical sites. This funding will be continued under the Transportation Equity Act for the 21st Century of 1998 (TEA-21).
34. Personal comments, Dan McGuiness, November 1998.

Chapter 21

❦ ❦

Easements and Public Access on the Ice Age National Scenic Trail

Christine Thisted

The Ice Age National Scenic Trail is one of seven national scenic trails located throughout the United States.[1] Meandering through thirty-one Wisconsin counties along a terminal moraine left by the glacier nearly 10,000 years ago, it affords excellent views of Wisconsin's spectacular glacial landscape (Photograph 21.1).

Management of the Ice Age Trail is by a cooperative alliance between the National Park Service, the Wisconsin Department of Natural Resources, and the private nonprofit Ice Age Park and Trail Foundation.[2] Each partner to the agreement has a specific set of responsibilities with respect to the trail, including corridor planning, protection of private lands, and construction and maintenance, as well as promotion and overall administration.

When completed, the trail will wind for over 1,000 miles across Wisconsin (Figure 21.1).[3] Approximately 700 miles will traverse private lands, and the remainder will cross public lands. Acquiring the rights necessary to intersect these private lands, among some of Wisconsin's most desirable lands for residential development, will be complicated. Over 25 percent of the state's population lives within ten miles of the Ice Age Trail, creating intense competition for land and forcing real estate prices through the sky. Paradoxically, the forces that create demand for residential properties and inflate the price of land give birth to an increased demand for outdoor recreation opportunities such as the Ice Age Trail. At the same time, these forces erect economic barriers to land being set aside for such uses, making a literal catch-22.

Imagine if the Department of Transportation attempted to build a highway from New York City to Jacksonville, Florida, without powers of eminent domain. Because of their limited budget, it must accomplish the job with a staff of seven and a half million dollars a year in matching funds for land pur-

Photograph 21.1. Wisconsin's spectacular glacial landscape: Farm with eskers formed from glacial deposits.
File photo: IAPTF

chases from the government (where the match is to be raised by the local "Friends of the DOT"). Interestingly, this is not unlike the situation on the Ice Age Trail, where much of the responsibility for acquiring private land interests for the trail has fallen on the nonprofit partner.

Unfortunately, the National Park Service does not have the authority to purchase lands for the trail.[4] Legislative authority has been granted to the Wisconsin Department of Natural Resources for land acquisitions on the trail, but appropriations for any large-scale purchases have yet to be made.[5] A few local units of governments have helped, yet the range of acquisition responsibilities along the trail remains largely that of the foundation.[6]

From 1958 to 1998, the Ice Age Trail principally traversed public lands. On occasion, a handshake agreement with individual landowners allowed a few miles of the trail to cross private lands, but these agreements could be revoked at any time.[7] Recognizing the assailable nature of this method, the Ice Age Park and Trail Foundation embarked upon a long-term protection strategy to acquire easements and fee title interests on private land over which the trail could be built.

By 1999, the foundation had raised over $2 million from private and municipal sources, a total matched by $1.7 million from the Knowles-Nelson Stewardship Program.[8] These funds have helped the foundation to purchase fee title to fifteen parcels and access easements on five parcels. In addition, the

Figure 21.1. Ice Age National and State Scenic Trail.
Source: Christine Thisted, IAPTF

Foundation has acquired title to fourteen parcels and twenty-six easements without the use of stewardship funds.[9] The result is the permanent protection and creation of nearly twenty miles of trail.[10]

It is unlikely that the foundation will ever have enough money to acquire private land along the entire length of the proposed trail. Therefore, until the

Photograph 21.2. Devil's Lake. Perhaps Wisconsin's most famous and beloved
lake, formed when glacial deposits plugged up a meltwater channel on both the
north and south sides of the lake. The Ice Age Trail passes through Devil's Lake
State Park.
Source: IAPTF

government partners in the Ice Age Trail venture are able to participate more
fully in acquiring land for the trail, the foundation will need to use its limited
financial resources as shrewdly as possible. For now, that means concentrating on acquiring larger interests in those parcels of land that best illustrate the
state's glacial history, while protecting the remaining areas in a minimal fashion with 200-foot-wide corridor (Photograph 21.2).[11]

Some may say that without larger involvement in acquisition by the government the trail will never be completed. To others, the challenge makes
it even more interesting. Regardless of how one views it, for the Ice Age
Park and Trail Foundation to succeed in permanent trail development on
private lands, a positive attitude coupled with the ability to establish a creative, landowner-oriented approach to acquisition are needed. Many times,
acquiring the right-of-way across private land through an access easement
is the best way to satisfy the requirements of the trail, the landowner, and
the law.

Easements, however, are not always the first choice method for protecting
the land. Along with the benefits are liabilities. Such easements are expensive;
often their appraised values are nearly equal to that of the fee. In addition,

monitoring becomes more than an annual obligation, which in turn drives up management costs and the need for adequate defense funds.[12] Finally, there is always the possibility that successive landowners may not be interested in a public right-of-way across their land, and real estate agents who do not understand an easement of this type may choose to simply ignore it.[13]

Easement Benefits

Flexibility

The greatest benefit of using an easement as a method of creating a corridor is the flexibility it affords both landowners and the foundation. For a number of reasons, landowners are not always interested in selling fee title to their land. The land may have been in their family for years and they may wish to pass it on to their heirs, for example. They may also wish to continue living on the property, or they may be holding it as an investment. Easements provide a mechanism for landowners to continue to own their land while accommodating the needs of the Ice Age Trail. In some instances, landowners may only be willing to sell or donate a 50- to 250-foot strip for the actual public use corridor. In other instances, landowners are interested in protecting an area larger than that needed for the trail corridor.

When a landowner wishes to protect an entire parcel, the foundation may acquire an easement protecting the entire tract with defined areas of public access. In such cases, however, the foundation must be cautious because its mission first and foremost is to secure public access. Although habitat protection and farmland protection are worthy goals, they are not central to the foundation's mission and cannot be allowed to drain limited financial and staff resources. It is possible to address multiple goals at the same time with one easement, but the more comprehensive the protection, the more cumbersome the monitoring. Until quite recently, actively attempting to accomplish multiple conservation goals with an easement has not been considered.[14] It is possible, however, that such multiple-purpose easements will become part of a necessary strategy for land protection. Many landowners, even those who are conservation-minded, perceive public access as a liability, not an asset, giving them little reason to participate in the Ice Age Trail project. The foundation can provide an incentive to reluctant landowners if it can address the landowner's protection goals at the same time it can meet the needs for public access. From the foundation's standpoint, by acquiring development rights to a large area in unison with some form of public access to provide a corridor for the trail, the foundation will be able to provide a trail with the highest scenic amenity possible.

Recycling Limited Funds

Easements have been created for the Ice Age Trail in a buy, protect, and resell program. Through this program, the foundation purchases a larger tract, places easements for the trail corridor on part of it, sets aside a building lot or two, and then returns the property to the market. This strategy has been very successful for the foundation,[15] and the benefits are many. At a minimum, the program allows the foundation to recover money put into the purchase. On occasion, such transactions even make a profit if land values are increasing rapidly enough. In addition, it has proven easier to sell a property encumbered with an easement on 75 out of 80 acres, for example, than to convince an existing landowner to place an access easement over a property. This method of protection, which some trail partners are concerned will facilitate fragmentation of the landscape, should be used with sensitivity. At this time, however, it remains one of the best methods of protection in that it allows the foundation to recycle limited funds.

Local Zoning and Subdivision Regulations

Another major advantage to using easements is that they allow the foundation and the landowner to protect a small corridor of land without having to go through the process of land subdivision and the attendant legalities. In many jurisdictions along the trail, landowners wanting to convey fee title to a 200-foot strip to the foundation, even along the boundary of an existing parcel, must proceed as if they are subdividing the land. The nuisance and expense of seeking approvals for platting and rezoning involve considerable expenditures of time and money and would be a sizable request to make of a landowner donating or selling land for the trail. Yet, in protecting the same corridor with an easement, the fee ownership does not change, so the legalities involved in the process of subdivision do not apply.

Easement Disadvantages

Monitoring Demands

Without a doubt, the biggest drawback in using easements to secure access for the Ice Age Trail corridor is the need for persistent monitoring. All lands protected by easement present a massive responsibility to grantee organizations. Stretch this requirement over 1,000 miles and the task becomes nearly overwhelming. The number of private landowners involved, coupled with an extremely active land market involving numerous real estate transactions that are precursors to a changing landscape, place an enormous burden on the foundation's two-person field staff.

Building the Ice Age Trail is very much like assembling a 5,000-piece puzzle. The easiest approach is to assemble little sections of the puzzle here and there rather than spending hours searching for one missing piece in a particular section. Confident the missing piece or pieces will turn up eventually, one section may be left incomplete to begin assembling another. Similarly, rather than starting at one end of the trail and protecting contiguous parcels along the corridor's length, the foundation tends to acquire title and easements to a few parcels in one county and a few in another according to protection priorities set by the partnership. An opportunistic approach has largely driven the foundation in assembling the trail. Acquiring interests in parcels as they become available may require the foundation to purchase an easement on property that may not be used for the trail for years, knowing that the pieces around it will fall into place eventually.

On occasion, this process has caused considerable problems for several reasons. Essentially, these lands may go largely unmonitored as local volunteers focus efforts on sections of the trail that are developed rather than on easement lands that are set aside for future trail. In addition, when the trail can actually be opened on a property, there is an element of interest generated by the user in caring for the trail. Finally, foundation staff may live 300 miles from a particular easement property; consequently, these future trail lands may only be inspected once a year, if at all. Almost as important is that no one is monitoring what is happening to properties adjacent to the easement lands on which the utility and integrity of an easement might depend. As new residential and commercial subdivisions spring from nowhere seemingly overnight, there is constant fear that the effectiveness of easement-protected lands could be lost because an adjacent landowner may not be cognizant of its existence and debilitating encroachments may occur.

Unfortunately, paying attention to what current landowners, adjacent or principal, may decide to do with their land is only part of the job. Yet another issue is keeping track of the whereabouts of those who own the land the easement crosses. Prized for its bountiful hunting and fishing, land in northern Wisconsin is owned by many absentee landowners. Each day, land across the region changes hands, particularly when property values are on the rise and there is money to be made.

The easement will always contain language providing that all parties are given proper notice when changes in ownership occur. Yet having developed little or no personal relationship with the landowner due to staff constraints renders this provision largely ineffectual. Under this scenario of absentee landowners, limited staff, and attention to monitoring, chances are good that the land will change hands and notice will never be given. At this point, the only approach the foundation can take is to hope that the new landowners are aware of the easement, have a copy and understand it, were not lead to believe that living with the easement is optional, and think public hiking trails are a pretty good idea. Obviously, this method is not the best way to handle public access or land protection.

Management and Defense Funds

For most landowners, donating a conservation easement that protects the land surface is far different from donating an easement that allows public access as part of a hiking trail. In fact, it is often very difficult to convince a landowner to sell an easement for public access, let alone donate one. Almost instantly, questions about landowner liability for trail users and the effect of public access on a landowner's ability to sell the land are raised. Consequently, most trail easements acquired by the foundation have been purchased.

It has largely become common practice for land trusts to request a cash contribution from landowners to ensure that lands subject to an easement will be managed, monitored, and defended in court if necessary. In some cases, this donation is in addition to the donation of the easement itself. If the foundation acquires an easement as a donation from a landowner, that is normally the limit of a landowner's contribution. In general, asking for an additional cash donation for management and defense is simply not an option. This area must be tread softly; the last thing the foundation, or any land trust for that matter, wants is to get laughed away from the kitchen table and asked not to come back. This precarious set of conditions firmly places the responsibility of raising funds for management and defense of the easement with the holder. The ultimate result is a substantial increase in funding required to make the acquisition.

Conclusion

Easements are a valuable tool for protecting a corridor for the Ice Age Trail. They have been used and must continue to be used creatively yet wisely. They are most effective in two situations. In cases where the cumbersome and expensive process of platting would prohibit acquiring the fee title to a key parcel, easements may be the only way to gain necessary rights to land. In other cases, where large parcels are available, easements can be created in a buy-protect-resell process. In the latter instance, recovered funds may be recycled for further protection of the trail.

A principal difficulty with any easement lies in an organization's ability to provide adequate long-term care and monitoring. Organizations that hold easements must be prepared to deal with violations.[16] Without regular monitoring, the easement may not survive to see a single hiker.

If the restrictions necessitating an easement are absent and the capacity to manage and monitor is minimal, it may be more desirable to acquire fee simple interests rather than easements. To be certain, real property interests, whether in the form of an easement or fee ownership, should ideally be acquired when an organization has the capacity to manage those interests. If given a choice, however, it is much less risky to shirk management responsibilities as a landowner than it is to walk away from easement monitoring. After all, the result of an organization not restoring a prairie on the land it owns is not as problematic as the result of an organization failing to stop the construction of a garage in a fifty-foot trail corridor, nor as irreversible.

Perhaps such failings do not concern easements themselves but rather the overall assignment of roles within the partnership between the National Park Service, the Wisconsin Department of Natural Resources, and the foundation.[17] The Ice Age Park and Trail Foundation is currently responsible for acquiring easements on private lands, for constructing and maintaining the trail, and for the majority of its promotion. If the partnership roles remain unchanged and the foundation continues to shoulder trail protection, choices will have to be made. Either the foundation must change its nature and become more like a traditional land trust or it must focus on acquiring fee title to parcels. To do otherwise would be an irresponsible use of limited funds.

Notes

1. In 1968, Congress enacted the National Trails System Act (16 U.S.C. 1241 et seq.). The act immediately established the Appalachian National Scenic Trail (NST) and the Pacific Crest NST. In 1978, the Continental Divide NST was authorized, followed by the North Country NST and Ice Age NST in 1980, and the Potomac Heritage and Florida NST in 1983.

2. The Ice Age Park and Trail Foundation was established in 1958. Although the foundation's main mission is to support the work of over 2,100 volunteers who give more than 50,000 hours a year to the development and maintenance of the Ice Age Trail, the foundation also acts as the trail's land trust. Currently, over 4,000 people from thirty-eight states are members of the foundation.

3. The trail very generally follows the natural features that mark the furthest advance of the last continental glaciation, such as the terminal and interlobate moraines. The trail passes through thirty-one Wisconsin counties and numerous small villages and cities. At present, approximately 510 miles are open for public use.

4. The statutory language prohibiting the federal government from spending funds to acquire lands for the Ice Age Trail outside federal areas can be found in the Ice Age NST authorization itself (16 U.S.C.1241 et seq.).

5. In 1987, Wisconsin State Statutes, Chapter 23.17, designated the Ice Age Trail, as

provided for in 16 U.S.C. 1244(a)(10), plus land adjacent to each side of that trail designated by the Wisconsin DNR, as a State Scenic Trail to be known as the Ice Age Trail. Wisconsin State Statutes, Chapter 23.09(2)(d), gives the DNR approval to acquire lands for the Ice Age Trail.

6. The cities of Janesville and West Bend and counties of Waukesha and Dane have all purchased lands specifically for the Ice Age Trail.

7. These handshake agreements are essentially revocable licenses. Although money has never been exchanged, in a few cases labor by local volunteers was traded for the right to build the trail.

8. The Knowles-Nelson Stewardship Program is a ten-year program, created by the Wisconsin legislature, which ends on June 30, 2000. The program consists of twelve components that span a variety of conservation goals, including a component that grants funds to the Ice Age Park and Trail Foundation for the acquisition of a corridor for the Ice Age Trail (Wisconsin State Statutes, Chapter 23.09(2)(d)). The Wisconsin Department of Natural Resources administers the program. $500,000 is available as 50 percent grants to the foundation, which are matched with funds given by corporations, foundations, and individuals. To date, two municipalities—Dane County and the city of West Bend—have provided funds for part of the match. In these cases, after the foundation acquires the land, title is given to the municipality.

9. In some cases, parcels were acquired before funds for stewardship were available. In other cases, stewardship funds could not be used on some parcels because the interpretation of the rules did not allow grants to be given for parcels in counties without approved corridor plans. This interpretation recently changed.

10. The foundation owns property in ten Wisconsin counties: Chippewa, Columbia, Dane, Manitowoc, Marathon, Polk, Sauk, Taylor, Washington, and Waukesha. In total, approximately 1,450 acres have been protected, with 392 acres in easement and 1,059 acres owned in fee.

11. The National Park Service, Wisconsin Department of Natural Resources, and Ice Age Park and Trail Foundation make collective decisions on acquisition priorities.

12. Defense funds are set aside to cover costs of defending an easement if encroachments or other violations occur.

13. Obviously, because acquisition for the trail occurs only on a willing seller basis, the landowners who place easements on their property are comfortable with public access to their land. The problem is with successor landowners.

14. As the focus has historically been to protect a corridor only for the purposes of the Ice Age Trail, multiple-purpose easements have not generally been considered.

15. The foundation uses this strategy when it has enough money to make the initial purchase (stewardship money cannot be used in the case where the foundation will be reselling the property) and where the likelihood is high that a buyer who is willing to accept the easement will be found.

16. Alternatively, if defense funds are not established, lose the easement or accept the violation.
17. The partnership has recently started to look at other options for land protection, such as pursuing willing-seller acquisition authority for the National Park Service.

Chapter 22

☙ ❧

Conservation Easements in
the Ninth Federal Circuit

William T. Hutton, supervising author

*David Brown, Josh Butler, Timothy Chambers,
Michael Eden, Amy Humphreys-Chandler, David Levi,
Michael Malugani, Osha Meserve, David Shapiro,
and John Slaymaker*

Nine states, the seven westernmost in the coterminous United States along with the states of Alaska and Hawaii, comprise the Ninth Federal Circuit (Figure 22.1). Ecologically speaking, a more diverse group of states could not exist. Conditions in the states range from tropical rainforest to deserts, from seashore to mountain, from the equator to the pole. They do share some characteristics, however. Most have extensive areas where the population densities are extremely low. With the exception of Hawaii, they all possess large acreages of public lands within their boundaries, a fact that has fostered both a hostility toward the federal government and a misperception that there already exists a large protected estate. In several of the states, this misperception has fostered an attitude of indifference by landowners toward federal statutes aimed at encouraging private land protection. Yet, the states of California, Montana, Washington, and Oregon, for example, have long been involved in promoting protection efforts of private landowners, and several more have long histories in actively exercising their regulatory powers to protect land. The diversity of terminology used across the circuit in reference to land resources given protection is reflected in Table 22.1.

Alaska

Alaska's conservation easement enabling act, the Alaska Uniform Conservation Easement Act (AUCEA) enacted in 1989, is virtually identical to the Uniform Conservation Easement Act (UCEA). There are three differences between the AUCEA and the UCEA, but these differences add little in the way of substance to the UCEA and have not proven to be significant to creating conservation easements in Alaska. First, the AUCEA does not allow the state to create conservation easements by eminent domain.[1] Second, the AUCEA

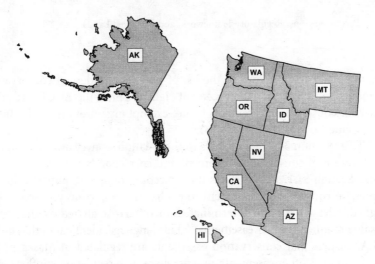

Figure 22.1. States comprising the Ninth Federal Circuit.
Credit: J. A. Gustanski

Table 22.1. What Conservation Easements Protect in the Ninth Federal Circuit

STATE	UCEA	HOLDER'S PURPOSES INCLUDE	HOLDER'S PURPOSES ARE:	NATURAL	SCENIC	OPEN SPACE	AGRICULTURAL	SILVICULTURAL	FOREST	RECREATIONAL	AIR QUALITY	WATER QUALITY/WATER AREA	HISTORICAL	ARCHITECTURAL	ARCHEOLOGICAL	PALEONTOLOGICAL	CULTURAL	CONSERVATION OF LAND	PROTECTING NATURAL RESOURCES	SPECIAL NOTES
Alaska	U	X[a]		X	X	X	X		X	X	X	X	X	X	X		X		X	[a] "empowered to"
Arizona	U	X		X	X	X	X		X	X	X	X	X	X	X		X		X	
California	N	[b]	X	X	X	X	X	X		X				X						[b] "primary purpose"
Hawaii	N	[c]																		[c] "whose original purpose is designed to facilitate the purpose of this chapter"
Idaho	U	X		X	X	X	X		X	X	X	X	X	X	X				X	
Montana	N	[d]																		[d] "original purpose designate to further purpose of this" wildlife habitat
Nevada	U	X		X	X	X	X		X	X	X	X	X	X	X		X		X	
Oregon	U	X		X	X	X	X		X	X	X	X	X	X	X		X		X	
Washington	N	X[e]		X									X						X	[e] "One of the holder's principal purpose; also scientific research"

U = Conservation easement legislation directly influenced by UCEA.

N = Conservation easement legislation absent or not directly influenced by UCEA.

adds nonprofit corporations to the list of potential holders of conservation easements and third-party enforcement rights.[2] Third, the AUCEA requires holders of conservation easements be tax-exempt organizations under Internal Revenue Code Section 501(c)(3).[3]

AUCEA Section 34.17.010 relates to the creation, conveyance, acceptance, and duration of conservation easement and corresponds to section 2 of the UCEA. Section 34.17.010(a) states that "except as otherwise provided in this chapter, a conservation easement may be created, conveyed, recorded, assigned, released, modified, terminated, or otherwise altered or affected in the same manner as other easements."[4] This language, identical to that of the UCEA, ensures that conservation easements are regulated in Alaska in the same manner as other easements, except where such regulation conflicts with the AUCEA.[5] Table 22.2 details how states across the Ninth Federal Circuit have addressed issues of assignability, conveyance, modification, and termination.

Section 34.17.010(b) states that "a right or duty in favor of or against a holder and a right in favor of a person having a third-party right of enforce-

Table 22.2. Permissible Terminations, Modifications, and Assignment of Conservation Easements in the Ninth Federal Circuit

State	UCEA	Released	Terminated	Termination by Court (Under the Principles of Law and Equity)	Termination by Taking	Abandoned	Termination by Merger	Modified	Modified by Court	Assignable	Special Notes
Alaska	U	X	X	X				X	X	X	
Arizona	U	X	X	X[a]				X	X[a]	X	[a] Requires consideration of public interest
California	N									X	
Hawaii	N										
Idaho	U	X	X	X				X	X	X	
Montana	N										
Nevada	U	X	X	X				X	X	X	
Oregon	U	X	X	X				X	X	X	
Washington	N										

U = Conservation easement legislation directly influenced by UCEA.
N = Conservation easement legislation absent or not directly influenced by UCEA.

ment may not arise under a conservation easement before the conservation easement is accepted by the holder and the acceptance is recorded."[6] This language differs slightly from the UCEA, although not significantly, and has the same effect, making clear that neither the holder of a conservation easement nor the holder of a third-party enforcement right has any rights prior to the recordation of their acceptance.[7]

Section 34.17.010(c) states that "except as provided in AS 34.17.020(b), a conservation easement is unlimited in duration unless the instrument creating the conservation easement provides a limitation on duration."[8] This section is slightly different from the UCEA, which states only that "a conservation easement is unlimited in duration unless the instrument creating it otherwise provides is not significant because both acts allow the creation of conservation easements that exist in perpetuity."[9] Table 22.3 reflects the disparities across the Ninth Federal Circuit on the issue of easement duration. In Alaska, the duration of the conservation easement is subject to the qualification of section 24.17.020(b), which duplicates the language of UCEA section 3(b), stating that the act "does not affect the power of a court to modify or terminate a conservation easement in accordance with the principles of law and equity."[10] Therefore, in Alaska, the duration of conservation easements is subject to the authority of the state courts.[11]

Section 34.17.010(d) states that "an interest in real property in existence at the time a conservation easement is created is not impaired by the conserva-

Table 22.3. Duration of Conservation Easements in the Ninth Federal Circuit

STATE	PERPETUAL MANDATORY	PERPETUAL BY DEFAULT	TERM BY DEFAULT
Alaska		X	
Arizona		X	
California	X		
Hawaii	X		
Idaho		X	
Montana		N/A	N/A
Nevada		X	
Oregon		X	
Washington			X

Note: Montana's act precedes the UCEA by six years and departs in some key areas, particularly when describing what purpose conservation easements may serve and who may hold a conservation easement. See the section on Montana in this chapter.

tion easement unless the owner of the interest is a party to or consents to the conservation easement."[12] This language is identical to the language in its corresponding UCEA provision, UCEA section 2(d).[13]

Section 34.17.010(e) provides that "the state or a municipality may not establish a conservation easement on property by eminent domain," language not present in the UCEA.[14] The purpose of this provision is perhaps to assuage the fears of Alaskan landowners who have a historical antipathy toward state interference with property rights.[15]

Section 34.17.020 deals with judicial actions and is identical to the language of UCEA section 3.[16] This section identifies "categories of persons who may bring actions to enforce, modify or terminate conservation easements, quiet title to parcels burdened by conservation easements, or otherwise affect conservation easements."[17] It envisions that the need for such action will arise as the result of changed circumstances, making it impossible for the land use restrictions to achieve their intended purpose.[18]

Section 34.17.030, using language that is identical to UCEA section 4, removes "outmoded common law defenses that could impede the use of easements for conservation or preservation ends."[19]

Section 34.17.040 makes the AUCEA applicable "to an interest created on or after May 31, 1989, that complies with this chapter, whether designated as a conservation easement or as a covenant, equitable servitude, restriction, easement or otherwise."[20] The AUCEA also applies to other easements created before May 31, 1989. First, the AUCEA provisions were applied retroactively to all easements created before the act was passed that comply with its provisions unless such application would be unconstitutional.[21] Second, the AUCEA provisions were applied retroactively to easements created before May 31, 1989, that do not comply with the act but that complied with other state law.[22] In making the AUCEA retroactive, the legislature stated that such provisions do "not invalidate an interest, whether designated as a conservation or preservation easement or as a covenant, equitable servitude, restriction, easement, or otherwise, that is enforceable under the law of the state."[23] This language is nearly identical to the language of UCEA section 5.

Section 34.17.050, in language identical with UCEA section 6, states that it "shall be applied and construed to effectuate its general purpose to make uniform the laws with respect to the subject of the chapter among states enacting it."[24]

The final section of the AUCEA, section 34.17.060, deals with definitions and corresponds to section 1 of the UCEA. The AUCEA defines three terms that are central elements of conservation easements. A "conservation easement" is a nonpossessory interest of a holder in real property imposing limitations or affirmative obligations to retain or protect natural, scenic, or open space values of real property, ensure its availability for agricultural, forest, recreational, or open space use, protect natural resources, maintain or enhance air or water quality, or preserve the historical, architectural, archaeological, or cultural aspects of real property.[25]

This language is somewhat more restrictive than the language used in the UCEA. The UCEA indicates that the "purposes" of the limitations and obligations of the easement "include" those listed in the statute.[26] Table 22.4 highlights the variation of language across the circuit compared with the UCEA. The permissible purposes listed in the AUCEA are the same as those listed in the UCEA. The more restrictive language of the AUCEA, however, indicates that in Alaska, the purpose of the conservation easement must be one that is listed in the statute. In the AUCEA, a purpose of conservation easements on real property is to "ensure its availability for agricultural, forest, recreational, or open space use."[27] In the UCEA, purposes of conservation easements sim-

Table 22.4. How Conservation Easements Protect in the Ninth Federal Circuit

STATE	UCEA	NEGATIVE RIGHTS	AFFIRMATIVE RIGHTS	NONPOSSESSORY INTEREST	RESTRICTION	EASEMENT	COVENANT	CONDITION	EQUITABLE SERVITUDE	INTEREST IN LAND	INCORPOREAL RIGHT	INTEREST IN PROPERTY	CONTRACTUAL RIGHT	SPECIAL NOTES
Alaska	U	X	X	X	X	X	X	X	X					
Arizona	U	X	X	X	X	X	X	X	X					
California	N	X			X	X	X	X				X		Massachusetts model
Hawaii	N				X		X	X						
Idaho	U	X	X	X	X	X	X	X	X					
Montana	N	X										X		
Nevada	U	X	X	X	X	X	X	X	X			X		
Oregon	U	X	X	X	X	X	X	X	X			X		
Washington	N				X	X	X					X		

U = Conservation easement legislation directly influenced by UCEA.
N = Conservation easement legislation absent or not directly influenced by UCEA.

ply include "assuring its availability" for such uses.[28] Use of the word *ensure* rather than *assure* may indicate that in Alaska, qualifying for status as a conservation easement is subject to a higher standard than required by the UCEA.

Under the AUCEA, a "holder" is defined as a

> governmental body empowered to hold an interest in real property under the laws of the state or the United States [or] a nonprofit corporation, charitable corporation, charitable association, or charitable trust exempted from taxation under 26 U.S.C. 501(c)(3) and empowered to retain or protect the natural, scenic, or open space values of real property, ensure the availability of real property for agricultural, forest, recreational, or open space use, protect natural resources, maintain or enhance air or water quality, or preserve the historical, architectural, archaeological, or cultural aspects of real property.[29]

This language differs significantly from the UCEA by adding "nonprofit corporations" to the list of potential holders of conservation easements and by adding a requirement that the holder of the conservation easement be exempt from taxation under section 501(c)(3) of the Internal Revenue Code. Furthermore, the Alaskan statute removes the language "the purposes and powers of which include," limiting the possible purposes and powers that inhere to the holder of a conservation easement to those listed in the statute. Table 22.5 identifies the variants that occur in language pertaining to eligible easement holders across the circuit.

A "third-party right of enforcement" is "a right provided in a conservation easement to enforce any of its terms granted to a governmental body, nonprofit corporation, charitable corporation, charitable association, or charitable trust that is not a holder."[30] This language adds "nonprofit corporation" to the list of possible third-party holders defined in the UCEA. As can be seen in Table 22.6, variation exists across the states of the Ninth Federal Circuit on the issue of third-party rights of enforcement.

For several reasons, only a few conservation easements have been created in Alaska to date. There is considerably less opportunity in Alaska for private landowners to take advantage of some of the tax benefits of conservation easements because in many parts of Alaska there is no property tax.[31] Generally speaking, an ethic in favor of conserving the natural resources of the state is absent.[32] However, this seems to be changing over time.[33] Many landowners are unable to finance the stewardship obligation that usually accompanies the donation of a conservation easement.[34] Having home-

Table 22.5. Who May Hold Conservation Easements in the Ninth Federal Circuit

STATE	UCEA	GOVERNMENT	CHARITABLE TRUST	CHARITABLE ASSOCIATION	CHARITABLE CORPORATION	SECTION 501 (c)(3) TAX-EXEMPT ORGANIZATION	SPECIAL NOTES
Alaska	U	X	X	X	X	X	"nonprofit corporation"
Arizona	U	X	X		X		"trustee of charitable trust"
California	N	X	X		X	X	"tax exempt nonprofit organization"
Hawaii	N	X[a]	X		X	X[b]	[a] "public body" [b] 501(c) organization
Idaho	U	X	X	X	X		
Montana	N	X	X		X	X*	"qualified private organization" 501(c) organization
Nevada	U	X	X	X	X		
Oregon	U	X[c]	X	X	X		[c] modified UCEA
Washington	N	X	?		X	X	"nonprofit nature conservancy corporation"

U = Conservation easement legislation directly influenced by UCEA.
N = Conservation easement legislation absent or not directly influenced by UCEA.

Table 22.6. Comparison of Third-Party Enforcement Rights in the Ninth Federal Circuit

STATE	UCEA	THIRD-PARTY ENFORCEMENT	NO STATUTORY REFERENCE
Alaska	U	X	
Arizona	U	X	
California	N		X
Hawaii	N		X
Idaho	U	X	
Montana	N		X
Nevada	U	X	
Oregon	U	X	
Washington	N		X

U = Conservation easement legislation directly influenced by UCEA.
N = Conservation easement legislation absent or not directly influenced by UCEA.

steaded their property in the 1950s and 1960s, many landowners are not in a position to contribute a significant amount of cash.[35] Consequently, most conservation easement donations are made by owners of land without any financial contribution in situations where such contributions are not necessary, such as lands adjacent to state parks where a government entity manages the land.[36] A final obstacle to creating conservation easements in Alaska is that assessors and appraisers in Alaska are not familiar with conservation easements.[37]

Before enactment of the AUCEA, there were no conservation easements in Alaska.[38] Since 1989, approximately fifteen conservation easements have been created and are held by four land trusts.[39] Undoubtedly, if public sentiment in favor of protecting the environment continues to increase and if the legislature can effectively address the issues of tax incentives and stewardship contributions, the AUCEA will continue to provide an effective vehicle for creating conservation easements in Alaska.

Arizona

Although most of Arizona's citizens support conservation, land trusts have encountered substantial difficulty acquiring conservation easements, in part because of a general misperception that substantial amounts of land are already preserved. The proconservation sentiment, however, allowed Arizona to adopt enabling legislation very similar to the UCEA in 1985, four years after the Uniform Commission adopted the UCEA.[40]

Like the UCEA, the Arizona legislation presumes that conservation easements are perpetual unless a limited duration is specified in the document creating the easement.[41] Also like the UCEA, the Arizona legislation provides that conservation easements are to be treated like other forms of easements for purposes of ownership.[42] Finally, in contrast to the conservation easement legislation in other states, Arizona only requires a "holder" of a conservation easement to be either a governmental entity or a charitable corporation or trustee of a charitable trust dedicated to preservation purposes.[43] To gain federal income or gift and estate tax benefits, however, the donee must be a qualified organization under section 170(h) of the Internal Revenue Code.

Although Arizona adopted most of the UCEA virtually verbatim, some deviations were made to ensure that it conformed to local conditions. Arizona made both substantive and minor detailed modifications to the UCEA. Although the substantive modifications represent theoretical splits from the UCEA, the detail-oriented additions represent a need for greater formality in ensuring conservation easements would be treated as real property interests under existing state law.

Substantive Changes

Arizona law requires that all conservation easements must be the result of a voluntary arrangement.[44] Thus, state law specifically precludes actions by the government through its sovereign powers to condemn, zone, or regulate subdivisions to create a conservation easement.[45] This provision marks a sharp break from the UCEA, which has no such prohibitions.

Second, Arizona omitted from its enabling legislation section 5(b) of the UCEA that allows the provisions of the act to be retroactively applied. Although retroactive application would allow those conservation easements in existence before the enactment of legislation to enjoy protection under the law, Arizona elected to operate on a prospective basis.

Added Formalities

Most of the differences between the UCEA and the Arizona legislation reflect a need for formalities in any transaction involving real property interests. First, Arizona law requires that the owner of the property burdened by the easement, the holder of the easement, and any person or entity with a third-party right of enforcement be named as parties in any judicial action.[46] Second, conservation easements are only valid after they have been recorded with the appropriate county recorder.[47] By adding this provision, Arizona guaranteed actual notice of real property transactions to all interested parties. Third, the holder of a conservation easement must give consent before any right to enforce the provisions of the easement is assigned to another party.[48] Fourth, conservation easements are subject to the application of other state laws.[49] A conservation easement has "the same rights as any other recorded interest in real property."[50] Fifth, conservation easements are subject to eminent domain, and thus the state may take a conservation easement just as it may take other interests in private real property. Finally, conservation easements are treated like all other interests in real property under the laws relating to adverse possession and to recording interests in real property.[51]

Conclusion

Although private individuals do not own much of the land in Arizona, the state is still ripe for conservation easement activity. Coupled with activity surrounding the state trust land, conservation easements provide a means of preserving the large amount of undeveloped land remaining in Arizona. The key for conservation groups is to overcome the public misperception that enough land is already preserved.

California

California is ecologically rich and diverse, containing majestic mountains, fertile valleys, coastal forests, and breathtaking bays, rushing rivers, picturesque lakes, and estuaries.[52] In addition, California is the most populous state in the union, with approximately 32 million people.[53] Conservation easements, firmly supported by the legislature, serve as a way to preserve the state's natural resources from unbridled development.[54]

Open space, far from being solely an aesthetic concern, substantially contributes to the quality of California's air, water, and soil.[55] Inefficient development of open spaces or urban sprawl stains the land and squanders California's natural resources.[56] If current population and development trends continue, 1 million acres of California's Central Valley farmland will be converted to urban uses by the year 2040.[57] Through public controls on land use and through private conservation easements, using a carrot and a big stick approach, California's state and local legislatures have attempted to preserve the state's natural resources.

The rapid growth of urban centers has increased the value of the open lands surrounding California's cities.[58] Landowners in these areas, faced with increases in the market value of their land and in their property taxes and seeing an opportunity for substantial economic rewards, sold their farms to developers, who swiftly converted the agricultural to urban uses.[59] California's legislature addressed the issue in several ways, especially, for the purposes of this chapter, enacting of Civil Code sections 815 through 816, the current California Conservation Easement Act.

Comparison of California's Conservation Easement Act with the UCEA

California's Conservation Easement Act contains many of the same basic provisions as the UCEA written in 1981.[60] California's provisions are more specific and restrictive than the UCEA, but these restrictions do not seem to have hindered the creation of conservation easements in California.

The first difference between the two statutes is that California includes findings and a specific declaration that the voluntary conveyance of conservation easements to qualifying nonprofit organizations is encouraged.[61] The UCEA includes no findings, but its prefatory note indicates the same purposes.[62]

The statutes characterize conservation easements differently. California refers to such an easement as a "limitation in a deed."[63] The UCEA, on the other hand, defines a conservation easement as a "nonpossessory interest of a holder in real property" and specifies that the easement may impose affirmative obligations in addition to limitations.[64] This difference leaves open for interpretation the question of whether conservation easements in California may impose affirmative duties on the grantor. In addition, the California statute expressly states that easements are binding on successive owners and perpetual in duration.[65] The UCEA characterizes them as "unlimited in duration unless the instrument creating it provides otherwise."[66] Thus, the UCEA allows easements of shorter duration, although the tax benefits to the donor would not be applicable under current tax statutes unless the easement is perpetual.[67]

California's legislation professes fewer purposes for which conservation easements may be created than does the UCEA. California's act has an exclusive and short list of valid purposes only "to retain land predominantly in its natural, scenic, historical, agricultural, forested, or open-space condition."[68] The UCEA contains a more inclusive listing.[69] With the exception of "scenic," the UCEA includes all California's purposes and several other useful purposes such as archeological, cultural, recreational, protecting natural resources, and maintaining or enhancing air or water quality.[70] California's exclusive list has not prevented either the creation of the broad variety of conservation easements or their enforcement throughout the state.

The UCEA provides more protection for the easement holder than does California's act. The UCEA requires that the holder of an interest created by an easement must accept and then record the acceptance of that interest.[71] Thus, no easement duties may be imposed on a person without his or her agreement. California only specifies that the instrument creating or conveying the easement describe the particular characteristics of the easement, leaving open the possibility that a person could be burdened by easement duties without acquiescing to them.[72] The UCEA also explicitly limits valid easements to those instances in which the "owner of the interest is a party or consents."[73] The California statute, on the other hand, states that "interests not transferred and conveyed by the instrument shall remain in the grantor of the easement."[74] This provision may assure potential grantors that they will retain all interests that they do not grant in the easement, but it seems superfluous.

California is stricter than the UCEA regarding the type of entity that may hold a conservation easement. In California, a tax-exempt nonprofit organization qualified under 501(c)(3) of the Internal Revenue Code, "which has as its primary purpose the preservation, protection, or enhancement of land in its natural, scenic, historical, agricultural, forested, or open-space condition or use," may hold conservation easements.[75] Under the UCEA, the charity need not qualify as a tax-exempt organization, making the list of possible organizations long.[76] In California, state or local government entities authorized to hold title to real property may also hold conservation easements as long as the issuance of an entitlement is not conditioned on the granting of the easement.[77] The UCEA simply allows any government entity able to hold an interest in real property to hold a conservation easement.[78]

The California act provides for broad enforcement of the terms of easements. California establishes a virtual per se standing by abolishing various common-law requirements for easements.[79] California also allows the grantor or owner of the easement to seek injunctive relief for mere threats of violations of the easements or its terms.[80] In such cases, the state provides monetary damages to the holder of a conservation easement for loss of "scenic, aesthetic, or environmental value to the real property subject to the easement."[81] Finally, a court is permitted to award reasonable attorney fees to the prevailing party for the costs of litigation.[82]

Notably, both the California act and the UCEA are silent on the issue of modifying and terminating easements. Attempting to ensure that all conservation easements are perpetual, references to the manner in which a conservation easement may cease to exist are lacking.[83] This lack of legislative direction allows the courts more discretion than is appropriate.[84]

Wide Diversity Among California's Conservation Easements

All conservation easements in California serve the particular interests of the parties involved in their creation. Only the provisions of the enabling legislation, the natural attributes of the site, and the imaginations of the creators limit the types of easements found in California. One hundred and twenty-three land trusts in the state protect about 543,650 acres of land, many involving the use of conservation easements.[85]

Differences in topography and population density account for much of the variation between conservation easement programs in California's fifty-eight counties. Even in the fairly small northern central coast area of California, where landforms are similar, the land trusts' approaches to conservation easements vary greatly.

In Napa County, just north of San Francisco, the main thrust of conservation easements is to limit development and preserve the agrarian, grape-growing, and wine-making economy. In Napa County, many easements held by the Napa County Land Trust simply limit any development of the land or limit the possible use of the land. In other counties with less development pressures, conservation easements may be more focused on particular resource protection, such as the Pacific Forest Trust in Mendocino County.

The local population's attitude also affects what entities create and hold conservation easements. For instance, in Mendocino County, widespread distrust of government means that private land trusts negotiate and hold easements. In Sonoma County, however, although private land trusts hold the easements, the negotiations occur via a quasi-governmental entity.

Room for Improvement in California's Conservation Easement Program

Better Intercounty Coordination. Although reasons exist for county-by-county autonomy of land trust operations, coordination between counties could improve response to intercounty concerns. For instance, when important wildlife species travel across several counties, better intercounty communication and coordination could ensure a strategy to acquire the necessary easement to protect its habitat. In addition, a statewide monitoring and record-keeping program could compile and distribute useful information to land trust organizations. Such a program would only be successful, however, if it did not burden the free-market individualistic approach to conservation easements that makes them such a valuable tool.

Compatibility with Need for Affordable Housing. Land trusts are acquiring easements in areas where housing is scarce and expensive. Unfortunately, an inherent quality of conservation easements is to preclude the building of housing in undeveloped areas, which creates conflict with California's growing demand for housing in and around urban centers. One possible solution to this dilemma is for land trusts to contemplate building houses on land burdened by conservation easements. Making land available for residential construction in a less sensitive portion of a property could provide the funds necessary for habitat improvements in other parts of the property or for monitoring the easement. Alternatively, where a landowner already plans to develop land, a land trust's involvement in the process can make that development more ecologically sensitive. For such landowners, placing an easement on the property may offer significant tax advantages.

Conclusion

Since their legislative beginnings in 1979, conservation easements have contributed to land preservation in California. Counties all over the state have experimented with this valuable conservation tool and have made strides to perfect its use. With the competing demands of a growing population and the need to protect natural resources, the successes and failures of conservation easements are sure to be of great concern to all Californians.

Hawaii

The state of Hawaii adopted enabling legislation in 1985 recognizing conservation easements as valid and enforceable property interests.[86] No case law interpreting these statutory provisions exists at this time.

Definitions and Purposes

The Hawaii legislation defined a conservation easement as "an interest in real property created by deed, restrictions, covenants, or conditions, the purpose of which is to preserve and protect land predominantly in its natural, scenic, forested or open-space condition."[87] Similar to the unqualified preservation purpose requirement found in the UCEA, the Hawaiian legislation does not expressly state that conservation easements may be created to protect cultural resources or air and water quality.

In 1996, the Hawaii legislature amended its definition to permit conservation easements that preserve and protect historic properties, traditional and family cemeteries, and "the structural integrity and physical appearance of cultural landscapes, resources, and sites which perpetuate indigenous native Hawaiian culture."[88]

Eligible Holders

The UCEA allows governmental bodies and charitable organizations having a conservation purpose, regardless of their status as exempt organizations under any tax law, to hold a conservation easement.[89] Hawaii requires holders of conservation easements to be public bodies and organizations that are exempt under section 501(c) of the Internal Revenue Code and that facilitate preservation purposes.[90]

Duration

The UCEA gives the parties to a transaction creating a conservation easement freedom to determine the period of time during which their mutual obligations are enforceable. Section 2(c) of the UCEA, however, provides a default rule in favor of perpetuity if the instrument does not otherwise specify its duration.[91] In contrast, the legislation adopted by Hawaii mandates that a conservation easement "shall be perpetual in duration."[92]

Alienability

Like the UCEA, the Hawaii statute provides that conservation easements are freely transferable property interests, declaring void the common-law characteristics of such easements, easements in gross.[93] Any instrument creating, assigning, or otherwise transferring a conservation easement must be recorded in the proper bureau of conveyances or land court.[94] Conservation easements may be transferred to a public body or charitable organization with a preservation purpose "by purchase, agreement, donation, devise, or bequest."[95]

Enforcement and Remedies

Third-Party Right of Enforcement. The Hawaii statute does not provide for a third-party right of enforcement. Because it was enacted four years after the UCEA was accepted, it must be presumed that the legislators did not intend to allow third parties to obtain rights to enforce conservation easements in which they have no property interest.

Injunctive Relief. The UCEA merely provides for actions "affecting a conservation easement" without specifying the remedies available to those suffering injury when the terms of the easement are violated.[96] The comments to the UCEA, however, contemplate "actions to enforce, modify or terminate conservation easements, quiet title to parcels burdened by conservation easements, . . . [and suits] in cases where the easements also impose duties upon holders and these duties are breached by the holders."[97] Under the Hawaii statute, grantors and holders of conservation easements may initiate proceedings for injunctive relief to prevent "actual or threatened injury to or impairment of a conservation easement, or actual or threatened violations of its terms."[98]

Money Damages. In addition to injunctive relief, the Hawaii statute allows the *holder* of a conservation easement to recover monetary damages for any injury to the easement, the interest protected by the easement, or any other damages flowing from the violation of the terms of the easement.[99] In assessing damages, the holder may take into account "in addition to the cost of restoration, the loss of scenic, aesthetic, or environmental value to the real property subject to the easement, and other damages."[100] Because valuation of an easement's scenic, aesthetic, or environmental qualities is in some measure a subjective determination, the proper assessment of money damages in the event of injury or violation will no doubt prove difficult.

Attorneys' Fees. Hawaii legislation expressly gives courts the power to award to the party prevailing in litigation that involves a conservation easement the costs of such litigation, including reasonable attorneys' fees.[101]

The Current State of Hawaiian Land Trusts and Conservation Easements[102]

The land trust movement in Hawaii is encouraged by a group of small yet dedicated volunteers in the local communities of the islands. The trusts are scattered throughout the state and receive contributions of conservation easements primarily from landowners interested in preserving their community and preempting urban sprawl. The continued viability of land trusts in Hawaii, however, is severely handicapped by both a lack of community support for the preservation movement, leading to an inadequate financial base for land trusts promoting charitable contributions, and state zoning laws.

Much of the agricultural land in Hawaii is held by a few landowners, most of whom value the possibility of future development and are not familiar with conservation easements. The state's real property tax law favors agricultural lands, providing no tax incentives for conservation purposes. Thus, lack of community support for the preservation movement frustrates land trusts in Hawaii.

State law defines four major zoning categories: (1) conservation, (2) agricultural, (3) rural, and (4) urban. The state government manages lands zoned conservation, agricultural, and rural. County governments are responsible for managing land zoned urban. What results is a system of centralized state land use control in which local, community-based land trusts have difficulty surviving.

Under regulations adopted by the state's Land Use Commission, zoning authorities cannot withhold a residential building permit on agricultural lands for a "farm" residence if the parcel consists of at least 2 acres. A second "farm" dwelling will be allowed if there is almost any discernible agricultural activity on the land. According to Fred Rohlfing of the Maui Open Space Trust, Hawaiian landowners commonly sprinkle their parcels with false agricultural intent to obtain permits for second dwellings. The situation is further aggravated by the state's failure to perform any follow-up review to ensure that the lands are, in fact, being used for agricultural purposes. Accordingly, these second "farm" dwellings soon become nonfarm-related rental units, or "gentlemen's estates." This process of development takes place without the necessity of a public hearing to obtain any community views.

Agricultural zoning does not distinguish between lands that are truly agricultural and those that are only marginally agricultural. Consequently, much land that might otherwise be classified as rural remains classed as agriculture and hampered by agricultural land use restrictions. Individuals involved in the land trust movement have initiated a campaign to encourage the state legislature to allow county governments to manage rural and agricultural lands.

Such local control over these lands would give communities greater flexibility to further their own goals free from the permissive state zoning regulations, allowing environmentally minded communities the ability to "cluster" development and preserve areas of open-space land. This campaign, however, has met with little success.

Idaho

In 1988, the Idaho legislature enacted the Idaho Conservation Easement Act.[103] The Idaho act was modeled on the UCEA and apparently on the Nevada Conservation Easement Act of 1986.[104] No case has been litigated in its history.

The Idaho act differs from the UCEA in a number of important respects. Perhaps the most notable difference is a provision essentially denying any real property tax benefit from a reduction in assessed value on land burdened with a conservation easement. The statute states that "the granting of a conservation easement . . . shall not have an effect on the market value of property for ad valorem tax purposes. . . . The market value shall be computed as if the conservation easement did not exist."[105] Individual counties have the authority to waive this provision, although only one, Blaine County in the Sawtooth Valley, has done so to date. This type of provision, although unusual, is not unique to Idaho.[106] Although most conservation easements are created largely to take advantage of federal income and estate tax benefits, the prohibition of this benefit may deter some property owners from granting conservation easements.

In keeping with Idaho's well-known individualist spirit, the act makes clear that no conservation easement may encumber the property of an unwilling owner. Section 55-2107 states that a "conservation easement pursuant to this chapter shall not be created through eminent domain proceedings. . . . "[107] Similarly, section 55-2102, subsection 4, modeled on the UCEA, requires that the owner of the real property be a party to or consent to a conservation easement before such easement may impair that property interest.[108]

The Idaho act deleted the phrase "unless the context otherwise requires" from the first sentence of section 1 of the UCEA defining the various purposes for which a conservation easement may be created. The deletion of this phrase from the Idaho statute may limit the instances in which conservation easements can be created, but the limited experience in applying the Idaho act means that the importance of this deletion is currently unknown.

Despite this limitation of the Idaho act, agriculture is specifically listed as a proper purpose for a conservation easement.[109] This relatively common purpose for conservation easements indicates Idaho's interest in balancing preservation with the use of the land to further the state's economy and of the highly agricultural nature of much of the state's remaining privately owned land.

The Idaho act applies only to interests created after its effective date of July 1, 1988.[110] It differs in form, but not in substance, from the UCEA, adding a requirement that the "instrument creating the conservation easement shall state it was created under the provisions of this chapter."[111] The act states, however, that this "chapter does not invalidate any interest . . . that is enforceable under other law of this state."[112] Failure to meet this requirement apparently would not defeat all easements but would simply defeat the application of the Idaho act to that particular easement.

Local Experience

Some of the oldest conservation easements in the mountain states occur in Idaho. Many precede specific conservation easement legislation. In the early 1970s, the Idaho congressional delegation, including Senator Frank Church, succeeded in getting federal appropriations allowing the U.S. Forest Service to purchase and hold conservation easements in the Sawtooth Scenic Area in central Idaho. Those bipartisan actions, primarily intended to protect fish and wildlife habitat and scenery, were driven by exploding subdivisions, especially in the Sun Valley area, still a focus for land trust activity today. Today, approximately 18,000 acres are encumbered with seventy-nine easements, easily the largest block of conservation easements in the state.[113]

Today there are also eight private land trusts in Idaho, holding conservation easements to about 8,315 acres.[114] Although the acreage protected by conservation easement is a relatively small amount in a state as large as Idaho, it represents significant conservation efforts because, as is the case in many of the states comprising the Ninth Federal Circuit, Idaho has a large amount of publicly owned land.[115]

Widespread understanding and acceptance of private land trusts is still developing in Idaho. Until recently, there was a great deal of confusion about land trusts and other nonprofit conservation organizations on the part of many landowners, confusion that bred considerable suspicion of those in existence. For a number of years, the small and inexperienced Idaho land trusts struggled with credibility problems. Recently, however, they and conservation easements have overcome this difficulty and their numbers have grown exponentially. The Teton Regional Land Trust, one of the two land trusts that function at this time, nearly doubled the number of conservation easements in its portfolio in 1998 alone and now holds over 80 percent of all acreage under conservation easements held by land trusts in Idaho.[116]

There are two interrelated yet distinct reasons for this growth. One is an increasing awareness and acceptance of the idea of conservation easements through publicity, generally by word of mouth and specifically in various publications such as *Beef* magazine, and through sustained success. Second is that Idaho remains a very rural state, and thus the need for specific and complex conservation mechanisms, such as conservation easements, has not existed until quite recently.[117] Today, land trusts and conservation easement activity in the state are concentrated in areas that are experiencing population growth either of permanent residents such as in Boise and Ada County or of seasonal residents such as in Sun Valley and Ketchum. Approximately one-half of the state has no specific land trust coverage.[118] Nonetheless, as the population of Idaho remains around 1 million people, the whole state still only has one telephone area code, and the conservation easement movement is arriving well in time to manage growth and protect and conserve valuable open spaces, natural resources, and environmental assets.[119]

Nearly all the existing conservation easements in Idaho are connected to protecting and preserving agricultural land. Even the older easements are related to agriculture because the vast majority of the private lands in the state not already urbanized are used for agriculture. In general, the agriculture community is supportive of conservation easements. Individual farmers, many of whom are land rich and cash poor and obvious candidates for easement donations, are not comfortable donating easements and choose to participate only when easements are purchased from them either at full value or via a bargain sale. Frequently, as these individuals die, they bequeath lands burdened with high estate taxes, even high property taxes, to their similarly situated children, and the property is lost to farming. This is clearly a lose-lose situation and is one of the great publicity challenges of the local land trust movement.[120]

Key to the growth of Idaho's conservation easement movement is that the Idaho act denies a property tax break to owners of encumbered property. According to Carol Brown, a member of the board of the Wood River Land Trust near Ketchum, nearly every time she talks to potential easement grantors, they lament the lack of a property tax reduction. This particular tax break is important because it is an annual benefit, whereas other tax benefits associated with easements are limited. There is some sentiment toward legislative change, and there has recently been a legal challenge to the denial of the property tax benefit brought by property owners in Twin Falls County, in south-central Idaho, which remains unresolved. A change in the property tax characteristic of conservation easements is strongly opposed by most counties, especially those that are substantially composed of federal lands and already significantly strapped for revenue sources. There is also a sectarian aspect to the property tax debate. The generally more conservative rural areas oppose any change to benefit easement holders and encourage further protection of undeveloped lands, and the generally more liberal areas around Twin Falls, Boise, Sun Valley, and the University of Idaho in Moscow generally support such changes. The threat of legal challenge has gained the attention of some county tax commissions and tax assessors, and so this issue is likely to figure prominently in the near future.[121]

Conclusion

Conservation easement activity in Idaho is just beginning to increase, riding the coattails of population inflows as well as an increasing awareness and acceptance of them as a mechanism for land conservation and agricultural preservation. Because of the rapid growth in land trust activity, the skills and knowledge of experienced practitioners and organizations are in high demand, and regional alliances are beginning to form to provide these services. The property tax provision of the Idaho Conservation Easement Act currently stands as a significant impediment to the growth trend in conservation easements in the state, and the denial of a local assessment adjustment for property under conservation easement is *the* current issue of debate.

Montana

Montana's Voluntary Conservation Easement Act was enacted in 1975 to facilitate an ambitious growth management plan developed in the Blackfoot River area of Missoula County.[122] Landowners along the river hoped to gain some measure of control over increasing recreational use and development while protecting the pristine Blackfoot River. Conservation easements figured prominently in the plan but were not recognized by Montana law at the time. Consequently, the state legislature amended the existing Open Space Land Act, enabling individuals to create conservation easements. The amended act is now known as the Open Space Land and Voluntary Conservation Easement Act.[123]

Montana's act was enacted six years before the UCEA's acceptance, and its drafters foresaw many of the obstacles to conservation easements addressed subsequently in the UCEA. Montana's act departs from the UCEA in some key areas, particularly when describing what purpose conservation easements may serve and who may hold a conservation easement.

Purpose

Under the UCEA, conservation easements may be created to serve a broader range of purposes than under Montana law. Conservation purposes explicitly provided for in the UCEA but absent from the Montana code include the protection of agricultural lands and preservation of land with historical or cultural value.[124] In the Montana code, conservation easements are limited to preserving "open space, native plants or animals, biotic communities, geological or geographical formations of scientific, aesthetic, or educational interest."[125] The broader scope of the UCEA clearly provides land trusts with more conservation opportunities. For example, conservation easements are often granted over agricultural lands to preserve open space. If the property owner wants to level land in anticipation of planting crops or to build a barn, the open-space purposes of the easement may be at risk. The UCEA avoids this dilemma by including the preservation of agricultural lands as a conservation purpose.

Who May Hold a Conservation Easement

Montana's Voluntary Conservation Easement Act only allows organizations that meet the tax-exempt requirements of Internal Revenue Code section 501(c) to hold conservation easements.[126] Public bodies are also qualified to hold conservation easements.[127] In contrast, the UCEA empowers any charitable corporation, association, or trust whose purposes include protecting the "natural, scenic or open space values of real property" to hold a conservation easement.[128]

Duration of Conservation Easements

Under Montana law, the easement may be granted in perpetuity or for a renewable term of not less than fifteen years.[129] The UCEA provides that conservation easements are unlimited "unless the instrument creating it otherwise provides."[130] Of course, if the donor wants the conservation easement treated as a charitable contribution for federal income tax purposes, the easement must meet the requirements of Internal Revenue Code section 170(h) that the conservation easement be granted "in perpetuity."[131] Thus, any interest granted for a particular period, however long a period, precludes the donor from qualifying for a charitable contribution deduction on the federal income tax, and hence such donations appear unattractive. This is intentional; conservation goals can only be served by permanent protection.

Third-Party Right of Enforcement

The UCEA permits the original parties to a conservation easement to assign enforcement rights to any third party meeting the requirements for conservation easement holders.[132] Montana's statute does not allow any such assignment of enforcement right. Thus, in Montana, only the original easement holder may enforce the terms of the easement.[133]

Validity of Conservation Easements

Conservation easement acts are often referred to as enabling statutes, reflecting the principal purpose of the acts to free conservation easements from the common-law impediments to such real property interests. As a result, the Montana act provides that no conservation easement shall be unenforceable due to "lack of privity of estate or contract or lack of benefit to particular land or on account of . . . not being an appurtenant easement or because such easement is an easement in gross," all common-law restrictions to easements.[134] Conservation easements may be assigned under Montana law, but only to assignees who are qualified to hold conservation easements.[135] Montana's enabling statute has worked well so far. The Montana Land Reliance reports no history of a common-law challenge to a conservation easement.

Current Issues for Montana's Land Trusts

Third-Party Mineral Rights. The potential federal income tax benefits of conservation easements are often a key consideration for a potential donor. Accordingly, whether or not a conservation easement qualifies as a charitable gift is essential to its creation and donation. The standard for treatment as a charitable contribution is contained in Internal Revenue Code section 170(h). Section 170(h) allows a conservation easement to qualify as a charitable deduction even if the donor reserves the mineral rights as long as the donor is committed to protecting the conservation interest of the easement, agreeing to use subsurface methods only to extract minerals.[136] If a third party holds the mineral rights, a conservation easement may still qualify for charitable contribution treatment as long as the probability of surface mining is "so remote as to be negligible."[137]

Minerals figure prominently in Montana's economy. Mining for copper, gold, and silver remains profitable in Montana, and the state's reserves are the largest in the nation. Therefore, third-party mineral rights are frequently attached to potential conservation easement land. If the donor wishes to deduct the grant as a charitable contribution, a remoteness test must be commissioned to determine whether the probability of surface mining is so remote as to be negligible.

A certified independent geologist must be hired to perform this test. The first step is a survey of the mineral deposits in the area. If the survey reveals the existence of mineral deposits in merchantable quantities below the surface, the test is virtually over. When the survey of a potential easement donation in the Powder River area of eastern Montana revealed coal deposits ten feet below the surface, for example, the test was halted and the proposed donation was abandoned. If the survey does not reveal merchantable deposits, the geologist makes an on-site visit and makes a conclusion whether surface mining will or will not occur.

Existing gravel pits present a significant problem for a land trust seeking to place conservation easements on ranch lands in Montana. Many ranchers interested in donating conservation easements insist that they be able to continue extracting gravel from existing pits to maintain roads. Although importing gravel from any other source is very expensive for most ranchers, the continued extraction of gravel is almost certain to conflict with the Internal Revenue Code section 170(h) prohibition on surface mining. There may be an issue as to whether the right to extract gravel qualifies as a "mineral interest," but land trusts would be well advised to avoid a likely fatal collision with an auditor for their donors by keeping gravel pits out of conservation easements. Unfortunately, many would-be donations are lost to this problem. For example, the Montana Land Reliance reports recently losing several hundred acres along the Yellowstone River because of it.

Conclusion

Because Montana's legislation predates the UCEA, comparisons between it and the UCEA may not shed much light on how successful the UCEA has been. The Montana legislation has been successful, however. The Montana Land Reliance has managed to protect over 300,000 acres under the Voluntary Conservation Easement Act, prompting one member to remark "if it ain't broke. . . ."[138]

Nevada

In 1983, the Nevada legislature enacted its version of the UCEA that mirrors it in all principal aspects.[139] The main reason for adopting such a statute was to be consistent with other states enacting similar legislation. At the time that the legislature was considering the act, Nevada was experiencing a rapid increase in population, and with it came an increase in development that likely helped to push this legislation forward.[140]

Differences between the language used in Nevada's conservation easement statute and the UCEA do not change the UCEA in any substantive way. For instance, NRS 11.430(1)(C) allows "an action affecting an easement for conservation [to] be brought by *a third person with a right of enforcement* although the UCEA section 3(a)(3) allows such an action by *"a person having a third-party right of enforcement"* (emphasis added). The Nevada statute also rearranges the UCEA sections. For example, the Nevada statutes begin with the Uniformity of Application and Construction, or section 6 of the UCEA, whereas the UCEA begins with the definitions that appear in NRS 111.410. These changes by the Nevada legislature only have the effect of making the UCEA easier to navigate.

The Nevada legislature added a clause allowing a court to terminate or modify an easement. NRS 111.420 (3) states that "an easement for conservation is unlimited in duration unless: (a) The instrument creating it otherwise provides or (b) a court orders that the easement be terminated or modified, according to subsection 2 of NRS 111.430." Section 2 of the UCEA, the model for NRS 111.420, states that "except as provided in Section 3(b), a conservation easement is unlimited in duration unless the instrument creating it otherwise provides." Although UCEA section 2 does refer to another section, section 3(b) of the UCEA, which allows a court to "modify or terminate a conservation easement," does not expressly provide for the court's power, as does NRS 111.420. Nevada's conservation easement legislation twice expressly provides that a court can step in to modify or terminate a conservation easement, whereas the UCEA only mentions the court's power once.

Conservation easements have yet to become widely used in Nevada for a variety of reasons. One of the main reasons is that, unlike Nevada's neighboring states of Montana, Wyoming, and Idaho, where agricultural land is abundant, there is almost no agricultural land available in the state.[141] The absence of such land in other parts of the Ninth Federal Circuit providing an important impetus for conservation easements hampers the efforts to promote their use. Most of Nevada is desert, and preserving desert is not as seductive as protecting agricultural land. Although there are ranches in northern Nevada, there have been few attempts to promote conservation easements among the ranch owners.[142]

In addition, only a few land trusts exist in Nevada, and most people are simply not aware of conservation easements. The Nevada Land Conservancy is beginning to educate citizens of the benefits of land protection and conservation easements, but to date these efforts have been minimal.[143]

The federal government owns almost 90 percent of the land in Nevada. This high percentage of public land is another reason for the lack of land trusts and conservation easements that focus on privately owned land. Most efforts to preserve land have focused on persuading the federal government to manage their lands for the purposes articulated in the conservation easement legislation. With the federal government owning such a vast majority of the land, the emphasis has been, and will continue to be on getting land from the government.[144] In fact, the lack of private land in the state makes landowners reluctant to give up their real property rights without getting something in return. Consequently, the American Land Conservancy acquires land through land exchanges.[145]

In southern Nevada, there are two additional reasons for the lack of conservation easements. In this part of the state, the recent great increase in population has caused conservation groups to focus on coping with the rapid growth rather than obtaining land or easements. Many individuals are new to the area and may possess little incentive to preserve the land because they have yet to develop a commitment to the area and the community.[146]

Oregon

Oregon's conservation easement enabling legislation, first enacted in 1967, limited the potential class of easement holders to counties, cities, and park and recreation districts.[147] A 1975 amendment expanded the class of holders to include nonprofit conservation organizations.[148] In 1983, Oregon Revised Statutes 271.715–271.795, which incorporated the UCEA of 1981, supplanted these provisions.[149] The Oregon statute added important provisions to the UCEA, ensuring that all easements to be held by government agencies would be subject to public hearings and a public interest determination, limiting the use of eminent domain and authorizing agencies to promulgate rules. The statute also authorized land encumbered with conservation easements to receive preferential property tax assessment, even tax exemption. The statute also established "highway scenic preservation easements." Complementing the conservation easement enabling legislation are two other statutes, one to designate free-flowing Oregon rivers and the other to a designated portion of the Willamette River.

Public Interest Determination

ORS 271.725, concerning the "acquisition and creation of conservation or highway scenic preservation easements," incorporates the whole of UCEA section 2. ORS 271.725 section (1), however, provides that specifically listed agencies may acquire conservation easements "in any area within their respective jurisdictions wherever and to the extent that a state agency or the governing body of the county, city or park and recreation district determines that the acquisition will be in the public interest." The term *public interest* is not further defined, and nonprofit organizations are specifically excluded from this requirement.

Notice and Hearing Requirement

ORS 271.735 requires that government agencies provide notice and hold public hearings before acquiring easements.[150] These provisions are partially at odds with the rationale of the UCEA drafters who, in their prefatory comments, recommend "not subjecting conservation easements to a public ordering system," fearing that

> the requirement of public agency approval adds a layer of complexity, which may discourage private actions. Organizations and property owners may be reluctant to become involved in

the bureaucratic, and sometimes political, process which public agency participation entails.[151]

Oregon's exemption of charitable organizations from this "layer of complexity" recognizes the UCEA drafters' intent. The provision seems to
acknowledge the suggestion in the UCEA that there is "assurance that the Act
will serve the public interest" because such organizations are "[not] likely to
accept [easements] on an indiscriminate basis" and, in any event, "federal tax
statutes and regulations . . . rigorously define the circumstances under which
easement donations qualify for favorable tax treatment."[152] Like the UCEA,
the Oregon enabling statute does not require charitable organizations to have
federal Internal Revenue Code 501(c)(3) status to hold conservation easements.[153] Rather, as explained in the commentary to UCEA section 1, "the
word 'charitable' . . . describes organizations that are charities according to
the common law definition regardless of their status as exempt organizations
under any tax law."[154]

Agencies: Eminent Domain and Rulemaking

The UCEA "neither limits nor enlarges the power of eminent domain," recognizing that the scope of the condemnation power is determined by other
applicable state law.[155] By contrast, in ORS 271.725, government agencies are
limited to acquiring conservation easements through "purchase, agreement
or donation, but not by exercise of the power of eminent domain, unless
specifically authorized by law."[156] This wording differs from the powers given
agencies under the Willamette River Greenway Program, described below, but
is consistent with the scenic easement provisions of the Oregon Scenic Waterways System.[157] The phrase "unless specifically authorized by law" is not
defined further. ORS 271.775 also provides that authorized government agencies "may make and enforce reasonable rules, regulations, orders or ordinances governing the care, use and management of its conservation easements."

Taxation

ORS 271.785 provides that property subject to a conservation easement first
"shall be assessed on the basis of the real market value of the property less any
reduction in value caused by the conservation easement" and second that
"such an easement shall be exempt from assessment and taxation the same as
any other property owned by the holder." In practice, however, private
landowners reportedly have trouble in getting their properties reassessed in
conformance with this provision, particularly in rural counties.[158]

Highway Scenic Preservation Easements

Provisions for highway scenic preservation easement, "the purposes of which include retaining or protecting natural, scenic or open space values of property," are included in the conservation easement statute.[159] Such easements, although similar to conservation easements, may only be acquired by government agencies, "in land within 100 yards of state, county or city highway rights of way" and "only in lands that possess significant scenic value in themselves and contribute to the overall scenic beauty of the highway."[160]

Willamette River Greenway Program

Codified at ORS 390.310–390.368 is a complex statutory framework for establishing and maintaining "a natural, scenic, historical and recreational greenway upon lands along the Willamette River to be known as the Willamette River Greenway."[161] The state Parks and Recreation Department is authorized to acquire "scenic easements" designed to "preserve the vegetation along the Willamette River and the natural and scenic qualities of the lands subject to such easements."[162] In contrast to both the conservation easement enabling legislation and that establishing the Scenic Waterways program, the Greenway act authorizes the department to "acquire such easements by any method, including but not limited to the exercise of eminent domain."[163] The department may not acquire easements for public access and on working farmlands using this power.[164] The Greenway program is not active due to insufficient funding in the 1990s, itself a product of the resistance from some members of the agricultural community.[165]

Oregon Scenic Waterways System

Applicable to "many of the free-flowing rivers of Oregon . . . and lands adjacent to [them]" is a statewide system, authorized by statute, to preserve selected rivers and river segments "in a free-flowing condition" and to "protect and preserve the natural setting and water quality of . . . such rivers and fulfill other conservation purposes."[166] The state Parks and Recreation Department is authorized to acquire scenic easements and has "the right to control the use of related adjacent land, including air space above such land, for the purpose of protecting the scenic view from waters within a scenic waterway."[167] The Department cannot acquire such easements through condemnation, although it can condemn related adjacent land.[168]

Land Trusts in Oregon

There are ten section 501(c)(3) land trusts in Oregon, four with full-time staffs.[169] The state Nature Conservancy, using conservation easements primarily to protect lands that abut their fee-owned lands, holds ten to twelve easements of them. Two of these were purchased, and the rest were donated.[170] The conservation easement enabling statutes appear to be working well in practice; neither land trusts nor conservation easements, however, are as numerous in Oregon as they are in the neighboring states of Washington and California.[171] R. Pinto, of the Oregon Office of The Nature Conservancy, suggests several reasons, including the lower disposable incomes of residents in Oregon compared with neighboring states and less public exposure to the rapid development of large tracts of open lands that occurs in these neighboring states. He also suggests that the public relies heavily on the effectiveness of Oregon's land use statutes, such as those promoting urban growth boundaries, in protecting natural and open space values.[172]

Washington

The state of Washington enacted measures to protect its lands long before the issue was addressed in the UCEA. In 1970, the state legislature enacted the Open Space Tax Act. The act stated that it was "in the best interest of the state" to maintain and preserve the existence of open space lands in their current state and "to assure the use and enjoyment of natural resources and scenic beauty for the economic and social well-being of the state and its citizens."[173] The main objective of this legislation was to minimize the economic pressure placed on owners of open space and agricultural property and to encourage owners to retain such land in its current state.[174]

The state legislature has enacted numerous other statutes designed to carry out this broad mandate.[175] One of these is a statute equivalent to the UCEA that prescribes the purchase, in perpetuity, of future development rights pertaining to any open-space land, farmland, agriculture land, or timberland.[176] Like the Open Space Tax Act, this legislation was enacted a decade before the adoption of the UCEA.

The Basic Legislative Requirements

Washington's statute authorizes a broad range of government entities and private parties, including nonprofit historic preservation and nature conservation corporations, to acquire property interests necessary to protect or limit the future use of open space and agricultural lands thus providing for their public use or enjoyment.[177] These property interests, collectively called "conservation futures," encompass fee simple or any lesser interest, including conservation easements.[178] Nonprofit organizations must meet the tax-exempt charitable organization standards prescribed by Internal Revenue Code section 501(c)(3).[179] In addition, the Washington statute requires that the nonprofit must have as one of its principal purposes the conservation of natural resources, the conservation of open space, or the facilitation of scientific research.[180] There is no requirement that the nonprofit organization have been in operation for a minimum number of years. Acquisition of conservation futures may occur in several ways, including purchase, lease, and donation; they may not be acquired by eminent domain.[181] The statute does not address whether property burdened by a conservation future may be condemned.

Compared with the UCEA: Contrasting and Common Elements

As provided in the UCEA, land subject to a conservation future may be sold or assigned, but such conveyance is subject to the terms of the conservation agreement.[182] All such interests must be perpetual.[183] Notably, Washington State has no conflicting legislative marketable title act. Furthermore, the common-law restraint on alienation provision applies only if the restraint is unreasonable or violates public policy.

No reference is made in current statutory law to the common-law distinction between appurtenant or "in gross" easements and the nature of a conservation future. The original statute specifically upheld the validity of in gross interests, but the language was changed. The Washington statute does not refer to other common law issues regarding conservation easements. The legislature created a new property interest, the conservation future, and thus avoided the common law "easement" terminology.

There is no reference to third-party enforcement.

The Washington statute addresses a number of issues not covered in the UCEA. A conservation future can forbid, or at minimum restrict, the property owner from building or "improving" the land in any way.[184]

Mineral rights are mentioned as being a property interest to be acquired and held for preservation.

Taxes: Levies, Assessments, and Exemptions

Tax Measures to Effectuate the Use of Conservation Futures. The Open Space Tax Act gives municipalities the opportunity to levy a tax for the sole purpose of acquiring conservation futures. Taxes garnered may be placed in a conservation futures fund.[185] Several Washington counties have adopted such a tax. In Skagit County in 1997, $6.25 of the tax on a $100,000 home was dedicated to conservation futures acquisitions.[186] The validity of this legislation and the actions of one county were challenged in court. Plaintiffs argued, unsuccessfully, that because the county could substantially achieve the purpose of preserving open space through use of its police power without the use of public funds, the tax was akin to an unconstitutional gift of public funds.[187]

To further the purposes of the Open Space Tax Act, the legislature has allowed owners of agricultural, timber, and open-space land numerous tax exemptions and deductions. Conservation futures on designated agricultural lands held by nonprofit organizations are exempt from ad valorem real property taxation if the conservation futures are for an unlimited duration and prohibit all nonagricultural uses.[188] Conservation futures on open space lands are exempt from property tax under the two following circumstances. One is when the primary purpose of the land is either scientific research or educational opportunity for the public, the property is open to the public, and no party receives a pecuniary benefit.[189] The other is that conservation futures on forestland that are held by a designated governmental body are exempt from "special benefit assessments," those charges imposed on property owners for municipal services such as water supply, storm sewerage service, and road improvement and maintenance. Furthermore, any conservation future on forests that serves to protect against future nonforest use and conserves forests is exempt from special benefit assessments.[190]

Measures to Promote Preservation of Open Space Generally. The legislature has also exempted certain owners of agricultural, timber, and open-space properties, unencumbered by conservation futures, from beneficial assessments. The legislature reasoned that agricultural and forest industries are to be preserved and protected and thus should be exempt from special benefit assessments unless such lands benefit from or cause the need for the local improvement district.

The Open Space Tax Act prescribes that property tax assessments must reflect the goal of statewide open space preservation.[191] In addition, several other tax measures support preservation and protection goals. In support, the legislature cites Article VII, section 7, of the state constitution, which states that assessments of farms, agricultural lands, standing timber and timberlands, and other open space used for enjoyment of their scenic or natural beauty shall be based on current use. Such lands avoid assessment based on highest and best use or any potential future use. Furthermore, for purposes of determining the value of such lands, the statute prohibits comparing them with parcels that have been converted to nonagricultural, nonforest, or nonopen–space uses within five years of the sale.[192] In 1997, 11,574,810 acres of the state's agricultural, timber, and open space lands were assessed under this law and received an average 67 percent tax reduction.[193]

Additional legislation provides county land planning agencies the necessary authority to promulgate open-space plans in which they identify properties worth protecting. Once identified, the owner of such property may receive a reduction in property taxes.[194] Since 1992, over 3,500 acres in King

County have been enrolled in the program, and property owners have enjoyed a 50 to 90 percent reduction in taxes.[195]

All exemptions and special assessments are allowed as long as the property is maintained in its protected condition. Lands that are converted or otherwise fail to meet the requisite protection character will be subject to changes in tax responsibilities and may even be subject to rollback taxes.[196]

Incentives for Governmental Entities. In addition to the various incentives for private property owners, Washington has enacted numerous laws prescribing the use of conservation futures by governmental bodies. Specifically, the Department of Natural Resources provides funds and the authority to acquire real property rights, including conservation easements, for long-term management.[197] Numerous other municipal organizations, including cities, wildlife agencies, and conservation districts, are similarly authorized and directed to acquire real property interests for open-space preservation purposes, recreational purposes, and endangered species protection.[198] Finally, the state's comprehensive growth management plan encourages the use of "conservation easements and other innovative techniques" to manage growth in rural areas.[199]

Additional Statute

In 1979, the state legislature passed legislation that further strengthened the legitimacy of conservation easements, recognizing "interests in land for purposes of conservation, protection and preservation."[200] There are a few distinctions between the Open Space Tax Act of 1971 and this 1979 real property statute. First, the 1979 statute applies only to interests less than fee simple. Second, the statute provides that the interest may be appurtenant or "in gross." Last, the statute requires that the instruments for conveying such interests follow the form required by state law for all real property conveyances.[201] It is not clear why the legislature felt compelled to create yet another statute addressing conservation easements. It is clear, however, that the state is acutely aware of the need to preserve its open-space lands and continues to act affirmatively to fulfill this goal. It is also clear that the state's laws are facilitating the use of conservation easements. Washington currently has thirty to thirty-five local private land trusts holding conservation easements on approximately 12,000 to 21,000 acres.[202] In addition, governmental bodies and national organizations such as The Nature Conservancy own substantial acreage. These examples illustrate that through comprehensive legislation, Washington State has ensured that the conservation easement is a viable and beneficial instrument in protecting land.

Notes

1. Alaska Uniform Conservation Easement Act ("AUCEA") § 34.17.010(e) (West, 1998).
2. AUCEA §§ 34.17.060(2) and (3).
3. AUCEA § 34.17.060(2).
4. AUCEA § 34.17.010(a).
5. Uniform Conservation Easement Act ("UCEA") § 2(a) (West, 1998); UCEA § 2, Official Comment.
6. AUCEA § 34.17.010(b).
7. UCEA § 2, Official Comment.
8. AUCEA § 34.17.010(c).
9. UCEA § 2(c); UCEA § 2, Official Comment.
10. UCEA § 3(b).
11. AUCEA § 34.17.020(b).
12. AUCEA § 34.17.010(d).
13. UCEA § 2, Official Comment.
14. AUCEA § 34.17.010(e).
15. Interview with Randy Hagenstein of the Alaska chapter of Nature Conservancy, October 12, 1998.
16. AUCEA § 34.17.020(a); AUCEA § 34.17.020(b); UCEA § 3.
17. UCEA § 3, Official Comment.
18. UCEA § 3, Official Comment.
19. AUCEA § 34.17.030; UCEA § 4, Official Comment.
20. AUCEA § 34.17.040(a).
21. AUCEA § 34.17.040(b); UCEA § 5, Official Comment.
22. UCEA § 5, Official Comment.
23. AUCEA § 34.17.040(c).
24. AUCEA § 34.17.050.
25. AUCEA § 34.17.060(1).
26. UCEA § 1(1).
27. AUCEA § 34.17.060(1).
28. UCEA § (1).
29. AUCEA § 34.17.060(2).
30. AUCEA § 34.17.060(3).
31. Hagenstein interview. Approximately 20 percent of the acreage in Alaska is native allotment and thus is not subject to property or estate tax.
32. Hagenstein interview.
33. Hagenstein interview.
34. Hagenstein interview.
35. Hagenstein interview.
36. Hagenstein interview.
37. Hagenstein interview.
38. Hagenstein interview.
39. Hagenstein interview.
40. A.R.S. § 33-272C (1985).

41. A.R.S. § 33-272C (1985).
42. A.R.S. § 33-275.
43. A.R.S. § 33-271.
44. A.R.S. § 33-271.
45. A.R.S. § 33-271.
46. A.R.S. § 33-272C.
47. A.R.S. § 33-274A.
48. A.R.S. § 33-274B.
49. A.R.S. § 33-275.
50. A.R.S. § 33-275.
51. A.R.S. § 33-275.
52. See Thomas S. Barrett and Putnam Livermore, *The Conservation Easement in California 1* (Washington, D.C.: Island Press, 1983).
53. See Bank of America, *Beyond Sprawl: New Patterns of Growth to Fit the New California* (visited October 12, 1998) *http//www.bankamerica.com/community/comm_env_urban1.html>.
54. See Cal. Civ. Code §§ 815–816 (1998).
55. See Barrett and Livermore, 3.
56. See Barrett and Livermore.
57. See Henry Rodegerdts, "Land Trusts and Agricultural Conservation Easements," 13 *Natural Resources and Env't* 336 (1998).
58. See Rodegerdts, 9.
59. See Rodegerdts, 9–10.
60. UCEA (1996 and Supp. 1998).
61. See Cal. Civ. Code § 815.
62. See UCEA, Prefatory Note.
63. Cal. Civ. Code § 815.1.
64. UCEA § 1(1).
65. See Cal. Civ. Code § 815.1; see Cal. Civ. Code § 815.2(b).
66. See UCEA § 2(c).
67. IRC § 170(h)(2)(c) requires restrictions to be in perpetuity to qualify for federal income tax benefits; conservation easements, however, do not have to be in perpetuity to qualify for property taxes advantages in California. See Cal. Rev. & Tax. Code § 421.
68. See Cal. Civ. Code § 815.1.
69. See UCEA § 1(1) (using the phrase "purposes of which include").
70. See UCEA § 1(1).
71. See UCEA § 2(c).
72. See Cal. Civ. Code § 815.2(d).
73. UCEA § 2(d).
74. Cal. Civ. Code § 815.4.
75. Cal. Civ. Code § 815.3(a).
76. See UCEA § 1(2)(ii).
77. Cal. Civ. Code § 815.3(a).
78. See UCEA § 1(2)(i).

79. See Cal. Civ. Code § 815.7(a) such as privity of contract, benefit to a particular estate, or acknowledgment of enforcement in the creating instrument.

80. See Cal. Civ. Code § 815.7(b).

81. Cal. Civ. Code § 815.7(c).

82. See Cal. Civ. Code § 815.7(d).

83. See Barrett and Livermore, 32.

84. See Barrett and Livermore.

85. See Land Trust Alliance, *Land Trust Directory* (Washington, D.C.: Land Trust Alliance, 1998).

86. Haw. Rev. St. §§ 198-1–198-6 (1997).

87. Haw. Rev. St. § 198-1 (1985).

88. Haw. Rev. St. § 198-1 (1997).

89. UCEA § 1(2); Comment to § 1 of the UCEA, 1996 Main Volume.

90. Haw. Rev. St. § 198-3 (1997).

91. Section 2(c) states that "a conservation easement is unlimited in duration unless the agreement otherwise provides."

92. Haw. Rev. St. § 198-2(b) (1997).

93. Haw. Rev. St. § 198-2(a) (1997).

94. Haw. Rev. St. § 198-4 (1997).

95. Haw. Rev. St. § 198-3 (1997).

96. UCEA § 3(a).

97. Comment to § 3 of the UCEA, 1996 Main Volume.

98. Haw. Rev. St. § 198-5(b) (1997).

99. Haw. Rev. St. § 198-5(c) (1997).

100. Haw. Rev. St. § 198-5(c).

101. Haw. Rev. St. § 198-5(d) (1997).

102. The information contained in this section is based on telephone conversations with Fred Rohlfing, director of the Maui Open Space Trust, and Ken Boshay, former director of the now-defunct Kohala Foundation.

103. I.C. §§ 55-2101–2109 (Michie 1997).

104. Idaho was, as of 1997, one of seventeen states to have adopted the UCEA. See Melissa Baldwin, "Conservation Easements: A Viable Tool for Land Preservation," 32 *Land and Water Rev.* 89 (1997): 123 n.127.

105. I.C. § 55-2109.

106. See, e.g., Ala. Const. amend. 543 (1997) (no allowance for conservation easement for property tax assessment); but see, e.g., Mont. Rev. Code Ann. § 76-6-208 (1997); Ore. Rev. Stat. § 271.785 (1997) (valuation for property tax purposes reflects easement use restrictions).

107. I.C. § 55-2107. Idaho does, however, permit the state to hold a conservation easement otherwise acquired. See Constance M. Callahan, "Warp and Weft: Weaving a Blanket of Protection for Cultural Resources on Private Property," *Envtl. L.* 23 (1993): 1323, 1346.

108. I.C. § 55-2102(4). Largely, these provisions comport with constitutional prohibitions against uncompensated takings of private property. See, e.g., *Lucas v. South Carolina Coastal Council,* 505 U.S. 1003 (1992). Partial takings, however,

such as an easement that leaves a property owner with at least some residual value, are not necessarily prohibited under the Constitution or federal case law; thus, in this respect, Idaho goes an extra step toward protecting the property rights of private landowners. See id.

109. See I.C. § 55-2101(1).
110. I.C. § 55-2105.
111. I.C. § 55-2105(1).
112. I.C. § 55-2105(2).
113. Chris Herrman, western regional director, Land Trust Alliance, October 12, 1998; Carol Brown, U.S. Forest Service, October 13, 1998.
114. Land Trust Alliance, Western Region, 1998 Census.
115. Idaho is comprised of approximately 53.5 million acres and is the eleventh largest state in the United States.
116. Mike Whitfield, director, Teton Regional Land Trust, October 13, 1998.
117. Idaho is populated by about 12 people per square mile on average, compared with California, for example, which is inundated by about 202 people per square mile.
118. See, e.g., Ala. Const. amend. 543 (1997) (no allowance for conservation easement for property tax assessment); but see, e.g., Mont. Rev. Code Ann. § 76-6-208 (1997); Ore. Rev. Stat. § 271.785 (1997) (valuation for property tax purposes reflects easement use restrictions).
119. Carol Brown, U.S. Forest Service, October 13, 1998.
120. Carol Brown, board member, Wood River Land Trust, October 13, 1998 (also of the U.S. Forest Service).
121. I.C. § 55-2102(4); Twin Falls County Farm Bureau.
122. Montana Code Annotated (M.C.A.) § 76-6-204 (1997).
123. Dye Knight, "Attorney's Guide to Montana Conservation Easements," 42 Mont. L. Rev. (1981): 21.
124. UCEA §1(1)(1981).
125. Montana Code Annotated (M.C.A.) § 76-6-204 (1997).
126. M.C.A. § 76-6-104(5)(1997).
127. M.C.A. § 76-6-201 (1997).
128. UCEA §1(1)(ii)(1981).
129. M.C.A. § 76-6-202 (1997).
130. UCEA § 2(c)(1981).
131. Internal Revenue Code § 170(h)(2)(C)(1997).
132. UCEA § 3(a)(3)(1981).
133. M.C.A. § 76-6-211(1) (1997).
134. M.C.A. § 76-6-210(2)(1997).
135. M.C.A. § 76-6-205 (1997).
136. I.R.C. 170(h)(5)(B)(i)(1997).
137. I.R.C. §170(h)(5)(B)(ii)(1997).
138. Thanks to John Wilson of the Montana Land Reliance, who provided essential information for this article.
139. Nevada's statutes 11.390–11.440.

140. Interview with Bill Whitney, Washoe County Open Space Program, September 1998.
141. Whitney, interview, September 1998.
142. Whitney, interview, September 1998.
143. Interview with Alicia Reban, Nevada Land Conservancy, October 1998.
144. Whitney, interview, September 1998.
145. Interview with Amy Hellman, American Land Conservancy, October 1998.
146. Whitney, interview, September 1998.
147. 1967 Or. Laws ch. 318, cited in "Note: Conservation Easements in Oregon: Abuses and Solutions," 14 *Envtl. L.* 555 at 559 n31.
148. 1975 Or. Laws ch. 511, cited in "Note: Conservation Easements in Oregon: Abuses and Solutions," 14 *Envtl. L.* 555 at 560 n39.
149. ULA Cons Easement §§ 1–6 (West 1998).
150. ORS 271.735 (1997).
151. ULA Cons. Easement Ref.s, Prefatory Note, 1996 Main Volume (West 1998).
152. ULA Cons. Easement Ref.s, Prefatory Note.
153. ORS 271.715 (1997).
154. ULA Cons. Easement § 1, Comment, 1996 Main Vol. (West 1998).
155. ULA Cons. Easement Ref.s, Prefatory Note, 1996 Main Vol. (West 1998).
156. ORS 271.725(1) (1997).
157. The Willamette River Greenway Program. ORS 390.310-390.368 (1997). The Oregon Scenic Waterways System ORS 390.805-390.925 (1997).
158. R. Pinto, Director of Land Protection, Oregon office of The Nature Conservancy, personal communication, October 26, 1998.
159. ORS 271.715(2) (1997).
160. ORS 271.725 (1997).
161. ORS 390.314(1) (1997).
162. ORS 390.332(1),(2) (1997).
163. ORS 390.332(2) (1997).
164. ORS 390.332(2) (1997).
165. R. Pinto, director of Land Protection, Oregon office of The Nature Conservancy, personal communication, October 26, 1998.
166. Codified at ORS 390.805-390.925, ORS 390.815 (1997).
167. ORS 390.805(4) (1997).
168. ORS 390.845(6), (7) (1997).
169. R. Pinto, director of Land Protection, Oregon office of The Nature Conservancy, personal communication of October 26, 1998.
170. R. Pinto, communication of October 26, 1998.
171. R. Pinto, communication of October 26, 1998.
172. R. Pinto, communication of October 26, 1998.
173. Wash. Rev. Code Ann. § 84.34.010 (West, WESTLAW through 1998).
174. *Van Buren v. Miller,* 22 Wash. App. 836, 592 P.2d 671 (1979).
175. Wash. Rev. Code Ann. §§ 84.34.010–920 (West, WESTLAW through 1998).
176. Wash. Rev. Code Ann. §§ 83.34.200–260 (West, WESTLAW through 1998).
177. Wash. Rev. Code Ann. § 83.43.210, government agencies include state or federal

agencies, cities or counties, metropolitan municipal corporations, and metropolitan park districts.

178. Wash. Rev. Code Ann. § 84.34.220.
179. See 26 U.S.C.A. § 501(c)(3) (West, WESTLAW through 1998).
180. Wash. Rev. Code Ann. § 84.34.250.
181. Wash. Rev. Code Ann. §84.34.210.
182. Wash. Rev. Code Ann. §84.34.220.
183. Wash. Rev. Code Ann. § 84.34.220.
184. Wash. Rev. Code Ann. § 84.34.220.
185. Wash. Rev. Code Ann. §§ 84.34.230–240.
186. Linda Ashton, "Groups, Government Works to Rescue Northwest Farmland from Urban Sprawl," *The News Tribune*, November 9, 1997, p. 4; available in 1997 WL 14535382.
187. *Louthan v. King County*, 94 Wash. 2.d 422, 617 P.2d 977 (1980).
188. Wash. Rev. Code Ann. § 84.36.500 (West, WESTMATE through 1998).
189. Wash. Rev. Code Ann. § 84.34.260 (West, WESTLAW through 1998).
190. Wash. Rev. Code Ann. § 84.33.27 (West, WESTLAW through 1998).
191. Wash. Rev. Code Ann. § 83.34.010.
192. Wash. Rev. Code Ann. § 84.36.500 (West, WESTLAW through 1998).
193. Linda Ashton, supra.
194. Wash. Rev. Code Ann. § 84.34.055 (West, WESTMATE through 1998).
195. Linda Ashton, supra.
196. Wash. Rev. Code Ann. § 84.34.300 (West, WESTLAW through 1998).
197. Wash. Rev. Code Ann. § 43.30.115, § 79.66 (West, WESTLAW through 1998).
198. See Wash. Rev. Code Ann. § 43.51.920, § 43.51.950, § 39.33.060, § 77.12.655 (West, WESTLAW through 1998).
199. Wash. Rev. Code Ann. § 36.70.070 (West, WESTLAW through 1998).
200. Wash. Rev. Code Ann. § 64.04.130 (West, WESTLAW through 1998).
201. Wash. Rev. Code Ann. § 64.04.130.
202. Land Trust Alliance, *National Directory of Conservation Land Trusts* (Washington, D.C.: Land Trust Alliance, 1995); Land Trust Alliance, National Land Trust Census (1998).

Chapter 23

☜ ☞

The Power of Conservation Easements: Protecting Agricultural Land in Montana

John B. Wright

Montana is where the myth of a pristine American West now resides. The expansive, spectacular landscape of the state is attracting growing numbers of immigrants wishing to inhabit the *idea* of Montana, that of an intact and elegant place, one that stays unspoiled as the rest of America is inexorably altered.[1] Instead, these pilgrims are placing intense development pressure on an actual geography that seldom matches their Edenic dreams. Lost open space is the main geographic symptom of this cultural transformation.

Sixty percent of the surface of Montana is privately owned. In western and central Montana, however, public ownership dominates, the federal and state governments owning as much as 85 percent, a landownership pattern that has created a unique challenge for conservationists. Although extensive public ownership protects a large part of the state from subdivision, such ownership focuses an array of powerful, often conflicting demands on the remainder that is in private hands. The greatest residential development pressure is found in river valleys and broad plains at the foot of the Rocky Mountains. Over 75 percent of the state's big game winter range and waterfowl habitats, day-to-day open-space and recreational areas, historic sites, and archeological treasures are found here.

Such development pressure on Montana's privately owned lands is not new. By 1973, over 500,000 acres of ecologically important agricultural land had been subdivided into tracts of less than 40 acres in size. Waves of lifestyle migrants quickly bought up many of these parcels and erected houses. In some counties, over 95 percent of all lots were being created without any land use planning oversight. Attempting to halt unplanned development, the Montana legislature enacted a Subdivision and Platting Act in 1974. This measure, however, turned out to be extremely weak and contained numerous loopholes. Environmentally concerned citizens began searching for alternative tools. Conservation easements were soon "discovered" and lauded as the state's saving grace. It would be years for this perception to become reality.

The Montana Land Reliance (MLR) was formed in 1976 as a statewide nonprofit land trust with a mission "to provide permanent protection for private lands that are ecologically significant for agricultural production, fish and wildlife habitat, and open space."[2] The goal was to prevent the subdivision of Montana's agricultural land base. Initially, Bill Long, Barbara Rusmore, and the other "pioneers" of the MLR, sought out diverse methods for carrying out the mission, including making cautious attempts to improve the economic viability of farming and ranching. The trust's approach, however, soon distilled to doing one thing extremely well: negotiating and receiving donated conservation easements. Today, this is the MLR's technique of choice.

The initial responses of Montana landowners to conservation easements ranged from loud opposition to bored disinterest. The MLR believed that unexpressed support for their mission existed, but only if they followed an unwaveringly apolitical course. Sides were not taken on environmental issues. Opponents were not vilified. Kitchen table conversations and grassroots networking were quietly used to build friendships around the state. In 1977, the MLR received their first easement, a 2,000-acre ranch embracing a long reach of the Big Hole River. This project made the tool visible in the agricultural community. More and more ranchers and farmers started coming forward to listen. Many found an ally in the trust: a group that could provide tangible help in dealing with income and estate tax problems. Some landowners chose to conserve their places. Over time, this straightforward, voluntary process brought astonishing results.

Today, the MLR is the most accomplished local and regional land trust in the United States. It holds 275 donated easements covering 278,643 acres of ecologically important agricultural land, more than any other land trust in the nation. More than half of this total acreage has been protected since 1996. In 1997 alone, the group received fifty-one easements totaling 53,000 acres.

During negotiations, MLR's personnel recognize the need for flexibility in easement design but strive for clear, unambiguous language in easement deeds. As a result, land use restrictions are spelled out in remarkably similar ways in all MLR documents. Although specific terms vary from one deed to another, their focus is to eliminate or substantially reduce residential development on particular parcels. Occasionally, additional housing is allowed to provide for the landowner's children or to provide the option of future income, but easement restrictions require that these houses be carefully sited within environmentally capable and visually screened "building envelopes."

Often such structures must be clustered in the existing ranch headquarters area. Commercial and industrial uses are typically prohibited, except for fly fishing or dude ranching enterprises. Destructive land use activities such as mining, clear-cutting forests, and stream channelization and the construction of telecommunications towers, solid-waste disposal sites, and new roads are routinely prohibited. Selective timber harvesting may be allowed to satisfy on-ranch needs, provided it is carried out according to previously established logging practices.

In their conservation easements, the MLR does not seek to restrict agricultural practices except in areas where there is severe overgrazing. Even here, the organization relies on annual monitoring visits and cordial, cooperative relationships to solve problems.[3] The group's intention is to use easements to *support* agriculture and not to interfere unduly with the daily management of the ranch. Given the abundance of wildlife on most working ranches in Montana, the MLR seldom requires a rancher to alter current practices. No attempt is made to further any sort of "green" or "organic" social agenda, and thus ranchers may be permitted to apply agrochemicals and control predators in a responsible manner. Genuine respect for the historic stewardship of private landowners is the fundamental tenet of how this trust operates. The MLR's philosophy is that the best "enforcer" of the easement terms is a caring, well-informed landowner. Accordingly, the trust gathers extensive and precise data as an easement is negotiated. Reports focus on qualifying the property for tax deductions and on providing baseline ecological data to enable the trust to assess ecosystem health, map existing improvements, and establish photo points for annual monitoring purposes. This process has worked well. The MLR has never had to go to court to enforce the terms of an easement.

Most of the MLR's easements arise from word-of-mouth praise for the trust's goals, skill in designing workable easements, knowledge of tax and estate planning, and a consistent pro-agriculture stance. The MLR has a strong reputation as an ally to farmers and ranchers, a trust one can turn to when estate tax and other issues arise. Wealthy newcomers also find support in the trust's environmental ethics, businesslike manner, and familiarity with income tax matters. Such an inclusive operating style largely explains the robustness of the MLR's easement program.

The MLR uses easements both opportunistically and strategically. In the early years, there was a strong need to protect qualified projects wherever they appeared so as to build credibility. As the MLR's accomplishments grew, however, it began to target Montana's key valley ecosystems in an effort to conserve entire landscapes rather than isolated remnants. Today, the "neighborhood conservation" projects around Yellowstone and Glacier National Parks and in the Boulder/Stillwater, Smith, Blackfoot, Swan, Nine Mile, and Bitter-root Valleys are outstanding examples of this approach (Photograph 23.1).

In the greater Yellowstone ecosystem, the MLR works with the Greater Yellowstone Coalition, The Nature Conservancy, the Gallatin Land Trust, and the Jackson Hole Land Trust to create buffers, corridors, and linkages to maintain the biological integrity and scenic beauty of Yellowstone National Park, the world's first national park.[4] The trust has acquired easements on 115,000 acres of lower-elevation private lands in the valleys surrounding the park (Photograph 23.2), protecting over 53,000 acres through twenty-three easements in the Madison Valley "neighborhood" alone. These lands are an ecological extension of the park, providing critical habitat for elk, deer, moose, bison, grizzly bear, wolves, and migrating waterfowl. These easements create corridors of wildlife habitat, linking private ranchland with public federal national parks, forests, and wilderness areas and state wildlife management sites. Donors of the easements, designed to maintain current land use, range from multigenerational Montana ranch families to wealthy, lifestyle migrants in love with fly fishing.

Individual easements serve several of the conservation purposes identified

Photograph 23.1. Blackfoot River conservation easement corridor. Easements are held by both The Nature Conservancy (TNC) and the Montana Land Reliance (MLR).
Photo credit: Jack Wright

Photograph 23.2. Views of Paradise Valley ranchland conservation easement.
Easements are held by both TNC and MLR.
Photo credit: Jack Wright

in state and federal legislation.[5] The MLR now protects over 537 miles of
stream and river frontage habitats. Some 41,000 easement acres are used as
hay meadow, cropland, or range for livestock. About 237,000 acres of range-
and forestlands have been saved from development. Nearly 103,000 acres of
elk habitat are now secured. The unique beauty that abounds on such protected lands can only be imagined by those who have not visited Montana
(Photograph 23.3).

   The growth in the size and accomplishments of the MLR offers the following points for conservation easement practitioners:

 1. Organizations negotiating, holding, and enforcing donated conservation
    easements need to establish a clear mission. The MLR established a sin-
    gular ambition—to receive donated conservation easements on ecologi-
    cally important agricultural land—and its ambitious current five-year
    plan reflects its confidence in the future of conservation easements.[6] The
    MLR has never purchased development rights, arguing that to do so
    would undermine the donated easement program and set up a false eco-
    nomic expectation in landowners. Fee acquisitions remain rare, although
    the trust will occasionally buy property at imminent risk from develop-
    ment or provide equity-based operating loans to aid ranchers to stay in
    business. These arrangements are, however, temporary. The trust quickly

Photograph 23.3. Montana's unique beauty. Mission Valley conservation easement held by MLR.
Photo credit: Jack Wright

finds buyers for land it purchases, buyers who are willing to donate conservation easements over the land to the trust.

2. The success of any land trust depends on the relationship between the landowner and the trust. This relationship is founded on the organization's people skills and a respect for the landowner. The MLR is a field-based land trust that sends its staff to meet at the landowner's home, preferring that negotiations for conservation easements be personal and as informal as possible. A fence-line chat is preferred to an office meeting, thus reinforcing the voluntary nature of easement work and building long-term friendships. It also creates the best marketing device of all: a local landowner willing to introduce the MLR to his or her neighbors.

3. MLR procedures are streamlined and extremely well organized. All easement documents are standardized to the maximum extent possible. Title reports, State Historic Preservation Office searches, baseline inventories, appraisals, and other tasks are completed rapidly due to the group's extensive experience.

4. Negotiating conservation easements may not be inexpensive. Success requires skilled, well-paid personnel. In 1997, the trust employed a staff of twelve spread out among their Helena, Bigfork, and Billings offices and operated on a budget of $478,973. In addition, the trust maintains two funds, a $2.5 million land protection fund and a $1.6 million education

and research fund. Income from the land protection fund is used to defend and protect lands already under easement and for stewardship projects, easement monitoring, and completing easement with donors who cannot afford to pay transaction costs. Income from the education and research fund is used to educate the public about the use and benefits of conservation easements and other land use and protection matters.

The MLR is very competitive about the easements it seeks to acquire, and critics point to instances of being cut out of deals. Although the MLR has on occasion captured a coveted easement client from another trust, it generally strives to coordinate its actions with local land conservation organizations. Occasional turf conflicts are inevitable between a statewide group such as the MLR and smaller local and regional trusts, however. Some have complained about the MLR's fixation on easement acreage figures. Although the MLR does stress its tote board, it is hard to find fault with the quality of lands it protects. The trust is extremely adept at negotiating conservation easements and is envied by other land trusts not only in Montana but throughout the nation. Conservationists in Montana have solid respect for the group's accomplishments and indicate that it does not much matter who gets the job done as long as it gets done.

Some criticism surfaces about the assembly line nature of MLR easements,

Photograph 23.4. Big Sky country.
Photo credit: J. A. Gustanski

in particular the drafting of terms before baseline data are fully compiled. The end of the year rush hits all land trusts hard, and only time will tell whether oversights have been made during the crafting of easement restrictions. This sort of problem is the byproduct of accomplishment; the preparation of fifty easements a year demands using standard documents and routine procedures.

The achievements of the MLR demonstrate the power of conservation easements in protecting ecologically rich agricultural lands in the American West. A fortunate melding of skills and aspirations has resulted in extraordinary, bounteous success, yet beyond all this tallying, an emotional connection to the land still lies at the heart of the MLR's easement work. Rancher Richard Hammond of Fishtail offered this reminder: "By gifting a conservation easement to the Montana Land Reliance, our family has the opportunity to maintain our heritage—the legacy of hard work and independent spirit in the wide open spaces of Big Sky country" (Photograph 23.4).

Notes

1. During the 1990s, Montana has grown from 799,000 residents to nearly 900,000, a 12.5 percent increase and a fifty-five-year doubling time. One-quarter of this growth is from California in-migrants alone.
2. Montana Land Reliance brochure (Sept. 1998).
3. A large measure of ranching knowledge goes into monitoring and enforcing any easement, such as knowing that drought years sometimes bring grazing impacts that are reversed by a return to normal precipitation levels. A large measure of this kind of ranching knowledge goes into monitoring and enforcing any easement.
4. The Nature Conservancy is a national land trust whose mission is to preserve plants, animals, and natural communities that represent the diversity of life on Earth by protecting the lands and waters they need to survive. The Greater Yellowstone Coalition works to protect the greater Yellowstone ecosystem, a vast array of public and private lands that include Yellowstone and Grand Teton National Parks. The Gallatin and Jackson Hole Land Trusts work to preserve open space and the scenic, ranching, and wildlife values of their given regions by assisting landowners who wish to protect their land in perpetuity.
5. Montana Code Annotated (M.C.A.) § 76-6-204 (1997); UCEA § 1(1)(1981).
6. By 2002, it expects to negotiate easements on an additional 250,000 acres, including more than 75,000 acres in the greater Yellowstone ecosystem and another 400 miles of stream and river frontage. In Montana, 23,000 agricultural landowners control nearly all the private land in the state. The median age of these people is 60. By 2020, as much as one-third of Montana's private land will have gone through estate proceedings. The MLR envisions using easements to protect a sizable portion of these lands.

Chapter 24

❦ ❦

Saving Special Places: How a Land Trust Used Emerging Technology to Address Conservation Priorities

Brian Stark

The city of San Luis Obispo, California, has adopted the goal of creating a greenbelt around the city; a ring of undeveloped open space surrounding the built environment (Figure 24.1). The purpose of the greenbelt is to retain a buffer between San Luis Obispo and its neighboring communities while preserving the community's small-town character. Because the greenbelt area is outside the city's planning boundary, the open space program will rely on the voluntary participation of landowners. One method the city will use to secure the greenbelt is land acquisition, either by purchasing fee title to land or through conservation or agricultural easements.

Acquisition programs require both a financing mechanism and a process to evaluate conservation priorities. The city council retained the Land Conservancy of San Luis Obispo County to assist in setting conservation priorities and formed a separate committee to investigate funding options to support acquisitions.[1] The priority-setting process developed by the conservancy was outlined in a publicly released report entitled "Saving Special Places: A Study of Resource Values in the San Luis Obispo Greenbelt."[2]

The priority-setting process established through this study is based on property ownership, willing landowners, environmental and scenic resources, and community values listed in the city's General Plan. The city of San Luis Obispo has embraced this methodology and used it to justify several recent acquisitions. Members of the community have also accepted this process and use the information provided to weigh conservation opportunities. This chapter describes the methods that the conservancy used to evaluate open-space protection priorities.

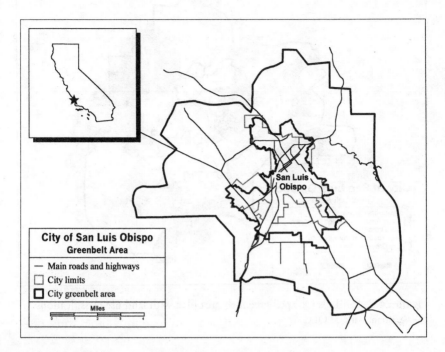

Figure 24.1. Regional map with greenbelt area boundaries.
Credit: Brian Stark, San Luis Obispo Land Conservancy (SLOLC)

Land Ownership Inventory

The Land Conservancy began this project by mapping current property ownership patterns in the greenbelt area.[3] This process assisted in identifying key landowners and understanding development trends in the greenbelt area. This map was also useful in contacting landowners and identifying those interested in conveying their property. Both public and private property were mapped, with particular attention paid to lands that were already protected by land use restrictions and conservation easements and to large areas under single ownership, which offer unique conservation opportunities. Through this process, it was discovered that over one-half (57 percent) of the greenbelt was already protected for the near future (Figure 24.2). The conservancy was then able to focus conservation efforts on the remaining lands.

One important characteristic of greenbelt ownership is that very few landowners own a large portion of the land. Roughly, fourteen people (Figure 24.3) own 55 percent of the greenbelt area. The long-term success of the greenbelt program will require close working relationships with these people.

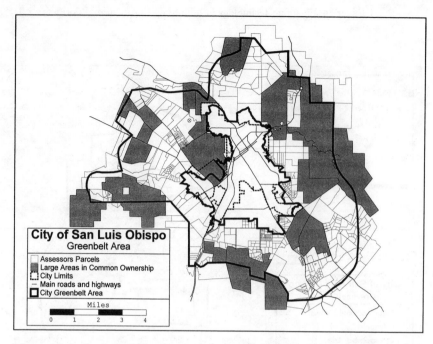

Figure 24.2. San Luis Obispo's greenbelt area plan with land use classifications.
Credit: Brian Stark, SLOLC

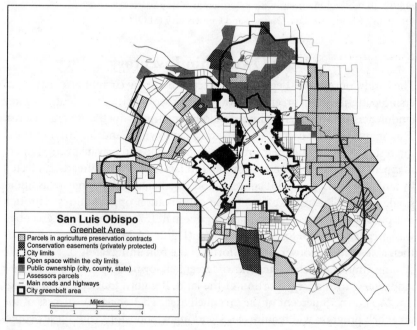

Figure 24.3. Landownership in greenbelt area.
Credit: Brian Stark, SLOLC

Each of these landowners was contacted individually, and two of the fourteen landowners were involved in acquisitions made under this program. In addition, constructive dialogue has been opened with several others.

The land ownership inventory revealed important information for targeting the search for conservation opportunities. The next steps were to find voluntary partners and assess the conservation values of available lands.

The Process: Identifying Landowner Interest and Community Values

Following the ownership inventory process, the conservancy set out in search of landowners who would become our voluntary partners. Landowners were contacted through mailed surveys, community meetings, news articles, and workshops hosted by the conservancy.

Community Survey

The city parks director mailed a letter to 183 of the 485 private landowners in the greenbelt area, asking their interest in conveying title to their property or a conservation easement to the city. Included in the survey were landowners whose property was likely to contain open-space resources and was not currently protected.[4] Excluded from the mailing were those whose lots were committed to development or have little conservation potential.[5] Also excluded were landowners whose property was already encumbered with a conservation easement.

Fifty landowners answered the survey, a 28 percent return rate. Twenty-seven indicated that they were not interested in participating, seventeen responded that they might be interested but would like more information about conservation easements before they decided their level of interest, and six indicated an interest in participating but still wanted more information regarding easements. Those who were not interested and those who did not return the survey were removed from the process. Those requesting more information about conservation easements were invited to a workshop held by the Land Conservancy.

In addition to the mailed survey, Land Conservancy staff attended several public and private meetings with organized community groups to describe the greenbelt program and to solicit interested landowners. Several additional landowners stepped forward following these meetings to participate in the program. Finally, a prominent newspaper article outlined the program and lead to two additional landowners' participation.

As a result of these efforts, ten parcels where the landowner was interested in participation were identified as currently available. Each landowner then met with Land Conservancy staff to evaluate the options of fee acquisition and conservation easements.

Community Values Assessment

During the public meetings and several public festivals, members of the public were asked to mark maps for areas they considered to be most desirable for open space enjoyment and permanent protection. Newspaper articles also brought citizens into the Land Conservancy office to mark maps. This information was later considered in the resource evaluation and used by city officials to gage public values on certain landscapes.[6]

Resource Mapping

The next step was to provide information that would help city officials in deciding which parcels should be protected, considering the city's limited funding. The San Luis Obispo General Plan lists resources the community wants to protect with a greenbelt, and the conservancy began by mapping as many of these resources as possible. Evaluation of the available parcels with respect to these resources and development of a method to organize this vast amount of information followed. The conservancy used a geographic information system (GIS) to organize the necessary information, creating a map and database with which to view entire landscapes as well as individual parcels. It is important to note that the computer analysis was not intended as the sole determinant of acquisition priority; rather, it is a tool to help city leaders understand their conservation choices and provide a method to fairly assess properties with a consistently applied methodology.

Identifying Resources

The first step in assembling information was to clarify which resources the city considered important. This step was made simple thanks to a comprehensive resource list contained in the city's General Plan. Some of these resources, such as stream corridors, are well understood, and community members relate to them. Other listed resources, such as "rural character," were more problematic and posed difficulties in mapping. This mapping project therefore is weighted toward those resources that can be definitively located geographically.

Information concerning resource location and specific resource attributes were then sought for mapping and analysis. Note that information was not available for each listed resource. This analysis concentrates on the data that were available.

Some resource information was already available in a digital form and thus could be readily used in a GIS analysis.[7] Other resources were mapped by converting paper maps into a digital format through a process called digitizing.[8] Three specific resources, wildlife corridors, historically significant areas, and scenic gateways into the city, have not been mapped locally. These resources were added to the final resource database at a later stage.

Mapping Methods

Natural and cultural resources are normally mapped as separate maps (layers), one for each resource. GIS technology lets one combine the maps and view them together; creating a more holistic view of greenbelt resources. It would take many maps, however, to describe all the resources described in the open-space element. A map combining all these resources would look rather confusing (Figure 24.4). Too much information can therefore pose a problem when analyzing multiple resources. To organize this information into a usable form, the conservancy aggregated the resource information from the many individual map layers into a single layer that depicted landscapes (Figure 24.5). This method is referred to as a "landscape unit" approach.[9]

Once the landscape units were complete, each individual resource data layer was overlaid over these units and the acreage of intersection was calcu-

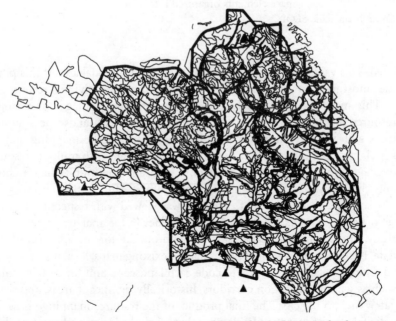

Figure 24.4. Map reflecting confusion created by individual layers of information. *Credit:* Brian Stark, SLOLC

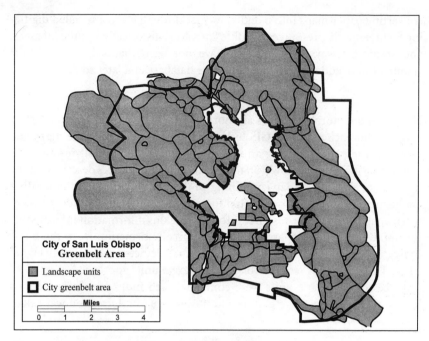

Figure 24.5. Open-space elements organized into a landscape unit map.
Credit: Brian Stark, SLOLC

lated. This value was then placed in a landscape unit database. At this point, the landscape units could be queried for one or more individual resources.

This mapping approach has several important advantages over single-resource mapping. First, the landscape units represent landscape scale features with which community members can identify. The mapping method kept landscapes intact, rather than fragmenting them with multiple resource overlays. When it came time to acquire land, the community had a choice between known landscapes such as the "South St. Hill" or the "airport area." The second advantage is that each unit was viewed with respect to the same set of resource layers. This ensured consistency in the analytical phase of the study. Finally, the landscape scale was appropriate for the addition of new data. Because some resource values had no existing maps, local historians and wildlife experts were enlisted to code each landscape unit for certain values, such as wildlife migration corridors, historically significant areas, and scenic gateways into the city. The final product of the resource mapping phase was a digital map of greenbelt landscapes that was linked to a database describing the listed resources that could be found in each. In addition, the GIS technol-

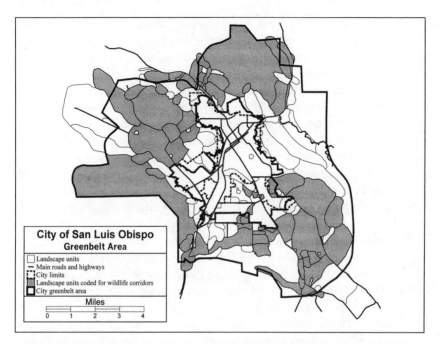

Figure 24.6. Greenbelt area map reflecting landscape units coded for wildlife corridors.
Credit: Brian Stark, SLOLC

ogy allowed questions to be asked of the model and the answers displayed graphically. For example, one might ask for all the landscapes containing wildlife habitat and migration corridors, and the computer will prepare a map illustrating these landscapes (Figure 24.6).

Property Evaluation

The final step in the process was to evaluate the resource information in a way that would help city officials prioritize acquisition opportunities and make choices between available properties. The evaluation methods used information from the landscape database to evaluate the available parcels.[10] The report only presented the evaluation information for the available parcels.[11]

The conservancy chose not to assign numerical rankings to landscapes because there was no common scale among the natural and cultural resources it was evaluating for comparing their relative values. In addition, there were significant policy issues to be decided regarding the value of a wildlife area, for example, as opposed to a strictly scenic resource. Rather, the analysis was presented using three different interpretations of the resource information that included consideration of various resource types. These were the number of resources, the importance of the resources, and the potential for valuable resource restoration.

The first rating was the number of analyzed resources that could be found within the landscape unit, called the magnitude method of evaluation. When acquiring land, the city may wish to maximize the number of resources they protect. The first product was a map of landscapes ranked in four scales of magnitude.[12] Once complete, the magnitude value was applied to the available parcels (see note 9). This method is important but rather simplistic. There may be lands that have very few resources, but those resources may be very rare or unique. These resources would be overlooked in the magnitude model, so complementary methods were also applied.

The importance evaluation complements the magnitude evaluation. The rating was on a scale of one to five. The importance of an area is based on a number of subjective variables, including the quality of resources, restoration potential, proximity to protected lands, unique views, scale of features, presence of historic features, input received at public meetings, and threat of development. Landscape areas containing parcels with a potential for linking existing open space, areas containing rare, unique, or historic resources, and areas receiving high marks for importance from the public were given higher ratings. Ratings were also higher for areas containing important resources that were under a current threat of development. The importance rating for the landscape unit was then applied to the available parcels, and the parcels were checked for consistency with the importance value. The result was a map of available parcels ranked in one of five importance categories.

The importance evaluation includes some degree of subjectivity. This point was clearly explained in the documentation provided to the city and the public, and the importance ratings were not disputed by any parties. Like other land trusts, the conservancy spends a great deal of time getting to know the surrounding lands and the people that live on and around them. All the information collected routinely regarding conservation opportunities in the community made its perspective on landscape and parcel importance easy to justify.

The final evaluation method was resource potential, which was applied only at the parcel level and which consisted of notes regarding restoration potential on the available lands. This preliminary research was undertaken in the event that a degraded parcel was offered at a low price and restoration of the parcel could result in a valuable piece of the greenbelt. The resource potential notes were presented in the text of the report rather than in map form.

Results

The process of identifying open space values and acquisition opportunities involved an inventory of land ownership, mapping of important resources and community values, and development of an evaluation system. The three evaluation methods provided ratings for the number of resources, the importance of those resources, and a preliminary investigation of restoration opportunities for the ten available parcels in the San Luis Obispo greenbelt. The information developed sparked a lively public debate over which of the parcels were the best acquisition opportunities.

Following several city council study sessions, the city decided to begin negotiations with four landowners. They chose to work with multiple landowners for two reasons. First, in case negotiations failed with any of them, the city would still have other landowners who were in an advanced level of the negotiating process. Another reason was to keep landowners from raising prices during this phase by maintaining the possibility of competition for limited resources.

Negotiations led to two acquisitions. One was fee title acquisition of a 90-acre parcel on the side of a mountain on the edge of town. The mountain is the primary community landmark and can be seen from the entire town. The parcel also had seventy lots that could have been developed, and it adjoined protected open space. Prior to conveying fee title, the landowner conveyed a conservation easement over the land to the Land Conservancy to ensure that it would be preserved. This acquisition was very popular, and the land is now in unimproved public use.

The second acquisition was a conservation easement over 1,500 acres of open space in the outer greenbelt. This easement protects an entire subbasin of an important watershed and includes oak woodlands habitat, habitat for numerous wildlife species, and two rare plant species. This acquisition was less popular in the greater community, probably because it lies out of view for much of the community. Those interested in wildlife habitat preservation, however, found this easement to be very valuable.

Since the initial acquisitions, the city's greenbelt acquisition program has continued, as has the use of the landscape model. One additional property that links previously existing open space areas and provides for public use has been secured. The city is also in negotiations with four other landowners. The city has retained the Land Conservancy to assist in acquisitions, and each candidate parcel is reviewed in the model described above. Each time a greenbelt parcel becomes available, it can be quickly checked for which landscape it lies in and the relative value of the landscape. Since 1995, the program has preserved 1,670 acres.

Notes

1. The Land Conservancy of San Luis Obispo County is a private, nonprofit land trust with a mission to preserve open space and lands with sensitive environmental resources located in San Luis Obispo County, California. Incorporated in 1984, the Land Conservancy has been active in preservation and restoration of pine forests, endangered species habitats, coastal dunes, riparian corridors, and rapidly fragmenting agricultural lands. The conservancy has three full-time and three part-time staff with backgrounds in land-use planning, landscape architecture, real estate transactions, biology, hydrology, and geographic information systems technology.

2. *Saving Special Places: A Study of Resource Values in the San Luis Obispo Greenbelt Area* (San Luis Obispo, Calif.: The Land Conservancy of San Luis Obispo County, June 1995).

3. Mapping for this project was undertaken on computers using Atlas GIS software. A geographic information system (GIS) is a powerful mapping tool that is becoming more available to the nonprofit sector and the public at large. A GIS allows features on maps to be linked to databases (attribute information) for analysis. Conversely, a GIS allows attribute information from one or more databases to be mapped graphically. Through the use of GIS software, graphically mapped ownership parcels were "linked" to the county tax assessor's database. The assessor's database provided information about property ownership, development level, agricultural preservation contracts (a promise to keep land in agriculture in exchange for tax reduction), and improved values all at the click of a mouse.

4. A list of these resources is presented in the city's General Plan.

5. "Committed to development" refers to lots that were already mostly developed (information from county assessor's database and field inspections). Limited conservation potential refers to those lots that were surrounded by development and not consistent with the formation of a continuous greenbelt and those that were smaller than 1 acre. In cases where a small yet important resource was known to exist on a small parcel, the owners were contacted.

6. The budget given for the project did not allow for expansive public input. It is recommended that more public meetings are held and that efforts be made to include a more diverse cross section of the community in determining community values. Many communities use questionnaires and community visioning processes to determine values. The model described in this chapter can easily accommodate this information.

7. Gathering digital data for a project of this type can be challenging. Although a great deal of data were available, the data came in a variety of formats. There are many different GIS programs in use today, and each GIS software package stores data differently. Thus, much of the information needed to be converted for use in Atlas GIS. Conversion between program formats can be tedious, but it has become much simpler in the last few years.

8. Digitizing refers to assigning geographic coordinates to a graphic image so that it can be displayed in the same geographic space with other digitized maps for an

area. Digitizing can be done with a digitizing tablet and puck. The feature to be digitized is traced over the target feature with the puck, while the coordinate grid in the tablet assigns real geographic coordinates.

9. Land Conservancy staff through extensive recognizance of the greenbelt area prepared the landscape unit map. Homogenous landscape units were drawn onto U.S. Geological Survey topographical quadrangle maps and later digitized for use in the GIS. The landscape units were delineated by consideration of their "sense of place," a term long used by geographers to refer to the unique set of tangible and intangible elements that determine the "feel" of a place. Draft copies of this map were circulated among local resource experts to confirm the applicability of these units for resource analysis.

10. Due to possible inaccuracies encountered by aggregating data into different areal units, it is not entirely accurate to apply the value of a landscape unit *directly* to an assessor parcel. For example, if a landscape unit contains a riparian corridor, it cannot be assumed that every assessor parcel within that unit has a riparian corridor. This statistical problem was mitigated to a large extent by site visits and map confirmation of resource locations for the available parcels.

11. We concentrated on available parcels to avoid placing values on land that was not available because there was concern among landowners that a property's value might be affected by its listing as desirable for open space. The first concern was to respect the privacy of landowners who were not interested in the program

12. Any assessment of priorities based on a quantitative measure is dependent on which information is inventoried. If, for example, the database contained twelve columns of data on wildlife and only one on scenic quality, the results would be heavily weighted in favor of wildlife values. This situation is largely the case with this study.

Chapter 25

Neighborhood Conservation Easements at Entrance Mountain on Orcas Island in Washington State

Robert Myhr

This chapter summarizes how 325 acres in contiguous parcels of scenic mountainside and wildlife habitat of Entrance Mountain on Orcas Island in the San Juan Islands of Washington State were placed under neighborhood conservation easements (Photograph 25.1). Eleven different parties protected the land through a series of fourteen transactions over nine and a half years. Today, the Entrance Mountain project continues to expand.

The Organization: The San Juan Preservation Trust[1]

The San Juan Preservation Trust is a private, nonprofit, 501(c)(3), conservation land trust serving the islands of San Juan, Skagit, and Whatcom Counties in Washington State. Founded in 1979, the trust is governed by a nineteen-member volunteer board of trustees from eight islands in the archipelago. A three-person, part-time, paid staff manages the programs of the trust throughout the San Juan Islands from its office on Lopez Island. Financial support is from voluntary contributions from more than 1,200 memberships.

Fundamental Programs of the Preservation Trust

There are four fundamental programs of the San Juan Preservation Trust:

1. Acquisition of land and conservation easements, primarily through donations, to preserve the natural values and scenic landscapes of the islands
2. Stewardship of conservation interests in land held by the trust and for government agencies (on a fee-for-service basis), including baseline documentation and ongoing monitoring work
3. Education on the necessity for and techniques of voluntary land conser-

Photograph 25.1. Orcas Island's Entrance Mountain viewed from East Sound.
Source: Bob Myhr, San Juan Preservation Trust file photo

vation through lectures, slide shows, field trips, newsletters, brochures, videos, posters, and books
4. Fund-raising from individuals, foundations, and businesses to support annual operating expenses, special projects, and the trust stewardship and endowment funds, special funds set aside to defend the interests in land held by the trust in perpetuity

As of July 31, 1998, the San Juan Preservation Trust held 117 conservation easements and owned twenty-three parcels in the San Juan Islands. Of these 140 holdings on twelve different islands, 339 acres are conservation land owned by the trust and 7,068 acres are conservation easements, including over fourteen miles of waterfront. Areas protected include productive farmland and forests, undisturbed natural shoreline, freshwater and saltwater wetlands, and wildlife habitat. The trust also holds one historic preservation easement.

The trust works with other agencies to support local conservation goals. The trust works with the San Juan County Land Bank, a government land conservation agency, and with land trusts in Skagit and Whatcom Counties. Cooperative efforts include joint publications, frequent staff consultation, and identification of key acquisition priorities. The trust has also participated in projects with the state Department of Ecology, the State Department of Wildlife and Natural Resources, the Federal Bureau of Land Management, The Nature Conservancy, and the San Juan Islands Audubon Society.

The Location: San Juan Islands of Washington State

The San Juan Islands are often referred to as the gems of Washington State. Located in the extreme northwestern corner of the state and bordering Canada, the 743 islands—at low tide—are the tops of mountains that remained after the glaciers that cut the Puget Sound Trough retreated some 14,000 years ago. The islands are famous for their spectacular scenic beauty and the presence of an abundance of wildlife. The islands, despite growth and change, have outstanding native wild plant, bird, and animal habitats. They attract hundreds of thousands of tourists each year. Outdoor recreation, vacation homes, and retirement living have replaced traditional industries of fishing, logging, and farming.

The islands are quite small in total land area. Total acreage in San Juan County is 114,000 acres, with about 100,000 of these acres in private ownership. There is a strong interest in conservation throughout the community from both residents and vacation homeowners. Because of strong community support for private voluntary land conservation, the San Juan Preservation Trust now holds conservation interests in approximately 7 percent of the private land in San Juan County. One factor in the trust's success has been a program that encourages neighborhood conservation easements.

Neighborhood Conservation Easements

Two of the most serious problems facing land conservation in the San Juan Islands have been the rapid increase in real estate values and the disappearance of large blocks of undivided land. Although a few large blocks do remain, many of the larger land parcels have already been broken up for sale in smaller pieces as the value of land continues skyrocketing as a result of rapidly increasing demand for vacation and retirement homes. Many of these subdivided blocks of land still have large portions of the smaller parcels, *if pieced back together,* that merit conservation of their natural and scenic values. One way to bring these large portions back together is through neighborhood conservation easements, a series of small-area conservation easements from adjoining neighbors. These conservation easements are assembled together, over time, to protect the natural and conservation values originally associated with a larger block of land in the now-subdivided neighborhood.

The San Juan Preservation Trust now has a series of neighborhood conservation easement projects. They include scenic road projects on adjoining properties on Lopez and San Juan Islands and the projects blocking up portions of conservation forestland on Guemes and Orcas Islands. One project that has nearly been completed is the trust's Entrance Mountain project on Orcas Island.

Identification of the Project

In 1985, the San Juan Preservation Trust had identified several key areas around the San Juan Islands that merited conservation or preservation. The bigger issue was, How do we do it? The trust already owned 38 acres of bald eagle habitat on San Juan Island gifted in the trust's first transaction back in 1981. It also held conservation easements on 520 acres of traditional farmland. Nevertheless, there was so much more conservation work to be done, especially with the increasingly rapid disappearance of large blocks of conservation lands.

One of the things that the trust did not want to do was to target areas publicly, because few, if any, property owners want their land to be targeted. Instead, the trust had to identify, *for internal purposes,* key areas that the board and the staff judged to be important for wildlife or scenic purposes. There were several ways to identify these areas, including a 1975 survey of key private lands with natural values prepared by The Nature Conservancy, the "Metsker's map" of private holdings prepared by a local mapmaking company, an informal survey of board members, and recommendations from members and the general public of key lands meriting conservation in the islands. (Subsequently, in 1990, the trust jointly commissioned an open space and conservation study with the San Juan County Planning Department that became the blueprint for work of the new San Juan County Land Bank, which started in 1991.)

The list was overwhelming, and it included many more properties than the trust could possibly protect quickly. Nevertheless, it presented a great many parcels or areas to work on for conservation easements. One important area was Entrance Mountain on Orcas Island. The board of the San Juan Preservation Trust identified Entrance Mountain as highly visible and a significant landmark in the San Juan Islands that merited conservation. The 1975 Nature Conservancy inventory of natural areas on private lands in San Juan County also cited Entrance Mountain as a priority area of countywide significance because of its natural and scenic values. Owners of the mountain—the local resort, local developers, and larger property owners—were contacted in the early 1980s. They expressed mild interest in conservation easements, but chose not to act at that time, perhaps because the program was still in its infancy in the islands.

Entrance Mountain on Orcas Island

Entrance Mountain on Orcas Island, often referred to as the Camel Back, is the prominent dual peak that marks the entrance to East Sound. It is a landmark mountain on the San Juan Islands Ferry Corridor Greenway, the relatively undeveloped shoreline along the ferry route that winds its way through the islands. The ridge is also a significant habitat for bald eagles, and there is an active nest on the side of the mountain. (The San Juan Preservation Trust has a special "preserve habitat" poster of a mature bald eagle and chick at the nest on trust-preserved conservation easement land photographed by world-famous wildlife photographer Art Wolfe.) Along the shore is a haul-out site for river otters. Other wildlife include black-tailed deer, raccoons, pileated woodpeckers, turkey vultures, red-tailed hawks, peregrine falcons, and great blue herons. The mountain is also habitat for rare plant species such as the phantom orchid, brittle cactus, and leafless pyrola.

Open upper slopes of mountains of the San Juan Islands that jut up from the sea were gradually disappearing. New residential buildings were appearing on mountainsides, changing scenic views and affecting wildlife habitat. It was a compelling project because of its natural values, its visibility, and its symbolic value as a focal mountain in the archipelago.

One of the more daunting aspects of the Entrance Mountain "puzzle" was the pattern of ownership. One family owned the 122-acre southern face of the mountain. Trust approaches to the family in the early 1980s encountered a strong interest in conservation, but probably because the trust was still in its relative infancy, the family appeared to have a wait-and-see attitude toward a conservation easement.

The western portion of Entrance Mountain had been owned by the Moran estate dating back to the beginning of the nineteen century when a Mr. Moran, on the advice of his medical doctors, left his successful shipbuilding business in Seattle to rest on Orcas Island for health reasons. On Orcas, his health improved, he constructed a beautiful mansion, and he lived a long and pleasant life. A portion of his estate was given to Washington State and became Moran State Park, one of the finest in the state. The remainder was sold to a resort and real estate developer who used the original mansion (as it still is today) for his main lodge at famous Rosario Resort. Cabins and apartments were added next to the lodge and near the boat docks at the marina. Some of the immediately surrounding land was subdivided into hundreds of small building lots for vacation homes in the early 1950s and 1960s. By the mid-1970s, however, large tracts of the original Moran estate that had not been given to the state park or subdivided remained in the hands of the resort developer.

Most of this western portion of Entrance Mountain remained undivided in the early 1980s, although residential subdivision was gradually "creeping" southward from the main resort. Being more difficult terrain, it was less easy to subdivide and sell off in small lots than other parts of the original estate.

One of the resort developers more industrious managers, Jim Dahl, was very familiar with and loved the land (Photograph 25.2). He also saw the potential for land development and subdivision and purchased more than 120 acres from the resort. He proceeded to do his own subdivision into approximately 15-acre parcels with property lines stretching up the mountain. Along with his surveyor, he thought that larger parcels would be favored by the islands' real estate market more than smaller 5-acre tracts. According to local subdivision rules, he could have divided the land into 5-acre parcels, but he chose not to. Future owners could, if they wished, subdivide the 15-plus-a-fraction acre parcels so carefully laid out by the surveyor. Dahl, however, did not advocate that. He liked that there was an active bald eagle nest near his properties. He also realized the value of larger parcels for seclusion and quiet for vacation homes.

After Dahl had sold several of the parcels, he learned of the land conservation program of the San Juan Preservation Trust, now barely six years old and

Photograph 25.2. Successful real estate developer, Jim Dahl, turned successful advocate for conservation.
Source: Bob Myhr, San Juan Preservation Trust file photo

still working to educate the community about conservation easements. As he learned more about the program, he suggested that his development plans for the west face of Entrance Mountain might have been different. All the work of the development over many years had been done, however, and he was not about to undo it. He did, however, become convinced that he could help preserve the face of the Entrance Mountain from further development. Portions of the lots at the lower elevations could have one house, but the upper reaches should be preserved and kept totally wild for their scenic and habitat values. The successful real estate developer then became a successful advocate for conservation among his clients and purchasers of his land.

The Initial Transactions

When Dahl approached the trust, the trust was prepared to work with him to initiate a neighborhood conservation easement program on Entrance Mountain. The trust had already determined in earlier studies that Entrance Mountain was a priority neighborhood for protection for its scenic and habitat values. The trust, however, approached the project cautiously because it did not feel that it should just take one or two easements. It did not want to protect just one or two isolated parcels. Instead, it wanted an indication that more easements would be forthcoming to protect a much larger area. Dahl understood that position, and he indicated that he would personally work with the trust to secure more easements on Entrance Mountain.

Therefore, the trust agreed with Dahl that it would move ahead with the project if, working together, they could encourage several easements to come in about the same time. The trust did consider that idea of assembling several easements in escrow, but there was also a concern that doing so might delay the project and that it would never get started. In the final analysis, the process was initiated with four conservation easements and anticipated at least four additional easements before the year's end. These eight easements provided the core base for the overall protection. They were accomplished over an eight-month period in the sequence identified in Figure 25.1.

The transaction process for the initial easements followed a pattern that Dahl and the trust anticipated would accomplish the goal of piecing together protection for at least a key part of the mountain. Dahl agreed to donate three of the first six conservation easements on parcels that he owned or was about to sell to third parties. He also agreed to contact several other owners in the neighborhood to whom he had previously sold property and to encourage them to join in the protection of the upper portions of the mountain. All the land placed under easements was to be left forever wild as native plant and animal habitat. No structures of any kind were permitted. Walking trails on

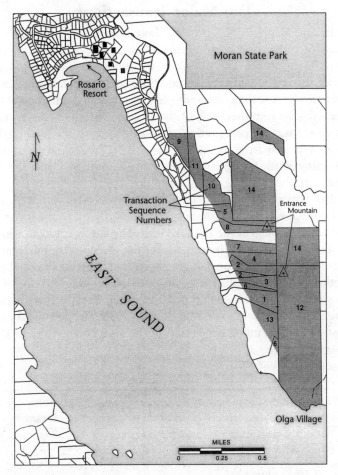

Figure 25.1. Map reflecting sequence of conservation easement transactions.
Source: Bob Myhr
Credit: Cartography Lab, University of Minnesota

the property were permitted, but placement of signs, mining, timber harvesting, camping, and other uses were all prohibited. The upper reaches of Entrance Mountain would become an easement-protected nature preserve. To provide for long-term stewardship and monitoring of the preserve, Dahl and the other donors each agreed to donate to the San Juan Preservation Trust Stewardship Fund. The amount of the tax-deductible contribution for each parcel was determined by a percentage of the before-easement assessed fair market value of the property.

Two Major Transactions

After the initial phase, the process slowed to a crawl, but momentum remained and other people expressed interest as they learned of the effort to preserve the mountain. The success of the initial stage of the process ultimately set the stage for two major additions to the block of protected land. These occurred more than four and seven years *after* the initiation of the project (see Table 25.1, transactions 12 and 14). In 1991, the 122-acre conservation easement was the culmination of nearly ten years of efforts by the trust (initiated separately from the smaller 15-acre neighborhood parcels) to protect the entire south-facing slope of Entrance Mountain. Under the terms of this easement, the entire 122 acres, except for a small weekend cabin near the shore, shall remain forever wild. In essence, the successes with transactions 1 through 11 helped to demonstrate substantial progress to the conservation-minded family owners of the 122-acre tract. The family could now have confidence that the trust would indeed succeed in preserving the mountain, especially with their participation. Long supporters of the trust's work, they could now enthusiastically add their key acreage to the project.

The second major transaction occurred when Rosario Resort and all its remaining land were sold to new investors in 1995. The new managers chose to divest all the remaining large tracts in the resort ownership. In 1996, the

Table 25.1. Summary of Acquisitions on Entrance Mountain

Transaction No.	Date	Acres	Person
1	5/22/87	5	#2
2	6/9/87	12	Dahl
3	6/9/87	8	Dahl
4	7/21/87	10	#3
5	9/24/87	10	#4
6	12/18/87	5	Dahl
7	12/18/87	9	#5
8	1/28/88	9	#6
9	12/5/89	9	#7
10	12/14/90	10	#8
11	7/15/91	10	#9
12	9/10/91	122	#10
13	11/9/94	16	Dahl
14	12/1/96	90	San Juan County Land Bank
TOTAL	9.5 years	325 acres	11 individual parties

San Juan County land bank purchased two key parcels totaling 90 acres on Entrance Mountain. The land bank did not exist when the Entrance Mountain project was initiated in 1987. Funded by a 1 percent real estate excise tax paid by all purchasers of land in the county after 1990, the local government land bank has the funds to *purchase* land and conservation easements. It is a valuable complement to the trust's private program of *donated* land and conservation easements. Although totally separate entities, the trust and the land bank work in close consultation. When the resort properties came up for sale, the land bank was fully aware of the Entrance Mountain project and had the funds to acquire the 90 acres that were available by purchase but not by donation. (A portion next to the resort that bordered Cascade Lake in Moran State Park, but not really part of the mountain, was sold to the trust for public land and subsequently sold to the state to add to the park.)

The Future at Entrance Mountain

The San Juan Preservation Trust monitors at least annually all the conservation interests it holds on Entrance Mountain. Currently, although several of the 15-acre parcels have been sold to new owners, there have been no violations of the terms of the conservation easements. The trust sends each new owner a welcome letter and outlines the nature and purposes of the restrictive covenants on the owner's land. There has been an amendment to one of the conservation easements to allow for the construction of a wildlife pond, a use not anticipated in the original easement but well in keeping with purpose of protection and enhancement of wildlife habitat. Most new owners welcome the trust's role and become members of the land trust. Indeed, the trust anticipates future additions to the neighborhood preserve through both donated conservation easements and gifts from estates. The neighborhood conservation easement area will continue to expand and preserve Entrance Mountain for generations to come.

Lessons Learned

Land trusts must have specific and clearly defined goals of (priority lands) that merit conservation. The goals to preserve these priority lands may be much more than can be immediately accomplished, but they provide guidance for proactive work with landowners and for unexpected opportunities that may arise.

Conservation or preservation of a neighborhood area worthy of protection need not happen all at once. It can be a cumulative process that feeds on its own successes.

It is important to have a core-starting group of three to four parcels. One isolated parcel may not be enough to begin, but with a core mass of three or four parcels, a firm base may be established that can lead to more conservation easements among the group.

It is important to have a neighborhood advocate, independent from the land trust itself, who understands and can help tell other neighbors about the community advantages of conservation easements and how they work.

An area worthy of protection has to have meaning for the community. It must be a key piece of habitat or important scenic parcel that the entire community can identify with, not just neighboring landowners.

Various incentives affect various property owners in different ways. Some are interested in land preservation for its own sake; others are interested but need the carrots of the tax codes as added incentives.

It is not mandatory to "escrow" a series of neighborhood easements to accomplish the goal. It may be desirable to pull in reluctant landowners, but it can be done without it.

It is important to have a neighborhood advocate, independent of the land trust itself, who understands and can help sell other neighbors on the advantages to the community from conservation easements and how they work.

Success can help lead other conservation agencies to join in the effort, especially government agencies that may have funds to purchase land and conservation easements that the land trust cannot acquire by donations.

Finally, and perhaps one of the most important lessons for programs that rely primarily on donated conservation easements or gifts of land, it is imperative to have patience and a willingness to take time to complete the project. An essential part of the process is educating all owners involved. Once they understand, they can join in the project, and do so enthusiastically.

Note

1. The San Juan Preservation Trust is dedicated to helping people protect the wildlife, scenery, and traditional way of life of the unique San Juan Islands through the preservation and careful use of land. The trust is dedicated to preserving scenic open spaces, forests, agricultural lands, habitats, vital wetlands, and shorelines in the San Juan Islands. The trust serves landowners who wish to protect the special features of their lands through voluntary private action. The trust offers the community and future generations a legacy of unique natural areas and open spaces. It counsels property owners on preservation techniques available to them and on tax benefits that might be available from donations of land or easements. The trust is a private, nonprofit, tax-exempt corporation founded by local residents and governed by a local board of trustees representing all the islands.

Chapter 26

❦ ❧

Conservation Easements in the Tenth Federal Circuit

Heidi A. Anderson, William M. Silberstein,
Matthew B. Cobb, and Kelly Kindscher

A massive influx of new residents from other states into the states of the Tenth Federal Circuit, which includes Colorado, Kansas, New Mexico, Oklahoma, Utah, and Wyoming (Figure 26.1) is creating tremendous land use conflicts. Douglas County, Colorado, ranks as one of the fastest-growing counties in the United States, and Grand Junction, Colorado, was considered the fastest-growing city under 100,000 just a few years ago. As a result, farmland in many of the states is being swallowed up by urban, suburban, and exurban development. Prime agricultural land in Colorado, for example, is disappearing at an average rate of 1,700 acres a week.[1] Having a rich history in farming and ranching, these states are known for their natural scenic beauty, attracting millions of tourists and generating billions of dollars in revenue. The continued loss of open space poses a threat to the quality of life of the residents. The destruction of agricultural land threatens the livelihood of a large segment of the population and the economic and cultural heritage of entire states.

The Uniform Conservation Easement Act (UCEA), adopted by the Uniform Commission in 1981, presented an opportunity for these states to preserve their heritage, remain economically stable, and maintain their desirability both as a place to live and as a place to visit. This chapter provides a comparative study of the legislation in each state in the Tenth Federal Circuit and the UCEA, describing their current practices, obstacles to, and successes in obtaining conservation easements as well as the future of conservation easements. The UCEA prompted similar legislation in Utah, New Mexico, and Kansas.[2] Colorado already had conservation easement legislation, enacted in 1976.[3] Wyoming and Oklahoma, on the other hand, are still without conservation easement enabling legislation. See Table 26.1 for a compar-

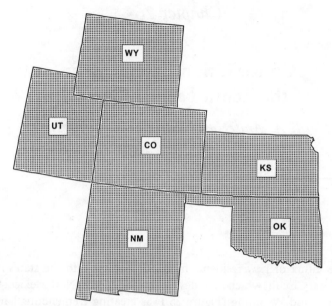

Figure 26.1. States comprising the Tenth Federal Circuit.
Credit: J. A. Gustanski

ative treatment of conservation easement enabling laws across the Tenth Federal Circuit.

The lack of conservation easement enabling legislation has severely curtailed the formation of land trusts and conservation easement transactions in Oklahoma. In Wyoming, however, where there also is no conservation easement enabling legislation, the lack of such legislation has not been an obstacle to the two land trusts active there because they have used a common law rule to create and enforce conservation easements. Significantly, the existence of conservation easement statutes in Colorado and Utah has fostered the enactment of related legislation for the preservation of agricultural and open land.[4] In Colorado, the presence of strong policies and conservation easement enabling laws has served as an impetus for much of the recent land trust activity across the state.

Colorado

The Colorado legislature enacted a Conservation Easement Act in 1976, five years before the Uniform Commission adopted the UCEA.[5] Likely forces behind this action were a resident population and a legislature sensitive to the growth occurring in Colorado and a desire to preserve the state's agricultural

Table 26.1. Comparison of Statutory Language and Terminology in the Tenth Federal Circuit

Comparison of Statutory Language	UCEA	Colorado	Kansas	New Mexico	Utah
Description of Interest					
Nonpossessory interest	X	X	X	X	
Easement	X	X	X	X	X
Restriction	X		X	X	X
Equitable servitude	X		X	X	
Covenant	X		X	X	X
Articles of dedication					
Condition					X
Interest in land		X			X
Easement of view					
Easement in structures					
Obligation					
Affirmative duty	X		X	X	
Negative duty (limitations/restrictions)	X		X	X	
Holder's access to ensure compliance					X
Public use permitted by contract					
Management to preserve, maintain, or enhance					
Protected Subject Matter					
Natural values	X	X	X	X	X
Natural beauty					
Scenic values	X	X	X		X
Open-space values	X	X	X	X	X
Wetland area					
Agricultural resources	X	X	X	X	X
Wooded condition					
Habitat for fish					
Habitat for plants		X			
Habitat for wildlife		X			X
Forest resources	X	X	X	X	
Recreational resources	X	X	X	X	X
Natural resources	X		X	X	
Natural area		X			
Geological resources					
Natural diversity					
Biological resources		X	X		
Scenic resources			X		
Archeological resources		X			
Horticultural resources					
Silvicultural resources					
Visual effect					
Audible effect					
Atmospheric effect					
Air quality	X		X		
Water quality	X		X		
Historic aspects	X	X	X		
Architectural aspects	X	X	X		
Historical resources			X		
Facade/external appearance					

(continues)

Table 26.1. Continued

Comparison of Statutory Language	UCEA	Colorado	Kansas	New Mexico	Utah
Cultural aspects	X	X	X		X
Historical value on designated registers		X			
Cultural heritage					
Structures		X			
Permissible Conservation Easement Holder					
Authorized governmental body	X	X	X		X
Charitable corporation	X	X	X	X	
Charitable association	X		X	X	
Charitable trust	X		X	X	
Authorized tax-exempt section 501(c) charitable organization		X			X
Permissible Third-Party Enforcer					
Governmental body	X		X		
Charitable corporation	X		X	X	
Charitable association	X		X	X	
Charitable trust	X		X	X	
Beneficiary					
Real property owner	X				
Conservation easment holder	X	X			
Authorized third party	X				
Person authorized by law	X				
Legal and equitable principles unaffected	X				
Representatives, heirs, and assigns					
Creation, Conveyance, Acceptance, and Duration					
Same as other easements	X		X	X	
Same as other interests in land					
Holder's acceptance prerequisite to enforcement	X		X	X	
Recordation of acceptance prerequisite to enforcement	X		X	X	X
Notify assessor					
Duration unlimited	X	X			X
Duration for life of another					
Duration of owner's life			X		
Duration as stated	X	X		X	X
Written consent of subsurface right required					
Fee simple					
Acquisition by donation					X
Acquisition by purchase					X
Cancel after 10 years if not needed and tax repaid					
Enforcement					
Injunction		X			X
Action at law		X			X
Equitable action		X			
Civil action		X			
Specifically enforceable					

Comparison of Statutory Language	UCEA	Colorado	Kansas	New Mexico	Utah
Superior Interests					
Existing interest absent	X		X	X	
Surrounding coal mining operation				X	
Surrounding coal transportation					
Innocent bona fide purchaser protected					
Eminent domain not impaired			X	X	
Defenses Specifically Eliminated					
Not appurtenant	X	X	X	X	
Assignability	X	X	X		
Imposes a negative burden	X		X		
Imposes affirmative obligations	X		X	X	
Benefit does not touch/concern real property	X		X	X	
No privity of estate	X		X	X	
No privity of contract	X	X	X	X	
Frustation of purpose					
Applicability of Statute					
Nontermination for violation of conservation easement terms					
Interest created after effective date of statute	X	X	X		
Permissible interests created before effetive date	X	X	X	X	
Does not invalidate other lawful interest	X	X	X	X	
In countries over 200,000 people					
In approving county/municipality					
Uniformity of Application and Conservation					
Applied to effectuate uniform law	X		X		
Construed to effectuate uniform law	X		X		
Tax Valuation					
Tax at eased value for tax-exempt organizations		X			
Public body tax exemption					

heritage. Because the Colorado legislation preceded the UCEA, the wording is not parallel. It does contain many of the same requirements for creating, terminating, and enforcing conservation easements, however. Uniquely, Colorado requires that any nongovernmental entity be in existence for a period of at least two years before becoming eligible to accept conservation easements.[6] On its face, this restriction may appear to be an obstacle to obtaining conservation easements, but proponents of this measure argue that it ensures that an organization is committed to preserving the land rather than merely creating tax shelters for donors. Opponents of the measure argue that two years is a long time to wait, given the rapid spread of development that consumes thousands of acres of Colorado's agricultural land and open space each year and fearing that land that may have been otherwise protected by a legitimate new land trust will be lost to development before the two-year waiting period is over. Colorado's statute, like Utah's, requires the easement grantee be a governmental entity or a charitable organization exempt under section 501(c)(3) of the Internal Revenue Code.[7] Proponents of this requirement argue that it forces land trusts to achieve the level of sophistication as an organization necessary to comply with the lengthy and detailed IRS regulations. Opponents argue that linking the Colorado statute to a federal statute is risky, first, because changes in the federal tax code will necessarily result in changes to Colorado's conservation easement legislation by default, and second, because in any litigation involving conservation easements, Colorado state courts will be in the position of interpreting the federal tax code, which is a highly complex series of regulations, that they may be poorly equipped to handle.[8] The Colorado statute is silent on the issue of third-party enforcement rights, so whether a third party could enforce a conservation easement is unknown. To avoid the problems that might arise when a holder is not capable of enforcing the easement, easements may be set up with a coholder who will take on the duties of the primary holder when the primary holder cannot meet his or her obligations. A key piece of Colorado property tax legislation protects agricultural land and open space by allowing land assessed for agricultural purposes to continue being taxed as agricultural land even though it is no longer used for agricultural purposes, if the landowner places a conservation easement on the land.[9] Should landowners violate the easement, the Colorado Department of Revenue may retroactively assess the land at its fair market value, holding the landowners responsible for back taxes.

The Colorado constitution makes conservation and preservation of open space a priority. In 1992, following a citizens' initiative, Colorado voters added Article 27 to the Colorado state constitution to allow state lottery dollars to be dedicated to the Great Outdoors Colorado (GOCO) trust fund for the purpose of preserving, protecting, and enhancing the state's wildlife, parks, rivers, trails, and open spaces.[10] The GOCO Trust Fund, currently $10 million to $20 million per year, is disbursed in several ways: as grants to state agencies and local governments to acquire and manage open space; for recreational facilities, including the building and maintenance of trails; for education; and for preserving critical wildlife habitat. In addition, GOCO uses a portion of the lottery dollars to sponsor "legacy projects" conservation projects of regional or statewide significance. By February 1998, the GOCO Trust Fund had awarded in excess of $111 million for over 900 projects.[11] Local governments are encouraged to match the funding provided by the GOCO grant, and many municipalities have increased both property and sales taxes to fund land acquisition programs. Funds raised both locally and through GOCO grants are generally passed on to land trusts to facilitate both conservation easement purchases and future monitoring requirements.

Many of the Tenth Federal Circuit states perceive conservation easements as a provider of tax shelters for the rich who have recently purchased trophy ranches. Two Colorado organizations, dedicated to preserving Colorado's ranching community, are trying to dispel this perception. The Colorado Cattlemen's Agricultural Land Trust was created in 1995 with the exclusive intent of preserving agriculture and helping landowners keep agricultural land in production.[12] The drive behind the creation of this particular land trust was the loss of 4.8 million acres of agricultural land from 1959 to 1992.[13] Another small grassroots organization in the high mountain valley of Gunnison, the Gunnison Legacy Fund, was founded to help local ranchers deal with concerns about development gobbling up prime agricultural land. Through estate planning assistance and purchase of development rights with monies from the GOCO Trust Fund, the Gunnison Legacy Fund helps families ensure that their ranches can be passed intact to the next generation. The ranchers receive money they desperately need in these times of agricultural economic recession, and their property taxes are stabilized, both now and for future generations. In exchange, the land trusts receive conservation easements, and the public gets a beautiful scenic valley dotted with cows and hay fields, not condominiums and golf courses. Colorado has over thirty-five legally recognized land trusts, of which slightly more than half hold conservation easements. As of the end of 1996, approximately 107,500 acres are held in conservation easements (Table 26.2).

The funds available from the GOCO Trust Fund are slated to double after 1998. It is expected that this increase in funds will foster a period of dramatic growth in both the number of land trusts and the amount of land protected through conservation easements. The amendment to the constitution and the change in property tax legislation has changed the path of Colorado's future. Where the continued decline of available agricultural land and open space once seemed irreversible, there is now renewed faith that Colorado's heritage can be preserved.

Kansas

In 1992, the Kansas legislature passed conservation easement enabling legislation, which closely patterns the UCEA.[14] Several other statutes preceded it, however. The first piece of legislation that dealt with conservation easements was passed in 1987; it allowed only governmental entities to hold easements

Table 26.2. Active Land Trusts in the Tenth Federal Circuit

Land Trusts	Acres Preserved Under Easement
Colorado	
American Farmland Trust	12,487
Aspen Center for Environmental Studies	193
Aspen Valley Land Trust	3,400
Clear Creek Land Conservancy	577
Colorado Cattlemen's Agricultural Land Trust	20,000
Colorado Open Lands	6,702
The Conservation Fund	1,920
Crested Butte Land Trust	132
Douglas County Land Conservancy	1,315
Eagle Valley Land Trust	60
Estes Valley Land Trust	2,218
La Plata Open Space Conservancy	1,955
Larimer Land Trust	215
Mesa County Land Conservancy	13,440
The Nature Conservancy	45,790
The Palmer Foundation	3,056
The Rocky Mountain Elk Foundation	33,117
The San Miguel Conservation Foundation	320
Southwest Land Alliance	4,021
Valley Land Conservancy	517
Yampa Valley Land Trust	4,762
Subtotal	156,197
Kansas	
Kansas Land Trust	1,572
The Nature Conservancy	40
Subtotal	1,612
New Mexico	
Albuquerque Conservation Trust	647
Arroyo Hondo Land Trust	219
Forest Trust	7,103
The Nature Conservancy	245,666
Rocky Mountain Elk Foundation	2,800
Santa Fe Conservation Trust	647
Taos Land Trust	1,370
Subtotal	258,452
Oklahoma	
The Nature Conservancy	145
Subtotal	145
Utah	
Summit Land Conservation Association	3,000
The Nature Conservancy	260
Subtotal	3,260
Wyoming	
Jackson Hole Land Trust	9,101
The Nature Conservancy	128,200
Subtotal	137,301
TOTAL	555,595

Note: A variety of sources, including the Land Trust Alliance, Colorado Open Lands, and phone call verification were used to gather the data in the table. It is accurate as of December 31, 1997.

for a narrow range of purposes. Then, in 1991, the Kansas Land Trust, work-ing with legislators in Douglas County and other eastern counties, attempted to broaden the statute to incorporate language from the UCEA. The thrust of this effort was to make substantive changes that would allow nonprofit orga-nizations "with a conservation purpose" to hold easements and to expand the law's scope to include the protection of natural, scenic, agricultural, histori-cal, and archeological lands. The bill did not pass in its first year. A consor-tium of agricultural lobbying groups that influence all natural resources and environmental issues in the state legislature charged that the bill was being pushed by "tree huggers" (although it was pointed out that there were not a lot of trees to protect in the state) and "Sierra Clubbers." During the summer of 1991, the Kansas Farm Bureau studied the proposed legislation. With the assistance of the Kansas Land Trust, the bureau realized that under existing legislation, a landowner had the right to plow or destroy native prairie but no right to protect native prairie or, in fact, any agricultural land for the future. One incident, controversial and highly publicized, in which a developer pur-posely plowed a native prairie, habitat for two endangered species, high-lighted the current status.[15] Both the bureau and the Kansas Land Trust agreed that the bill offered in the previous legislative session should be sup-ported because it would preserve farmland, preserve the land as private prop-erty, and keep it on the tax rolls; besides, the granting of an easement is totally voluntary. The bill passed in 1992, despite a significant challenge from the Kansas homebuilder's association. The association asserted that the measure would tie up potentially developable lands. As enacted, the legislation deviates from the UCEA, as easements are limited to the lifetime of the grantor unless specific language provides otherwise.[16] There has been no other conserva-tion- or preservation-inspired legislation in the state. The use of conservation easements has been slow to catch on in Kansas, having only been used by three entities, the Kansas Department of Wildlife and Parks (eighty-one ease-ments), the Kansas Land Trust (four easements), and The Nature Conser-vancy (one easement). The Kansas Department of Wildlife and Parks has gen-erally used easements to protect riparian areas and winter nesting sites of bald eagles along the Kansas River near Lawrence. The Kansas Land Trust has pro-tected 200 acres of land with conservation easements, including two native tallgrass prairies containing the federally protected Mead's milkweed and agricultural and range lands adjacent to the Konza prairie in the Flint Hills. The Konza prairie is owned by The Nature Conservancy and managed by Kansas State University. The Kansas chapter of The Nature Conservancy also holds a conservation easement on forested and agricultural areas along the Blue River in Johnson County, near the Kansas City suburban fringe.

In Kansas, the greatest interests in conservation easements have come from landowners who have conservation as their primary motivation, rather than tax benefits. For the majority of lands in Kansas, there is only a nominal or no increase in value for land other than for basic agricultural purposes. Development pressures are growing, however, particularly in the Kansas City to Topeka corridor and in the Wichita area. As a result, easements will likely play an increasing role in open-space and natural areas protection.

New Mexico

The New Mexico Land Use Easement Act was adopted in 1991, ten years after UCEA.[17] The push behind the adoption of the law was increased development pressures, combined with the need for estate tax planning and citizen support for open space.[18] The language of the statute closely parallels that of the UCEA. The statute also conforms to the state's general easement legislation by establishing rules for creation, conveyance, and enforcement, although it specifically provides for the validity of such easements, which deviate from common law principles. The statute does not bind itself to the criteria described in the federal income tax code, which defines those entities that may hold conservation easements. Essentially, any nonprofit corporation, association, or trust whose purpose or authority allows it to retain or protect open space or natural resources may hold easements under the law.[19] An easement donor, however, may not claim any federal tax benefits unless the easement is donated to a "qualified organization" under the federal tax code.[20] Another important distinction in the New Mexico law that sets it apart is the definition of a "land use easement," which deviates from the UCEA in that it does not expressly provide for the protection of air and water quality.[21] Practitioners familiar with New Mexico easement laws were unable to offer explanation for this important omission and, the Uniform Commission did not address the omission in its comments. The UCEA provides that all conservation easements will be held in perpetuity unless otherwise stated in the easement. The New Mexico statute, however, requires that language in the easement document specify the term of the easement.[22] Although such a requirement has the potential to create problems, some New Mexico practitioners argue that the statutory language gives them necessary flexibility and the ability to write valid easements for varying periods of time, which encourages landowners to consider placing conservation easements on their land.[23] Land conservationists, quite naturally, claim that this flexibility is detrimental to the goal of perpetual conservation and preservation. The UCEA allows conservation easements to be assigned to another holder without jeopardizing the validity of the easement. The New Mexico statute is silent on the issue, although it is common practice for land trusts in the state to include a provision for assigning the easement in the event that the land trust is no longer capable of performing its contractual obligations under the easement.[24] The government's ability to acquire a conservation easement or to terminate its existence through the use of eminent domain is not covered by the UCEA. The New Mexico statute expressly prohibits such action, as does Utah's statute.[25] This section of the law fundamentally restricts the state's ability to use eminent domain to create a conservation easement. The statute is silent, however, on whether the state government could condemn land encumbered by an easement.

Finally, the statute adds a special provision regarding those lands affected by the New Mexico Surface Mining Act and the federal Surface Mining Control and Reclamation Act of 1977.[26] The provision states that the conservation easement legislation shall not deny the right of the surface owner to consent to surface mining or interfere with extraction of minerals. On its face, this provision seemingly allows surface mining on land held under a conservation easement. The true effect, however, is that if the conservation easement document expressly prohibits mining, then mining is preempted and thus only creates a problem if the drafters of the easement fail to expressly prohibit mining.[27] Such an oversight is potentially fatal to both the landowner and to land trusts. In essence, it may prevent the landowner from receiving a tax deduction for donating the easement if, at a later date, the IRS determined that the original intent of the easement donation was to reserve the right to mine the land.[28]

Like many states in the West, New Mexico has what is commonly referred to as preferential property tax legislation.[29] The purpose of the legislation is to preserve greenbelts in rapidly growing suburban areas where property values have rocketed in recent years. By allowing lands principally dedicated to agricultural and forestry production to be valued according to their use, rather than as land being held for development, this goal is accomplished. Recently, tax assessors have tried to limit its application while landowners have tried to expand it, in part to reduce their soaring property tax bills.[30] A 1997 amendment to the legislation appears to have tipped the balance in favor of the landowners. Now, land that has been taxed at the lower agricultural or forest use rate for at least one of the last three tax years is presumed to still qualify for that assessment, without need for annual inspection to verify current use.[31]

New Mexico, like many of its sister states, has been experiencing significant development pressures. Although the use of conservation easements has been limited since adoption of the conservation easement legislation, at least one land trust director expects to see their use double, or possibly triple, by the end of 1998.[32]

A lack of funding remains the biggest obstacle to organizations acquiring conservation easements in New Mexico. Although a majority of easements held by local land trusts are donated by landowners, not all landowners are positioned to make such contributions. Moreover, landowners are often required to contribute additional funds to the land trusts to cover the costs of annual monitoring. Unlike some other western states, New Mexico is ill equipped to provide any funding. New Mexico's economy is one of the poorest in the nation, ranking in the ninetieth percentile among all states for revenue. Most municipalities simply do not have funds available to purchase easements or to acquire other interests for open space.³³ One exception is home rule counties and municipalities that have the authority to pass sales tax levies to acquire open space.

Landowner perception has been another significant obstacle for conservation easements in New Mexico. In general, they are not well received by landowners who fear that, by giving up development rights to their land, they are virtually giving up the use of their land entirely, for any purpose. New Mexico land trusts are busy with community outreach programs to better educate citizens and inform them of the potential benefits.

Overly restrictive zoning codes in some areas of New Mexico present yet another hurdle for conservation easements. Due to extensive limitations imparted through zoning, some landowners have had to fight to obtain the federal tax benefits for donating a conservation easement.³⁴ For example, in Santa Fe, zoning restrictions limit development to such an extent that landowners have no development rights either to sell or donate as an easement. Although the end result may be ultimately the same in that the land gets protected, it may only be temporary at best because zoning codes can and do change, and rezoning requests may be honored, whereas conservation easements typically are perpetual.³⁵

Oklahoma

Perhaps because of a large amount of tribal and federal lands and a variety of extractive industries, Oklahoma, unlike most of the other states in the Tenth Federal Circuit, does not have conservation easement enabling legislation. Furthermore, all attempts to adopt the UCEA have faced insurmountable opposition from the Oklahoma Independent Producer's Association, which believes that conservation easements could impede or restrict mining rights. The most recent attempt was on March 9, 1998, when the Oklahoma Senate passed Senate Bill 1253 containing all the major provisions set out in UCEA. The bill went on to the House Judiciary Committee, where it died on March 26, 1998.

Although Oklahoma has been slow to adopt conservation easement enabling legislation, several different types of easements have been used by state agencies to protect wildlife. The Oklahoma Wildlife Conservation Commission through the Wildlife Heritage fund may acquire easements.[36] These easements are held for specific purposes described in state statutes, including: "management of game animals, protected animals and birds, and recreation and management of public hunting, fishing, areas for public use."[37]

A related important piece of state legislation is the Scenic Rivers Act. This act enables the Scenic Rivers Commission, Oklahoma Tourism and Recreation Department, and Oklahoma Wildlife Conservation Commission to acquire, develop, and maintain public access points or park areas in or near scenic river areas by acquiring easements and fees from willing sellers.[38] The act, which prohibits the state from using its power of eminent domain, was adopted to encourage the preservation of areas designated as scenic river areas in their natural scenic state.

The federal Wetlands Reserve Program has been an active conservation tool in both Oklahoma and Kansas. This program, available in all states, helps to preserve wetlands on private property by offering financial incentives to landowners. Landowners retain title to their land and grant one of three easement options to the government. In the first instance, an easement may be permanent, in which case the U.S. Department of Agriculture (USDA) pays the landowner the entire cost of any wetland restoration that may be necessary. A second option is a long-term, thirty-year easement, in which case the easement can be acquired by the USDA for 75 percent of the cost of a permanent easement and the USDA pays 75 percent of any wetland restoration costs. Finally, the landowner may enter into a minimum ten-year restoration cost-share agreement. Under this arrangement, the land is not encumbered by an easement and the USDA pays only for 75 percent of the restoration costs.

Despite Oklahoma's failed attempts to pass enabling conservation easement legislation, the state has maintained strong support for a variety of wildlife conservation practices. Perhaps related to the failure to pass state enabling legislation is that the state also lacks an active nonprofit corporation that falls under the general land trust umbrella. The presence of such an organization may facilitate not only the holding of conservation easements, but could help to educate people across the state and lobby for such legislation.

Utah

Utah's conservation easement enabling legislation, the Land Conservation Easement Act, was adopted in 1985, four years following adoption of the UCEA.[39] The statute deviates in many ways from the UCEA and other Tenth Federal Circuit states' legislation. Reading more like a set of procedures than a statute, it lays out, step by step, the requirements for acquiring, creating, conveying, terminating, and enforcing conservation easements. Neither the UCEA nor other states' legislation contains this same amount of specificity. The final deviation from the UCEA and other Tenth Federal Circuit states is the statement that conservation easements cannot be acquired by eminent domain. The rationale for the inclusion of this restriction may lie in the western property rights' philosophy that the government should not interfere with private property rights, and this statement was necessary to get the legislation passed.[40]

A most significant and atypical part of Utah's legislation is the requirement that an easement recipient, usually a land trust or other qualified entity, must advise the easement grantor on all three of the following:

1. The types of conservation easements available
2. The legal aspects of each type
3. The suggestion that the grantor seek advice of legal counsel prior to granting the easement[41]

This requirement seems to have had minimal impact on the volume of easements in the state; Utah Open Lands, the only land trust in the state that holds such easements, reports that no one has ever backed out of obtaining an easement as a result of the requirement.[42]

Under the statute, the holder, or a third-party assignee, may enter the property at any time to enforce compliance with the easement document and may enforce the easement against the grantors or their successors or assignees. Action may be taken through injunction or for the purposes of obtaining monetary compensation.[43] In addition, the easement holder may enter the land to enforce compliance with the terms of the easement.[44] The UCEA does not contain similar requirements. Like the Colorado legislation, the Utah statute requires that holders of conservation easements be a charitable organization as defined in section 501(c)(3) of the tax code.[45] The UCEA does not contain a similar provision. Beyond discussion of the requirements of acquiring an easement, the Utah statute sets forth other methods through which a conservation easement may be acquired (purchase, gift, grant, lease, etc.). Neither the UCEA nor other states' legislation contains this degree of specificity. In accordance with the statute's theme of providing step-by-step guidance for establishing conservation easements, the statute clearly defines what must be included in the easement document itself, including the legal description, a statement of purpose, and the termination date where provided, or a statement that the easement is perpetual.[46] Like the New Mexico legislation then, the Utah statute leaves open the duration of conservation easements. Utah practitioners, however, view this situation as a threat to the viability of the easement, as opposed to a feature that adds flexibility (the view expressed by the New Mexico practitioners).[47]

Utah has two other important pieces of legislation that relate to the preservation of undeveloped land. The first is the Agricultural Preservation Area legislation. This act allows landowners to create an agricultural protection area (APA) for land currently used for agriculture and agricultural products, including crops, livestock, and livestock products, "with a reasonable expectation of making a profit."[48] This legislation does not provide permanent protection, however, because the landowner may petition for land to be added to or withdrawn from the established APA.[49] In addition, municipalities may annex the land and reassess its viability as preserved agricultural land[50] or use its powers of eminent domain to condemn the land in an APA, with the approval of the local legislative body.[51]

The second piece of legislation, the Farmland Assessment Act, also promotes the conservation of undeveloped land.[52] Under this act, land that is currently being used for agricultural purposes and has been so used for the previous two years may be assessed based on its value as agricultural land as opposed to its highest and best use.[53] The act contains a disincentive provision that encourages landowners of such land to keep land in its agricultural use. If land ceases to be used for agriculture, the landowner is required to pay a rollback tax penalty for the time that he or she received the preferential assessment based on the agricultural use.[54] Land that may later become restricted through a conservation easement is exempt from the rollback tax provision.[55] Should such an easement be terminated in the future, however, the rollback tax will be applicable unless the land reverts back to agricultural use.[56]

The use of conservation easements in the state of Utah has been fairly limited to date, but an increasing population and subsequent development pressures are likely to prompt an increase in their use. A report from the Utah Governor's Office of Planning and Budget indicated that from 1995 through 1997, the state lost approximately eight square miles of open land a year. This number is projected to increase to nine square miles a year by 2008. Utah legislators are being called upon to increase their efforts to preserve Utah's open space and improve deteriorating recreational facilities.[57] Specifically, the citizens of Utah want state legislators to develop a funding mechanism to purchase conservation easements. In response to these concerns, a recent bill in the Utah State House of Representatives proposed an increase in sales tax to be dedicated to a fund for preserving agricultural land.[58] The bill was narrowly defeated. The death knell for the bill was an amendment to the bill calling for a ten-year cap on conservation easement duration.[59] The fight is not over, however.

Wyoming

The state of Wyoming does not have a conservation easement enabling act, although there have been several attempts to pass such legislation. Key factors influencing the failed attempts include major philosophical differences between principal actors, such as the conservationists and the stock growers, a lack of coordination between the supporters of the conservation easement bills, and resistance to the requirement that an easement be perpetual.[60]

In the absence of statutory authority, landowners in Wyoming have used a common-law rule to create and enforce conservation easements.[61] When an organization acquires an easement on a parcel of land, it also acquires fee title to a small parcel (typically 1 acre) adjacent to the land over which it holds the easement. Thus, the conservation easement is appurtenant and not an easement in gross and therefore becomes enforceable under common law. Conservation easements constructed in this way are subject to the same tenets of common law that provide for modification or termination of an easement (e.g., equitable powers, the hardship doctrine, and the doctrine of changed circumstances) as are referred to in the UCEA.[62]

The two land trusts that are active in Wyoming, the Jackson Hole Land Trust and The Nature Conservancy, have been able to operate successfully without conservation easement enabling legislation, securing the donation of many conservation easements. Nevertheless, conservationists within the state continue to press for enactment of enabling legislation.

Not unlike Colorado, New Mexico, and Utah, Wyoming also has a "preferential" property tax law. The Wyoming law allows agricultural land, "land employed for the previous two years and currently employed for the purpose of obtaining a monetary profit from agricultural use," to be assessed at a lower fair market value than lands held for development.[63] The intent of Wyoming's legislation mirrors that of other states in that the lower assessed value is aimed at enabling farmers and ranchers to continue farming and ranching. In Wyoming, however, there are two unfortunate realities that, despite the existence of preferential tax laws, continue to threaten agricultural lands. First, given the depressed agricultural economy, many farmers have found it difficult to generate sufficient income to pay even the lower property tax. This situation is particularly true in areas where development pressures are most intense.[64] Second, when land is no longer being used for agriculture, it is assessed at fair market value. Thus, when aging landowners are not able to continue farming and ranching operations and the land is no longer used for agriculture, it reverts to being taxed at its fair market value. In addition, when a landowner dies and the heirs do not intend to continue agricultural operations on the land, the heirs will become liable for significant property and estate taxes. As a result, a large portion of the land in areas where development pressure is most intense and where open space is most urgently needed is divided into smaller parcels and sold to pay estate taxes.

The state of Wyoming is actively trying to attract people and businesses,[65] which may, in part, account for the inability to get conservation easement legislation passed.[66] The open space in some areas of Wyoming, most notably the northwestern portion of the state near Yellowstone and Jackson Hole, has been under population pressure for some time. Not surprisingly, Jackson Hole is home to one of the state's most active land trusts. The Jackson Hole Land Trust holds a significant number of conservation easements that protect some 9,000 acres. Organizations in the northwestern part of the state have made efforts to sponsor conservation easement legislation, but their efforts have been thwarted by a state legislature sharply divided over philosophies on growth. As is the case in many western states, funding is the biggest obstacle to nonprofit land trusts obtaining conservation easements in Wyoming. Most land trusts do not have the financial resources for easement purchases; therefore, landowners must donate them. Given the current agricultural market conditions, there is little incentive for a landowner to donate land in exchange for a tax deduction when he or she has not generated enough income to be offset by the tax break. This lack of monetary incentive to donate easements, coupled with a general lack of understanding of how easements work, the benefits they may provide, and the lack of conservation easement enabling legislation, continues to hamper the land conservation movement in the state.[67] Despite the state's prevailing desire to protect land and preserve the state's farming and ranching heritage, the movement is likely to progress slowly unless both landowners and legislators can be sufficiently educated and spurred to create effective legislation.

Conclusion

The UCEA has served as an effective model for conservation easement enabling legislation in the Tenth Federal Circuit to date and will continue to do so for the remaining states without enabling acts. In three of the states that comprise this circuit, language from the state conservation easement enabling acts contains many provisions similar to those contained in the UCEA. Colorado's enabling legislation, which preceded UCEA, is remarkably similar. Kansas adopted the provisions of UCEA almost word for word, whereas Utah expanded on the principles established in UCEA to provide more details regarding procedure.

Conservation easement enabling legislation has been important to the facilitation of conservation easement transactions in Colorado, Utah, New Mexico, and Kansas. In Wyoming, the lack of enabling legislation has not been an obstacle to the two land trusts operating there. An additional benefit of conservation easement enabling legislation in Colorado and Utah has been the enactment of related property tax legislation aimed at preserving agricultural and open land.

Although the use of conservation easements in some of the states in the Tenth Federal Circuit has been limited, citizens of all the states have a deeply rooted desire to protect what remains of open space and agricultural land. A universal obstacle seems to be the lack of funding available to land trusts for the acquisition and monitoring of easements. Aside from Colorado's Great Outdoors Colorado Trust Fund, land trusts in most of the states in the district cite a lack of funds as the principal reason why there are not more conservation easements. Several states are trying to pass legislation dedicating property or sales tax revenue to be used to protect open space through the purchase of conservation easements. To date, most conservation easements are donated by landowners in exchange for tax benefits, but in the West, many farmers and ranchers do not make sufficient income to take advantage of these tax benefits. Hence, there is a need for a funding source that would allow farmers and ranchers to be paid up front to forgo development opportunities.

Many landowners in the Tenth Federal Circuit states lack sufficient understanding of how conservation easements work and what their benefits are, creating yet another obstacle to the success of conservation easements. Landowners are reluctant to give up development rights because they are unable to differentiate such rights from the other property rights they possess and enjoy. This lack of understanding has resulted in at least one state refusing to adopt adequate easement legislation. The education of landowners is a critical step toward the success of conservation easements in the western states.

Notes

1. Eric Pooley, "Gunnison, Colorado, Cows or Condos," *Time,* July 7, 1997, p. 81.
2. UCEA (1981); Utah Code Ann. §§ 57-18-1–7 (1953) (1994 repl.); K.S.A. §§ 58-3810–3817 (1994); N.M. Stat. Ann. §§ 47-12-1–6 (1991).
3. Colo. Rev. Stat. § 38-30.5-101 (1997).
4. Colo. Rev. Stat. §§ 37-1-102–103 (1997); Utah Code Ann. § 59-2-503 (1996 repl.).
5. Colo. Rev. Stat. §§ 37-1-102–103 (1997).
6. Id. § 38-30.5-104.
7. Colo. Rev. Stat. § 38-30.5-104 (1997); Utah Code Ann. § 57-18-3 (1953) (1994 repl.).
8. Interview with Federico Cheever, associate professor, University of Denver College of Law (March 25, 1998).
9. Colo. Rev. Stat. §§ 39-1-102–103 (1997).
10. Colo. Const. of 1876, art. XXVII (1992).
11. Great Outdoors Colorado Fact Sheet, February 1998.

12. Colorado Coalition of Land Trusts Newsletter, *Colorado Cattlemen's Agricultural Land Trust: Preserving Land For Agriculture* (spring 1996).
13. Colorado Coalition of Land Trusts Newsletter (spring 1996).
14. K.S.A. § 58-3810 (1994).
15. "Ignoring Pleas of Environmentalists, Kansas Man Digs Up Virgin Prairie," *New York Times*, November 23, 1997, p. B18.
16. Michael J. Davis, "Survey of Kansas Law: Real Property," 41 *Kan. L. Rev.* 669, 689 (1993).
17. N.M. Stat. Ann. §§ 47-12-1–6 (1991).
18. Interview with Tracy Connor, Esq., February 26, 1998.
19. N.M. Stat. Ann. § 47-12-2(A).
20. I.R.C. §§ 170(h)(1)–(3), 170(b)(1)(A)(v)–(vi) (1997).
21. N.M. Stat. Ann. § 47-12-2(B).
22. Id. § 47-12-3(D).
23. Interview with James B. Alley Jr., Esq., Rubin, Katz, Salizar, Alley and Rouse, P.C., February 17, 1998.
24. Interview with James B. Alley Jr.
25. N.M. Stat. Ann. § 47-12-6(C).
26. N.M. Stat. Ann. § 47-12-6(D).
27. Interview with Tracy Connor.
28. I.R.C. § 170(h)(5)(B) (1997). A conservation easement must be held exclusively for conservation purposes. No surface mining is permitted.
29. N.M. Stat. Ann. § 7-36-20 (1978) (1995 rpl.).
30. Interview with James B. Alley Jr.
31. Interview with James B. Alley Jr.
32. Interview with Clare Swanger, Director, Taos Land Trust, February 24, 1998. Currently, there are ten recognized land trusts in the state of New Mexico.
33. Interview with Clare Swanger.
34. Interview with James B. Alley Jr.
35. Interview with James B. Alley Jr.
36. 29 Okl. St. Ann. § 4-134 (1991).
37. 29 Okl. St. Ann. § 4-134(B)(1) and (2) (1991).
38. 82 Okl. St. Ann § 1454 (1991).
39. Utah Code Ann. §§ 57-18-1 et seq. (1953) (1994 repl.).
40. Interview with Wendy Fisher, Utah Open Lands, April 9, 1998.
41. Utah Code Ann. § 57-18-4(4).
42. Interview with Wendy Fisher.
43. Utah Code Ann. § 57-18-6(1), (2).
44. Id. § 57-18-6(3).
45. Id. § 57-18-3.
46. Id. § 57-18-4(3).
47. Interview with Tom Bergeren, Esq., Bancott and Bangley, P.C., March 3, 1998.
48. Utah Code Ann. § 17-41-101.
49. Id. § 17-41-306(2)(A).

50. Id. § 17-41-306(3).
51. Id. § 17-41-405.
52. Utah Code Ann. § 59-2-503 (1953) (1996 rpl.).
53. Id. § 59-2-503(1) and (2).
54. Id. § 59-2-506(1)(a).
55. Id. § 59-2-506(1)(b).
56. Id. § 59-2-506(1)(b)(iii) and (c).
57. Karl Cates, "What Trail Is Nature On? Harm to Utah's Environment May Be Unavoidable," *Desert News,* February 1, 1998, p. 3.
58. Karl Cates, "What Trail Is Nature On?" p. 4.
59. Interview with Wendy Fisher, Utah Open Lands, March 5, 1998.
60. Jackson Hole Land Trust Memorandum, March 18, 1997, "Conservation Easement Bill Exit Memo," unpublished.
61. Andrew Dana and Michael Ramsey, "Conservation Easements and the Common Law," 8 *Stan. Envtl. L.J.* 2, 3 (1989). Common-law conservation easements typically prohibit negative perpetual in gross servitudes because they impair alienability and prevent property from being put to its highest and best use. The common law recognizes two types of easements: appurtenant and in gross. In gross easements are rarely upheld or recognized in a court of law.
62. Dana and Ramsey.
63. Wyo. Stat. Ann. § 39-2-103 (1997).
64. In fact, even this measure is insufficient in some instances. The agricultural economy of Wyoming and other western states has been in a slump for several years, and farmers and ranchers cannot even afford the lower tax assessments.
65. Interview with Dave Larson, February 12, 1998.
66. Interview with Dave Larson.
67. Interview with Storey Clark, former director, Jackson Hole Land Trust, February 17, 1998.

Chapter 27

❧ ❧

The Santa Fe Conservation Trust: Protecting Northern New Mexico's Complex Land Tenure Patterns

John B. Wright

Some of the country's most complex land tenure patterns and some of the most bitter land use conflicts today occur in northern New Mexico. As a consequence, the Santa Fe Conservation Trust (SFCT) works to acquire conservation easements in one of the most challenging cultural settings imaginable (Figure 27.1). The origins of these patterns and disputes can be traced back to the mid-1880s. Before the area became part of the United States with the Treaty of Guadalupe Hidalgo in 1848, title to some 35 million acres had already been granted by Spanish and Mexican governors and military commandants to individuals and communities, including the Pueblo Indian groups.[1] The history of the land grants continues to influence the geography of northern New Mexico. The memory of the land grant dealings remains fresh and part of the modern psychological makeup, especially of the Hispano residents. To this day, billboards reading "Tierra o Muerte"—Land or Death—are common in rural areas. In mystical Santa Fe, as waves of wealthy Anglo in-migrants arrive, the conflicts over land tenure, development, and open space conservation has now taken center stage.[2]

The SFCT was incorporated in 1993 with the mission of "serving the community of greater Santa Fe by preserving open spaces, traditional landscapes, and trails." Despite overwhelming cultural impediments, significant progress has been made. In its short history, the SFCT has received twenty-one conservation easements covering some 18,000 acres. Their projects are distributed all over the region and demonstrate a broad range of easement applications.

The trust holds conservation easements on two large, contiguous ranches on both sides of a 3 1/2-mile stretch of the Gallinas River southeast of Santa Fe. This 9,805-acre expanse abuts the Las Vegas National Wildlife Refuge and

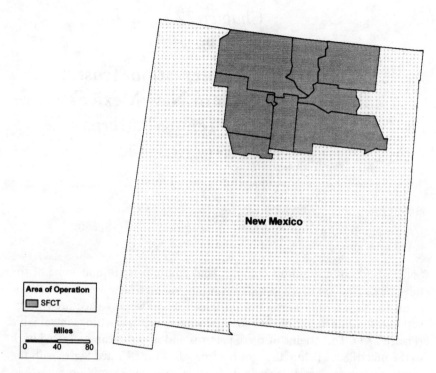

Figure 27.1. Map of region covered by the Santa Fe Conservation Trust.
Credit: J. A. Gustanski

acts as an ecological extension of that key waterfowl reserve (Photograph 27.1). The land use restrictions contained in these easements are typical of SFCT deeds. The Anglo fee owners cannot greatly alter the current agricultural practices and may not subdivide the property for residential development. They may build an additional 50-acre ranch headquarters area to facilitate management, however.

The SFCT holds an easement on the historic, 832-acre Los Trigos Ranch near Pecos National Monument southeast of Santa Fe. The ranch, bounded on the north and south by the Santa Fe National Forest and astride the Pecos River, possesses considerable historic value (Photograph 27.1). Located on a key trading route between the Pecos Indians and tribes of the Great Plains, no doubt the Spanish explorers Coronado and Onate passed through the property. Ruts made by the wheels of wagons using the Santa Fe Trail and the abandoned roadbed of Route 66 are still visible. During the Civil War, troops were deployed here. The easement protects these historic values as well as vital habitat for big game, fish, and waterfowl in what the SFCT hopes will

Photograph 27.1. Vast ranch landscape provides key ecological extensions to waterfowl reserve on Pecos River. Conservation easements held by the Santa Fe Conservation Trust.
Photo credit: Jack Wright

become an extensive and unique corridor of protected lands. The most unusual easement restriction requires the use of movable fencing to keep cattle away from the river's bed and banks.

The trust holds five connected easements, 6,000 acres, in Rio Arriba County, the scene of many conflicts between Aglos and Hispanos over land grants. Only very limited residential development is allowed on these properties, and fencing that would impede wildlife movement is prohibited. As a consequence of these easements, the lands serve as a wildlife migration corridor between the Rio Chama Wilderness and the Abiquiu Reservoir (Photograph 27.2).

The Galisteo Basin project is one of the SFCT's most intriguing use of conservation easements. This semiarid landscape contains more paleo-Indian ruins and artifacts than any other site in the United States. The Archeological Conservancy and the SFCT have a visionary plan to save and study these resources.[3] Although five easements totaling over 900 acres have been acquired in the basin, the project is being used largely as a rationale for an extensive series of voluntary land exchanges between private parties and the Bureau of Land Management. The ultimate goal of the SFCT and the Arche-

Photograph 27.2. Rio Chama, Santa Fe Conservation Trust area of interest.
Photo credit: Jack Wright.

ological Conservancy is to protect the entire southern basin from the tide of residential development spreading south from Santa Fe.

The SFCT's greatest activities have concentrated on Atalaya Mountain, Santa Fe's forested backdrop, the site of many current land use conflicts. In 1993, the SFCT negotiated its first conservation easement on 50 acres of highly visible habitat, an action that prompted widespread community support for more significant actions. The SFCT aided Santa Fe County in preventing a proposed housing project on the mountain by structuring a land exchange between the Bureau of Land Management and the developer who provided alternative land on which the housing project could occur. It plans to help other land exchanges, one of which may create an urban wilderness area connecting Santa Fe's residents with the Santa Fe National Forest. The SFCT continues trying to acquire more easements on Atalaya Mountain, but it is currently encountering resistance from a key landowner. A buyout or land exchange may have to be used. This situation reveals how donated conservation easements may not be an effective land protection tool, particularly in instances in which a vital single property is being targeted.

The SFCT has a strong commitment to trails in the Santa Fe area, restoring a road scar on the mountain's face and thus creating a spectacular trail to the summit. In 1997, it brokered an agreement between Santa Fe County and the Santa Fe Southern Railway Company that created a perpetual twenty-foot-wide easement along the railroad line right-of-way from Santa Fe to the small hamlet of Lamy, 11 1/2 miles away. This easement, limiting the right-of-way as a trail, cost $100,000. Santa Fe County and the state of New Mexico each contributed $45,000 to the acquisition cost of the easement, and the remaining $10,000 came from the SFCT.

One of the most frequent criticisms of donated conservation easements that seek to restrict future land use is that owners of property will not voluntarily give up the possibility of future financial returns. Although often true, enough exceptions now exist to mute such criticism. A classic example involved a 19-acre parcel of native vegetation inside the city of Santa Fe itself. This tract offered spectacular views of the Sangre de Cristo and Jemez Mountains and was appraised at an astonishing $4.2 million, more than $221,000 per acre (Photograph 27.3). Still, the owner decided to live in her home and enjoy the beauty surrounding it, donating a conservation easement over the entire parcel to the SFCT to prevent further development. The acreage can be sold by her heirs, but no subdivision can occur.[4]

Conservation easements may play an important role in a community's existence, initiating other actions. In the small village of Tesuque, a landowner donated to the SFCT a conservation easement on 1.924 acres that he used to grow a small amount of hay. Importantly, this parcel of land lay along the community's acequia (irrigation ditch) that, in rural New Mexico, is more than a mere water delivery system; it brings individuals living in the communities together, reinforces community cultural and conservation values, and supports the ideal of communal stewardship.[5] The SFCT believes that the continued existence of functioning acequias is crucial in maintaining traditional ways of land and life in rural New Mexico, just as crucial as pro-

Photograph 27.3. Spectacular Sangre de Cristo Mountains.
Photo credit: National Park Service files.

tecting the ecological characteristics of particular parcels of land through conservation easements.

Successful negotiations for donated conservation easements are still mostly driven by the tax benefits received by the donor. In the western part of the United States, easements reduce land values by 30 to 50 percent. In particular places such as Aspen, Jackson Hole, and Santa Fe, it may be higher. Getting the IRS to accept such diminution in value as an income tax deduction, however, can be difficult, and the SFCT has created a unique procedure to help. The trust contracts with a consultant to prepare a development plan for a property on which negotiations for an easement are taking place. In the plan soils and slopes are analyzed, access and services are assessed, and a design for the maximum allowable development density under existing local plans is prepared. Great pain is taken to make this mock platting as realistic and legally defensible as possible. Once easement terms have been negotiated, the development plan is given to an appraiser, who makes a determination of the before and after value of the property. Using such a procedure, donors of easements to the SFCT now receive an "official" opinion that the value of the property has been diminished by 70 to 80 percent, greatly increasing the financial incentive to landowners. The average cost of a development plan is about $2,500, but it is money well spent by a landowner, who might double his or her tax savings. Thus far, the IRS has not challenged any of these appraisals.

The Santa Fe Conservation Trust has one staff member and an annual budget of $125,000. Half its budget comes from memberships and half from foundations. Dale Ball has been the trust's executive director since its inception in 1993. Ball sees easements as simply one of the many tools available for solving conservation problems. This perspective is essential for trusts operating in both rural and urban fringe settings. Flexibility and creativity demand that no single technique is appropriate in all cases. The SFCT, however, holds conservation easements on 18,000 acres, owns only 7 acres, and has used land exchanges and trail easement purchases somewhat sparingly. Donated conservation easements remain central to the day-to-day operation of the trust.

New Mexico's fractious cultural geography has not severely impaired the operation of the Santa Fe Conservation Trust, but all the SFCT's easements have been donated by Anglos. There are many reasons that no Hispano landowners have yet come forward to conserve their property: mistrust stemming from the past thefts of land grants, small parcel sizes, a real or imagined lack of estate tax exposure, little income to shelter, and the need to retain all development value as an emergency savings amount. Many Hispanos argue that they are already conserving the land by passing it to their children. Restricting the value of that legacy simply makes no sense for most families.

Signs of change are appearing, however. As the value of property continues to rise, estate tax problems are beginning to hit rural "land rich, cash poor" Hispanos. The Taos Land Trust has begun receiving donated easements from Hispano landowners. For now, though, the SFCT and other local groups are still mostly doing business with Anglos who own large tracts.

The complex land tenure pattern of northern New Mexico (Photograph 27.4) may soon grow even more so. Congress has now called for hearings on past land grant injustices. Hispano families and individuals can now come forward with claims for federal land. Tierra o Muerte—Land or Death—may soon become more than a rallying cry. If Hispanos are actually granted land back from the government, they will face massive income and estate tax bills. Conservation easements are a natural solution for preventing a second loss of the land base, not to covert chicanery but to the tax man. Perhaps common ground can at last be recognized as groups like the Santa Fe Conservation Trust come forward to help. Easement use in New Mexico reminds practitioners of the importance of historical and human geography. Attention to such basic matters is critical if easements are to build confidence in a shared future, a future that is biologically and culturally diverse, an undiscovered country of social and environmental healing.

Photograph 27.4. Northern New Mexico, a dramatic and fractious physical and cultural landscape.
Photo credit: J. A. Gustanski

Notes

1. Many of the grants made during the Spanish colonial period (1607–1820) consisted of a central settlement where each family could build a house and farm a small plot irrigated by an acequia (ditch). This core was surrounded by a large ejido (common area) where all villagers could harvest timber, graze livestock, and communally use other resources. Many of the grants made during the Mexican era (1821–1848) tended to be sitios (ranch) grants embracing immense expanses of forest and rangeland.

   Article 8 of the Treaty of Guadalupe Hidalgo in 1848 promised that the United States would honor these land grants. The United States quickly realized that the best forests, soils, minerals, and water resources were in the hands of rural Hispanos. Over time, the inexactness of ownership records—including only the vaguest of property descriptions, a rejection of the legality of commonly owned ejidos, and at times blatant racism—resulted in most of these valuable lands being taken from the original grantees. Some 33 million acres were lost. Some was acquired by ricos (wealthy speculators) and sold off to Anglos; some became part of the public domain.

2. In the 1960s, activist Reis Tijerina and individuals residing on current grants came into armed confrontations with police, and the National Guard was called out to track down *valientes* (militants) based in rural towns like Tierra Amarilla. The Valdez Condo War broke out over a wealthy Anglo's plans to build a large resort community on former *ejido* land. *La Raza* (the people) succeeded in blocking this development, and their action is recounted in the *Milagro Beanfield War*.

3. The Archaeological Conservancy is a national, nonprofit organization established in 1980 by concerned conservationists and archeologists to identify, acquire, and permanently preserve the most significant archeological sites in the United States so that they may be studied and enjoyed by future generations. Although a number of important sites throughout the nation are protected as government parks or preserves, a majority of significant sites are located on private lands and remain unprotected. The Archaeological Conservancy endeavors to ensure their preservation primarily through the acquisition of lands holding these sites.

   The Archaeological Conservancy receives funding from a variety of sources, including individuals, and today has a membership totaling more than 14,000. The conservancy has maintained a dynamic role in educating the public about archeological site destruction and the need to preserve limited archeological resources. It remains the only national nonprofit organization actively acquiring and preserving archeological sites. (Information courtesy of the Archaeological Conservancy, October 1998.)

4. Conservation easements really are about ethics and emotional bonds with place.

5. The *mayordomo* (ditch master) organizes work crews to clean out the acequia each spring, inspects it during the summer, and acts as the mediator in disputes between individuals using the water.

Part III

Conservation Easements:
A Future for Protected Lands
and the Challenges Ahead

Chapter 28

❧ ❧

Land Trusts and Conservation Decision Making: The Integrated Land Conservation Decision-Support Model

Julie Ann Gustanski

To protect or not to protect is ultimately the question. Given limited human and financial resources, land trusts are frequently faced with choices. These choices present several important questions. Are we making sound decisions in the lands we choose to protect? What is current community sentiment toward the lands under consideration? What are the social and economic implications for the community if the lands are protected or are left available for development? To what extent do we try to integrate the choices or decisions about protecting lands in our community with local and regional long-range plans? These are questions that private nonprofit land trusts and their public counterparts are increasingly having to answer, yet the tools to adequately and judiciously answer them do not currently exist.

As previous chapters amply demonstrate, a mélange of legislation and programs is now in place across the nation to protect a diversity of land resources. At the heart of many of these efforts are the more than 1,200 local and regional land trusts that either facilitate the protection of lands through tools like conservation easements or in supplement to public agency efforts. Although such efforts generally receive broad public support, no formal examination to explore the interwoven linkages between social and economic values, policies sanctioned through our laws and the land conservation has been made, until now. Appropriately, the *land trust lens* is used to aid in the development of a tool designed to incorporate ethics (social values) and economics.[1] The integrated land conservation decision support model (ILCDS) has been developed to assist land conservation organizations and agencies in making sound judgments on the protection of limited land resources, using an integrated decision-making approach (Figure 28.1). Extending beyond traditionally used ecological constraints, ILCDS's synthesized system incor-

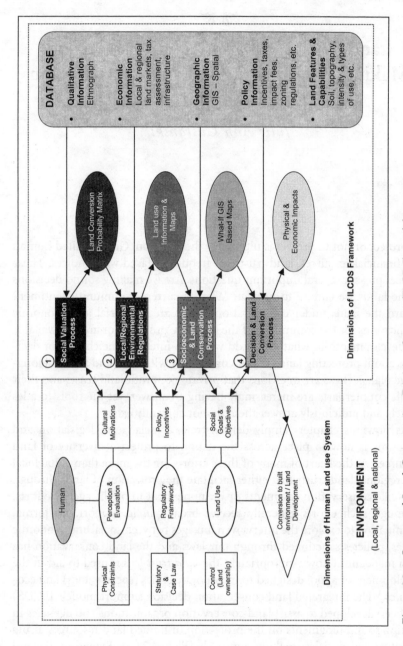

Figure 28.1. Integrated Land Conservation Decision Support (ILCDS) model structure.

Source: J. A. Gustanski (1998)

porates both qualitative and quantitative information required to evaluate the protection of privately held land in an intergenerational context.

The ILCDS model provides a comprehensive, flexible, and user-friendly software framework for mounting social, economic, land resource, and policy information and for examining alternative conservation development scenarios. It is intended that the ILCDS model be as flexible in facilitating the decision-making process as conservation easements are in their diverse applicability to protecting land resources.

In coming to a more comprehensive understanding of the nation's land trusts and implications for such an instrument, a 10 percent sample of land trusts from across the United States were questioned.[2] More than 150 professionals from 139 organizations across the United States and Britain were interviewed to identify a range of objectives, covered in greater detail later. Figure 28.2 shows the geographic distribution of interviews conducted across the United States.

Ninety-six of the 120 interviews for the United States, or 80 percent, were conducted between July and October 1996. To maintain uniform standards and consistency in the personal interview process the twenty-four remaining interviews were completed between September 1997 and June 1998 on miscellaneous conference and business-related trips to the United States.[3] Across the interview population, a standardized question set was consistently presented through a structured interview process (Appendix 28C).

Open-ended questions were selected because they provide flexibility, encourage cooperation and rapport, and allow for a truer assessment of what the participant actually believes. In addition, open-ended situations can elicit unexpected responses, which may enrich the understanding of relationships and hypotheses. (Cohen and Manion, 1989). Times of interviews ranged from fifty-five minutes to two hours and twenty minutes.

The results of the interviews carried out with conservation professionals in both the United States (120) and the United Kingdom (19) indicate a strong desire to use a more integrated framework to facilitate the decision-making process. Ninety-six percent of the 139 organizations interviewed felt that their land conservation efforts would ultimately be enhanced through the use of decision-support software that extends beyond traditional ecological and criteria constraints by using and integrating qualitative social and economic information.[4] Interviews were both regenerative and productive, and extended insights into potential uses of such a model were gained. Among potential uses and benefits of the ILCDS model most frequently cited by land conservation professionals were (1) to facilitate decisions between competing parcels; (2) to assist in garnering public support; (3) to help leverage project specific funding from the community; (4) to influence political support; (5)

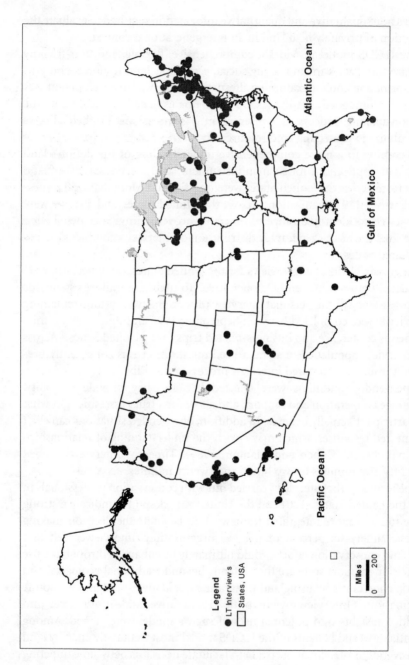

Figure 28.2. Distribution of U.S. land trust interviews (1996–97).
Phase III Expert Interviews: Public Attitudes Toward Land and Conservation (1997), J. A. Gustanski

Legend
● LT Interviews
☐ States, USA

Atlantic Ocean

Gulf of Mexico

Pacific Ocean

Miles
0   200

to provide a system of checks and balances on community support, values, and attitudes; (6) to provide useful information to be coordinated with other tools (e.g., Land Evaluation Site Assessment systems, ranking criteria, soils, ecological); (7) to provide tangible data on the largely intangible factors; and (8) to guide proactive decision making on current and future land protection work in the region.

This chapter presents the transdisciplinary approach based on current research carried out in the United States and United Kingdom on the complex and interdisciplinary relationship of the *ethics-economics-policy* paradigm (Figure 28.3).[5] The paradigm is set in a land conservation framework viewed from the little explored private lands perspective. The paradigm acknowledges that a suite of complex factors—including social, economic, and policy characteristics—interact with their environmental counterparts to drive land use changes. The ILCDS model is developed through assessment of the paradigm and is intended to integrate its various agents: economic efficiency, social equity (between and within generations), behavioral models of resource use, and other patterns of human and economic development. The fundamentals of the paradigm are framed, operational dimensions are for-

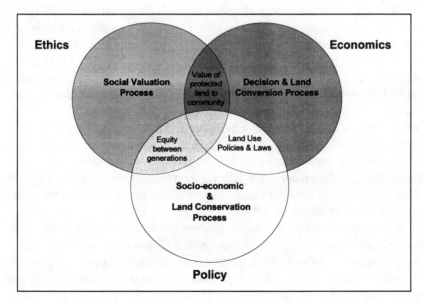

Figure 28.3. The ethics-economics-policy paradigm and land use decision-making context.
Source: J. A. Gustanski

malized (e.g., land resources, sustainability, community, environment), and their integration into the model are examined in context.[6]

Land

Land. This single word has any number of connotations. It signifies solid ground, the physical environment at large, a rural farmstead, an urban industrial site, public and private property. For some, it holds deep personal meanings. This diverse association of ideas about land shows the extent to which the concept is interwoven with culture and points clearly to differences in the ways in which land is perceived and valued in American society. These differences in turn give rise to some very difficult land use issues and conflicts.

Across the country, millions of acres of *private* land have been protected, yet there remains no documented measure to support its important role, thereby leaving a substantial gap in our understanding of the balance, connections, expectations, and obligations between landscape and society. Understanding the connections between theory, research, and analysis is in many ways similar to understanding the paradigm at hand: Each area functions to accomplish a different piece of the overall puzzle. In the context of land conservation, the social constructs, economic implications, and various policies do not and cannot occur in isolation from one another.

Throughout the preceding chapters, authors have focused on efforts of state and federal governments in the United States to strengthen both legislative protection and policy guidance on the conservation of the land. The recent changes to tax law via Taxpayer Relief Act of 1997, together with modifications to the American Farm and Ranch Protection Act, are recent examples.[7] Although such measures reflect strong public opinions and support for the protection of land, there is a lack of substantive evidence to support the assertion that, other than encouraging tourism, for example, conservation does contribute significantly to the long-term social and economic well-being of our communities. This, in part, is the impetus behind this research and forms the foundation for what follows. Every effort was made to provide depth and balance, drawing together views of the public, conservation professionals, and academic expertise.

At the heart of the conundrum is that the regulations, policies, ordinances and plans that govern the use of private land focus on *how* the land will be developed, not *if* it should be developed. The essential purpose of regulation is therefore not to conserve land but to see to it that developments are of the desired type and intensity, that design criteria are met, that local infrastructure can handle the increased load, and that the effects on services and taxation are considered. For any number of reasons, the traditional paradigm operating through regulatory attempts to force people to protect land often falls far short of intended goals. Principal among these is the failure of officials to face the reality that conservation has more to do with socioeconomics and psychology than with planning theory and law.

What, then, is required of land conservation leadership into the twenty-first century? The emerging metaphysics of conservation is a call to ethical responsibility, focusing squarely on the values that are a requisite to a just and sustainable world. These "values" should not be confused with mere individual preferences. They arise naturally and continuously from the act of human participation in community and in nature.

Therefore, the challenge is to comply with different, interdependent targets of sustainability and development, keeping the future of the planet in mind. This challenge calls for the design and application of multidisciplinary models such as the ILCDS and the definition of consistent and operational terms of sustainability. Accessibility of such decision-support tools is a critical factor. Accessibility as generally defined here pertains to both cost and ease of use. If such tools are so complex that only their creators are able to use them efficiently, they will be of little value to the organizations, which such information will ultimately benefit. The ILCDS model was specifically designed with input from the land trust community and with their interests in mind.

Through analysis of the paradigm, the objective here is to lay forth the conceptual framework and development of the ILCDS decision-support tool to enable those involved in the conservation of land resources to (1) proactively plan for the future, (2) justify particular decisions made, and (3) use information obtained in garnering public and political support.

Issues of Land Ownership: An Overview

In any discussion relating to the protection of land resources, one must ultimately look to its ownership. In the United States, some 60.2 percent of the land base is privately owned. The remaining acres are held in various states of public ownership, with approximately 31.1 percent held by the federal government and 8.7 percent held by either state, county, or municipal governments (Table 28.1).

With a nationwide average of something less than 40 percent of the total land mass held in public ownership, one might ask, Why, then, has the conservation of land resources historically been expected to be a function of government rather than of private landowners? Although outside the boundaries under examination, this question must stay in the frontline of our consciousness during our explorations. It is also important to remind ourselves that there are two important tenants that pertain to traditional legal and social notions of private landownership. First, owners of land are entitled to do what they wish with their land and have no individual responsibility for its

Table 28.1. Public vs. Private Land Ownership in the United States (rounded averages)

Total Land Area	2,323 million acres
Total Land Area Federal Ownership	726 million acres
Percentage of Total Land Area	31.25
Total Land Area State Ownership	197 million acres
Percentage of Total Land Area	8.48
Nongovernment-Owned Land	1,400 million acres
Percentage of Total Land Area	60.26

Note: Lands under federal ownership as reflected in the table include national forests, national parks, Bureau of Land Management (BLM) lands, lands under the jurisdiction of the Bureau of Indian Affairs, national wildlife refuges, historic and cultural sites and wilderness areas.

Source: Statistics were derived and averaged using various resources, including: U.S. Bureau of the Census, *Statistical Abstract of the United States: 1991*, 11th ed. (Washington, D.C.: U.S. Government Printing Office, 1991) p. 201; U.S. Department of the Interior, U.S. Fish and Wildlife Service, *Annual Report of Lands Under the Control of the U.S. Fish and Wildlife Service as of September 30, 1994*, (Washington, D.C.: U.S. Government Printing Office, 1994); Department of the Air Force, *Military Real Property Controlled as Installations* (Washington, D.C.: U.S. Government Printing Office, 1994); U.S. Department of the Interior, Bureau of Indian Affairs, *Branch of Real Property Management Acreage Held in Trust for Individual Indians and Indian Tribes, by State, in 1995* (Washington, D.C.: U.S. Government Printing Office, 1995); U.S. Department of the Interior, National Park Service, Land Resources Division, *Master Deed Listing: Listing of Acreages by State as of 9/30/94* (Washington, D.C.: U.S. Government Printing Office, 1994), and *Land Ownership: Information on the Acreage, Management, and Use of Federal and Other Lands* (Letter Report) 03/13/96 (Washington, D.C.: GAO/RCED-96-40).

stewardship, although they are limited by federal, state, and local laws and by some narrow restrictions in the common law. Second, owners are entitled to dispose of land—that is, pass land from one owner to another—unencumbered by restrictions on its use. Together, these elements have allowed many owners of private property to look after their land only to the extent that it is required for their own activities on it.

These historical attitudes toward the environmental movement and land protection efforts in the United States have essentially had the effect of requiring governments to respond by setting aside land to be held in its natural state or for a variety of recreational and open-space uses. To the extent possible, governments have addressed concerns about a host of environmental and land use impacts by limiting potentially damaging activities, including unwanted development, principally through regulation. A shift in interests and public attitudes has occurred in the 1980s and 1990s, however. New demands have been placed on the protection of privately owned lands, an interest that plays an important role in complementing government efforts to protect land resources. This interest in the protection of private land and the concept of stewardship has invoked community participation in land stewardship efforts and has set a steady path for increased involvement in organizations such as land trusts across the country.

This increased interest in protecting privately held lands has occurred for a number of reasons:

1. Economic development has resulted in sprawling development patterns. This development has effectuated the destruction of forests, agricultural and historical lands, wetlands, and other ecologically important lands to the point of near elimination in some regions of the United States. Conservation becomes imperative, a "now or never" proposition, a literal reality.

2. The market value of private land, particularly in urban areas, has risen dramatically at the same time that government's fiscal resources have been depleted.

3. Many people who have acquired land in the past are now trying to make plans for the future, wanting to ensure that some of or all their land is protected.

4. Environmental awareness has generally increased.

5. With the pressures of urbanization, it is apparent that undeveloped land that is left to an owner's beneficiaries—no matter how well intentioned those beneficiaries are—will come under intensive pressure for development if protection measures are not taken now.

Theoretical Issues

When considering the dimensions of the paradigm at hand, it must be acknowledged that human-influenced landscapes are strongly affected by the integration of social, economic, environmental, and political factors that influence land use decision making. These economic, social, and natural systems operate within an overall ethical perspective that is not always clearly rationalized or articulated. Table 28.2 shows the primary interacting value properties relevant to the multifaceted concept.

The key question in the conservation of land resources is whether or not a particular parcel of land should be protected. At virtually every level, land use decision making calls for resource professionals to make choices between varied interests. In an effort to make sound choices, past practices have commonly involved assigning market values to objects and activities as a means

Table 28.2. Values in the Ethics-Economics-Policy Paradigm

Dimensions	Social and Ethical	Socioeconomic	Environmental and Ecological	Sociopolitical
Land Resources	Access, conservation of resources, stewardship	Exploitation, use of resources	Natural resources, water, air, bioecological systems	Education, human resources, population
Sustainability	Ecocentrism, ideology, justice, stewardship	Employment, carrying capacity, inter- and intra-generational equality	Biodiversity, quality, ecological continuity	Community health and welfare
Community	Shared values, coexistence, trust	Employment, poverty, need, choice	Biodiversity, natural amenities	Empowerment, identity, cognition, participation

of choosing the best option; the logic is that which is worth the most must be the best. Tangible goods and services are given values based on their contribution to humanity's growth, development, or success; the more a particular end fulfills human wants and needs, the more valuable it is. This market valuation facilitates decisions by the ranking of one choice over another.

Other important questions within the context of private land conservation, although not specifically addressed within this volume, include:

- How can those benefits produced by land conservation efforts that are not directly in the price of land and constituent environments protected be valued?
- What, if any, role is played by "anchor" parcels of protected private lands?
- What contribution can protected private lands make to the local or regional economy?
- What scale of land conservation and urban or suburban regeneration is required to generate a potential for satisfying lifestyle demands that, in turn, reinforce the success of private land conservation efforts by attracting people to existing developed core areas over suburban or rural developments?
- What role does conservation play in contributing to the image of our communities?

Decision makers faced with important questions such as these are beginning to realize that monetary valuation alone often unfairly favors commercial interests while failing to incorporate values that do not readily lend themselves to the market system (e.g., intrinsic, aesthetic, spiritual). Many problems are now seen as being as much value based as they are fact based, and sound decisions are seen as requiring knowledge of not only relevant facts but also meaningful values.[8] Values can be used to make judgments or to specify the relationship between things. Rational values involve standards for truth, moral values address standards for conduct, aesthetic values identify standards for appreciation, and spiritual values seek standards for meaning.

Humanity values land and its diverse resources not only because they provide services to people (e.g., food, recreation), but also for altruistic or ethical reasons. Public policies or individuals can control the flow of these services, creating different benefits and costs. For example, an acre of wetland may trade in the real estate market on the basis of its value for commercial or residential development, but this value is likely to be significantly different from its value as wildlife habitat, as a means of controlling floods, or as a groundwater aquifer-recharging mechanism. Because these services exhibit the neoclassical economics-defined characteristics of externalities, common property, and public goods, market forces cannot be relied upon for them to reach either their highest valued use or their true social value attributes. This economically recognized failure of the market system to allocate and price environmental services and resources correctly creates the need for other means of measuring values to accurately guide decision making.[9]

Although decision makers set policy frameworks, it is in local communities and by and large on private property that action takes place. Taken on a case-by-case basis, various actions may not appear particularly significant, yet taken together they will both shape and determine the future sustainability of the community. The ethics-economics-policy paradigm invokes the need to listen to the views of people who are most directly affected by changes to land use and the landscape of their communities as well as those who are responsible for the management and protection of land resources and their diverse ecosystems. Doing so will lead to the development of land conservation incentives and techniques that are more likely to succeed in promoting the conservation of land resources and in ensuring a more sustainable future.

Method

To address the integration of the paradigm's agents, an accurate measure of expectations and obligations possessed by individuals within society is necessary. Appropriately, this research employed a multiphased survey approach to assess current public sentiments toward land and conservation.[10] This survey work was vital to interpreting the qualitative information pertaining to social philosophies on the conservation of land.

Phase I: Focus Groups

To identify key issues, a series of twelve semistructured focus groups from the United Kingdom and United States were conducted. Questions were designed to obtain critical information as to the realm of land and conservation issues at the forefront of concern in the general populace. Qualitative data obtained from focus group sessions was analyzed using Ethnograph[11] (see Appendix 28A for the focus group question set). Although thousands of miles, many states, and an ocean apart, the similarities in group discussions and issues raised were significant (Table 28.3). These findings were later introduced in an "issue set" that accompanied the mail survey in phase II (see Appendix 28B for the survey). Table 28.3 identifies the location of urban and suburban focus groups held.

Table 28.4 reflects the sixteen most frequently referenced land use and environmental concerns from phase I focus group findings. The table also gives representative percentages of phase II survey respondents in the United States and United Kingdom who felt that the issues identified in the focus-

Table 28.3. Focus Group Locations

Urban Session Locations	Rural/Suburban Session Locations
Edinburgh, U.K.	East Fortune, U.K.
Dundee, U.K.	Tayport, U.K.
Newcastle, U.K.	Durham, U.K.
St. Paul, Minnesota	Lake Elmo, Minnesota
Greater Philadelphia, Pennsylvania	Centerville, Pennsylvania
San Jose, California	Scots Valley, California

Table 28.4. Public Attitudes Toward Land and Conservation

Issue	United States (%) Very Serious or Serious	Britain (%) Very Serious or Serious
Pollution	96.7	98.7
Water quality	96.5	94.8
Hazardous waste disposal	93.0	94.4
Forests and deforestation	87.6	86.3
Land conservation	87.3	88.2
Traffic and transportation	87.1	97.8
Recycling	86.0	85.4
Nuclear energy	84.3	88.8
Destruction of habitat	84.1	86.2
Exploitation of natural resources	83.8	84.9
Poor planning and mismanagement of land	83.8	81.9
Population	81.5	87.1
Urban and suburban sprawl	78.0	85.4
Farming methods and sustainability	76.1	79.7
Wetlands	70.8	55.6
Preservation of historic sites	54.3	56.4

group sessions were either "very serious" or "serious" issues for society as they pertain to land use and conservation.

Phase II: Mail Survey

The mail survey, "Public Attitudes Toward Land Use and Conservation," was administered in Britain and in the United States in July and August 1996, respectively. Information derived from focus groups together with information distilled from other surveys and interviews with appropriate officials and organizations aided survey development. Surveys were distributed to a stratified random sampling of people aged eighteen or over, with an equal distribution by gender, geographical location, and socioeconomic profiles in each country.

The survey contained questions about the familiarity with land use, conservation, and environmental issues; ranking of social, land use, and related environmental problems; willingness to pay for conservation measures; and socioeconomic information.

Phase III: Expert Interviews

Over 150 individuals from 139 land conservation organizations across Britain and the United States were interviewed. Interviews occurred between July and October 1996 and between September 1997 and June 1998 (see Appendix 28C for Interview Questions). Interviews were intended to identify a range of issues, including (1) "measures" of success, (2) primary conservation methods or tools used, (3) attitudes held and expressed by the general public, (4) decision-making processes and procedures employed by organizations, and (5) reflections on the use and usefulness of the proposed ILCDS model and the need for a more holistic approach or instrument to facilitate decision making.

Evidence from phase III interviews indicates that approximately 96 percent of those conservation professionals interviewed felt strongly that the land protection efforts of their organizations would be enhanced if they had the advantage of information gained through the use of a decision-support system as that presented by the ILCDS model.

Phase IV: Model Development and Site Implementation Tests

Future research will center on full-scale model development. The model will be used on case study sites using an interactive, GIS-based land use planning support system to assist in projecting future implications and evaluating the likely impacts of policy choices and assumptions determined by the ethics-economics-policy paradigm. Distillation of information from phases I, II, and III enable the derivation of a formal measure that may be interpreted as the "policy" component key to the foundation of the model.

Results

In both focus groups and the subsequent mail survey, it was found that one source of frustration or anxiety over the protection of local or regional landscapes is related to both the players and the process. Generally, people felt that there was a lack of community participation in the decision-making process, resulting in "lack of connection and knowledge about local issues" and "apathy."

Participants in both focus groups and the mail survey were often unclear about their individual and collective or community roles and responsibilities within the process, one that is predominantly defined by vast bodies of laws, regulations, and rules. Findings also indicate support for viewing the ethics-economics-policy paradigm through the land trust lens; respondents overwhelmingly vested their trust for information delivery on land use and conservation issues with private, nonprofit conservation organizations over government-driven public agencies (Table 28.5).

The forgoing, not being the focus of this chapter, serves simply to illustrate the magnitude of perceptions and values held by the general population. From a social and cultural perspective, the ownership and use of land have formed the visions and perspectives of people across the United States. Con-

Table 28.5. Level of "Trust" by Institution Type

Institutional Framework	United States (%)	
	Most	*Least*
Nonprofit environmental and conservation organizations	57.8	1.6
Scientific	19.0	1.4
Government agencies (Department of Environment, Department of Natural Resources, etc.)	10.1	12.4
Friends	4.7	11.9
Industry	4.4	31.1
Local or municipal authorities	2.6	11.7
Media (newspaper/television/radio, etc.)	0.9	8.0
Advertisements	0.5	20.8

temporary debates over landowner's rights and landownership are explicit manifestations of deep-seated feelings for the land. Whether expressed as a national pride in the landscape and wildlife or rage at the desecration of the land, the concerns are real and are widely expressed.

The remainder of the chapter focuses on the integration of the various properties fundamental to the ethics-economics-policy paradigm and the ILCDS model in the context of private land conservation.

Framing the Paradigm for Land Conservation Decision Making

Figure 28.4 conceptualizes the challenges and complexity of traditional decision-making processes surrounding the ethics-economics-policy paradigm in a land trust context.

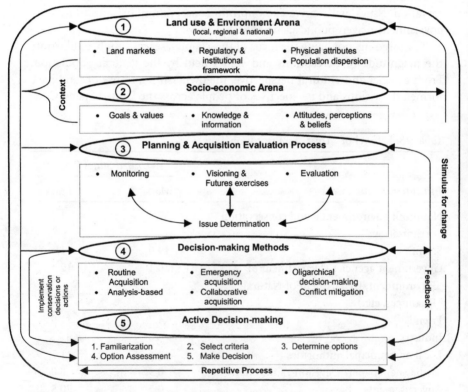

Figure 28.4. Land trust decision-making environment.
Source: J. A. Gustanski

Land Use and Environmental Arena
(Local, Regional, National)

Within the first arena is the state of land use and the environment (local, regional, and national). This arena envelopes four broadly defined conditions:

Land markets, availability of land, and development pressures: Ultimately through the interaction of supply and demand, land will transfer to its highest and best use as determined by the market. As the total supply of available land is fixed, land prices are often regarded as being determined by demand alone.

Regulatory and institutional framework: In its broadest understanding, institutions are simply patterns of expected human behavior that are enforced by both positive and negative social sanctions. Decision making with regard to the protection of land and other natural resources is shaped and reinforced by both our formal and informal political institutions, statutes, economic, and community institutions.

Population dispersion, habitat fragmentation, ecological succession, and so forth: The considerations driving decision making in this arena include questions about present populations and their distribution (human, plant, and animal), associations with one another, and shifts in structure and species composition based on fragmentation or connectivity due to natural and anthropogenic factors.[12]

Physical (land use and changes in land use): The transformation of land uses is important to all human issues that involve land. From forestry to economics to biodiversity and conservation to sociology and soil science, all expressly acknowledge and act within a dynamic landscape.[13]

Socioeconomic Arena

Within the second arena are the socioeconomic underpinnings (political institutions, economic systems, goals, attitudes and values, and so forth), the very fabric of our communities. Processes effect change within both arenas. The state of land use and the environment, the more predictable of the two, shifts on its own as well as under the coercion of human influences. In the socioeconomic arena, the changes that occur are predominantly ad hoc, idiosyncratic, and more often than not outside anyone's control, although everyone within a community is a contributor to cultural shifts and value changes.

Both the land use and environment and the socioeconomic arenas are products of social manufacture. Reality percolated through social constructions of words, notions, ideas, values, beliefs, and courses of action, resulting in "values" placed on the protection of land and other natural resources. It may even be argued that people socially construct the environmental issue set, of which land use and conservation issues are major components.

The use of focus groups provided names or labels for such an issue set (e.g., transportation, urban sprawl, forests and deforestation, destruction of wildlife habitat, preservation of historic sites, exploitation of natural resources, population) (see Appendix 28B). Incorporation of the issue set into the mail survey enabled respondents to indicate who they believe is responsible for causing the problems (e.g., developers, greed of consumer oriented society, industry) and who should be responsible for providing solutions to such problems (e.g., government, industry, developers, nonprofit organizations, public at large). The survey also helped to identify "who" respondents, a generic stratified cross section of the population identified as the stakeholders with respect to the negative consequences of the problem and costs affiliated with providing solutions. The socioeconomic constructs specify how various problems relate to each other and are identified as follows.

Goals and values: Goals that drive environmental decision making in a land use context often include public participation, development control, land conservation, and community stability. Broad values that drive decision making include issues of stewardship, sustainability, intergenerational equity, and economic stability (see Table 28.2).

An interesting characteristic of multidisciplinary discussions about the protection of environmental resources, such as land, is that each discipline has a perception that the resource has a "value" defined in terms of the concerns of that discipline, and this value is in some sense distinct from "economic value." In part, this idea follows from the perception that economic value is the same as market price. Most scientists and those working in the land conservation field are acutely aware, however, that market prices often capture very little of the value that such resources have in supporting human activity.

The breadth of the legislation that has been enacted since the era of environmental enlightenment in the United States reflects how shifts in predominant cultural values can work to guide the regulatory and policy framework. In coming to an understanding in the context of decision making, "values" must be examined in light of their effect on policy dedicated to the protection of land resources.

Attitudes toward time, goods, nature, and market vary. In shifting toward this realization, it is suggested that what we might, for example, call nature is, in fact, a projection of social values and order on the environment. One can observe as many "natures" as societies and as many "natures" as value systems. Similarly, attitudes toward goods, time, market, and conservation of land as an element of nature vary from one place to another and presumably vary over time. These perceptions are at the inception of any analysis of the interactions between humans and their complex relationship with the land.

The concept of value relies on a determination of importance that frames the basis for preference. This preference is achieved through our behavior, which includes decisions that ultimately transform the landscape. Individual value systems are rooted on an extremely elaborate aggregation of cultural orientation, experiences, and religious influences, to name a few factors. Economists believe that these values can be and are expressed in market-based monetary systems. Experience, however, reveals that market-based monetary systems are intrinsically flawed by presuming people become better off by satisfying existing preferences and not by developing their preferences. Costanza provides a clear example of this:

> While humans may appear to only directly value the "charismatic mega vertebrates" ... such a valuation implies an indirect valuation for the components of the ecosystem that supports these high profile species. For example, humans may value watching raptors and are unaware or indifferent toward pocket gophers. But if pocket gophers are a critical part of the raptor food supply then humans have derived value for their habitat. The ecological inter-relationships necessary to support the high profile species may mean the entire ecosystem must be protected.[14]

Knowledge: Both existing and new information, which may be either common or scientifically proven knowledge pertaining to the land use and environment issues and the social structure of the community fall into this category.

Perceptions, attitudes, and beliefs: These concepts primarily describe people's views of their current environmental and socioeconomic context and how they envision how the world works. Phases I, II, and III provided further explanations about the complexity of the land use decision-making arena.

Planning and Acquisition Evaluation Process

The basic process of decision making, in the context of land use, lends the functions of oversight and guidance. The first, community visioning or futures activities, contributes to the last, determination of issues. Decision processes are implemented based on the outcomes of the associated diagnostic processes. It is constructed of the following subparts: (1) community visioning or futures appraisal activities (assist in forecasting future local and regional economic situation); (2) monitoring the physical, bioecological, and human processes; (3) evaluating population dispersion, new infrastructure demands, and so forth; and (4) determining the issues.

Land protection and affiliated measures appear to be somewhat better aligned with sets of diagnostic categories that can be directly linked to the decision-module encompassing the process and action of decision making than do other categories of environmental concern (e.g., siting of landfills, groundwater contamination). Attributes of conservation are generally viewed as environmentally positive, and there are at least a handful of ecologically based diagnostic techniques that can be linked in part to the decision-making process and ultimately to actions taken. Thus, an important research task is to assess existing "evaluation tools" to determine the applicability or compatibility with a system more directly related to the social and economic contexts.

Decision-Making Methods

Interviews held with land conservation trusts identified six general forms of decision-making processes aligned with land or conservation easement acquisition processes. For ease of analysis, these were later classified as

- Routine acquisitions
- Emergency acquisitions
- Analysis-based acquisition and conservation decisions
- Oligarchical decision making
- Collaborative acquisition
- Conflict mitigation

Each decision method is implemented in different ways.

These methods of decision making are not, however, unique to issues of land conservation. They all take place within the larger context of institutional and social systems, especially the individual values and beliefs as well as the aggregated norms and knowledge of those most interested in the decision at hand. The decision-making processes are also affected by, and in turn may affect, the structures of the institutions participating in the decision: land trusts and other bodies involved in guiding the use and conservation of a community's land resources as well as contextual institutional activities as retrospective evaluation or community visioning. None of the methods exists as a discrete type; rather, various methods are likely to act in combination, simultaneously or over time. For example, an analysis-centered method may be in support of an elite corps method that may in turn precipitate a conflict-mitigation method. Despite the fluid nature of individual processes and due to their interaction with one another and with context, this typology is a useful construct for clarifying not only where such decision making stands today, but also where it is likely to go in the future.

In the past, and coinciding with a period of vast expansion of land trusts and their land protection efforts, the first four methods have been dominant. Among these processes, the analysis-based and oligarchical methods have been predominant for controversial conservation projects, those associated with significant costs and potential long-term consequences. Since the early 1990s, the concept of collaborative action and learning has received widespread attention as a way to deal with highly complex issues where immediate and tangible values are diverse.

Active Decision Making

The attributes form the substantive phases and activities guiding the land trust's decisions. The following stages are concurrent with other compositions found in the decision-making literature. The proposed framework is slightly different from other formulations, however, in that the identified universal actions are viewed more as the edifice of diverse methodologies to decision making and not merely stages in a penetrating number crunching process. The five stages are (1) familiarize (proposed project issues), (2) select criteria, (3) determine options, (4) assess options, and (5) make decisions.

Elements fundamental to the paradigm include

- Assessment of the community values toward protection of private land
- Cross-disciplinary analysis of land conservation's social and economic benefits
- Assessment of inter- and intragenerational equity issues

Development of the ILCDS model used relative survey, focus group, and interview findings to establish a format useful to those working with the day-to-day complexities of protecting important private land resources.

The Ethics-Economics-Policy Paradigm

The regional dynamics in human-influenced landscapes are strongly affected by the integration of social, economic, and political factors that influence land use decision making. The land use decision-making process as conceived through the integrative ethics-economics-policy paradigm is expanded here to identify the ILCDS component modules and their roles.

The model is developed on the premise that market processes, ethical responsibilities, human institutions, landowner knowledge, and ecological processes influence private lands and the conversion or protection thereof. Therefore, both the sustainability of those lands proposed for protection and those in the position of making land use decisions will benefit from the integration of ethics and economics in facilitating and enhancing the decision-making process.

The structure adopted for ILCDS model consists of four subject modules linked by a common database: (1) social valuation process, (2) local and regional environmental regulations and land use laws, (3) socioeconomic and land conservation process, and (4) decision and land conversion process. The modules and submodules within the conceptual diagram are obviously not mutually exclusive. Figure 28.5 expands the operational framework of ILCDS

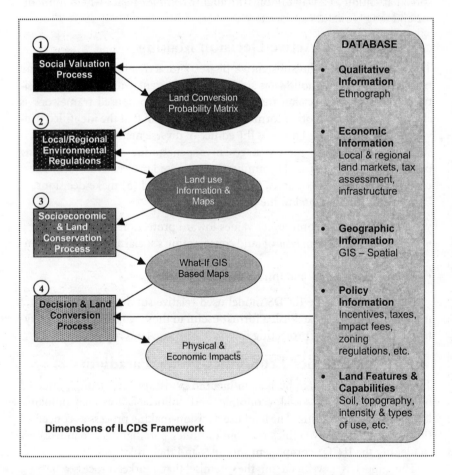

Figure 28.5. Expanding the dimensions of the ILCDS model framework.
Source: J. A. Gustanski

presented in Figure 28.1. It illustrates principal points and provides a foundation for the description of module components.

The first module is that of the social valuation process (Figure 28.6). It contains the socioeconomic models used to derive conversion probabilities associated with land development. These probabilities are computed as a function of (1) preexisting information about environmental and land conservation, (2) characteristics of land ownership, (3) population density, (4) attitudes toward land and conservation, (5) access and transportation costs, and (6) infrastructure costs (roads, sewer and water, schools and other public services, etc.).

The second module contains the local and regional environment information (Figure 28.7) involved in determining the community value of a particular landscape computed as a component of the (1) development pressure and land availability, (2) local and regional land markets, (3) planing process, (4) political structure, and (5) land protection and conservation policies. The land use conversion model resides in the first ILCDS module. It receives as its inputs the conversion probability matrix determined from the social valuation module and accesses the same database of driving variables. It is

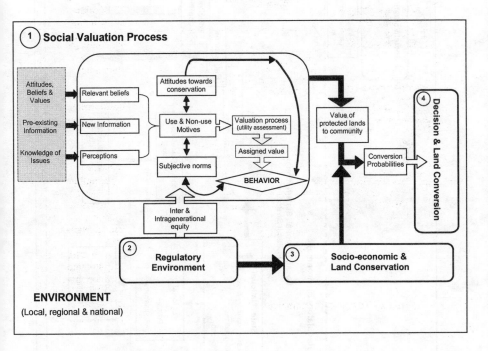

Figure 28.6. ILCDS social valuation process module.
Source: J. A. Gustanski

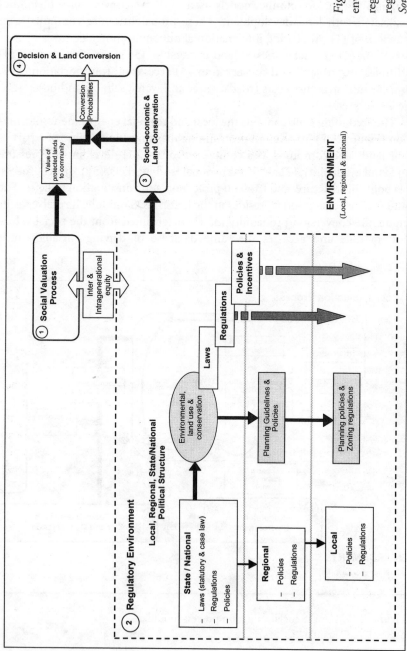

Figure 28.7. Regulatory environment: Local and regional environmental regulations.
Source: J. A. Gustanski

intended that a single iteration of the land use conversion model will produce a land cover map that reflects the community's ethical and economic motivations behind the land use decision-making process as represented in the conversion probability matrix.

Figure 28.8 reflects how land conversion probability is determined in the ILCDS model. The hypothetical landscape presented here is typical of the urban-suburban fringe. To make the job here easier, numbered tracts 1 through 4 are designated as farmland. Tract 1, a small parcel, is some distance from a major highway and is physically separated by a wooded creek bottomland area. Abutting tract 1 is tract 2, which is larger, intersected by a seasonal creek, and visible from the highway. Tract 3 adjoins tract 2, is smaller than tract 2, and is somewhat physically separated from the highway by an area of woodland and open space (although it is in close proximity to a newer suburban residential development and the landowner has subdivided off three, 3-acre residential lots that each contain one single-family residence). Farmland tract 4 is relatively small, has three house lots ranging from 4 to 8 acres, and is physically separated from the other farms by the highway; it is in close proximity to the northern edge of the urban area, although to some extent the river provides a natural buffer zone. The motivating conversion variables will function differently for each tract, depending on the specific nature of the relationship between the tract and the variables. For example, tracts 3 and 4 are under greater development pressures due to their proximity to urban infrastructure (e.g., water and sewer), a main highway, and higher population densities and employment centers. In addition, both farms are of a size that as independent units are not likely to be economically viable over the long term. Tracts 1 and 2 are more likely to be held in agriculture over the long term due to location, size, other physical features, and landowner demographics that reduce the likelihood of conversion in the near future.

Although most land conservation decisions are not so simplistic, for purposes here suppose that the local land trust is faced with the difficult choice of protecting one of the four tracts. The following example speaks to the development and use of the land conversion matrix as an important function of the ILCDS model.

Tract 1: Conversion probability 81, moderate to high
- Removed from urban infrastructure, although proposed new road would enhance access
- Questionable long-term economic viability due to size
- Current zoning: agriculture; enrolled in preferential tax assessment program, tax low
- Elderly farmer, no children, would like to ensure that the land remains in agricultural or open space

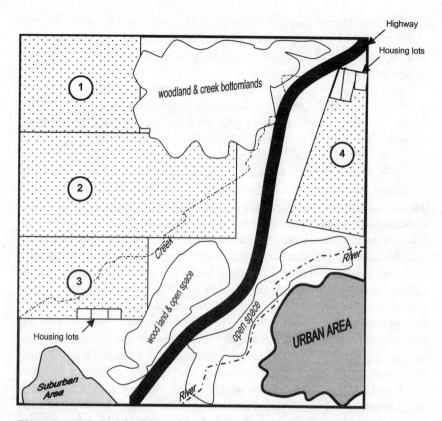

Figure 28.8. ILCDS land conversion probability: A hypothetical model.
Source: J. A. Gustanski

Tract 2: Conversion probability 37, low

- Distanced from urban infrastructure
- Economically viable farm
- Current zoning: agriculture; enrolled in preferential tax assessment program, tax low
- Young farmer seeking to expand land holding and enlarge operation in the long term

Tract 3: Conversion probability 96, very high

- Near urban and suburban infrastructure
- Declining profitability of farm due to size and performance of agricultural markets

- Current zoning: rural residential 1-acre minimum lot size; taxes moderate due to location, enrolled in preferential tax assessment program
- Frustrated aging farmer

Tract 4: Conversion probability 92, high
- Near urban infrastructure
- Not profitable for past two years due to tract size and agricultural markets
- Current zoning: rural residential 3-acre minimum lot size, not enrolled in preferential tax assessment program, taxes high
- Middle-aged executive/farmer; farming is not primary occupation

Conversion probabilities are derived as functions of the social valuation process, regulatory environment, and socioeconomic modules. GIS is used to make spatial calculations between those parcels under consideration and drivers of land use conversion. Assigned values in the form of probabilities are then fed into the decision-making and land conversion process module, where they are again integrated with *parcel specific* data pertaining to motivating factors (e.g., land tenure and management, environmental and socioeconomic factors).

The socioeconomic and conservation objectives defined in the third module (Figure 28.9) use the land cover maps produced by the land use conversion module to estimate impacts to selected resource-supply and planning process variables. These variables include the spatial arrangement of land uses and historical changes due to human impacts. Potential resource-supply variables include land values, available land, development pressures, land use regulations, and incentives. For simulations of land conversions, output maps reflecting predicted changes in land use over variable time and scales can be generated.

Graphical tools such as these can prove invaluable to land trusts in evaluating the long-term course of specific land conservation decisions as well as providing communities with information that can help guide the entire land use planning process.

In the fourth module, land use decisions and conversion information derived from the three other modules and interactive land cover maps generated to estimate impacts to the local or regional land base are used to project long-term inter- and intragenerational physical and economic impacts of various land use decisions (Figure 28.10). The fourth module effectively uses a development pressure grid that is integrated with associated variables from motivating factors, impact assessment, and the planning process. Evaluations can then be performed at ten-, and twenty-year intervals to evaluate the longer-term local and regional economic impacts of various land conservation decisions.

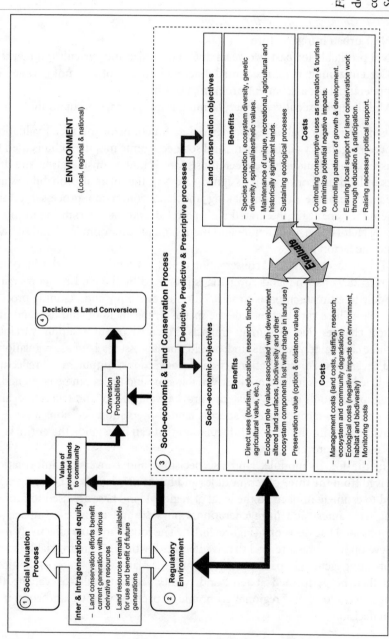

Figure 28.9. ILCDS decision and land conversion process.
Source: J. A. Gustanski

Figure 28.10 Decision & Land Conversion Module

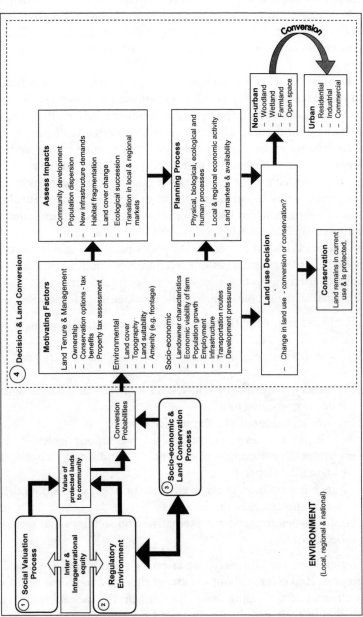

Figure 28.10. ILCDS socioeconomic and land conservation objective module.
Source: J. A. Gustanski

481

Conclusion

Decisions concerning land use and the environment always involve costs and benefits, some with monetary values and some without. In an ideal world, decisions are made where the benefits outweigh the costs. In situations such as the conservation of land, however, where real-world decisions affect not only the immediate resource but the connected community as well, monetary and nonmonetary values must be incorporated into the whole decision-making process.

The great irony of the challenges facing the protection of privately held land resources is that the workings of natural phenomena—the ecological facts of life—are utterly unconcerned with human illusions about our control over nature, our destiny, values, biases, and concerns. The failure to appreciate the distance encompassed by this ironic gap is one reason we are in the current position of urgency to correct and reevaluate entire values systems, those that have led to decades of sprawling development patterns in the name of economic growth and development and to the current turning-point trends. To surmount this breach, we must bridge the gap in understanding the human-land relationship and discard long-held illusions of separateness from the land. The ethics-economics-policy paradigm enables an enhanced consciousness that capacitates our recognition of both individual and community connections to this most elemental natural resource.

The challenge in context, then, is the development of a process that

1. Facilitates clear definitions of the land conservation decisions under consideration
2. Aids in determining or recognizing common community goals and values
3. Facilitates assimilation of values, both monetary and nonmonetary, into the decision-making process
4. Involves all stakeholders (community at large)
5. Coordinates the views of those affected by decisions made
6. Integrates the perspectives of experts (e.g., land trusts, planners, farmers, ecologists, developers)
7. Averts blind reliance on single attribute or linear decision models in the face of complex nonlinear decisions
8. Facilitates determination of alternatives and solutions that serve to optimize the whole

In this light, the ethics-economics-policy paradigm as embodied in the conceptual ILCDS is not about a matter of right decisions or wrong decisions; it is a matter of facilitating those charged with the use and conservation of lands within their jurisdiction in sound decision making. Choices should contribute to individual community goals, be aligned with the values of the people who live and work there, and not detract from their ultimate purpose of protecting the communities sense of place.

Through advancements in technology, policy, and our own understandings of the multitudes of connections that exist at every level, we have become more and more sophisticated in our efforts to protect the lands that provide meaning to the places where we live and work. As we devise new ways of advancing land conservation goals set out in various laws and policies, the use and guidance provided by integrated decision-support tools such as the ILCDS will take both land trusts and conservation tools as the conservation easement into the future.

Notes

1. The need for local input and participation in land conservation measures and assessment of benefits generated is a critical component to the success of the more than 1,200 land trusts throughout the United States and the 130 or more such organizations in the United Kingdom. The land trust model restores a level of local responsibility for managing the bioecological resources of the community that have traditionally been removed from the local people and transferred to central government agencies in offices in distant cities. In the past, abrogation of these responsibilities has frequently removed local communities from the decision-making process, resulting in local communities being not only removed from the process, but left with a deep-seated apathy.

2. At the time the interviews were conducted, some 1,110 organizations were known to exist in the United States. The base sample consists of 114 U.S. organizations from across the country. The research for which this data set was developed was set to rigorous academic standards as part of my Ph.D., in which I look to private land conservation in the United States and United Kingdom to evaluate the ethics-economics-policy paradigm and develop the ILCDS model.

   Having worked for many years in land conservation for public, nonprofit, and private organizations, I became increasingly aware and interested in the ways in which various communities perceive the benefits of privately protected lands. This is particularly interesting considering the fact that those lands protected through the use of conservation easements, do not often allow for any form of public access or may provide only limited visual access. How, then, do we effectively communicate the *value* of private land conservation? After years of talking with local farmers and legal bar associations, radio and television personalities, and politicians at every level, the message that seemed to stick universally was one that could be put to numbers, something tangible in the here and now, something people could use to both individually and collectively "assess" the benefits of private land conservation. It was not that people did not feel sympathetic to the loss of wildlife habitat or that they necessarily liked the sprawling patterns of development that had engulfed their communities; rather, it was the abstraction of protecting lands that would remain in private ownership through legal instruments and organizations with which they were unfamiliar.

One event I recall as clearly as if it were yesterday. One evening I spoke at a community meeting about the various tax and community benefits of protecting land using conservation easements, and a man from the audience stood to ask, "Who are the beneficiaries?" Before I could respond, he followed with, "How do we know there are benefits to our community? How do we know what they are? Are they economic and are they community-wide, or are they for just a few individual landowners?" These are all valid questions, I thought to myself. Decisions are not generally supported by abstract information. People like to feel they are doing something "good," something they have reason to believe will positively contribute to the place where they live and work, but they want more than something that is simply "warm and fuzzy."

This episode and many ones like it put my current research in motion.

3. J. A. Gustanski, *Empirical Evidence from U.S. Land Trusts Supporting the Development of ILCDS Model to Guide Land Protection Efforts* (submitted for publication).

4. In each country, I personally interviewed about a 10-percent sample of organizations known to exist at the time the data collection was undertaken. For the United States, 120 organizations were interviewed; for the United Kingdom, 19.

5. For our purposes of this chapter, the focus is on the information relative to U.S. land conservation organizations, except where reference to a British counterpart seems logical.

6. Although notions of sustainable development and sustainability are fundamental concepts in any discussion on the conservation of natural resources, they remain vague. I choose not to engage in this discourse, however, and instead depend on intuitive understandings. In human systems, sustainability suggests reproducibility of the social unit, through satisfactory economic performance. Related to the human system, the ecological dimension extends our use; that is, ecological sustainability intimates reproducibility of the resident ecosystem. Thus, when taken as a term of sufficient abstraction so as to include natural and human dimensions, sustainability suggests harmonious long-term relationships between human systems and the environment.

7. Section 2031(c); passed into law in August 1997.

8. T. A. More, J. R. Averill, and T. H. Stevens, "Values and Economics in Environmental Management: A Perspective and Critique," *Journal of Environmental Management* 48, no. 4 (1996): 397–409.

9. A. M. Freeman, "The Measurement of Environmental and Resource Values," *Theory and Method* (Washington, D.C.: Resources for the Future), p. 516.

10. Survey methods were focus groups, mail surveys, and interviews and were uniformly administered in both the United States and Britain.

11. *The Enthnograph*, vol. 4.0, a computer program designed to facilitate the analysis of data collected in qualitative research (Amherst, Mass.: Qualis Research Associates, 1995).

12. R. F. Noss, M. A. O'Connell, and D. D. Murphy, *The Science of Conservation Plan-*

ning: Habitat Conservation under the Endangered Species Act (New York: Columbia University Press, 1997).

13. Richard T. T. Forman, *Land Mosaics: The Ecology of Landscapes and Regions* (Cambridge: Cambridge University Press, 1997).

14. R. Costanza, *Ecological Economics: The Science and Management of Sustainability* (New York: Columbia University Press, 1994), p. 18.

ᗩ ᗯ

PHASE 1: Focus Group Discussion Guidelines

Public Attitudes Toward Land and Conservation in the United States and the United Kingdom

Topic 1: Role As an Individual

1. To what extent do you feel a personal responsibility to ensure that certain features of the land are protected for future generations?
2. What lands or landscapes do you feel are most important to protect? .
3. Is there anything you feel you could do to help provide solutions? (or) Do you feel that there is not a lot that can be done?

Topic 2: Land Use Concerns and Issues

1. What do you consider to be the three most significant land use concerns?
    (a) On the local level?
    (b) On the state or regional level?
    (c) On the national level?
    (d) On the international level?
2. In your own experience, what do you feel are the three greatest threats to the countryside or open space?
3. Where do you get the majority of your information or views on such issues?

Topic 3: Quality of Life

1. How do these factors or issues affect the quality of your life?
2. How do these factors or issues affect the quality of life for the community as a whole?

Topic 4: Role of Various Players

1. What do you feel that government (at any level) could be doing to more adequately address such land use issues?
2. To what extent is there a role for voluntary or nonprofit conservation organizations in helping to address such issues?
3. To what extent is there a role in the current educational system for developing a greater appreciation of land use issues?

❧ ❧

Phase II: Mail Survey: Public Attitudes
Toward Land and Conservation

INSTITUTE *of* ECOLOGY *and* RESOURCE MANAGEMENT

The University of Edinburgh
School of Agriculture Building
West Mains Road
Edinburgh EH9 3JG

Fax +44 (0)131 667 2601
Telephone +44 (0)131 667 1041

14 August 1996

Dear Participant,

Your Opinions on Land Use & Conservation

I am trying to find out some important facts on how people feel about the land, specifically their relationship with it and how they feel about conservation. You have been randomly selected to participate in this study. Your participation is very important. The accuracy of the results and further research depends on the responses, from people like yourself, to this survey.

I would be very grateful if you can help me by giving about 15 minutes of your time to complete the following survey form. The information provided will be kept strictly **confidential** and will be used only by myself for the purposes of my research.

Please use the enclosed prepaid envelope to return the questionnaire. Even if you only partially complete the survey, I am still interested in your responses.

I would like to have your personal views. Please do not ask anyone else to complete the form on your behalf or assist you with the form, or I will not have a true cross section of opinions.

Thank you for your assistance and time.

Sincerely,

Julie Ann Gustanski
Ph.D. Candidate
Institute of Ecology & Resource Management

A Part of The University of Edinburgh DIVISION of BIOLOGICAL SCIENCES
The INSTITUTE incorporates Schools of AGRICULTURE (Professor C T Whittemore Head of Institute) ECOLOGICAL SCIENCES
(Professor P G Jarvis & Professor J Grace) FORESTRY (Dr D C Malcolm) and RESOURCE ECONOMICS (Professor J B Dent)

Public Attitudes Toward Land and Conservation

YOUR OPINIONS:

1.   **Do you live in the country, a village, a town or a city?** *Check one.*
○ Country (on a farm)   ○ Larger town
○ Country (not on a farm)   ○ Suburb
○ Village or Borough   ○ City
○ Small town or Township

For Questions 2-8, PLEASE USE THE ENCLOSED "ISSUE SET".
For each question Check (✓) the box that best matches your answer.
You will not need to use all boxes provided

2.   **Of the 16 environmental and land use issues shown, how much would you say you know about each of these issues?** If you have not heard of a particular issue then Check appropriately below.

	1	2	3	4	5	6	7	8	9	10	11	12	13	14	15	16
A great deal																
Quite a lot																
Some																
Nothing at all																
Not heard of																

For those Issues you identified as "Not heard of" in Question 2,
PLEASE DO NOT USE THEM AGAIN.

3.   **How much do you think each issue shown directly affects you?** *Check as appropriate.*

	1	2	3	4	5	6	7	8	9	10	11	12	13	14	15	16
A great deal																
Quite a lot																
Not very much																
Not at all																

4.   **Which of the Issues shown, do you think are most serious for society as a whole?** *Check as appropriate.*

	1	2	3	4	5	6	7	8	9	10	11	12	13	14	15	16
Very serious																
Quite serious																
Not very serious																
Not at all serious																

5.   **How concerned do you personally feel about each of these issues?** *Check as appropriate.*

	1	2	3	4	5	6	7	8	9	10	11	12	13	14	15	16
Very concerned																
Quite concerned																
Not very concerned																
Not at all concerned																

6.   **Some people think there is quite a lot that can be done about these issues, while others think that there is not a lot that can be done and we just have to live with them. WHAT DO YOU THINK?**

	1	2	3	4	5	6	7	8	9	10	11	12	13	14	15	16
Quite a lot could be done																
Just have to live with																
Don't know																

**For Questions 7 and 8 use only those Issues you have placed in the
'QUITE A LOT COULD BE DONE' GROUP.**

7. These are the problems that <u>you think a lot could be done about.</u> Who should take the lead in doing something about them? *Check* the box you think *best* represents who should take the lead in doing something about these issues.

	1	2	3	4	5	6	7	8	9	10	11	12	13	14	15	16
We all should/Public at large																
World governments																
Central government (state or national)																
Local authorities/government																
Developers																
Industry																
Non-profit/Voluntary Organizations																
Farmers/other owners of land																
Others																
Write in Who																

8. If you had the power to improve just <u>one</u> of these which would it be?

Write in the ID Number ____

Questions 8.1 - 8.4 deal only with the issue you have just selected.

8.1 What are your feelings as to the primary causes of this problem? WRITE IN: _____
_____
_____

8.2 In your opinion, who is responsible for causing this problem? *Check all that apply.*

- ☐ We all are
- ☐ Central government
- ☐ Local authorities
- ☐ Developers
- ☐ Industry
- ☐ Farmers / Ranchers
- ☐ Other landowners
- ☐ Others (write in)_____

8.3 What should be done about the issue you have selected? WRITE IN: _____
_____
_____

8.4 Who should pay? (for the protection/to improve/for that). *Check only one.*

- ☐ We all should
- ☐ Central government
- ☐ Local authorities
- ☐ Developers
- ☐ Industry
- ☐ Farmers / Ranchers
- ☐ Other landowners
- ☐ Others (write in)_____

THE ISSUE SET CAN NOW BE PUT AWAY.

9. **Have land uses in your area changed much in recent years?** For example: the number of people living there, number of houses, economy of the area, decrease in number of farms or open lands, etc. Do you think this area has:

- ☐ Changed a lot   (Go to Question 9.1)
- ☐ Changed a little   (Go to Question 9.1)
- ☐ Not changed much   (Go to Question 10)
- ☐ Not changed   (Go to Question 10)

9.1 In what way has it changed? WRITE IN: _____
_____

9.2 In your opinion has this been a good thing for the area in general? *Check one.*

- ☐ Very Good
- ☐ Fairly Good
- ☐ Neither Good nor Bad
- ☐ Fairly Bad
- ☐ Very Bad

10. **The following statements are about the loss of land due to new residential and commercial development in your area.** *Check* the box that best represents the extent to which you agree or disagree with each statement.

	Strongly Agree	Agree	Neither	Disagree	Strongly Disagree
a. Development should only be allowed on the edge of built-up areas.	❑	❑	❑	❑	❑
b. No further development should be allowed in this area.	❑	❑	❑	❑	❑
c. Parks and open space should be part of all new developments.	❑	❑	❑	❑	❑
d. Development should be allowed only on available sites <u>within</u> existing built-up areas.	❑	❑	❑	❑	❑
e. There has already been too much development in this area.	❑	❑	❑	❑	❑
f. This area would benefit from more development.	❑	❑	❑	❑	❑
g. This area would benefit from a long term planning for future development.	❑	❑	❑	❑	❑
h. The car is the primary reason for development in rural areas and open space.	❑	❑	❑	❑	❑

11. **Rank the THREE (1-3) you feel are the greatest threat to natural and open space areas in your area?** *One (1) being the greatest threat.*

—— Industrial smoke & fumes
—— Pollution of water
—— Farming practices
—— Urban & suburban sprawl
—— Housing development
—— Detachment from the land
—— Litter/Waste disposal
—— Highways, freeways & other road building
—— Commercial/Industrial Development
—— Poor land planning/resource management
—— Greed/Attitudes
—— People moving to rural areas/accessibility
—— Something else (WRITE IN) _____

12. **The following statements are about open space in your region.** *Check* the box that best represents your level of agreement or disagreement with each of the following statements.

	Strongly Agree	Agree	Neither	Disagree	Strongly Disagree
a. Modern farming methods damage the rural environment.	❑	❑	❑	❑	❑
b. To protect open space and natural areas we will have to limit the number of visitors.	❑	❑	❑	❑	❑
c. Too much is already done to protect open space.	❑	❑	❑	❑	❑
d. The government should pay more in incentives to owners of land to protect open space lands.	❑	❑	❑	❑	❑
e. Industry should be responsible for the clean-up of industrial eyesores in rural areas.	❑	❑	❑	❑	❑
f. Policies protecting farmland from development should be stronger.	❑	❑	❑	❑	❑

ISSUE SET

Issue 1
Traffic / Transportation

Issue 2
Urban Sprawl /
Development in Open
Space & Rural areas

Issue 3
Farming Methods &
Sustainability

Issue 4
Hazardous Waste
Disposal / Landfills

Issue 5
Land Conservation

Issue 6
Destruction of
Wildlife Habitat

Issue 7
Nuclear Energy

Issue 8
Exploitation of Natural
Resources

Issue 9
Forests & Deforestation

Issue 10.
Mismanagement of Land
Resources / Poor Land
Use Planning

Issue 11
Preservation of Historic
Sites / Areas

Issue 12
Pollution
(air, land & water)

Issue 13
Wetlands

Issue 14.
Water Quality

Issue 15
Recycling

Issue 16
Population

491

g. Unrestricted public access imposes a burden on farmers and other owners of land. ❑ ❑ ❑ ❑ ❑

h. Farmers and other owners of land should look after rural lands. ❑ ❑ ❑ ❑ ❑

i. More facilities are needed for recreational visitors to rural open spaces. ❑ ❑ ❑ ❑ ❑

j. Much can be learned about protecting open space lands by looking to other countries. ❑ ❑ ❑ ❑ ❑

k. Everyone should look after open space. ❑ ❑ ❑ ❑ ❑

l. Policies protecting open space could be stronger. ❑ ❑ ❑ ❑ ❑

m. Lands providing habitat for rare or endangered species are the most important lands to protect. ❑ ❑ ❑ ❑ ❑

n. Lands protected through government payment schemes should allow public access. ❑ ❑ ❑ ❑ ❑

o. More emphasis should be placed on protecting historical landscapes. ❑ ❑ ❑ ❑ ❑

p. Everyone should have access to recreational areas ❑ ❑ ❑ ❑ ❑

q. More areas of the U.S. should be set aside as National Parks so that they are protected from development? ❑ ❑ ❑ ❑ ❑

13. **Would you personally be willing to pay more in taxes** *(local or property)* **if you knew that the funds would be used within your area to create new or improve existing parks, trails or open space corrido for public use?** *Check one.*

❑ Yes (Go to 13.1)　　　　❑ No (Go to 14)　　　　❑ Don't know (Go to 14)

13.1 **How much more taxes would you be willing to pay for such improvements in your area?** *Check one.*

❑ Between 0 and 10%
❑ Between 11% and 25%
❑ Between 26% and 40%
❑ Between 41% and 60%
❑ Up to 70%
❑ Up to 80%
❑ Up to 100% more
❑ Do not know

14. **Do you think there is a greater role for non-profit/voluntary environmental and conservation groups to play in protecting land and other natural resources?** *Check one.*

❑ Yes　(Go to 14.1)　　　　❑ No　(Go to 14.2)　　　　❑ Don't know　(Go to 15)

14.1 **If Yes, What role(s) do you think such non-profit conservation organizations should play in land and natural resource protection?** *Check all that apply.*

❑ Owning & maintaining lands for public use
❑ Holding partial interests or legal restrictions on lands to prevent future development
❑ Helping with local and/or regional planning and conservation issues
❑ Helping with community education and information on land and conservation issues
❑ Promoting sound land use and environmentally friendly development
❑ Promoting farming methods that are environmentally friendly
❑ Helping to develop long term plans and regulations for land use
❑ Education through schools
❑ Monitoring and enforcing land use and environmental regulations
❑ Assessment and survey of land and other natural resources
❑ Inventory and recording of plants, animals, geologic and historic conditions, and other resource features
❑ Creating trails, greenbelts, parks and other recreational areas for public use
❑ Publishing information on conservation for the public
❑ Conducting research on new ways to protect land resources

❑ Other (write in): _____

_____

14.2 **If No, explain what role you see for such organizations.** (write in):

_____

_____

15. **How much would you be willing to contribute <u>annually</u> to such voluntary/non-profit conservation organizations to perform the roles you have just identified?** *Check one.*

$0 ___ $15 ___ $30 ___ $50 ___ $75 ___ $100 ___ **Other** _____

16. **Have you ever personally contributed to a non-profit conservation or environmental organization either as a one time donation or through a membership?** *Check one.*

❑ Yes (Go to 16.1) ❑ No (Go to 16.2) ❑ Can't recall (Go to 16.3)

16.1 **In general do you believe that the group(s) you have supported, have made progress towards protecting land or the environment and that this has had a positive effect on your area?** *Check one.*

❑ Yes (Go to 16.2) ❑ No (Go to 16.3) ❑ Don't know (Go to 16.3)

16.2 **Do you feel the work of such groups is important to your quality of life?** *Check one.*

❑ Yes (Go to 16.3) ❑ No (Go to 16.3) ❑ Don't know (Go to 16.3)

16.3 **As applicable in: (16.1) Will you continue to support the work of such non-profit organizations? <u>OR</u> (16.2 or 16.3) Will you consider supporting the work of such groups in the future?** *Check one.*

❑ Yes ❑ No ❑ Don't know

EDUCATION & GENERAL INFORMATION:

17. **Do you think that children in school are taught too much about land conservation issues, too little, or about the right amount?** *Check one.*

❑ Too much (Go to 17.1) ❑ Right amount (Go to 17.1)
❑ Too little (Go to 17.1) ❑ Don't know (Go to 18)

17.1 **Do you think, for the general public there is too much information about the environment, too little information or about the right amount?** *Check one.*

❑ Too much (Go to 18) ❑ Right amount (Go to 18)
❑ Too little (Go to 17.2) ❑ Don't know (Go to 18)

17.2 **You think there is generally too little information about the environment. What would you like to see done?** (write in)_____

_____

18. **Where do you get most of your information about land use and conservation issues?** (write in) _____

_____

19. **Which <u>ONE</u> of these would you trust MOST and which would you trust the LEAST to tell you about land use and conservation issues?** *Check only one box for each column.*

MOST	LEAST	
❑	❑	Non-profit Environmental & conservation organizations
❑	❑	Government agencies as Dept. of Natural Resources or the Environment, etc.
❑	❑	Local or municipal authorities
❑	❑	Friends
❑	❑	Scientists
❑	❑	Advertisements
❑	❑	Industry
❑	❑	Media/News
❑	❑	Other WRITE IN: _____

20. **Listed below are some things that people have said about land use and conservation issues, you may have even heard comments such as these.** *Check the box that best represents your level of agreement or disagreement with each statement.*

	Strongly Agree	Agree	Neither	Disagree	Strongly Disagree
a. We should find the money to protect important lands by being prepared to pay higher taxes.	❏	❏	❏	❏	❏
b. Industry should be prevented from causing damage to land and the environment even if this leads to higher prices.	❏	❏	❏	❏	❏
c. It is up to all of us as individuals to help protect the land by changing our behavior and attitudes towards this resource.	❏	❏	❏	❏	❏
d. We should find the money to protect the environment by being prepared to pay more for products that are environmentally and ecologically friendly.	❏	❏	❏	❏	❏
e. New jobs should be created even if this sometimes causes damage to the land and the environment.	❏	❏	❏	❏	❏
f. Nothing should be spent on protecting the land or the environment because we can not afford it.	❏	❏	❏	❏	❏
g. Individuals should pay to have recreational access to natural and open space areas in order to protect it.	❏	❏	❏	❏	❏
h. Companies that seriously harm the land or the environment should be shut down.	❏	❏	❏	❏	❏
i. The government could do a lot more than it does at the moment to protect important lands.	❏	❏	❏	❏	❏
j. The protection of land for future generations would be better off in the hands of a non-governmental organization.	❏	❏	❏	❏	❏
k. The government should find the money to protect the environment by spending less on other things	❏	❏	❏	❏	❏

If you AGREE or STRONGLY AGREE with 20k above, go to 21. **All** others go to 22.

21. **What should the government spend less on in order to find money to protect the environment? Should it spend less on:** *Check as appropriate:*

	YES	NO
Defense		
Health care		
Social services		
Law enforcement		
Aid to the 3rd world		
Aid to industry		
Aid to farmers		
Transportation		
Education		

22. **Below is a list of actions. Please indicate whether, in the last 12 months you have done them at least once a week (F), at least once a month (Occ), several times a year (R), not at all (NAA) or never do this (N/A).** *Check as appropriate.*

	F	Occ	R	NAA	N/A
a. Walked in the woods or along the shore	❏	❏	❏	❏	❏
b. Purchased one product over another because it was better for the environment	❏	❏	❏	❏	❏

c.	Picked up other people's litter	❏	❏	❏	❏	❏
d.	Taken bottles, plastic or aluminum to the bottle bank/recycling center or put out for pick up	❏	❏	❏	❏	❏
e.	Bought a magazine concerned with nature or other 'green' issues	❏	❏	❏	❏	❏
f.	Watched a television program about nature or the environment	❏	❏	❏	❏	❏
g	Cut down on the amount of car travel you do for environmental reasons	❏	❏	❏	❏	❏
h	Requested information about 'green' issues	❏	❏	❏	❏	❏
i	Cut down on the use of electricity, oil or gas in your home	❏	❏	❏	❏	❏
j	Joined a conservation or 'green' organization	❏	❏	❏	❏	❏
k	Avoided using pesticides on your garden or lawn	❏	❏	❏	❏	❏
l.	Donated money to environmental, conservation or other 'green' causes	❏	❏	❏	❏	❏
m.	Taken paper to a collection point for recycling or put out for pick up	❏	❏	❏	❏	❏
n.	Became active in community environmental issues	❏	❏	❏	❏	❏
o.	Backed political candidate(s) who supported 'green' issues	❏	❏	❏	❏	❏

23.   **Are you a member of any organization concerned with the environment, wildlife, nature, planning, fishing, hunting, or open space?** *Check all that apply.*

Earth Watch	❏
National Wildlife Federation	❏
Audubon Society	❏
Friends of the Earth	❏
Greenpeace	❏
The Nature Conservancy	❏
World Wildlife Fund	❏
Environmental Defense Fund	❏
State or local Sportsman's Club/Association	❏
Sierra Club	❏
American Farmland Trust	❏
Local/regional land trust or conservancy	❏
Local/regional hiking club	❏
Other similar organizations - (please, list all)	❏

_____

_____

CLASSIFICATION:

The last few questions will enable me to analyze the answers statistically and ensure that all persons in the US are fairly represented. **As stated earlier all information and responses will be held strictly confidential.**

24.   **Sex:**   ❏ Male   ❏ Female

   24.1   Which of these age groups do you fall into? *Check one*

   ❏ 18 - 24   ❏ 25 - 34   ❏ 35 - 44   ❏ 45 - 64   ❏ 64+

   24.2   What is the highest level of education you have obtained? *Check one.*

   ❏ Primary   ❏ Secondary   ❏ Trade or Vocational   ❏ University or College   ❏ Post-graduate

   24.3   How many people in the following age groups are in your household, including yourself? Write in the number in each age group.

   0 - 4 _____
   5 - 10 _____
   10 - 17 _____
   18 - 24 _____
   25 - 34 _____

```
35 - 44    _____
45 - 64    _____
65+        _____
```

24.4   **Do you:**

❑ own your house
❑ rent from council/housing assn.
❑ rent from a private landlord
❑ Other (WRITE IN) _____

24.5   **How long have you stayed/lived in this area?**   WRITE IN _____ years

24.6   **In what area of the Country do you live?**   ZIP CODE _____

24.7   **How many cars/vans or other motor vehicles are available in your household?** *Check one.*

```
0      ❑
1      ❑
2      ❑
3      ❑
More   ❑
```

25.   **Is the chief wage earner in the household:** *Check one.*

Working (full or part-time)   ❑ (Go to Q25.2)

Retired/not working (but with private pension or other means)   ❑ (Go to Q25.2)

Unemployed less than two months   ❑ (Go to Q25.2)

Unemployed over two months   ❑ (Go to Q25.1)

Retired/not working (but on State pension or benefit only)   ❑ (Go to Q25.1)

25.1   **Is there another wage earner in the household?** *Check one.*

❑ Yes (Go to Q25.2)   ❑ No

25.2   **Occupation of 'Head' of Household/Chief Wage Earner.** (Write in full description of current or last main job, and profession/industry)

Job: _____

Profession/Industry: _____

If you have any additional comments you would like to add, please use this page.

Comments:_____

_____

Thank you for your time!

❦ ❦

Phase III: Expert Interview Questionnaire

Question Set

1. How is the "success" of your organization measured?
2. What are the principal land protection tools, techniques, or mechanisms used by your land trust?
3. What are the most prevalent attitudes or perceptions about land conservation efforts that one might encounter in your area?
4. Does your land trust use any decision-making tool, ranking device, or other criteria to assist with making decisions in land protection efforts?
5. Would a tool, such as the ILCDS model outlined, be useful to your organization in guiding long-term land protection efforts?
6. In what ways do you see such a tool being used to benefit your land protection work?

Chapter 29

❦ ❦

Reflections on Patterns and Prospects
of Conservation Easement Use

John B. Wright

The fundamental strength of conservation easements is their flexibility. The preceding chapters well illustrate some of the unique roles easements are playing in open-space conservation across the country.

Their applications of easements are diverse, and, beyond the statutory impediments discussed elsewhere in this volume, their future use seems limited only by the creativity and patience of practitioners. The dominant themes illustrated in this book are (1) the tension between the permanence and amendability of easement restrictions, (2) the use of easements in conservation strategies, (3) the advantages of cooperative partnerships, (4) the role of limited development in easement designs (and as a fund-raising technique for land trusts), (5) the benefits of systematic procedures, and (6) the necessity of comprehending the cultural geography of landscapes we wish to conserve.

The examples also expose a tactical point: Conservation easements are but one tool in a broad array of tools and techniques employed by land trusts, one that gained great momentum in the 1990s and is often but not always appropriate for solving a land protection problem. Where planning regulations or restrictive covenants are too weak and fee simple acquisitions are impossible or infeasible, the sound devise of conservation easements may be the most pragmatic option.

Dennis Collins's chapter (chapter 9) on enforcement problems with an easement in Pennsylvania, however, offers a cautionary tale of how trouble can arise when a grantor requests significant changes in easement terms years after filing. Every easement design requires both extreme care and due diligence, from the negotiation phase through to the actual wording. Advising grantors of the marketability of restricted land is one such issue worthy of repeated exploration. Collins reminds us that even when we employ great care in drafting easement language and creating professional conservation management plans, circumstances and hearts change. What do we do when a landowner wants to weaken easement terms, build more structures, and disturb the landscape? Collins shows that we must be fully prepared to answer those questions. In our haste to "save" that next property, we simply must pause long enough to create easements that have the greatest chance of lasting. In the case Collins describes, the lack of easement enabling legislation in Pennsylvania compounded by the ambiguity of key language within the easement resulted in a substantial weakening of the restrictions. The lessons learned by the land trust were many, mostly that fair, clearly written terms give an easement the greatest potential for endurance and that vague overly zealous terms may be vanquished in court, particularly when the land trust has neither the money nor the will to engage in litigation.

Being human, it is not unthinkable that landowners who grant easements may change their minds about restrictions. Practitioners must enter negotiations with a commitment to discuss and evaluate all possible future uses of the land. In our rush to craft the most stringent restrictions, we must take care not to create time bombs that may well detonate the reputation of the land trust involved. The best foundation from which to address this comes from having a strong, clear mission statement as an organization and preparing a sufficiently detailed baseline report of the land in question. If the baseline report verifies that a certain restriction is necessary to protect key ecological or open space resources and that these are crucial to fulfilling the organizations' mission, we must enter negotiations willing to walk away from the project if that restriction is not included. If the baseline document reveals that a certain level of development or disturbance is compatible with larger conservation goals, we can enter negotiations willing to bend. In every case, easement architects should include only those restrictions required to guarantee the perpetual protection of the land. If the landowner then has a change of heart or cannot market the land to their satisfaction, the trust can at least respond from a position of strength. Perhaps the happiest outcome might result from the trust assisting the landowner in locating a conservation buyer. The benefits of such a strategy far outweigh those of legal proceedings.

Several of the case studies explored how easements can be used to realize conservation strategies. Land trust practitioners have long understood the need to operate both opportunistically—deal with grantors who walk in the door—and strategically by targeting key lands for protection. In chapter 24, Brian Stark shows how a geographic information system (GIS) was used in San Luis Obispo, California, to map property ownership within a proposed greenbelt. Although such approaches have now become somewhat common in the academic setting, more open space planners and land trust staff members need to become adept at using GIS applications to advance their work. Stark shows how a computer system was used both to locate properties and to store and analyze their resource attributes to rank them for acquisition. A community values survey was then integrated into the program to assess public concerns such as aesthetics. It is inferred that lands of lesser importance might be protected by conservation easements rather than by expending public funds on direct purchases. This level of evaluation is increasingly important even in the age of ever-larger conservation bonds being passed by government entities. There is simply not enough money to buy all open space lands. A GIS can be of great assistance in establishing where conservation easements will offer sufficient protection. Where systematic or developed public use is required and where an extraordinary level of land use control is needed, land purchases rather than easements may be required. To implement conservation strategies at the local and regional level successfully, such reasoned analysis is essential for the optimum allocation of both land and financial resources.

Land conservation projects often contain significant historic and architectural dimensions. Seth McKee's case study (chapter 6) of a villa landscape in the scenic Hudson River valley provides much useful material on the interplay of geography, landscape painting, and heritage tourism. McKee suggests how a comprehensive yet flexible approach enabled a mixed application of conservation easement terms, architectural standards, and agricultural plans to protect the viewshed. Any one approach would have been insufficient on its own to protect the Olana viewshed properly. Firm positions were replaced by a rational willingness to alter initial designs to improve the economic viability of the landowners. The result was exceedingly productive: a vineyard was expanded and 5-acre building envelopes were paired with sensitive architectural requirements. In essence, conservation was seen not as "preservation" but as stewardship and responsible use. McKee shows the futility of trying to "freeze" a landscape in an arbitrarily defined "historic period." Rather, landscapes can and should be allowed to evolve without sacrificing historic structures, scenic beauty, and geographic importance. The goal should be to conserve the essence and integrity of a meaningful place, not to reify the false glories of an imagined past.

Robert Myrh's case study from the San Juan Islands (chapter 25) illustrates the patience required to complete conservation strategies. With fourteen transactions in more than nine years, Myrh reminds us of the necessity for setting internal priorities (because publicity is often the enemy of delicate negotiations) and of the need to cumulatively achieve goals by working with a key landowner to achieve community trust through time. This same essential message is derived from Randolph Brown's detailed example (chapter 13) from the Great Smoky Mountains, but here, private planning schemes were devised that accommodated limited development to make the conservation element work for the landowner. Now largely complete, the resulting landscape is one that maintains a strong historic connection to rural Appalachian culture. In chapter 7, Leslie Reed-Evans offers the similar instruction from her case study near Mount Greylock, in Massachusetts, yet in this case, a new wrinkle emerged. The nonprofit organization actively participated in the design and development process to ensure that limited housing and conservation remained compatible. In addition, this model shows how sensitive limited developments can generate funds that a land trust can apply to other open space protection efforts.

These examples reveal the power of strategically targeting key lands. As subdivision, land clearance, and other perturbations increasingly fragment landscapes, conservation strategies aimed at protecting large collective blocks of land and linear corridors of open space are ever more critical for meaningful success to occur. The lessons derived from such fields as conservation biology, landscape ecology, historic preservation, environmental planning, and indeed agricultural economics all converge on a single fact: Small, isolated tracts of undeveloped land are insufficient to secure ecological health, agricultural continuity, and the solace of open spaces so profoundly needed by human beings.

In this light, cooperative projects involving several land trusts and public agencies are often proving the most feasible approach to conserving regional landscapes. Mark Ackelson describes how four land trusts are collaboratively working to conserve the blufflands along portions of the Upper Mississippi River. Organized by the Iowa Natural Heritage Foundation and funded by the McKnight Foundation, an alliance of trusts is now in place. Beyond the strata of organization is a simple concept: use GIS technologies to analyze data, involve all land trusts and public agencies such as the U.S. Fish and Wildlife Service where appropriate, and coordinate all land protection activities. As the number of land trusts continues to rise in the United States, this type of effort must become the norm if counterproductive competition for easement donations is to be avoided. Acrimony between land trusts now simmers beneath the surface of the seemingly unified "land trust community" in some places. Ackelson shows how such psychodrama can be avoided by defining roles and sharing the abundant work before us. He also reveals the importance of low-interest loans from national organizations such as the Conservation Fund.

Truly cooperative conservation efforts involve multiple dimensions, requiring participation at every level, from local trusts to international organizations. In chapter 13, Charles Roe explores long-term efforts to protect the scenic character of the Blue Ridge Parkway. In doing so, he amply demonstrates how shortsighted efforts in the past have resulted in the need to reprotect some lands. The National Park Service conserved portions of the 469-mile-long parkway corridor during the 1930s and 1940s using "short form scenic easements." Yet because of vague language, lack of participation, local governmental resistance, misunderstanding, and a failure to enforce easement provisions, far fewer lands have been protected than expected. Today, the Conservation Trust of North Carolina (CNTC) is one of the major nonprofit players in securing the robust protection of the Blue Ridge Parkway corridor. In addition to the $1.3 million CNTC effort, a coalition of conservationists, business people, and government agencies are also involved. Donated conservation easements are now being actively solicited and received. The recent donation of an easement on 17,000 acres (and fifteen miles of the parkway) is heartening. The sobering lesson for practitioners, however, is that such actions may not have been necessary if the initial National Park Service easement effort had been more systematically applied. Those first easements came quickly but were not nearly as durable and effective as once believed. The National Park Service is now joining land trusts all along the Blue Ridge Parkway to craft lasting conservation easements before more key lands are lost to development.

Tom Quinn shows in chapter 20 how land trusts played a role in community leadership during ongoing efforts to create a farm and river greenway on Wisconsin's St. Croix River. This watershed is undergoing an all too familiar conversion from a relatively natural farming landscape to a suburban smurge of homesites, shopping centers, and strip developments. Two land trusts, numerous government agencies, several foundations, and the Boy Scouts of America are now cooperatively creating a vision for conserving the best of what remains of the St. Croix National Scenic River corridor and adjacent farmlands. The Englewood Property, a 1,120-acre tract, was secured for $1.7 million raised by these partners. A management plan for the stewardship of the property is being prepared. Quinn believes that the larger outcome of this project is community cohesion and shows how relationships built during the Englewood project are now continuing. The important point is that conservationists and farmers are now personally allied. With that long overdue alliance in place, the future of the watershed looks promising. Land trust work is built on human trust. Once that difficult hurdle is crossed, tools such as conservation easements can then attain more widespread application. In chapter 18, Linda Mead's account of Tom Bailey's experience along the Mackinaw Headlands reveals the same message: Land trusts can bring communities together to forge a better future. Whether the goal is protection of 25 acres of productive land in a New England village, a 600-acre estate, or an entire watershed, cooperative projects involving community action are often the most effective strategy.

Yet there are cases where largely independent action is the best course. The story of the Montana Land Reliance (MLR) in chapter 23 demonstrates how a clear mission, fieldwork, streamlined professional easement procedures, and a skilled, well-paid staff can result in extraordinary success. It is interesting that no single conservation easement done by MLR stands out as particularly unusual, which is testimony to their agility in scooping projects and moving things along in a timely manner. Although every easement involves detailed and sometimes lengthy negotiations, this trust has protected some 280,000 acres by being clear, cordial, and direct with landowners. The MLR now completes about fifty easements per year, which requires that they have many irons in the fire. Too many land trusts believe that all their time must be spent on one or two properties, even when progress is glacially slow or the landowner seems uninterested. The MLR operates from both a strategic and opportunistic vantage, allowing it to systematically target and complete projects within various watersheds and giving it the flexibility to take on worthwhile projects as opportunities present themselves. Perhaps thinking big comes naturally in Big Sky country.

The Santa Fe Conservation Trust (SFCT), detailed in chapter 27, is a highly accomplished group. Their successes have involved not only donated easements, but land purchases, trail projects, and archeological conservation. Large measures of these achievements have resulted from a comprehension of the complex, often fractious historical and cultural geography of New Mexico. Although all the conservation easements held by the SFCT were donated by Anglo landowners, this landscape has a large and long-standing Hispano population. The continuing repercussion from centuries-long disputes over land tenure makes for unique challenges, but the first Hispano-donated easements are now starting to come in, testimony to the time involved in unraveling not only the complexities of land trust work but of other cultures. Although New Mexico is clearly a more dramatic case than many, it underscores a vital, often missing element in conservation easement training: a basic knowledge of the cultural geography of the place where we live. Easement negotiations involve understanding the personal, financial, familial, and psychological needs of landowners. It seems clear that cultural geography plays a role in forming the ideals and expectations of people. In cultural regions such as Hispano/Indian/Anglo New Mexico, Mormon Utah, Cajun Louisiana, Scandinavian Minnesota, and Yankee Maine, it seems obvious to learn the beliefs and histories of people. Every landscape has its own distinct cultural geography that shapes notions of land and life. Those wishing to successfully negotiate conservation easements would be wise to set aside the tax codes and legal briefs for a moment and pick up a book on the cultural and historical geography of the landscape they are trying to save.

Any collection of case studies can only represent a larger whole. Yet the these chapters provide much needed context and timely updates on how easements are being applied across the country. The details of these examples undoubtedly touch on similar successes and difficulties being experienced.

The many associations that tend to the affairs of cattle and sheep raisers, wheat and soybean growers, and farmers and ranchers of every sort simply must be brought on board if easements are to succeed in conserving entire landscapes. There is no way for this logical outcome to be easy. Sometimes, there are decades of mistrust to overcome. Although conservation easements have little to do with environmentalism and the "shutting down" of agriculture, a perceptual barrier still exists in some regions. There are no local land trusts in farming states such as Oklahoma and far too few in the Great Plains. Utah has one—with all that farmland and ranchland—only one. Even in Montana, with the success of the Montana Land Reliance, there are many ranchers who simply do not trust urban-based, nonagriculture people. Still, the tide is slowly turning. The Colorado Cattleman's Association has formed its own land trust and now holds more than a dozen conservation easements; this same group loudly opposed conservation easements in the media. In southern New Mexico, ranchers who have a visceral hatred of planning regulations and "open space" are now forming the Southern Rockies Agricultural Land Trust, which will place 7,000 acres under easement in 1999. There is room for trusts of every ideological and political stance and for easements that protect land owned by people of all kinds. The entire point of easements and land trust work is to find the common ground of agreement. If we work only with those who share our ecological or aesthetic sensibilities, there is little chance we will truly succeed in saving landscapes.

The essential points revealed in the case studies are profoundly important. We must design easements that are fair, flexible and strong, amendable when necessary, but stout enough to dissuade overaggressive landowners from trying to retrieve development rights already foregone. Most often, we need to function strategically and in cooperation with other trusts or in alliances of groups sharing the same intentions. Easement procedures must be systematic, professional, and thorough, with a careful balance of individual attention and daily routine to complete projects in a timely manner. We need to open our eyes to historic and cultural geography, to the fascinating human story of settlement dreams and modern worries that surrounds us. Finally, we must meet with agricultural organizations and enlist their support and become trusted neighbors. All of these actions must be taken for conservation easements to become even more widely accepted and effective.

The Uniform Conservation Easement Act

The Uniform Conservation Easement Act was approved by the National Conference of Commissioners on Uniform State Laws in 1981. Included with the Uniform Act are a series of notes or comments prepared by the commissioners. The Prefatory Note contains an explanation of the entire act. The individual sections that were adopted are followed by additional comments explaining the reasons for their existence.

Prefatory Note

The Act enables durable restrictions and affirmative obligations to be attached to real property to protect natural and historic resources. Under the conditions spelled out in the Act, the restrictions and obligations are immune from certain common law impediments which might otherwise be raised. The Act maximizes the freedom of the creators of the transaction to impose restrictions on the use of land and improvements in order to protect them, and it allows a similar latitude to impose affirmative duties for the same purposes. In each instance, if the requirements of the Act are satisfied, the restrictions or affirmative duties are binding upon the successors and assigns of the original parties.

The Act thus makes it possible for Owner to transfer a restriction upon the use of Blackacre to Conservation, Inc., which will be enforceable by Conservation and its successors whether or not Conservation has an interest in land benefited by the restriction, which is assignable although unattached to any such interest in fact, and which has not arisen under circumstances where the traditional conditions of privity of estate and "touch and concern" applicable to covenants real are present. So, also, the Act enables the Owner of Heritage Home to obligate himself and future owners of Heritage to maintain certain aspects of the house and to have that obligation enforceable by Preservation, Inc., even though Preservation has no interest in property benefited by the obligation. Further, Preservation may obligate itself to take certain affirmative actions to preserve the property. In each case, under the Act, the restrictions and obligations bind successors. The Act does not itself impose restrictions or affirmative duties. It merely allows the parties to do so within a consensual arrangement freed from common law impediments, if the conditions of the Act are complied with.

These conditions are designed to assure that protected transactions serve defined protective purposes (Section 1(1)) and that the protected interest is in a "holder" which is either a governmental body or a charitable organization having an interest in the subject matter (Section 1(2)). The interest may be created in the same manner as other easements in land (Section 2(a)). The Act also enables the parties to establish a right in a third party to enforce the terms of the transaction (Section 3(a)(3)) if the possessor of the right is also a governmental unit or charity (Section 1(3)).

The interests protected by the Act are termed "easements." The terminology reflects a rejection of two alternatives suggested in existing state acts dealing with nonpossessory conservation and preservation interests. The first removes the common law disabilities associated with covenants real and equitable servitudes in addition to those associated with easements. As statutorily modified, these three common law interests retain their separate existence as instruments employable for conservation and preservation ends. The second approach seeks to create a novel additional interest which, although unknown to the common law, is, in some ill-defined sense, a statutorily modified amalgam of the three traditional common law interests.

The easement alternative is favored in the Act for three reasons. First, lawyers and courts are most comfortable with easements and easement doctrine, less so with restrictive covenants and equitable servitudes, and can be expected to experience severe confusion if the Act opts for a hybrid fourth interest. Second, the easement is the basic less-than-fee interest at common law; the restrictive covenant and the equitable servitude appeared only because of then-current, but now outdated, limitations of easement doctrine. Finally, nonpossessory interests satisfying the requirements of covenant real or equitable servitude doctrine will invariably meet the Act's less demanding requirements as "easements." Hence, the Act's easement orientation should not prove prejudicial to instruments drafted as real covenants or equitable servitudes, although the converse would not be true.

In assimilating these easements to conventional easements, the Act allows great latitude to the parties to the former to arrange their relationship as they see fit. The Act differs in this respect from some existing statutes, such as that in effect in Massachusetts, under which interests of this nature are subject to public planning agency review.

There are both practical and philosophical reasons for not subjecting conservation easements to a public ordering system. The Act has the relatively narrow purpose of sweeping away certain common law impediments which might otherwise undermine the easements' validity, particularly those held in gross. It is the intention to facilitate private grants that serve the ends of land conservation and historic preservation; moreover, the requirement of public agency approval adds a layer of complexity which may discourage private actions. Organizations and property owners may be reluctant to become involved in the bureaucratic, and sometimes political, process which public agency participation entails. Placing such a requirement in the Act may dissuade a state from enacting it for the reason that the state does not wish to accept the administrative and fiscal responsibilities of such a program.

In addition, controls in the Act and in other state and federal legislation afford further assurance that the Act will serve the public interest. To begin with, the very adoption of the Act by a state legislature facilitates the enforcement of conservation easement serving the public interest. Other types of easements, real covenants and equitable servitudes are enforceable, even though their myriads of purposes have seldom been expressly scrutinized by state legislative bodies. Moreover, Section 1(2) of the Act restricts the entities that may hold conservation and preservation easements to governmental agencies and charitable organizations, neither of which is likely to accept them on an indiscriminate basis. Governmental programs that extend benefits to private donors of these easements provide additional controls against potential abuses. Federal tax statutes and regulations, for example, rigorously define the circumstances under which easement donations qualify for favorable tax treatment. Controls relating to real estate assessment and taxation of restricted properties have been, or can be, imposed by state legislatures to prevent easement abuses or to limit potential loss of local property tax revenues resulting from unduly favorable assessment and taxation of these properties. Finally, the American legal system generally regards private ordering of property relationships as sound public policy. Absent conflict with constitutional or statutory requirements, conveyances of fee or non-possessory interests by and among private entities is the norm, rather than the exception, in the United States. By eliminating certain outmoded easement impediments which are largely attributable to the absence of a land title recordation system in England centuries earlier, the Act advances the values implicit in this norm.

The Act does not address a number of issues which, though of conceded importance, are considered extraneous to its primary objective of enabling private parties to enter into consensual arrangements with charitable organizations or governmental bodies to protect land and buildings without the encumbrance of certain potential common law impediments (Section 4). For example, with the exception of the requirement of Section 2(b) that the acceptance of the holder be recorded, the formalities and effects of recordation are left to the state's registry system; an adopting state may wish to establish special indices for these interests, as has been done in Massachusetts.

Similarly unaddressed are the potential impacts of a state's marketable title laws upon the duration of conservation easements. The Act provides that conservation easements have an unlimited duration unless the instruments creating them provide otherwise (Section 2(c)). The relationship between this provision and the marketable title act or other statutes addressing restrictions on real property of unlimited duration should be considered by the adopting state.

The relationship between the Act and local real property assessment and taxation practices is not dealt with; for example, the effect of an easement upon the valuation of burdened real property presents issues which are left to the state and local taxation system. The Act enables the structuring of transactions so as to achieve tax benefits which may be available under the Internal Revenue Code, but parties intending to attain them must be mindful of the specific provisions of the income, estate and gift tax laws which are applicable. Finally, the Act neither limits nor enlarges the power of eminent domain; such matters as the scope of that power and the entitlement of property owners to compensation upon its exercise are determined not by this Act but by the adopting state's eminent domain code and related statutes.

Section 1. Definitions.

As used in this Act, unless the context otherwise requires:

(1) "Conservation easement" means a nonpossessory interest of a holder in real property imposing limitations or affirmative obligations the purposes of which include retaining or protecting natural, scenic, or open-space values of real property, assuring its availability for agricultural, forest, recreational, or open-space use, protecting natural resources, maintaining or enhancing air or water quality, or preserving the historical, architectural, archaeological, or cultural aspects of real property.

(2) "Holder" means:
   (i) a governmental body empowered to hold an interest in real property under the laws of this State or the United States; or
   (ii) a charitable corporation, charitable association, or charitable trust, the purposes or powers of which include retaining or protecting the natural, scenic, or open-space values of real property, assuring the availability of real property for agricultural, forest, recreational, or open-space use, protecting natural resources, maintaining or enhancing air or water quality, or preserving the historical, architectural, archaeological, or cultural aspects of real property.

(3) "Third-party right of enforcement" means a right provided in a conservation easement to enforce any of its terms granted to a governmental

body, charitable corporation, charitable association, or charitable trust, which, although eligible to be a holder, is not a holder.

Comment.
Section 1 defines three central elements: What is meant by conservation easements; who can be a holder; and who can possess a "third-party right of enforcement." Only those interests held by a "holder," as defined by the Act, fall within the definitions of protected easements. Such easements are defined as interests in real property. Even if so held, the easement must serve one or more of the following purposes: Protection of natural or open-space resources; protection of air or water quality; preservation of the historical aspects of property; or other similar objectives spelled out in subsection (1).

A "holder" may be a governmental unit having specified powers (subsection (2)(I)) or certain types of charitable corporations, associations, and trusts, provided that the purposes of the holder include those same purposes for which the conservation easement should have been created in the first place (subsection (2)(ii)). The word "charitable," in Section 1(2) and (3), describes organizations that are charities according to the common law definition regardless of their tax status as exempt organizations under any tax law.

Recognition of a "third-party right of enforcement" enables a party to structure into the transaction a party that is not an easement "holder," but which, nonetheless, has the right to enforce the terms of the easement (Sections 1(3), 3(a)(3)). But the possessor of the third-party enforcement right must be a governmental body or a charitable corporation, association, or trust. Thus, if Owner transfers a conservation easement on Blackacre to Conservation, Inc., he could grant to Preservation, Inc., a charitable corporation, the right to enforce the terms of the easement, even though Preservation was not the holder, and Preservation would be free of the common law impediments eliminated by the Act (Section 4). Under this Act, however, Owner could not grant a similar right to Neighbor, a private person. But whether such a grant might be valid under other applicable law of the adopting state is left to the law of that state. (Section 5(c).)

Section 2. Creation, Conveyance, Acceptance and Duration.

(a) Except as otherwise provided in this Act, a conservation easement may be created, conveyed, recorded, assigned, released, modified, terminated, or otherwise altered or affected in the same manner as other easements.

(b) No right or duty in favor of or against a holder and no right in favor of a person having a third-party right of enforcement arises under a conservation easement before its acceptance by the holder and a recordation of the acceptance.

(c) Except as provided in Section 3(b), a conservation easement is unlimited in duration unless the instrument creating it otherwise provides.

(d) An interest in real property in existence at the time a conservation easement is created is not impaired by it unless the owner of the interest is a party to the conservation easement or consents to it.

Comment.

Section 2(a) provides that, except to the extent otherwise indicated in the Act, conservation easements are indistinguishable from easements recognized under the pre-Act law of the state in terms of their creation, conveyance, recordation, assignment, release, modification, termination, or alteration. In this regard, subsection (a) reflects the Act's overall philosophy of bringing less-than-fee conservation interests under the formal easement rubric and of extending that rubric to the extent necessary to effectuate the Act's purposes given the adopting state's existing common law and statutory framework. For example, the state's requirements concerning release of conventional easements apply as well to conservation easements because nothing in the Act provides otherwise. On the other hand, if the state's existing law does not permit easements in gross to be assigned, it will not be applicable to conservation easements because Section 4(2) effectively authorizes their assignment.

Conservation and preservation organizations using easement programs have indicated a concern that instruments purporting to impose affirmative obligations on the holder may be unilaterally executed by grantors and recorded without notice to or acceptance by the holder ostensibly responsible for the performance of the affirmative obligations. Subsection (b) makes clear that neither a holder nor a person having a third-party enforcement right has any rights or duties under the easement prior to the recordation of the holder's acceptance of it.

The Act enables parties to create a conservation easement of unlimited duration subject to the power of a court to modify or terminate it in states whose case or statute law accords their courts that power in the case of easement—see Section 3(b). The latitude given the parties is consistent with the philosophical premise of the Act. However, there are additional safeguards; for example, easements may be created only for certain purposes and may be held only by certain "holders." These limitations find their place comfortably within similar limitations applicable to charitable trusts, whose duration may also have no limit. Allowing the parties to create such easements also enables them to fit within federal tax law requirements that the interest be "in perpetuity" if certain tax benefits are to be derived.

Obviously, an easement cannot impair prior rights of owners of interests in the burdened property existing when the easement comes into being unless those owners join in the easement or consent to it. The casement property thus would be subject to existing liens, encumbrances, and other property rights (such as subsurface mineral rights) that preexist the easement, unless the owners of those rights release them or subordinate them to the easement. (Section 2(d).)

Section 3. Judicial Actions.

(a) An action affecting a conservation easement may be brought by:
    (1) an owner of an interest in the real property burdened by the easement;
    (2) a holder of the easement;
    (3) a person having a third-party right of enforcement; or
    (4) a person authorized by other law.
(b) This Act does not affect the power of a court to modify or terminate a conservation easement in accordance with the principles of law and equity.

Comment.

Section 3 identifies four categories of persons who may bring actions to enforce, modify, or terminate conservation easements, quiet title to parcels burdened by conservation easements, or otherwise affect conservation easements. Owners of interests in real property burdened by easements might wish to sue in cases where the easements also impose duties upon holders and these duties are breached by the holders. Holders and persons having third-party rights of enforcement might obviously wish to bring suit to enforce restrictions on the owners' use of the burdened properties. In addition to these three categories of persons who derive their standing from the explicit terms of the easement itself, the Act also recognizes that the states other applicable law may create standing in other persons. For example, independently of the Act, the attorney general could have standing in his capacity as supervisor of charitable trusts, either by statute or at common law.

A restriction burdening real property in perpetuity or for long periods can fail of its purposes because of changed conditions affecting the property or its environs, because the holder of the conservation easement may cease to exist, or for other reasons not anticipated at the time of its creation. A variety of doctrines, including the doctrines of changed conditions and *cy pres*, have been judicially developed and, in many states, legislatively sanctioned as a basis for responding to these vagaries. Under the changed conditions doctrine, privately created restrictions on land use may be terminated or modified if they no longer substantially achieve their purpose due to the changed conditions. Under the statute and case law of some states, the court's order limiting or terminating the restriction may include such terms and conditions, including monetary adjustments, as it deems necessary to protect the public interest and to assure an equitable resolution of the problem. The doctrine is applicable to real covenants and equitable servitudes in all states, but its application to easements is problematic in many states.

Under the doctrine of *cy pres,* if the purposes of a charitable trust cannot be carried out because circumstances have changed after the trust came into being or, for any other reason, the settlor's charitable intentions cannot be effectuated, courts under their equitable powers may prescribe terms and conditions that may best enable the general charitable objective to be achieved while altering specific provisions of the trust. So, also, in cases where a charitable trustee ceases to exist or cannot carry out its responsibilities, the court will appoint a substitute trustee upon proper application and will not allow the trust to fail.

The Act leaves intact the existing case and statute law of adopting states as it relates to the modification and termination of easements and the enforcement of charitable trusts.

Section 4. Validity.

A conservation easement is valid even though:

(1) it is not appurtenant to an interest in real property;

(2) it can be or has been assigned to another holder;

(3) it is not of a character that has been recognized traditionally at common law;

(4) it imposes a negative burden;

(5) it imposes affirmative obligations upon the owner of an interest in the burdened property or upon the holder;

(6) the benefit does not touch or concern real property; or

(7) there is no privity of estate or of contract.

Comment.

One of the Act's basic goals is to remove outmoded common law defenses that could impede the use of easements for conservation or preservation ends. Section 4 addresses this goal by comprehensively identifying these defenses and negating their use in actions to enforce conservation or preservation easements.

Subsection (1) indicates that easements, the benefit of which is held in gross, may be enforced against the grantor or his successors or assigns. By

stating that the easement need not be appurtenant to an interest in real property, it eliminates the requirement in force in some states that the holder of
the easement must own an interest in real property (the "dominant estate")
benefited by the easement.

Subsection (2) also clarifies common law by providing that an easement
may be enforced by an assignee of the holder.

Subsection (3) addresses the problem posed by the common law's recognition of easements that served only a limited number of purposes and its
reluctance to approve so-called "novel incidents." Easements serving the conservation and preservation ends enumerated in Section I(1) might fail of
enforcement under this restrictive view. Accordingly, subsection (3) establishes that conservation or preservation easements are not enforceable solely
because they do not serve purposes or fall within the categories of easements
traditionally recognized at common law.

Subsection (4) deals with a variant of the foregoing problem. The common
law recognized only a limited number of "negative easements"—those preventing the owner of the burdened land from performing acts on his land
that he would be privileged to perform absent the easement. Because a far
wider range of negative burdens than those recognized at common law might
be imposed by conservation or preservation easements, subsection (4) modifies the common law by eliminating the defense that a conservation or
preservation easement imposes a "novel" negative burden.

Subsection (5) addresses the opposite problem—the unenforceability at
common law of an easement that imposes affirmative obligations upon either
the owner of the burdened property or upon the holder. Neither of those
interests was viewed by the common law as true easements at all. The first, in
fact, was labeled a "spurious" easement because it obligated the owner of the
burdened property to perform affirmative acts. (The spurious easement was
distinguished from an affirmative easement, illustrated by a right-of-way,
which empowered the easement's holder to perform acts on the burdened
property that the holder would not have been privileged to perform absent
the easement.) Achievement of conservation or preservation goals may
require that affirmative obligations be incurred by the burdened property
owner or by the easement holder or both. For example, the donor of a facade
easement, one type of preservation easement, may agree to restore the facade
to its original state; conversely, the holder of a facade easement may agree to
undertake restoration. In either case, the preservation easement would
impose affirmative obligations.

Subsection (5) treats both interests as easements and establishes that neither would be unenforceable solely because it is affirmative in nature.

Subsections (6) and (7) preclude the touch and concern and privity of
estate or contract defenses, respectively. Strictly speaking, they do not belong

in the Act because they have traditionally been asserted as defenses against the enforcement not of easements but of real covenants and of equitable servitudes. The case law dealing with these three classes of interests, however, had become so confused and arcane over the centuries that defenses appropriate to one of these classes may incorrectly be deemed applicable to another. The inclusion of the touch and concern and privity defenses in Section 4 is a cautionary measure, intended to safeguard conservation and preservation easements from invalidation by courts that might inadvertently confuse them with real covenants or equitable servitudes.

Section 5. Applicability.

(a) This Act applies to any interest created after its effective date which complies with this Act, whether designated as a conservation easement or as a covenant, equitable servitude, restriction, easement, or otherwise.

(b) This Act applies to any interest created before its effective date if it would have been enforceable had it been created after its effective date unless retroactive application contravenes the constitution or laws of this State or the United States.

(c) This Act does not invalidate any interest, whether designated as a conservation or preservation easement or as a covenant, equitable servitude, restriction, easement, or otherwise, that is enforceable under other law of this State.

Comment.

There are four classes of interest to which the Act might be made applicable:

(1) those created after its passage which comply with it in form and purpose;

(2) those created before the Act's passage which comply with the Act and which would not have been invalid under the pertinent pre-Act statutory or case law either because the latter explicitly validated interests of the kind recognized by the Act or, at least, was silent on the issue;

(3) those created either before or after the Act which do not comply with the Act but which are valid under the state's statute or case law; and

(4) those created before the Act's passage which comply with the Act but which would have been invalid under the pertinent pre-Act statutory or case law.

It is the purpose of Section 5 to establish or confirm the validity of the first three classes of interests. Subsection (a) establishes the validity of the first class of interests, whether or not they are designated as conservation or preservation easements. Subsection (b) establishes the validity under the Act of the second class. Subsection (c) confirms the validity of the third class independently of the Act by disavowing the intent to invalidate any interest that does comply with other applicable law.

Constitutional difficulties could arise, however, if the Act sought retroactively to confer blanket validity upon the fourth class of interests. The owner of the land ostensibly burdened by the formerly invalid interest might well succeed in arguing that his property would be "taken" without just compensation were that interest subsequently validated by the Act. Subsection (b) addresses this difficulty by precluding retroactive application of the Act if such application "contravenes the constitution or laws of this state or the United States." That determination, of course, would have to made by a court.

Section 6. Uniformity of Application and Construction.

This Act shall be applied and construed to effectuate its general purpose to make uniform the laws with respect to the subject of the Act among states enacting it.

Twenty states and the District of Columbia have adopted the Uniform Conservation Easement Act.[1] (See chapter 4, Introduction to Legal Analysis.)

Whether a state has adopted the major provisions of the UCEA can be difficult to determine through casual observation. Some states have departed from the title and have even omitted the term "Uniform." The statutory citation for the UCEA varies as the state amends and renumbers the legislation. The General Statutory Notes includes such variations also a variety of information relating to the enactment of the UCEA.[2] Some states have altered the language of the uniform act to suit their particular circumstances, their political history and legal traditions, especially their approaches to private real property rights and land uses targeted in the UCEA. "Not infrequently a jurisdiction will substantially adopt the major provisions of a Uniform Act, and, yet, depart form the official test in such a manner that the various instances of substituted, omitted, and added matter cannot clearly be indicated."[3]

Notes

1. Uniform Laws Annotated, Master edition (St. Paul, Minn., West Publishing, 1968), 1998 pocket part 10.
2. Uniform Laws Annotated note 1, p. v.
3. Uniform Laws Annotated note 1, p. v.

Appendix B

ᔕᔕ

Grant of Conservation Easement and Declaration of Restrictive Covenants

This Grant of Conservation Easement and Declaration of Restrictive Covenants (hereinafter referred to as the "Grant and Declaration") is made and declared this _____ day of _____ _____, 19____, by and between _____ (hereinafter called "Grantor") and the WILDLANDS CONSERVANCY, INC., 601 Orchid Place, Emmaus, Pennsylvania 18049-1637, a Pennsylvania nonprofit corporation (hereinafter referred to as the "Grantee")

WITNESSETH:

WHEREAS, Grantor is the owner of all that certain tract of land located in Albany Township, Berks County, Pennsylvania, as is more fully described on Exhibit "A" attached hereto (hereinafter referred to as the "Property"); and

WHEREAS, the Property is a relatively natural area or environment in which a significant fish, wildlife, plant community or similar ecosystem ordinarily lives; and

WHEREAS, the Property consists of open-space and other environmental and ecological values the preservation of which is in furtherance of the conservation policy set forth by the United States of America, the Commonwealth of Pennsylvania, the County of Berks, and Albany Township; and

WHEREAS, Grantor is desirous of preserving the natural state of the Property for the scenic enjoyment of the general public and of conserving and protecting the Property and surrounding lands from soil erosion, water pollution, natural disruption, development (residential [except as permitted herein] commercial and/or industrial) and other occurrences which might interfere with the beauty and unique character of the Property as it exists in its natural and scenic state or threaten the wildlife thereon; and

WHEREAS, Grantor is also desirous of protecting the riparian habitat, vegetation and wildlife, and wetland habitat, vegetation and wildlife; and

WHEREAS, Grantor is also desirous of imposing certain limitations and restrictions on the use and development of the Property so that the Property's unique and natural character will be preserved and the riparian and wetland areas will be protected; and

WHEREAS, the specific conservation values of the Property are documented in an inventory of relevant features of the

Property, dated _____ and kept on file at the offices of
the Grantee (hereinafter referred to as the "Baseline
Documentation"), which consists of reports, maps, photographs,
and other documents that the parties agree provide, collectively,
an accurate representation of the Property at the time of this
grant and which is intended to serve as an objective information
baseline for monitoring compliance with the terms of this grant;
and

WHEREAS, Grantor and Grantee jointly have prepared a plan
for the future conservation, preservation and protection of the
values documented in the Baseline Documentation dated _____
and kept on file at the offices of the Grantee (hereinafter
referred to as the "Conservation Plan") attached hereto as
Exhibit B and incorporated herein by reference, which consists of
plans and requirements for future management of the Property; and

WHEREAS, Grantee is a public charity exempt from Federal
income taxes under section 501(c)(3) of the Internal Revenue Code
of 1986 and is organized and operated substantially or primarily
for conservation purposes.

NOW, THEREFORE, and for and in consideration of the mutual
promises herein contained and for the further consideration of
the sum of One ($1.00) Dollar in hand paid by Grantee to Grantor,
the receipt of which is hereby acknowledged, the parties hereto,
intending to be legally bound hereby, do mutually grant, convey,
covenant, agree and declare as follows:

1.   Grantor hereby grants and conveys unto Grantee an
Easement in Gross for the purpose of preserving the natural state
of the Property for scenic enjoyment of the general public and of
conserving and protecting the Property and surrounding lands from
soil erosion, water pollution, natural disruptions and other
occurrences which might interfere with the beauty and unique
character of the Property as it exists in its natural and scenic
state, or threaten the wildlife thereon, and to protect the
riparian and wetland areas, subject to the qualifications, terms
and conditions hereinafter set forth.

2.   In order to accomplish the intent of the Easement set
forth in paragraph 1 above, Grantor hereby covenants and agrees
with Grantee that the Property shall remain in its present
natural and scenic state subject to the qualifications,
conditions and terms hereinafter mentioned, and shall not be the
subject of residential (except as permitted herein), commercial
or industrial development. In furtherance of the foregoing,
Grantor hereby declares and imposes the following restrictions
upon the use and enjoyment of the Property:

A.   No residential (except as permitted herein),
commercial and/or industrial activities, including, but not

limited to, the construction or erection of public roads, driveways, parking lots, pipe lines and poles shall be conducted or permitted on the Property, and the use of the Property as a site for any major public utility installations such as electric generating plants, electric power substations, high tension electric power transmission lines, gas reservoirs, sewage treatment plants, microwave relay stations, telephone exchanges, or nuclear generating plants shall be prohibited.

B.   Further subdivision of the property for commercial and/or industrial purposes shall be prohibited. Certain portions of the Property have previously been subdivided and are referred to by lot numbers as shown on the subdivision plan known as Subdivision Plan for Whirlwind Farm, Albany Township, dated April 9, 1990, and filed with Albany Township (hereinafter referred to as the "Subdivision Plan") attached hereto as Exhibit B.

C.   Grantor and Grantee agree to the following:

(i) Grantor reserves the right to have one, single-family residence and accessory buildings such as a garage and/or storage shed on that portion of the property identified as Lot 2 Tract A or Lot 5 (but not both) on the Subdivision Plan. The stone-and-frame barn existing on Lot 2 Tract A at the time of this grant may not be converted to a residence if any other residence exists on Lot 2 Tract A or Lot 5. Should the barn be converted into a residence, then no other residence may be built on Lot 2 Tract A or Lot 5.

(ii) Any sewage-treatment facility for any residence located on Lot 2 Tract A or Lot 5, including but not limited to a septic field, sand mound, or other sewage-treatment facility (excepting approved self-composting toilets) shall be located on that area designated as Lot 5 on the Subdivision Plan.

(iii)   Accessory buildings such as garages and storage sheds may be erected in the immediate vicinity of such single-family residence, provided that the total ground area covered by such single-family residence and accessory buildings shall not exceed four thousand (4,000) square feet.

(iv) Driveways and parking areas necessary for access and parking at such single-family residence may be constructed on the Property.

D.   All rights reserved by Grantor pursuant to the preceding Paragraph C shall be subject to the following conditions and limited as follows:

(i)   No construction or erection shall be undertaken at any place on the property where such construction or erection would destroy or impair the scenic enjoyment of the

view by the general public. For the purpose of insuring that any
construction or erection shall not impair or destroy the scenic
qualities of the property, no construction or erection (except as
permitted in Paragraph C above) shall be undertaken without
Grantor first having obtained site and building plan approval
from Grantee. Grantor need not seek approval of Grantee for any
interior remodeling or repair.

      (ii) No construction or erection (except as
permitted in Paragraph C above) shall be undertaken without
Grantor first having obtained site and building plan approval by
the Grantee.

      E. No signs, billboards or outdoor advertising
structures shall be constructed or displayed on the Property
other than one sign not exceeding four feet by four feet (4' x
4') for each of the following purposes:

      (i) To state the name of the Property and the
name and address of the occupant;

      (ii) To advertise an activity, permitted under
the provisions of this Agreement; and

      (iii) To advertise the Property for sale or
rental. Provided, however, that this subparagraph D shall not
limit the right of the Grantee to display on the Property, at its
discretion, a small marker or sign evidencing the ownership of
the Easement granted herein, provided the same is approved by
Grantor in writing.

      F. Dumping of soil, trash, ashes, garbage, waste,
sewage or other unsanitary or offensive material on the Property
shall be prohibited. No material may be stored which will be
hazardous to health or safety by reason of being poisonous or
flammable except as may be used in customary agricultural
operations.

      G. Quarrying, excavation or removal of rock, minerals,
gravel, sand, topsoil or other similar materials from the
Property shall be prohibited, except as permitted in Paragraph C
above.

      H. Timber lands shall be managed by Grantor in
accordance with sound forestry practices and trees may be
selectively cut from time to time in such a manner as will not
alter the character of such land as forest lands. Grantor shall
be entitled to the proceeds from the sale of any trees cut in
accordance herewith.

    3. Rights of Grantee. To accomplish the purpose of this

Easement, the following rights are conveyed to the Grantee by this Easement:

A. To preserve and protect the conservation values of the Property;

B. To enter upon the Property at reasonable times in order to monitor Grantor's compliance with and otherwise enforce the terms of this Easement;

C. To prevent any activity or use of the Property inconsistent with the purpose of this Easement and to require the restoration of such areas or features of the Property that may be damaged by any inconsistent activity or use, pursuant to Paragraph 4;

D. To conduct, only with permission of Grantor, such public programs on, and tours of, the Property as it deems appropriate.

4. Grantee shall have the right to seek any legal action or remedy at law or in equity to enforce the provisions set forth herein and granted hereunder, including, but not limited to, the right to require restoration of the Property to its condition at. the time of this Granted Declaration (subject to the rights reserved herein to Grantor). Grantee shall have the right to recover any legal fees incurred in such action from the Grantor or the Grantor's successors.

5. Grantor reserves unto Grantor in title to the Property, all rights, privileges, powers and immunities in respect to the Property, including, without limitation, the right of exclusive possession and enjoyment subject only to the restrictions and easements set forth in, and the terms and covenants of, this Grant and Declaration. Grantor further reserves the right to grant other qualified organizations the non-exclusive right of access to and the use and maintenance of the Property for purposes approved by Grantor not inconsistent with the provisions of this Grant and Declaration.

6. Grantee shall be under no obligation to maintain the Property or pay taxes or assessments thereon.

7. The provisions of this Grant and Declaration shall run with and bind the land described in Exhibit "A" in perpetuity.

8. Grantee may not subsequently transfer the Easement created by this Grant and Declaration, whether or not for consideration, unless:

A. The Grantee, as a condition of the subsequent transfer, requires that the conservation purposes which this

Grant and Declaration is intended to advance, shall continue to be carried out; and

B.   Subsequent transfers shall be restricted to organizations qualifying, at the time of the subsequent transfer, as eligible donees of qualified conservation contributions under section 170(h) of the Internal Revenue Code of 1986 and any amended or successor internal revenue laws of the United States.

9.   If circumstances arise in the future such as render the purpose of this Easement impossible to accomplish, this Easement can only be terminated or extinguished, whether in whole or in part, by judicial proceedings in a court of competent jurisdiction, and the amount of the proceeds to which Grantee shall be entitled, after the satisfaction of prior claims, from any sale, exchange, or involuntary conversion of all or any portion of the Property subsequent to such termination or extinguishment, shall be determined, unless otherwise provided by Pennsylvania law at the time, in accordance with paragraph 10 below.   Grantee shall use all such proceeds in a manner consistent with the conservation purposes of this grant.

10.   This Easement constitutes a real property interest immediately in Grantee, which, for the purposes of paragraph 9 above, the parties stipulate to have a fair market value determined by multiplying the fair market value of the Property unencumbered by the Easement (minus any increase in value after the date of this grant attributable to improvements) by the ratio of the value of the Easement at the time of this grant to the value of the Property, without deduction for the value of the Easement, at the time of this grant.   The values at the time of this grant shall be those values used to calculate the deduction for federal income tax purposes allowable by reason of this grant, pursuant to Section 170(h) of the Internal Revenue Code of 1954, as amended.   For the purposes of this paragraph, the ratio of the value of the Easement to the value of the Property unencumbered by the Easement shall remain constant.

11.   Any general rule of construction to the contrary notwithstanding, this Easement shall be liberally construed in favor of the grant to the effect the purpose of this Easement and the policy and purpose.   If any provision in this instrument is found to be ambiguous, an interpretation consistent with the purpose of this Easement that would render the provision valid shall be favored over any interpretation that would render it invalid.

12.   If any provision of the Easement, or the application thereof to any person or circumstance, is found to be invalid, the remainder of the provisions of this Easement, or the application of such provision to persons or circumstances other

than those as to which it is found to be invalid, as the case may
be, shall not be affected thereby.

13.   The provisions of this Agreement shall inure to and be
binding upon the heirs, executors, administrators, devisees,
successors, and assigns, as the case may be, of the parties
hereto.

14.   This Agreement is made by virtue of a resolution of the
Board of Directors of Grantee, duly passed at a meeting thereof
duly and legally held on the _____ day of _____, 19____.
The Grantee does hereby constitute and appoint Veronica
Sorrentino to be its attorney, for and in its name, and as and
for its corporate act and deed, to acknowledge this Agreement
before any person having authority under the laws of the
Commonwealth of Pennsylvania to take such acknowledgment, to the
intent that the same may be duly recorded.

IN WITNESS WHEREOF, Grantor has executed this Agreement, and
Grantee has caused this Agreement to be signed by its President,
and its corporate seal to be hereunto affixed, duly attested by
its Secretary, the day and year first above written.

_____   _____
                      Witness   Grantor

ATTEST: WILDLANDS CONSERVANCY, INC.

_____   BY:_____

                (SEAL)

CONSERVATION PLAN

for the property of

This Conservation Plan has been prepared by Wildlands
Conservancy, 601 Orchid Place, Emmaus, Pennsylvania 18049-1637
for the purpose of carrying out the provisions in the Grant of
Conservation Easement and Declaration of Restrictive Covenants
(hereinafter referred to as the "Grant and Declaration") between
_____ and Wildlands Conservancy.

The Conservation Plan applies to all the property of_____
_____ as described in Exhibit "A" in the Grant and Declaration
(hereinafter referred to as the "Property"). It is agreed that
the Conservation Plan will be carried out by the Property owner,
so that the specific conservation values of the Property
documented in the Baseline Documentation referred to in the Grant
and Declaration and kept on file in the office of the Grantee may
be protected and preserved.

A complete physical description and inventory of the
Property may be found in the Baseline Documentation. The
principal conservation values are the streams and wetlands, as
well as the scenic quality of the property. There are other
features also worthy of preservation and protection.

In order to protect the streams and wetlands, the following
conditions apply:

1. No building, construction, or earth disturbance of any
kind shall be permitted within fifty (50) feet of any stream or
wetland, nor within any wetland, as described in the Baseline
Documentation, except that as respects repairs, renovations,
and/or additions to buildings existing on the Property at the
time of grant of this Conservation Easement, or any future
building permitted by the terms of this Conservation Easement, or
for the construction of a swimming pool or pond on Lot 2 Tract B
or Lot 2 Tract A or Lot 5, such fifty (50) foot restriction is
modified so as to allow building, construction or earth
disturbance up to the limit of any wetland or stream area as
described in the Baseline Documentation.

2. No vehicles of any kind, nor any farm machinery or
equipment shall be allowed to cross Kistler Creek except at the
ford presently existing at the date of this Conservation Plan and
as shown in the Baseline Documentation. Emergency vehicles are
excepted.

3. No vehicles of any kind, including farm machinery or equipment shall be permitted to cross the unnamed stream flowing in a northerly direction across Lot 2 Tract A and Lot 2 Tract B into Kistler Creek excepting by means of the private lane defined on the Baseline Documentation.

4. No bridges, except light-duty foot bridges, shall be constructed anywhere on the Property for any purpose.

5. No domestic animals, such as, but not limited to, cattle, sheep, goats, swine, etc., shall be permitted to enter the wetlands on the Property for any purpose. If any animal husbandry takes place on the Property, fencing shall be placed in such a manner as to restrain domestic animals as described above from entering the streams and wetlands at any time, except as provided in Paragraph 6 below.

6. No domestic animals such as described in Paragraph 5 above shall be permitted to cross Kistler Creek except at the ford described in Paragraph 2 above. Any such crossing shall be supervised so that such animals do not remain in the creek longer than the time necessary to immediately and directly cross the creek.

7. No such domestic animals shall be permitted to cross the unnamed stream described in Paragraph 3 above at any time, nor shall such animals be permitted access to this unnamed stream for purposes of obtaining water.

8. No animal waste of any kind shall be permitted to directly enter Kistler Creek, the unnamed stream, or the wetlands on the Property.

9. As respects Paragraphs 5, 6, 7 and 8 above, none of the restrictions shall apply to domestic horses or other domestic equine species. As respects horses and/or other equine species, no more than a combined total of 4 such equine animals shall be permitted on the Property at any time.

10. No chemicals of any kind, including, but not limited to, pesticides, insecticides, inorganic agricultural fertilizers, etc., shall be applied on or under the land, or in the air above the areas designated as streams, wetlands or buffer zones in the Baseline Documentation. Every effort should be made to prevent runoff from agricultural lands from entering any of these area.

11. No improvement of any kind shall be made to the existing ford on Kistler Creek except the minimum necessary to safely permit the passage of such farm vehicles and machinery as are needed to carry out agricultural practices on that portion of the property north of Kistler Creek.

12. No household sewage effluent or grey water of any kind shall be permitted to flow into Kistler Creek or the unnamed stream, or the wetlands on the Property.

13. Hedge rows and tree lines existing on the Property as of the date of this Conservation Plan shall not be disturbed, so as to protect wildlife and habitats for wildlife, excepting that the tree line parallel to the private lane between Lot 2 Tract A and Lot 5 may be removed from Kistler Valley Road southward to the southernmost boundary of Lot 5.

14. Grantor shall not enter into any wetland area with any form of mechanized equipment without prior permission of Grantee.

I agree to, and accept, the restrictions and recommendations contained in this Conservation Plan.

Signed _____   Date _____

Witness _____   Date _____

AMENDMENT TO CONSERVATION PLAN

        THIS AGREEMENT made this _____ day of August, 1992, by
and between WILDLANDS CONSERVANCY, INC., 601 Orchid Place,
Emmaus, Pennsylvania 18049 (hereinafter referred to as "Grantee")
and _____ and

_____

(hereinafter referred to as "Grantors").
                    WITNESSETH:
        WHEREAS, Grantors and Grantee have entered into a Grant
of Conservation Easement and Declaration of Restrictive
Covenants, with a Conservation Plan attached thereto as Exhibit
"B," and recorded in the office of Berks County Recorder of
Deeds, Misc. Vol. 2184 page 1082, and incorporated therein by
reference, dated the 21st day of December, 1990; and
        WHEREAS, The original grantor, _____ , has
sold a portion of the Property to, _____ ; and
        WHEREAS, the new owner, _____ desires
his portion of the Property to be subject to this agreement; and
        WHEREAS, the parties hereto now deem it necessary and
appropriate to amend the terms, conditions and provisions of the
Conservation Plan, as more fully set forth hereinafter.
        NOW, THEREFORE, intending to be legally bound hereby,
the parties hereto agree as follows:
    1. Paragraph #9 of page #2 of the Conservation Plan shall be
amended to read as follows: "As respects Paragraphs 5, 6, 7, and
8 above, none of the restrictions shall apply to domestic horses
or other domestic equine species. As respects horses and/or

other equine species, such equine animals shall be permitted at a density no greater than one horse per eight acres of (eased) Property and no more than a combined total of four such equine animals shall be permitted on the Property at any time."

2. All terms, conditions, provisions, and conditions of the Grant of Conservation Easement and Declaration of Restrictive Covenants, and the Conservation Plan attached thereto, not changed or modified by this Agreement are hereby ratified and confirmed.

3. This Agreement shall be binding upon and inure to the benefit of the respective successors and assigns and the parties hereto.

4. This Agreement shall be governed by and construed in accordance with the laws of the Commonwealth of Pennsylvania, without regard to the conflict-of-laws principles thereof.

IN WITNESS WHEREOF, the parties hereto have caused this Agreement to be executed as of the date and year first above written.

WITNESS/ATTEST: GRANTEE:

BY: _____   BY: _____
                                        Name:
                                        Title:

WITNESS/ATTEST: GRANTOR:

BY: _____   BY: _____

WITNESS/ATTEST: GRANTOR:

BY: _____   BY: _____

STATE OF   :
                            : SS.
COUNTY OF   :

    On this ___ day of _____, 19___, before me a
Notary Public, the undersigned officer, personally appeared

_____

known to me (or satisfactorily proven) to be the person(s) whose
name(s) is/are subscribed to the within instrument, and
acknowledged that he/she/they executed the same for the purposes
therein contained.

         In witness whereof, I hereunto set my hand and official
seal.

                         _____
                                Notary Public

STATE OF   :
                                     :   SS.

COUNTY OF   :

On this ___ day of _____, 19___, before me a Notary Public, the undersigned officer, personally appeared

_____

known to me (or satisfactorily proven) to be the person(s) whose name(s) is/are subscribed to the within instrument, and acknowledged that he/she/they executed the same for the purposes therein contained.

In witness whereof, I hereunto set my hand and official seal.

_____
Notary Public

```
STATE OF                        :
                                :  SS.
COUNTY OF                       :


       On this ___ day of _____, 19___, before me a

Notary Public, the undersigned officer, personally appeared

_____, who acknowledged himself/

herself to be the _____ of _____,

a corporation, and that he/she, as such _____,

being authorized to do so, executed the foregoing instrument for

the purposes therein contained by signing the name of the

corporation by himself/herself as _____.

           In witness whereof, I hereunto set my hand and official

seal.



                              _____
                                   Notary Public
```

Appendix C

❦ ❦

Table of Cases

California
Erickson v. Bank of California, 97 Wash. 2d 246, 643 P.2d 670 (1982).

Massachusetts
Parkinson v Board of Assessors of Medfield, 398 Mass. 112 (1986).

Springfield Preservation Trust, Inc. v. Springfield Historical Commission, 380 Mass. 159 (1980) (dismissal for lack of jurisdiction, but good discussion).

New York
Bleier v. Board of Trustees of Village of East Hampton, 191 A.D.2d 552, 595 N.Y.S.2d 102 (2d Dept. 1993).

Delaware
Edgell v. Divver, 402 A.2d 395 (Del. Ch. 1979).

Guy v. State, 438 A.2d 1250 (Del. Super. 1981).

Richard Paul, Inc. v. Union Improvement Co., 91 A.2d 49 (Del. 1952).

Rivas & Rivas, Inc. v. River Road Swimming Club, 180 A.2d 282 (Del. Ch. 1962).

Woods v. Maciey, 148 A.2d 544 (1959).

New Jersey
Borough of Englewood Cliffs v. Estate of Allison, 69 N.J. Super. 514 (App. Div. 1961).

Boss v. Rockland Elec. Co., 468 A.2d 1055 (N.J. 1983).

Eggleston v. Fox, 232 A.2d 670 (N.J. Super. 1967).

Faircloth v. Baumgartner, 84 A.2d 545 (1951).

Gardner v. New Jersey Pinelands Commission, 593 A.2d 251 (N.J. 1991).

Hyland v. Fonda, 129 A.2d 899 (N.J. Super, App. Div. 1957).

Kline v. Bernardsville Assn., Inc., 631 A.2d 1263 (N.J. Super. App. Div. 1993).

Kruvant v. 12-22 Woodland Avenue Corporation, 350 A.2d 102 (N.J. 1975), citing Thompson on Real Property, ß440 (1961 Replacement).

Leasehold Estates, Inc. v. Fulbro Holding Co., 136 A.2d 423 (N.J. Super. 1958).

Pennsylvania
Appeal of Pfirrmann, 437 A.2d 1336 (Pa. Commw. 1981).

Brodt v. Brown, 172 A.2d 152 (1961).

Burnier v. Dept. of Env. Resources, 611 A.2d 1366 (1992).

Burns v. Baumgardner, 449 A.2d 590 (1982).

531

Iorfida v. Mary Robert Realty Co., Inc., 539 A.2d 383 (Pa. Super. 1988).

McLennan v. United States, 994 F. 2d 839 (Fed. Cir. 1993).

Northwestern Lehigh School District v. Commonwealth Agricultural Lands Condemnation Approval Board, 578 A.2d 614 (1990).

Ozehoski v. Scranton Spring Brook Water Service Co., 43 A.2d 601 (Pa. Super. 1945).

Piper v. Mowris, 351 A.2d 635 (1976).

Reed v. Reese, 374 A.2d. 665 (1977).

Sigal v. Manufacturers Light & Heat Co., 299 A.2d 646 (Pa. 1973).

Southall v. Humbert, 685 A.2d 574 (Pa. Super. 1996).

Vogel v. Haas, 322 A.2d 107 (1974).

Zettlemoyer v. Transcontinental Pipe, 657 A.2d 920 (Pa. 1995).

North Carolina

Springs Partnership v. County of Macon, 339 S.E.2d 681 (N.C. Ct. App. 1986).

Michigan

Indian Garden Group v. Resort Twp, Michigan Tax Tribunal Docket No. 157,543.

Iowa

Bormann v. Board of Supervisors in and for Kossuth County, 584 N.W.2d 309 (Iowa 1998).

Minnesota

Madson v. Overby et al., 425 N.W.2d 270 (Minn. App., 1988).

Preferential taxation and conservation: see, for example, *Barron v. Hennepin County,* 488 N.W.2d 290 (Minn. 1992); *Walthall vs. County of Wadena,* 1985 Minn. Tax LEXIS 107 (Minn. Tax Court, 1985); *Haasken vs. County of Carver,* 1994 Minn. Tax LEXIS 50 (Minn. Tax Court, 1994); *Eisinger et al. vs. County of Washington,* 1992 Minn. Tax LEXIS 104 (Minn. Tax Court, 1992).

North Dakota

United States v. Albrecht, 364 F. Supp. 1349 (D. ND 1973).

United States v. Johansen, 93 F.3d 459 (8th Cir. 1996).

South Dakota

Donovan v. City of Deadwood, 538 N.W.2d 790 (1995).

Lucas v. South Carolina Coastal Council, 505 U.S. 1003 (1992).

Washington

Louthan v. King County, 94 Wash. 2d 422, 617 P.2d 977 (1980).

Van Buren v. Miller, 22 Wash. App. 836, 592 P.2d 671 (1979).

Bibliography

゛ァ ୧

Ackermann, Bruce A. *Private Property and the Constitution.* New Haven, Conn.: Yale University Press, 1977.

Alyward, B. "Appropriating the Values of Wildlife and Wildlands." In *Economics for the Wilds: Wildlife, Diversity and Development,* edited by T. M. Swanson and Edward B. Barbier, Washington, D.C.: Island Press, 1992.

"America's New Boomtowns." *U.S. News & World Report,* 11 April 1994, 62–69.

Appalachian Land Ownership Task Force. *Who Owns Appalachia? Landownership and Its Impact.* Lexington: University Press of Kentucky, 1983.

Arnold, Terri F., "Condemnation and Conservation Easements." In *The Back Forty Anthology: Selected Letters from the Newsletter of Land Conservation Law,* edited by William T. Hutton. San Francisco: The Hyperion Society, Haskings College of the Law, 1995.

Arrow, Kenneth J., and Anthony C. Fisher. "Environmental Preservation, Uncertainty, and Irreversibility." *Quarterly Journal of Economics* 88 (1974): 312–319.

Ashton, Linda. "Groups, Government Works to Rescue Northwest Farmland from Urban Sprawl." *News Tribune,* 9 November 1997.

Baldwin, Melissa. "Conservation Easements: A Viable Tool for Land Preservation." *Land and Water Law Review* 32 (1997): 89–123.

Barbier, E. B. "Sustainable Use of Wetlands—Valuing Tropical Wetland Benefits: Economic Methodologies and Applications." *Geographical Journal* 159 (1993): 22–32.

Barde, J. P., and D. W. Pearce, eds. *Valuing the Environment: Six Case Studies.* London: Earthscan Publications, 1991.

Barrett, Thomas S., and Putnam Livermore. *The Conservation Easement in California.* Washington, D.C.: Island Press, 1983.

Bean, Michael J., and David S. Wilcove. "The Private-Land Problem." *Conservation Biology* 11, no. 1 (1997): 1–2.

Beatley, Timothy. "The Role of Expectations and Promises in Land Use Decisionmaking." *Policy Sciences* 22 (1989): 27–50.

———. *Ethical Land Use.* Baltimore: Johns Hopkins University Press, 1994.

Bennet, Andrew F. "Conservation and Management on Private Land: Facing the Challenge." In *People and Nature Conservation: Perspectives on Private Land Use and Endangered Species Recovery,* edited by Andrew F. Bennett, Gary Backhouse, and Tim Clark. Chipping Norton, UK: Surrey Beatty and Sons, 1995.

Bialecki, Gregory. "What Must the Taking Authority Pay for Land Subject to a Conservation Easement?" *The Back Forty* (July/August 1990): 6.

———. "Eminent Domain Takings of Land Subject to Conservation Easements." *The Back Forty* (September 1990): 8–9.

Blackie, Jeffrey A. "Do Conservation Easements Last Forever? Conservation Easements and the Doctrine of Changed Conditions." *The Back Forty* (July/August 1990): 1–5.

Blackstone, William. *Commentaries on the Laws of England. A Facsimile of the First Edition of 1765–1769.* Chicago: University of Chicago Press, 1979.

Bockstael, Nancy. "Modeling Economics and Ecology: The Importance of a Spatial Perspective." *American Journal of Agricultural Economics* 78 (1996): 1168–1180.

Brenneman, Russell L., and Sarah M. Bates, eds. *Land-Saving Action: A Written Symposium by 29 Experts on Private Land Conservation in the 1980s.* Washington, D.C.: Island Press, 1984.

Brothers, Gene, and Rachel J. C. Chen. *Economic Impact of Travel to the Blue Ridge Parkway, Virginia and North Carolina.* Raleigh: Department of Parks, Recreation and Tourism Management, North Carolina State University, 1995–96.

Browne, Kingsbury, Jr., and Walter G. Van Dorn, "Charitable Gifts of Partial Interests in Real Property for Conservation Purposes." *Tax Lawyer* 29 (1975): 69–93.

Bruce, Jon W., and James W. Ely, Jr. *The Law of Easements and Licenses in Land,* rev. ed. Boston: Warren, Gorham and Lamont, 1995.

Callahan, Constance M. "Warp and Weft: Weaving a Blanket of Protection for Cultural Resources on Private Property." *Environmental Law* 23 (1993): 1323–1351.

Cates, Karl. "What Trail Is Nature On? Harm to Utah's Environment May Be Unavoidable." *Desert News* (1 February 1998), 3.

Chenchile, Richard A. "Introduction to Environmental Decision Making." In *Environmental Decision Making: A Multidisciplinary Perspective,* edited by R. Chenchile and Susan Carlisle. New York: Van Nostrand Reinhold, 1991.

Cocker, A., and C. Richards, eds. *Valuing the Environment: Economic Approaches to Environmental Evaluation.* London: Belhaven Press, 1992.

Cohen, Louis, and Lawrence Marion. *Research Methods in Education,* 3rd ed. London: Routledge, 1989, 141–167.

Colorado Coalition of Land Trusts Newsletter. *Colorado Cattlemen's Agricultural Land Trust: Preserving Land for Agriculture.* Spring 1996.

Common Ground, The Newsletter of the Wisconsin Farmland Conservancy 3, no. 2 (Fall 1997).

"Conservation Easements in Oregon: Abuses and Solutions." *Environmental Law* 14 (1983–84): 555–583.

"Counties Get Creative in Efforts to Preserve Open Space." *Minneapolis Star Tribune,* 20 November 1998.

Covington, George M. "Conservation Easements: A Win/Win for Preservationists and Real Estate Owners." *Illinois Bar Journal* 84 (1996): 629–633.

Crabtree, J. Robert, P. M. K. Leat, J. Santiarossa, K. J. Thomson, and K. M. Lee. "The Economic Contribution and Potential of Nature Conservation." University College London/Joint Nature Conservation Council, working paper (1992), p. 21.

Culliton, Thomas J., M. A. Warren, T. R. Goodspeed, D. G. Remer, C. M. Blackwell, and J. J. McDonough III. *Fifty Years of Population Change along the Nation's Coasts, 1960–2010.* Rockville, Md.: U.S. Depatment of Commerce, National Oceanic and Atmospheric Administration, 1990.

Dallas Morning News. *1994–95 Texas Almanac and State Industrial Guide.* Dallas: Dallas Morning News, 1995.

Dana, Andrew, and Michael Ramsey. "Conservation Easements and the Common Law." *Stanford Environmental Law Journal* 8 (1989): 2–45.

Daniels, Tom L. "Policies to Preserve Prime Farmland in the USA: A Comment." *Journal of Rural Studies* 6, no. 3 (1990): 331–336.

———. *Farmland Preservation Report* 4, no. 10 (July 1994).

Daniels, Tom, and Deborah, Bowers, *Holding Our Ground: Protecting America's Farms and Farmland.* Washington, D.C.: Island Press, 1997.

Davis, Michael J. "Survey of Kansas Law: Real Property." *Kansas Law Review* 41 (1993): 727–757.

Densham, P. "Spatial Decision Support Systems." In *Geographic Information Systems: Principles and Application,* edited by David J. Maguire, Michael F. Goodchild, and David Rhind, 403–412. New York: Wiley, 1991.

Diehl, Janet, and Thomas H. Barrett. *The Conservation Easement Handbook: Managing Land Conservation and Historic Preservation Easement Programs.* San Francisco: Trust for Public Land and Land Trust Exchange, 1988.

Dixon, J. A., and P. B. Sherman. *Economics of Protected Areas: A New Look At Benefits and Costs.* London: Earthscan Publications, 1990.

Doscher, Paul, and Sylvia Bates. "Merging Ownership of Conservation Easements with Fee Interests: The Experience of the Society for the Protection of New Hampshire Forests." *The Back Forty* (August 1991): 1–4.

Dunwell, Frances F. *The Hudson River Highlands.* New York: Columbia University Press, 1991.

Fisher, Anthony C., John V. Krutilla, and Charles J. Cicchetti. "The Economics of Environmental Preservation: Further discussion." *American Economic Review* 64 (1974): 1030–1039.

Fishwick, Paul A. *Simulation Model Design and Execution* Englewood Cliffs, N.J.: Prentice Hall, 1995.

Flicker, John R. "Conservation Easements" *Hennepin County Lawyer* (January–February 1976): 24–25.

Forests Forever. Concord: New Hampshire Conservation Institute and Society for the Protection of New Hampshire Forests, 1995.

Garrett, K.H. "Conservation Easements: The Greening of America." *Kentucky Law Journal* 73 (1984–85): 255–273.

Ginsberg, William R. "The Destructibility of Conservation Easements through Merger." *The Back Forty* (August 1991): 5–8.

———. "Marketable Title Acts: Traps for the Unwary." *The Back Forty* (May/June 1992): 8–10

Gobster, Paul H., and Aldo Leopold. "Ecological Esthetic": Integrating Esthetic and Biodiversity Values." *Journal of Forestry* 93, no. 2 (1956): 10.

Grimaldi, Ann, Kelly Moffat, and Eric Singleton. "Back-Up Enforcement of Conservation Easements." *The Back Forty* (September 1991): 1–6.

Gustanski, Julie A. *Protecting Unique Land Resources: Tools, Techniques, and Tax advantages. A Handbook for Pennsylvania Landowners* Mt. Wolf, Penn.: 4Ever Land Conservation Associates, 1997.

————. "Land Trusts and Private Land Conservation: A Trans-Atlantic Comparative Analysis of the Ethics-Economic-Policy Paradigm." From paper presented at "Who Owns America II?," Land Tenure Center conference, Madison, WI, June 1998.

Gustanski, Julie A., Gareth Edwards-Jones, and Roderick Squires. "The Ethics-Economics-Policy Paradigm: Foundations from an Integrated Land Trust Conservation Decision-Support Model." Urban Ecosystems: Kluwer Press (in press).

Hanink, D. M. "The Economic Geography in Environmental Issues: A Spatial-Analytical Approach." *Progress in Human Geography* 19, no. 3 (1995): 372–387.

Healey, Patsy. *Collaborative Planning: Shaping Places in Fragmented Societies.* London: Macmillian, 1997.

Henle, Klaus. "Biodiversity, People and a Set of Important Connected Questions." In *Nature Conservation 4: The Role of Networks,* edited by Dennis A. Saunders, John L. Craig, and Elizabeth M. Mattiske, 161–174. Chipping Norton, Surrey Beatty and Sons, 1996.

Heskin, Allan David. *The Struggle for Community.* Boulder, Colo.: Westview Press, 1991.

Hough, Michael. *Out of Place: Restoring Identity to the Regional Landscape.* New Haven, Conn.: Yale University Press, 1990.

Huggett, Richard J. *Modelling the Human Impact on Nature.* Oxford: Oxford University Press, 1993.

Hurst, James Willard. *Law and Economic Growth: The Legal History of the Lumber Industry in Wisconsin, 1836–1915.* Cambridge, Mass.: Belknap Press of Harvard University Press, 1964.

Hutton, William T., and Walter T. Moore. "Easements in the Wake of Catastrophe: The Legal Fallout." *The Back Forty* (April 1991): 1–7.

"Ignoring Pleas of Environmentalists, Kansas Man Digs Up Virgin Prairie." *New York Times,* November 1997, B18.

International Union for the Conservation of Nature. *Caring for the Earth: A Strategy for Sustainable Living.* Gland, Switzerland: IUCN, 1991.

Johnson, Warren. *Muddling Toward Frugality.* San Francisco: Sierra Club Books, 1978.

Knight, Robert M., and Nancy K. Moe Dye. "Attorney's Guide to Montana Conservation Easements." *Montana Law Review* 42 (1981): 21–65.

Lancaster County Agricultural Preserve Board. *1997 Farm Sales Analysis.* Lancaster, Pa.: Lancaster County Planning, March 1998.

"Life in Lancaster County." Lancaster New Era, 21 March 1995, 1.

Lewis, Peirce F. "Axioms for Reading the Landscape, Some Guides to the American Scene." In *The Interpretation of Ordinary Landscapes,* edited by Donald W. Meinig, 11–32. New York: Oxford University Press, 1979.

Lindbloom, Charles. "The Science of Muddling Through." *Public Administration Review* (Spring 1959): 79–88.

Meltz, Robert, Dwight H. Merriam, Richard Merriam, and Richard M. Frank. *The Takings Issue: Constitutional Limits on Land Use Control and Environmental Regulation.* Washington, D.C.: Island Press, 1998.

Minnesota–Wisconsin Boundary Commission. *Lower St. Croix River Stewardship Study.* 1994. Hudson, WI: Minnesota–Wisconsin Boundary Commission.

Morrish, William R., and Catherine R. Brown. *Planning to Stay: Learning to See the Physical Features of your Neighborhood.* Minneapolis: Milkweed Editions, 1994.

Nash, Roderick, ed. *The American Environment, Readings in the History of Conservation.* Reading, Mass.: Addison-Wesley, 1968.

Nation Archives and Records Administration, Office of the Federal Register. "Standards for Rehabilitation and Guidelines for Rehabilitating Historic Buildings." *Title 36 Code of Federal Regulations, part 67.*

Natural Resources Conservation Service. *Soil Survey of Lancaster County, Pennsylvania.* Washington, D.C.: Government Printing Office, 1985.

Natural Resources Journal 15 (1975).

Nichols, John. *The Milagro Beanfield War.* New York: Ballantine, 1976.

Norton, B. G. "On What We Should Save: The Role of Culture in Determining Conservation Targets." In *Systematics and Conservation Evaluation,* Systematics Association, Special Volume 50, edited by Peter L. Forey, Christopher J. Humphries, and Richard I. Vane-Wright. Oxford: Oxford University Press, 1994.

Pearce, David W. *Economic Values and the Natural World.* London: Earthscan Publications, 1993.

Pearce, David W., and R. Kerry Turner. *Benefits Estimates and Environmental Decision Making.* Paris: OECD Publication 9792081, 1992.

Pooley, Eric. "Gunnison, Colorado, Cows, or Condos." *Time* (7 July 1997), 81.

Richter, Tobin M. "Conservation Rights in Illinois—Meshing Illinois Property Law with Federal Tax Deduction Requirements." *Illinois Bar Journal* 71, 1 (1983): 430–437.

Robinson, J. "Modeling the Interactions between Human and Natural Systems." *International Social Sciences Journal* 43 (1991): 629–647.

Rodegerdts, Henry. "Land Trusts and Agricultural Conservation Easements." *Natural Resources and Environment* 13 (1998): 336.

Ryan, James. *The Master Plan for Olana State Historic Site.* M.A. thesis, State University of New York–Oneonta, 1984.

Sagoff, Mark. *The Economy of the Earth: Philosophy, Law, and the Environment.* Cambridge, Mass.: Cambridge University Press, 1988.

Saupe, William, and Janet Eisenhauer. "The Wisconsin Family Farm Surveys." In *Status of Wisconsin Farming,* edited by Frederick Butell, 30–43. Madison: University of Wisconsin, Deptartment of Agricultural Economics, August 1994.

Small, Stephen J. "The Tax Benefits of Donating Easements in Scenic and Historic Property." *Real Estate Law Journal* 7 (1979): 304–319.

———. "Working with the 1980 Amendments to the Internal Revenue Code." In *Land-Saving Action,* edited by Russell L. Brenneman and Sarah M. Bates. Washington, D.C.: Island Press, 1984.

————. *The Federal Tax Law of Conservation Easements.* Bar Harbor, Maine: Land Trust Exchange, 1986.

————. *The Federal Tax Law of Conservation Easements,* Second Supplement. Washington, D.C.: Land Trust Alliance, 1995.

————. *Preserving Family Lands, Book II.* Boston: Landowner Planning Center, 1997.

————. *Preserving Family Lands, Book I,* 3rd ed. Boston: Landowner Planning Center, 1998.

Stark, Brian. *Expanded Initial Study for the Agriculture and Open Space Element, San Luis Obispo County General Plan.* San Luis Obispo, Calif.: San Luis Obispo County, 1995.

————. *Saving Special Places: A Study of Open Space Values in the San Luis Obispo Greenbelt.* San Luis Obispo, Calif.: City of San Luis Obispo, 1995.

————. *San Luis Obispo Creek Watershed Hydrologic Survey.* San Luis Obispo, Calif.: Land Conservancy of San Luis Obispo County, 1996.

Thompson, George. *Commentaries on the Modern Law of Real Property,* 1961 replacement volume. Indianapolis: Bobbs-Merrill, 1961.

Turner, Billie L., and William B. Meyer. "Global Land Use and Land-Cover Change: An Overview." In *Changes in Land Use and Land Cover: A Global Perspective,* edited by W. B. Meyer and B. L. Turner, 3–10. Cambridge: Cambridge University Press, 1994.

U.S. Bureau of the Census. *Statistical Abstract of the United States,* 11th ed. Washington, D.C.: Government Printing Office, 1991.

U.S. Department of Agriculture. *1992 Census of Agriculture.* Washington, D.C.: Government Printing Office, 1992.

U.S. Department of the Interior, National Park Service. *Blue Ridge Parkway Land Protection Plan.* Asheville, N.C.: National Park Service, 1994.

Webster, C. "GIS and the Scientific Inputs to Planning: Part 2, Prediction and Prescription." *Environment and Planning: Planning and Design* 21 (1994): 145–157.

Wilbanks, Stephanie J. "Qualified Conservation Contributions: Analysis of Proposed Regulations." *Virginia Tax Review* 3 (Winter 1984): 323–345.

Wilson, Edward O. "Biodiversity, Prosperity, and Value." In *Ecology, Economics, Ethics: The Broken Circle,* edited by Frank H. Bormann and S. R. Kellert, 3–10. New Haven, Conn., and London: Yale University Press, 1991.

Wright, John B. *Rocky Mountain Divide: Selling and Saving the West.* Austin: University of Texas Press, 1993.

About the Contributors
❧ ❦

Mark Ackelson is president of the Iowa Natural Heritage Foundation (INHF). He has directed INHF's land protection projects and regional resource planning projects for sixteen years, helping to turn more than 400 miles of abandoned railroad rights-of-way into recreational trails. He was a cofounder of the Land Trust Alliance and served as chairman of the board for three years.

Heidi A. Anderson is currently a third-year law student at the University of Denver College of Law. Heidi was a legal intern for the law firm of Isaacson, Rosenbaum, Woods & Levy, P.C. in Denver, Colorado, and worked on this project under the supervision of William Silberstein.

David Bezanson is a GIS analyst in Austin, Texas, and a volunteer with the Natural Area Preservation Association, a land trust that works to protect native habitat throughout Texas. David is currently completing a master's degree in geography at the University of Texas.

Randolph Y. Brown is executive director of the Foothills Land Conservancy. He previously served as the executive director of the Chattanooga (Tennessee) Nature Center and as a fund-raising assistant in The Nature Conservancy's Wyoming Field Office.

T. Heyward Carter Jr. is president of the Lowcountry Open Land Trust, Inc. He is a partner with the law firm of Evans, Carter, Kunes & Bennett, P.A., in Charleston, South Carolina, specializing in estate planning and probate matters.

Mathew B. Cobb is a licensed attorney in the state of Kansas. He graduated from the University of Kansas School of Law, served as a legal intern with the Kansas Land Trust, and is currently working on an LL.M. at the University of Edinburgh, Scotland.

Dennis G. Collins is with the Wildlands Conservancy in Emmaus, Pennsylvania, where he has served as the director of Land Protection since 1980. He is responsible for the identification of conservation lands of the conservancy. He negotiates all conservation easements, fee acquisitions, and transfers of property to governmental agencies. In 1997 alone, the conservancy preserved more than 2,400 acres valued at over $2 million, and in 1998 added another 2,700 acres to its total, which now reaches just less than 30,000 acres.

Jerry Cosgrove, an attorney, is director of American Farmland Trust's, New York Field Office in Saratoga. He grew up on his family's dairy farm in central New York. He is a graduate of the Cornell College of Agriculture and Life Sciences and the Cornell Law School. He joined American Farmland Trust in 1992 and now directs its Northeast

Field Office, covering New York and New England. At the trust, he works on farmland conservation issues, including land use, conservation easements, estate planning, and environmental regulations.

Tom Daniels is a professor in the Department of Geography and Planning at the State University of New York at Albany. He is the former director of the Lancaster County Agricultural Preserve Board in Lancaster, Pennsylvania, and recently coauthored the book, *Holding Our Ground: Protecting America's Farms and Farmland* (Washington, D.C.: Island Press, 1997). *Note:* The statements in this paper are those of the author and not of the Agricultural Preserve Board or the Lancaster County Commissioners.

Beth Davis is a third-year law student at the University of Georgia School of Law.

Laurie Fowler is an environmental attorney who serves as counsel to many Georgia land trusts. She is the director of Public Service and Outreach at the University of Georgia's Institute of Ecology and is on the faculty of the law school. She is the author of *Conservation Easements: A Natural Resource Protection Tool* published by the Georgia Department of Natural Resources in 1999.

Julie Ann Gustanski earned a Ph.D. from the University of Edinburgh (U.K.). She also holds the following degrees: M.E.M., Duke University, Natural Resource Economics and Policy; M.Phil. and LL.M., Urban Design and Regional Planning and Planning Law, University of Edinburgh, U.K.; B.S., environmental policy and law, University of Minnesota. She is president and cofounder of 4Ever Land Conservation Associates, a certified planner, and an environmental economic consultant with the United Nations Development Programme. Formerly she was both the director of Buck County, Pennsylvania's farmland preservation program and the executive director of a land trust in south-central Pennsylvania, and she has worked to secure protection of more than 80,000 acres of land since 1987.

Scott Hitch is a third-year law student at the University of Georgia School of Law.

William T. Hutton is the supervising author of chapter 22. He is a professor of law at Hastings School of Law in California, where students in his Land Trust Seminar produced this chapter. The contributors by state are as follows: (Alaska) Josh Butler; (Arizona) Michael Malugani; (California) Osha Meserve and David Shapiro; (Hawaii) Michael Eden; (Idaho) David Levi; (Montana) Timothy Chambers; (Nevada) David Brown; (Oregon) John Slaymaker; and (Washington) Amy Humphreys-Chandler. He also serves as tax counsel to the Trust for Public Land, editor-in chief of *The Back Forty,* and counsel with the law firm of Coblentz, Patch, Duffy & Bass in San Francisco.

Kelly Kindscher holds a joint appointment as a scientist with the Kansas Biological Survey and assistant professor in the Environmental Studies Program and the Departments of Botany and Systematics and Ecology at the University of Kansas.

W. Leighton Lord III is a partner with the law firm of Nexsen Pruet Jacobs & Pollard, LLP, specializing in specializing in real estate finance law.

Karin Marchetti is a lawyer, speaker, and educator who has devoted her practice in Maine to voluntary land conservation techniques, taxation of conserved land, and land trust issues. As general counsel to Maine Coast Heritage Trust since 1987 and as a consultant to other organizations, she has been instrumental in the planning and drafting of several hundred easements and acquisitions.

Todd D. Mayo of Winer and Bennett in Nashua, New Hampshire, practices in the areas of estate planning, business planning, and nonprofit organizations. He is a member of the Massachusetts and New Hampshire bars and a contributing editor of *The Back Forty*.

Seth McKee is currently Scenic Hudson's director of Land Projects and has worked as land projects manager of Scenic Hudson, Inc., since 1991. Before joining Scenic Hudson, he worked in land stewardship for The Nature Conservancy's North Carolina chapter. He has a master's degree in regional planning from the University of North Carolina at Chapel Hill. At Scenic Hudson, he oversees a new farmland protection pilot project, negotiates acquisitions of land and conservation easements, and builds constituencies for the stewardship of protected lands. He is cochair of the town of New Paltz Environmental Conservation Commission and is a member of the steering committee of the Outdoor Coalition of New York, a coalition of environmental organizations, hunting and fishing enthusiasts, and recreational user groups.

Linda J. Mead is executive director of Delaware and Raritan Greenway, Inc., in Princeton, New Jersey, and has been working to secure protected land since 1989. Linda interviewed Tom Bailey, executive director of the Little Traverse Conservancy, who provided information for this case study.

Larry E. Meuwissen is an attorney at his own firm in Minneapolis. He recently has served as an administrative judge, where his principal responsibilities were to determine eligible claimants under the White Earth Land Settlement Act of 1986. For the better part of his professional career, he has been in private practice in the Minneapolis–St. Paul metropolitan area. He also served nine years as an U.S. Department of Justice trial attorney in Washington, D.C. He is admitted to practice before Minnesota State Supreme Court (1974), U.S. Supreme Court (1980), District of Columbia Court of Appeals (1986); U.S. Court of Appeals for the Federal Circuit, the Eight and Eleventh Circuits, U.S. States Tax Court, and U.S. Court of Federal Claims. He has been involved with both founding and serving on boards of a number of nonprofit organizations in the Twin Cities.

Robert Myhr has been executive director of the San Juan Preservation Trust in the San Juan Islands of Washington State since 1985. He served on the board of directors of the Land Trust Alliance from 1990 to 1996. He is familiar with conservation issues worldwide from his experience in university research and teaching, international business, and consulting.

Hans Neuhauser is director of the Georgia Land Trust Service Center, a project of the Georgia Environmental Policy Institute. He is a former chair of the board of the Land

Trust Alliance, currently serves on the National Land Trust Council, and is involved with a number of land trusts in Georgia.

Brian Ohm combines his training in law with his interest in planning and policy as a professor within the Department of Urban and Regional Planning at the University of Wisconsin, Madison. His current areas of research include the reform of land use enabling legislation, the law of takings, nonregulatory devices for land use control, and the interaction between law and planning. Professional activities include serving as a member of a local commission overseeing the implementation of Wisconsin's first farmland purchase of development rights program and service on a number of boards of nonprofit organizations involved in land use and environmental planning issues. He formerly practiced in Minnesota, where he was an attorney for the Metropolitan Council in the Twin Cities. He is licensed to practice law in Minnesota and Wisconsin.

Melanie Pallone teaches college-level criminal justice and is consultant to several local environmental and conservation groups on legal and public relations matters. She currently works as an interviewer and investigative newswriter for a weekly environmental radio program entitled "The Allegheny Front," airing on WYEP 91.3 FM, serving western Pennsylvania. As former assistant legal counsel and director of public policy for the Western Pennsylvania Conservancy, she practiced contract and real estate issues for the nonprofit land trust and advocated issues of conservation policy on its behalf. She previously served as project assistant with the Pennsylvania Department of Environmental Protection's southwest regional office. She began her legal career as an assistant district attorney in the Pittsburgh area, after having served as a judicial clerk. She received her J.D. from the University of Pittsburgh School of Law.

Chalmers W. Poston, Jr. is an attorney with the law firm of Evans, Carter, Kunes & Bennett, P.A., in Charleston, South Carolina. Formerly a trial attorney with the Internal Revenue Service, he specializes in tax matters.

Tom Quinn is the executive director of the Wisconsin Farmland Conservancy. The conservancy is a regional land trust concerned with protecting the character of the rural countryside, that mix of diversified farms, natural areas and forests, and small towns that makes rural Wisconsin a special place. The conservancy's programs work with landowners and farmers to develop individual land protection plans and provide assistance to local governments in establishing land protection programs and policies. The conservancy has a special focus on linking land protection and sustainable economic development.

Leslie Reed-Evans has been the executive director of the Williamstown Rural Lands Foundation since 1990. Projects during her tenure have focused on preservation of community character, farmland, and rare species habitat protection and recreational access. The conservation and limited development project described here was her first major project with the foundation. She is a well-known area naturalist and leader of bird, wildflower, and natural history walks in all seasons.

Sharon E. Richardson is the director of land protection of the Lowcountry Open Land Trust, after serving as executive director for two years. In her time at the land trust, she has designed conservation easements for more than thirty families to protect almost 10,000 acres of land in coastal South Carolina. She is also vice president of the Charleston Natural History Society. Before joining the land trust, she was long-range planner for Beaufort County and was responsible for the adoption of the River Protection Overlay District for the Outstanding Resource rivers in coastal Beaufort County. She has worked in conservation with her husband, Bruce Richardson of the U.S. Fish and Wildlife Service Coastal Program, since 1997 in South Carolina and Vermont. She has a master's in public administration from the University of Vermont and a B.A. from Middlebury College.

Charles E. Roe is executive director of the Conservation Trust for North Carolina, a statewide, private, nonprofit organization dedicated to helping communities, landowners, private nonprofit land trusts, and public agencies protect natural and undeveloped lands. Former manager of the state of North Carolina's Natural Heritage Program for fourteen years, he is consultant to and board member of numerous state conservation organizations as well as the national Land Trusts Alliance. He holds a master's degree in regional planning from the University of North Carolina, Chapel Hill; an M.A. in American history/environment and public policy from Indiana University, Bloomington; and a B.A. in history/political science and geography from Western Illinois University.

John F. Rohe practices law in Petoskey, Michigan. He is the author of *Michigan Construction Liens* published by Lexis Publishing, is a contributing author to *AmJur,* wrote *A Bicentennial Malthusian Essay* published by Rhodes and Easton, and wrote the Model Conservation Easement used by land trusts in Michigan.

William M. Silberstein is recognized as one of Colorado's leading experts in land conservation law and open-space preservation. His practice includes conservation easements and limited developments, and representation of land trusts and landowners.

Stephen J. Small is a tax attorney at his own firm in Boston. Before going into private practice, he was an attorney in the Office of the Chief Council for the Internal Revenue Service, Washington, D.C. There he was involved in writing the federal income tax regulations on conservation easements. He advises landowners around the country on federal income and estate tax planning to help them preserve their valued family lands. He has given lectures, seminars, workshops, and speeches across the country and has published several books on the conservation of family lands. He is the author of *The Federal Tax Law of Conservation Easements,* published by the Land Trust Alliance in 1985. He holds a J.D. and an LL.M. in taxation from Georgetown University Law Center, an M.S. in journalism from Northeastern University, and a B.A. in English from Yale University. He is a member of the Massachusetts and District of Columbia Bars.

Roderick H. Squires holds a B.A. and Ph.D. in geography from the University Durham, U.K. He is currently an associate professor in the department of geograp at the University of Minnesota. He teaches courses in physical geography and b geography, stressing the interdependence of earth's systems, and environmental qu ity, land ownership, and land use, stressing the role of humans in those systems. F writings include articles on conservation, the public land survey, submerged lan and American Indian landownership

Brian Stark is the watershed programs director/GIS manager at the Land Conservan of San Luis Obispo County, California. He holds an M.A. in geography from Califc nia State University, Chico, and a B.S. in social sciences from California Polytechr State University, San Luis Obispo. Currently, he is involved in riparian restoration a water quality monitoring for the San Luis Obispo Creek watershed. His most rece publications include *San Luis Obispo Creek Watershed Hydrologic Survey* (Land Co servancy of San Luis Obispo County, 1996); *Saving Special Places: A Study of Op Space Values in the San Luis Obispo Greenbelt* (City of San Luis Obispo, 1995); a *Expanded Initial Study for the Agriculture and Open Space Element, San Luis Obis County General Plan* (San Luis Obispo County, 1995).

Christine Thisted is the executive director of operations for the Ice Age Park and Tr Foundation. Since October 1995, she has worked with over 2,000 volunteers fro around Wisconsin as well as federal, state, and local units of government to plan, bu and maintain the Ice Age National Scenic Trail. She holds an M.S. in urban a regional planning from the University of Wisconsin, Madison.

John B. Wright has worked with land trusts since 1980 on more than seventy-five co servation easement projects and a land exchange that created the Rattlesnake Nation Recreation and Wilderness Area. He holds a Ph.D. in geography from University California, Berkeley. Currently, he is a professor of geography at New Mexico Sta University, where he codirects the planning program. Previously, he was director planning for Mineral County, Montana, an independent land use planner, and a co servation consultant. He is widely published and the author of a book on land trus entitled *Rocky Mountain Divide: Selling and Saving the West* (Austin: University Texas Press, 1993).

Index

❦ ❦